Culture and Politics

Culture and Politics
A Reader

Edited by Lane Crothers and Charles Lockhart

St. Martin's Press
New York

CULTURE AND POLITICS: A READER
Copyright © 2000 Lane Crothers and Charles Lockhart. All rights reserved. Printed in the United States of America. No part of this book may be used or reproduced in any manner whatsoever without written permission except in the case of brief quotations embodied in critical articles or reviews. For information, address St. Martin's Press, Scholarly and Reference Division, 175 Fifth Avenue, New York, N.Y. 10010.

ISBN 0-312-22543-1 (cloth)
ISBN 0-312-23300-0 (paper)

Library of Congress Cataloging-in-Publication Data to be found at the Library of Congress.

First edition: July 2000

10 9 8 7 6 5 4 3 2 1

To Aaron Wildavsky, Scholar and Teacher

CONTENTS

Acknowledgments ix
Permissions xi
Editors' Introduction xv

PART I: CONCEPTS AND APPLICATIONS

Introduction 1
1. The Study of Political Culture, Gabriel A. Almond 5
2. A Cause in Search of Its Effect, or What Does Political Culture Explain? David J. Elkins and Richard E. B. Simeon ... 21
3. Culture and Identity in Comparative Political Analysis, Marc Howard Ross ... 39
4. The Startling Ability of Culture to Bring Critical Inquiry to a Halt, Patricia Nelson Limerick ... 71

PART II: CULTURE AND GLOBALIZATION

Introduction 75
5. Socialism and the Ideological Dimensions of Globalization, Manfred B. Steger ... 79
6. The Clash of Civilizations? Samuel P. Huntington ... 99
7. Singapore and the "Asian Values" Debate, Donald K. Emmerson ... 119

PART III: POPULAR CULTURE

Introduction 129
8. Deep Structures: Polpop Culture on Primetime Television, Allen McBride and Robert K. Toburen ... 133

9. The Symbolic Annihilation of Women by
   the Mass Media, Gaye Tuchman   150
10. Deep Play: Notes on the Balinese Cockfight, Clifford Geertz   175

PART IV: CIVIL SOCIETY AND SOCIAL CAPITAL

Introduction   203
11. The Politics of Virtue Today: A Critique and
    a Proposal, Shelley Burtt   207
12. Bowling Alone: America's Declining Social
    Capital, Robert D. Putnam   223
13. Making Social Science Work Across Space and Time:
    A Critical Reflection On Robert Putnam's
    Making Democracy Work, Sidney Tarrow   235

PART V: SOCIAL MOVEMENTS, COLLECTIVE IDENTITY,
AND POLITICAL CULTURE

Introduction   249
14. Culture and Social Movements, Doug McAdam   253
15. Cultural Power and Social Movements, Ann Swidler   269
16. Cultural Conflict in America, James Davison Hunter   284

PART VI: CULTURE AND POLITICAL CHANGE

Introduction   303
17. A Culturalist Theory of Political Change, Harry Eckstein   307
18. Does Latin America Exist? (And Is There a Confucian Culture?),
    Ronald Inglehart and Marita Carballo   325
19. Patterns of Response, Samuel P. Huntington   348

PART VII: CULTURE AND RATIONALITY

Introduction   359
20. Social Norms and Economic Theory, Jon Elster   363
21. Socioeconomics and the New "Battle of Methods":
    Toward a Paradigm Shift? Richard Swedberg   381
22. Rationality and Interpretation: Parliamentary Elections in
    Early Stuart England, John Ferejohn   393

Notes   413
Index   435

ACKNOWLEDGMENTS

No project can ever be accomplished without the help, assistance, and patience of innumerable people. Our debt is sufficiently wide and deep that we apologize in advance for likely failing to recall accurately and acknowledge here all the valuable contributions that others have provided.

First, we express our gratitude to Richard Ellis of Willamette University. We sought Richard's advice regularly when this project was first under way, and it was freely given and invaluable. Richard's suggestions live on in the organization and even the title of this volume. In particular, his careful consideration of how to present the various ideas that form this volume has been crucial to shaping its finished version. We are extremely pleased to have this opportunity to recognize his generous help.

Earlier in our lives we benefited from the knowledge and inspiration of numerous scholars. In particular, Gabriel Almond and Sidney Verba, whose many works are cited repeatedly throughout this volume, made political culture a central component of political science and of our careers. Similarly, the influence of Richard Pride at Vanderbilt University brought an excitement to the subject that proved impossible to resist; without his influence, this project literally would not have come to life. Aaron Wildavsky also taught us how to conceptualize the political ramifications of culture in a different way that is exceptionally useful and has stimulated our thought and our fascination with political culture.

We derived much benefit as well from the active support and suggestions of Manfred Steger at Illinois State University. His careful reading of the manuscript in its early phases contributed much to its final form. Jamal Nassar and Tom Eimermann, both of Illinois State University as well, are also due great thanks for their unflagging professional support and personal friendship. The extraordinary insight and inspiration as well as the generous support of these various scholars and colleagues brighten our lives beyond measure.

Additionally, a number of people and organizations ably facilitated this project in a variety of critical practical ways. Robert Putnam, whose "Bowling

Alone" appears in this volume, intervened personally so as to allow us to reprint this important article. Sarah Walcynski and the staff of LILT (the Lab for Integrated Learning and Technology) at Illinois State University were patient and helpful throughout this project. Rob Miller's inexhaustible hours of patient scanning brought this book into a useful form. Eric Schuller of Illinois State University was extremely helpful as well. We greatly appreciate their crucial assistance.

We also owe a debt of gratitude to our families, whose support and insight helped us to shape this volume and stay the difficult course of the project. A special thanks is owed to Jean Giles-Sims, whose casual question regarding the content of this book led to the inclusion of an important component. We thank you all.

Finally, we want to thank the various authors, journals and presses whose works are presented in this volume.

As always, while those cited here have helped make this a better work, its flaws are entirely ours.

PERMISSIONS

Gabriel Almond, *A Discipline Divided*, pp. 138-156, copyright © 1990 by Sage Publications. Reprinted by permission of Sage Publications, Inc.

David J. Elkins and Richard E. B. Simeon, "A Cause in Search of Its Effect, or What Does Political Culture Explain," *Comparative Politics*, 11 (January 1979). Reprinted with permission of *Comparative Politics*, where the article first appeared.

Marc Howard Ross, "Culture and Identity in Comparative Political Analysis," pp. 42-80 in *Comparative Politics: Rationality, Culture, and Structure*, edited by Mark I. Lichbach and Alan S. Zuckerman. (New York: Cambridge University Press, 1997). © Mark Irving Lichbach and Alan S. Zuckerman 1997. Reprinted with the permission of Cambridge University Press.

Patricia Nelson Limerick, "The Startling Ability of Culture to Bring Critical Inquiry to a Halt," *Chronicle of Higher Education* (October 24, 1997): A76. Reprinted with permission of the author.

Manfred Steger, "Socialism and the Ideological Dimensions of Globalization." Adapted from M. Steger, *Globalism:The New Market Ideology* (New York: Rowman and Littlefield, forthcoming 2001). Reprinted with permission of the author.

Samuel Huntington, "The Clash of Civilizations." *Foreign Affairs* 72 (3): 22-49. Reprinted by permission of *Foreign Affairs*, (1993). Copyright 1993 by the Council on Foreign Relations, Inc.

Donald Emmerson. "Singapore and the 'Asian Values' Debate." *Journal of Democracy* 6.4 (1995): 95-105. © 1995. The Johns Hopkins University Press and National Endowment for Democracy.

Allen McBride and Robert K. Toburen. "Deep Structures: Polpop Culture on Primetime Television," *Journal of Popular Culture* 29 (Spring 1996): 181-200. Reprinted with permission.

Gaye Tuchman, "The Symbolic Annihilation of Women by the Mass Media." "Introduction," from *Hearth and Home* by Gaye Tuchman, A. Kaplan Daniels and J. Benet. Copyright © 1978 by Oxford University Press, Inc. Used by permission of Oxford University Press, Inc.

Clifford Geertz, "Deep Play: Notes on the Balinese Cockfight," reprinted with permission of *Dædalus,* Journal of the American Academy of Arts and Sciences, from the issue entitled "Myth, Symbol, and Culture," Winter 1972, Vol. 101, No. 1.

Shelley Burtt. 1993. "The Politics of Virtue Today: A Critique and a Proposal." *American Political Science Review* 87 (2): 360-68. Reprinted with permission.

Robert Putnam. "Bowling Alone." *Journal of Democracy* 6:1 (1995): 65-78. © 1995. The Johns Hopkins University Press and National Endowment for Democracy.

Sidney Tarrow. 1996. "Making Social Science Work Across Space and Time: A Critical Reflection on Robert Putnam's *Making Democracy Work.*" *American Political Science Review* 90 (2): 389-97. Reprinted with permission.

Doug McAdam, "Culture and Social Movements." From *New Social Movements: From Ideology to Identity* edited by Enrique Laraña, Hank Johnston, and Jospeh R. Gusfield. Reprinted by permission of Temple University Press. © by Temple University. All rights reserved.

Ann Swidler, "Cultural Power and Social Movements." In *Social Movements in Culture,* edited by Hank Johnston and Bert Klandermans (University of Minnesota Press, 1995). Copyright © 1995 by the Regents of the University of Minnesota.

Ann Swidler, "Cultural Power and Social Movements." In *Social Movements in Culture,* edited by Hank Johnston and Bert Klandermans (UCL Press, 1995). Reprinted with permission of UCL Press.

James Davison Hunter, "Cultural Conflict in America." From *Culture Wars: The Struggle to Define America* by James Davison Hunter. Copyright © 1991 by Basic Books, A Division of HarperCollins. Reprinted by permission of Basic Books, a member of Perseus Books, L. L. C.

Harry Eckstein. 1988. "A Culturalist Theory of Political Change." *American Political Science Review* 82 (2): 789-804. Reprinted with permission.

Ronald Inglehart and Marita Carballo. "Does Latin America Exist? (And Is There A Confucian Culture?): A Global Analysis of Cross-Cultural Differences." *PS: Political Science and Politics* 30 (1): 34–47. Reprinted with permission.

Samuel Huntington, pp. 64–75 of *American Politics: The Promise of Disharmony.* Reprinted with permission of the publisher from *American Politics: The Promise of Disharmony* by Samuel Huntington, Cambridge, Mass: Harvard University Press, Copyright © 1981 by Samuel Huntington.

Jon Elster, "Social Norms and Economic Theory," *Journal of Economic Perspectives* 3 (4): 99–117. Reprinted with permission.

Richard Swedberg, "Socioeconomics and the New 'Battle of the Methods': Towards a Paradigm Shift?" Reprinted from *Journal of Socio-Economics,* Vol. 19, 1990, with permission from Elsevier Science.

John Ferejohn, "Rationality and Interpretation: Parliamentary Elections in Early Stuart England," from *The Economic Approach to Politics* by Kristen Renwick Monroe. Copyright 1991 by Kristen Renwick Monroe. Reprinted by permission of Addison-Wesley Educational Publishers Inc.

EDITORS' INTRODUCTION

Culture and Politics: A Reader deals successively with ten questions central to culture's application to the social sciences, most particularly political science. As several of the authors included in the *Reader* point out, theorists have been using culture to explain social and political life for over 2,000 years (e.g., Almond 1990). So, the first question is: What is culture? Part I examines this question both by surveying a number of views and by focusing on three in particular. When theorists speak of culture, especially political culture, they generally refer to certain mental predispositions that people hold: particular beliefs about how the world works, certain values that they honor, and various practical commitments to which they subscribe. For instance, since the Enlightenment period (late seventeenth- through eighteenth-century), people in Western societies frequently have believed that humans can acquire the capacity to control the natural environment and shape their social environments through reason. Further, they have increasingly valued their fellow humans as unique people all capable of contributing (unequal increments of progress) to this project. Valuing their fellow humans for their unique capacities has, in turn, fostered social commitments to more extensive efforts aimed at developing peoples' talents under conditions of fair equality of opportunity.

Some theorists extend the denotations of "culture" so that they encompass not only mental predispositions but also various actions that stem from these orientations as well as at least some of the social consequences of these actions, such as the construction and maintenance of distinctive political institutions. So supporters of the Enlightenment often became public advocates for the universal development of human talents and, eventually, supporters of public school systems. Further, some theorists think primarily in terms of culture's contributions to shaping peoples' patterns of attending to and interpreting the world around them; whereas other theorists focus more on culture's contributions to building social ties (i.e., a shared identity) among adherents. Clearly, concepts of culture vary among social analysts. In fact, this *Reader* offers only a sampling of this variety.

While culture has long been employed by prominent theorists to explain various aspects of social and political life, it is fair to ask (question two): How successful is it relative to alternative schemata? Indeed, culture has faced increasing competition from alternative explanatory devices, particularly across the last century. Rational choice analysis (see Part VII) has become particularly influential, initially in economics and increasingly in political science. Studies demonstrating how the differing structures of various institutions shape the activities of people who live and work within them have also gained ground vis-à-vis cultural explanations. We examine issues about the relative capacities of culture and institutions to explain political life in parts IV and VI.

These concerns are examples of a broader, third question: How does the world work? that we raise in part II. In the aftermath of the cold war and its fierce Soviet-American rivalry that provided a clear international order, analysts disagree about the character of the international system. Some see societies worldwide converging on one or another aspect of the single remaining superpower, the United States. Various views focus on the dominance of American popular culture, democracy, and particularly the necessity of societal practices converging to survive the progressive penetration of a single global market. By this last interpretation, market capitalism provides a culture or ideology that explains the most significant trends in the contemporary international system (Cox 1999).

Yet other analysts perceive the contemporary world becoming increasingly diverse as various regional cultures or civilizations progressively go their own way in the absence of the organizing influence of the Soviet-American rivalry. Huntington (1993) sees increasing diversity among rival civilizations as leading to more frequent and severe conflict activity along the "fault-lines separating cultural regions." His view is particularly ominous from an American perspective since he foresees the United States (and Western Europe) losing a long-term conflict of "the West against the rest" in which "the rest" become more modern, and thus technologically capable, but not more "Western" in the sense, for instance, of supporting personal liberty and individual rights.

Thus far we have been following the implicit assumption that everyone adheres to a culture (or cultures). Yet it is still common to refer to some people as "cultured," with the implication that others are not. This practice raises a distinction basic to part III. In this context, those who are cultured have acquired familiarity with and appreciation for certain art forms (e.g., Mozart, Cézanne, or Shakespeare), activities (lawn tennis, fencing, or polo), or patterns of consumption (Armagnac, balsamic vinegar, or roasted squab with foie gras). Other people then lack this "high" culture and were once thought of (by the cultured at any rate) as "uncultured." The dramatic increases in economic prosperity of the last century, particularly since World War II, as well as the significant social leveling associated with democracy have helped to further an alternative way of conceiving those whose habits fit poorly with conceptions of high culture. These people may adopt various aspects of "popular" culture (e.g., Stephen King, the National Football League, and Fenway Franks).

Part III picks up on this trend by asking question four: What is the social and especially the political significance of popular culture? The readings in this part examine whether certain themes of popular culture reflect or, alternatively, help to shape broader concerns of political culture generally such as attitudes toward authority or the status of women in society.

Democracy's widespread popularity since the late 1980s and the concomitant concerns, especially among American political scientists, for consolidating recent democratic gains in the form of increasingly liberal (in a classical John Locke/Adam Smith sense) democracy have raised the profile of pair of additional questions involving culture. Many prominent social theorists have argued that specific political institutional arrangements (monarchy, liberal democracy fascism, etc.) arise from particular types of political cultures and require these distinctive cultures for their maintenance. So question five is: Does culture foster and sustain political institutions, or does the reverse occur, or do both processes contribute to a symbiotic relationship? Putnam with Leonardi and Nanetti (1993) recently has advanced considerable evidence that he regards as supporting cultural shaping of institutional arrangements. Yet others argue, sometimes drawing on the same data (Tarrow 1996), that the reverse occurs. Surely in a broad sense both are correct. Different cultures help to shape and sustain distinctive institutional arrangements, and institutions, in turn, socialize both people who work within them and succeeding generations of citizens who grow up among the institutions (frequently in relative ignorance of alternatives) to acceptance and support. Relations between culture and institutions are interactive and mutually supportive. Without institutions of particular types, the adherents of rival cultures have no means for shaping human experience in accordance with their distinctive beliefs and values, and without suitable cultures, particular institutional forms have no justifications in terms of beliefs and values. But we have much to learn—and the readings in part IV contribute to our learning—about these reciprocal causal flows.

Acknowledging that culture helps to shape political institutions leaves open question six: Precisely what culture or cultures help to consolidate new democracies facing a range of difficult circumstances? Classical authors disagreed among themselves on this point, and the range of disagreement has grown in the past half century. The cultural preconditions that some analysts perceive as required are viewed by other theorists as unrealistic or even destructive of practical democratic development efforts. Our part IV, entitled "Civil Society and Social Capital" (the latter being a term that Putnam and a few others use roughly synonymously with the former) explores these arguments.

Relations between culture and various forms of political change provide the central concerns of parts V and VI. Part V focuses on the seventh question: How does culture contribute to the formation of various social movements (such as those that convulsed the United States in the late 1960s and early 1970s) that are often the visible agents of change? While broad societal changes are frequently prompted, at least in part, by various historical contingencies (wars, depressions, etc.) that confront people with distressing social dislocations of various sorts, culture may shape both the manner in which resources are mobilized in support of social movements and the specific goals that these movements seek to realize. For instance, Dr. Martin Luther King, Jr., sought to link the African American civil rights movement of the 1960s to prominent egalitarian and individualistic strands of American experience that retained a high profile in Americans' consciousness. Thus King hoped to mobilize a substantial portion of the American population in support of his goals. King frequently drew on Jesus' activities as recorded in the Bible to stress egalitarian themes such as extending equally good treatment to all as well as on Jefferson's (Lockean) language in the Declaration of Independence about the equality of "all men" and the similar rights they hold.

Just as surely as King employed these cultural icons in support of his objectives, his objectives were themselves molded by the relative egalitarianism of Puritan Christian experience in America as well as the individual rights tradition of the English settlers who initially directed our society's development. So while it is likely that a number of unanticipated technical and social changes associated with the World War II explain the timing of this civil rights movement, both King's successful mobilization strategy and the central goals of the movement were clearly linked to the most basic egalitarian and individualistic cultural influences in American history.

Yet culture is widely perceived as static, a stable shelter in a world in which change is constant and nearly pervasive. So more generally, then, arises question eight: Can culture contribute to political change? This is, of course, the central issue of part VI. It is helpful, in addressing this question, to visualize societies not as monolithic collections of persons with similar cultural identities (i.e., national character) but as having substantial internal variations or distinctive "subcultures." Even better, we might, for the moment at least, consider the rival ideologies or worldviews that we routinely recognize as dividing most, if not all, societies as indices of distinctive cultures. That is, ideologies serve as shorthand measures for the selective attention and interpretation activities of cultures, less well, perhaps, with respect to cultures' identity-bestowing contributions. So, for instance, Huntington's conceptualization of several European societies (e.g., the Federal Republic of Germany) into three historically sequential regimes—*ancien,* liberal, and socialist—translates fairly accurately into a contemporary Germany in which three rival cultures, organized by different political parties, contend: the Christian Democratic Union/Christian Social Union (CDU/CSU) representing hierarchy, the Free Democratic Party (FDP) representing individualism, and the Social Democratic Party of Germany (SPD) and the Greens representing egalitarianism (Huntington 1981, 42-44 and 113).

With this vision of "multicultural" societies in mind, culture's contributions to political change are eased without violating Eckstein's (1988) prohibition on individuals shifting from one cultural perspective to another. One possibility is examined by Inglehart (1997). He argues that, as general socioeconomic conditions shift, the relative frequencies of various cultures within a society's population change. Further, as democratic societies become composed increasingly of "postmodernists" and less thoroughly of "modernists," the nature of their public issues, the character of their political party systems, and the substance of their public policies also change. Cultural change produces a variety of political innovations, including new or revised political institutions. As was the case in part IV, other authors argue that institutional changes are responsible for cultural changes. In general, this is true. But Inglehart's argument both fits and specifies more carefully our earlier suggestion that the relationship between culture and institutions is symbiotic. He contends that new socioeconomic circumstances produce cultural change, which in turn prompts innovations in political institutions.

Huntington (1981) offers another idea as to how cultures might contribute to political change. He suggests that the efforts a culture engages in to realize its values in practical political ways may go through relatively long-term cycles of multiple phases which vary in the types and amount of activity. While a culture's view of desirable circumstances remains relatively stable, the energy and political will to push hard for bringing this vision to fruition waxes and then wanes across a multi-decade cycle as a culture's adherents are exhausted by their generation's round of political activism.

Our final part, Part VII, deals with relations between culture and rationality. Question nine involves this issue: Do culture and rationality represent rival or complementary explanations of social life? We argue for the complementary option. This response leads directly to question ten: How are culture and rationality complementary elements of social and political explanation? We think that rationality is appropriately understood as instrumental, a concern for the efficient realization of consistent ends: preference implementation. Culture, in contrast, is—as we have seen—a preference formation device. Peoples' varying experience with the way the world works and what their fellow humans are like leads them to adopt distinctive beliefs and values and to derive from these rival objectives and practical political interests. Surely the processes of preference formation and implementation are complementary rather than contradictory activities. Some rational-choice theorists realize this (e.g., North 1990). But even among these analysts, the beliefs and values that underlie the egoistic and (materially) hedonistic "economic men" frequently assumed in applications of their theory (assumptions similar to those of liberal individualism) often are privileged as being "natural" to humans in a way that the group-oriented beliefs and values discussed by Aristotle and Rousseau are not (Ferejohn 1991, 279-305).

Each of the parts of this *Reader* offer a (generally three-item) selection of "classic" articles examining various aspects of the issues we have introduced here and related concerns. Collectively, these articles provide an excellent introduction to culture and its application to the social sciences. In each part one of the articles represents a practical application of the ideas introduced either in the introduction or the part's other articles. Generally, this is the last article in the part, although in part IV the second article, by Putnam, serves this purpose. The part introductions also include a "References and Further Readings" section that can direct subsequent research. Finally, the part introductions contain all of the citations for each of the reading introductions that follow.

References

Almond, G. 1990. *A discipline divided: Schools and sects in political science.* Newbury Park, CA: Sage Publications.

Cox, H. 1999. The market as God. *Atlantic Monthly* 283 (March): 18-23.

Eckstein, H. 1988. A culturalist theory of political change. *American Political Science Review* 82: 789-804.

Ferejohn, J. 1991. Rationality and interpretation: Parliamentary elections in early Stuart England. In *The Economic Approach to Politics: A Critical Reassessment of the Theory of Rational Action,* edited by K. R. Monroe. New York: HarperCollins.

Huntington, S. 1981. *American politics: The promise of disharmony.* Cambridge, MA: Harvard University Press.

———. 1993. The clash of civilizations? *Foreign Affairs* 72: 22-49.

Inglehart, R. 1997. *Modernization and postmodernization: Cultural, economic and political change in 43 Societies.* Princeton, NJ: Princeton University Press.

North, D. 1990. *Institutions, institutional change and economic performance.* New York: Cambridge University Press.

Putnam, R., with R. Leonardi, and R. Y. Nanetti. 1993. *Making democracy work: Civic traditions in modern Italy.* Princeton, NJ: Princeton University Press.

Tarrow, S. 1996. Making social science work across space and time: A critical reflection on Robert Putnam's Making democracy work. *American Political Science Review* 90: 389-97.

PART I

Concept and Applications

Introduction

A prominent political culture theorist laments that "the term *culture*, unfortunately, has no precise, settled meaning in the social sciences" (Eckstein 1988, 801). The three readings in this part all offer different definitions of culture, particularly political culture. Yet it is not clear that, overall, the absence of a settled meaning is a problem. The resulting "heuristic openness" (Kaplan 1964) enables researchers to employ different specific meanings in order to explain various specific dependent variables. What is important, as Elkins and Simeon suggest in chapter 2, is this specificity rather than the adoption of one settled definition.

Although various theorists conceive of political culture differently, a range of commonly applied conceptions can be delineated. For most researchers culture centers on certain mental orientations or predispositions: peoples' beliefs, values, and affective commitments. Yet various scholars employ these common foci differently. Some (Eckstein 1988) emphasize culture as a scheme of selective attention and interpretation. Others (Ross, chapter 3 herein) stress the contributions to identity that these mental predispositions provide. While these distinctive orientations share a focus on culture as interpretative schemata, the former perspective often lends itself more easily to incorporation into a social science designed to produce empirical generalizations. Generally, scholars recognize beliefs, values, and affective commitments as predispositions to action. But they differ on the firmness of linkages between mental orientations and action and also as to whether actions resulting from cultural predispositions are appropriately included as culture. For instance, Almond (chapter 1, herein) perceives firmer linkages and evinces a greater willingness to count actions as culture than Elkins and Simeon (1979). Further, some scholars (Thompson, Ellis, and Wildavsky 1990) include the distinctive social institutions that arise from the actions deriving from rival cultural orientations as culture or at least as closely related cultural indices. That is, while specific institutional structures are certainly distinct from mental predispositions and actions, certain versions of the former are closely tied to specific variations of the latter. Other researchers (Ross 1997) perceive relations between mental orientations and social institutions as less firm and specific and thus think of the latter as—at best—cultural artifacts rather than culture itself.

Almond, in chapter 1, reminds us that social analysts have employed culture as an explanatory variable minimally since Plato and Aristotle. Prominent thinkers of the modern period (e.g., Machiavelli, Montesquieu, Rousseau, and Tocqueville) also relied on cultural explanations. In contemporary social science Almond was the fountainhead of a vibrant, post–World War II, culture-based, social-science initiative that included a number of the most prominent political scientists of the time (Almond 1956; Almond and Coleman 1960; Almond and Verba 1963; Almond and Powell 1966; Eckstein 1961; LaPalombara 1964; Lipset 1963; Pye and Verba 1965; Weiner 1967). The theoretical roots of this initiative lay among the great sociologists (e.g., Max Weber, Emile Durkheim) of the late-nineteenth and early-twentieth centuries. Across the 1950s and 1960s, this initiative formed the central thrust of the study of comparative politics and applied political culture theory to a variety of problems, most prominently political development. Moreover, scholars who employ culture continue to do high-profile work in political science (Verba et al. 1987; Verba, Nie, and Kim 1978; Almond and Verba 1980; Eckstein 1996, 1988; Inglehart 1997, 1988, 1977; Lipset 1996, 1991, 1-45, 1990; Putnam with Leonardi and Nanetti 1993, 1988; Thompson, Ellis, and Wildavsky 1990).

Nonetheless, political culture theory has lost ground since the early 1970s to alternative forms of political analysis. Even on what is arguably its "home turf" of comparative politics, Lichbach and Zuckerman (1997) see political culture theories currently as only one of three preeminent theoretical approaches, including rational-choice theory and institutional analysis, and arguably the least influential of the three. Part VII of this *Reader*, "Culture and Rationality," introduces aspects of the ongoing controversies between political culture theories and rational-choice theory. (See as well the related excellent set of articles in *Political Psychology* 1995.) Parts IV and VI, "Civil Society and Social Capital" and "Culture and Political Change," provide an introduction to issues central to the dispute between political culture theories and institutional analysis.

Political culture theories share a focus on people's cognitive perceptions, basic values, and affective or emotional commitments (Verba 1965, 512-60). That is, these theories argue that people's views about how the world works, their senses about the values and practical objectives that it is appropriate to pursue in such a world, and the commitments to particular forms of political institutions that it thus makes sense to accept explain much about the character of social life. This general idea has intrigued social analysts since Plato. Yet against the increasingly rigorous epistemological standards of contemporary social science, the linkages between these beliefs, values, and practical commitments and various political behaviors and consequences have come under increasing scrutiny. Ross's excellent review of various criticisms of political culture theories in chapter 3 helps to reveal the directions in which its practitioners must strive for increasingly rigorous analysis. Encouragingly, Ross concludes that at least some versions of political culture theory are compatible with and can contribute to a social science of empirical generalizations. Yet as Limerick suggests in chapter 4, in the hands of "poststructuralists" in particular, culture has been employed in sweeping imprecise ways that serve more to disrupt than to sustain careful analysis.

References and Further Readings

Almond, G. 1956. Comparative political systems. *Journal of Politics* 18: 391-409.
———. 1990. The study of political culture. In *A discipline divided: Schools and sects in political science.* Newbury Park, CA: Sage Publications.
Almond, G., and J. Coleman. 1960. *The politics of developing areas.* Princeton, NJ: Princeton University Press.
Almond, G., and G. B. Powell, Jr. 1966. *Comparative politics: A developmental approach.* Boston: Little, Brown.
Almond, G., and S. Verba. 1963. *The civic culture: Political attitudes and democracy in five nations.* Princeton, NJ: Princeton University Press.
Almond, G., and S. Verba, eds. 1980. *The civic culture revisited.* Boston: Little, Brown.
Eckstein, H. 1961. *A theory of stable democracy.* Princeton, NJ: Center of International Studies, Princeton University.
———. 1988. A culturalist theory of political change. *American Political Science Review* 82: 789-804.
———. 1996. Culture as a foundation concept for the social sciences. *Journal of Theoretical Politics* 8: 471-497.
Elkins, D., and R. E. B. Simeon. 1979. A cause in search of its effect, or what does political culture explain? *Comparative Politics* 11: 127-145.
Inglehart, R. 1977. *The silent revolution: Changing values and political styles.* Princeton, NJ: Princeton University Press.
———. 1988. The renaissance of political culture. *American Political Science Review* 82: 1203-1230.
———. 1997. *Modernization and postmodernization: Cultural, economic and political change in 43 societies.* Princeton, NJ: Princeton University Press.
Kaplan, A. 1964. *The conduct of inquiry: Methodology for behavioral science.* San Francisco: Chandler.
Lane, R. 1992. Political culture: Residual category or general theory? *Comparative Political Studies* 25: 362-387.
LaPalombara, J. 1964. *Interest groups in Italian politics.* Princeton, NJ: Princeton University Press.
Lichbach, M., and A. Zuckerman, eds. 1997. *Comparative Politics: Rationality, Culture, and Structure.* New York: Cambridge University Press.
Limerick, P. N. 1997. The startling ability of culture to bring critical inquiry to a halt. *Chronicle of Higher Education* (October 24): A76.
Lipset, S. M. 1963. *The first new nation: The United States in historical and comparative perspective.* New York: Basic.
———. 1990. *Continental divide: Values and institutions of the United States and Canada.* New York: Routledge.
———. 1991. American exceptionalism reaffirmed. In *Is America different? A new look at American exceptionalism,* edited by B. E. Shafer. Oxford: Oxford University Press.
———. 1996. *American exceptionalism: A double-edged sword.* New York: Norton.
Political Psychology. 1995. 16 (1): 1-198.
Putnam, R., with R. Leonardi, and R. Y. Nanetti. 1988. Institutional performance and political culture: Some puzzles about the power of the past. *Governance: An International Journal of Policy and Administration* 1: 221-242.
———. 1993. *Making democracy work: Civic traditions in modern Italy.* Princeton, NJ: Princeton University Press.
Pye, L., and S. Verba, eds. 1965. *Political culture and political development.* Princeton, NJ: Princeton University Press.
Ross, M. H. 1997. Culture and identity in comparative political analysis. In *Comparative politics: Rationality, culture, and structure,* edited by M. Lichbach and A. Zuckerman. New York: Cambridge University Press.
Thompson, M., R. Ellis, and A. Wildavsky. 1990. *Cultural theory.* Boulder, CO: Westview.

Verba, S. 1965. Comparative political culture. In *Political culture and political development,* edited by L. Pye and S. Verba. Princeton, NJ: Princeton University Press.

Verba, S., S. Kelman, G. Orren, I. Miyake, J. Watanuki, I. Kabashima and G. D. Ferree, Jr. 1987. *Elites and the idea of equality: A comparison of Japan, Sweden, and the United States.* Cambridge, MA: Harvard University Press.

Verba, S., N. Nie, and J. Kim. 1978. *Participation and political equality: A seven nation comparison.* New York: Cambridge University Press.

Weiner, M. 1967. *Party building in a new nation: The Indian National Congress.* Chicago: University of Chicago Press.

CHAPTER 1

The Study of Political Culture

Gabriel A. Almond

Originally published in A Discipline Divided: Schools and Sects in Political Science, *1990.*

READING INTRODUCTION

Gabriel Almond, the "dean" of contemporary political culture theory, begins by showing that culture—people's cognitions, values, and affective commitments—has been central to important explanations of social life for over two thousand years. Moreover, he argues, the terribly destructive "irrational" events of twentieth century (in particular, World Wars I and II and the Holocaust) have underscored the importance of culture, in contrast to rationality, for explaining social life. Indeed, the efficacy of culture in this regard was bolstered at mid-century with developments in measurement theory, social survey techniques, and statistical analysis. Almond explores the origins of contemporary political culture theory, dismissing its critics perhaps too quickly. But his survey of contemporary political culture theory is sure-handed and optimistic about the centrality of future applications to the development of social science.

READING TEXT

The Prehistory of Political Culture Theory

The effort to explain politics and public policy by political culture theory goes back to the very origins of political science. The Greek and Roman historians, poets, and dramatists comment on the ways in war and peace of the Spartans, Athenians, Corinthians, Parthians, Caledonians, Judeans, and the like. The concepts and categories we use in the analysis of political culture—subculture, elite political culture, political socialization, and culture change—are also implied in ancient and classical writings. The great families and tribes of Athens and Rome had their founder deities, their sacred fires, their traditions, and their civic-political propensities. In the ancient kingdom of Israel at least four elite political cultures were in conflict: the relatively cosmopolitan royal court engaged in war and diplomacy, pitted against the prophets and their supporters affirming and perfecting the Sinaitic revelations and covenant; and the Jerusalem priesthood and temple officialdom pitted against the surviving local cult leaders of the "high places."

The notion of political culture change is one of the most powerful themes of classical literature. Each Greek city-state had its memory of an austere Solonic or Lycurgan past by which to measure the corrupt present. The Catos were celebrators of the frugal, martial, and civic virtues of the early Roman republic. The Greeks had a cyclical theory of political change, and explained the rise and fall of political constitutions in social psychological terms.

Plato (n.d.), in *The Republic,* argues that "governments vary as the dispositions of men vary, and that there must be as many of the one as there are of the other. For we cannot suppose that States are made of 'oak and rock' and not out of the human natures which are in them" (445). There is no stronger argument for the importance of the process of political socialization than Plato's: "Of all animals the boy is the most unmanageable, inasmuch as he has the fountain of reason in him not yet regulated; he is the most insidious, sharp witted, and insubordinate of animals. Wherefore he must be bound by many bridles." Mothers and nurses, fathers, tutors, and political officials all have the obligation to guide and coerce the incorrigible animal into the path of civic virtue.

Aristotle is a more modern and scientific political culturalist than Plato, since he not only imputes importance to political cultural variables, but explicitly treats their relationship to social stratification variables on the one hand and to political structural and performance variables on the other. He argues that the best attainable form of government is the mixed aristocratic-democratic form in a society in which the middle classes predominate. He says:

> The middle amount of all the good things of fortune is the best amount to possess. For this degree of wealth is the readiest to obey reason. . . . And the middle class are the least inclined to shun office and to covet office, and both of these tendencies are injurious to states. . . . those who have an excess of fortune's goods, strength, wealth, friends, and the like, are not willing to be governed. . . . they have acquired this quality even in their boyhood from their homelife, which was so luxurious that they have not gotten used to submitting to authority even in schools, while those who are excessively in need of these things are too humble.

A society in which the middle class is small produces a state "consisting of slaves and masters, not of free men, and of one class envious and another contemptuous of their fellows. This condition is very far removed from friendliness, and from political partnership," which Aristotle believed to be the cultural basis of the best and most lasting form of government (Aristotle 1932, 329-331).

Plutarch (n.d.), in his biography of Lycurgus, reports how the Spartan lawmaker proposed the engineering of the Spartan character from the moment of birth, so to speak, counseling the women to bathe their newborn sons in wine rather than in water, in order to temper their bodies. The nurses of Sparta used "no swaddling bands; the children grew up free and unconstrained in limb and form, and not dainty or fanciful about their food; not afraid in the dark, or of being left alone; and without peevishness, or illhumour, or crying" (62).

Machiavelli, Montesquieu, and Rousseau, among others of the later political theorists, contribute to the political culture tradition. Machiavelli and Montesquieu draw lessons from Roman history on the importance of moral and religious values and upbringing for the formation of the Roman character, which in turn explained the steadfast course and remarkable performance in war and in peace of the Republic. With expansion and riches, and the admixture of other cultural strains, came the debasement and collapse of this great empire. But both of these scholars, while emphasizing political cultural and socialization themes, tended to treat them anecdotally and illustratively rather than analytically, as did Plato and Aristotle.

The terms that Rousseau (n.d.) used to identify political culture are *morality, custom,* and *opinion*. He treats these as a kind of law more important than law properly speaking, a kind of law that is

> engraved on the hearts of the citizens. This forms the real constitution of the State, takes on every day new powers, when other laws decay or die out . . . keeps a people in the ways it was meant to go and insensibly replaces authority by the force of habit. I am speaking of morality, of custom, above all of public opinion. (41)

Tocqueville's analysis of American democracy and of the origins of the French Revolution are among the most sophisticated treatments of these themes. In *Democracy in America* (1945) he points out:

> The manners of the people may be considered as one of the great general causes to which the maintenance of a democratic republic in the United States is attributable. I here use the word customs with the meaning which the ancients attached to the word *mores* for I apply it not only to manners properly so called—that is, to what might be termed the habits of the heart—but to the various notions and opinions current among men and the mass of those ideas which constitute their character of mind. I comprise under this term, therefore, the whole moral and intellectual condition of a people. (299)

Tocqueville had a similarly keen sense of political subculture. His analysis of the political attitudes of the French peasantry, bourgeoisie, and aristocracy on the eve of the revolution is a similar masterpiece of political culture analysis (see Tocqueville 1955).

The Enlightenment, Liberalism, and Marxism

If the notion of political culture has in some sense always been with us, how do we explain its sudden popularity in the 1960s and the proliferation of research dealing with it in recent decades? We suggest that the failure of enlightenment and liberal expectations as they related to political development and political culture set the explanatory problem to which political culture research was a response, and the development of social theory in the nineteenth and twentieth centuries, and of social science methodology after World War II (particularly survey methodology), provided the opportunity for solving this problem. The intellectual challenge plus the theoretical developments and methodological inventions explain the emergence of this field of inquiry in its modern form.

By the second half of the nineteenth century these beliefs in intellectual, material, and moral progress, stimulated by the Industrial Revolution, strengthened by the success of political and social reforms in Britain and by the American example, and fortified by the development of evolutionary ideas in biology, took on a sense of inevitability. For liberalism the study of political culture was pointless since all the indicators pointed to the rise of educated, civically oriented, participant societies. Political culture was not problematic. Similarly, for Marxism political culture was not problematic. Marx was surely in the tradition of the enlightenment, save that he arranged the theoretical variables differently and viewed the historical process in dialectic rather than incremental terms. Instead of intellectual improvement pressing forward material and political-moral progress in a benign sequence, material improvement produces three political subcultures: an exploitative and ever concentrating capitalist class; an exploited, propagandized, and coerced working class; and an enlightened organization of revolutionaries. The end result is a universal enlightenment culture and society of mass welfare, rationality, and creativity.

There was, of course, a skeptical and cynical school—Mosca, Pareto, Michels, and others—that attacked both the Marxist and liberal varieties of enlightenment expectations, picturing in their stead a future of permanent elitist exploitation and authoritarian rule based on a different set of psychological and sociological premises. While in England and the United States the more sanguine enlightenment view predominated, there were scholars and publicists such as Graham Wallas (1921) and Walter Lippman (1922) who also challenged the easy assumption of growing mass rationality. But in the decades from the mid-nineteenth century until World War I the processes of enlightenment seemed to be going forward, and the concern with cultural patterns seemed to be in abeyance.

The Rise of Modern Political Culture Research

The enormity and irrationality of World War I, the rise of fascism, more particularly the rise of Nazism, and the climactic destructiveness of World War II thoroughly shattered these complacent expectations. The effort to find an intellectual solution to these tragic historical puzzles—both the theories and the methods—came primarily out of American social science in the first decades after World War II. In the aftermath of the war, social science was primarily an American enterprise. It had been enriched by German and Italian scholarly refugees who brought with them their sociological, social psychological, and psychoanthropological traditions. We ought not to forget this strong European and particularly German influence on political culture research.

There were three intellectual components that led into political culture research: the sociological tradition of Weber, Durkheim, Mannheim, Parsons, and others; the social psychological tradition of Graham Wallas, Walter Lippman, William McDougall, E. L. Thorndike, Paul Lazarsfeld, and others; and the psychoanthropological tradition stemming originally from Freud and including Theodore Adorno, Max Horkheimer, Else Fraenkel-Brunswik, Nevitt Sanford, Ruth Benedict, Margaret Mead, Harold Lasswell, Alex Inkeles, Daniel Levinson, and many others.

But most important in the rise of modern political culture research was the development of survey research methodology and technology. As is often the case in the history of science, progress is stimulated more by the development of new technical and empirical capabilities than by substantive theories and hypotheses. Theories remain speculations unless there are rigorous methods of validating them. The revolution in survey research technology had four main components: (1) the development of increasingly precise sampling methods, making it feasible to gather representative data on large populations; (2) the increasing sophistication of interviewing methods to assure greater reliability in the data derived by these methods; (3) the development of scoring and scaling techniques, making it possible to sort out and organize responses in homogeneous dimensions and relate them to theoretical variables; and (4) the increasing sophistication of methods of statistical analysis and inference, moving from simple descriptive statistics to bivariate, multivariate, regression, and causal path analysis of the relations among contextual, attitudinal, and behavioral variables. The invention of survey research technology may be compared to the invention of the microscope, making possible a strongly increased and accurate resolution of biological data in the one, and of social, psychological, and political data in the other.

Three decades after these early developments it is clear that political culture has found its way into the conceptual vocabulary of political science. It is part of the explanatory strategy of political science. It is the occasion for a persisting polemic in the discipline—not as prolific as the pluralism polemic, but quite respectable in the quantitative sense. There are perhaps some 35 or 40 book-length treatments of political culture of an empirical and theoretical sort, perhaps 100 article-length treatments in journals and symposia, and more than 1,000 citations in the literature.

A respectable part of the talent of the profession has been involved in these polemics, including Samuel Beer, Samuel Barnes, Brian Barry, Archie Brown, Dirk Berg-Schlosser, Harry Eckstein, Richard Fagen, Ronald Inglehart, Max Kaase, Dennis Kavanagh, Joseph LaPalombara, Robert Lane, S. M. Lipset, Herbert McCloskey, Carole Pateman, Robert Putnam, Lucian Pye, Irwin Scheuch, Robert Tucker, Aaron Wildavsky, and Stephen White. The broad theme that runs through this literature is the importance of values, feelings, and beliefs in the explanation of political behavior. Political values, feelings, and beliefs are not the simple reflections of social and political structure; nor are they reducible to rational choice individualism. The political content of the minds of citizens and political elites is more complex, more persistent, and autonomous than Marxism, liberalism, and rational choice theory would suggest.

The first social science response to the "German problem" was a psychocultural one. The phenomena of German politics seemed to invite the sciences of the irrational and the nonrational to join forces in efforts to explain them. There is a shelf full of books and journal articles interpreting National Socialism and the "German problem" in psychocultural terms. Psychocultural theory interprets German politics (and Japanese, American, Russian, French, and British politics) in terms of family structure and childhood socialization. It was the German patriarchal authoritarian family that explained the mix of servile obedience and externalized hostility that produced German nationalism, ethnocentrism, and anti-Semitism. There was little room in this psychocultural interpretation of German politics for adult experience, for the impact of history, and for autonomous cognitive processes.

In this extreme form the psychocultural approach was soon discredited and rejected. We do not read Schaffner's *Fatherland* (1948) and Rodnick's *Post-War Germans* (1948) anymore. But its stress on the importance of subjective factors in political explanation survives in two research "programs"—leadership studies that continue to emphasize personality factors, and political culture research that is concerned with group propensities and that is based to a substantial extent, though not entirely, on survey research.

Political culture theory defines political culture in this fourfold way: (1) It consists of the set of subjective orientations to politics in a national population or subset of a national population. (2) It has cognitive, affective, and evaluative components; it includes knowledge and beliefs about political reality, feelings with respect to politics, and commitments to political values. (3) The content of political culture is the result of childhood socialization, education, media exposure, and adult experiences with governmental, social, and economic performance. (4) Political culture affects political and governmental structure and performance—constrains it, but surely does not determine it. The causal arrows between culture and structure and performance go both ways.

Critiques of Political Culture Theory

Political culture theory has been attacked from some four different perspectives. One line of argument, advanced by Brian Barry (1970), and Carole Pateman (1980), attributes to political theory a determinist thrust, assuming that political socialization produces political attitudes, which in turn cause political behavior and underlie political structure. Barry and Pateman make the case that causality can and does work the other way—that institutions and performance influence attitudes. The early advocates of political culture explanation also recognized that causality worked both ways, that attitudes influenced structure and behavior, and that structure and performance in turn influenced attitudes. This was essentially a straw-man polemic.

The Marxist critique, reflected in the work of Jerzy Wiatr (1980) and others, holds that attitude change results from economic and social structural change; in other words, the causal logic works from class structure to political attitudes, political behavior, and structure. Political attitudes have a structurally necessary content, and hence have little independent or autonomous explanatory power. This argument is no longer seriously advanced by contemporary Marxists, who have discovered in recent decades that politics and the state have a degree of autonomy, and that ethnicity, nationality, and religion do not easily give way to resocialization.

A third line of criticism, stemming mainly from students of communism—Richard Fagen (1969), Robert Tucker (1973), Stephen White (1979, 1984), and others—suggests that it is inadmissible to separate political attitudes from behavior. To restrict the concept of political culture to its psychological aspect amounts to a radical "subjectification" of the phenomenon. Such a separation gives a conservative propensity to political culture theory. It understates the malleability of attitudes in response to structural change. In contrast to the first and second arguments, this point of view preserves the political culture concept, but modifies its content to include behavior. What is overlooked in this critique is the fact that separating the psychological dimension from the behavioral one enables us to ascertain what these relationships really are. Failure to separate them prevents us from exploring the complexities of the relation between political thought and political action.

A fourth line of criticism was advanced by the rational choice or "methodological individualist" school of thought. Ronald Rogowski (1974) and Samuel Popkin (1979) argue that political structure and behavior can be explained by the short-run material interest calculations of political actors. In some versions of this theoretical approach there is no place for values, norms, feelings, and more complex cognitive components. History, memory, and cultural context have no explanatory power. A simple plugging in of rational choice in any political situation gives one all the explanatory power one needs. Others in this school employ the rational choice assumption simply as a heuristic device, as a way of deriving hypotheses systematically and cumulatively, and recognize the explanatory power of cultural and sociological variables.

Persistence and Change in Political Culture

The literature of contemporary political culture scholarship is focused on the experience of three regions: (1) the political culture of advanced industrial societies; (2) the role of political culture in the development of communist societies; and (3) the role of political, economic, and religious culture in the modernization of Asian countries. The first theme really consists of two parts: (a) a literature dealing with findings related to *The Civic Culture* (Almond and Verba 1963), and a literature dealing with the theme of changing political culture in advanced industrial societies associated primarily with the work of Ronald Inglehart and Samuel Barnes.

Since the publication of *The Civic Culture* in 1963 there have been a substantial number of follow-up studies of political attitudes in the United States, Britain, West Germany, and Italy. Indeed, there have been more than two decades of surveys. Some of these data are included in *The Civic Culture Revisited* (Almond and Verba 1980). From these and other sources we can get some kind of impression of how stable political culture is, and of the factors that may transform it.

Recent studies of American political culture—including Lipset and Schneider's *The Confidence Gap* (1983), based on several hundred opinion surveys conducted in the United States since the 1940s—show a serious decline in trust and confidence in American political, economic, and social leadership and institutions. The high confidence and legitimacy reported in *The Civic Culture* seem to have been replaced by skepticism as to the effectiveness and integrity of American political, military, economic, and other leaderships. While none of this evidence supports a crisis of legitimacy, surely the United States in the 1980s no longer has the confident civic culture of the early 1960s. And, suggesting how volatile these indicators of trust are, after several years of the Reagan administration, a follow-up study (Lipset and Schneider 1985) showed that economic improvement and better leadership morale had reduced this alienation and distrust significantly.

As far as Britain is concerned, Dennis Kavanagh (1980), in *The Civic Culture Revisited,* speaks of a "decline in the deferential and supportive elements" in British political culture in the period from 1960 to 1980. But he points out that there is more dissatisfaction with performance than with the system as a whole. He says that "recent years of slow economic growth have led to greater social tensions, group rivalries, and growing dissatisfaction with incumbent authorities" and that "traditional bonds of social class, party, and common nationality are waning, and with them the old restraints of hierarchy and deference" (170).

Kendall Baker, Russell Dalton, and Kai Hildebrandt (1981), in their analysis of German survey data from the 1950s through the 1970s, document a thorough transformation of German political culture from the apolitical passive pattern pictured in *The Civic Culture,* to the prodemocratic, politicized, and participation-oriented culture of the 1970s and 1980s. Thus the declining civic culture in the United States and Britain and the emerging civic culture in West Germany show political culture to be a relatively soft variable, significantly influenced by historical experience and by governmental and political structure and performance. The trauma of National Socialism, a cunningly engineered governmental and political structure, and an effective economy seem to have produced a stable democracy in Germany. On the other hand, the Vietnam War, the counterculture, and Watergate have seriously undermined the civic culture in the United States; poor economic performance and declining international prestige have also reduced the legitimacy of British political institutions.

The plasticity of political culture in the advanced industrial societies is also suggested by the empirical studies of Ronald Inglehart (1975, 1989), Samuel Barnes and Max Kitase (1979), and their collaborators. Inglehart demonstrates, from a set of surveys he administered in Europe and the United States over a period of more than a decade in the 1970s and early 1980s, that generational changes in the advanced industrial democracies have transformed the policy or issue cultures of these democracies, and that these new issues have begun to modify their party systems. In its first version, Inglehart's theory held that the generations born in Europe and the United States in the post–World War II period up to the mid-1970s had experienced continued peace, rapid economic growth, rising educational opportunities, and increased media exposure. This political socialization tended to downplay the salience of the older issues of economic, political, and military security that had influenced the attitudes of previous generations, and gave salience to a new set of participatory, quality-of-life, and environmental issues. Later, Inglehart's and other surveys during the "stagflation" years of the later 1970s and early 1980s reported a return of economic anxiety, but the newer quality-of-life attitudes survived as well. Barnes and Kaase (1979), in their five-country study of attitudes toward political action, pursuing Inglehart's lead, demonstrate that this new political culture of advanced industrial societies also includes changes in attitudes toward political action—the readiness to resort to unconventional modes of political participation such as demonstrations, marches, sit-ins, and the like, in addition to the conventional modes of political participation. Thus a combination of historical experience and changed political socialization patterns—generational and period effects—have significantly altered the political culture of the advanced democracies.

In his most recent book, Inglehart (1989) draws a balance between continuity and change in the development of European values and attitudes, based on a longitudinal series of surveys extending over more than 15 years:

> Surveys carried out repeatedly over many years show enduring crossnational differences in levels of overall life satisfaction, happiness, political satisfaction, interpersonal trust, and support for the existing social order. These attributes are part of a coherent syndrome, with given nationalities consistently ranking relatively high (or relatively low) on all of them. High or low scores on this syndrome have important consequences for the political and social behavior of given peoples, shaping the prospects for viable democracy, among other things. As we have seen, large cross-cultural differences in this syndrome of attitudes persisted throughout the period from 1973 through 1988; and fragmentary additional evidence suggests that these differences can be traced back into the 1950s. (1)

Inglehart then goes on to point out that there have also been remarkable changes in European attitudes. Thus attitudes in Italy show less distrust than has been true of the past. And he points to the remarkable changes in German political attitudes in the last two decades, associated with rising standards of living and good governmental performance.

If these recent studies of political culture in Europe and the United States suggest that it can change relatively quickly in response to changed circumstances and experience, studies of political attitudes in communist countries suggest the persistence of certain aspects of political culture in the face of very powerful transformative efforts (see, e.g., Almond 1983; Brown 1984; Brown and Gray 1977; White 1979, 1984). Unfortunately, there is little good survey research available on the political culture of the communist countries, but there is some; and there are other kinds of data from which students of communist countries are able to draw inferences. This literature argues that despite the systematic efforts of communist movements to penetrate, manipulate, organize, indoctrinate, and coerce over a period of several decades, nothing like "socialist man" has emerged. Nationalist feelings have survived in substantial strength, cultural and religious identities persist with great vitality. In countries like Czechoslovakia, which at an earlier time had democratic traditions, these traditions seem to persist, ready to pop out, whenever history makes this possible. In Poland there may very well be stronger liberal currents today than existed in the years of its independence. The communist experience with political culture approximates a set of "crucial case studies" in Eckstein's (1975) sense. If a monopoly control of the media of communication, a monopoly or near monopoly of organization, penetrative police controls, and the like cannot transform values and attitudes, then some explanatory power must be assigned to political culture and the socialization processes that maintain it.

A third set of historical developments—the extraordinary rate of economic growth of the East Asian Confucian countries in contrast with other Asian countries influenced by Islam and Hinduism—also suggests the importance of culture in the shaping of economic and political behavior. Hofheinz and Calder (1982) make the argument that the emphasis on loyalty, education, mutuality, and respect for authority in these areas rests on the norms of Confucianism. Spengler (1980) attributes a market-oriented entrepreneurialism in Japan to Confucian social thought. Bellah (1957) argues that the religious values of the Tokugawa period affected the economic takeoff of the Meiji restoration era. Winston Davis (1987) summarizes some of this literature, offering a modified version of Weber's theory of the relation between the economic ethics of religions and economic growth. Rather than viewing religious ethics as necessary conditions of economic growth, Davis argues that they may influence economic growth, either by facilitating or tolerating it or by obstructing the development of attitudes and values conducive to economic discipline and performance. The questions we ought to ask, according to Davis, are not of the either/or sort; rather, we should ask, "Has religion motivated economic change? Has it tolerated change? Has it promoted a quiescent acceptance of the social costs imposed by development?" (226). Davis makes a qualified case for the contribution of Confucianism to the strong economic growth propensities of the East Asian countries.

Lucian Pye (1985), in a wide-ranging and imaginative study of culture and politics in Asia, shows how Confucianism, Hinduism, and Islam contribute, though in different ways, to paternalistic, "familistic," consensual, and clientelistic political patterns throughout East, Southeast, and South Asia. He argues that the Asian area may have its own patterns of modernization, that education and economic growth need not necessarily lead to democratization, or, if they do, then it might have these paternalistic, consensual, and clientelistic propensities.

The unanticipated reversal of modernization and the emergence of populistic Islamic fundamentalism in Iran and elsewhere in the Middle East similarly argues the strength of traditional political culture and socialization variables.

The Present State of Political Culture Theory

The historical record at first glance would seem to be ambiguous. Political culture on the one hand can change relatively quickly; on the other hand it would seem to be able to take quite a pounding without changing very much. What can we learn from these historical experiences, and from the research that has accumulated in the last several decades, about two of the fundamental questions raised by political culture theory: first, the stability of political culture, its persistence and autonomy, and hence its explanatory significance in political explanation; and second, the relative importance of the factors affecting political culture, in particular the relative importance of early childhood, adult workplace, community, and media experience, and direct experience of political and governmental performance?

On the stability or persistence of political culture, the data we now have suggest that political moods, such as trust in political incumbents and confidence in political and social institutions, seem to be quite changeable, varying with the effectiveness of the performance of these leaders, officers, and agencies. Basic political beliefs and political values are more resistant, though still subject to change. Thus in the United States and Britain in the 1960s and 1970s trust in leaders and confidence in political, economic, and social elites declined sharply. But the evidence did not show any serious attrition in the basic legitimacy of American and British political and social institutions, despite the poor economic and governmental performance experienced in both countries.

The transformation of basic German political attitudes seems to have been accomplished as a consequence of three major causes: (1) the most powerful historical experiences affecting people directly (military collapse, bombing, occupation, partition, forced migration, international humiliation); (2) imaginative constitutional engineering (an electoral system biased in favor of the larger political parties, the constructive vote of nonconfidence, federalism); and (3) a remarkable political and policy performance producing a "miracle" of reconstruction and growth. It is impossible to separate out and assign a specific weight to the role played by changes in basic cultural patterns produced by changes in family structure, childhood socialization, and adult resocialization. All that we can say is that these factors together have produced a changed political culture in West Germany, characterized by democratic and regime legitimacy and a participant political culture.

In the United States the decline of trust and confidence and of consensual politics seems also to have been overdetermined by a costly and demoralizing defeat in the decade-long Vietnam War, by racial conflict on a major scale, by major changes in American social and cultural norms brought about in part by the "counterculture," and by the demoralizing scandals of the Nixon administration. But these powerful impacts have not significantly undermined the legitimacy of American institutions—governmental, political, and economic.

Thus our evidence shows that basic political beliefs such as regime legitimacy have considerable stability. Only catastrophes seem to be able to affect these attitudes in short periods of time; otherwise the rate of change is relatively slow.

Finally, most resistant to change are attitudes, identities, and value commitments associated with ethnicity, nationality, and religion. These are primordial values and commitments that seem to be almost indestructible. It is these primordial values and commitments, and the socialization processes that maintain them, that explain the failure of the Soviet Russian and communist efforts to transform the political cultures of the Eastern European countries, and even in Russia, particularly outside the Great Russian area. But the resistance of political cultures in Eastern Europe is not limited to national, ethnolinguistic, and religious identities. It is argued that in Czechoslovakia liberal political attitudes persist in even greater strength than in the precommunist period; and in Poland it seems that liberal political attitudes are now widespread where there were none before. Political learning cannot be reduced to simple reactivity.

The theory of political socialization has made some progress in the last decades. Generally speaking, there is evidence that family authority has changed in a participatory direction. It is difficult to determine how much of an independent contribution such changes as these may have made to the democratization of political culture in industrial societies, since so many other influences were operative in the same direction during those decades. The evidence also shows that increasing educational levels in advanced industrial societies have raised the proportion of politically efficacious citizens, and transformed the political cultures of advanced industrial societies in a participatory direction (Hyman 1975).

One of the most significant changes in the political socialization process is the emergence of the electronic media, particularly television. Studies of voting behavior in the United States in the late 1940s and 1950s produced the "two-step flow of communications" theory of Katz and Lazarsfeld (1955). This theory held that the impact of the mass media on attitudes and behavior was mediated by opinion elites—trusted individuals, clergymen, teachers, older family members, and the like. The messages transmitted by the media were interpreted by these opinion leaders, and it was presumed that ordinary people were protected from mass manipulation.

Television has weakened the hold of opinion leaders and has accentuated the importance of the mass media in the shaping of values and attitudes. The greater access that television has to the senses and the rise of influential television commentators and interpreters, according to Austin Ranney (1983), have eroded the importance of the intimate, face-to-face opinion leader, with important consequences for family, community, interest group, and political party cohesion. Sidney Verba and his collaborators (1988), in their recent study of attitudes of elites in the United States, Sweden, and Japan, demonstrate that in all three of these countries the various leading groups of politicians, bureaucrats, business leaders, labor leaders, and the like describe the media as being at the very highest level of political influence. In Verba and Orren's (1985) earlier study of elite attitudes in America, the media were viewed by other elites not only as influential, but as *too* influential. Thus the changing character of the media seems to have changed the relationship between political elites and publics in advanced industrial societies. The amount of discretion accorded to leaders has been reduced; political styles and skills have been transformed.

It is also apparent from German and French political experience that constitutional and political-structural engineering may have significant effects on political culture. German constitutional arrangements have ensured that Bonn was not a repeat of Weimar. Surely German political stability over more than three decades, which is in substantial part attributable to constitutional arrangements, has made an important contribution to the legitimacy of the German system. Similarly, the French experiments with mixed "presidential-parliamentary government" and its electoral system have made an important contribution to the stability and effectiveness of the Fifth Republic, and have reduced French political cynicism and alienation.

Thus the political culture theory that survives today is not the familistic, childhood, and "unconscious"-dominated set of ideas of the 1940s, but rather a theory that emphasizes the cognitive-level attitudes and expectations influenced by the structure and performance of the political system and the economy. But if much of it is fluid and plastic, there are persistent and stable components, such as basic political beliefs and value commitments, and primordial attachments that affect and constrain our political behavior and our public policy.

A System, Process, and Policy Approach to Political Culture

There have been a number of polemics about the content of political culture. What are its components, and how do they relate one to the other? The Fagen-Tucker-White thesis would move us away from conceptual disaggregation, toward a more inclusive concept. Lowell Dittmer (1977) attacks the prevailing definition of political culture as the "subjective perception of an objective political reality" as a blurred conception not distinguished from "political structure on the one hand and political psychology on the other" (581). He proposes a sharper focus for the definition of political culture within the framework of a semiological systems approach. But he acknowledges that the theoretical superiority of such an approach has still to be demonstrated.

In my work with G. Bingham Powell, we have argued that if political culture is the subjective dimension of the political system, then it must be a divisible set of orientations toward the various structures and aspects of the political system (Almond and Powell 1978). Members of the political system have knowledge of these various parts and structures; they have feelings toward them, and they judge or evaluate them according to various norms. Thus from the separation of the political system into the three levels of system, process, and policy, it follows that every political system has a system, process, and policy culture. System culture consists of knowledge, feelings, and evaluations vis-a-vis the political authorities, the role incumbents; knowledge, feelings, and evaluations toward the regime, that is, the institutional structure; and knowledge, feelings, and evaluations toward the nation. Thus when we talk about the legitimacy of a political system we have to specify whether we are talking about the leaders and the officialdom, the regime, the nation, or some combination of these.

Process culture consists of the knowledge, feelings, and evaluations members of the political system have toward the self as political actor, and toward other political actors, including other political groupings such as parties and interest groups, and specific political and governmental elites. Policy culture consists of the knowledge, feelings, and evaluations members of the political system have toward the outputs of the system—its internal policies (extractive, regulative, and distributive) and its external policies (military, diplomatic, economic).

Disaggregating political culture in these systemic terms enables us to explore the logical or interactive structure of political culture. It may lead us to remedy some of the conceptual shortcomings spelled out by Lowell Dittmer, on the one hand, and at the same time to avoid some of the turgidity of semiology, on the other. It is clear that these three levels of political culture are closely related. At one relatively simpleminded level, it is clear that dissatisfaction with policy outputs is likely to lead to dissatisfaction with the political authorities responsible for those outputs. Dissatisfaction with the political process is likely to lead to dissatisfaction with the regime. Sustained dissatisfaction with policy outputs may, in some kinds of political systems, lead to a change in the political authorities, just as sustained dissatisfaction with the political process may lead to regime or structural change. Deteriorating performance either at the process or the policy level in countries that include separate ethnic components, may over time lead to a decline in national legitimacy and the rise of autonomy and secessionist movements as in Great Britain, Canada, Spain, and other countries in recent years.

On the other hand, satisfactory and responsive policy and process performance may over time increase the legitimacy of political authorities, of regimes, and of nations. There is something like a process of capital accumulation and depletion in this interaction between process and policy performance and system legitimacy.

Treating political culture in terms of these three levels illuminates some aspects of political strategy. Threats to a regime by virtue of process dissatisfaction may be dealt with directly, as was the case in the process of democratization in Britain in the nineteenth century. The bargaining process turned not on the either/or question of universal suffrage, but rather on limited enfranchisements, step by step, that were responsive to the most mobilized sections of the population. The Bismarck strategy in Germany bought off popular demands for full enfranchisement on the part of the middle and working classes by shrewd policy inducements—welfare policy for the working class, trade policy for the industrialists and large landowners, and an aggressive foreign policy for everyone. This Bismarckian strategy of using distributive policy as a way of mitigating and containing demands for participation has been followed in a number of contemporary Third World countries—in particular South Korea and Taiwan.

A systemic approach to political culture research, along such lines as these, has the virtue of keeping it firmly grounded in the structure and performance of the political system. It lends itself to formal, logical analysis, and generates interesting hypotheses on important aspects of politics.

References

Almond, G. A. 1983. Communism and political culture theory. *Comparative Politics* 13 (January).
Almond, G. A., and G. B. Powell. 1978. *Comparative politics: System, process, policy.* Boston: Little, Brown.
Almond, G. A., and S. Verba, eds. 1963. *The civic culture.* Princeton, NJ: Princeton University Press.
———. 1980 *The civic culture revisited.* Boston: Little, Brown.
Aristotle. 1932. *Politics,* translated by H. Rackhani. London: Heineman.
Baker, K., R. Dalton, and K. Hildebrandt. 1981. *Germany transformed.* Cambridge, MA: Harvard University Press.
Barnes, S., and M. Kaasc. 1979. *Political action: Mass participation in five western democracies.* Beverly Hills, CA: Sage.
Barry, B. 1970. *Sociologists, economists and democracy.* London: Macmillan.
Bellah, R.N. 1957. *Tokugawa religion.* Boston: Beacon.
Brown, A., ed. 1984. *Political culture and communist studies.* New York: M. E. Sharpe.
Brown, A., and J. Gray, eds. 1977. *Political culture and political change in communist states.* New York: Holmes & Meier.
Davis, W. 1987. Religion and development: Weber and the East Asian experience. In *Understanding political development,* edited by M. Weiner and S. Huntington. Boston: Little, Brown.
Dittmer, L. 1977. Political culture and political symbolism. *World Politics* 30 (July).
Eckstein, H. 1975. Case studies in political explanation. In Vol. 7 of *Handbook of political science,* edited by F. Greenstein and N. Polsby. Reading, MA: Addison-Wesley.
Fagen, R. 1969. *The transformation of political culture in Cuba.* Stanford, CA: Stanford University Press.
Hofheinz, R., and K. Calder. 1982. *The East-Asian edge.* New York: Basic Books.
Hyman, H. 1975. *The enduring effects of education.* Chicago: University of Chicago Press.
Inglehart, R. 1975. *The silent revolution: Changing values and political style among western publics.* Princeton, NJ: Princeton University Press.
———. 1989. *Changing culture.* Princeton, NJ: Princeton University Press.
Katz, E., and P. Lazarsfeld. 1955. *Personal influence: The part played by people in the flow of mass communication.* Glencoe, IL: Free Press.
Kavanagh, D. 1980. Political culture in Britain: The decline of the civic culture. In *The civic culture revisited,* edited by G. Almond and S. Verba. Boston: Little, Brown.
Lipset, S. M. 1985. The confidence gap: Down but not out. Unpublished manuscript.
Lipset, S. M., and W. Schneider. 1983. *The confidence gap.* New York: Free Press.
Pateman, C. 1980. The civic culture: A philosophical critique. In *The civic culture revisited,* edited by G. Almond and S. Verba. Boston: Little, Brown.
Plato, n.d. *The works of Plato,* translated by Jowett. New York: Dial.
Plutarch, n.d. *The lives of the ancient Greeks and Romans,* translated by J. Dryden. New York: Random House.
Popkin, S. 1979. *The rational peasant.* Berkeley: University of California Press.
Pye, L. W. 1985. *Asian power and politics: The cultural dimensions of authority.* Cambridge, MA: Belknap Press of Harvard University Press.
Ranney, A. 1983. *Channels of power.* New York: Basic Books.
Rodnick, D. 1948. *Post-war Germans.* New Haven, CT.: Yale University Press.
Rogowski, R. 1974. *Rational legitimacy.* Princeton, NJ: Princeton University Press.
Rousseau, J. J. N.d. *The social contract.* New York: Carlton House.
Schaffner, B. 1948. *Fatherland: A study of authoritarianism in the German family.* New York: Columbia University Press.
Spengler, J. 1980. *Origins of economic thought and justice.* Carbondale: Illinois University Press.
Tocqueville, Alexis de. 1945. *Democracy in America.* New York: Knopf.
———. 1955. *The old regime and the French Revolution.* Garden City, NY: Doubleday.
Tucker, R.C. 1973. Culture, political culture, and communist society. *Political Science Quarterly* (June).

Verba, S. 1965. Germany: The remaking of political culture. In *Political culture and political development*, edited by L. Pye and S. Verba. Princeton, NJ: Princeton University Press.
———. 1988. *Elites and the idea of equality*. Cambridge, MA: Harvard University Press.
Verba, S., and G. Orren. 1985. *Equality in America: The view from the top*. Cambridge, MA: Harvard University Press.
Wallas, G. 1921. *Human nature in politics*. New York: Knopf.
White, S. 1979. *Political culture and Soviet politics*. London: Macmillan.
———. 1984. Political culture in communist states. *Comparative Politics* 14 (April).
Wiatr, J. 1980. The civic culture from a Marxist sociological perspective. In *The civic culture revisited*, edited by G. Almond and S. Verba. Boston: Little, Brown.

CHAPTER 2

A Cause in Search of Its Effect, or What Does Political Culture Explain?

David J. Elkins and Richard E. B. Simeon

Originally published in Comparative Politics 11 *(2), 1979.*

READING INTRODUCTION

Elkins and Simeon are less specific than Almond (in chapter 1) and Ross (in chapter 3) about defining political culture. But by way of clarification, they provide us with a series of topics that political cultures routinely address. They are also careful to distinguish between a narrow conception of culture (e.g., certain mental predispositions) and the behaviors or political institutions (what other analysts sometimes call cultural artifacts) that may stem from them. More important, they alert us for the need to be careful in applying political culture theory to the explanation of social phenomena and warn us against unrealistic expectations. In the process, they produce several caveats.

First, they encourage scholars employing culture to specify clearly both what they mean by culture as well as what dependent variables they perceive culture, in this sense, as explaining. Second, they argue that cultural explanation is inherently comparative in nature. That is, culture helps us to explain, for instance, why people with similar education, income, and job status in two different societies hold sharply different beliefs about certain matters. Third, culture and social structure (Elkins and Simeon use "structure" to refer to both demographic patterns and political institutions) exist in a symbiotic relationship. Thus matters that we reasonably consider cultural (e.g., people's beliefs how the world works—that humans are equal in essential respects) help to form and sustain particular political institutions (e.g., liberal democratic adherence to basing political legitimacy on free elections). Yet institutions also socialize the people who work within them as well as succeeding generations of youngsters who grow up accepting them. So institutions foster and support cultures as well. Thus Elkins and Simeon conclude that cultural and structural explanations are both likely to be necessary for explaining any range of social phenomena. Finally, they stress what they call the "passive" character of culture. By this they mean that, while the assumptions they associate with culture predispose people in particular directions, purposive action in these directions does not necessarily follow.

Rather, various sorts of (frequently structural) facilitating conditions may be required for moving from assumptions to action. Elkins and Simeon think that some of the dependent variables to which culture has been applied in the past are too broad and vague to admit to cultural explanation, but—with their caveats in mind—they share Almond's optimism that culture can be helpful in explaining the character of political institutions, including public policies, and thus in contributing to social science.

READING TEXT

Political culture is one of the most popular and seductive concepts in political science; it is also one of the most controversial and confused. The reaction against the concept stems primarily from exaggerated claims made on its behalf. Neither the view which ascribes the operation of a political system to its political culture nor the view that the political culture is irrelevant merits a lengthy discussion. Instead, we offer two separate contributions in this article. We propose a definition of political culture which we believe overcomes certain deficiencies charged to previous definitions. We also outline the logical status of political culture as a component in the explanation of political phenomena. While we prefer to use our definition of the concept in conjunction with our strategy of explanation, the latter stands on its own. Regardless of how the concept of political culture has been defined, there are limits to its explanatory usefulness; clarifying these limits specifies the remaining areas in which the concept should prove valuable. This task requires that we avoid two common failings in political analysis. First, there is the failure to specify clearly and precisely the dependent variable. What is to be explained—by political culture or, indeed, by any other factor? Second, there is the need to avoid the common but disconcerting tendency to shift dependent variables in mid-analysis.

Political Culture: An Overview

Political culture consists of assumptions about the political world.[1] If a person acts on the assumptions which are widely shared in his collectivity, he will "pass" as a legitimate political actor.[2] An "outsider" who holds quite different views on the nature of the political game, on proper modes of conduct, and on goals and strategies will be identifiable as deviant; he will not "pass."

Assumptions about the political world focus attention on certain features of events, institutions, and behavior, define the realm of the possible, identify the problems deemed pertinent, and set the range of alternatives among which members of the population make decisions. Political culture, then, is a shorthand expression for a "mind set" which has the effect of limiting attention to less than the full range of alternative behaviors, problems, and solutions which are logically possible. Since it represents a "disposition" in favor of a range of alternatives, by corollary another range of alternatives receives little or no attention within a particular culture. Most people in any culture, therefore, will take for granted a particular course of action or consider only a few alternatives. That they choose from a restricted set will, for most of them, remain below the threshold of consciousness, because they seldom encounter individuals who take for granted quite different assumptions.

The range of assumptions or unconscious premises coexisting within a culture may be extremely narrow, highly consistent, and strongly interrelated—as might characterize a traditional, relatively isolated tribe. Or, the culture may encompass a very wide range of contrasting views, not necessarily consistent or compatible, perhaps not even interrelated, but rather divided into "water-tight compartments" as may be the case with so-called consociational democracies. However, we do not suggest that culture consists of all the assumptions held by all the members of a group. There is no requirement that everyone share a given belief. For practical purposes, we can ignore assumptions held only by very small proportions of the population. We consider below the special relevance, however, of some minorities, especially elites.

This conception of political culture owes much to recent anthropological writers. In his review of significant theoretical work on culture, Roger Keesing (1974) has shown that a common theme—cultures as "ideational codes"—runs through the literature, a theme found in the work of such diverse scholars as Ward Goodenough, Claude Levi-Strauss, Clifford Geertz, and David Schneider. Drawing also on Chomsky's distinction between linguistic *competence* and *performance,* Keesing sums up the general view of culture as

> shared in its broad design and varying between individuals in its specificities. . . . It is his *theory of what is fellows know, believe and mean,* his theory of the code being followed, the game being played, in the society into which he was born. . . . But note that the actor's "theory" of his culture, like his theory of his language, may be in large measure unconscious. (89)[3]

What "theory" may be found in anyone's head is not, by our conception or by Keesing's, culture. Culture is interpersonal, covering a range of such theories. Not everyone shares the same theory of his culture, and not everyone knows all aspects of his culture: "Thus a cultural description is always an abstracted composite" (Keesing 1974, 89).

Geertz makes a similar point when he writes that "culture is best seen not as complexes of concrete behavior patterns—customs, usages, traditions, habit clusters— . . . but as a set of control mechanisms—plans, recipes, rules, instructions (what computer engineers call 'programs')—for the governing of behavior" (Geertz in Keesing 1974, 87). While a distinction like this is helpful, we emphasize that we restrict culture to a particular type of control mechanism—assumptions or premises. Culture is thus distinct from other types of more explicit control mechanisms.

Several closely related consequences follow from this perspective. It implies a particular unit of analysis. Political culture is the property of a collectivity—nation, region, class, ethnic community, formal organization, party, or whatever. Individuals have beliefs, values, and attitudes but they do not have cultures.

But what kinds of collectivities have cultures? Most of the writing on political culture focuses on national cultures, as when Almond and Verba compare the cultures of five nations. Some studies focus on territorially defined units at the subnational level, such as the political cultures of American states or Canadian provinces (Simeon and Elkins 1974). Less frequently, we find studies of the cultural attributes of other social groupings: the "culture of poverty," "working class culture," "elite political culture," religious subcultures, and the like. We argue that culture may refer to any or all of these. Students of culture who wish to refine its utility as an explanatory concept must develop precise means of identifying the culture-bearing unit in different situations. We propose such a strategy in conjunction with our exposition of the logic of cultural explanation.

If a scholar is interested in culture primarily in a descriptive sense, he may specify *a priori* which collectivity interests him and then proceed to describe the patterns of assumptions within it. But if we use culture as an explanation, we must identify what it is about these collectivities which leads to the distinctive patterns of assumptions. Thus, for nations, we must ask whether their collective experience is important or whether the internation difference stems from the varying proportions of particular groups, each with its own unique experiences. If it is the latter, then our attention should shift to an enquiry about the cultural attributes of the subnational collectivities rather than the national one. Conversely, if our focus were on religious groups, but we found that Catholics in one nation differed strongly in political behavior from Catholics in another, then we would be led to hypothesize the nation as the relevant culture-bearing unit; and it would be national rather than religious cultures to which we would look for explanation. (We oversimplify for expository neatness; it may happen that both national and religious cultures are important.)

Hence, explanations based on national cultures can be persuasive only after we have ruled out some structural and institutional explanations. Structure can refer, among other things, to the different proportions of individuals possessing certain positions or social characteristics: income levels, ethnicity, age, gender, urbanization, and so on.[4] Societies can vary either in the proportions of people found in each category, or in the views held by people within similar categories, or both. If an internation difference disappears when structural proportions are controlled or "partialled out," then we have a structural explanation, not a cultural one, because the difference is accounted for by the relative size of a group in different nations (Rosenberg 1962). National culture is at work only when people in the same social categories, but in different nations, hold different assumptions. When a structural control eliminates the differences, then that control variable identifies a collectivity whose cultural attributes may be important. Whether the researcher is content to label "religion" or "class" or "ethnicity" as the explanation, rather than pursuing this investigation further, is a matter of choice. The distinction between structural and cultural, then, can be seen in either of two ways: as a means of ruling out some cultural explanations, or as a means of identifying which collectivities should be seen as bearers of the culture and hence potential components of a cultural explanation.

There is a useful rule of thumb in such cases: keep your eye on the dependent variable. If we examine a particular phenomenon on which two nations differ, then an explanation which "reduces" that difference to relative proportions of groups in each nation halts the search for further explanations. If we ask further why those nations have such different proportions of these groups, we have shifted to a different dependent variable, and we may hypothesize cultural phenomena as an explanation. At some stage in the analysis of any internation dissimilarity, both of these outcomes are likely to occur. That is, eventually we can reformulate most differences in structural terms, and eventually we will be tempted or forced to explain structural features in cultural terms. In this sense, it may be a matter of semantics whether explanations are called cultural or something else. By keeping clearly in mind the precise dependent variable, however, the primary explanation of that feature will either be structural (i.e., a matter of proportionalities) or not. This gives us a rule for labeling the explanation as cultural or structural; but even if it must be called structural, note that such an explanation identifies a potential culture-bearing unit.

"Structure" may also be used in a second sense, to refer not to the distribution of individuals across social, economic, or demographic categories, but rather to political institutions. Unlike proportionalities, these are collective phenomena, rather than aggregations of individuals. For example, the extent of party competition or the availability of a large number of interest groups may affect citizens' sense of political efficacy: the more competition, for example, the more valuable they feel their votes to be. Here again, if such institutional features account for the intergroup differences, we would not make a claim for the explanatory power of political culture. At the next stage of analysis, however, the presence or absence of certain institutions might be the dependent variable; cultural explanation could prove important in those cases.

One cannot assess the relative importance of structural and cultural explanations within a single collectivity since these are confounded. After the relevant comparisons have demonstrated the importance of cultural factors, however, the fact that assumptions are distributed in particular proportions accounts in cultural terms for certain kinds of political characteristics. Therefore, the question should not be "are cultural explanations possible?" but rather "at what stage of analysis are they most useful?"

Political culture defines the range of acceptable possible alternatives from which groups or individuals may, other circumstances permitting, choose a course of action. Except in the limiting case in which everyone shares precisely the same assumption, culture does not explain the particular choices which individuals make. Its explanatory power is primarily restricted to "setting the agenda" over which political contests occur. Other factors must explain the choice of a particular element of the subset identified in that culture. These supplementary factors include personality, role, self-interest, and so on, at the individual level, or simply the relative power of organized groups at the societal or collective level of analysis.[5]

Since the actual choice an individual or a group makes within the acceptable range of the culture is explained by other factors, many criticisms of political culture lose their force. Likewise, the difficulty of establishing the causal link between political culture and variables it presumably explains, a problem many commentators have noted, is lessened when one can restrict the types of dependent variables and when one can specify more clearly the content of political culture.

In summary, the most significant feature of our approach is its sharp distinction between political culture as a descriptive category and as an explanation. Political culture as descriptive of a collectivity entails only that the group exhibits a given range and distribution of (largely unconscious) assumptions about its political life. Cultural *explanations,* on the other hand, utilize this information in conjunction with structural features to account for *the differences between collectivities* on certain dependent variables. The use of culture for explanation, therefore, must always be comparative.

Political Culture As Assumptions

It would be presumptive to provide a detailed classification of the types of assumptions which constitute political culture. Difficult as it may be to step out of socially engendered outlooks, we nevertheless offer a tentative list of types of assumptions and some examples. We hope thereby to stimulate others to make their own examination of the range of assumptions underlying political life in diverse groups. Some of the types of assumptions which seem likely to provide fruitful grounds for cultural description and comparison include the following:

1. Assumptions about the orderliness of the universe. These will necessarily be very general.
2. Presumptions about the nature of causality. Is the world random? Are events foredestined? Inevitable? Are human agents more or less important than impersonal material causes?
3. What are the principal goals of political life?
4. Should one try to maximize gains, or to minimize losses? In other words, what assumptions are made about the relative payoffs of optimistic or pessimistic strategies?
5. Who belongs to one's political community? Is it a vaguely bounded community, or is it one marked by sharp "we-they" distinctions? Do the boundaries vary with types of situations, or are they more or less unchanging? To whom or to what does one owe any obligation?
6. What types of events, actions, or institutions are deemed political (as opposed to economic, social, etc.), or is a sharp line drawn at all? Is "the political" a positively or negatively valued domain?
7. Assumptions about others—their trustworthiness, public spiritedness, etc.—and about how one should relate to them.

This list should be sufficient to indicate that the content of political culture considered as assumptions which narrow the range of alternative actions that are possible or desirable—diverges radically from the attitudes, affect, and personality traits usually included in most previous definitions (Lane 1962; Putnam 1971).

Some of the assumptions are very general. They involve broad views of the nature of the world and not just of political life. An example of such a fundamental view is whether or not events have systematic causes or whether they are largely fortuitous or accidental. Individuals who assume that any given event has an identifiable set of causes will feel and act quite differently from people who believe that things "just happen" or that humans cannot explain or modify them.

To make an assumption about the causative status of the universe, or at least of human affairs, will surely color one's view of events and limit one's attention to certain aspects to the exclusion of others. A fatalistic outlook, or one posited on the superior knowledge of certain elites, limits one's view of effective political action largely to propitiation of deities or to supplication of leaders.

Similarly, is politics seen as a zero-sum game or as an expandable-sum game? Each of these outlooks has a different implication for one's willingness to seek solutions through compromise with political "enemies." Of course, we do not suggest that a person always views politics in only one way, but we suspect that for most people one view predominates. To the extent that there is agreement on one view, this should affect the kinds of political rhetoric to which a group responds and the kinds of leadership it finds congenial or inspiring. The distribution of zero-sum rather than expandable-sum assumptions should vary widely between collectivities; and these variations should be associated with marked contrasts in how different populations play the game of politics.

The causal status of any assumption is permissive rather than deterministic. By this we mean that persons or groups making the assumption do not automatically engage in a particular action; the final action depends as well on the existence of relevant institutions or leadership. The assumption opens the possibility of action, and it disposes the members of the group sharing it to certain actions more than to others. Mobilization of a group in support of a compromise worked out by political leaders will be made easier if politics, generally, is not a zero-sum game.

A concept such as political efficacy also embodies some basic assumptions. The positive correlation between agreement with statements like "I believe my elected representative pays attention to my opinions" and the degree of political activity depends on the widespread acceptance of several assumptions about political and social life: that participation is available to people like themselves; that it is legitimate or good to participate; and that political participation can, and often does, have an effect on outputs. All these assumptions may be false, but citizens' belief in them is what counts. Finally, feelings of efficacy rest on a generally nonfatalistic view of the world: trying to influence political events leads to in increased likelihood of the desired effect. The contrary views are that one should leave well enough alone to avoid making things worse and that things happen no matter what one does.

Note again the permissive nature of these assumptions. None of the assumptions requires persons making them to undertake any action, but they predispose individuals in certain directions; whether they perform these actions will depend on opportunities afforded them by political institutions and by their position in the social structure. Similarly, failure to make these assumptions does not mean that such people will engage in no political activity; it does mean, we believe, that such actions will be performed for different reasons, such as loyalty to a leader.

The efficacy example refers to a very general orientation to politics. But exploration of underlying assumptions may also illuminate much more concrete issues of public policy. For example, Ronald Manzer (1975) has traced the evolution of Canadian public priorities in economic and social policy. He shows how they are related to prevailing theories of the social and economic order held by dominant elites. He argues that the principles underlying policymaking are similar to the paradigms of scientific communities in that they summarize the world view of policymaking elites and they limit the appropriate set of policy instruments (35). Similarly, in *The Gift Relationship,* Richard Titmuss (1971) shows how the differing ways Britain and the United States provide blood for medical purposes stem from differences in fundamental assumptions about the obligations of citizens to each other, about the definition of community, and the like.

Culture and Personality

The view that a culture can be described in terms of modal or majority personality or character types conflicts with our approach because of our emphasis on the range and distribution of traits rather than on the mode or average (Inkeles and Levinson 1969). Similarly, the content of culture differs markedly from personality, since it refers to basic premises of action or guiding assumptions about the world, while personality refers to behavior patterns or to behavioral dispositions.[6]

That culture and personality obviously interact and that they may both be inferred from interviews and survey questionnaires blur the line of demarcation. Of course, other methods may be used to assess either culture or personality, as we suggest below, but the use of individual responses easily leads some scholars to think of cultures in terms of the proportions of individual personality types in the collectivity. Our notion of political culture as a property of collectivities precludes such an approach. Instead, one should examine the interaction between psychological and cultural dimensions seen independently. The best approach regards personality as an individual's characteristic strategies of adaptation to his environment and inner needs. Culture thus becomes a part of his environment.

Personality traits and their organization, of course, influence which elements within a culture an individual is most likely to internalize and express, although this is also fashioned partly by social position and role set. For example, a great many of Richard Nixon's personal attributes and beliefs (politics is war, enemies are to be destroyed, etc.) are closely related to many themes in the range of American culture.[7] His personality found support within the culture, and he appropriated from the culture those features he found most congenial. In the same way, orientations found among Barber's "active-positive" presidents (politics is fun, men are generally good, etc.) are also recurring themes in American culture. "Positive" and "negative" personalities, then, respond to different elements within the broad range of variants in American political culture and select some but deny or ignore others.

This perspective highlights another important way in which culture and personality relate to each other. In cultures with a very limited range of assumptions, there is less scope for individual variation based on personality to influence political behavior. The relative homogeneity of the political culture, by offering only one or a few viable alternatives, severely constricts the play of personality. In a large, complex, broad-range culture, on the other hand, we can expect to find many different—even contradictory—strands which grant great latitude to different personality types to pursue different adaptive strategies legitimately. In such societies, personality, role, and social position play a larger part than culture in determining the exact forms of political behavior, although culture still "sets the agenda."

On the other hand, even in diverse collectivities, actors may find themselves constrained by the roles they play and by the expectations and assumptions characteristic of others in their social milieu. The effect of culture on individual behavior may thus develop in two ways: through internalization as a result of socialization and character formation, or through the imposition of external social constraints. One cannot function successfully in society while remaining too far outside the norms, assumptions, and expectations of other people with whom one must deal regularly.

Personality and culture are conceptually distinct, but often intimately related, dimensions of empirical situations. Personality, role, and social structure mediate the relationship between culture as a range of options and concrete individual behavior patterns. As explanations, these concepts supplement rather than compete with each other.

Structural, Institutional, and Cultural Explanations

Structural and institutional explanations pose the major alternatives to explanation by political culture. We use the term "structural" in several special senses. Structures may signify regularized patterns of behavior, especially in formal or informal organizations; these we will call "institutions." Structural explanations, however, may also be conceptualized in terms of proportions of individuals. Social classes may also be institutions, but social class as a structural explanation consists of the relative proportions of a collectivity which fall into the different social classes. Such proportions or variables pose important threats to cultural explanations, because the experiences they represent are believed to be important determinants of behavior and attitudes in their own right and because they are easily confounded with political culture as a distributional characteristic of a collectivity.

An example from Almond and Verba's well-known (1963) study will illustrate our position. They demonstrate very large differences among five nations in sense of political competence. These differences in competence may stem from distinct national cultures or from the fact that the nations differ in such matters as proportion of educated people. In fact, the latter is the case: virtually all the internation difference is accounted for when education is controlled. In our terms, then, the explanation is a structural one: it is the pattern or proportion of structural positions that varies within this set of countries. We entertain a cultural explanation for the difference only when persons in similar structural positions possess divergent orientations. In fact, Almond and Verba (1963) present such a case: large internation differences in *how* people would attempt to influence government—by individual or cooperative action—persist even after relevant controls (191).

When controls for social or demographic categories reduce to insignificance the intercollectivity differences on the dependent variable, the explanation should be termed a structural one. If, on the other hand, such controls reveal that people with similar structural positions diverge between collectivities on the dependent variable, then either there are structural variables which have not been examined (or have been inadequately measured or controlled), or there are *cultural* differences which account for the observed intergroup variation.

There are several reasons for thinking that it will be even more difficult to sort out institutional from cultural influences than it was for the structural variables mentioned above. Institutional features, like cultural ones, are collective characteristics rather than simple aggregates. They are thus much harder to measure and quantify. There will also be many instances of complex interaction between institutional and cultural influences, insofar as both factors serve the function of setting an agenda. Nevertheless, as with proportionalities, we suggest that the institutional effects should be partialled out first. That is, if differences between collectivities exist, we should begin by looking for an institutional explanation. If differences exist, despite institutional similarity, then our confidence that the explanation is cultural is increased.[8]

This two-stage approach may be unnecessarily severe. No one type of explanation is generally better than another. Our concern here is entirely practical. To the extent that structural or institutional variables are simpler, more easily measured, more widely applicable, or more universally understood than cultural variables, it makes sense to try them first.

Most important, the strategy we have underlined constitutes an appropriate search procedure for locating the structures and institutions which are the relevant culture-bearing units. What accounts for the existence of particular policies, attitudes, or behaviors in one collectivity rather than another? If it is the proportion of people with a given characteristic (religion, ethnicity, age, education), or if it is the presence or predominance of a given institution (bureaucracy, political party, electoral system), then that property or institution identifies the culture-bearing units *for that dependent variable*.[9] An explanation of that property or institution will involve, at one remove, the same type of analysis, and so on with the causes of that cause. Each step in the analysis has two possible outcomes: the relevant collectivities explain the differences on the dependent variable, or the demonstration that they do not explain the differences reveals the most likely culture-bearing unit. Hence, at the point of departure, one may not have a cultural explanation; but explaining the pattern of structural proportions or institutional forms which mark the culture "carriers" will eventually lead to an explanation we would designate as cultural.

Inference and Evidence

Several characteristics of political culture pose special problems for measuring and describing it. First, it is often hard to disentangle from structural and psychological variables. Second, it is an abstract concept, not a concrete thing. It cannot be directly seen, heard, or touched; therefore it must be inferred from other clues. Third, for most of the members of a society, culture is unconscious, inexplicit, taken for granted; hence we cannot easily ask people about it directly. Fourth, while individuals participate in a culture, as a collective attribute of society, we do not describe a culture by simply aggregating all the individuals. How then do we find it?

One might begin by asking why we should use a hypothetical construct to explain anything. First, the social sciences have had considerable success with several hypothetical constructs: personality, attitude, role, power, and so on. Nor are the social sciences unique in this regard; gravity is a central hypothetical construct in physics, and yet no physicist knows what it is. Second, if one believes everything has a cause, and if other plausible causes cannot be found, it is reasonable to postulate a construct such as political culture. Thus, after controls for structural and institutional variables, political culture is postulated to account for limitations in the range of options, norms, and behaviors to be found in a population.

Individuals manifest or express their political culture without generally being aware of it. Political cultures consist largely of unconscious assumptions, so taken for granted that, except for a few rare and sensitive individuals, members of a culture seldom have occasion to question them. Cultural norms are likely to become explicit and openly debated only in times of rapid change, spectacular violation of the norms, and the like. "Unconscious" is thus used here not in the Freudian sense of "repressed," but as "taken for granted." Each person assumes that everyone else shares the same belief; or an assumption is so basic to people's outlook that it is literally impossible for them to conceive how it could be different. One would become conscious of such assumptions only when they are challenged; given the homogeneity of the primary groups in which most people participate, such challenges are infrequent.

This feature of culture poses some advantages and some difficulties for research. The advantage is that when interviewing or observing respondents, it is harder for them to "fake" or to give self-serving and pragmatic answers. Similarly, the responses are less likely to be facile, short-run responses to transitory contemporary political phenomena. The disadvantage is, of course, that it becomes difficult to elicit the underlying assumptions. Apart from the general techniques of inference we have mentioned, four other strategies are likely to overcome the difficulty. First, some individuals in the society are likely to be thrust into positions in which they encounter different assumptions; they may thus be led to greater awareness of the premises of their own actions.

Political leaders are an example. Moreover, certain groups or individuals are likely to be especially sensitive observers or critics of their own culture: poets, novelists, journalists, and so on. In addition, rebels, members of "countercultures," or malcontents may often be able to tell us a great deal about a culture; we can learn as much from those who reject a system of assumptions as from those who have learned and internalized it. Hence, students of culture should concentrate some of their resources on such specialized respondents.

Second, the principle of confrontation and comparison with different groups suggests that it would be fruitful to study individuals who have moved from one society to another. One could begin by studying exchange students. What strikes them as odd, inexplicable, different, or discomforting about the other group? What did they have to learn or unlearn in order to "pass"?

Third, cultural assumptions may be clear only in contrast to those of another culture. We argued above that cultural explanations logically entail comparative research. Here we suggest a practical consequence of this requirement—by comparing and contrasting, we become aware of what has been taken for granted. Hartz, for example, would probably never have formulated his theory about the Lockean foundations of American liberalism without his comparative research on England and other societies (Hartz 1955, 1964).

Fourth, experimental techniques can play a central role in the study of cultures (Elkins 1976). Since assumption about the political world are generally taken for granted by their carriers, one cannot ask directly about them as though they were consciously held opinions on political issues. One must elicit them in carefully structured and controlled situations, or one must "read between the lines" when analyzing documents or behavior. One must, therefore, guard against the possibility that an investigator will impute ideas, assumptions, or meanings to ambiguous responses, statements, or behavior. One safeguard is to use laboratory experiments to test hypotheses about cultural assumptions and their casual status.

Such experiments alone cannot provide a complete methodology for the analysis of political culture. Interviews, surveys, field observation, historical analysis, documents, literary materials, and many other sources should also be used. Some source materials—especially novels, public rhetoric, ceremonies, and social and political criticism—may be especially fruitful for formulating hypotheses about the presence of fundamental assumptions of the culture, while other materials or methods may be necessary to determine the extent to which these assumptions are widely shared and to test hypotheses about their causal influence on behavior or attitudes. It is in regard to this last task that we feel experimental devices will prove most essential.

Some will argue that experiments are useless for studying political culture because they are so far removed from the complex intertwining of elements in the real world. This degree of abstraction, of course, is precisely their main attraction. Because we create the conditions and manipulate their administration, we know which precedes which, and thus we can settle more satisfactorily questions of casual priority.

Experimentation has several advantages. For one thing, situations of conflict between values, norms, or people can be created expressly to see how conflicts are resolved. Such situations in the real world may appear so infrequently or covertly that they can be studied only by devious means. Those which appear frequently may be confounded with other features of social life so that certainty about bases of choice may result only from limiting the number of variables. Second, experimental conditions favor the creation of situations which are deliberately ambiguous. The "instinctive" reaction to ambiguity may reveal the hidden assumptions at the core of political culture. The study of optical illusions has provided evidence of the usefulness of this approach (Segall, Campbell, and Herskovits 1966). Third, once one has formulated hypotheses about the nature of the assumptions in the culture, one can vary them experimentally to assess their effect on other variables.

Finally, experimental settings present ideal opportunities for the testing of questions, items, and formats for survey research and interviews. In the laboratory situation, one can vary wording, instructions, and interviewer characteristics systematically in an effort to improve research devices for eliciting these subtle assumptions in the wider population in which one has a primary interest. In this way, experimental findings may be used as pretests for survey research. Conversely, experiments might be utilized subsequent to survey research; when assumptions are known to be common in a population, experiments will help to clarify their possible causal influence on perception, cognition, or action.

Despite serious methodological obstacles, political culture can be studied by normal social science techniques. Many deficiencies of previous research derive from a failure to use enough different techniques. Hypothesis formation requires a playful and broad-ranging familiarity with anecdotal material as well as systematic research. Estimates of the extensiveness of assumptions, norms, beliefs, and behavior require survey research and personal interviewing. Tests of hypotheses about the causal status of cultural assumptions, and in some cases measurement of assumptions, can most effectively occur in laboratory settings.

What Does Political Culture Explain?

Consider the restrictions we have imposed on the concept of political culture as explanation. First, we have argued that it is a collective property of groups such as nations or classes. What it may explain are differences between groups in the range of options considered by the population in deciding on a course of action. Second, political culture is a "second-order" explanation, appropriately applied only after institutional and structural explanations have been ruled out or in conjunction with such explanations. Structural and institutional features may be shown to be relevant "culture bearers," but alone they do not constitute cultural explanations. Third, because the implicit assumptions which form its content are taken for granted, it constitutes a largely unconscious perceptual screen which determines how one views or understands a situation.

Given these restrictions, what is the logic of cultural explanation, and to what range of dependent variables might it be usefully applied? First, it must be comparative. Logically, culture cannot be used to explain variations within the unit, since by definition all groups within the unit share in the culture. For culture to be used within a nation, then, the culture-bearing units must be subnational groups. The only other condition in which culture can be used within nations is when comparisons are made over time. Thus, one might hypothesize that changes in the range of basic assumptions between one period and the next help account for other political changes. Here, of course, the logic of comparison is maintained.

Second, culture as an explanation is seldom direct and seldom operates alone. Rather, it is generally permissive and almost always acts in conjunction with other variables. This is largely because the culture is defined by the range of assumptions found in the society. Hence, one cannot infer or predict directly from cultural assumption to individual attitude, individual act, or collective decision. Such an inference requires that the assumption or belief combine with particular information, goals and interests, personality needs, and the like. The cultural assumptions provide the lens through which these more proximate political forces are assessed; they influence what kind of interpretation will be placed on political forces, but alone they cannot account for the result. The broader the range of assumptions found within a culture, the more weight must be given to noncultural factors, since there will be fewer cultural constraints; to put it another way, the larger the number of items on the agenda, the larger the role of noncultural decision factors.

Political culture should seldom be seen as competing with other variables, but as a complement to them. Which other variables it most powerfully interacts with depends largely on what sorts of things we want to explain. If we are interested in individual attitudes, the focus will be on the interrelationships of culture, personality, and social position. If we are interested in public policy, the emphasis will be on which groups, occupying what part of the cultural range, are most influential.

What elements of political life seem most and least amenable to cultural explanation? Cultural factors have often been used to understand very broad system characteristics: stability, democracy, authoritarianism, and level of economic or political development. While relationships between such dimensions and assumptions about the political world are plausible, we propose that this level of analysis should not remain a preoccupation of students of culture, because, as dependent variables, such phenomena are simply too broad and vague.[10] The wide sweep of so much writing on culture seems to invite application to equally sweeping dependent variables. But if it is to be a useful concept, culture needs to be much more clearly specified and so must the dependent variables it is designed to explain.

At a second level, some scholars have pointed to culture to explain individual attitudes and behavior, but we doubt that it can do so alone. Political culture is an important part of individual action insofar as it provides the repertoire or range of options available. Thus an "authoritarian personality" in one culture is likely to behave differently from one in another culture—in the language and symbols he uses, the objects of his attention, and so on (Sniderman 1975). This is one reason why instruments designed to measure authoritarianism in one society may be ineffective or misleading in another. We have already noted how political culture may affect the sense of efficacy as a motive for action. Other psychological states which culture might also foster include: feelings of frustration at being unable to do what seems obvious according to cultural assumptions; feelings of guilt or shame at doing or contemplating things which are not natural or ideal for that culture; and feelings of confusion which result from performing actions one believes right or natural, but which have contrary or puzzling effects because one's allies or opponents operate on different assumptions (Merton 1957). The investigation of culturally induced feelings of this sort might be particularly fruitful in cases where members of different cultural groups come into contact: the interaction of French- and English-Canadians in a bicultural civil service; confrontations between bureaucrats and citizen protest groups; and international negotiations.[11] When different cultural groups interact, the results may be incomprehension, frustration, inability to cooperate, misunderstanding of each other's signals, failure to agree, and so on. Thus, political culture plays a part in explaining the actions people undertake, and it also explains in part the value they place on these actions and the feelings they have about them.

Brian Barry (1970) contrasts the "sociological" approach to individual behavior (by which he mainly means Parsonian value analysis) with an "economic" approach in which self-interest and utility maximization are the central assumptions. Although he argues that the economic approach contrasts with the more culturally oriented sociological approach, in our terms, culture enters into both. Self-interest and the idea of a utility calculus are themselves cultural concepts. Similarly, cultural assumptions will affect the kinds of factors which enter into any assessment of benefits and costs. Knowledge of the culture will also be necessary to predict the reactions of others to what one does. The value of game theory as a tool of comparative analysis is that it consists of an extremely simple set of cultures where few assumptions are made and those are explicit (Elkins 1976).

At a third level, political culture is likely to help explain certain characteristics of political institutions. One might distinguish between institutions in the sense of formal statutory or constitutional creations and their actual operation. Culture may play a part in both senses. The structural differences between British cabinet and American presidential government may reflect very different assumptions about authority and sovereignty. Once an institution exists, the culture may play a more obvious role in whether and how people realize it. Political culture also helps to sustain institutions through a process of consensual validation. What we mean by institutionalized behavior, after all, is a pattern of interactions which are highly repetitive and mutually intelligible, precisely because people in that milieu operate on similar assumptions and take for granted that these behaviors and opinions are correct. Indeed, this is just what Parsons and other action theorists mean by "structure": interactions are structured or institutionalized only to the extent that they reflect internalized patterns of normative or cultural expectations (Parsons and Shils 1962). Without shared assumptions—such as the norm of reciprocity—it is hard to see how an institution like the United States Congress could function at all. This again suggests the close interaction between cultural and institutional forces, which makes them difficult to disentangle in practice. Over the long run, institutions modify the range of assumptions of those who operate them and those who are affected by them. But in the short run, cultural assumptions are likely to have a role in specifying the operation of institutions. For this reason, cultural data may be fruitful in predicting the effects of institutional and organizational changes.

Political culture has been less attractive to students of policy analysis and policymaking than to other political scientists. But our stress on culture as setting the agenda and as reducing the range of alternatives to be considered suggests that cultural explanations of policy should be explored more fully, especially in comparative settings. For example, in his study of differences in the extent of public ownership and breadth of the welfare state, Anthony King (1973) concludes that "ideas," rather than institutions, interest, or demands, best explain the variations. Culture is unlikely to be of much help in explaining why alternative *A* was chosen over alternative *B*—but it may be of great help in understanding why A and B were considered, while no thought was given to *C, D,* or *E.*

We might distinguish here between two aspects of the study of policy formation: first, the procedures or processes through which policy is debated and decided; and second, the substance or content itself. In a procedural sense, culture would affect the ways policymakers interact and their style of behavior: what forms of behavior are legitimate; what criteria (scientific, religious, etc.) should be applied to policies; how the policy field is perceived (as consensual or conflictual, zero- or variable-sum); who is permitted to participate; or the balance between voluntarism and coercion. Theodore Lowi's (1967) discussion of the "public philosophy," Alexander George's (1969) and others' analysis of the "operational code," Robert Putnam's (1971) examination of elite political cultures, and Michel Crozier's (1964) "bureaucratic phenomenon" are all studies of the impact of cultural factors on the policy process. In this area, as in all the other aspects of politics discussed here, it must be assumed that cultural factors would collaborate with institutions, group interests, and many other variables.

In a substantive sense, culture may help to explain the scope and content of government activity. These depend partly on the distribution of assumptions about the role of the state, about the desirable balance between public and private activity, and about collective versus individual decisions. In particular policy areas, the assumptions and theories prevalent among relevant decision makers would be paramount. For example, in explaining international differences in social welfare policies, we would want to know what assumptions were held by elite members about the causes of poverty, the characteristics of the poor, and so on. Again, culture interacts with other factors. It is closely related to the more explicit policy statements embodied in ideologies.

The influence of culture may be more direct in some policy areas than in others. Environmental constraints on resources and opportunities and the common character of problems may ensure that even when policymaking procedures differ greatly between collectivities, the results are much the same. This may be true in such areas as fiscal policy. At the other extreme, cultures may allow a great deal of freedom. Policy with respect to abortion, criminal justice, or drug use might more fully reflect cultural assumptions than "objective" environmental constraints. In substantive policy, culture remains primarily permissive: it does not determine precisely what will be done; it conditions the range of issues to which attention will be devoted; it influences the way those issues will be defined; and it limits the range of options considered within a given issue domain.

Although we consider political culture a useful explanatory tool, our goal has been to elucidate its role by severely restricting the types of things it should explain. In particular, we suggest that it be reserved for explaining political differences between collectivities, when structural and institutional explanations can be shown to be insufficient. By corollary, cultural, institutional, and structural explanations are not competitors, but collaborators; all are needed for a full understanding of why collectivities exhibit different institutional arrangements, why their institutions work in various ways, and why individuals believe and act in particular fashions. The notion of explanation must therefore be understood to be more complex than is implicit in most of the literature on political culture. Instead of asking whether institutions cause culture or culture causes institutions, we should look for their joint effects.

References

Almond, G., and S. Verba. 1963. *The civic culture.* Princeton.
Barry, B. 1970. *Sociologists, economists, and democracy.* London.
Crozier, M. 1964. *The bureaucratic phenomenon.* Chicago.
Elkins, D. J. 1976. Experimental political culture. Paper presented to the International Political Science Association, Edinburgh, Scotland.
George, A. 1969. The operational code: A neglected approach to the study of political leaders and decision-making. *International Studies Quarterly* 13 (June): 190-222.
Hartz, L. 1955. *The liberal tradition in America.* New York.
Hartz, L., ed. 1964. *The founding of new societies.* New York.
Inkeles, A., and D. Levinson. 1969. National character: The study of modal personality and sociocultural systems. In *The handbook of social psychology,* 2d ed., Vol. 4, edited by G. Lindzey and E. Aronson. Reading, MA.
Keesing, R. 1974. Theories of culture. In *Annual review of anthropology,* Vol. 3, edited by B. Siegel, et. al. Palo Alto.
King, A. 1973. Ideas, institutions, and the policies of governments. *British Journal of Political Science* 3: 291-313, 409-423.
Lane, R. 1962. *Political ideology.* New York.
Lowi, T. 1967. The public philosophy: Interest-group liberalism. *American Political Science Review* 61 (March): 5-24.
Manzer, R. 1975. Public policies in Canada: A developmental perspective. Paper presented at the Canadian Political Science Association, Edmonton, Alberta.
Merton, R. K. 1957. Social structure and anomie. In *Social theory and social structure,* rev. ed. New York.
Parson, T., and E. A. Shils, eds. 1962. *Toward a general theory of action.* New York.
Putnam, R. 1971. Studying elite political culture: The case of "ideology." *American Political Science Review* 65 (September): 651-681.
Rosenberg, M. 1962. Test standardization as a method of interpretation. *Social Forces* 41 (October): 53-61.

Segall, M., D. Campbell, and M. Herskovits. 1966. *The influence of culture on visual perception.* Indianapolis.
Simeon, R. E. B., and D. J. Elkins. 1974. Regional political cultures in Canada. *Canadian Journal of Political Science* 7 (September): 397-437.
Sniderman, P. 1975. *Personality and democratic politics.* Berkeley.
Titmuss, R. 1971. *The gift relationship: From human blood to social policy.* New York.

CHAPTER 3

Culture and Identity in Comparative Political Analysis*

Marc Howard Ross

Originally published in M. Lichbach and A. Zuckerman,
Comparative Politics: Rationality, Culture, and Structure, 1997.

READING INTRODUCTION

Ross's lengthy article represents a thorough and broad-ranging assessment of contemporary political culture theory. (See also Lane 1992.) After defining culture somewhat differently from either Almond or Elkins and Simeon (as a system of meaning and identity), Ross takes up four topics in turn. First, he outlines five distinctive contributions that political culture theories make to the study of comparative politics. Second, he isolates five central themes of contemporary political culture applications. Third and perhaps most interesting, he culls five important criticisms of political culture theories from the contemporary literature of comparative political analysis. Fourth, Ross shows how political culture theories might enrich studies focusing on topics beyond explicitly political subjects (e.g., government institutions) such as the economy. Like Almond as well as Elkins and Simeon, Ross concludes that political culture theory holds much promise for helping us to explain social life in a fashion consistent with the demands of empirical social science.

READING TEXT

Introduction

In this essay I argue that two distinct, but not unrelated, features of culture are relevant to comparative politics. First, culture is a system of meaning that people use to manage their daily worlds, large and small; second, culture is the basis of social and political identity that affects how people line up and how they act on a wide range of matters. Culture is a framework for organizing the world, for

---

* I wish to thank the organizers and participants in the Symposium on Theory in Comparative Politics for their comments on my presentation. In addition, Donald Campbell, Katherine Conner, Barbara Frankel, Carol Hager, Phil Kilbride, Mark Lichbach, and Alan Zuckerman offered detailed comments on earlier versions of this chapter.

locating the self and others in it, for making sense of the actions and interpreting motives of others, for grounding an analysis of interests, for linking collective identities to political action, and for motivating people and groups toward some actions and away from others. At the same time, two caveats are in order: One is that to be useful culture cannot be defined so broadly as to include all behaviors, beliefs, institutions—in short, any domain of life—although it is appropriate to consider the cultural dimensions of specific domains; two, the effects of culture on collective action and political life are generally indirect, and to fully appreciate the role of culture in political life, it is necessary to inquire how the impact of culture interacts with interests and institutions.

It should not be surprising that cultural analyses in comparative politics take many forms, for unlike rational choice theory, cultural approaches are less clear about exactly what domains of politics to examine, and there is even less of a consensus concerning the methods and tools to employ.[2] Lichbach distinguishes between subjective and intersubjective views of culture—the subjective emphasizes how individuals internalize individual values and attitudes that become the object of study, while the intersubjective focuses on the shared meanings and identities that constitute the symbolic, expressive, and interpretive part of social life. I argue here for the merits of a postmodern intersubjective understanding of culture (with attention to subjective elements). This strong view of culture is completely compatible with the belief that comparison is central to the social science enterprise (while not denying its complexities), although this is not the position some radical interpretivists hold. In making this argument here, an important task is to situate important or exemplary works in the field in terms of crucial questions that cultural approaches to politics address. However, this essay is not a review article, and there are many additional studies that would be included if reviewing the field were my goal.

This essay offers an opportunity to emphasize (even advocate) what an intersubjective cultural approach can contribute to comparative politics. In contrast to rational choice approaches, which are well entrenched in the discipline, and institutional approaches, which have dominated the field in one form or another since its inception, cultural contributions to political analysis are relatively rare and far less developed. Few graduate students take culture very seriously, and if one peruses the annual list of dissertations in comparative politics over several years, it is difficult to place cultural analyses in the trinity of comparative politics, as the editors of this volume have done.

It is not hard to identify the reasons why studies that give culture a central role are rare in comparative politics. Most basically, culture is not a concept with which most political scientists are comfortable. For many, culture complicates issues of evidence, transforming hopes of rigorous analysis into "just so" accounts that fail to meet widely held notions of scientific explanation. Culture violates canons of methodological individualism while raising serious unit of analysis problems for which there are no easy answers. Culture to many, neo-Marxists and non-Marxists alike, seems like an epiphenomenon offering a discourse for political mobilization and demand-making while masking more serious differences dividing groups and individuals. Finally, employing the concept of culture puts political scientists into a series of controversies over which proponents of cultural analysis in anthropology themselves are deeply divided.[3] Each of these objections is more or less addressed in this essay, and while I do not argue that they are unimportant, I do not view them as sufficiently damaging to warrant throwing the baby out with the bath water.

Cultural analysis of politics takes seriously the postmodern critique of behavioral political analyses and seeks to offer contextually rich intersubjective account of politics that emphasize how political actors understand social and political action (Merelman 1991). In cultural analyses, for example, interests are contextually and intersubjectively defined, and the strategies used to pursue them are understood to be context-dependent. Central to cultural analysis is the concept of interpretation. The interpretations of particular political significance are built from the accounts—stories if one prefers—of groups and individuals striving to make sense of their social and political worlds, and I use the term to refer both to the shared intersubjective meanings of actors[4] and to the explicit efforts of social science observers to understand these meanings and to present them to others (Taylor 1985). Shared interpretations of actors—worldviews—are important in any cultural analysis as they offer an important methodological tool, along with an examination of rituals and symbols, for examining both systems of meaning and the structure and intensity of political identity.

This essay has four parts. The first discusses five contributions the concept of culture defined as a system of meaning and identity make to comparative political analysis: culture frames the context in which politics occurs; culture links individual and collective identities; culture defines the boundaries between groups and organizes actions within and between them; culture provides a framework for interpreting the actions and motives of others; and culture provides resources for political organization and motivation. The second part examines five central themes (some might say approaches) in cultural analyses of politics: culture and personality studies; the civic culture tradition; culture and political process (an approach that originated in anthropology); political ritual; and culture and political violence. Third, I identify five critiques of cultural studies of politics: unit of analysis issues; the problem of within-culture variation; the difficulty of distinguishing culture from social or political organization; the static nature of culture and explaining political change; and the need to identify underlying mechanisms that suggest "how culture works." The fourth section examines the role of interpretation in cultural analysis as an effort to link the contextually rich political details found in particular political settings (be they small communities or countries) to general domains of political life such as authority, community, and conflict. I discuss the concept of psychocultural interpretations and their methodological relevance in the comparative study of culture and politics for understanding processes such as ethnic and national identity construction. I conclude that culture is too often ignored as a domain of political life and that cultural analyses can enrich the ways we conceptualize areas such as political economy, social movements, and political institutions in a number of ways, often complementing the insights derived from interest and institutional approaches.

Culture and Cultural Analyses of Politics

Culture

Culture, a central concept in anthropology, has been defined in a wide variety of ways that variously emphasize culture as social organization, core values, specific beliefs, social action, or a way of life (Kroeber and Kluckhohn 1952). Most contemporary analyses, however, begin, as I do here, with Geertz's definition of culture as "an historically transmitted pattern of meaning embodied in symbols, a system of inherited conceptions expressed in symbolic forms by means of which men communicate, perpetuate, and develop their knowledge about and attitudes towards life" (1973b, 89).[5] This view emphasizes culture as public, shared meanings; behaviors, institutions, and social structure are understood not as culture itself but as culturally constituted phenomena (Spiro 1984). Culture from this perspective is a worldview that explains why and how individuals and groups behave as they do, and includes both cognitive and affective beliefs about social reality and assumptions about when, where, and how people in one's culture and those in other cultures are likely to act in particular ways (see also Berger 1995).[6] For purposes of political analysis, I want to emphasize that shared understandings occur among people who also have a common (and almost invariably named) identity which signals distinctions between the group and outsiders. Culture, in short, marks "a distinctive way of life" characterized in the subjective we-they feelings of cultural group members (and outsiders) and is expressed through specific behaviors (customs and rituals)—both sacred and profane—which mark the daily, yearly, and life cycle rhythms of its members and reveal how people view past, present, and future events and understand choices they face (Berger 1995). Cultural metaphors have both cognitive meaning, which describes group experience, and high affective salience, which emphasizes the unique intragroup bonds—almost like a secret code—that set one group's experience apart from that of others.

It should be pointed out that in a shared meaning and identity system the fact that different individuals and groups understand each other does not imply agreement that widely held meanings are necessarily acceptable to all. Rather, meaning and identity, control over symbols and rituals, and the ability to impose one interpretation rather than another on a situation are frequently bitterly contested (Scott 1985). In this same vein, Laitin (1988) contends that culture highlights points of concern to be debated (589) and not just areas of agreement. Sharing a culture does not mean that people are necessarily in agreement on specifics, only that they possess a similar understanding of how the world works.

Placing the concept of culture at the center of analysis affects the questions asked about political life (Brysk 1995; Merelman 1991, 45). For example, an interest in distinctive worldviews and identity leads to questions about how differences in worldviews might explain such phenomena as the emergence of certain leaders and reactions to them, the organization of political decision making, social movement mobilization, or perception of external threats. At the same time, an interest in culture and cultural difference discourages inquiry into the role of rational self-interest in political choice making, for such questions presume that interest maximization is more or less invariant across cultures and does not need a theory of cultural variation to explain what is viewed as constant (Wildavsky 1987).

My goal is to suggest how cultural analysis enhances our understanding of politics, not to comprehensively review the field, which defined broadly, could include every study that includes a cultural variable in a regression equation on the one hand to the most hermeneutically informed textual analysis on the other. Here I emphasize work that gives a central role to the concept of culture as a system of meaning and identity, and in the next few pages I suggest core questions in comparative political analysis that profit from attention to the concept of culture. Underlying my presentation is the belief that most political scientists have not thought a great deal about culture; that many consider it an epiphenomenon to be explained away rather than to be incorporated into theories and explanations; and that many who do invoke culture define it so thinly that they do not develop analyses of cultural dynamics that are terribly insightful.[7]

Culture Frames the Context in which Politics Occurs
Culture orders political priorities (Laitin 1986, 11), meaning it defines the symbolic and material objects people consider valuable and worth fighting over, the contexts in which such disputes occur, the rules (both formal and informal) by which politics takes place and who participates in it. In doing so, culture defines interests and how they are to be pursued. For example, anthropologist Napoleon Chagnon (1967) invokes the cultural importance of the value of fierceness *(waiteri* complex) to explain the prevalence of high warfare among Yanomano communities; political scientist Edward Banfield (1958) explains the absence of political participation and civic society in southern Italy in terms of a cultural pattern he calls amoral familism; and political scientists Gabriel Almond and Sidney Verba (1963) explain differences in political attitudes and patterns of participation among the United States, Great Britain, Germany, Italy, and Mexico in terms of differences between participant, subject, and parochial political cultures. To understand the cultural framing of politics, consider how culture influences beliefs about, and the organization of, community, authority, and conflict (Ross 1988).

Cultural understandings are at the core of the definition of political communities since people in a community share, in Geertz's (1973b) words, "schematic images of the social order," common meanings which Taylor (1985, 39) says are the basis of community. Communities are distinct, but also nested, entities. People are invariably part of more than one community and develop multiple loyalties whose interrelationship can take a variety of forms. Authority in any political community is culturally constituted and consists of regularized procedures that members of a community consider more or less legitimate—meaning that they have been arrived at by a procedure they consider fair, although the issue may continue to be highly contested—for distributing tangible and symbolic goods. The establishment of legitimate authority is a historical process for a community (Arendt 1958) and a psychological one for individuals, linking people through a sense of common fate captured in the historical accounts people in a community share. The establishment and maintenance of political authority is often explained in cognitive and cost-benefit terms and threats of coercion but also involves ritual activity, including religious action, which connects people's everyday experience and anxiety to those of the collectivity (Edelman 1964; Kertzer 1988; Shils and Young 1953; Turner 1957, 1968). Conflict occurs in virtually all communities, and all cultures have norms about what is reasonable to fight about and how conflicts are to be managed. Cultures shape conflict, defining what is appropriate social action, how the motives of others should be understood, and what is worth fighting about (Ross 1993a). Thus, at the same time, culture constitutes the social order and is a tool for domination, and conflict over the nature and make-up of the political community and authority within it are regular features of political life.

Culture Links Individual and Collective Identities
Culture offers an account of political behavior that makes particular actions more or less likely and connects the fate of individuals and the group. The crucial connection at work is that of identification, which renders certain actions reasonable and removes alternatives that on other grounds might be equally plausible. Individual and collective action, this view suggests, are motivated, in part, by the sense of common fate people in a culture share and involve two distinct elements: the strong reinforcement between individual and collective identity that renders culturally sanctioned behavior rewarding and the sense that outsiders will treat oneself and other members of one's group in similar ways.

Identification dynamics involve the construction of internal images of the external world out of the developmental and historical experiences group members share. Many objects of identification are associated with primary sensations such as smell, taste, and sound that acquire intense affective meaning and only later acquire a cognitive component. People sharing cultural attachments have common experiences that facilitate the developmental task of incorporating identity into one's own sense of self. Anderson (1991) writes of imagined communities, which can link the person and collective identities. The process of within-group identity formation overemphasizes what it is that group members actually share. It gives greater emotional weight to the common elements, reinforcing them with an ideology of linked fate. It overvalues the uniformity within groups, emphasizing both affectively and cognitively the common elements individuals share, and exaggerating differences with outsiders (Turner 1988). Deviations from the norm are selectively ignored or negatively reinforced as incompatible with group solidarity and its myth of shared historical experiences.

It should be stressed that culture is only one basis for linking individual to social identity. It can be a particularly powerful one, however, in situations of threat and uncertainty because cultural attachments are connected to very primary feelings about identity. While much of our language, in western thought generally and psychoanalysis in particular, emphasizes an inherent conflict between the group and the individual, an emphasis on identity draws attention to which social attachments are an integral way of strengthening individual identity (Turner 1988).

Culture Defines Group Boundaries and Organizes Actions Within and Between Them
As culture defines identity groups, it also specifies expectations, patterns of association within and between groups. Consider such basic questions as who lives with whom, who spends time together, to whom one is most attached emotionally, who controls scarce resources, how property is transferred between generations, and how work is organized. The world's cultures provide very different answers to each of these questions, but most important the evidence shows that how any group answers any of these questions has significance for how people act and expect others to behave (Levinson and Malone 1981; Naroll 1970).

Cultural definitions of social groups—whether they are defined by kinship, age, gender, or common interests—entail clear expectations about how people are to act, even when these definitions are continually contested (Greif 1994; Scott 1985). How such social categories and groups are defined and the rules that regulate their behavior vary cross-culturally. Cultural norms regarding intergroup relations (here we can consider relations between groups in the same culture such as age or ritual groups, or groups from different cultures) can be highly elaborate. Cultures differ in how and when they restrict (and how they enforce such restrictions on) relations, but few are silent on these questions.

People don't often think about the social origin of groups with which they identify, for most groups are seen as natural, often biological in character, when in fact they are cultural and political constructions whose "reasonableness" needs to be regularly reasserted and taught to succeeding generations (Anderson 1991). Weber (1976), for example, shows how the nineteenth-century French state, through the institutionalization of a national education system, investment in transportation, and universal male military service, created a sense of national identity out of a myriad of regional loyalties.[8] All cultures, of course, provide specific, but not always explicit, socialization regarding in-group and out-group distinctions. Cultural learning involves messages about groups' motives, their behavior, and how one is to act toward members of each category.

Cross-culturally, the rigidity of social distinctions is highly variable, and variation in the permeability of boundaries means that functioning categories are both contextual and changing over time. This is clearly seen in the literature on "situational ethnicity," which shows how distinctions among groups can depend upon what other groups are in a social environment and what the particular political stakes are in a conflict. In East Africa, for example, speakers of *Kiluhya*, whose homeland is in western Kenya, gradually developed a political and social identity as Luhya people through contact with other ethnic communities in Nairobi, Mombasa, Kampala, and other urban centers since 1900. Earlier, however, their identity was primarily as Martgoli, Busia, or Samia, more localized Baluhya subgroups.

Culture Provides a Framework for Interpreting the Actions and Motives of Others
Actions, like words, are highly ambiguous, and making sense of them requires a shared cultural framework to assume that the message that is sent is similar, if not identical with, that which is received. Few behaviors are so universal that they require little or no interpretation. The work on the cross-cultural (and even

cross-species) interpretability of specific facial gestures (Ekman, Friesen, and Ellsworth 1972; Masters and Sullivan 1989), while fascinating, is also testimony to how few domains of human action are coherent outside of a shared cultural framework. Because most political and social action is complex, a capacity to decode only facial and other obvious physical gestures doesn't get one very far in understanding political life. It also provides little assistance in placing action in a broader context—one that includes motives, which offer an account of what someone has done but, in addition, says why they acted as they did.

Motives are central to cultural analysis because they offer a mechanism to link individual action to a broader social setting (D'Andrade and Strauss 1992). This contrasts with Geertz's focus on "inspecting events" and making sense of actors' interpretations of them but his rejection of the idea that we should examine mental structures (1973a, 10-12). D'Andrade's (1992) cultural analysis of motives develops the notion of a schema (not unlike what I am calling worldviews), "a conceptual structure which makes possible the identification of objects and events" (28). Schemas, he argues, are culturally acquired and produce "motivational strivings." He emphasizes the importance of understanding the context-dependent nature of schemas as interpretive devices and the need to spell out how they are acquired. Both D'Andrade and Strauss argue that we need to see cultures as "both the public actions, objects and symbols that make shared learning possible . . . and the private psychological states of knowledge and feeling without which these public things are meaningless and could not be recreated" (Strauss 1992, 6).[9]

In many ways motives in cultural analysis are much like interests in rational choice theory. In statements such as "They were motivated by fear of their ancestors and so they sacrificed half of their livestock" or "The blips had an interest in weakening the military capability of their enemy," both motives and interests offer a "reasonable" account of why individuals or groups behave in a certain way. Yet there are also significant differences in the use of motives and interests as explanatory mechanisms that are central to the difference between cultural and rational choice explanations. Most basically, while interests are assumed to be more or less transparent (some would say given) and universal, motives are knowable only through empirical analysis of particular cultural contexts.[10] As a result, while turning to interests suggests that more or less any human group would behave the same way in a certain situation, an emphasis on motives focuses on explaining variation in behavior across groups. Wildavsky (1987) argues that rational choice theorists make a serious error in taking interests as a given. In fact, he says, an empirically based cultural analysis reveals systematic variation in interests across cultures.

In an analysis of intracultural behavior, the difference between motives and interests is not always consequential, for in fact when interests are shared they can operate like motives, offering a readily available account of why people behave as they do. However, when we consider cross-cultural encounters, the difference between interests and motives can be more significant. Consider the statement above that a group of people motivated by fear of their ancestors and therefore sacrificed half their domestic animals. To people in another culture in which such fears are unknown, they are not plausible motives for action, and such behavior is not comprehensible. Trying to transform such an explanation into an interest statement ("They had an interest in not making the ancestors angry") still begs the question of why the group understands the world in terms of "fear of the ancestors." Only an analysis that seeks to explain why this motive is important in one culture but not another is adequate here.

Interest accounts of political action are imperialistic, dominating other explanations and insisting in what is often a tautological fashion that whatever action occurs can be understood in terms of individual (or group) interest maximization. The power of interest explanations lies in their hypothesized connection between thought and action; their weakness, however, is that they begin with action and then identify interests that are consistent with the pursuit of such action. All too infrequently is there an effort made to see if actors themselves make the same connections. More interesting from a cultural perspective is the almost complete absence of concern with the nature of specific interests in interest theories.[11] To the extent that groups and individuals are seen as having invariant interests, such as the maximization of wealth or political power, this question is somewhat interesting. However, to the degree to which interests vary from culture to culture, the matter of what constitutes crucial political interests for groups or individuals is worthy of serious empirical study. Cultural explanations, as a result, do not deny the relevance of interests but see them as contextually defined and one motive among many. Even though it views interests as cultural constructions rather than objectively identifiable universals, cultural theory can complement rational choice and other interest theories. Its different emphasis does not necessarily lead to competing propositions that put the two theories in conflict with each other; rather, cultural theory's concern with the construction of interests addresses an issue about which interest theories have little to say.

In cross-cultural encounters people most often make sense of other groups' behavior, i.e., attribute motives to them, by drawing on their own cultural worldview. However, it is worth pointing out that cultural worldviews provide two contrasting strategies for encounters with outsiders. One is to apply the rules of one's own culture because they are, after all, what is best known (and often all that is known), believing that outsiders will respond as insiders do. The second is to search for different rules, assuming that outsiders share few motives with people in one's own culture, hence will respond in "heathen" ways and are likely to take advantage of any weakness shown to them—for they will not follow what are viewed as "civilized norms." The first strategy is that of generalization, whereas the second is one of differentiation.[12]

Few people ever subject shared cultural frameworks to self-conscious analysis, since most people deeply internalize cultural assumptions and hence rarely articulate them consciously or view them as problematic. Yet even in times of stress there is a widespread (if not universal) ethnocentric tendency to suggest that "there is something wrong" with a person who fails to offer or misreads an obvious cultural signal and to take such behavior as evidence that something is "wrong" with that person or of the inferiority of the other group. For the most part, culturally shared worldviews are protected, and people will go to great lengths to resist changes that challenge their core elements.

Culture Provides Resources for Political Organization and Mobilization
Culture offers significant resources that leaders and groups use as instruments of organization and mobilization (Brysk 1995; Edelman 1964; Kertzer 1988; Laitin 1986). For example, Tilly has developed the concept of repertoires of collective action referring to "a limited set of routines that are learned, shared, and acted out through a relatively deliberate process of choices. Repertoires are learned cultural creations" (1995, 26; also see Tilly 1986; Traugott 1995; McAdam, Tarrow, and Tilly 1997). Anthropologist Abner Cohen (1969, 1974, 1981) spells out more generally the political uses of culture, emphasizing the importance of cultural organizations (formal or informal groups organized around specific cultural practices such as a religious or age group) as a political tool in situations where "normal politics" is not possible for one reason or another; in fact, the theory is much more widely relevant. In Cohen's analysis of Hausa traders in Ibadan (Nigeria) and Creoles in Freetown (Sierra Leone), the two were small minorities, so that using electoral strategies to pursue their economic and political goals would have likely resulted in massive defeats. Instead, the two groups organized around cultural issues—a religious revival focused on the Tijaniyyi brotherhood in the case of the Hausa, and Freemasonry for the Creoles. In each case these cultural responses to changing political situations provided intense within-group interaction and social exchange that prevented the loss of control over long-distance trade in the case of the Hausa and protected the Creoles's domination of the state's administrative elite.

Frequently groups use cultural organizations (not always consciously, as Cohen points out) to achieve goals that cannot be pursued directly. Cohen (1969) identifies six political problems addressed by cultural organizations that bolster group solidarity and effective mobilization (Cohen 1969, 201-10). (1) Such organizations help define a group's distinctiveness, meaning its membership and sphere of operation within the context of the contemporaneous political setting, through myths of origin and claims to superiority; descent and endogamy; moral exclusiveness; endo-culture; spatial proximity; and homogenization (201-4). (2) Cultural organizations meet the political need for intense internal communications among the group's constituent parts (205). (3) Cultural organizations offer mechanisms for decision making involving some formulation of general problems confronting the group and taking decisions about them (206). (4) They provide authority for implementing decisions and for speaking, where appropriate, on behalf of the group (207). (5) Cultural organizations can provide a political ideology often rooted in the language of kinship and ritual, which gives legitimacy to power and converts it into authority (208-10). (6) Finally, cultural organizations meet the need for discipline, through ceremonials and rituals that connect the ideology to current problems of the community (210-11).[13]

In discussing religion, the prototypical cultural basis for political organization, Cohen points out that:

Religion provides an ideal "blueprint" for the development of an informal political organization. It mobilizes many of the most powerful emotions which are associated with the basic problems of human existence and gives legitimacy and stability to political arrangements by representing these as parts of the system of the universe. It makes it possible to mobilize the power of symbols and the power inherent in the ritual relationship between various ritual positions within the organization of the cult. It makes it possible to use the arrangements for financing and administering places of worship and associated places for welfare, education, and social activities of various sorts, to use these in developing the organization and administration of political functions. Religion also provides frequent and regular meetings in congregations, where in the course of ritual activities, a great deal of informal interaction takes place, information is communicated, and general problems are formulated and discussed. The system of myths and symbols which religion provides is capable of being continuously interpreted and reinterpreted in order to accommodate it to changing economic, political and other social circumstances. (1969, 210)

Although Cohen's analysis is about the coping strategies of small cultural minorities, it is clearly relevant to understanding how leaders of large ethnic groups (often, but not always, majorities) have come to, and held onto, political power. African politics since the 1960s provides many examples of mobilization around cultural symbols and fears, and so do European settings such as Northern Ireland, France with a strong antiimmigrant, antiforeigner party, and Germany with its numerous outbreaks of antiforeigner violence. It is, however, in Eastern Europe and the former Soviet Union where we perhaps have the most to learn about the political manipulation of cultural symbols and rituals and their sometimes disastrous consequences. Here we must ask why the appeals to Serbian, Armenian, or Hungarian identity are all so powerful. However, as Campbell (1983) has suggested, any such answer that relies on mechanisms of individual benefit only makes sense if we can also account for the strength of individual attachments to groups such as those defined in cultural terms.

Cultural Analyses of Politics

Although one could make a cogent argument that cultural analyses are among the oldest works of political analysis, here I discuss a selected number of more recent studies that illustrate key concepts and methods associated with a cultural approach in comparative politics. My focus here is on approaches that give a central role to the concept of culture, not ones in which one or two cultural variables appear but are neither theoretically significant nor well developed. I discuss five different (but not necessarily mutually exclusive) approaches that are important because of their widespread influence within comparative politics and/or because of their potential to provide important insights. Under each I discuss a few important studies that illustrate the approach, without suggesting they are the only, or best, examples of it.

Culture, Personality, and Politics
The merging of the theoretical perspectives of psychoanalysis and cultural anthropology in the 1940s and early 1950s provided a framework linking a macro- and micro-level phenomena to explain cross-cultural differences in behavior. A popularized branch of this work, national character studies, combined Ruth Benedict's (1934) view that cultures were highly patterned with psychoanalysis' stress on the importance of infant and child socialization to offer profiles (some would say caricatures) of large countries, such as Japan, Russia, and the United States, to explain, among other things, their political institutions and political styles (Benedict 1946; Gorer and Rickman 1946; Mead 1942). Emphasizing (often with weak data) the link between socialization (defined in terms of a country's modal patterns), personality (often not directly measured), and political behavior, these studies offered sweeping generalizations about American individualism, Japanese militarism, and Russian totalitarian rule. Within a few years, a wide range of critiques emerged emphasizing problems in these works, including assumptions of within-country homogeneity, lack of evidence linking key elements in the theory, and its inability either to account for political change or to speak to the zigs and zags in political life in the countries under study. Clearly, transferring culture and personality theory and methods from small-scale preindustrial societies to the largest modern, industrial nations was not successful on either theoretical or methodological grounds.[14]

However, two political scientists, Lucien Pye (1962) and Edward Banfield (1958), found sufficient merit in the approach that they borrowed from it in two widely read, influential studies, while trying to address some of the most trenchant critiques of national character research. Pye, in an ambitious study of Burma in the 1950s, sought to explain the country's search for national identity. Keenly aware of the criticism that the personalities of political elites might be significantly different from those of the mass public and the need to study personality directly, Pye produced data on the crucial psychological variables through in-depth psychoanalytic interviews with Burmese elites. Emphasizing identity issues in an Eriksonian framework, Pye developed the link between the problems of individual identity among the elites he interviewed and Burmese nation-building. Development, he concluded, was not just about economic policies and institution-building but was intimately linked to the worldviews and psychological capacities of a country's elites.

Banfield developed a far less psychoanalytic framework to examine the absence of collective social or political action among peasants in a town in southern Italy where on self-interest grounds an outsider might expect to find it. His answer was that amoral familism, the rule that one can only trust and cooperate with the members of one's immediate family, is taught from an early age and supported in a variety of domains of daily life. Wider cooperation fails to gain a toehold because no one can imagine that cooperation will be reciprocated or sustained. Consequently, the culture of amoral familism is a powerful configuration (as Ruth Benedict might have used the term) and difficult to overcome despite the likely benefits from doing so.

The Civic Culture Tradition

Without a doubt, when most political scientists think about cultural analysis of politics, Almond and Verba's *The Civic Culture* (1963) quickly comes to mind. Utilizing data collected from large national samples in five countries—the United States, Britain, Germany, Italy, and Mexico—the authors sought to explain different levels of support for, and participation in, democratic political practices. Almond and Verba identify three distinctive political cultures—the participant, subject, and parochial—which differ in the attitudes citizens express toward the political system, trust in political authorities, beliefs concerning the efficacy of individual and collective political actions, and levels of political involvement. Thus, individual subjective attitudes and behaviors are the basis for assigning individuals to patterns, and the distribution of a country's individuals determines where the country is categorized in Almond and Verba's scheme. As a result, Almond and Verba's indicators of political culture cohere far more loosely than the constituent parts of culture do for Benedict, Geertz, and most anthropologists (Merelman 1991, 52; see also Almond 1980).[15]

Although the civic culture data are more or less consistent with the authors' theory, there are large questions that remain from a study using individual level survey data to discuss national political patterns, such as how to explain the sometimes large numbers of people who do not fit a country's dominant pattern, the role of weak conception of culture that emerges from their individualistic approach, and the relationship between political and other domains of culture (Verba 1980). The relatively low correlations among attitudes, the very small number of respondents who fit ideal-typical patterns, and the subjective, but not intersubjective nature of survey data mean that survey evidence alone is insufficient to describe the existence and significance of cultural meaning systems. In contrast, Merelman's (1991) comparative study of political culture in the United States, Canada, and Britain is based on a richer view of culture as a system of meaning and includes intersubjective cultural data derived from television programs, corporate publications, textbooks, and magazine ads along with survey data.[16]

Nonetheless, survey research in literally dozens of countries has produced hundreds of studies in the civic culture tradition, including another large-scale study in which Verba and his colleagues examined political participation in seven countries (Verba, Nie, and Kim 1978). Perhaps, however, Inglehart (1977, 1988) is the political scientist who has most faithfully carried out work in the civic culture tradition, emphasizing culture in interpreting cross-national survey data using the yearly Euro-Barometer surveys. For example, he has explained in cultural terms the strong political and life-style differences between individuals who emphasize what he calls materialist and postmaterialist values, i.e., emphasis on order and the economy versus participation and free speech. Arguing that political scientists often develop explanations that give short shrift to cultural factors, Inglehart links the strength of a syndrome of attitudes he calls civic culture—personal life satisfaction, political satisfaction, interpersonal trust, and support for the existing social order—to democratic stability and economic development (1988).

Finally, although it does not rely on survey data as exclusively as Almond and Verba or Inglehart, Putnam's (1993) work on the political differences in the civic cultures in northern and southern Italy is also squarely in this tradition. To the survey evidence he presents, Putnam also adds data on governmental performance, aggregate economic and political participation data, and interviews with political elites. Using these different data, Putnam argues that democracy and democratic innovations are most effective where there is a strong tradition of civic participation. When he examines alternative explanations for the relative success of Italian regionalization in 1976, he argues that those regions in which civic participation has flourished for perhaps the past 800 years are most likely to be those in which effective regional governments developed, whereas in regions without such cultural traditions (such as the one Banfield studied), the governments are less effective.[17]

Culture and Political Process: The Extended Case
Although political anthropology has existed as a field for decades, only a few political scientists have found its theoretical insights or methods of great interest (Barkun 1968; Bates 1983; Easton 1959; Friedrich with Horwitz 1968; Laitin 1986; Masters 1964). Much of this is probably due to the field's emphasis on documenting variations in political structure in human communities. Among these works one finds Fortes and Evans-Pritchard (1940), who provide detailed descriptions of eight African states and stateless societies in which kinship forms the basis of political organization and who argue strongly that politics does not require a state with a monopoly over the means of legitimate force, as Weberians have argued. Others illustrate the complex ways in which different societies deal with leadership succession, political decision making, and conflict management (Goody 1966; Kuper and Richards 1971; Pospisil 1971). Cross-cultural studies in this tradition examine patterns among political variables and relations between them and social, economic, and ecological factors (Murdock 1949; Ross 1986, 1988). From the point of view of cultural approaches to comparative politics, most structural studies in political anthropology, while documenting differences among societies, do not pay much explicit attention to culture per se.

In contrast to structural studies, works that put political process at their core have greater theoretical and methodological relevance for comparative politics. Initially developed by Max Gluckman and his followers in field research in southern Africa (and later known as the Manchester School), these studies focused on explaining how and why particular political outcomes occur, providing rich details about political conflict in which culture's role is at center stage (Gluckman 1942; Mitchell 1956; Epstein 1958; Turner 1957, 1968; Cohen 1969, 1974). These studies, which particularly influenced Africanists, offered a deeply contextualized account of particular events or problems to develop broad middle range theory that is especially useful in comparative political analysis.[18] For example, in one study, Victor Turner (1957) analyzed how the Ndembu of Zambia cope with the strong conflicting structural demands between their norms of political succession and postmarital residence. He argued that strong cross-cutting ties in their society provide the basis for the extensive use of ritual, which emphasizes what members share and integrates a group that often finds itself bitterly divided on other grounds. Abner Cohen, whose work was discussed in detail above, argues that culture provides a strategic, although not necessarily conscious, basis for political mobilization of groups whose positions cannot be defended through more conventional political means. An examination of ethnic mobilization in the last decade in Eastern Europe (and elsewhere) shows the power of his analysis, which few political scientists have examined, and offers a theoretical context for explaining the behavior of political leaders whose ability to survive in multicultural contexts is uncertain.

The extended cases of interest here are those that use culture to explain why and how a political conflict takes the course it does. For example, Scott (1985) analyzes the responses to irrigation and the institutionalization of double cropping in Sedaka, a village in Malaysia, in terms of how the richer and poorer rice farmers understand the demands of traditional norms and obligations in light of new opportunities and challenges. His study includes several detailed cases, one concerning the village gate and another involving a politically motivated village improvement scheme, that are especially effective at showing how the competing interests are manifest within a culturally homogeneous village. Scott demonstrates that it is only because the villagers' shared understandings are so great that small actions that an outsider might easily miss can contribute to the continuing battle over access to resources.

Political Ritual and Identity

Before Murray Edelman published *The Symbolic Uses of Politics* (1964), few political scientists gave much serious thought to issues of political symbolism and ritual. Since then, comparativists ignore it at their peril. Edelman's core argument was simple but important. Politics, he said, is a passing parade of symbols to which we react on two levels: the cognitive, which involves the information any symbol communicates; and the affective, which consists of powerful feelings political symbols can invoke. The ability of leaders to provide symbolic reassurance to the masses allows organized groups to take the lion's share of material benefits for themselves. Edelman and the many people he influenced more indirectly have made the study of political symbolism and ritual central to analyses of political institutions and dynamics. For our point of view here, this work is crucial because it shows how cultural frameworks render political symbols and rituals significant in a wide range of settings and to a wide number of political dynamics (Brysk 1995).

Whereas earlier analyses, for example, emphasized elections as citizen choice making, a more cultural analysis would also pay attention to how political parties and candidates, in their quest for power, use culturally shared metaphors and culturally rooted fears in their appeals to citizens. Policy positions or candidate choices, we now understand, are not just about the issue preferences of individuals; we also must ask how such orientations are or are not consonant with shared cultural understandings and identities. The invocation of symbols and use of rituals do not just indicate points of consensus; they are also efforts to overcome contradictions in situations of disjunction (Kurtz 1991, 149).

This richer understanding of politics' cultural roots has produced an interest in how political rituals create (rather than just reflect) meanings and shape actions (Gusfield 1966). There is attention to high-visibility political rituals such as the torchlight marches in East Germany in the waning days of the old regime in 1989, and how participation in these events provided the courage for citizen participation under a regime that earlier made such action unthinkable. More generally, political transitions, such as the changes in Eastern Europe or in South Africa between 1990 and 1994, can only be explained effectively when we make sense of the interaction between substantive change and ritual action.

An even stronger position is that political rituals are particularly critical to constructing political reality for most people (Edelman 1988; Kertzer 1988, 77-101) and that the power to control ritual is important. Indeed, ritual is an important means of influencing people's ideas about political events, political policies, political systems, and political leaders. Through ritual, people develop their ideas about what are appropriate political institutions, what are appropriate qualities in political leaders, and how well the world around them measures up against these standards (Kertzer 1988, 79). In short, rituals are important instruments of control and from a Gramscian point of view are central mechanisms for obtaining and maintaining power. Detailed analyses of meaning-construction rituals would examine social movements as well as the mass media, which increasingly for citizens of mass democracies provide not only access to core knowledge but also the framework for making sense of it (Dayan and Katz 1992).

Political rituals offer meaning in ambiguous, uncertain situations and are crucial to the dynamics of identity construction and maintenance, particularly in periods of change. In bringing certain people together, culturally rooted rituals simultaneously exclude others. Powerful political rituals are those that utilize culturally rooted metaphors and meanings to offer a vision of reality; often this involves pitting one group against another by raising fears and threats to the point that people are all too ready to undertake strong action in the name of the group.

Culture and Political Conflict
In many analyses culture plays a central role in explaining the level and form of political conflict and violence. Culture in these analyses provides a system of meaning to make sense of the actions and motives of opponents and a mechanism for building and maintaining identity. Within-group worldviews are reinforced as groups increase in-group solidarity and out-group hostility increases. Not all cultural mobilization in conflict situations leads to violence, however, and one important comparative question concerns when this turn to violence occurs and when it does not.

For example, Laitin (1995a) offers a controlled comparison emphasizing culturally constituted differences in social organization to explain the high use of political violence in the Basque protest in Spain and its relative absence in nearby Catalonia. He identifies as a significant difference between these subcultures relative importance of autonomous male groups with strong norms of honor in the small towns in the Basque region and their relative absence in Catalonia. When these small, local male groups engage in protest that produces some limited and mainly symbolic successes, violence becomes self-sustaining.[19] As a result, the differences in the use of violence between the regions are not a function of objective differences or relative deprivation within them but of the cultural organization of each community, which affects the likelihood that the ethnic revivals in each community will turn to violence.

Ross (1993a) provides a more general cross-cultural analysis to explain differences in levels and targets of conflict and violence. He finds that psychocultural variables—low warmth and affection in child rearing, harsh socialization, and male gender identity conflict—were excellent predictors of a society's overall level of violence, while social structural factors, such as the strength of cross-cutting ties or the presence of exclusive male groups, determined whether targets were within the same society, in another society, or both. He goes on to argue that cultural worldviews determine how groups see outsiders and the motives attributed to them. In addition, the culture of conflict is a crucial determinant not just of a group's level of conflict but also of how conflict is managed when it occurs (Ross 1993b).

Raymond Cohen demonstrates how culture provides a framework through which political leaders understand the actions and words of others in his examination of how cultural assumptions complicate the task of diplomatic negotiations. First through an analysis of Egyptian-Israeli negotiations over time (1990), and then through an examination of how cultural miscommunication has affected U.S. negotiations with Mexico, Egypt, China, India, and Japan, Cohen (1991) suggests that differences in time frames and in the importance of context, language, and individualistic versus collectivist ethos all are important in either inhibiting or facilitating negotiated efforts to deal with international issues. Focusing only on "substance," he contends, leads to serious missed opportunities and failures where successes might have emerged.

Finally, culture is central in the ethnic and identity disputes that have seemingly proliferated in recent years. In intransigent conflicts between groups with very different systems of meaning and distinct identities, cultural factors easily become the focal point of many conflicts when they are central to the parties' definition of the dispute (Ross 1997). In such situations, each group readily sees itself as a threatened minority whose very existence is precarious (Horowitz 1985). Frequently, in conflicts such as the one in Northern Ireland, differences are framed so that central elements of one culture are seen as powerful threats to the other; in these cases one can only imagine a resolution that addresses these culturally rooted fears head-on (Mulvihill, Ross, and Schermer 1995).

Critique of Cultural Analyses of Politics

Cultural studies of politics have been subject to a number of important criticisms about which proponents cannot remain silent. Perhaps the most significant problems arise over methodological issues such as the vagueness of culture as a unit of analysis or the issue of within- versus between-cultural variation. Others are concerned with the vagueness of the concept of culture and the difficulty in distinguishing culture from related concepts such as social organization, political behavior, and values. Some are worried that, since culture suggests relatively fixed, unchanging patterns of behavior, it is not terribly useful in accounting for changes in behavior and beliefs, a key feature of most contemporary political systems. Finally, there is concern that cultural analyses are not sufficiently explicit concerning the mechanisms linking culture and political action. Each of these criticisms is worth some brief comments. However, it should be clear that my view is that none of these problems is fatal and that in the cultural approach to comparative politics, like those rooted in interests or institutions, the best way to address the conceptual and methodological problems is through a multimethod search for convergence rather than abandonment of the theory.

Unit of Analysis Issues
Defining the unit of analysis precisely—be it voters, states, wars, or international organizations—is one of the first lessons of most methods seminars in political science. "What is a culture?" some political scientists ask, meaning "How do I know one when I see one?" since culture is not a unit of social or political organization with readily identifiable boundaries. Furthermore, the imprecision of common language use makes it very unclear what are a culture's key properties. As a result we hear references to western culture, French culture, Breton culture, rural Breton culture, etc. Where does the parsing stop? Conceptually the best answer is that the appropriate level of analysis depends on what one wants to explain. However, this is not always an easy-to-use methodological guide in empirical research.

Huntington offers a similar answer when he describes a range of what he calls cultural entities starting with villages and moving to regions, ethnic groups, nationalities, religious groups, and civilizations. Each has distinct cultural features that distinguish it from similar units in other cultural entities. The key for him is that the civilization is "the highest grouping of people and the broadest level of cultural identity people have short of that which distinguishes humans from other species" (1993, 24). Following Horowitz (1985), he says that the level of cultural identity that is the most salient at any moment depends upon where someone is and what they are doing with whom.

The unit of analysis problem is about what constitutes the core of a culture and also how to identify its edges (Barth 1969). Where does one culture stop and another begin? Since cultures, unlike states or political parties, are not formal units of organization, creating them as independent units of political analysis can be troubling indeed. While this may seem like a devastating critique to some, it is just as true that neither states nor voters are as independent as our political and methodological theories lead us to believe. For purposes of most analyses we emphasize the independence of all these units. What is probably more useful is to be more sophisticated about interaction effects and the influence of one unit upon another.[20]

Probably the best answer to these methodological problems is to begin with the recognition that cultural identity is layered and situationally defined.[21] People hold multiple identities, some identities partially overlap, and the group boundaries can shift across issues. Despite the methodological problems this can present, we cannot ignore culture if we think it is important, and we should make decisions about units of analysis based on what we are trying to explain rather than on abstract criteria intended to identify a set of cultural units akin to a list of all UN member states.[22] In addition, there are a number of other procedures we can use to define cultural units in particular pieces of research. For example, we can use operational criteria such as asking people how they identify themselves and others and use social consensus about particular cultural groups and their boundaries. The point is that the task for research is to identify relevant groupings in whatever situation is under study. The fact that people can have multiple identities or that identities can change over time does not invalidate such analysis, it just makes the research more complicated. Good longitudinal data on socially defined cultural identities might be of real importance, for example, in understanding the breakdown of Yugoslavia and its recent civil war.

Political culture research in the Almond and Verba tradition ought to solve the problem by defining culture as the aggregate of individual orientations. Almond and Powell, for example, define political culture as "the pattern of individual attitudes and orientations towards politics among members of a political system" (1966, 23). Reducing culture to the sum of individual attitudes is hardly adequate, however, ignoring both the context in which particular attitudes are held and the shared understandings that organize clusters of intersubjective orientations (Merelman 1991). Culture, as a result, is no longer a system of meanings and identity; rather, it is simply a frequency distribution on a set of single attitude items—a kind of machine with totally interchangeable parts. While studying individuals is one way that we can understand culture, as both Taylor (1985, 37) and Geertz (1973a) argue, culture is not the property of single individuals, for it is rooted in social practice and shared understandings, and survey data alone cannot build a rich understanding of political culture. This explains why survey data alone are inherently limited as a tool for studying political culture; they must be used in conjunction with other data to provide a coherent portrait of any single culture or comparisons between cultures.

Within-Culture Variation Can Be Substantial

It often seems easy to say what members of formal groups have in common. But what exactly do people of a given culture share? My answer is shared meanings and a common identity. Operationally, this can be ambiguous, however, for we know that people who themselves identify with a culture (or any organized group) may also differ in terms of values, lifestyles, political dispositions, religious belief and practice, and ideas about common interests. In addition, Strauss (1992, 10-11) cautions that while there may be some variation in schemas (what I have been calling worldviews) across individuals in the same culture, even those with very similar schemas may not internalize exactly the same things, and that the ambiguity of metaphor produces variation in responses. However, this is not necessarily any more a problem in dealing with culture than with other units (or even intra-individual variation in behavior or attitudes over time). LeVine (1984, 68) argues that emphasizing culture as common understandings of the symbols and representations they communicate does not mean there is necessarily a problem with within-cultural variation in thought, feeling, and behavior.

A second answer is that often what is more crucial politically than agreement on content is that people share a common identity, although this still leaves open the question of different degrees of identification and differences in the actions people are willing to undertake in the name of that identity. Shared identities mean that people see themselves as similar to some people and different from others and are open to potential mobilization on the basis of these differences. What an emphasis on identity stresses, once again, is that the relevant critical aspects of cultural similarity and difference are defined in specific political contexts. It is also the case that often what people believe they share may be at odds with reality because perceptions of cultural homogeneity overemphasize what is actually shared, minimizing within-group while stressing between-group differences. In this dynamic, in-group conformity pressures will lead people both to selectively perceive greater within-group homogeneity on critical characteristics than actually exists and to generate greater actual homogeneity and group conformity in situations where perceived threats to the culture are great.

Distinguishing Culture from Other Concepts

Some uses of the concept of culture, such as much of the early work on national character, defined culture so broadly as to include society, personality, values, and institutions. In fact, nothing was excluded.[23] The very broad use of the concept of culture is also seen among social scientists emphasizing culture as a source of the social integration of a society. This perspective, probably clearest in functional theory in British social anthropology, would use culture to refer both to distinct elements of social organization and to the "fit" between different parts of a cultural system and the integration of the whole. The problem here is not the concept of culture but the way it is used. As noted above, the current anthropological focus is on culture meaning systems distinct from social structure and behavior. D'Andrade (1984) makes this particularly clear in his description of culture "as consisting of learned systems of meaning, communicated by means of natural language and other symbol systems, having representational, directive, and affective function, and capable of creating cultural entities and particular senses of reality. Through these systems of meaning, groups of people adapt to their environment and structure interpersonal activities" (116). I find Spiro's (1984) clear distinction between culture as a system of meaning, and what he calls "culturally constituted elements," referring to social structure, behaviors, beliefs, rituals, etc., particularly helpful here.

Spiro's (1984) distinction between culture and culturally constituted elements allows us to distinguish between cultural meanings and identity on the one hand and structure, behaviors, and individual beliefs on the other. Structure, from this perspective, is reflective of (and to some extent derived from) culture, but it is independently measurable, and an important empirical question concerns the conditions under which the correspondence between culture and various culturally constructed elements is high and when it is not. We also can examine hypotheses about change and examine how culture, structure, and other phenomena do and do not shift in patterned ways. Last, the distinction makes it feasible to compare societies in which the correspondence between culture and social structure are high and those in which they are low to test hypotheses about the impact of consistency on such things as citizen satisfaction with government, political involvement, and political stability.

Culture and Change
Cultures are commonly viewed as slow-changing entities. How, then, can the concept of culture help comparativists deal with issues of political change, especially relatively rapid developments such as the end of military rule in many Latin American states during the 1980s or the breakup of the Soviet empire?

Three points are worth making. First, cultural analyses are no better than any other partial theories, such as interest or institutional ones, available in comparative politics. There are some phenomena for which each is most powerful, and some aspects of change are not best explained in cultural terms. Second, and interestingly, while it is not clear that cultural theories would have explained the fall of the Soviet empire very well (many other comparative political theories share this feature), a political cultural analysis is probably a good deal better at accounting for the ebb and flow of politics in the region since 1989 than many of its rivals (Fleron 1996). Particularly in unstructured, changing settings, cultural interpretations and assumptions about the motivation of others can be especially important in accounting for political processes in which there are few or no institutionalized procedures to guide action. Third, few contemporary views see culture as a static, unchanging phenomenon marked by fixed beliefs and unalterable practices (Eckstein 1988). Rather, emphasis on the interactive, constructed nature of culture suggests a capacity to modify beliefs and behaviors, and for important shifts in the salience of particular cultural understandings and their connections to other cultural elements (Goode and Schneider 1994; Merelman 1991).

Culture can play a significant role in political change despite the fact that culture itself does not change rapidly, if, and when political demands are articulated through culturally meaningful accounts, which sharpen goal articulation and mobilize supporters. Defining culturally legitimate possible alternatives both builds support and can challenge a regime. Brysk (1985) argues that this is particularly powerful when it involves reframing elements of identity in a way that mobilizes supporters, produces agenda change, and challenges the legitimacy and authority of existing policies and institutions (580-2).

The Mechanisms Underlying Cultural Explanations
Asking "how culture works" raises two different questions: (1) How does the organization of any particular culture produce the specific effects attributed to it? and (2) why are appeals to cultural identity so powerful that people are willing to take high risks in their name? The first is about the organization of culture and the second about its mobilizing power.

Theories that give culture a central explanatory role must specify how the effects attributed to culture come about. It is not good enough to simply say, "They did it because they're Germans." While this statement implies that non-Germans (such as the Japanese or French) would have behaved differently, adding a clause to this effect doesn't really enhance the explanation a great deal. Only when one starts to say why Germans are likely to behave in a certain way that is different from how Americans behave (in what is presumed to be an equivalent situation) do we begin to have an adequate explanation that pays attention to the content of culture and also says something about how it is learned and reinforced (Andrade 1992; Strauss 1992).[24] Indeed this was a central concern of early political culture research, although few were very impressed with the adequacy of explanations it provided. Learning and reinforcement involve institutional contexts in which a person (child or adult) practices, and then masters, key behaviors, infusing them with emotional significance.[25]

Social experiences within institutions such as schools, religious organizations, kin groups, and later in work and leisure settings all provide cultural messages that are selectively reinforced. It is certainly the case that the messages from different domains are not always fully consistent. Sometimes there is a difference in emphasis; at other times there is an outright contradiction, e.g., peer groups and families don't necessarily give adolescents the same messages. However, what are most important from a cultural perspective are the beliefs, customs, rituals, behaviors, expectations, and motives that are internalized by individuals and widely shared among people in a culture even though they may also, at the same time, be highly contested. For example, Scott's (1985) study of a small rice-growing village in Malaysia shows how people can share meanings while at the same time compete over how specific elements are to be weighted and in what situations specific cultural elements are most relevant. Culture is about what is held in common and regularly reinforced; there is a reward for "getting it right" and a cost—which most people are willing to pay at times—for not doing so. Finally, it should be noted that cultural learning is not necessarily very conscious, occurring when individuals in institutional roles pass on culturally sanctioned beliefs and behaviors to others. Through these experiences culture prepares people to make sense of—to interpret—the world and act "effectively" in it.

The power of culture—the ability to mobilize action in its name—requires explanation, for it is not always the case that people can or will exhibit solidarity around cultural identity just because a leader (or anyone else) asserts that there is an external threat. Cultural mobilization builds on fears and perceived threats that are consistent with internalized worldviews and regularly reinforced through high in-group interaction and emotional solidarity. Such worldviews are expressed in daily experiences as well as significant ceremonial and ritual events that effectively restate and renew support for a group's core values and the need for solidarity in the face of external foes (Kertzer 1988). In potentially threatening situations, the ability of a group to organize collective action, which can range from unified voting to political demonstrations and violent action, is tied to the plausibility of a specific worldview—although the view itself does not produce direct effects. Rather, these must be mediated through institutions

(Laitin 1986, 1995a). The resonance between the definition of a situation and group-based action is often not explicit, as Abner Cohen's (1969) analysis points out. Nonetheless it is effective when group members act in unified ways in the face of perceived threats. Closer examination of the dynamics of psychocultural interpretation in the next section suggests additional specific mechanisms at work.

The Centrality of Interpretation in Cultural Analyses of Politics

At the core of contemporary intersubjective approaches to culture and politics is the concept of interpretation. Culture in the Geertzian, postmodern view is a system of meaning and identity that accounts for why and how people in any particular setting act as they do, in contrast to the idea of culture as a set of norms or behaviors that directly shape action. This culture-as-meaning-and-identity perspective gives a central role to interpretation, the making of meaning from the ambiguous and fragmented elements of daily life (Darnton 1985; Taylor 1985). While there is widespread agreement that a subjective, meaning-centered conception of culture is richer than more mechanistic or material views, there is also fundamental disagreement concerning the goals of cultural explanations of politics. More humanistically oriented political (and other social) scientists emphasize the role of particular contextual and historical forces that shape meaning for actors. Their concern is with the uniqueness of each context as actors understand it, and they have little interest in accounting for patterns of similarity and difference across settings. This emphasis on the uniqueness of each cultural context and its particular meaning for actors readily leads to the conclusion that any search for generalization is pointless, for the only generalizations that might be offered are uninteresting. At the same time, this radical interpretivist view denies the value of any comparison at all and is not the one I develop here (Edgerton 1992, 23-45).[26]

In contrast, more socially scientifically oriented investigators, while accepting the intersubjective and subjective character of culture, seek to identify the mechanisms that link culture and action, and to identify regularities in cultural behavior across settings. One approach found in psychological anthropology draws on both psychoanalytic and cognitive theories to explain how culture affects behavior (e.g., D'Andrade 1992; Spiro 1987). It emphasizes, for example, how individuals absorb, process, and modify cultural knowledge (information, affect, images) to develop images of the world, and how these images affect collective and individual action.

Here I discuss the conceptual and methodological importance of interpretations, arguing that they are key tools for understanding culture and politics. The rich accounts found in the images of the world's people point to key concerns, assumptions about how social and political relations are organized, and views about the possibilities for political action. These images of the world are obtainable, in part, through public and private accounts. However, simply presenting the transcripts of individuals' stories is insufficient for a number of reasons, including the important one that texts do not speak for themselves and without an intermediary they often make no sense to an outsider (Scott 1985, 138-41). Rather, the comparativist needs to frame accounts in both a cultural and comparative context and highlight the crucial elements (Kohli et al. 1995, 44-5).[27] Laitin (1988) says that connecting culture and action requires detailed, local, ethnographic knowledge and experience. Without a rich contextual understanding, it is too difficult to derive much significance from the detailed, highly contextualized interpretations of the world that hardly ever speak for themselves.[28]

The interpretations of interest here are accounts of the world that people within a culture widely share (or at least easily understand).[29] Elsewhere I use the term psychocultural interpretations to describe how shared interpretations are acquired through individual-level psychological (and social-psychological) mechanisms that are widespread in a culture (Ross 1993a, 1995).[30] Psychocultural interpretations are the basis on which people in a culture understand the world and link specific worldviews to political action, offering rich data for comparative political analyses.

Psychocultural interpretations offer plausible accounts of the world, emphasizing the motives of different actors and reinforcing those features that distinguish one's own group from others. When supported by one's social world, these plausible accounts offer psychic and social protection from the ambiguities and uncertainties of existence, reinforcing social and political bonds within groups. The power of psychocultural explanations lies in their shared social character, not those idiosyncratic features that distinguish one person's account from another's. As Taylor (1985) writes, "They are not subjective meanings, the property of one or some individuals, but rather inter-subjective meanings which are constitutive of the social matrix in which individuals find themselves and act" (36).

At the core of psychocultural interpretations are internalized, shared orientations rooted in the earliest social relationships that help people in a culture make sense of the inherently ambiguous, highly charged events that characterize their lives (Ross 1995). Psychocultural interpretations draw attention not just to what people do to each other but also to what one group of people think or feel that another group of people are doing, trying to do, or wanting to do. In a context of suspicion and uncertainty, not only actions but also presumptions about the intentions and meanings behind the actions play an important role. This is crucial, for in few political situations do external events provide clear explanations for what is occurring; to develop these, individuals turn to internal frameworks which then shape subsequent behavior.

While participants in any dispute can often tell someone "just what the conflict is about," this precision is often illusory, and political scientists often see this precision as evidence of flawed decision making and/or faulty information processing. However, it is more useful to view these "errors as important data about the social dynamics. In many situations, different parties don't always agree about what a conflict is about, when it started, or who is involved, for they operate from (but are not aware of) alternative frames of references that shape their actions. Many disputes, whether they are between families in a community or nations in the world, involve parties with a long history, which, of course, includes long lists of accumulated grievances that can be trotted out and appended to newer ones as political conditions shift (Scott 1985). In many situations, complex conflicts are about a range of issues that are not of equal interest to all parties. For example, Hager (1995) offers a particularly clear case in her examination of conflict in West Berlin over energy policy, which she examines in terms of both the public policy considerations and the democratization issues concerning the legitimation of citizen roles in decision making on technologically complex matters. Decision makers saw the issues as technical ones needing conflict management, while citizen groups emphasized the legitimation of citizen participation.

The same factors that push actors to make a sense of a situation also lead to cognitive and perceptual distortion, because the desire for certainty is often greater than the capacity for accuracy. Not only are disputants likely to make systematic errors in the "facts" underlying interpretations, but the homogeneous nature of most social settings and cultural amplifiers reinforces these self-serving mistakes. What is most crucial, however, about interpretations of politics is the compelling, coherent account they offer to the parties in linking discrete events to general understandings. Central to such interpretations is the attribution of motives to parties. Once identified, the existence of such motives seemingly makes it easy to "predict" another's future actions, and through one's own behavior to turn such predictions into self-fulfilling prophesies. In this sense, it is appropriate to suggest that rather than thinking about particular objective events that cause conflicts to escalate, we ought to be thinking about the *interpretations* of such events that are associated with escalation and those that are not.[31]

Psychocultural interpretations are found in the stories parties recount about past experiences, present difficulties, and future aspirations. These accounts are valuable for revealing how participants think about and characterize their political worlds. In fact, as we listen to them it is important to consider the extent to which stories from different groups or factions differ without necessarily directly contradicting each other, as each selects key events in its effort to gain supporters and to make sense of its actual experience (Scott 1985).[32]

This can be seen vividly in stories about long-standing ethnic conflicts that contain the culturally rooted aspirations, challenges, and deepest fears of communities. Volkan (1988) uses the term "chosen trauma" to refer to a specific experience that comes to symbolize a group's deepest threats and fears through feelings of helplessness and victimization (1991, 13). Volkan and his collaborators provide many examples of such events including the Turkish slaughter of Armenians, the Nazi holocaust, the experience of slavery and segregation for African Americans, and the Serbian defeat at Kosovo by the Turks in 1389.[33] If a group feels too humiliated, angry or helpless to mourn the losses suffered in the trauma, Volkan suggests that it then incorporates the emotional meaning of the traumatic event into its identity and passes on the emotional and symbolic meaning from generation to generation.[34] In escalating intergroup conflicts, the key metaphors, such as the chosen trauma, serve both as a rallying point and as a way to make sense of events that evoke deep fears and threats to existence (Horowitz 1985; Kelman 1978, 1987). Only when the deep-seated threats these stories represent are addressed, he suggests, is a community able to begin to formulate a more peaceful future with its enemies.

Psychocultural interpretations reflect but also strengthen the boundary between in-groups and out-groups. The process of telling and listening to—validating[35] if you will—stories of past traumas and glories strengthens the link between individual and group identity and emphasizes how threats to the group are also threats to individual group members. In long-term intransigent conflict, strong threats to identity are an essential part of the conflict dynamic, and any efforts to defuse such a situation must take seriously the stories that participants recount, and the perceived threats to identity. The point, after all, is not whether participants' accounts are true or false from some objective point of view but that they are meaningful to the parties involved.

Interpretations play a central role in the construction of ethnic and national identities (Anderson 1991; Brubaker 1996; Gellner 1983; Hobsbawm and Ranger 1983; Smith 1986; Tambiah 1986). The examination of interpretations over time is a tool for understanding the contested nature of history and for discerning how one account comes to be accepted as "what really happened" while other plausible stories of the past are rejected. Interpretations of the past are found in how people talk and write about it but are also found in the public rituals and myths built around key events in the national (or ethnic) past. The rituals and myths are significant because of the meanings and metaphors surrounding a group's history that they communicate and reinforce, and because of the political mobilizing potential they have in the hands of political entrepreneurs.

Interpretations as a Methodological Tool

At the core of cultural analyses of politics are people's accounts of their daily worlds. Comparative researchers of all persuasions easily recognize many of the forms in which such accounts appear, such as formal written materials, historical documents, public discourse, government records, law cases, systematic observations, and survey data. In addition, the rich accounts often needed in cultural analysis can only be obtained through ethnographic field research (Laitin 1988; Ross and Ross 1974); in-depth interviews and life histories; structured interviews; extended case analysis of trouble cases; popular culture (Merelman 1991); and public and semipublic myths and rituals. Certainly the process analysis Migdal, Tarrow, and Zuckerman all advocate is central to cultural analysis with its emphasis on interpretations.

The central goal of the culture as a meaning and identity perspective is to understand from the point of view of actors in a particular context why certain actions are undertaken and others are not. What this entails is developing a plausible account—and in the process examining rival accounts of action and showing why they are not as good. There can be a huge gap, however, between the elements in the stories actors offer and how a comparativist understands political action, just as there is a great difference between the content of a patient's dreams and the psychoanalyst's interpretation of how the elements fit together and the dreams' overall significance. Bridging the two requires calling on cultural understandings and building interpretations that both make sense to cultural insiders and can be appreciated by outsiders.[36]

With a few rare exceptions, the most successful work linking culture and politics will not rely on only one source of data or a single tool for data analysis. Our most interesting theories are complex and highly contingent and cannot be simply accepted or rejected on the basis of one crucial piece of evidence, as is the case in some natural sciences. Instead, we need to obtain areas of convergence between independent data collected using a wide range of methods in order to have confidence in a set of findings, as Campbell and Fiske (1959) advocated. Exclusive reliance on one type of data to study the interplay of culture and politics, as is found in some survey researchers such as Inglehart (1988), inevitably produces a thin, almost content-free sense of culture and points to few dynamics of how culture produces the political effects it does. Instead, a more useful approach is one such as Scott's (1985) or Laitin's (1986, 1995a) in which a range of evidence is marshaled to explain a phenomenon that is not self-evident: the presence of everyday, but not overt, resistance among third-world peasants; the absence of bitter conflict between Christians and Moslems in western Nigeria; or why in Spain, the Basque revival has been violent while under very similar circumstances, the Catalonian one was not. Another successful instance of bringing together a range of data is Merelman's (1991) comparison of liberal democratic cultures in the United States, Britain, and Canada, which analyzes television programs, corporate publications, textbooks, and magazine ads along with survey data.

Conclusion

Culture is a worldview offering a shared account of action and its meaning and providing people with social and political identities; it is manifested in a way of life transmitted (with changes and modifications) over time, and embodied in a community's institutions, values, and behavioral regularities. Politics, I have argued, occurs in a cultural context that links individual and collective identities, defines the boundaries between groups and organized actions within and between them, provides a framework for interpreting the actions and motives of others, and provides resources for political organization and mobilization. Cultural accounts of politics emphasize how, through shared intersubjective meanings, actors understand and act in their daily worlds. Beginning with context-dependent accounts—worldviews—cultural analysis constructs plausible interpretations of political life that both seem reasonable to local actors and make sense to outsiders.[37]

I have argued for a "strong" view of culture and against the notion that it can be more simply approached in terms of specific values that people in a community hold. In fact, the significance of the presence or absence of consensus on any single item is often unclear without an analysis of the context. Culture as a system of meaning is not at all incompatible with strong disagreement on particular attitudes (Laitin 1988), and it is often those points of disagreement that are of real political significance and shed light on "tough" problems facing a society. For example, the bitter divisions in some European countries over questions such as the treatment of immigrants or further European political or economic integration are powerful points of tension involving complicated, alternative cultural constructions of what it means to be French or German or British. As a result, a cultural analysis might utilize survey data to document the nature of divisions in a country on these questions, but it would go a good deal further, trying to make sense of why and how they are important to people, the connections between these issues and political and personal identity, and the significance of bitterly contested political meanings and actions within a common cultural framework.

In principle, cultural analysis can enhance our understanding of politics in a number of domains. McAdam, Tarrow, and Tilly (this volume)* describe important cultural contributions in the field of contentious politics and offer a model of how structural, interest, and cultural perspectives can complement each other in explaining significant political phenomena. Seeing social movements as both carriers and makers of meaning, they suggest, enriches older, more developed structural and resource mobilization perspectives. Cultural analyses emphasize framing of action and increase our understanding of the definition of political opportunities and the repertoires of action that are found in different settings. A focus on narrative structuring and symbolic politics expands our capacity to explain collective action in terms of changing preferences, changing identities, and changing responses to resources (Brysk 1995, 567).

Attention to culture would certainly address one of the most widely cited weaknesses of rational choice theory, its inattention to context-specific interests and cross-cultural differences in how interests are conceptualized and articulated. More broadly, political economy might be an area that would benefit from more explicit attention to cultural questions, as Hall (this volume) suggests. For example, political economists have long documented differences in equality of resource distribution across countries, noting places like Scandinavia and Sri Lanka where inequalities are relatively low. While there is certain amount of lip service paid to "cultural differences" in these cases, a more profound analysis would inquire into cultural conceptions of social justice, linked fate, and perhaps the relationship between the individual and the collectivity. Similarly, there are probably strong cultural factors involved in explaining cross-national differences in the locus of decision making and control over the economy. Where economic theory would emphasize efficiency, it may be that culture is much more salient in determining not only how a country resolves such an issue but also how it implements economic and political programs.

Political institutions are another obvious candidate for more culturally oriented research, although such studies are certainly not totally absent. Many students of American legislatures, for example, have found culture particularly helpful in explaining their internal operation (Matthews 1962; Muir 1982). The "folkways" of the U.S. Senate that Matthews identifies to explain its functioning in the 1950s are both specific norms affecting any individual senator's

---

*In original work.

behavior and also a system that cannot simply be understood in terms of its individual elements or the degree to which any senator thinks a particular norm is appropriate. Similarly, as Crozier (1964) demonstrated so effectively, culture can shape the behavior of both public and private bureaucracies, and a cultural model sharply contrasts with explanations derived from a more universal, rational-actor, bureaucratic routinization model.

Finally, conflict is cultural behavior, since culture shapes what people fight about, how they fight, with whom they fight, and how the conflict ends (Avruch 1991; Ross 1993b). Both group goals and group actions are linked to cultural notions of appropriate behavior in the development and pursuit of goals. As a result, culturally shared rules can guide behavior even in the absence of strong institutions to enforce them. Conflict involves both the pursuit of culturally defined competing interests and the parties' divergent interpretations and threats to identity. These interpretations offer alternative metaphors about what is at stake in a conflict and the intensity of the dispute. Only when we examine the cultural meanings from the point of view of the participants can we make sense of why any conflict took the particular course it did.

References

Almond, G. A. 1980. The intellectual history of the civic culture concept. In *The civic culture revisited*, edited by G. Almond and S. Verba. Boston: Little, Brown.
Almond, G. A., and S. Verba. 1963. *The civic culture: Political attitudes and democracy in five nations.* Princeton, NJ: Princeton University Press.
Almond, G. A., and G. B. Powell. 1966 *Comparative politics: A developmental approach.* Boston: Little, Brown.
Anderson, B. 1991. *Imagined communities: Reflections on the origin and spread of nationalism.* London: Verso.
Arendt, H. 1958. What is authority? In *Nomos 1: Authority,* edited by K. Friedrich. Cambridge, MA: Harvard University Press.
Avruch, K. 1991. Introduction: Culture and conflict resolution. In *Conflict resolution: Cross-cultured perspectives,* edited by K. Avruch, P. W. Black, and J. A. Scimecca. New York: Greenwood Press.
Banfield, E. C. 1958. *The moral basis of a backward society.* New York: The Free Press.
Barkun, M. 1968. *Law without sanctions: Order in primitive societies and the world community.* New Haven, CT: Yale University Press.
Barth F., ed. 1969. *Ethnic groups and boundaries.* Boston: Little, Brown.
Bates, R. H. 1983. The centralization of African societies. In *Essays on the political economy of rural Africa,* edited by Robert H. Bates. New York: Cambridge University Press.
Benedict, R. 1934. *Patterns of culture.* Boston: Houghton Mifflin.
———. 1946. *The chrysanthemum and the sword.* Boston: Houghton Mifflin.
Berger, B. M. 1995 *An essay on culture: Symbolic structure and social structure.* Berkeley: University of California Press.
Brubaker, R. 1996. *Nationalism reframed: Nationhood and the national question in the new Europe.* Cambridge: Cambridge University Press.
Brysk, A. 1995. "Hearts and minds": Bringing symbolic politics back in. *Polity* 27:559-585.
Campbell, D. T. 1983. Two distinct routes beyond kin selection to ultrasociality: Implications for the humanities and social sciences. In *The nature of prosocial development: Theories and strategies,* edited by D. L. Bridgeman. New York: Academic Press.
Campbell, D. T., and D. W. Fiske. 1959. Convergent and discriminant validation through the multitrait-multimethod matrix. *Psychological Bulletin* 56: 81-105.
Cecil, R. 1993. The marching season in Northern Ireland: An expression of politico-religious identity. In *Inside European identities: Ethnography in Western Europe,* edited by S. Macdonald. Ann Arbor, MI: Berg Publishers.
Chagnon, N. 1967. Yanomamo social organization and warfare. In *War: The anthropology of armed conflict and aggression,* edited by M. Fried, M. Harris, and R. Murphy. Garden City, NY: Natural History Press.

Cohen, Abner. 1969. *Custom and politics in urban Africa.* Berkeley: University of California Press.

———. 1974. *Two-dimensional man: An essay on the anthropology of power and symbolism in complex society.* Berkeley: University of California Press.

———. 1981. *The politics of elite culture.* Berkeley: University of California Press.

Cohen, R. 1990. *Culture and conflict in Egyptian-Israeli relations.* Bloomington, IN: Indiana University Press.

———. 1991. *Negotiating across cultures: Communication obstacles in international diplomacy.* Washington, DC: USIP Press.

Crozier, M. 1964. *The bureaucratic phenomenon.* Chicago: University of Chicago Press.

D'Andrade, R. G. 1984. Cultural meaning systems. In *Culture theory: Essays on mind, self, and emotion,* edited by R. A. Schweder and R. A. LeVine. Cambridge: Cambridge University Press.

———. 1992. Schemas and motivation. In *Human motives and cultural models,* edited by R.G. D'Andrade and C. Strauss. Cambridge: Cambridge University Press.

D'Andrade, R. G., and C. Strauss. 1992. *Human motives and cultural models.* Cambridge: Cambridge University Press.

Darnton, R. 1985. *The great cat massacre and other episodes in French cultural history.* New York: Basic Books.

Dayan, D., and E. Katz. 1992. *Media events: The live broadcasting of history.* Cambridge, MA: Harvard University Press.

Easton, D. 1959. Political anthropology. In *Biennial review of anthropology,* edited by B. J. Siegel. Stanford, CA: Stanford University Press.

Eckstein, H. F. 1988. A culturalist theory of political change. *American Political Science Review* 82: 789-804.

Edelman, M. 1964. *The symbolic uses of politics.* Urbana: University of Illinois Press.

———. 1988. *Constructing the political spectacle.* Chicago: University of Chicago Press.

Edgerton, R. B. 1992. *Sick societies: Challenging the myth of primitive harmony.* New York: Free Press.

Ekman, P., W. V. Friesen, and P. Ellsworth. 1972. *Emotion in the human face.* Elmsford, NY: Pergamon Press.

Epstein, A. L. 1958. *Politics in an African urban community.* Manchester: Manchester University Press.

Fleron, F. L., Jr. 1996. Post-Soviet political culture in Russia: An assessment of recent empirical investigations. *Europe-Asia Studies* 48.

Fortes, M., and E. E. Evans-Pritchard. 1940. *African political systems.* Oxford: Oxford University Press.

Friedrich, C. J., with M. Horwitz. 1968. The relation of political theory to anthropology. *American Political Science Review* 52: 536-545.

Geertz, C. 1973a. Thick description: Toward an interpretive theory of culture. In *The interpretation of cultures.* New York: Basic Books, Harper Torchbooks.

———. 1973b. Religion as a cultural system. In *The interpretation of cultures.* New York: Basic Books, Harper Torchbooks.

Gellman, M. 1942. *Analysis of a social situation in modern Zululand.* Manchester:Manchester University Press.

Gellner, E. 1983. *Nations and nationalism.* Ithaca, NY: Cornell University Press.

Gluckman, M. 1942. *Nations and nationalism.* Ithaca, NY: Cornell University Press.

Goode, J., and J. A. Schneider. 1994. *Reshaping ethnic and racial relations: immigrants in a divided city.* Philadelphia: Temple University Press.

Goody, J. 1966. *Succession to high office.* Cambridge: Cambridge University Press.

Gorer, G., and J. Rickman. 1946. *The great people of Russia.* London: Creset Press.

Greif, A. 1994. Cultural beliefs and the organization of society: A historical and theoretical reflection on collectivist and individualist societies. *Journal of Political Economy* 102: 912-950.

Gusfield, J. R. 1966. *Symbolic crusade: Status politics and the American temperance movement.* Urbana: University of Illinois Press.

Hager, C. J. 1995. *Technological democracy: Bureaucracy and citizenry in the German energy debate.* Ann Arbor: University of Michigan Press.

Hobsbawm, E., and T. Ranger. 1983. *The invention of tradition.* Cambridge: Cambridge University Press.

Horowitz, D. L. 1985. *Ethnic groups in conflict.* Berkeley: University of California Press.

Huntington, S. P. 1993. The clash of civilizations. *Foreign Affairs* (Summer): 22- 49.

Inglehart, R. 1977. *The silent revolution in Europe: Changing values and political styles among Western publics.* Princeton, NJ: Princeton University Press.

———. 1988. The renaissance of political culture. *American Political Science Review* 82: 1203-1230.

Inkeles, A., and D. J. Levinson. 1968. National character; the study of modal personality and sociocultural systems. In *Handbook of social psychology.* Vol. 2, edited by G. Lindzey. Cambridge, MA: Addison-Wesley.

Kelman, H. C. 1978. Israelis and Palestinians: Psychological prerequisites for mutual acceptance. *International Security* 3: 162-186.
———. 1987. The political psychology of the Israeli-Palestinian conflict: How can we overcome the barriers to a negotiated solution? *Political Psychology* 8: 347-63.
Kertzer, D. 1988. *Ritual, politics and power.* New Haven, CT: Yale University Press.
Kohli, A., et al. 1995. The role of theory in comparative politics: A symposium. *World Politics* 48: 1-49.
Kroeber, A. L., and C. Kluckhohn. 1952. *Culture: A critical review of concepts and definitions.* Papers of the Peabody Museum of American Archeology and Ethnology, 47, Vol. 1.
Kuper, A., and A. Richards, eds. 1971. *Councils in action.* Cambridge: Cambridge University Press.
Kurtz, D. V. 1991. Strategies of legitimation and the Aztec state. In *Anthropological approaches to political behavior,* edited by F. McGlynn and A. Tuden. Pittsburgh: University of Pittsburgh Press.
Laitin, D. 1986. *Hegemony and culture: Politics and religious change among the Yoruba.* Chicago: University of Chicago Press.
———. 1988. Political culture and political preferences. *American Political Science Review* 82: 589-593.
———. 1995a. National revivals and violence. *Archives Europeennes de Sociologie* 36: 3-43.
———. 1995b. The civic culture at 30. *American Political Science Review* 89: 168-173.
LeVine, R. 1973. *Culture, behavior and personality.* Chicago: Aldine.
———. 1984. Properties of culture: An ethnographic view. In *Culture theory: Essays on mind, self, and emotion,* edited by R.A. Schwader and R. LeVine. Cambridge: Cambridge University Press.
Levinson, D., and M. Malone. 1981. *Toward explaining human culture: A critical review of the findings of worldwide cross-cultural research.* New Haven, CT: HRAF Press.
Mack, J. 1983. Nationalism and the self. *Psychohistory Review* 2: 47-69.
Masters, R. D. 1964. World politics as a primitive political system. *World Politics* 16: 585-619.
Masters, R. D., and D. Sullivan. 1989. Nonverbal displays and political leadership in France and the United States. *Poltical Behavior* 11: 121-153.
Matthews, D. 1962. *US Senators and their world.* New York: Norton.
McClelland, D. C. 1961. *The achieving society.* Princeton, NJ: Van Nostrand.
Mead, Margaret. 1942. *And keep your powder dry.* New York: Morrow.
Merelman, R. 1991. *Partial visions: Culture and politics in Britain, Canada, and the United States.* Madison: University of Wisconsin Press.
Mitchell, J. C. 1956. *The Kalela dance: Aspects of social relationships among urban Africans in northern Rhodesia.* Rhodes-Livingstone Institute Papers No. 27. Manchester: Manchester University Press.
Muir, William K., Jr. 1982. *Legislature: California's school for politics.* Chicago: University of Chicago Press.
Mulvihill, R. F., M. H. Ross, and V. L. Schermer. 1995. Psychocultural interpretations of ethnic conflict in Northern Ireland: Family and group systems contributions. In *Group Process and Political Dynamics,* edited by M. F. Ettin, J. W. Fidler, and B.D. Cohen. Madison, CT: International Universities Press.
Murdock, G. P. 1949. *Social structure.* New York: The Free Press.
Murray, H. C. 1938. *Explorations in personality.* New York: Oxford University Press.
Naroll, R. 1970. What have we learned from cross-cultural surveys? *American Anthropologist* 72: 1227-1288.
Paige, K., and J. Paige. 1981. *The politics of reproductive ritual.* Berkeley: University of California Press.
Pospisil, L. 1971. *The anthropology of law: A comparative theory.* New York: Harper & Row.
Przeworski, A., and H. Teune. 1970. *The logic of comparative social research.* New York: John Wiley.
Putnam, R. 1993. *Making democracy work: Civic traditions in modern Italy.* Princeton, NJ: Princeton University Press.
Pye, L. 1962. *Politics, personality and nation building: Burma's search for identity.* New Haven, CT: Yale University Press.
———. 1991. Political culture revisited. *Political Psychology* 12: 487-508.
Regan, P. M. 1994. War toys, war movies and the militarization of the United States, 1900-85. *Journal of Peace Research* 31: 45-58.
Ross, J., and M. H. Ross. 1974. Participant observation in political research. *Political Methodology* 1: 63-88.
Ross, M.H. 1986. Female political participation: A cross-cultural explanation. *American Anthropologist* 88: 843-858.
———. 1988. Studying politics cross-culturally: Key concepts and issues. *Behavior Science Research* 22: 105-129.

———. 1993a. *The culture of conflict: Interpretations and interests in comparative perspective.* New Haven, CT: Yale University Press.
———. 1993b. *The management of conflict: Interpretation and interests in comparative perspective.* New Haven, CT: Yale University Press.
———. 1995. Psychocultural interpretation theory and peacemaking in ethnic conflicts. *Political Psychology* 16: 523-544.
———. 1997. Cultural contributions to the study of political psychology and ethnic conflict. *Political Psychology* 18: 299-326.
Ross, M. H., and Homer, E. L. 1976. Galton's problem in cross-national research. *World Politics* 24: 1-28
Scheper-Hughes, N. 1982. *Saints, scholars and schizophrenics: Mental illness in rural Ireland.* Berkeley: University of California Press.
Schweder, R. A., and R. A. LeVine, eds. 1984. *Culture theory: Essays on mind, self, and emotion.* Cambridge: Cambridge University Press.
Scott, J. 1985. *Weapons of the weak: Everyday forms of peasant resistance.* New Haven, CT: Yale University Press.
Shils, E., and M. Young. 1953. The meaning of the coronation. *Sociological Quarterly* 1: 63-81.
Smith, A. D. 1986. *The ethnic origin of nations.* Oxford: Basil Blackwell.
Spiro, M. E. 1984. Some reflections on cultural determinism and relativism with special reference to emotion and reason. In *Culture theory: Essays on mind, self, and emotion,* edited by R.A. Schweder and R.A. LeVine. Cambridge: Cambridge University Press.
———. 1987. Culture and human nature. In *Culture and human nature: Theoretical papers of Melford E. Spiro.* Chicago: University of Chicago Press.
Strauss, C. 1992. Models and motives. In *Human motives and cultural models,* edited by R. G. D'Andrade and C. Strauss. Cambridge: Cambridge University Press.
Tambiah, S. 1986. *Sri Lanka: Ethnic fratricide and the dismantling of democracy.* London: I. B. Tauris.
Tarrow, S. 1996. Making social science work across space and time: A critical reflection on Robert Putnam's *Making Democracy Work. American Political Science Review* 90: 389-397.
Taylor, C. 1985. Interpretation and the sciences of man. In *Philosophy and the Human Sciences,* Vol. 2. Cambridge: Cambridge University Press.
Thompson, M., R. Ellis, and A. Wildavsky. 1990. *Culture theory.* Boulder, CO: Westview Press.
Tilly, C. 1986. *The contentious French: Four centuries of popular struggle.* Cambridge, MA: Harvard University Press.
———. 1995. Contentious repertoires in Great Britain, 1758-1834. In *Repertoires and cycles of collective action,* edited by M. Traugott. Durham, NC: Duke University Press.
Traugott, M., ed. 1995. *Repertoires and cycles of collective action.* Durham, NC: Duke University Press.
Turner, J. 1988. *Rediscovering the social group: A self-categorization theory.* Oxford: Basil Blackwell.
Turner, V. 1957. *Schism and continuity in an African society.* Manchester: Manchester University Press.
———. 1968. Mukanda: The politics of a non-political ritual. In *Local-level politics,* edited by M. J. Swartz. Chicago: Aldine.
Verba, S. 1980. On revisiting the civic culture: A personal postscript. In *The civic culture revisited,* edited by G. A. Almond and S. Verba. Boston: Little, Brown.
Verba, S., N. Nie, and Jue-on Kim. 1978. *Participation and political equality: A seven-nation comparison.* Cambridge: Cambridge University Press.
Volkan, V. D. 1988. *The need to have enemies and allies: From clinical practice to international relationships.* New York: Jason Aronson.
———. 1991. On chosen trauma. *Mind and Human Interaction* 3: 13.
———. 1996. Bosnia-Herzegovina: Ancient fuel of a modern inferno. *Mind and Human Interaction* 7: 110-127
Wallace, A. F. C. 1970. *Culture and personality.* 2d ed. New York: Random House.
Weber, E. 1976. *Peasants into Frenchmen: The modernization of rural France, 1870-1914.* Stanford, CA: Stanford University Press.
Whiting, B. B. 1980. Culture and social behavior: A model for the development of social behavior. *Ethos* 8: 95-116
Wildavsky, Aaron. 1987. Choosing preferences by constructing institutions: A cultural theory of preference formation. *American Political Science Review* 81: 3-21.

CHAPTER 4

The Startling Ability of Culture to Bring Critical Inquiry to a Halt

Patricia Nelson Limerick

Originally published in Chronicle of Higher Education, *October 24, 1997.*

READING INTRODUCTION

Limerick agrees with the authors of the three previous selections that culture can be useful for explaining social life. But, like Elkins and Simeon, she urges us to be cautious with respect to cultural explanations that lack clear specification of the explanatory and dependent variables and the linkages between them. She underscores her brief argument with vivid contemporary examples, drawn primarily from the poststructuralist literature, in which she finds culture employed vaguely to serve any purpose authors require.

READING TEXT

For many of us of a certain age, the concept of culture was our key to the kingdom, the device that decoded mysteries and resolved riddles. Since the 1970s, the idea of culture has become a powerful lens for scrutinizing society, equally effective at helping and, as has become clear recently, hindering our understanding of human thought and action.

Graduate school, everyone agrees, has a "culture" all its own. Twenty-five years ago, I was as impressed as I was irritated by one highly assimilated convert to that milieu, who used ritual repetition as her adaptive strategy. Whatever the book under discussion, this student could be relied on to declare, like a doctor delivering very grim news, that the author had come down with a very bad case of "reification."

In my hometown of Banning, Cal., we did not use words like reification, and I did not know its meaning. Worse, as a point of inverted cultural pride, I assumed that most polysyllables were invented and used primarily to veil intellectual emptiness. In hindsight, I should have paid attention; I should have gone to the dictionary and read "reify: to treat an abstraction as substantially existing, or as a concrete material object." Then I might have realized that my fellow student had provided a warning particularly applicable to that soon-to-be-omnipresent word "culture."

In the years since I was in graduate school, both scholars' and the public's considerations of American history have been refreshed and reinvigorated in ways familiar to every reader. To paraphrase St. Paul in I Corinthians: "Now abideth race, class, and culture." We are better for this, and yet it is necessary to add: "And the most reified of these is culture." Proceeding down the slippery slope from reifying to anthropomorphizing, I believe that culture is now asking to be set free from authority and constraints we have attached to it.

I remember vividly the burst of illumination that the concept of culture delivered—and can still deliver. For me personally, books such as Anthony F. C. Wallace's 1969 *Death and Rebirth of the Seneca* turned the lights on, and books such as Keith H. Basso's *Wisdom Sits in Places* have kept them on. Without the concept of culture, the behavior of an unfamiliar group—the Seneca people and their enthusiasm for war, which Wallace examined, and the Apache people and their capacity to hold sustained conversations consisting entirely of place names, which Basso studied—seemed like anomalous and mysterious fragments. The idea of culture connected the dots, revealing the underpinnings that tied practices to meaning, that made mystery understandable and anomaly explicable.

Culture offered comparable illumination for the study of white Americans. Without culture as an analytic concept, every white scholar was at risk of looking at the behavior of whites in various settings and seeing only "normality." My own favorite example of this is the 1996 book *Nuclear Rites,* by the anthropologist Hugh Gusterson, an ethnographic study of nuclear-weapons designers at Lawrence Livermore Laboratories. Gusterson analyzes taken-for-granted matters—How do employees at weapons plants live with secrecy? What role does ritual play in a designer's first test of his own weapons?—and leaves his readers with a deepened appreciation of the complexity—and the logic—of work on weapons, a very distinctive category of human behavior.

So thank heavens for culture! It helped scholars unlock the maze of historical understanding and walk free.

But then, of course, in the manner of human beings, after a brief, wonderfully expansive stroll, we set to work constructing the *next* maze. By the end of the 1980s, we had our new labyrinth pretty much built. And a key phase in that building was the reification of culture. Many of us seemed to forget that it was a tool for understanding, not a "concrete material object."

Once culture was reified, its surfaces became opaque, more effective at absorbing light than at directing it. Instead of being usefully employed as an explanation or as a causal factor, culture developed a startling ability to bring inquiry to a halt.

Let me use an example easy to observe in undergraduates studying the history of the American West. Why did white men kill Cheyenne and Arapaho women and children in the Sand Creek Massacre in 1864? Because, many students will respond, the culture of the time permitted and encouraged, maybe even required, white Americans to do so. The fact that many white Americans spoke out *against* the killing of Indian women and children vanishes from the picture. With culture as a freestanding, self-determining force of its own, human agency disappears, and automatons march around following culture's inflexible orders.

It is no wonder that many people outside academe have made enthusiastic use of this reified concept of culture. Forced to reckon with enormous accumulations of radioactive waste from the days of nuclear weapons production, the Department of Energy has become an ardent user of the term. Why did the staff at the Nevada Test Site fail to warn people downwind of radioactive fallout? Why did officials at the various weapons plants adopt such careless mechanisms for storing waste? According to many former and present officials, the Atomic Energy Commission and its successor agency, the D.O.E., had a certain, unfortunate but understandable, "institutional culture."

Of course, officials now are earnestly engaged in trying to change that culture, but everyone knows that cultures are very stubborn entities, and that one cannot expect miracles. This assertion that "my culture made me do it" proves to have remarkable power as a defense strategy and a mechanism for dissolving responsibility.

In escaping from monographs and journal articles and heading out into the world, like Dr. Frankenstein's manufactured but very willful monster, culture these days pays no attention to even the most forceful invitations to return to the lab and quit tearing up the town.

One of the most injurious powers of the culture-monster is its talent for erasing very basic questions about power and economic dominance in the United States. Here scholars have proved to be the monster's unwitting allies. In many recent studies, scholars have adopted an approach that comes close to being a formula: Study a particular group and highlight the ways in which that group—be it an ethnic group, a group of women, a group of workers—has determined its own cultural destiny. Note and celebrate a series of cultural successes by the group, the ways in which its members have managed—despite the constraints imposed upon them—to maintain or redefine their family structures, religious practices, processes of self-governance, forms of expression, and personal identities.

In a book following this pattern, whether the group under discussion is made up of Indian people or Mexican Americans after the Conquest, African Americans in slavery or segregation, women under patriarchy, or immigrant workers doing degraded or ill-rewarded labor, the bulk of the book—the chapters on family, community, religion, internal governance, ritual, art, literature, music, and identity—will be full of good news. Sitting alone, almost quarantined from the rest of the text, is the chapter on *economics,* in which it turns out that this group, for all its ability to maintain its culture, got trounced economically.

Culture thus has let us evade the fact that some groups have remained powerless. "Winning all the cultural battles and losing the economic war" is how Tracy Ainsworth, a graduate student at the University of Colorado, has characterized this approach. While there is no question that faith, family, and community offer tremendous comfort against economic hardship, a reified culture has become the consolation prize, the compensation awarded by scholars to neutralize the bitter reality that one group took from another group the control of its land and labor.

By focusing on the culture of those who have been overpowered in history, we have allowed those who sought and exercised coercive power to avoid responsibility for their actions.

Then there is the problem of overaccented difference. The process of reification has made cultures into cohesive, hard-surfaced units, inside which we picture groups of people as living and thinking in separate worlds. Excited by the recognition of how well the concept of culture has worked to explain difference—an excitement matched by the discovery of how much we can learn about the experiences of people formerly excluded from the historical record—we have let the concept of culture evolve into a powerful piece of earthmoving equipment, digging away at what might have been common ground.

In the process, we have helped cut the ground out from under intergroup empathy, compassion, fellow feeling, and understanding. And yet one of the most important tracks of current scholarship explores the ways in which close examination shows an individual culture to be a patchwork of influences and elements adopted from different cultures. In a thousand different ways, we are encountering patterns that do little to support the notion of cultural purity and separation—whether it is the Christian elements incorporated in the 19th–century Ghost Dance movement among some Indian peoples and, later, in the Native American Church, or the gifted use of the white-dominated media by Indian activists such as Russell Means; whether it is the mestizo identity of Mexicans and Mexican Americans or the mixed white-and-black line of descent of most African Americans today.

The greatest public service that scholars studying the United States could perform now would be to spread this recently forged scholarly vision of interrelatedness, of our intertwined destinies, beyond the walls of academe. Even if some people in the United States want separate and pure cultures, identities, and histories, they are about 500 years too late.

The concept of culture has taken human beings a long way down the road toward seeing each other "face to face." But our situation in the 1990s inspires one to turn again to St. Paul's eloquence: "Now we see each other through a glass, darkly; now I know in part." His invocation of a future time of understanding—"But then shall I know even as also I am known"—is not a world apart from the hope for understanding that the concept of culture once made possible.

Free the concept from its captivity in reification, and the faith can live again.

PART II
Culture and Globalizaton

Introduction

"Globalization" is a term that has become widely used to refer to a plethora of developments: social (e.g., converging consumption patterns), technological (e.g., computers and the internet), economic (e.g., growing international capital flows), and political (e.g., people perceiving themselves less as U.S. citizens than as members of transsocietal identity groups such as women, Hispanics, or venture capitalists) (Castells 1998; Jameson and Miyoshi 1998). In this introduction we examine a narrower range of globalization issues that focus on the political-economic position of the United States in the post–cold war world.

During the cold war, relations among states were generally clear-cut. The United States led one collection of societies that included the advanced-industrial, capitalist democracies. The Soviet Union led another group of socialist societies. Societies struggling to attain industrial development formed a "third world." Some developing societies allied themselves, at least loosely, with the United States (e.g., much of Latin America); while a few (e.g., Cuba) maintained close ties with the Soviet Union. Still others were unaligned, but these societies were relatively unusual and, with rare exceptions (e.g., China), they had modest influence on an international system dominated by competition between two "superpowers."

Since the collapse of the Soviet Union and the consequent end of the cold war, the bases for and character of relations among societies have been open to a greater range of interpretation. One loose category of interpretations frequently is referred to in terms of a process various scholars envision: globalization. While the views of different authors contributing to this school of thought vary, collectively they are distinguished by perceiving various forms of convergence occurring among societies. These authors contend that, in the absence of competition between two superpowers representing sharply different social systems, the world's societies are moving—with varying speed and certainty to be sure—toward the model provided by the world's remaining superpower: the United States (Fukuyama 1992).

Frequently this convergence, like the competition that preceded it, is portrayed in ideological or cultural terms. Some scholars emphasize various aspects of American popular culture, such as Coca-Cola or McDonald's, which seem to be taking hold nearly everywhere. Others point to the shift toward democracy that has occurred across the last decade. In Latin America, Eastern Europe, the former Soviet Union, selectively in East Asia (e.g., South Korea and Taiwan), and here and there in Africa democratic forms of government are much more in evidence than they were fifteen years ago (Held 1995). Perhaps most frequently, convergence is thought of in terms of the increasingly global penetration of modern technology and market economies. The Internet and other aspects of contemporary technology facilitate the rapid movement of information and capital around the world, so that it is sometimes nearly as easy and more profitable for a corporation to have its three divisions located in Seattle, Lima, and Jakarta as to have them all in Seattle. In this vision the economies of virtually all societies—and thus the societies themselves—are being reshaped in progressively similar ways by the competitive market forces of increasingly global capitalism (Cox 1999). These forces reward economic efficiency, and advocates of this view foresee the gradual demise of various traditional (and characteristically economically inefficient) local patterns of life as well as some more modern practices (e.g., the relatively generous welfare states of Western Europe) that are designed to smooth social problems related to capitalist development. Our first chapter in this part, by Manfred B. Steger, provides an introduction to and critical commentary on globalization as market ideology or culture.

Other analysts see an entirely different situation. Rather than growing convergence on a single model, they perceive that the aftermath of the cold war has opened the way for greater diversity. Whereas most societies previously found it difficult to avoid having their policies shaped by the dominant Soviet-American competition, they now find it much easier to develop their own distinctive orientations (Moynihan 1993). So, while convergence conceptions either foresee a decline in international conflict or, minimally, a displacement of this conflict from military activities to economic competition, diversity analysts predict various forms of what Samuel P. Huntington in chapter 6 calls a "clash of civilizations." (See Huntington 1993, 1996; also Eisenstadt 1981). Further, like Kennedy (1987), diversity analysts often visualize the U.S. position as in decline, rather than acquiring increased preeminence as convergence theorists often portray it. Huntington (1996, 26-27), for instance, perceives eight civilizations or cultures: Western (Western Europe and North America), Latin American, African, Islamic, Sinic (Chinese), Hindu, Orthodox (Slavic), and Japanese. Moreover, he contends that the Islamic and Sinic civilizations are on the rise, while Western civilization is in relative decline.

One way of evaluating the contrasting claims of the convergence and diversity schools of thought is to examine particular issues. The democratizing trend of the last decade or so offers a rich example. Zakaria (1997) reminds us that Western democracies characteristically combine and attempt to balance two distinct and potentially contradictory goals: (classical Lockean) liberalism in terms of securing various civil and property rights and democracy in terms of empowering (in varying degrees) popular majorities. He calls such democracies "liberal democracies," and contrasts them with both illiberal democracies (e.g., contemporary Yugoslavia) and liberal autocracies (e.g., Hong Kong prior to its reversion to China). Zakaria contends that most new democracies are illiberal rather than liberal, so that the shift toward democracy is less encouraging for Western culture, whose foundation rests on individual rights, than many analysts appear to think. This point raises the issue of whether there are any universal human rights (Bauer and Bell 1999; Mayer 1999; Van Ness 1999). Minimally, liberal democracies appear to support different human rights than do some other societies.

Contrasting meanings of democracy arise as well in what has become known as the "Asian values" dispute (Bauer and Bell 1999; Zakaria 1994). As Hitchcock (1994) shows in his study of corporate executives, when Americans speak of democracy, they generally have liberal democracy—with its deep concern for securing various individual rights and liberties—implicitly in mind. Accordingly, concepts such as "personal freedom" and "the rights of individuals" are important values and represent high priorities for them. Yet when Hitchcock interviewed corporate executives from a variety of Asian societies, they placed higher priority on values such as "an orderly society" and "preserving harmony for the group," values in which their American counterparts showed little interest.

In chapter 7, Donald K. Emmerson argues that "democracy" may take on one meaning in a society in which substantial proportions of the citizenry are more concerned with social order and harmony than with personal freedom and the rights of individuals and a sharply different meaning in a society in which the citizens hold the reverse preferences. Thus, while he sensibly rejects the view that "Asians" believe one thing and Americans another, he allows that pursuit of democracy may result in different governing practices in Asia and North America since rival values often prevail, particularly among the political elites of these two regions.

References and Further Readings

Bauer, J., and D. Bell, eds. 1999. *The East Asian challenge for human rights.* New York: Cambridge University Press.
Bozeman, A. 1975. Civilizations under stress. *Virginia Quarterly Review* 51: 1-18.
Castells, M. 1998. *End of the millenium.* London: Basil Blackwell.
Cox, H. 1999. The market as God. *Atlantic Monthly* 283 (March): 18-23.
Donnelly, J. 1989. *Universal human rights in theory and practice.* Ithaca, NY: Cornell University Press.
Eckstein, H. 1988. A culturalist theory of political change. *American Political Science Review* 82: 789-804.
Eisenstadt, S. N. 1981. Cultural traditions and political dynamics: The origins and modes of ideological politics. *British Journal of Sociology* 32: 155-181.
Emmerson, D. K. 1995. Singapore and the "Asian Values" debate. *Journal of Democracy* 6 (4): 95-105.
Fukuyama, F. 1992. *The end of history and the last man.* New York: Free Press.
Held, D. 1995. *Democracy and global order: From modern states to cosmopolitan governance.* Stanford, CA: Stanford University Press.
Hitchcock, D. 1994. *Asian values and the United States: How much conflict?* Washington, DC: Center for Strategic and International Studies.
Huntington, S. 1993. The clash of civilizations? *Foreign Affairs* 72 (3): 22-49.

———. 1996. *The clash of civilizations and the remaking of world order.* New York: Simon and Schuster.

Inglehart, R. 1997. *Modernization and postmodernization: Cultural, economic and political change in 43 societies.* Princeton, NJ: Princeton University Press.

Jameson, F., and M. Miyoshi, eds. *The cultures of globalization.* Durham, NC: Duke University Press.

Kennedy, P. 1987. *The rise and fall of the great powers: Economic change and military conflict from 1500-2000.* New York: Random House.

Lewis, B. 1990. The roots of Muslim rage: Why so many Muslims deeply resent the West and why their bitterness will not be easily mollified. *Atlantic Monthly* 266 (September): 60-72.

Mahbubani, K. 1998. *Can Asians think?* Singapore: Times Books International.

Mayer, A. E. 1999. *Islam and human rights: Tradition and politics,* 3rd ed. Boulder, CO: Westview.

Moynihan, D. 1993. *Pandaemonium: Ethnicity in international politics.* New York: Oxford University Press.

Putnam, R., with R. Leonardi, and R. Y. Nanetti. 1993. *Making democracy work: Civil traditions in modern Italy.* Princeton, NJ: Princeton University Press.

Ricoeur, P. 1986. Introductory lecture. In *Lectures on ideology and utopia,* edited by G. H. Taylor. New York: Columbia University Press.

Steger, M. 1999. Socialism and the ideological dimensions of globalization. Adapted from M. Steger, *Globalization as market ideology.* New York: Rowman and Littlefield, forthcoming.

———. Forthcoming. *Globalization as market ideology.* New York: Rowman and Littlefield.

Thompson, M., R. Ellis and A. Wildavsky. 1990. *Cultural theory.* Boulder, CO: Westview Press.

Triandis, H. 1995. *Individualism and collectivism.* Boulder, CO: Westview.

Van Ness, P., ed. 1999. *Debating human rights: Critical essays from the United States and Asia.* London: Routledge.

Zakaria, F. 1994. Culture is destiny: A conversation with Lee Kuan Yew. *Foreign Affairs* 73: 109-126.

———. 1997. The rise of illiberal democracy. *Foreign Affairs* 76: 22-43.

CHAPTER 5

Socialism and the Ideological Dimensions of Globalization

Manfred B. Steger

Adapted from Globalism: The New Market Ideology, *forthcoming 2001.*

READING INTRODUCTION

Steger focuses on a worldwide triumph of a market capitalism version of globalization. Following Ricoeur (1986), Steger portrays market ideology similarly to what we would call a culture, a version of individualism. That is, he argues that capitalist ideology/culture offers, first, a partial vision of reality. He stresses that, because this vision is partial, it is distorted. We add that all visions of reality are partial and thus distorted at least with respect to particular phenomena. Second, capitalist ideology/culture legitimates its partial view of the world. Third, it offers its adherents integration through means such as providing a shared identity based on common social activities that develop from similar patterns of selectively attending to and interpreting how the world works. Steger sees this identity as essentially "consumerist," combining elements of what we called the popular culture and market capitalism versions of globalization in our introduction to part II. Steger sees this culture as having effectively vanquished the version of socialism that was embodied in the Soviet Union and similar societies. But he thinks the shallowness of this consumerist ideology is vulnerable to an alternative version of socialist egalitarianism stressing the civil, political, and socioeconomic rights of individuals.

READING TEXT

In an influential essay published ten years ago during the rapid disintegration of the Eastern Bloc, Francis Fukuyama (1989), a resident scholar at the RAND corporation in Washington, D.C., argued that Western liberal democracy and capitalism had won an irreversible victory over all their ideological competitors, most importantly, over socialism. According to Fukuyama and his supporters, the collapse of Soviet-style communism proved that the socialist idea was no longer viable, and history, understood in Hegelian terms as a struggle over political ideas, was over. The world's nations were inexorably moving to adopt market economies, and liberal democracy was swiftly becoming the only viable political order—the only recognized language of legitimate authority.

Ten years later, Fukuyama's hubristic vision of a "post-historical era" has not been realized. After all, the breakdown of communism has not delivered to the people of Eastern Europe the democratic promises of freedom, equality, and solidarity. Contrary to the expectations of Western neoliberal economists like Jeffrey Sacks, the hailed "transition to democracy" in various Eastern European countries has turned out to be a long and painful process with no end in sight—a far cry from the Western promises of quick results through a brief period of "shock treatments." In addition, global capital has to contend with the devastating economic crisis in Asia, and the gap between wealthy countries in the northern hemisphere and the poor South has steadily widened. Finally, the sweeping pronouncements of a "Third Wave" of global democratization ring hollow as we witness the rise of new forms of nationalist, ethnic, and religious violence around the world. In the United States, too, in spite of its supposedly booming economy and Wall Street's soaring stock market, the wages of working people have been stagnating. Most newly created job can be found in the low-paying service sector, and disparities in wealth and well-being are ever more pronounced. For example, in the 1960s, CEOs of large corporations earned thirty times as much money as the average worker, while in the 1990s, top executives received salaries and bonuses that were two hundred times higher than those of the workers who actually produced the corporations' record profits.

At the same time, however, Fukuyama's rhetoric of casting liberal capitalism as the only remaining game in our age of globalization has been eagerly embraced by nearly all Western political leaders. Even "New Laborites" like Tony Blair and Gerhard Schröder are defending "necessary" budget cuts and austerity measures by referring to the power exerted by "global economic pressures." As Mustafa Koc (1994) points out, the surging popularity of the concept of globalization has a lot to do with the rising fortunes of the neoliberal discourse advocating supply-side government programs in different parts of the world since the late 1970s. In the United States, President Bill Clinton tirelessly emphasizes that his neoliberal trade policies—virtually identical to respective Republican proposals—are based upon the "inexorable imperatives" to "grow the economy" and to "globalize free markets."

Predicated upon Fukuyama's pronouncement of the "end of socialism," neoliberal mantras and formulas have contributed to the rise of a powerful globalization ideology which extols the alleged virtues of the market and its role in creating economic efficiency, conditions of individual freedom, and prosperity for all. It is not rare to find academic textbooks on the subject of globalization which open with sweeping statements such as this one: "Globalization, privatization and liberalization have become dominant forces shaping societies and economies the world over. With the fall of communism and the decline of socialism in most parts of the world, these processes have accelerated in the 1990s" (Rao 1998, 1). As theologian Harvey Cox (1999) points out in a recent article, this neoliberal interpretation of globalization driven by omniscient and omnipotent market forces is frequently expressed in quasi-religious language which "assigns to The Market a wisdom that in the past only the gods have known. It knows our deepest secrets and darkest desires." This worship of the market has become stronger than at any point in this century, demanding constant sacrifices from working people in the form of inevitable corporate downsizing, cuts in welfare services, and business's growing ability to evade public accountability.

"Free market" and "democracy" have become virtually synonymous terms whose alleged compatibility often goes unchallenged in public discourse. In spite of the increasing penetration of civil society by the logic of consumerism, the images and sound bites of globalization as market ideology promise prosperity, personal choice, respect for cultural diversity, and political stability through the wondrous workings of the entrepreneurial spirit and global commerce freed of governmental regulation. This neoliberal version of globalization promises to uphold every person's inalienable and sacred right to wear Michael Jordan–endorsed Nikes; to protect the daily ritual of devouring billions and billions of Big Macs; to secure the watching of seemingly endless variations of the same Hollywood movie or TV sitcom; to make available to all consumers the Microsoft and IBM-constructed lanes of the information superhighway; and to extend to all peoples the privilege of listening to Madonna's latest mass-marketed record.

In this essay, I will make the argument that the concept of "globalization" increasingly reflects the slogans of a market ideology that defends, normalizes, and extends the privileged position and interests of global capital. Seeking to saturate the public discourse with their version of globalization, the market ideologists of globalization find themselves in the position of holding a unique rhetorical advantage over those dissenting voices who want to make global capital democratically accountable. Gleefully pointing to the collapse of the Soviet Union and lumping it together with any socialist or radical-democratic project, the advocates of the free market effectively suppress, isolate, and combat their dwindling critics by labeling them indiscriminately as adherents to the "failed ideology" of a bygone era. Rather than responding to the various arguments of progressive critics that reveal the systemic distortions of the new market ideology, neoliberal forces continue to beat up on the communist corpse in order to avoid or detract from more substantive and issue-oriented debates. In this way, the acolytes of the market deemphasize the potential of the globalization process for radical, democratic politics and instead present their economic and political agenda as the only viable and "realistic" vision for a global future.

Offering a critical reading of these strategies, this paper examines the various functions of ideology and their relation to the neoliberal discourse on globalization. This does not mean that I consider "globalization" merely as an imagery construct or a rhetorical package without foundations in material reality. In fact, my focus on the discursive and ideological character of globalization recognizes the interconnectedness of social institutions, concrete political practices and historical processes, and selective ideological interpretations of these processes (Koc 1994). I begin this essay with a brief introduction of influential perspectives on the subject of globalization, followed by a general exploration of the meanings and functions of ideology. Next, I connect my discussion of ideology to some concrete illustrations of the ideological maneuvers and rhetorical strategies employed by neoliberal market ideologists in their desire to present an image of "globalization" that reflects their own political and economic agenda. I close the paper by speculating on the possibilities of resisting these powerful ideological maneuvers. In this context, I am particularly interested in examining whether socialism, understood as a political and ideological project to extend democracy and further global distributive justice, has indeed come to an end, or whether it can still inspire people to generate alternative visions of a democratic global society.

Dimensions of Globalization

It seems appropriate that any general discussion of globalization should be prefaced by a cautionary statement: Cross-regional transfers of resources, technology, and culture did not start in the last two centuries, but the earliest beginnings of globalizing tendencies can be traced to the political and cultural interactions that sustained ancient empires such as Persia, China, and Rome. Andre Gunder Frank (1998), for example, offers in his recent book the provocative thesis that systematic, global interconnections reach as far back as 5,000 years. Rejecting Eurocentric accounts of globalization as ideological masks of domination, he points to the central role of Asian civilizations in the global economy up to about 1800. Appropriately, Frank advances his thesis by acknowledging that each historical era represents a unique constellation of interacting social forces and by noting that there are many factors that make globalization in the late twentieth century different from its ancient roots, or even from its relatively recent nineteenth century precursor.

As Stephen Gill (1997) observes, the term "globalization," referring to a very recent development, has come to be used with increasing frequency by scholars, politicians, businesspeople, and the media. Many academics have chosen to focus primarily on globalization as an economic phenomenon and the ways in which innovative technologies, new transport systems, and post-Fordist production processes have intensified the global exchange of capital, labor, commodities, and services.[1] According to James Mittelman (1997a), some of the main economic manifestations of globalization include "the spatial reorganization of production, the interpenetration of industries across borders, the spread of financial markets," and the "diffusion of identical consumer goods to distant countries (2).

In recent years, however, scholars have begun to recognize that the concept of globalization invites multiple levels of analysis: economics, politics, society, culture, and ideology. Such accounts explore the compression of time and space and the stretching of social relationships across the fixed political borders of nation-states within a theoretical framework that allows for the interrelatedness of economic and noneconomic factors. Pointing to the fundamentally multidimensional character of globalization, such perspectives also encourage the development of analytical models which emphasize existing links between social action and reaction and between human agency and structural constraints/

opportunities.² Roland Robertson (1992), for example, developed a culturally centered, cognitive theory which rejects a monolithic "systems approach" in favor of an understanding of globalization as a multidimensional "field" which contains multiple aspects of social life together with multiple centers of action and multiple players.

Moreover, Robertson and other writers on the subject have emphasized that globalization is not an all-encompassing social trend but a complex mixture of processes in which universalist and particularist impulses exert their power in often contradictory ways, producing conflicts and disjunctures such as the recent revival of regional nationalisms and the strengthening of local identities.³ Popularized in Benjamin R. Barber's international best-seller *Jihad vs. McWorld: How Globalism and Tribalism are Reshaping the World,* the most striking features of these polarizing tendencies is the coexistence of powerful processes of cultural differentiation with perhaps even stronger homogenizing forces such as the "Americanization" of the world. On the other hand, scholars like Ulf Hannerz (1992) identified in the emerging "global culture" new zones of "hybridization" which are defined as regions where meanings and meaningful forms derive from different historical sources that were originally separated from one another in space, but have come to mingle extensively.

As Robert Holton (1998) points out, multidimensional approaches to globalization like those of Robertson and Barber frequently suffer from a number of shortcomings. For example, the general commitment to multidimensionality is not always followed through in practice, notably by the failure to connect culture with political economy. Also, the cognitive emphasis tends to obscure issues of power and inequality. On the other hand, the great advantage of approaches to globalization that stress the importance of political and cultural ideas lies in their attention to the ideological realm of words and images and to its role in the construction of a particular interpretation of what it means to live in the "global village." Moreover, such studies in ideology must invariably deal with normative issues posed by globalization processes, most importantly the question of how the concept of globalization comes to be imbued in public discourse with particular norms and values.

My own analysis of globalization as a market ideology tied to the "end of socialism" makes the case for the interpenetration of culture and economy, in the sense that the logic of capitalism favors selective ideological interpretations of globalization processes just as much as ideological interpretations defend and strengthen the economic power of capital. Following Robert Holton's definition of globalization, I pay particular attention to the dissemination of particular cognitive and normative frameworks by which people come to understand and relate to the compression of time and space. As a result, they accept certain meanings of the "new world order," acting overwhelmingly in accordance with and sometimes in violation of its alleged "imperatives." In my view, then, a substantive exploration of "globalization" in the late twentieth century ought to involve both a normative-philosophical study of the meanings and functions of ideology and an analysis of the large transnational structures that form the subject matter of political economy or international relations.

Ideology: Elements and Functions

Most writers on the subject of ideology have stressed its role as a coherent body of shared images, ideas, values, beliefs, and ideals which provide individuals and social groups with a coherent, if systematically simplified, overall orientation in time and space, in means and ends (Erikson 1968; Sargent 1993). In an excellent essay on the historical development of the concept of ideology, Terrell Carver (1998) emphasizes the connection between ideology and politics, arguing that ideology is neither a template against which something is or is not an ideology, nor is it a recipe stating how to make an ideology correctly. "Rather," he writes, "it is an agenda of things to discuss, questions to ask, hypotheses to make. We should be able to use it when considering the interaction between ideas and politics, especially systems of ideas that make claims, whether justificatory or hortatory" (9).

In other words, there exists a specific place for ideology in politics, because politics is the dimension where "agendas of things to discuss" become linked to particular power interests. Ideology is therefore always political because it is ultimately about the many ways in which power is exercised, justified, and altered. Hence, globalization as market ideology represents the attempt at setting a public "agenda of things to discuss" by the particular power interests of capital. Lets us consider the following generic statement, randomly selected from several articles on globalization published in popular business magazines: "Globalization is a process inherently incompatible with socialism, because it is about the free exchange of capital, labor, products, services, and information, and the spread of democratic values throughout the world." Favoring a particular representation of "reality," this statement reflects a system of ideas connected with the power interests of neoliberal forces. It offers its readership a carefully circumscribed "agenda of things to discuss" which contains the following ideological elements:

1. An "explanation" of the socioeconomic phenomenon of globalization couched in supposedly neutral "scientific" terms emphasizing the "naturalness" and "factuality" of an "objective process."
2. Standards of normative evaluation: although globalization is an "objective process," its effects are nonetheless beneficial: therefore, globalization is "good" and socialism is "bad."
3. A guide and compass for action: global capitalism reflects an inherently valuable and superior way of ordering the world and is therefore worthy of popular support. Thus, "democratic" political regimes should facilitate the globalization process understood in those terms. People ought to support "free exchange" and the spread of "democracy" throughout the world, and therefore oppose socialism.
4. A simplification of complex social reality: the key terms "free," "exchange," "capital," and "democracy" are never explained and are put together in such a way as to elicit positive associations with the "free market." Particular power interests are presented as general interests.

Integrating most of these elements and functions into a comprehensive conceptual framework, Paul Ricoeur (1986) offers a useful model of ideology. Drawing on Marx, he characterizes the first functional level of ideology as *distortion,* that is, as the production of an inverted image of reality. Distortion hides the contrast between things as they appear in ideas and things as they play themselves out on the plane of material reality. In other words, ideology assembles a picture of the world based on a peculiar mixture which represents and distorts the real process of life. At the same time, Ricoeur disagrees with Marx's notion that distortion explains all there is to ideology; for the French philosopher, distortion is only one of the functions of ideology, representing the surface level of a phenomenon which contains different functions at progressively deeper levels.

Discussing the work of Max Weber, Ricoeur identifies *legitimation* as the second function of ideology. Two factors are involved here: the claim to legitimacy by the ruling authority and the belief in the order's legitimacy granted by its subjects. Accepting Weber's motivational framework stressing social action, Ricoeur focuses on ideology's function of mediating the gap between belief and claim. Ricoeur emphasizes that the discrepancy between claim and belief is a permanent feature of political life, asserting that it is ideology's permanent role to provide the needed supplement to belief to fill this gap.

Ricoeur's model is completed in his description of the third level—ideology as *integration*. Agreeing with Clifford Geertz's emphasis on the symbolic structure of action, Ricoeur claims that, on the deepest level, ideology plays a mediating, integrative role in the social realm. Thus, ideology creates, preserves, and protects the social identity of a person and/or a group. In this constitutive function, ideology provides the symbols, norms, and images that go into the process of assembling and holding together a group's identity. In this sense, ideology assumes a conservative function in both senses of that word. Ideology preserves identity, "but it also wants to conserve what exists and is therefore already a resistance. Something becomes ideological—in the more negative meaning of the term—when the integrative function becomes frozen, when it becomes rhetorical in the bad sense, when schematization and rationalization prevail. Ideology operates at the turning point between the integrative function and resistance" (Ricoeur 1986, 266; Taylor 1986).

Ricoeur's model provides a helpful analytical sketch for my own discussion of globalization as market ideology. It also supports my emphasis on the interpenetration of cultural, political, and economic dimensions of reality. As Ricoeur points out, ideology has to do with the character of human action as being mediated, structured, and integrated by symbolic systems. Thus, in exploring neoliberal representations of globalization, it makes good sense to resist divorcing interpretation and practice. Anchored in material reality, globalization is both a social process and a rhetorical package. Accepting Ricoeur's argument that social imagination can be constitutive of social reality itself, my discussion of globalization as market ideology rejects, therefore, the classical Marxist paradigm which situates ideology within a rigid model of historical materialism that assigns the "economic base" primary power over the "ideological superstructure."

Globalization as Market Ideology

Distortion

Globalization as market ideology serves the interests of global capital by feeding the media with a steady stream of distorted images of complex social processes. Multinational corporations and banks, the principal agents of economic globalization, present to society the workings and consequences of globalization processes in idealized—that is, sanitized—form. In its distortive function, then, the neoliberal rhetoric of globalization veils existing power interests and therefore conveys an image of globalization that often stands in opposition to social reality. For example, dominant liberal capitalist forces have been hailing globalization as the process based on the benign and ever-growing forces of technology, innovation, and science. Such commentators hardly mention the unequal distribution and impact of these technologies within developed countries as well as between the first world and the third world. Furthermore, they tend to remain silent on other serious ramifications of a market-oriented global capitalist economy: environmental degradation, the exploitation of third world labor, lack of free organizing ability for trade unions, human rights violations (particularly free speech), the loss of national sovereignty to transnational corporations, and the international coordination of fiscal and monetary policies by the International Monetary Fund, the World Bank, and General Agreement on Tariffs and Trade that disproportionally benefit the wealthy Group of Seven nations.

Instead, the proponents of globalization as market ideology argue that the superior design of the capitalist production process reflects "more realistic" assumptions about human nature and the preconditions of democracy. In their view, the creation of the world market and its global consumers—the lucky inhabitants of the so-called global village of the twenty-first century—has eclipsed all inferior political ideologies, particularly traditional or socialist systems. While paying lip service to some forms of cultural diversity, the neoliberal ideologists of globalization nonetheless support the emergence of a common cultural framework defined by CNN, MTV, Disney, Coca-Cola, Microsoft, and other multinational players on our "Planet Hollywood."

Indeed, global capital encourages the reflexive adoration of the "free market" in order to tip public opinion in its favor and convince political actors and their constituencies (who may not yet be fully aware of the full political and social consequences) that they should support even more drastic deregulation measures (Böröcz and Smith 1995; Scott 1997). To be sure, the success of this strategy depends on the ability of neoliberal forces to persuade their audiences that there is no alternative to the liberal-economic globalization. As Phil Condit, chairman and CEO of the Boeing Company put it, "Market economies work. We certainly have a great case study with the comparison between the world's largest planned economy, the Soviet Union [which had ceased to exist seven years before Mr. Condit's speech], and the world's largest market economy, the United States." Thus, in addition to constantly defining their project against the "failure of socialism," neoliberals present the "liberalization of global markets" as both an "inevitable" process (because it is driven by economic forces that cannot be stopped) and a "desirable" development (because it supposedly benefits both rich and poor nations). Stephen Gill's (1997) observation nicely captures the pivotal role of these two essential elements that drive the process of ideological distortion:

> Globalization is broadly represented in conventional political discourse in the OECD [Organization for Economic Cooperation and Development] countries as inevitable, if not desirable. Indeed, this discourse is reflected and reinforced worldwide by the global spread of transnational media corporations, which are often controlled by politically conservative neoliberals (e.g., Rupert Murdoch's News International). The message is reinforced by increasingly persuasive advertising and sponsorship, which stress the virtues of individualism and consumption associated with cultural and sporting events, such as the World Cup soccer tournament. In this sense, the discourse of globalization is ideologically convenient for transnational capital, although some firms (e.g., in the military industries) may fear the advent of increasing competition and the loss of state subsidies and forms of protection that underpin their profitability. (211)

Robert W. Cox (1997) concurs with Gill's assessment: "Globalization began to be represented as a finality, as the logical and inevitable culmination of the powerful tendencies of the market at work. The dominance of economic forces was regarded as both necessary and beneficial. States and the interstate system would serve mainly to ensure the working of market logic" (23).

It is not difficult to extract from the mainstream media a large number of statements on globalization which seek to convince their audiences that the direction of causality in the process runs from economic development—portrayed as the "inevitability" of deregulation and free markets—to political response. In other words, globalization is presented as an objective or neutral diagnosis rather than as an ideology contributing to the emergence of the very conditions they claim to analyze. At the 1996 World Economic Congress in Washington, DC, Joan E. Spiro, Under Secretary of State for Economic, Business and Agricultural Affairs in the Clinton administration, argued that efforts to resist the powerful technological and economic forces behind globalization were ultimately futile. However, Under Secretary Spiro did not consider this to be a bad thing, because open trade and investment on a global scale would ensure that "the benefits of globalization will spread to all corners of the world and to all sectors of society."

Similarly, Peter Sutherland (1998), chairman of the Overseas Development Council as well as chairman and managing director of Goldman Sachs International and chairman of British Petroleum, frequently emphasizes in his speeches the "inevitable dynamic" behind the rise of the "new world of global markets and instant communication," adding that "globalization's effects have been overwhelmingly good. Spurred by unprecedented liberalization, world trade continues to expand faster than overall global economic output, inducing a wave of productivity and efficiency and creating millions of jobs." To resist these developments would not only be futile but positively dangerous, since "the costs of being left behind by globalization are usually much greater than the losses caused by instability." George David (1997), CEO of United Technologies, shares Sutherland's opinion: "The wealth generation in emerging markets is going to happen whether we like it or not." Emphasizing that "we" need to "ensure the continued success of this globalizing agenda," David assures his audiences that "we are at an optimistic time in our world: the barriers between nations are down, economic liberalism is decidedly afoot and proven to be sound, trade and investment are soaring, income disparities between nations are narrowing, and wealth generation globally is at record high levels, and I believe likely to remain so."

Unfortunately, neither David nor Sutherland reveals the ideological assumptions behind his key concepts, because distortion thrives on vagueness and stereotyping. Who exactly is "we"? Who "proved" liberalism "sound"? What does "sound" mean? What about the overwhelming evidence that income disparities between nations are actually widening at a quicker pace than ever before in human history? Why withhold the global distribution patterns of wealth generated? Of course, the whole point of distortion is to generate and stabilize a discourse of globalization which serves the interests of transnational capital. To that end, neoliberal commentators must "normalize" the idea that a "healthy enterprise culture" can only be achieved through "market discipline." According to this neoliberal myth, markets strengthen the virtues of prudence, realism, responsibility, good governance, and social progress, and, in partly spontaneous fashion, give shape and direction to a liberal-capitalist world order (Gill 1997).

The final component of this ideological distortion is reflected in frequent assertions that economic globalization is a "natural" process anchored in the impersonal, objective logic of the market and is therefore uncontrollable by any one group or person. As Robert Hormats (1998), vice chairman of Goldman Sachs International, puts it: "The great beauty of globalization is that no one is in control. The great beauty of globalization is that it is not controlled by any individual, any government, any institution." Again, the negative consequences of the "liberalization" of global markets are either bypassed altogether or presented as "necessary" and "episodic dislocations" which will soon give way to "quantum leaps in our productivity" (Meehan 1997). While considering the problems created by such dislocations "legitimate concerns," Newt Gingrich is nonetheless quick to add that the "reality" of globalization is better reflected in "a rising general standard of living for everybody." Ignoring the contradiction of admitting to the negative consequences of "dislocations" and yet including "everybody" into the pool of globalization's beneficiaries, Gingrich launches into a masterpiece of ideological distortion:

> That is people overall are generally better off than they have ever been—but in the short run, in a period of great transition those who are more successful pull away, and get even wealthier faster. But the historical pattern is that everybody else begins to catch up over time, and I think if you know what you are doing you don't become a have not, and if you don't

know what you are doing transferring welfare to you does not solve the problem. We've got to find a way to have more people understand the information age and participate in it.

In the end, this impressive process of diverting from and hiding the real human costs of globalization becomes advertised as "economic liberalization." Such ideological maneuvers would not be possible without what Benjamin Barber (1995) has called the profit-oriented "infotainment telesector" which redefines for the masses existing economic, political, and social realities according to the imperatives of capital. Ideology emerges as "videology," the product of popular culture driven by expansionist commercial interests which incessantly instill in their audience the values, needs, and wants required for global markets to succeed. This is the wonderful world of television, film, shopping malls, and theme parks in which rapacious market strategies are advanced in the name of democratic free choice and individual self-realization. The riveting private lives and heart-rending troubles of celebrities like O. J. Simpson, Bill Clinton, JonBenet Ramsey, Oprah Winfrey, Michael Jackson, Princess Diana, and Arnold Schwarzenegger are interwoven with commercials that are just as entertaining as these life stories themselves. In fact, they become more "real" and newsworthy than the actual global reality of poverty, inequality, displacement, and environmental degradation brought on by the supposed triumph of globalization.

By many measures, corporations are today more central players in global affairs than nations. Serving the imperatives of multinational corporations to increase their market shares and maximize sales, the infotainment telesector is in the business of shaping the minds and souls of its audiences. Never mind actual economic and social conditions; whoever controls global information and communications can conjure up an ideal world of the global village inhabited by beautiful people living long and fulfilling lives as shopoholics. The effect of all this has been to both generate an abiding illusion about the "naturalness" and "inevitability" of unbridled markets and to promote its alleged benefits through the spread of a one-dimensional public discourse. In this way, the neoliberal discourse on globalization functions as a powerful ideological distortion.

Legitimation

On the second level, ideology functions as a set of ideas and values that justify and legitimate forms of domination by bridging the creditability gap that exists in all systems of authority. In the case of globalization, liberal-capitalist systems seek to generate a popular belief in the "benefits of the market" in order to bolster their claims to legitimacy. In order to maintain their strength, these popular beliefs constantly need to be fed with affirmative images and sound bites; it is ideology's permanent role to provide the discursive supplements to fill the credibility gap. Indeed, business executives and neoliberal politicians do their best to convince their audiences (mostly in advanced industrial countries) that free market globalization serves the interests of all groups in society. In a 1998 interview, Robert Hormats emphasized the rich "opportunities" opened up by globalization:

In my view, globalization is primarily about opportunity. It's about the opportunity to sell in many markets. It's about the opportunity to raise capital in many markets. . . . I think that globalization has dramatically increased the opportunities of people around the world. . . . In many parts of the world a lot of people are a lot better off because of a global market in which they can sell their goods. And consumers are a lot better off because they have access to goods from all around the world.

Concurring with Hormat's assessment, Alan Greenspan (1997), the chairman of the Federal Reserve Board, argued that "there can be little doubt that the extraordinary changes in global finance on balance have been beneficial in facilitating significant improvements in economic structures and living standards throughout the world." When asked to respond to obvious problems related to global labor practices, such as child labor or sweat shop conditions in various developing countries, Hormats (1998) replied with a personal story:

I was in Pakistan several years ago and saw an example of very young kids—I don't know—10- or 11-year-old kids who were working, helping their mothers to make rugs during the day. They did this after school. They went to school six hours and worked for four hours with their mothers make rugs, which is their only source of income. Well, to me, that was not abuse of those children. That was the only way their parents were going to get money and they were going to eat was if the kids helped their mothers make rugs. There are a number of societies where the only way people can earn enough money to live is to work at menial jobs, jobs in very large factories. They don't get paid much, that's true. But are we going to go in there and try to legislate what the workplace should be like or what wages should be like in these other countries? It would be nice if their lives could improve, if they could get more money but I don't think that's proper for American legislation or coercive pressures.

The picture of globalization Hormats wants to convey is clear: Americans shouldn't worry about child labor in the third world. Kids are simply helping out their mothers. Their pay may not be great, but if the global markets are left alone, everybody will eventually reap the benefits of globalization. Most importantly, business should not be expected to meet any social obligation.

Neoliberal attempts to strengthen the belief of lawmakers and the general public in the benefits of economic globalism are particularly evident in statements made at large conferences and public hearings on the subject. For example, in a 1999 hearing before the powerful U. S. Subcommittee on Trade of the House Committee on Ways and Means, Phil Condit, speaking as the chairman of the Business Roundtable Task Force on Trade and Investment, testified to the "enormous benefits" resulting from the "integration of global markets for capital." He urged lawmakers around the world to join business in its role as a "force for positive change in the global economy" and work for a trade agenda based upon a set of fundamental (neoliberal) principles. Speaking for the World Bank before a Global Symposium on globalization in 1996, managing director Caio K. Koch-Weser mixed his lecture on the benefits on the "globalizing markets" with thinly veiled warnings directed at "transition countries" in the former Eastern Bloc: "The challenge will be for them to take advantage of the favorable climate to move ahead with some of the tough reform measures that need to be taken to establish the basis for robust and sustained growth. . . . The message from early reformers and from elsewhere in the world is loud and clear: Good policies pay off." Obviously, "good policies" were those that attracted foreign investments regardless of the "tough" consequences of such policies reflected in rising unemployment, welfare cuts, and general human suffering.

The final and most obvious strategy by which globalization as market ideology generates popular support and legitimacy is through a thorough discreditation of its strongest competitors: traditionalism and socialism. The contest with precapitalist forms of traditionalism has been rather easily won because of the supposed cultural, political, and economic superiority of the West over so-called underdeveloped regions of the world. This claim has been a central feature of the dominant discourse of the last 500 years. Empirically, these claims of superiority have been backed up by the technological and scientific achievements of capitalism. Politically, one can point to the establishment of liberal democracy; and culturally, liberal capitalism shrewdly showcases the supposedly "universal" demand for the products of its Western culture industry: film, literature, music, and religion.

The battle with socialism turned out to be a much tougher case. As late as the 1970s, communist countries could make credible claims to being the more authentic representatives of globalization than capitalism. With the 1989 fall of the Soviet Union, however, the ideological edge has shifted decisively to the defenders of unbridled markets, and, as Fukuyama (1992) puts it, market-driven globalization processes have proven "that there has emerged something like a true global culture, centering around technologically-driven economic growth and the capitalist social relations necessary to produce and sustain it. . . . While not every country is capable of becoming a consumer society in the near future, there is hardly a society in the world that does not embrace the goal itself" (126).

Indeed, the strengthening of the legitimacy of values and beliefs in favor of such a global consumer society has been a main ideological task of globalization. Disney World and Dreamworks have linked hands with gigantic shopping malls to legitimize new forms of cultural colonialism which help generate and support the values necessary for the commodification of all aspects of human activity. In the new global village, we are told, the socialist revolution has become not only historically obsolete, but also entirely unnecessary: "[T]here are no more 'workers,' only consumers, no class interests, only a global pop culture that flattens economic contours" and eliminates the range of political alternatives (Barber 1995, 77). Bombarded by endless market propaganda, what else is left for the ordinary person but to support this "Brave New World" and its enticing ideology of fun?

Integration

According to Paul Ricoeur, ideology also functions as integration by creating, preserving, and protecting the identity of social groups. On one hand, this integrative function of ideology is important because it is allows a group to rally around its constitutive elements and historical memories in times of crisis and confusion, and thus provide a coherent framework for collective action. On the other hand, when the integrative function of ideology becomes rigid and frozen, it forecloses important opportunities of critical self-reflection and the imagination of social alternatives. Identity turns into dogma, serving as a cage of prejudice and bias rather than as a necessary point of departure anchored in a healthy sense of community. Applied to our topic, I argue that the market-oriented discourse on globalization seeks to create a one-dimensional consumer identity conducive to the logic of capital while still catering to popular attachments to a national identity.

Representing both TRW Inc. (a large Cleveland-based manufacturing and service company of high-tech products) and the Business Roundtable, chairman Joseph Gorman's remarks before Congress in 1997 represent a typical case of integrating "national" and "global" elements into an overarching market identity: While globalization is good for the world, it is even better for the United States. His ten-page statement is divided into several sections which bear the following titles: "To win in the global economy, the United States must lead liberalization efforts"; "International trade and investment agreements are still needed to open foreign markets for American companies and their workers"; "If the United States is not at the table, it can't play and it can't win"; "Success in the global economy is critical for the American economy, its companies, and its workers"; "The global economy is real, and the United States is part of it"; "Trade is good for our economy, good for business, good for workers, good for farmers, good for consumers"; "Because the United States is the world's most competitive nation, we have the most to gain from the global economy and from trade and investment liberalization"; "Developing countries in particular hold huge promise."

The interpretive possibilities arising from a critical discourse analysis of Gorman's testimony are almost limitless. Images of the world as a gambling table which can only be accessed by the best "players" are as telling as his neoimperialist desire to cash in on "promising" developing nations. As far as ideology's integrative function is concerned, Gorman's rhetoric seeks to persuade its audience that one's loyalty to market principles allows one to be both a "real American" and a "globalist." Moreover, while bitter class conflicts continue to be a very real phenomenon in the daily world of commodity production, the market rhetoric of the movers and shakers of global capital nonetheless conjures up a harmonious common identity around the "liberalization of trade." Businesspeople, workers, and farmers of the world, unite around your consumer identity!

In its ideological function of integration, globalization seems to favor the creation of a market identity "American-style" which is designed to eclipse most other components of personal, group, or class identity. As Steven Kline (1985) points out, global marketing efforts particularly attempt to provide young people with an homogenizing identity: the consuming "global teenager." Coca-Cola, Levi-Strauss, McDonald's, and Disney "have become the source of endless campaigns to enfranchise youth in the globalizing democracy of the market" (110). Why should mere consumers be interested in strengthening civic ties and work for global justice if such endeavors aren't profitable? Why show moral restraint and solidarity if "we," the consumers, are incessantly told that we can have it all? As pointed out above, while broadly endorsing happiness that comes with shopping and consuming, this market identity nonetheless takes on distinct cultural features, because "America" and "American culture" are best-selling commodities in the global marketplace. American films, American television, American software, American music, American fast food chains, American cars and motorcycles, American apparel, and American sports, to name but a few of those cultural commodities, have pervaded the world to such an extent that even ordinary Indonesians have become convinced that they, too, can become "cool" by drinking Coke instead of tea. In Budapest, people are breathlessly watching *The Cosby Show* on reruns, and the Russian version of *Wheel of Fortune* offers lucky winners Sony VCRs into which they can load their pirated versions of wildly popular American films (Barber 1995).

What makes the soft hegemony of American pop culture so dangerous is not necessarily its entertainment value but its one-dimensional market logic that transforms human beings into prisoners of commercialism. America's legendary image as the country of freedom, opportunity, and democracy appears increasingly in the figure of the mall-addicted bargain-hunter who boldly shops where nobody has shopped before. Television commercials tell us that in our global village everybody can be healthy, wealthy, glamorous, victorious, sexy, and energetic—in other words, American. After all, who doesn't want to have just plain fun American style? Never mind that the doors of the temples of consumption are closed to the majority of the world's population. The reality of AIDS, starvation, inequality, and genocide enters popular culture only to the extent that it can be commodified in Hollywood films like *Philadelphia* and *Schindler's List*. The woes of the world are evaluated according to how they impact business transactions. In fact, won't all the old problems caused by clashing political ideologies eventually be solved by the creation of an all-encompassing market identity? Can't even powerful phenomena like ethnonationalism eventually be tamed and "civilized" by the neoliberal siren call of market globalism?

Resisting the Ideology of Market Globalism: The End of Socialism?

In this essay, I have sought to show how globalization works as market ideology simultaneously on three levels. It distorts material reality and simplifies the many contradictory processes of globalization; it legitimates neoliberal social institutions by fostering a belief in the operations of the free market and its supportive political regimes; it engenders the integrative identity of the "consumer"—and defends it by evoking the menacing image of socialism as a "failed experiment." In short, globalization as market ideology threatens to become an unquestioned orthodoxy which is taking on a life of its own and comes to exercise an objective compulsion over actors (Altvater and Mahnkopf 1997).

So what is to be done? The answer to this question depends, of course, on one's ideological position. Although there have been recent attacks on the neoliberal vision of globalization by such successful capitalists as the British businessman James Goldsmith and the Hungarian American financier George Soros, for most defenders of globalization as market ideology not much needs to be done, for the "collapse of socialism" has vindicated the wisdom of neoclassical economics. Blaming the "Left" for policy mismanagement, welfare state arrangements, inflation, and unemployment, the spokespersons of neoliberalism argue that future efforts should be directed toward global deregulation, privatization, and the further expansion of transnational markets. In joining the ranks of remaining progressive voices, this author would argue that globalization as market ideology undermines democratic values and individual autonomy. To be sure, we need *some* market mechanisms to enhance productivity and generate goods, but markets must be held socially accountable and limited by democratic political institutions connected to the values of the French revolution: liberty, equality, and solidarity. Indeed, "market socialists" like John Roemer (1994) have long proposed and defended a new economic model that combines the efficiency of the market system with socialism's commitment to equality. Yet if we allow the market to become sovereign over politics, culture, and civil society, we are in danger of exchanging the democratic vision of public choices made by a critical, educated citizenry with the rhetoric of consumer choice.

Can the ideological hegemony of a neoliberal discourse of globalization still be challenged in the name of a socialist project which aims at the extension of democracy and the realization of global distributive justice? Can socialism still inspire people to generate alternative visions of the global society? Or has socialism indeed come to an end? Common sense at the close of the twentieth century would seem to dictate an affirmative answer to this question. The "Iron Curtain" in Eastern Europe has long disappeared, the Soviet Union has dissolved, Castro's Cuba is on the brink of collapse, and Chinese "communism" looks more and more like Singapore-style authoritarianism with a decidedly capitalist face. The admired "Third Way" of Scandinavian social democracy looks increasingly like "neoliberalism-lite," abandoning its commendable goals of full employment, rising real wages, and large welfare transfers. Caught in a world-wide transition from nationally organized to globally integrated capitalism, the nation state–based "Keynesian socialism" of twenty years ago has found itself in a losing battle with the new globalism of multinational corporations and expanding stock exchanges.

Still, we should be careful not to embrace Francis Fukuyama's (1989) triumphant end-of-history argument. After all, his hasty proclamation of the "final" and "irreversible" victory of liberal democracy over *all* its ideological competitors disregards the instructive historical lessons of the last four centuries, which taught us that sometimes even the most horrendous blows to allegedly "dying" political and religious traditions cannot prevent their successful reconstitution. Much in the same vein, let us not forget that modern political theorists and historians of ideas have been known to indulge their intellectual hubris in premature announcements of the certain "deaths" of various sociopolitical systems. In this respect, Hegel and Marx are just as guilty as Spengler and Nietzsche.

Yet it is my firm conviction that the ideas contained in Marxist socialism of both the "classical German" and the "Soviet" varieties have lost their ability to offer a viable alternative to the neoliberal discourse of globalization. I understand "Marxist socialism" to mean, first and foremost, two things: those ideological features commonly associated with the doctrine of Marx and Engels, such as the centrality of class struggle, the emancipatory role of the proletariat, the materialist conception of history, the emphasis on "dialectical science," and the vision of totalizing a "communist world outlook" (Engels); and, second, a political program of action best summarized in the formula of "socialization of the means of production plus planned economy plus one-party rule." For anyone who takes seriously the interconnection between theory and practice claimed in Marx's famous *Theses on Feuerbach,* it has become obvious that serious flaws in the design have doomed Marxist practice just as much as the despotic political practice of authoritarian collectivism in "real existing socialist countries" have discredited the theory. It would go beyond the confines of this essay to examine in some detail the reasons for the failure of Marxism. I have engaged in such a discussion elsewhere, arguing that, in addition to lacking insight into the role of power and coercion, Marxism's deterministic teleology bypasses and downplays crucial questions of individual liberty, ethics, and political morality (Steger 1997).

Does the decline of Marxism taint all future projects bearing the name "socialism"? Not necessarily. However, the crimes of Marxist regimes have taught us that "socialism" should only refer to a transcendental, moral ideal and not to a "dialectical science." The "socialist goal" is only possible as a *principle* of cooperation; it cannot point to an objective *telos* in the future. The failure of Marxist socialism to acknowledge the status of socialism as a moral ideal illuminates its inability to consciously embrace a language of human rights. Indeed, radical democrats ought to welcome the demise of Marxist socialism, for it allows older, *ethical* variants of socialism to reassert themselves. Perhaps we ought to look at the history of socialism in a different way, realizing that Marxism represented a long, regrettable deviation from an earlier nineteenth-century socialism which saw itself as the necessary social evolution of classical liberalism, guided by basic humanitarian ideals.

Hence, the core question of socialism remains pertinent in the twenty-first century of globalization: How can we reconcile growing social, political, and economic interdependence with peace, liberty, and democracy? Without indiscriminately collapsing social democracy into a new, ruthless market liberalism of the global age, the possible renewal of the socialist tradition calls for the rediscovery of non-Marxist socialist currents and their historical connections to a radical liberalism. In my view, the most appropriate vehicle for such a political program remains the language of international human rights, which best articulates progressive demands: the expansion of personal rights at the expense of property rights, thus making socially consequential power accountable to the will of all citizens. As long as the world continues to be torn apart by wars, ethnic hatred, and growing disparities in wealth and well-being, the timeless ideals of socialism will take root in those social thinkers and reformers who settle for the more modest role of mediating between different systems of thought. Even if future historians will be able to show that the term "socialism" itself had become utterly discredited by the late twentieth century, I am still convinced that its timeless ideals will survive—perhaps in an alternative discourse on globalization which emphasizes political and economic democracy, world peace, and global social justice.

As Stephen Gill (1997) has suggested, one might argue that neoliberal forms of globalization have already engendered new forms of resistance which contain a range of political alternatives: "Some of these challenges entail different conceptions of globalization, based on democratization of an emerging global civil society and a renovated form of authority and governance at the global level" (212). In order to strengthen these tendencies, radical democrats ought to commit themselves to the task of counterbalancing the globalization ideology of the unrestrained market with a system of ideas and values anchored in the ideals of social and distributive justice. Indeed, it is important to contest the reifying accounts of both the neoliberal and Marxist proponents of the globalization thesis which draw heavily on a Newtonian vision of mechanical economy driven by "iron" laws and tendencies. As Gill emphasizes, the Left needs to move from a rather economistic critique of neoliberalism to a new vision of world society that is less centered on materialist consumption and relentless competition: "This is a precondition for going beyond a purely economistic, defensive, and rather one-dimensional vision of politics to a more complete and comprehensive notion of a possible and desirable world order—a form of democratic globalization" (Gill 1997, 223).

In their role as educators, progressive academics must enter the ideological struggle over the global soul by making the case for democratic globalization which equally acknowledges the significant impact of structural forces, the importance of institutional and material capabilities, and the central role of voluntaristic collective action directed toward to the realization of world-wide human rights and greater equality. To enter this ideological struggle means to be critical of the dominant globalization ideology which extols the efficiency of free market, in the process distorting social reality, legitimizing domination and inequality, and creating one-dimensional consumer identities. It also means to support a Left internationalism which advocates the forging of connections and coalitions among the world's antisystemic movements organized around such important issues as environmental degradation, the decline of cities, racism, sexism, the lack of workplace democracy, and so on. The international women's movement represents perhaps the most impressive model for a successful struggle against the market logic of profitability at all costs. Guided by the ethical vision of solidarity and international sisterhood, women have been mobilizing worldwide around such issues as improving women's access to healthcare, the right to work, abortion rights, the elimination of gender hierarchies, workplace safety, and religious freedom (Ghils 1992; Moghadam 1996; Sassen 1998).

The creation of an alternative discourse of globalization that draws on the many voices of the Left is not an easy task, especially after the collapse of Marxist socialism. The emerging forms of transnational opposition to global capital are still no match for the latter's political and ideological ability to break resistance and shape identities conducive to their globalizing agenda. As James Mittelman (1997b) emphasizes, neoliberal globalization is at present the dominant force, and democratic globalization is a far less coherent counterforce. Anyone who seeks to debunk the ideological maneuvers of the hegemonic forces of neoliberalism or criticizes the growing global disparities in wealth and well-being must be prepared to accept to the label "socialist"—even if the source of the protest is something as simple as an ethical desire for social justice. Still, the realization of the extension of democratic principles into all spheres of social life begins with normative-philosophical debates on globalization and its discontents and culminates in the formulation of concrete strategies for action. Ordinary people need to let their governments know that they will not acquiesce to liberal-economic visions of globalization on the grounds that there exists no viable alternative. As Robert Holton (1998) points out, contrary to the postulates of free-market theology, globalization is not a process whose neoliberal direction has been determined for all time. Its foundations are political and ideological as well as economic and therefore far from stable. The necessary challenge to the hegemony of neoliberal ideology must therefore begin with a sustained wave of criticism directed at the notion that the unfettered globalization of markets represents an unambiguous social good.

References

Altvater, E., and B. Mahnkopf. 1997. The world market unbound. In *The limits of globalization,* edited by A. Scott. London: Routledge.
Barber, B. 1995. *Jihad vs. McWorld: How globalism and tribalism are reshaping the world.* New York: Ballantine Books
Böröcz, J., and D. Smith. 1995. Introduction: Late twentieth-century challenges for world-system analysis. In *A new world order? Global transformations in the late twentieth century,* edited by D. Smith and J. Böröcz. Westport, CT: Greenwood Press.
Carver, T. 1998. Ideology: The career of a concept. In *Ideals and ideologies: A reader,* 3rd ed., edited by T. Ball and R. Dagger. New York: Longman.
Condit, P. 1998. www.boeing.com/news/speeches/current/condit071598.html.
———. 1999. Statement before the Subcommittee on Trade of the Committee on Ways and Means, March 4. www.boeing.com/news/speeches/current/condit030499.html.
Cox, H. 1999. The market as God. *The Atlantic Monthly* (March).
Cox, R. W. 1997. A perspective of globalization. In *Globalization: Critical reflections,* edited by J. Mittelman. New York: St. Martin's Press.
Erikson, E. 1968. *Identity: Youth and crisis.* New York: W. W. Norton.
Frank, A. G. 1998. *ReORIENT: Global economy in the Asian age.* Berkeley: University of California Press.
Fukuyama, F. 1989. The end of history. *The National Interest* (Summer): 3-18.
———. 1992. *The end of history and the last man.* New York: Free Press.
George, D. 1997. The critics of globalization are wrong. Fortune Global Forum, Bangkok, Thailand, March 26. www.utc.com/ARCHIVE/bangkok.htm.
Ghils, P. 1992. International civil society. *Social Science Journal* 133: 417-433.

Gill, S. 1997 Globalization, democratization, and the politics of indifference. In *Globalization: Critical reflections,* edited by J. Mittleman. Boulder, CO: Lynne Rienner.

Gingrich, N. 1998. Interview with Danny Schlechter at the 1998 World Economic Forum in Davos, Switzerland. www.pbs.org/globalization/newt.html.

Gorman, J. 1997. Statement before the Subcommittee on Trade of the Committee on Ways and Means, March 18. fasttrack.org/track/congress/gorman.html.

Greenspan, A. 1997. The globalization of finance. October 14. www.cato.org/pubs/journal/cj17n3-1.html.

Hannerz, U. 1992. *Cultural complexity.* New York: Columbia University Press.

Holton, R. 1998. *Globalization and the nation-state.* New York: St. Martin's Press.

Hormats, R. 1998. Interview by Danny Schechter. February. www.pbs.org/globalization/hormats1.html.

Kline, S. 1995. The play of the market: On the internationalization of children's culture. *Theory, Culture and Society* 12.

Koc, M. 1994. Globalization as a discourse. In *From Columbus to con-Agra: The globalization of agriculture and food,* edited by Alessandro Bonanno et al. Lawrence, KS: University of Kansas Press.

Koch-Weser, C. K. 1996. Address to the XI Malente symposium, Lübeck, Germany, October 17. www.worldbank.org/html/extdr/extme/ckwsp005.htm.

Meehan, J. 1997. Globalization and technology at work in the bond markets. Speech given in Phoenix, AZ, March 1. www.bondmarkets.com/news/Meehanspeechfinal.shtml.

Mittleman, J. 1997a. The dynamics of globalization. In *Globalization: Critical reflections,* edited by J. Mittleman. New York: St. Martin's Press.

———. 1997b. How does globalization really work? In *Globalization: Critical reflections,* edited by J. Mittleman. New York: St. Martin's Press.

Moghadam, V. 1996. Feminist networks north and south: DAWN, WIDE and WLUML. *Journal of International Communication* 3.1 (July): 111-121.

Rao, C. P. Introduction. In *Globalization, privatization, and free market economy,* edited by C. P. Rao. Westport, CT: Quorom Books.

Ricouer, P. 1986. *Lecture on ideology and utopia.* ed. G. Taylor. New York: Columbia University Press.

Robertson, R. 1992. *Globalization: Social theory and global culture.* London: Sage.

Roemer, J. E. 1994. *A future for socialism.* Cambridge, MA: Harvard University Press.

Sargent, L. 1993. *Contemporary political ideologies: A comparative analysis.* Belmont, CA: Wadsworth.

Sassen, S. 1998. *Globalization and its discontents.* New York: Free Press.

Scott, A. 1997. Globalization: Social process or political rhetoric? In *The limits of globalization,* edited by A. Scott. London: Routledge.

Spiro, J. 1996. Remarks before the World Economic Development Congress, Washington, DC, September 26.

Steger, M. 1997. An autopsy of Marxist socialism. *Peace Review* 9.1: 25-31.

Sutherland, P. 1998. Expand the debate on globalization. *Time* (February 2). cgi.pathfinder.com/time/mag...02/special_report.expand_th25.html.

Taylor, G., ed. 1986. Editor's introduction. In *Lectures on ideology and utopia (Paul Ricoeur).* New York: Columbia University Press.

CHAPTER 6

The Clash of Civilizations?

Samuel P. Huntington

Originally published in Foreign Affairs 72 (3), 1993.

READING INTRODUCTION

Huntington contends that culturally based "civilizations" exert stronger holds on people than economic systems, levels of development, or even political systems. Clearly, he views culture and civilization as, at least partially and importantly, distinct from economic and political life, a view that many scholars of political culture (e.g., Inglehart 1997; Putnam with Leonardi and Nanetti 1993; Thompson, Ellis, and Wildavsky 1990; Eckstein 1988) would dispute. In his later expansion of this article's themes, Huntington focuses particularly on language and religion as clear indices of the distinctiveness of various civilizations (1996).

In the absence of constraints imposed by the Soviet-American cold war competition, Huntington offers several reasons for thinking that increasingly sharp conflict among at least the major contemporary civilizations is nearly inevitable (Bozeman 1975). These civilizations include the Western, Confucian, Islamic, Hindu, Slavic-Orthodox, and Latin American. In contrast to the advocates of globalization, Huntington perceives growing convergence within the regions of these various civilizations but increasingly clear lines of demarcation among the regions. In his view, long-standing fault lines separating different cultures are being reinforced in the process so that "kin-country" syndromes are replacing the political ideologies prominent during the cold war. Huntington thinks that the Islamic civilization, possibly because it lacks any single dominant state that can provide internal order, is particularly prone to conflict with rival civilizations.

Perhaps most alarming in Huntington's portrayal of the contemporary world is his sense that most other civilizations see the West as an enemy, thus leading to his characterization of the future as "the West versus the rest." While Huntington moderates this claim in his 1996 work, he continues to see a world that contrasts sharply with the visions of globalization. Not only does he see violent conflict as more likely, he perceives the United States (and Western Europe) as increasingly isolated against vastly more numerous opponents with rapidly increasing technological capacities. He finds an Islamic-Confucian "connection" or coalition particularly alarming in its propensity to become modern without becoming Western (Lewis 1990; Mayer 1999).

READING TEXT

The Next Pattern of Conflict

World politics is entering a new phase, and intellectuals have not hesitated to proliferate visions of what it will be—the end of history, the return of traditional rivalries between nation states, and the decline of the nation state from the conflicting pulls of tribalism and globalism, among others. Each of these visions catches aspects of the emerging reality. Yet they all miss a crucial, indeed a central, aspect of what global politics is likely to be in the coming years.

It is my hypothesis that the fundamental source of conflict in this new world will not be primarily ideological or primarily economic. The great divisions among humankind and the dominating source of conflict will be cultural. Nation states will remain the most powerful actors in world affairs, but the principal conflicts of global politics will occur between nations and groups of different civilizations. The clash of civilizations will dominate global politics. The fault lines between civilizations will be the battle lines of the future.

Conflict between civilizations will be the latest phase in the evolution of conflict in the modern world. For a century and a half after the emergence of the modern international system with the Peace of Westphalia, the conflicts of the Western world were largely among princes—emperors, absolute monarchs and constitutional monarchs attempting to expand their bureaucracies, their armies, their mercantilist economic strength and, most important, the territory they ruled. In the process they created nation states, and beginning with the French Revolution the principal lines of conflict were between nations rather than princes. In 1793, as R. R. Palmer put it, "The wars of kings were over; the wars of peoples had begun." This nineteenth-century pattern lasted until the end of World War I. Then, as a result of the Russian Revolution and the reaction against it, the conflict of nations yielded to the conflict of ideologies, first among communism, fascism-Nazism and liberal democracy, and then between communism and liberal democracy. During the Cold War, this latter conflict became embodied in the struggle between the two superpowers, neither of which was a nation state in the classical European sense and each of which defined its identity in terms of its ideology.

These conflicts between princes, nation states and ideologies were primarily conflicts within Western civilization, "Western civil wars," as William Lind has labeled them. This was as true of the Cold War as it was of the world wars and the earlier wars of the seventeenth, eighteenth and nineteenth centuries. With the end of the Cold War, international politics moves out of its Western phase, and its centerpiece becomes the interaction between the West and non-Western civilizations and among non-Western civilizations. In the politics of civilizations, the peoples and governments of non-Western civilizations no longer remain the objects of history as targets of Western colonialism but join the West as movers and shapers of history.

The Nature of Civilizations

During the Cold War the world was divided into the First, Second and Third Worlds. Those divisions are no longer relevant. It is far more meaningful now to group countries not in terms of their political or economic systems or in terms of their level of economic development but rather in terms of their culture and civilization.

What do we mean when we talk of a civilization? A civilization is a cultural entity Villages, regions, ethnic groups, nationalities, religious groups, all have distinct cultures at different levels of cultural heterogeneity. The culture of a village in southern Italy may be different from that of a village in northern Italy, but both will share in a common Italian culture that distinguishes them from German villages. European communities, in turn, will share cultural features that distinguish them from Arab or Chinese communities. Arabs, Chinese and Westerners, however, are not part of any broader cultural entity. They constitute civilizations. A civilization is thus the highest cultural grouping of people and the broadest level of cultural identity people have short of that which distinguishes humans from other species. It is defined both by common objective elements, such as language, history, religion, customs, institutions, and by the subjective self-identification of people. People have levels of identity: a resident of Rome may define himself with varying degrees of intensity as a Roman, an Italian, a Catholic, a Christian, a European, a Westerner. The civilization to which he belongs is the broadest level of identification with which he intensely identifies. People can and do redefine their identities and, as a result, the composition and boundaries of civilizations change.

Civilizations may involve a large number of people, as with China ("a civilization pretending to be a state," as Lucian Pye put it), or a very small number of people, such as the Anglophone Caribbean. A civilization may include several nation states, as is the case with Western, Latin American and Arab civilizations, or only one, as is the case with Japanese civilization. Civilizations obviously blend and overlap, and may include subcivilizations. Western civilization has two major variants, European and North American, and Islam has its Arab, Turkic and Malay subdivisions. Civilizations are nonetheless meaningful entities, and while the lines between them are seldom sharp, they are real. Civilizations are dynamic; they rise and fall; they divide and merge. And, as any student of history knows, civilizations disappear and are buried in the sands of time.

Westerners tend to think of nation states as the principal actors in global affairs. They have been that, however, for only a few centuries. The broader reaches of human history have been the history of civilizations. In *A Study of History,* Arnold Toynbee identified 21 major civilizations; only six of them exist in the contemporary world.

Why Civilizations Will Clash

Civilization identity will be increasingly important in the future, and the world will be shaped in large measure by the interactions among seven or eight major civilizations. These include Western, Confucian, Japanese, Islamic, Hindu, Slavic-Orthodox, Latin American and possibly African civilization. The most important conflicts of the future will occur along the cultural fault lines separating these civilizations from one another.

Why will this be the case?

First, differences among civilizations are not only real; they are basic. Civilizations are differentiated from each other by history, language, culture, tradition and, most important, religion. The people of different civilizations have different views on the relations between God and man, the individual and the group, the citizen and the state, parents and children, husband and wife, as well as differing views of the relative importance of rights and responsibilities, liberty and authority, equality and hierarchy. These differences are the product of centuries. They will not soon disappear. They are far more fundamental than differences among political ideologies and political regimes. Differences do not necessarily mean conflict, and conflict does not necessarily mean violence. Over the centuries, however, differences among civilizations have generated the most prolonged and the most violent conflicts.

Second, the world is becoming a smaller place. The interactions between peoples of different civilizations are increasing; these increasing interactions intensify civilization consciousness and awareness of differences between civilizations and commonalities within civilizations. North African immigration to France generates hostility among Frenchmen and at the same time increased receptivity to immigration by "good" European Catholic Poles. Americans react far more negatively to Japanese investment than to larger investments from Canada and European countries. Similarly, as Donald Horowitz has pointed out, "An Ibo may be . . . an Owerri Ibo or an Onitsha Ibo in what was the Eastern region of Nigeria. In Lagos, he is simply an Ibo. In London, he is a Nigerian. In New York, he is an African." The interactions among peoples of different civilizations enhance the civilization-consciousness of people that, in turn, invigorates differences and animosities stretching or thought to stretch back deep into history.

Third, the processes of economic modernization and social change throughout the world are separating people from longstanding local identities. They also weaken the nation state as a source of identity. In much of the world religion has moved in to fill this gap, often in the form of movements that are labeled "fundamentalist." Such movements are found in Western Christianity, Judaism, Buddhism and Hinduism, as well as in Islam. In most countries and most religions the people active in fundamentalist movements are young, college-educated, middle-class technicians, professionals and business persons. The "unsecularization of the world," George Weigel has remarked, "is one of the dominant social facts of life in the late twentieth century." The revival of religion, "la revanche de Dieu," as Gilles Kepel labeled it, provides a basis for identity and commitment that transcends national boundaries and unites civilizations.

Fourth, the growth of civilization-consciousness is enhanced by the dual role of the West. On the one hand, the West is at a peak of power. At the same time, however, and perhaps as a result, a return to the roots phenomenon is occurring among non-Western civilizations. Increasingly one hears references to trends toward a turning inward and "Asianization" in Japan, the end of the Nehru legacy and the "Hinduization" of India, the failure of Western ideas of socialism and nationalism and hence "re-Islamization" of the Middle East, and now a debate over Westernization versus Russianization in Boris Yeltsin's country. A West at the peak of its power confronts non-Wests that increasingly have the desire, the will and the resources to shape the world in non-Western ways.

In the past, the elites of non-Western societies were usually the people who were most involved with the West, had been educated at Oxford, the Sorbonne or Sandhurst, and had absorbed Western attitudes and values. At the same time, the populace in non-Western countries often remained deeply imbued with the indigenous culture. Now, however, these relationships are being reversed. A de-Westernization and indigenization of elites is occurring in many non-Western countries at the same time that Western, usually American, cultures, styles and habits become more popular among the mass of the people.

Fifth, cultural characteristics and differences are less mutable and hence less easily compromised and resolved than political and economic ones. In the former Soviet Union, communists can become democrats, the rich can become poor and the poor rich, but Russians cannot become Estonians and Azeris cannot become Armenians. In class and ideological conflicts, the key question was "Which side are you on?" and people could and did choose sides and change sides. In conflicts between civilizations, the question is "What are you?" That is a given that cannot be changed. And as we know, from Bosnia to the Caucasus to the Sudan, the wrong answer to that question can mean a bullet in the head. Even more than ethnicity, religion discriminates sharply and exclusively among people. A person can be half-French and half-Arab and simultaneously even a citizen of two countries. It is more difficult to be half-Catholic and half-Muslim.

Finally, economic regionalism is increasing. The proportions of total trade that were intraregional rose between 1980 and 1989 from 51 percent to 59 percent in Europe, 33 percent to 37 percent in East Asia, and 32 percent to 36 percent in North America. The importance of regional economic blocs is likely to continue to increase in the future. On the one hand, successful economic regionalism will reinforce civilization-consciousness. On the other hand, economic regionalism may succeed only when it is rooted in a common civilization. The European Community rests on the shared foundation of European culture and Western Christianity. The success of the North American Free Trade Area depends on the convergence now underway of Mexican, Canadian and American cultures. Japan, in contrast, faces difficulties in creating a comparable economic entity in East Asia because Japan is a society and civilization unique to itself. However strong the trade and investment links Japan may develop with other East Asian countries, its cultural differences with those countries inhibit and perhaps preclude its promoting regional economic integration like that in Europe and North America.

Common culture, in contrast, is clearly facilitating the rapid expansion of the economic relations between the People's Republic of China and Hong Kong, Taiwan, Singapore and the overseas Chinese communities in other Asian countries. With the Cold War over, cultural commonalities increasingly overcome ideological differences, and mainland China and Taiwan move closer together. If cultural commonality is a prerequisite for economic integration, the principal East Asian economic bloc of the future is likely to be centered on China. This bloc is, in fact, already coming into existence. As Murray Weidenbaum (1993) has observed,

> Despite the current Japanese dominance of the region, the Chinese-based economy of Asia is rapidly emerging as a new epicenter for industry, commerce and finance. This strategic area contains substantial amounts of technology and manufacturing capability (Taiwan), outstanding entrepreneurial, marketing and services acumen (Hong Kong), a fine communications network (Singapore), a tremendous pool of financial capital (all three), and very large endowments of land, resources and labor (mainland China).... From Guangzhou to Singapore, from Kuala Lumpur to Manila, this influential network—often based on extensions of the traditional clans—has been described as the backbone of the East Asian economy. (2-3)

Culture and religion also form the basis of the Economic Cooperation Organization, which brings together ten non-Arab Muslim countries: Iran, Pakistan, Turkey, Azerbaijan, Kazakhstan, Kyrgyzstan, Turkmenistan, Tadjikistan, Uzbekistan and Afghanistan. One impetus to the revival and expansion of this organization, founded originally in the 1960s by Turkey, Pakistan and Iran, is the realization by the leaders of several of these countries that they had no chance of admission to the European Community. Similarly, Caricom, the Central American Common Market and Mercosur rest on common cultural foundations. Efforts to build a broader Caribbean-Central American economic entity bridging the Anglo-Latin divide, however, have to date failed.

As people define their identity in ethnic and religious terms, they are likely to see an "us" versus "them" relation existing between themselves and people of different ethnicity or religion. The end of ideologically defined states in Eastern Europe and the former Soviet Union permits traditional ethnic identities and animosities to come to the fore. Differences in culture and religion create differences over policy issues, ranging from human rights to immigration to trade and commerce to the environment. Geographical propinquity gives rise to conflicting territorial claims from Bosnia to Mindanao. Most important, the efforts of the West to promote its values of democracy and liberalism as universal values, to maintain its military predominance and to advance its economic interests engender countering responses from other civilizations. Decreasingly able to mobilize support and form coalitions on the basis of ideology, governments and groups will increasingly attempt to mobilize support by appealing to common religion and civilization identity.

The clash of civilizations thus occurs at two levels. At the micro-level, adjacent groups along the fault lines between civilizations struggle, often violently, over the control of territory and each other. At the macro-level, states from different civilizations compete for relative military and economic power, struggle over the control of international institutions and third parties, and competitively promote their particular political and religious values.

The Fault Lines Between Civilizations

The fault lines between civilizations are replacing the political and ideological boundaries of the Cold War as the flash points for crisis and bloodshed. The Cold War began when the Iron Curtain divided Europe politically and ideologically. The Cold War ended with the end of the Iron Curtain. As the ideological division of Europe has disappeared, the cultural division of Europe between Western Christianity, on the one hand, and Orthodox Christianity and Islam, on the other, has reemerged. The most significant dividing line in Europe, as William Wallace has suggested may well be the eastern boundary of Western Christianity in the year 1500. This line runs along what are now the boundaries between Finland and Russia and between the Baltic states and Russia, cuts through Belarus and Ukraine separating the more Catholic western Ukraine from Orthodox eastern Ukraine, swings westward separating Transylvania from the rest of Romania, and then goes through Yugoslavia almost exactly along the line now separating Croatia and Slovenia from the rest of Yugoslavia. In the Balkans this line, of course, coincides with the historic boundary between the Hapsburg and Ottoman empires. The peoples to the north and west of this line are Protestant or Catholic; they shared the common experiences of European history—feudalism, the Renaissance, the Reformation, the Enlightenment, the French Revolution, the Industrial Revolution; they are generally economically better off than the peoples to the east; and they may now look forward to increasing involvement in a common European economy and to the consolidation of democratic political systems. The peoples to the east and south of this line are Orthodox or Muslim; they historically belonged to the Ottoman or Tsarist empires and were only lightly touched by the shaping events in the rest of Europe; they are generally less advanced economically; they seem much less likely to develop stable democratic political systems. The Velvet Curtain of culture has replaced the Iron Curtain of ideology as the most significant dividing line in Europe. As the events in Yugoslavia show, it is not only a line of difference; it is also at times a line of bloody conflict.

Conflict along the fault line between Western and Islamic civilizations has been going on for 1,300 years. After the founding of Islam, the Arab and Moorish surge west and north only ended at Tours in 732. From the eleventh to the thirteenth century the Crusaders attempted with temporary success to bring Christianity and Christian rule to the Holy Land. From the fourteenth to the seventeenth century, the Ottoman Turks reversed the balance, extended their sway over the Middle East and the Balkans, captured Constantinople, and twice laid siege to Vienna. In the nineteenth and early twentieth centuries as Ottoman power declined Britain, France, and Italy established Western control over most of North Africa and the Middle East.

After World War II, the West, in turn, began to retreat; the colonial empires disappeared; first Arab nationalism and then Islamic fundamentalism manifested themselves; the West became heavily dependent on the Persian Gulf countries for its energy; the oil-rich Muslim countries became money-rich and, when they wished to, weapons-rich. Several wars occurred between Arabs and Israel (created by the West). France fought a bloody and ruthless war in Algeria for most of the 1950s; British and French forces invaded Egypt in 1956; American forces went into Lebanon in 1958; subsequently American forces returned to Lebanon, attacked Libya, and engaged in various military encounters with Iran; Arab and Islamic terrorists, supported by at least three Middle Eastern governments, employed the weapon of the weak and bombed Western planes and installations and seized Western hostages. This warfare between Arabs and the West culminated in 1990, when the United States sent a massive army to the Persian Gulf to defend some Arab countries against aggression by another. In its aftermath NATO planning is increasingly directed to potential threats and instability along its "southern tier."

This centuries-old military interaction between the West and Islam is unlikely to decline. It could become more virulent. The Gulf War left some Arabs feeling proud that Saddam Hussein had attacked Israel and stood up to the West. It also left many feeling humiliated and resentful of the West's military presence in the Persian Gulf, the West's overwhelming military dominance, and their apparent inability to shape their own destiny. Many Arab countries, in addition to the oil exporters, are reaching levels of economic and social development where autocratic forms of government become inappropriate and efforts to introduce democracy become stronger. Some openings in Arab political systems have already occurred. The principal beneficiaries of these openings have been Islamist movements. In the Arab world, in short, Western democracy strengthens anti-Western political forces. This may be a passing phenomenon, but it surely complicates relations between Islamic countries and the West.

Those relations are also complicated by demography. The spectacular population growth in Arab countries, particularly in North Africa, has led to increased migration to Western Europe. The movement within Western Europe toward minimizing internal boundaries has sharpened political sensitivities with respect to this development. In Italy, France and Germany, racism is increasingly open, and political reactions and violence against Arab and Turkish migrants have become more intense and more widespread since 1990.

On both sides the interaction between Islam and the West is seen as a clash of civilizations. The West's "next confrontation," observes M. J. Akbar, an Indian Muslim author, "is definitely going to come from the Muslim world. It is in the sweep of the Islamic nations from the Maghreb to Pakistan that the struggle for a new world order win begin." Bernard Lewis (1990) comes to a similar conclusion:

We are facing a mood and a movement far transcending the level of issues
and policies and the governments that pursue them. This is no less than a
clash of Civilizations—the perhaps irrational but surely historic reaction of
in ancient rival against our Judeo-Christian heritage, our secular present,
and the world-wide expansion of both (60; see also Lewis 1992, 24-28).

Historically, the other great antagonistic interaction of Arab Islamic civilization has been with the pagan, animist, and now increasingly Christian black peoples to the south. In the past, this antagonism was epitomized in the image of Arab slave dealers and black slaves. It has been reflected in the on-going civil war in the Sudan between Arabs and blacks, the fighting in Chad between Libyan-supported insurgents and the government, the tensions between Orthodox Christians and Muslims in the Horn of Africa, and the political conflicts, recurring riots and communal violence between Muslims and Christians in Nigeria. The modernization of Africa and the spread of Christianity are likely to enhance the probability of violence along this fault line. Symptomatic of the intensification of this conflict was the Pope John Paul II's speech in Khartoum in February 1993 attacking the actions of the Sudan's Islamist government against the Christian minority there.

On the northern border of Islam, conflict has increasingly erupted between Orthodox and Muslim peoples, including the carnage of Bosnia and Sarajevo, the simmering violence between Serb and Albanian, the tenuous relations between Bulgarians and their Turkish minority, the violence between Ossetians and Ingush, the unremitting slaughter of each other by Armenians and Azeris, the tense relations between Russians and Muslims in Central Asia, and the deployment of Russian troops to protect Russian interests in the Caucasus and Central Asia. Religion reinforces the revival of ethnic identities and restimulates Russian fears about the security of their southern borders. This concern is well captured by Archie Roosevelt (1988):

> Much of Russian history concerns the struggle between the Slavs and the Turkic peoples on their borders, which dates back to the foundation of the Russian state more than a thousand years ago. In the Slavs' millennium-long confrontation with their eastern neighbors lies the key to an understanding not only of Russian history, but Russian character. To understand Russian realities today one has to have a concept of the great Turkic ethnic group that has preoccupied Russians through the centuries (332-333).

The conflict of civilizations is deeply rooted elsewhere in Asia. The historic clash between Muslim and Hindu in the subcontinent manifests itself now not only in the rivalry between Pakistan and India but also in intensifying religious strife within India between increasingly militant Hindu groups and India's substantial Muslim minority. The destruction of the Ayodhya mosque in December 1992 brought to the fore the issue of whether India will remain a secular democratic state or become a Hindu one. In East Asia, China has outstanding territorial disputes with most of its neighbors. It has pursued a ruthless policy toward the Buddhist people of Tibet, and it is pursuing an increasingly ruthless policy toward its Turkic-Muslim minority. With the Cold War over, the underlying differences between China and the United States have reasserted themselves in areas such as human rights, trade and weapons proliferation. These differences are unlikely to moderate. A "new cold war," Deng Xaioping reportedly asserted in 1991, is under way between China and America.

The same phrase has been applied to the increasingly difficult relations between Japan and the United States. Here cultural difference exacerbates economic conflict. People on each side allege racism on the other, but at least on the American side the antipathies are not racial but cultural. The basic values, attitudes, behavioral patterns of the two societies could hardly be more different. The economic issues between the United States and Europe are no less serious than those between the United States and Japan, but they do not have the same political salience and emotional intensity because the differences between American culture and European culture are so much less than those between American civilization and Japanese civilization.

The interactions between civilizations vary greatly in the extent to which they are likely to be characterized by violence. Economic competition clearly predominates between the American and European subcivilizations of the West and between both of them and Japan. On the Eurasian continent, however, the proliferation of ethnic conflict, epitomized at the extreme in "ethnic cleansing," has not been totally random. It has been most frequent and most violent between groups belonging to different civilizations. In Eurasia the great historic fault lines between civilizations are once more aflame. This is particularly true along the boundaries of the crescent-shaped Islamic bloc of nations from the bulge of Africa to central Asia. Violence also occurs between Muslims, on the one hand, and Orthodox Serbs in the Balkans, Jews in Israel, Hindus in India, Buddhists in Burma and Catholics in the Philippines. Islam has bloody borders.

Civilization Rallying: The Kin-Country Syndrome

Groups or states belonging to one civilization that become involved in war with people from a different civilization naturally try to rally support from other members of their own civilization. As the post-Cold War world evolves, civilization commonality, what H. D. S. Greenway has termed the "kin-country" syndrome, is replacing political ideology and traditional balance of power considerations as the principal basis for cooperation and coalitions. It can be seen gradually emerging in the post-Cold War conflicts in the Persian Gulf, the Caucasus and Bosnia. None of these was a full-scale war between civilizations, but each involved some elements of civilizational rallying, which seemed to become more important as the conflict continued and which may provide a foretaste of the future.

First, in the Gulf War one Arab state invaded another and then fought a coalition of Arab, Western and other states. While only a few Muslim governments overtly supported Saddam Hussein, many Arab elites privately cheered him on, and he was highly popular among large sections of the Arab publics. Islamic fundamentalist movements universally supported Iraq rather than the Western-backed governments of Kuwait and Saudi Arabia. Forswearing Arab nationalism, Saddam Hussein explicitly invoked an Islamic appeal. He and his supporters attempted to define the war as a war between civilizations. "It is not the world against Iraq," as Safar Al-Hawali, dean of Islamic Studies at the Umm Al-Qura University in Mecca, put it in a widely circulated tape. "It is the West against Islam." Ignoring the rivalry between Iran and Iraq, the chief Iranian religious leader, Ayatollah Ali Khamenei, called for a holy war against the West: "The struggle against American aggression, greed, plans and policies will be counted as a jihad, and anybody who is killed on that path is a martyr." "This is a war," King Hussein of Jordan argued, "against all Arabs and all Muslims and not against Iraq alone."

The rallying of substantial sections of Arab elites and publics behind Saddam Hussein caused those Arab governments in the anti-Iraq coalition to moderate their activities and temper their public statements. Arab governments opposed or distanced themselves from subsequent Western efforts to apply pressure on Iraq, including enforcement of a no-fly zone in the summer of 1992 and the bombing of Iraq in January 1993. The Western-Soviet-Turkish-Arab anti-Iraq coalition of 1990 had by 1993 become a coalition of almost only the West and Kuwait against Iraq.

Muslims contrasted Western actions against Iraq with the West's failure to protect Bosnians against Serbs and to impose sanctions on Israel for violating U.N. resolutions. The West, they alleged, was using a double standard. A world of clashing civilizations, however, is inevitably a world of double standards: people apply one standard to their kin-countries and a different standard to others.

Second, the kin-country syndrome also appeared in conflicts in the former Soviet Union. Armenian military successes in 1992 and 1993 stimulated Turkey to become increasingly supportive of its religious, ethnic and linguistic brethren in Azerbaijan. "We have a Turkish nation feeling the same sentiments as the Azerbaijanis," said one Turkish official in 1992. "We are under pressure. Our newspapers are full of the photos of atrocities and are asking us if we are still serious about pursuing our neutral policy. Maybe we should show Armenia that there's a big Turkey in the region." President Turgut Özal agreed, remarking that Turkey should at least "scare the Armenians a little bit." Turkey, Özal threatened again in 1993, would "show its fangs." Turkish Air Force jets flew reconnaissance flights along the Armenian border; Turkey suspended food shipments and air flights to Armenia; and Turkey and Iran announced they would not accept dismemberment of Azerbaijan. In the last years of its existence, the Soviet government supported Azerbaijan because its government was dominated by former communists. With the end of the Soviet Union, however, political considerations gave way to religious ones. Russian troops fought on the side of the Armenians, and Azerbaijan accused the "Russian government of turning 180 degrees" toward support for Christian Armenia.

Third, with respect to the fighting in the former Yugoslavia, Western publics manifested sympathy and support for the Bosnian Muslims and the horrors they suffered at the hands of the Serbs. Relatively little concern was expressed, however, over Croatian attacks on Muslims and participation in the dismemberment of Bosnia-Herzegovina. In the early stages of the Yugoslav breakup, Germany, in an unusual display of diplomatic initiative and muscle, induced the other 11 members of the European Community to follow its lead in recognizing Slovenia and Croatia. As a result of the pope's determination to provide strong backing to the two Catholic countries, the Vatican extended recognition even before the Community did. The United States followed the European lead. Thus the leading actors in Western civilization rallied behind their coreligionists. Subsequently Croatia was reported to be receiving substantial quantities of arms from Central European and other Western countries. Boris Yeltsin's government, on the other hand, attempted to pursue a middle course that would be sympathetic to the Orthodox Serbs but not alienate Russia from the West. Russian conservative and nationalist groups, however, including many legislators, attacked the government for not being more forthcoming in its support for the Serbs. By early 1993 several hundred Russians apparently were serving with the Serbian forces, and reports circulated of Russian arms being supplied to Serbia.

Islamic governments and groups, on the other hand, castigated the West for not coming to the defense of the Bosnians. Iranian leaders urged Muslims from all countries to provide help to Bosnia; in violation of the U.N. arms embargo, Iran supplied weapons and men for the Bosnians; Iranian-supported Lebanese groups sent guerrillas to train and organize the Bosnian forces. In 1993 up to 4,000 Muslims from over two dozen Islamic countries were reported to be fighting in Bosnia. The governments of Saudi Arabia and other countries felt under increasing pressure from fundamentalist groups in their own societies to provide more vigorous support for the Bosnians. By the end of 1992, Saudi Arabia had reportedly supplied substantial funding for weapons and supplies for the Bosnians, which significantly increased their military capabilities vis-à-vis the Serbs.

In the 1930s the Spanish Civil War provoked intervention from countries that politically were fascist, communist and democratic. In the 1990s the Yugoslav conflict is provoking intervention from countries that are Muslim, Orthodox and Western Christian. The parallel has not gone unnoticed. "The war in Bosnia-Herzegovina has become the emotional equivalent of the fight against fascism in the Spanish Civil War," one Saudi editor observed. "Those who died there are regarded as martyrs who tried to save their fellow Muslims."

Conflicts and violence will also occur between states and groups within the same civilization. Such conflicts, however, are likely to be less intense and less likely to expand than conflicts between civilizations. Common membership in a civilization reduces the probability of violence in situations where it might otherwise occur. In 1991 and 1992 many people were alarmed by the possibility of violent conflict between Russia and Ukraine over territory, particularly Crimea, the Black Sea fleet, nuclear weapons and economic issues. If civilization is what counts, however, the likelihood of violence between Ukrainians and Russians should be low. They are two Slavic, primarily Orthodox peoples who have had close relationships with each other for centuries. As of early 1993, despite all the reasons for conflict, the leaders of the two countries were effectively negotiating and defusing the issues between the two countries. While there has been serious fighting between Muslims and Christians elsewhere in the former Soviet Union and much tension and some fighting between Western and Orthodox Christians in the Baltic states, there has been virtually no violence between Russians and Ukrainians.

Civilization rallying to date has been limited, but it has been growing, and it clearly has the potential to spread much further. As the conflicts in the Persian Gulf, the Caucasus and Bosnia continued, the positions of nations and the cleavages between them increasingly were along civilizational lines. Populist politicians, religious leaders and the media have found it a potent means of arousing mass support and of pressuring hesitant governments. In the coming years, the local conflicts most likely to escalate into major wars will be those, as in Bosnia and the Caucasus, along the fault lines between civilizations. The next world war, if there is one, will be a war between civilizations.

The West Versus the Rest

The West is now at an extraordinary peak of power in relation to other civilizations. Its superpower opponent has disappeared from the map. Military conflict among Western states is unthinkable, and Western military power is unrivaled. Apart from Japan, the West faces no economic challenge. It dominates international political and security institutions and with Japan international economic institutions. Global political and security issues are effectively settled by a directorate of the United States, Britain and France, world economic issues by a directorate of the United States, Germany and Japan, all of which maintain extraordinarily close relations with each other to the exclusion of lesser and largely non-Western countries. Decisions made at the U.N. Security Council or in the International Monetary Fund that reflect the interests of the West are presented to the world as reflecting the desires of the world community. The very phrase "the world community" has become the euphemistic collective noun (replacing "the Free World") to give global legitimacy to actions reflecting the interests of the United States and other Western powers.[1] Through the IMF and other international economic institutions, the West promotes its economic interests and imposes on other nations the economic policies it thinks appropriate. In any poll of non-Western peoples, the IMF undoubtedly would win the support of finance ministers and a few others, but get an overwhelmingly unfavorable rating from just about everyone else, who would agree with Georgy Arbatov's characterization of IMF officials as "neo-Bolsheviks who love expropriating other people's money, imposing undemocratic and alien rules of economic and political conduct and stifling economic freedom."

Western domination of the U.N. Security Council and its decisions, tempered only by occasional abstention by China, produced U.N. legitimation of the West's use of force to drive Iraq out of Kuwait and its elimination of Iraq's sophisticated weapons and capacity to produce such weapons. It also produced the quite unprecedented action by the United States, Britain and France in getting the Security Council to demand that Libya hand over the Pan Am 103 bombing suspects and then to impose sanctions when Libya refused. After defeating the largest Arab army, the West did not hesitate to throw its weight around in the Arab world. The West in effect is using international institutions, military power and economic resources to run the world in ways that will maintain Western predominance, protect Western interests and promote Western political and economic values.

That at least is the way in which non-Westerners see the new world, and there is a significant element of truth in their view. Differences in power and struggles for military, economic and institutional power are thus one source of conflict between the West and other civilizations. Differences in culture, that is basic values and beliefs, are a second source of conflict. V. S. Naipaul has argued that Western civilization is the "universal civilization" that "fits all men." At a superficial level much of Western culture has indeed permeated the rest of the world. At a more basic level, however, Western concepts differ fundamentally from those prevalent in other civilizations. Western ideas of individualism, liberalism, constitutionalism, human rights, equality, liberty, the rule of law, democracy, free markets, the separation of church and state, often have little resonance in Islamic, Confucian, Japanese, Hindu, Buddhist or Orthodox cultures. Western efforts to propagate such ideas produce instead a reaction against "human rights imperialism" and a reaffirmation of indigenous values, as can be seen in the support for religious fundamentalism by the younger generation in non-Western cultures. The very notion that there could be a "universal civilization" is a Western idea, directly at odds with the particularism of most Asian societies and their emphasis on what distinguishes one people from another. Indeed, the author of a review of 100 comparative studies of values in different societies concluded that "the values that are most important in the West are least important worldwide" (Triandis 1990; see also 1989). In the political realm, of course, these differences are most manifest in the efforts of the United States and other Western powers to induce other peoples to adopt Western ideas concerning democracy and human rights. Modern democratic government originated in the West. When it has developed in non-Western societies it has usually been the product of Western colonialism or imposition.

The central axis of world politics in the future is likely to be, in Kishore Mahbubani's (1992) phrase, the conflict between "the West and the Rest" and the responses of non-Western civilizations to Western power and values. Those responses generally take one or a combination of three forms. At one extreme, non-Western states can, like Burma and North Korea, attempt to pursue a course of isolation, to insulate their societies from penetration or "corruption" by the West, and, in effect, to opt out of participation in the Western-dominated global community. The costs of this course, however, are high, and few states have pursued it exclusively. A second alternative, the equivalent of "band-wagoning" in international relations theory, is to attempt to join the West and accept its values and institutions. The third alternative is to attempt to "balance" the West by developing economic and military power and cooperating with other non-Western societies against the West, while preserving indigenous values and institutions; in short, to modernize but not to Westernize.

The Torn Countries

In the future, as people differentiate themselves by civilization, countries with large numbers of peoples of different civilizations, such as the Soviet Union and Yugoslavia, are candidates for dismemberment. Some other countries have a fair degree of cultural homogeneity but are divided over whether their society belongs to one civilization or another. These are torn countries. Their leaders typically wish to pursue a bandwagoning strategy and to make their countries members of the West, but the history, culture and traditions of their countries are non-Western. The most obvious and prototypical torn country is Turkey. The late twentieth-century leaders of Turkey have followed in the Attaturk tradition and defined Turkey as a modern, secular, Western nation state. They allied Turkey with the West in NATO and in the Gulf War; they applied for membership in the European Community. At the same time, however, elements in Turkish society have supported an Islamic revival and have argued that Turkey is basically a Middle Eastern Muslim society. In addition, while the elite of Turkey has defined Turkey as a Western society, the elite of the West refuses to accept Turkey as such. Turkey will not become a member of the European Community, and the real reason, as President Özal said, "is that we are Muslim and they are Christian and they don't say that." Having rejected Mecca, and then being rejected by Brussels, where does Turkey look? Tashkent may be the answer. The end of the Soviet Union gives Turkey the opportunity to become the leader of a revived Turkic civilization involving seven countries from the borders of Greece to those of China. Encouraged by the West, Turkey is making strenuous efforts to carve out this new identity for itself.

During the past decade Mexico has assumed a position somewhat similar to that of Turkey. Just as Turkey abandoned its historic opposition to Europe and attempted to join Europe, Mexico has stopped defining itself by its opposition to the United States and is instead attempting to imitate the United States and to join it in the North American Free Trade Area. Mexican leaders are engaged in the great task of redefining Mexican identity and have introduced fundamental economic reforms that eventually will lead to fundamental political change. In 1991 a top adviser to President Carlos Salinas de Gortari described at length to me all the changes the Salinas government was making. When he finished, I remarked: "That's most impressive. It seems to me that basically you want to change Mexico from a Latin American country into a North American country." He looked at me with surprise and exclaimed: "Exactly! That's precisely what we are trying to do, but of course we could never say so publicly." As his remark indicates, in Mexico as in Turkey, significant elements in society resist the redefinition of their country's identity. In Turkey, European-oriented leaders have to make gestures to Islam (Özal's pilgrimage to Mecca); so also Mexico's North American-oriented leaders have to make gestures to those who hold Mexico to be a Latin American country (Salinas' Ibero-American Guadalajara summit).

Historically Turkey has been the most profoundly torn country. For the United States, Mexico is the most immediate torn country. Globally the most important torn country is Russia. The question of whether Russia is part of the West or the leader of a distinct Slavic-Orthodox civilization has been a recurring one in Russian history. That issue was obscured by the communist victory in Russia, which imported a Western ideology, adapted it to Russian conditions and then challenged the West in the name of that ideology. The dominance of communism shut off the historic debate over Westernization versus Russification. With communism discredited Russians once again face that question.

President Yeltsin is adopting Western principles and goals and seeking to make Russia a "normal" country and a part of the West. Yet both the Russian elite and the Russian public. are divided on this issue. Among the more moderate dissenters, Sergei Stankevich (1992) argues that Russia should reject the "Atlanticist" course, which would lead it "to become European, to become a part of the world economy in rapid and organized fashion, to become the eighth member of the Seven, and to put particular emphasis on Germany and the United States as the two dominant members of the Atlantic alliance." While also rejecting an exclusively Eurasian policy, Stankevich nonetheless argues that Russia should give priority to the protection of Russians in other countries, emphasize its Turkic and Muslim connections, and promote "an appreciable redistribution of our resources, our options, our ties, and our interests in favor of Asia, of the eastern direction." People of this persuasion criticize Yeltsin for subordinating Russia's interests to those of the West, for reducing Russian military strength, for failing to support traditional friends such as Serbia, and for pushing economic and political reform in ways injurious to the Russian people. Indicative of this trend is the new popularity of the ideas of Petr Savitsky, who in the 1920s argued that Russia was a unique Eurasian civilization (Schneider 1993). More extreme dissidents voice much more blatantly nationalist, anti-Western and anti-Semitic views, and urge Russia to redevelop its military strength and to establish closer ties with China and Muslim countries. The people of Russia are as divided as the elite. An opinion survey in European Russia in the spring of 1992 revealed that 40 percent of the public had positive attitudes toward the West and 36 percent had negative attitudes. As it has been for much of its history, Russia in the early 1990s is truly a torn country.

To redefine its civilization identity, a torn country must meet three requirements. First, its political and economic elite has to be generally supportive of and enthusiastic about this move. Second, its public has to be willing to acquiesce in the redefinition. Third, the dominant groups in the recipient civilization have to be willing to embrace the convert. All three requirements in large part exist with respect to Mexico. The first two in large part exist with respect to Turkey. It is not clear that any of them exist with respect to Russia's joining the West. The conflict between liberal democracy and Marxism-Leninism was between ideologies which, despite their major differences, ostensibly shared ultimate goals of freedom, equality and prosperity. A traditional, authoritarian, nationalist Russia could have quite different goals. A Western democrat could carry on an intellectual debate with a Soviet Marxist. It would be virtually impossible for him to do that with a Russian traditionalist. If, as the Russians stop behaving like Marxists, they reject liberal democracy and begin behaving like Russians but not like

Westerners, the relations between Russia and the West could again become distant and conflictual.[2]

The Confucian–Islamic Connection

The obstacles to non-Western countries joining the West vary considerably. They are least for Latin American and East European countries. They are greater for the Orthodox countries of the former Soviet Union. They are still greater for Muslim, Confucian, Hindu and Buddhist societies. Japan has established a unique position for itself as an associate member of the West: it is in the West in some respects but clearly not of the West in important dimensions. Those countries that for reason of culture and power do not wish to, or cannot, join the West compete with the West by developing their own economic, military and political power. They do this by promoting their internal development and by cooperating with other non-Western countries. The most prominent form of this cooperation is the Confucian-Islamic connection that has emerged to challenge Western interests, values and power.

Almost without exception, Western countries are reducing their military power; under Yeltsin's leadership so also is Russia. China, North Korea and several Middle Eastern states, however, are significantly expanding their military capabilities. They are doing this by the import of arms from Western and non-Western sources and by the development of indigenous arms industries. One result is the emergence of what Charles Krauthammer has called "Weapon States," and the Weapon States are not Western states. Another result is the redefinition of arms control, which is a Western concept and a Western goal. During the Cold War the primary purpose of arms control was to establish a stable military balance between the United States and its allies and the Soviet Union and its allies. In the post-Cold War world the primary objective of arms control is to prevent the development by non-Western societies of military capabilities that could threaten Western interests. The West attempts to do this through international agreements, economic pressure and controls on the transfer of arms and weapons technologies.

The conflict between the West and the Confucian-Islamic states focuses largely, although not exclusively, on nuclear, chemical and biological weapons, ballistic missiles and other sophisticated means for delivering them, and the guidance, intelligence and other electronic capabilities for achieving that goal. The West promotes nonproliferation as a universal norm and nonproliferation treaties and inspections as means of realizing that norm. It also threatens a variety of sanctions against those who promote the spread of sophisticated weapons and proposes some benefits for those who do not. The attention of the West focuses, naturally, on nations that are actually or potentially hostile to the West.

The non-Western nations, on the other hand, assert their right to acquire and to deploy whatever weapons they think necessary for their security. They also have absorbed, to the full, the truth of the response of the Indian defense minister when asked what lesson he learned from the Gulf War: "Don't fight the United States unless you have nuclear weapons." Nuclear weapons, chemical weapons and missiles are viewed, probably erroneously, as the potential equalizer of superior Western conventional power. China, of course, already has nuclear weapons; Pakistan and India have the capability to deploy them. North Korea, Iran, Iraq, Libya and Algeria appear to be attempting to acquire them. A top Iranian official has declared that all Muslim states should acquire nuclear weapons, and in 1988 the president of Iran reportedly issued a directive calling for development of "offensive and defensive chemical, biological and radiological weapons."

Centrally important to the development of counter-West military capabilities is the sustained expansion of China's military power and its means to create military power. Buoyed by spectacular economic development, China is rapidly increasing its military spending and vigorously moving forward with the modernization of its armed forces. It is purchasing weapons from the former Soviet states; it is developing long-range missiles; in 1992 it tested a one-megaton nuclear device. It is developing power-projection capabilities, acquiring aerial refueling technology, and trying to purchase an aircraft carrier. Its military buildup and assertion of sovereignty over the South China Sea are provoking a multilateral regional arms race in East Asia. China is also a major exporter of arms and weapons technology. It has exported materials to Libya and Iraq that could be used to manufacture nuclear weapons and nerve gas. It has helped Algeria build a reactor suitable for nuclear weapons research and production. China has sold to Iran nuclear technology that American officials believe could only be used to create weapons and apparently has shipped components of 300-mile-range missiles to Pakistan. North Korea has had a nuclear weapons program under way for some while and has sold advanced missiles and missile technology to Syria and Iran. The flow of weapons and weapons technology is generally from East Asia to the Middle East. There is, however, some movement in the reverse direction; China has received Stinger missiles from Pakistan.

A Confucian-Islamic military connection has thus come into being, designed to promote acquisition by its members of the weapons and weapons technologies needed to counter the military power of the West. It may or may not last. At present, however, it is, as Dave McCurdy has said, "a renegades' mutual support pact, run by the proliferators and their backers." A new form of arms competition is thus occurring between Islamic-Confucian states and the West. In an old-fashioned arms race, each side developed its own arms to balance or to achieve superiority against the other side. In this new form of arms competition, one side is developing its arms and the other side is attempting not to balance but to limit and prevent that arms build-up while at the same time reducing its own military capabilities.

Implications for the West

This article does not argue that civilization identities will replace all other identities, that nation states will disappear, that each civilization will become a single coherent political entity, that groups within a civilization will not conflict with and even fight each other. This paper does set forth the hypotheses that differences between civilizations are real and important; civilization-consciousness is increasing; conflict between civilizations will supplant ideological and other forms of conflict as the dominant global form of conflict; international relations, historically a game played out within Western civilization, will increasingly be de-Westernized and become a game in which non-Western civilizations are actors and not simply objects; successful political, security and economic international institutions are more likely to develop within civilizations than across civilizations; conflicts between groups in different civilizations will be more frequent, more sustained and more violent than conflicts between groups in the same civilization; violent conflicts between groups in different civilizations are the most likely and most dangerous source of escalation that could lead to global wars; the paramount axis of world politics will be the relations between "the West and the Rest"; the elites in some torn non-Western countries win try to make their countries part of the West, but in most cases face major obstacles to accomplishing this; a central focus of conflict for the immediate future will be between the West and several Islamic-Confucian states.

This is not to advocate the desirability of conflicts between civilizations. It is to set forth descriptive hypotheses as to what the future may be like. If these are plausible hypotheses, however, it is necessary to consider their implications for Western policy. These implications should be divided between short-term advantage and long-term accommodation. In the short term it is clearly in the interest of the West to promote greater cooperation and unity within its own civilization, particularly between its European and North American components; to incorporate into the West societies in Eastern Europe and Latin America whose cultures are close to those of the West; to promote and maintain cooperative relations with Russia and Japan; to prevent escalation of local inter-civilization conflicts into major inter-civilization wars; to limit the expansion of the military strength of Confucian and Islamic states; to moderate the reduction of Western military capabilities and maintain military superiority in East and Southwest Asia; to exploit differences and conflicts among Confucian and Islamic states; to support in other civilizations groups sympathetic to Western values and interests; to strengthen international institutions that reflect and legitimate Western interests and values and to promote the involvement of non-Western states in those institutions.

In the longer term other measures would be called for. Western civilization is both Western and modern. Non-Western civilizations have attempted to become modern without becoming Western. To date only Japan has fully succeeded in this quest. Non-Western civilizations will continue to attempt to acquire the wealth, technology, skills, machines and weapons that are part of being modern. They will also attempt to reconcile this modernity with their traditional culture and values. Their economic and military strength relative to the West will increase. Hence the West will increasingly have to accommodate these non-Western modern civilizations whose power approaches that of the West but whose values and interests differ significantly from those of the West. This will require the West to maintain the economic and military power necessary to protect its interests in relation to these civilizations. It will also, however, require the West to develop a more profound understanding of the basic religious and philosophical assumptions underlying other civilizations and the ways in which people in those civilizations see their interests. It will require an effort to identify elements of commonality between Western and other civilizations. For the relevant future, there will be no universal civilization, but instead a world of different civilizations, each of which will have to learn to coexist with the others.

References

Lewis, B. 1990. The roots of Muslim rage. *The Atlantic Monthly.* (September): 60.

———. 1992. Untitled. *Time* (June 15): 24-28.

Mahbubani, K. 1992. The west and the rest. *The National Interest* (Summer): 3-13.

Roosevelt, A. 1988. *For lust of knowing.* Boston: Little, Brown.

Schneider, D. 1993. A Russian movement rejects western tilt. *Christian Science Monitor* (February 5): 5-7.

Stankevich, S. 1992. Russia in search of itself. *The National Interest* (Summer): 47-51.

Triandis, H. 1989. Cross-cultural studies of individualism and collectivism. Nebraska Symposium on Motivation, vol. 37: 41-133.

———. 1990. Untitled. *New York Times* (December 25): 41.

Weidenbaum, M. 1993. *Greater China: The next economic superpower?* St. Louis: Washington University Center for the Study of American Business, Contemporary Issues, Series 57: 2-3.

CHAPTER 7

Singapore and the "Asian Values" Debate

Donald K. Emmerson

Originally published in Journal of Democracy 6 (4), 1995.

READING INTRODUCTION

Emmerson's initial paragraphs provide an accessible and amusing contrast of the social values at issue in the "Asian values" debate. He and his Singaporean cab driver disagree about the relative merits of personal freedom and social harmony in an argument over the appropriateness of automobile speed governors. Emmerson acknowledges the long-standing nature of this debate as well as recent instances in Singaporean public life that help to keep it alive (e.g., the case of Michael Fay who was caned as punishment for vandalism). Yet he characterizes much opinion on the question of whether Asian and Western values differ as prone to commit one or the other of two fallacies.

One of these, which Emmerson associates with Kipling, suggests that (all) Asians subscribe to one set of values while (all) Westerners adhere to a distinct rival set. The alternative fallacy runs that (all) persons, both East and West, subscribe to a single set of values. Emmerson suggests, in contrast, that while citizens of Asian and Western societies subscribe to similar values, they frequently do so in different proportions. Thus, in Singapore one is more likely to run into the social harmony orientation toward automobile speed governors that Emmerson's cab driver holds than in Los Angeles. Likewise, in the latter city Emmerson's personal liberty position with respect to such governors is apt to be more common than the perspective of his cab driver (Triandis 1995).

Emmerson thus concludes that while no distinctively Asian values exist, the future character of democracy in Asia may well be different from the liberal democracy of the West since preferences for social harmony and order appear to be more prevalent than concerns for personal liberty and individual rights (Donnelly 1989; Mahbubani 1998).

READING TEXT

In the middle of a long night some years ago I found myself in Singapore, tired after a trans-Pacific flight, riding a taxi down the multilane straightaway from

Changi Airport into town. The highway at that hour was nearly empty and the police were nowhere in sight. Whenever the driver exceeded the speed limit, a mellifluous chime sounded from underneath his dashboard, ceasing only when he slowed down. The chime was then and still is required on all cabs in Singapore.

As the chime went on and off, I asked my driver jokingly whether, at traffic-free times like this, he had ever thought of disconnecting it. He was not amused. If he unhooked his chime, he told me, other cabs would follow suit. Soon everyone would speed. Accidents would break out all over the city, paralyzing traffic. He pictured Singapore sinking into lawless anarchy.

I begin with this anecdote because it reminds us that, in any society, some individuals are likely to value order and fear disorder more than others do. It follows that such order-valuing, disorder-fearing people may constitute a higher proportion of the citizenry of one society compared with another. If that is so, implementing representative democracy in these two societies could have different implications for human rights. An electorate that values individual rights, is accustomed to social order, and sees little or no contradiction between them could democratically enlarge personal freedom. But an electorate less confident of the capacity of its social order to withstand the conflicts that greater personal freedoms might entrain could, just as democratically, curtail them.

In my experience, an appreciation of social order is neither uniformly nor uniquely Asian. Nor do those Asians who place a high value on social order all behave the same way. My taxi driver's endorsement of the use of speed governors to keep other drivers from breaking the law was triggered by his having broken it himself—by speeding.

Yet even if there are no quintessentially Asian values, the debate about them must be taken seriously by students of "democracy" because it challenges us to consider what we mean by that term. For if differing societies may democratically implement differing views of the relative importance of social order versus individual rights, it follows that alongside rights-tilted or liberal democracies there could be nonliberal—or at any rate less liberal—variants of democracy that are, compared to their liberal counterparts, more order-inclined.

From Salamis to Singapore

The "Asian values" debate is not a formally organized oral disputation between two sides advancing contrary answers to the same question. It is a large, diverse, and ongoing array of written and oral pronouncements and exchanges that share some relevance to a set of questions about "Asian values"—their existence, their contents, and the implications of the answers to these first two questions for policy and behavior.

Answers to these core questions have been offered since the time of the ancient Greeks, when the word "Asia" first entered the vocabulary of a people resident in "Europe." From their initial contacts with the Persians in the mid-sixth century B.C., the Greeks began characterizing these "Asians." Thus originated a "Western" tradition of representing "Asia" that has been decried as "Orientalism" (Said 1978).

Images of democracy and dictatorship were central to this first stereotyping of Asia. In *The Persians,* first performed in 472 B.C. within a flourishing and self-confident Athenian democracy, the playwright Aeschylus contrasted the opulent tyranny of the Persians with the personal freedom of his fellow Greeks (Aeschylus 1970). In retrospect, this imputation of authoritarianism to Asia may be taken as the first recorded salvo in a "debate" that has been intermittently underway for almost 2,500 years.

Read through the admittedly distorting lens of late-twentieth-century concerns, Aeschylus's drama seems to prefigure current exchanges. The play takes place in the aftermath of the Athenians' bloody rout of the Persians at the battle of Salamis in 480 B.C. Just as the vanquishing of communism by democracy in the Cold War made possible a triumphalist championing of Western liberal values, so could this earlier victory be used to imagine the victorious Greeks, who invented democracy, projecting the spread of civilizing freedoms throughout barbarian Asia.

In Aeschylus's play the Greeks, in defeating the Persians, break the "honored rule" made by Zeus "that a single man should hold the whole of Asia . . . and dictate all its laws." The end of Persian tyranny turns "the mass of men" in Asia "loose and free in their speech"—their tongues can be "no longer kept in check." Free speech, Aeschylus implies, is not just an Athenian (Western) ideal. It is valued by all human beings.

Elsewhere in *The Persians,* while the battle of Salamis still rages, a "roar of Persian tongues" answers a Greek commander's appeal to his troops to repel the invader on behalf of freedom (Aeschylus 1970, 92, 76, 62). Aeschylus does not tell us what the Persians were shouting back at the Greek armada. That leaves us free to fantasize them defending their own undemocratic way of life against the Western faith that, deep down, all human beings want personal freedom—thus playing their part in the very first round of the "Asian values" debate.[1]

Much has happened on the road from Salamis to Singapore. The particulars of the "Asian values" debate have been repeatedly transformed over the last 2,500 years, and will continue to evolve. Interest in the subject will wax and wane, and may someday disappear. But only the still wildly implausible dissolving of perceived differences into a homogeneous world culture will eliminate the core questions—the existence, nature, and impact of supposedly Asian values—that have animated past versions of this controversy and will inspire future ones.

A Compliant Judiciary?

However ancient and dispersed the origins of disagreement over Asian values, the current phase of the debate may be described narrowly as a polemic of the 1990s conducted largely between Singaporeans and Americans. In 1993 in *Foreign Policy,* for example, Bilahari Kausikan, a Singaporean foreign ministry official, and Aryeh Neier, then head of Human Rights Watch, criticized and defended, respectively, what Kausikan termed "the Western approach to human rights" in East Asia (Kausikan 1993; Neier 1993).

Beyond words, deeds have exacerbated disagreement. It was one thing for Kausikan's foreign ministry colleague Kishore Mahbubani to assert in the spring of 1994 that Asians valued tough punishment for criminals. In the United States, he argued in contrast, a liberal preference for lenience had allowed wrongdoers to go unpunished, leaving Americans "in constant fear" of crime (Mahbubani 1994b). It was another matter, however, for Singapore, having convicted, jailed, and fined the American Michael Fay on vandalism charges, to punish him, that same May, with four strokes of the cane.

In October of that same year, in the *International Herald Tribune,* Mahbubani criticized Europeans for wrongly believing in the inevitability of liberal democracy while turning a blind eye to nearby political violence from Algeria to Bosnia. That "ring of fire," he wrote, was claiming more lives daily than were being lost in the entire Asian-Pacific region. East Asians, in contrast, were prospering, at peace, and soundly engaged with the larger world (Mahbubani 1994a).

A week later in the *Tribune,* a visiting American scholar at the National University of Singapore, Christopher Lingle, tried to debate Mahbubani. Democracy in Europe had at least assured public knowledge of the violence in North Africa and the Balkans, wrote Lingle. The same could not be said of East Asia, where censors still concealed the death toll from repression in Burma, East Timor, and Tibet. And those casualties did not include the Asian lives ruined by intolerant Asian regimes using subtler methods of repressing dissent, including "relying upon a compliant judiciary to bankrupt opposition politicians" (Lingle 1994b).

Lingle did not say which "intolerant regimes" were manipulating their judiciaries in this manner. But the Singapore police who promptly interrogated him thought he might have had Singapore in mind. Court proceedings ensued. In order to prove that Lingle had libeled Singapore's judiciary, Attorney General Chan Sek Keong was placed in the odd position of trying to prove that the American could only have had Singapore in mind. Chan noted that, from 1971 to 1993, 11 opposition politicians had been bankrupted by suits brought against them and won by government officials. In no other country had such a thing happened, Chan pointed out (Fernandez 1994, 2).

The attorney general insisted that these punishments were deserved. Yet by confirming the unique vulnerability of opposition politicians in Singapore he undermined his own case in the larger court of world opinion. If opposition figures had not been bankrupted by legal proceedings in other countries, could one seriously believe that such individuals in Singapore were by some quirk of nature uniquely malfeasant? As for the docility of Singapore's judiciary, far from refuting that imputation as slanderous, an easy court victory against Lingle risked being seen as confirming it. The government appeared more eager to punish Lingle, presumably to deter future criticism, than to show that Singaporean judges were in fact completely independent.

In January 1995 a Singaporean judge found Lingle and the *Tribune* guilty of contempt, fined them, and ordered them to pay the prosecutor's court costs. Lingle was unrepresented in the trial, having long since fled the city-state to avoid what he feared could have been a jail sentence. As evidence for that fear,

Lingle quoted Prime Minister Goh Chok Tong as threatening to "throw the book" at him were he found guilty (Lingle 1994b).[2]

In his article for the *Tribune*, Lingle had argued that Asia lacked any "tradition for promoting individual liberty or protecting individual rights." But in saying this he had undermined his own implied case for liberal democracy. For without cultural precedents to nourish it, how could a system based on respect for the individual survive? No less ironically, in prosecuting Lingle, Singapore's pro-"Asian values" government chose to defend a thoroughly Western concept—judicial independence—inherited from British colonial rule.

That the American defender of liberal democracy had implicitly acknowledged the existence of distinctively Asian values while the Singaporean exponent of Asian values had upheld an originally Western institution was more than merely ironic. It also suggested a way out of the impasse. For if within one side's viewpoint one could find a perception or preference common to the other's, the debate and its misleading polarity might be transcended—even if the trauma inflicted on Lingle could not.

Dynastic Politics?

Soon after its courts sought to cut off the Lingle-Mahbubani exchange, Singapore's government once again found itself pressed to debate the subject of Asian values. Upon learning that Prime Minister Goh Chok Tong had accepted an invitation to receive an honorary degree from Williams College in Massachusetts, local faculty members with objections to Singapore's record on human rights sought to arrange a debate at Williams between Goh and two critics of Singapore—Lingle and a prominent Singaporean dissident, former solicitor general Francis Seow.

In a *New York Times* column backing the idea of such a debate, William Safire (1995b) made his own view scathingly clear: "Despite oleaginous pretensions about a new Asian culture that transcends human rights," he wrote, Senior Minister Lee Kuan Yew, Prime Minister Goh, and "the dauphin"—Lee's son and deputy prime minister Lee Hsien Loong—"represent old-fashioned European totalitarianism" (A13). A week later, Goh's secretary replied by inviting Safire to debate Goh in Singapore. Safire rejected the idea of going to Singapore to appear before "a hometown Asian crowd" as "a set-up for a local racist triumph." He offered instead to argue the universality of democratic values with the creator of modern Singapore himself, Lee Kuan Yew, in Switzerland before an "unintimidated press"—provided Goh would agree to face Seow at Williams (Safire 1995b, A15). Safire, Lee's son promptly replied, had "chickened out" of debating Goh in Singapore (Reuter 1995).

Meanwhile, in a separate controversy, Goh and both Lees asked a Singapore court for $930,000 in damages from the *Tribune* for an August article by British journalist Philip Bowring criticizing the notion of Asian values (Reuter 1995).[3] In that piece, Bowring had attributed "dynastic politics" to Singapore, a charge understood by the Lees to mean that the son owed his position not to his abilities but to his father's influence (Bowring 1994). Earlier in the year, in a piece on what he called Singapore's "despo-nepotism," Safire had dismissed the senior Lee's claim that Asians valued society over the individual. One might as well argue that Asians were genetically preordained to be servile, wrote Safire—implying that only a racist could make a case for Asian values (Safire 1995c, A17).

Again there were constructive ironies at work. In his thoughtful debunking of extreme opinions on either side of the debate, Bowring had acknowledged that one might be able to identify a few values that were in fact more prevalent in Asia than in the West and vice versa. He had cited "family solidarity" as one plausibly Asian value. In this he agreed with Lee Kuan Yew, who had underscored the same value as fundamentally and uniquely characteristic of Sinitic societies such as China, Japan, Korea, and Vietnam (Zakaria 1994, 113). Conversely, in rejecting the "dynastic" label Lee implicitly agreed with Bowring that not every Asian value was unambiguously desirable and that sharp tensions could exist between different Asian values—notably, in this case, between kinship and merit as equally "Confucian" criteria of advancement.

Getting beyond polemics over Asian values means demolishing two straw men. The first of these we may call the Rudyard Kipling Fallacy: the obviously false notion that East is East, West is West, and never the twain shall overlap. It is absurd to affirm the existence of Asian values if by that we mean to ascribe a single set of beliefs to some 3.4 billion people—spread across dozens of countries, believing in different if not contradictory religions, speaking mutually unintelligible tongues—and to contrast that set with an altogether different list of Western values supposedly held by nearly a billion also diverse humans in Europe, the United States, and other places largely settled by Europeans.

Too often in the debate this straw man is knocked over with a flourish only to be replaced, by implication, with its polar opposite. With modest exaggeration we may call this equally romantic notion Rudyard Kipling's Other Fallacy: that there is one universal mode of moral conduct to which all 5.6 billion human beings adhere that entirely transcends all national or cultural differences.[4]

These two straw men—one might also call them ultra-Orientalism and ultra-universalism—form the least plausible ends of a spectrum of possibilities. It follows that we ought to move at least partway toward the complex and ambiguous middle of this continuum. We should be willing, that is, to relinquish the purity of our positions for the sake of making them more accurate.

The extreme understanding of "Asian values" as a unique set of preferences found only in Asia is untenable. But Asians do have some values, and certain Asians (and Westerners) have identified certain values as characteristically Asian. These observations imply a strategy for shifting constructively from the extremes of the "Asian values" debate toward the center by trying to determine what values Asians do hold and ascribe to one another.

Exploring Public Opinion

In a global study of managerial subcultures, business administrators in 38 countries were asked the following question:

Two people were discussing ways in which individuals could improve the quality of life:

A. One said: "It is obvious that if individuals have as much freedom as possible and the maximum opportunity to develop themselves, the quality of their lives will improve as a result."

B. The other said: "If individuals are continuously taking care of their fellow human beings, the quality of life will improve for everyone, even if it obstructs individual freedom and individual development."

Which of the two ways of reasoning do you think is usually best, A or B?

Countries were ranked by the percentage of respondents in each who agreed with proposition A—that maximum freedom and opportunity for individuals would improve the quality of their lives. In the resulting hierarchy of countries, nine of the ten most individualistic were Western—that is, located in Europe or mainly populated by descendants of Europeans—while five of the ten most communitarian were Asian. The contrast between Singaporeans and Americans was substantial: While 79 percent of the American sample took the individualist position—no country was more extreme—only 50 percent did so in Singapore (Trompenaars 1994, 51-53).

These results support neither the pure Orientalist nor the extreme universalist view. Contrary to the former, for example, individual freedom and opportunity were valued more highly in India than in France, equally popular in Japan and West Germany, and less highly valued in Switzerland than in Hong Kong. Contrary to the universalist thesis, the most communitarian and the most individualistic respondents were indeed more Asian and Western, respectively.

In the more authoritarian Asian states, directly questioning large numbers of people about their opinions can be a sensitive exercise. Partly to get around this difficulty, David Hitchcock (1994) asked 131 officials, scholars, businesspeople, and professionals from eight East Asian countries and the United States to select from a list of values not necessarily the ones that they themselves endorsed, but rather the ones that they considered were "critically important" to others in that particular country.[5]

On all major relevant differences between Asians and Americans, majorities of Asians took the supposedly Asian position, consistently ranking social stability as more important to their fellow citizens than personal liberty. Answers on the value of an "orderly society" differentiated the two groups the most. While 71 percent of the Asian respondents picked this value as critically important to others in their country, only 11 percent of the Americans did so. By differences of 54 and 51 percentage points, respectively, Asians were more inclined than Americans to pick "respect for learning" and "preserv[ing] harmony for the group" as critically important to their fellow citizens. By gaps of 50 and 49 points, Asians regarded "personal freedom" and "the rights of individuals" as less important to people in their own societies than Americans did. Especially striking were the differences between Singaporeans and Americans, which ranged from 67 to 82 percentage points. None of the 11 Singaporean informants listed personal freedom or individual rights as of critical importance to Singaporeans.

Yet Hitchcock's study did not confirm the ultra-Orientalist view. There were differences among Asians. For instance, on all five of the dimensions just quoted, between Singaporean and American rankings of key national values, the Thais saw their society more the way the Americans saw theirs. Purportedly Asian values were neither monolithic nor exclusive. Furthermore, Asians and Americans were in substantial agreement that "the accountability of public officials" and "decision by majority" were critically important to others in their societies; perceptual gaps on these values were only 4 and 11 percentage points, respectively. By this measure, democracy as a procedural system of public responsibility and choice would appear to have more attitudinal support in East Asia than the preference of classical liberalism for individual rights and freedoms over social order and group harmony. If this difference is real, it at least opens the possibility that in East Asia majoritarian democracy as a set of rules may have a brighter future than liberal democracy as a political culture. It would then be a matter of debate as to just how much less liberal a democracy can be before it no longer warrants being called a democracy at all.

Finally, if—and only if—Hitchcock's informants were able correctly to identify the value priorities generally prevalent in their societies, a modified Orientalist conclusion does emerge: For all its internal diversity, East Asian public opinion may indeed differ, though to varying extents, from the opinions of Americans in ways that are at least consonant with the assertion of Asian values.

The "Gullible-Other" Effect

But what if Hitchcock's respondents were wrong? He guaranteed their anonymity. Yet they still could have tailored their answers to fit an Asian-values-positing line. They could have done this insincerely by concealing what they knew to be the liberal preferences of the population. Perhaps they were afraid that local higher-ups who had asserted the existence of Asian values might discover their names and how they had answered Hitchcock's questions. Or, insofar as his Asian informants were themselves believers in the reality of Asian values, they could have sincerely misjudged their fellow citizens' views. And who but the Singaporean interviewees, living as they were under the close watch of authorities espousing a "Singapore School" of thought on the subject, could have been more liable to these pressures?

Yet Hitchcock's Singaporean informants knew him. Almost certainly they trusted him to keep their answers confidential. Nor did these respondents give him reason to think that they personally espoused the Asian values that they ascribed to the wider population. On the contrary, some of them seemed to Hitchcock to hold values that differed from those they were attributing to others. All of these respondents had enjoyed long and repeated exposure to the West. By implication, they may have been more "liberal" in outlook than the Singaporean public as perceived by them.

This raises a plausible anomaly: that, by and large, the people who make up Singapore's elite, including Hitchcock's respondents, may not themselves adhere to the Asian values that they attribute to—indeed, that some hope to inculcate in—ordinary Singaporeans. Thoroughly Westernized themselves, some of Singapore's opinion makers may sincerely fear the consequences for social stability should their own more liberal or "Western" values pervade the larger population. Implicit in this reasoning may be the idea that while "we the elite" can handle personal freedom, "they the masses" cannot.

One may respond to this idea by rejecting it out of hand on the ultra-universalist grounds that human nature is everywhere the same. But is it plausible to think that all humans will use personal freedom in the same way, regardless of circumstances? It would be more tenable to argue that, even though responses to freedom will vary, thus ensuring that the actual practice of democracy will differ from culture to culture to some degree, there may well be a tendency for elites to underestimate the ability of those in the rest of society to handle their freedom "responsibly."

Intriguing in this connection is the widely observed "third-person effect": the tendency of people to exaggerate the influence of mass communications on the attitudes and behavior of others (Davison 1983; Perloff 1993). A variation on this phenomenon might be called the "gullible-other" effect: the tendency of people to exaggerate the susceptibility of others to incitement. Why did the government of Singapore go to such lengths to punish the *International Herald Tribune* for carrying articles suggesting that the city-state's judiciary might be "compliant" and its politics "dynastic," if not to prevent the putatively credulous populace from being swayed by negative messages in the mass media?

More intriguing still is the possibility that the gullible-other effect may not be limited to elites. Consider my Singapore cab driver's fear of anarchy by example. Was it realistic of him to think that his own negative behavior—disabling the speed governor under his dashboard—would be contagious enough to cause mayhem and gridlock? Surely not. But if enough of the other cab drivers on the roads also overestimated the susceptibility of their colleagues, a shared misperception could have acquired its own behavioral truth, as drivers acted on their individually false but collectively effective assumptions.

Recent work on the popularity of censorship in Singapore suggests the operation of just such a pattern. In endorsing limits on freedom, many Singaporeans seem to use a double standard. I can handle morally or politically sensitive information, they seem to say, but censorship is needed because my neighbors cannot.

We may now expand the gullible-other effect into a general proposition: In any society, other things being equal, the more widespread the inclination to overestimate the susceptibility of others to incitement, the more official curbs on freedom are likely to be considered legitimate. This is only a hypothesis, but its implications are sobering. Optimism that democracy will spread around the world may not be realistic if by "democracy" we insist on meaning only its most uncompromisingly liberal or personal-freedom-maximizing kind.

In 1977, Singapore's then-foreign minister confessed to having "very serious doubts as to whether such a thing as 'Asian values' really exists. . . . It may exist as an image but it has no reality" (Rajaratnam 1977, 95). Most Asians may well prefer certain values more—or less—than most Westerners do, but wholly or solely Asian values are indeed more imaginary than real. Widely held images can, however, affect reality by helping make some arrangements more legitimate than others. In this sense, the controversy over Asian values is not a debate at all. It is a struggle for the future.

References

Aeschylus. 1970. *The Persians*. Translated with commentary by A. Podlecki. Englewood Cliffs, NJ: Prentice-Hall.
Bowring, P. 1994. The claims about "Asian" values don't usually bear scrutiny. *International Herald Tribune* (July 10): 4.
Davison, W. P. 1983. The third-person effect in communication. *Public Opinion Quarterly* 47 (Spring): 3.
Fernandez, W. 1994. Judge: Enough evidence for case against Lingle, four others. *Straits Times* (December 26): 2.
Hitchcock, D. 1994. *Asian values and the United States: How much conflict?* Washington, DC: Center for Strategic and International Studies.
Kausikan, B. 1993. Asia's different standard. *Foreign Policy* 92 (Fall): 24-41.
Lingle, C. 1994a. Singapore repression reveals regime's insecurity. *Daily Yomiuri* (December 2): 6.
———. 1994b. The smoke over parts of Asia obscures some profound concerns. *International Herald Tribune* (July 10): 4.
Mahbubani, K. 1994a. You may not like it, Europe, but this Asian medicine could help. *International Herald Tribune* (October 1, 2): 4.
———. 1994b. The United States: Go east, young man. *Washington Quarterly* 17 (Spring): 7.
Neier, A. 1993. Asia's unacceptable standard. *Foreign Policy* 92 (Fall): 42-51.
Perloff, R. 1993. Third-person effect research 1983-1992: A review and synthesis. *International Journal of Public Opinion Research* 5 (Summer): 167-184.
Rajaratnam, S. 1977. Asian values and modernization. In *Asian values and modernization*, edited by S. Chee-Meow. Singapore: Singapore University Press.
Reuter's. 1995. Singapore attacks opposition and U.S. columnist Safire. ClariNet Communications online. (July 24).
Safire, W. 1995a. Singapore's fear. *New York Times* (July 20): A15.
———. 1995b. Honoring repression. *New York Times* (July 10): A13.
———. 1995c. Singapoverty. *New York Times* (February 2): A17.
Said, E. 1978. *Orientalism*. New York: Pantheon.
Trompenaars, F. 1994. *Riding the waves of culture: Understanding diversity in global business*. Burr Ridge, IL: Irwin.
Zakaria, F. 1994. Culture is destiny: A conversation with Lee Kuan Yew. *Foreign Affairs* 73 (March-April).

PART III

Popular Culture

Introduction

Like other areas of culture addressed in this *Reader,* the study of "popular" culture is torn by deep issues. There is, for instance, a dispute over what popular culture *is.* Is it a manipulated "mass" culture, produced in media conglomerates and disseminated among the community's citizens by profit-seeking corporations? Or is it produced by its adherents: a set of beliefs, values, practices, and norms that emerge as people in particular communities interact and define the meaning of their lives? And of what importance are its distinctions from "high" culture (i.e., classical literature, art, and music—the legacy of a civilization's creative and intellectual enterprises that have stood the test of time)?

In general, studies in the area of popular culture take one of three paths: analyses of the concept of the "popular" and its utility for understanding and evaluating social and political life; methodological treatises in which questions are raised about how best to understand the "popular" and its meaning; and idiosyncratic studies of particular dimensions of ordinary people's culture that are argued to illustrate broader issues and values in society. While no brief introduction can provide a systematic review of these diverse applications of the popular culture concept, our analysis of these disputes is designed to provide a helpful context for the readings that follow.

To understand the notion of popular culture, it is necessary to recognize that the popular is being separated from something else (During 1993). After all, if culture were understood to be all the same thing, modifiers such as "popular," "political," or "high" would not be necessary. In simplest terms, popular culture is understood to be the beliefs, values, and affective commitments—particularly those displayed in various leisure activities—held and acted on by large numbers of ordinary people. "Popular" has historically been a pejorative term. Whereas the "better"—aristocratic, wealthy, educated—segments of society appreciated opera, symphonies, and poetry, the masses enjoyed melodrama, "pop" music, and serialized magazine stories. Such "low" pursuits were frequently held by intellectual elites to satiate the passions and desires of "the great unwashed"; they were certainly not construed by these elites as improving the soul or encouraging careful contemplation of duty, honor, country, or the divine. "Popular," then, meant debased as well as broadly enjoyed (Hoggart 1957; LeVine 1988).

Challenges to the idea that only great literature and other fine arts fostered appropriate values have developed across the last couple of centuries, particularly during the years following World War II. Studies of mass-produced music, magazines, newspapers, films, and eventually television programs began to show that these texts modeled beliefs, values, and affective commitments that people said they cared about and seemed to shape people's orientations toward democratic social life in the first place (During 1993; Riesman 1950; Thompson 1968; Whyte 1956). That is, these mass-produced popular programs appear both to emerge from as well as to reinforce culture, but their themes are distinct from and frequently at odds with some of the biases of high culture. Thus, in listening to rock songs about sexual promiscuity, younger people understand that these songs represented their desires. At the same time, such songs might give them license to undertake such activities when they previously might have refrained. Accordingly, researchers began to examine the ways in which particular programs and other popular phenomena—sports events, political campaigns, and so on—contributed to as well as derived from the broader context of social norms, values, and practices (Douglas 1975; Mercer 1995; Mukerji and Schudson 1991).

Additionally, there are methodological disputes about how best to analyze and interpret popular culture. In general, these disputes manifest a quantitative/qualitative division. For some, the only way appropriately to evaluate what is going on and determine what it means is to engage in statistical or other kinds of scientific operations—content analysis, survey research, and so on. Such analysis, they contend, is the best way to find out what people believe, how they interpret the ideals, values, and perspectives to which they are exposed; and how they use this information in their daily lives (Almond and Verba 1965; Devine 1972; Verba, Nie, and Petrocik 1980). Other scholars argue in favor of a more interpretive, ethnographic approach. For them, surveys say more about the researchers' culture than what ordinary people believe, care about, and act on. Thus, for these researchers, more focused interpretive studies ought to be undertaken in order to "unpack" the meaning of particular practices and explain how these events manifest broader cultural dynamics (Geertz 1973, 3-30; Merelman 1989; Wildavsky 1987).

There is general agreement in the following readings that the social values preferred by high culture are not generally better or safer than those of popular culture. Rather, these distinctive cultural expressions champion rival values. Each author uses popular programs and practices to illustrate broader cultural themes. Methodologically, one uses a content analysis/scientific approach, while the other two are more directly interpretive. Our primary concern in the selections that follow is to illustrate how broad cultural themes are embodied in specific popular practices, a point that these readings demonstrate admirably.

References and Further Reading

Almond, G., and S. Verba. 1965. *The civic culture.* Boston: Little, Brown.
Bourdieu, P. 1978. Sport and social class. *Social Science Information* 17 (6): 819-840.
Devine, D. 1972. *The political culture of the United States.* Boston: Little, Brown.
Douglas, M. 1975. *Implicit meanings.* London: Routledge and Kegan Paul.
During, S., ed. 1993. *The cultural studies reader.* New York: Routledge.
Geertz, C. 1972. Deep play: Notes on the Balinese cockfight. *Daedalus* 101(1): 1-37.
———. 1973. Thick description: Toward an interpretive theory of culture. In *The interpretation of cultures.* New York: Basic Books.
Hirsch, P. 1972. Processing fads and fashions: An organization-set analysis of cultural industry systems. *American Journal of Sociology* 77: 639-659.
Hoggart, R. 1957. *The uses of literacy.* New York: Penguin.
LeVine, L. 1984. William Shakespeare and the American people: A study in cultural transformation. *American Historical Review* 89: 34-66.
———. 1988. *Highbrow/Lowbrow: The emergence of cultural hierarchy in America.* Cambridge, MA: Harvard University Press.
McBride, A., and R. K. Toburen. 1996. Deep structures: Polpop culture on primetime television. *Journal of Popular Culture* 29: 181-200.
Mercer, K. 1995. Black hair/Style politics. In *Cultural Remix: Theories of Politics and the Popular,* edited by E. Carter, J. Donald, and J. Squires. London: Lawrence & Wishart.
Merelman, R. 1989. On culture and politics in America: A perspective from structural anthropology. *British Journal of Political Science* 19: 465-493.
Mukerji, C., and M. Schudson, eds. 1991. *Rethinking popular culture: Contemporary perspectives in cultural studies.* Berkeley: University of California Press.
Riesman, D. 1950. *The lonely crowd.* New Haven, CT: Yale University Press.
Thompson, E. P. 1968. *The making of the English working class.* New York: Penguin.
Tuchman, G. 1978. Introduction: The symbolic annihilation of women by the mass media. In *Hearth and home: Images of women in the mass media,* edited by G. Tuchman, A. K. Daniels, and J. Benet. New York: Oxford University Press.
Verba, S., N. Nie, and J. Petrocik. 1980. *The new American electorate.* Cambridge: Cambridge University Press.
Whyte, W. 1956. *The organization man.* New York: Simon & Schuster.
Wildavsky, A. 1987. Choosing preferences by constructing institutions. *American Political Science Review* 81: 3-21.
Williams, Rosalind. 1982. *Dream worlds.* Berkeley: University of California Press.

CHAPTER 8

Deep Structures: Polpop Culture on Primetime Television
Allen McBride and Robert K. Toburen

Originally published in Journal of Popular Culture *29, 1996.*

READING INTRODUCTION

McBride and Toburen investigate the ways that supposedly nonpolitical television programs, such as sit-coms and night-time dramas, manifest political cultural values. Using a scientific method known as content analysis, the authors rely on several "coders"—people trained to interpret television programming and identify events, actions, and themes according to a preestablished set of criteria. They focus on the way these programs handle authority, conflict, and conflict resolution. For example, coders examine whether authority figures are present and how they are treated by other characters (do other characters defer to authority, challenge it, etc.). Coders also focused on the degree to which conflicts are depicted, the end or goal of these conflicts, and how conflicts are resolved.

This analysis is then placed in a broader context through reliance on Daniel Elazar's three-part typology of American political culture. For Elazar, Americans cleave into three cultural types: individualists, moralists, and traditionalists. Individualists believe that people are personally responsible for their actions; that whatever happens is the individual's responsibility to handle. Traditionalists believe that ordinary people are properly subject to the authority of wiser, "better," people, and so believe that most people ought to accept their position in life without significant challenge. Finally, moralists believe that it is the responsibility of the broader society to protect and enhance the lives of ordinary citizens.

McBride and Toburen's examination of various television programs for the presence of authority figures and the ways conflict is represented and resolved reveals that the individualistic culture is the most commonly portrayed on television. This is consistent with other cultural analyses that have found a strong individualist bias in the United States. However, the analysis also finds strong moralist and traditionalist patterns in these programs, particularly in family relationships. Hence, evidence supports Elazar's theory and suggests that "nonpolitical" programming carries political implications.

READING TEXT

The September 21, 1992, cover of Time magazine carried a portrait of Candace Bergen, the star of the popular television program *Murphy Brown*. Ms. Bergen wore a campaign button supporting Murphy Brown for President, and the cover featured the title "Hollywood and Politics" in reference to an article that appeared within its pages. The article dealt with the controversy that captivated the media and public eye in the 1992 presidential campaign between "Murphy" and Vice-President Dan Quayle. This issue of Time chronicled the seepage between "fantasy and fact," between "entertainment and journalism," that occurs as a matter of course on American television. The editors and writers at Time were describing (and disparaging) a cultural reality that is disturbing to many Americans: that television has become the major player in disseminating and molding cultural values. It is our intention in this paper to explore the relationship between TV, culture, and politics (Morrow 1992).

We will argue that even the most innocuous, apolitical, entertainment programming has political content in the form of values, beliefs, and behaviors that are evidenced in what Richard Merelman (1989) refers to as "deep structures." Neither those who produce the programs, nor the viewers, may be aware of these underlying political messages, but the messages help to structure our political and nonpolitical relationships. We will use Daniel Elazar's (1984) American political subculture typology to help us identify the cultural patterns in the programming.

Political Culture and the Media

To the extent that human beings create their own world, they do so according to the values, beliefs, behaviors, and attitudes that play a central role in their culture, components of what has been called "cultural bias" (Thompson, Ellis, and Wildavsky 1991). Television is the most important cultural artifact in modern American society, replacing cave drawings and potsherds of preindustrial societies. The images that are saved and broadcast on magnetic tape provide clues about the cultural bias of our society in social, political, and economic terms.

Although the most apparent aspects of television entertainment programming are not clearly political, some types of programs have been examined for and do contain obvious political content. Public affairs programming, network news, campaign commercials and the coverage of the quadrennial political conventions are examples. These provide symbolic and ritualistic evidence of political culture by depicting our leaders, by mediating the political debate, and by presenting a forum for the anointed leadership to begin seeking power. But political content is not confined to non-entertainment programming. Police/detective shows and courtroom dramas, for example, often have clear political content which reflect and mold our individual notions of the American legal system. And even those programs which do not regularly contain explicit political content may contain such content in a latent form. Even more to the point for the purposes of this paper, they may promote certain politico-cultural values in a non-political context.

An example of both phenomena—occasional explicit political content and expression of more generalized political culture values—may be seen in the *Sesame Street* episode which aired November 4, 1992, the day after the Presidential election. On this post-election day program the daily morality tableau centered on the importance of voting. At issue was whether several of the *Sesame Street* regulars should purchase a box of crayons or some juice. The seven principals were divided on how to spend their combined money, forcing them to vote on which to purchase (a typical political economy problem of allocating scarce resources). After six persons had voted, there was a tie, leaving Telly Monster, a suitably named program regular, the responsibility for determining the outcome. The dramatic tension is created by Telly's inability to decide which side should benefit; his personal conflict is the result of not wanting any of his friends to lose. The tension is resolved when Gordon, a human program regular, advises Telly to vote his own conscience or interest. Telly then votes for the purchase of the crayons. Elmo, another Muppet regular and a member of the losing coalition, insists that he is still thirsty, and must have some juice. With the remainder of the money the group purchases one glass of juice which they all share, satisfying the needs of the entire community. While the tension created in the program is the result of concern for the "commonwealth," the resolution is pure individualism; as Telly votes his conscience the "hidden hand" safely conducts the ship of state to a peaceful harbor.

Most entertainment programming does not have the obvious political content (reference to the virtues of voting etc.) found in this episode of *Sesame Street*. However, many programs do develop some dramatic tension on the basis of conflicts that center on resource allocation, and because the allocation of resources is central to a definition of politics which is widely accepted by political scientists (Easton 1981), we regard such conflicts as political. Furthermore, the nature and object of any conflict, the social positions of the actors who influence its resolution, and the manner in which it is resolved have consequences for the development of political culture (Elazar 1984). Likewise, to the extent that television entertainment programs focus on resource allocation conflicts, we may say that such programs reflect and possibly influence American political culture.

Why should we focus upon culture? Students of political culture, including Elazar and George Gerbner, have provided evidence that culture has consequences for the way society is organized, for the way we interpret the world (what James Carey refers to as our "symbolic reality"), and upon behavior, at least as reported in the aggregate. Television is a medium of communication that universally reflects the values that are representative of our culture, and transmits them around the globe. To avoid the systematic study of television and popular culture seems to require more justification than does its pursuit.

Interest in the *cultural* effects of television beyond American borders has been substantial for a number of years. But while pundits and critics have, for some time, referred to television as the single most important purveyor of culture in our own society, political scientists have been slow to investigate the evident televised culture, except in limited ways, of which more below. Gerbner (1986) suggests that "institutional resistance" by those with high economic stakes and political interests may contribute to the lack of attention to television. Methodological problems inherent in conducting research without a sufficiently large comparison group (nonviewers) also contribute to the obstacles.

The reluctance of researchers to study the political culture of television entertainment programming may also be seen as one aspect of our reluctance to study our own culture generally (Carey 1988). Anthropologists regularly record the substance of culture in the "preindustrial societies" of the world, but they are less diligent in identifying cultural patterns in modern American culture. According to Carey, this is partially the result of the ideology of individualism and free will that permeates our culture. In other words, we view television as merely a form of entertainment with limited or no effect upon our beliefs, attitudes, and behavior. The "uses and gratification" theory (Rubin 1986), for example, posits that the effects of television viewing are selectively determined by the uses which the viewer makes of television fare. Researchers from this school base their research on the premise that the effects of television viewing are not generalized but are the outcome of self-mediated points of influence, a view that reflects an individualist ideology.

Those who have investigated political culture in the media have tended to limit their investigations to the effects of special programs (docudramas or infortainment for example) or movies (Adams et al. 1985; Ball-Rokeach, Grube, and Rokeach 1981; Feldman and Sigelman 1985; Lenart and McGraw 1989; Reiner 1981; Sigelman and Sigelman 1973-74) and these researchers have left a fairly rich research legacy suggestive of potential effects of prolonged television viewing, (see Combs for a general review and discussion of potential effects).

In contrast to the usual scholarly reluctance, George Gerbner and his research team have conducted a persistent, insightful, and systematic long term research program on television effects (1977, 1986, 1990). Their model and findings form the framework for research that is just beginning to develop in the area of political communication. Focusing on general viewing habits, instead of specific programs or news viewing, they have found, through an empirical process that they call "cultivation analysis," consistent evidence of media effects on specific types of attitudes, as well as on the development of "general values, ideologies and perspectives."

In this research report, we will describe a study that is similar to that of Gerbner et al. (1990) but that differs in three ways. The first difference between our research and that of Gerbner is the result of our interest in behavioral outcomes. We will suggest that televised political culture may be having an effect on the level of political participation, the decline of political parties, and antagonism toward welfare, for example. Second, we plan to focus upon the most popular programs on network television, as identified by Nielsen's rating for the 1991/92 viewing season, while Gerbner et al. (1990) examined the content of programs at all levels of popularity. Finally, we are interested in testing for the existence of a set of interrelated values associated with a specific definition of American political culture: Elazar's political culture typology.

Elazar suggests that American political culture can be divided into three unique subcultures—traditionalistic, individualistic, and moralistic—which roughly correspond to geographic regions of the United States. Traditionalistic subcultures are found largely in the South and are characterized by a traditional elite who are the primary actors in the political arena and who are expected to benefit from their own political activity. According to Elazar, elites are not noted for innovative behavior (they see their role as custodial) and the non-elite are likely to be politically passive (i.e. voter turnout will be low in these areas of the country) (Elazar 1984).

Persons from individualistic cultures view the political system as a marketplace which supplies certain goods that are unavailable from the private sector. Elazar (1984) describes the individualistic culture as follows: "In general, government action is restricted to those areas, primarily in the economic realm, that encourage private initiative and widespread access to the marketplace" (115). While public office is not reserved for a traditional elite as in the traditional culture, those who hold office in these areas of the country are also unlikely to be policy innovators. According to Elazar, office seekers and office holders pursue self-interest first and foremost with only limited concern for the public weal. Citizens in this type of culture, found most often in the Northeast, are more likely to participate in elections than are citizens in traditionalistic cultures; but, according to Elazar, politics is no place for amateurs.

The moralistic culture poses an interesting alternative to the individualistic and traditionalistic cultures. In moralistic areas of the country the politician and citizen alike are conscious of and participate in politics at all levels (this is the realm of the citizen politician), and the "common good" is presumed to be the goal of good government. Leaders are more likely to be innovators but are also more likely to be held to stricter moral accountability than in other parts of the country. Accordingly, there should be less corruption and fewer problems associated with conflict of interest by politicians. This type of culture is most likely to be found in New England and the upper Midwest. According to Elazar, persons from moralistic cultures are likely to be highly motivated by important political concerns, and, as a result, to be active politically (1984, 233).

In this first stage of our analysis, we undertake what Gerbner et al. (1990) refer to as "message system analysis." Our purpose is to determine if symptoms of moralistic, individualistic and traditionalistic cultures are evident in entertainment programming and, if so, which of them is most pervasive. We focus on two factors of basic political orientation, which we believe provide evidence of Elazar's political culture types in television entertainment programming. The two factors are authority and conflict. Questions concerning conflict and authority should elicit from coders evidence of what Merelman refers to as "deep structures"—themes and patterns of behavior and thought that are so embedded and interwoven into our culture that most of us remain totally unconscious of them.

We have chosen to measure authority by asking the following questions: are authority figures present, are they exercising authority, what sort of characteristics do they have, and how are they treated by other characters? Elazar uses authority to define his typology and to distinguish among the three cultural types. In the traditional model, authority figures should be most evident, they should bear responsibility for the exercise of authority, and others should accept their position in society as natural. In an individualistic culture, the role of the authority figure is more ambiguous. Individuals are expected to be responsible for their own actions: they should seek benefits from government, but the people who run government are expected to seek benefits for themselves rather than either to protect others or to seek benefits for the community. In individualistic cultures we would expect challenges to the authority figures as well. In the moralistic culture, "citizen-politicians" are more common, but they seek to protect the commonweal, rather than protecting the status quo or pursuing their own personal benefit. Authority figures should be even less clearly defined and should be less tolerated by other actors if the dominant culture is moralistic (Elazar 1984).

Like authority, conflict and conflict resolution should be uniquely manifested in each of the three cultural types. Questions we asked in order to characterize the treatment of conflict included: was there conflict in the program, what were the characteristics of the central antagonists in the conflict, for whom were benefits being sought, and how was the conflict resolved? In the traditional culture, conflict is more likely to be inter-institutional or between institutions and individuals, and resolution is most likely to occur by imposition from above. In the individualistic culture, conflict should be among individuals, and we would expect it to be resolved by the independent, competitive and bargaining behaviors of the characters. In the moralistic culture, conflict is turned toward cooperative resolution for the good of society.

Research Design

The TV programs that were selected for analysis were drawn from those being rebroadcast during the summer of 1992. We chose to analyze only programs that were the most popular (in the top 20 according to Nielsen) ("The Best"), and that were based upon a continuing storyline (resulting in the exclusion of *60 Minutes, 20-20, Unsolved Mysteries,* and *America's Funniest Home Videos*). The individual programs that were eventually coded were randomly selected from that pool of top 20 programs.

We used, as our coders, two black female graduate and three white female undergraduate students. Each student was given a set of instructions about the coding, and each also viewed a sample program with one of the researchers to insure that they were clear on how the coding was to proceed. They then coded one program, after which the researchers reviewed their coding sheets to insure that they were not experiencing any difficulties. Periodically throughout the coding process the researchers discussed the coding with the coders to maintain consistency. Coding was conducted independently, and coders were instructed to avoid discussing the coding with each other.

Findings

Each coder viewed and coded 20 programs. Seventeen of these programs were 30 minutes in length with the remainder having a length of one hour. With two segments coded per half-hour show and four segments per hour show, each coder coded approximately 46 segments, though the coders viewed each program in its entirety. The program names and their ratings are shown in Table 1.

Authority

Of the nearly 46 segments that were coded, our coders noted an average of twenty-seven in which an authority figure appeared. Not too surprisingly, given the nature of the programs, the "parent" was found to be the most common example of an authority figure, with the "boss" being a close second (Figure 1). There was little evidence of disagreement among the coders on this issue, though there were a few instances in which coders reported that neighbors and students acted as authority figures.

Not only were authority figures commonly present, they regularly attempted to wield their authority (an average of 21 segments were coded as such), though coders were less consistent on this issue than they were on the presence of authority. Authority holders were reported to be more likely to be domineering than cooperative, in the opinion of the coders, as they attempted to influ-

Table 1: Pool of Programs, Neilsen Ratings, Network, Frequencies*

Rating	Program Name	Network	Frequencies
2	*Roseanne*	ABC	10
3	*Murphy Brown*	CBS	5
4	*Cheers*	NBC	10
5	*Home Improvement*	ABC	11
6	*Designing Women*	CBS	0
7	*Coach*	ABC	5
8	*Full House*	ABC	11
10	*Murder, She Wrote*	CBS	4
11	*Major Dad*	CBS	7
13	*Evening Shade*	CBS	5
14	*Northern Exposure*	CBS	10
15	*A Different World*	NBC	9
16	*The Cosby Show*	NBC	5
17	*Wings*	NBC	0
18	*Fresh Prince of Bel-Air*	NBC	5
			97

*The Frequencies are based upon the total number of times that each of the listed programs was coded by a coder. The same episodes were coded more than once by different coders.

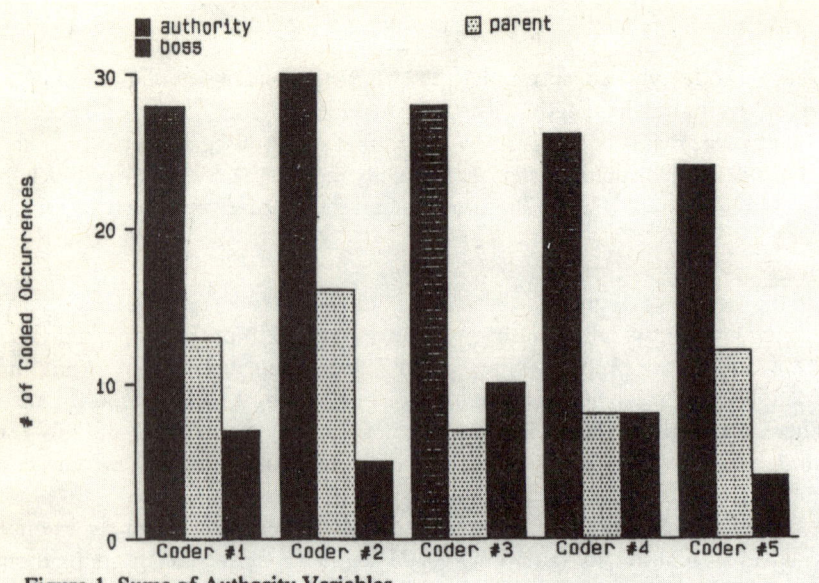

Figure 1. Sums of Authority Variables.

ence others (average number of segments = 11). The coders found authority was challenged about one-half of the time (mean = 9). Conversely, according to our coders, authority holders were successful in the exercise of their authority in an average of 18 segments, double the number in which their authority was challenged (Figures 2 and 3).

Conflict
All of the coders reported the presence of conflict (mean = 40) more often than they did the presence of authority, though the range of reported occurrences was large (32-47 segments) (Figure 4). Only four segments were coded by any of the coders as having no conflict whatsoever. These programs were *Full House* twice, *Major Dad* and *Cheers*.

Four dimensions were used to explore the nature of the apparent conflict. First, we asked coders to indicate who was involved in the conflict. The codeable categories included: internal conflict of one character, conflict between two or more individuals, conflict between one or more individuals and an institution, conflict between institutions. Internal conflict is exemplified by the following scenario: a young couple is planning their upcoming wedding. The man is marrying for the second time, after the death of his first wife, for whom, it becomes apparent, he retains strong feelings. During the course of the program, evidence of internal conflict on his part is represented by the frequent appearance of his former wife in the form of an apparition. His love for his fiancée is

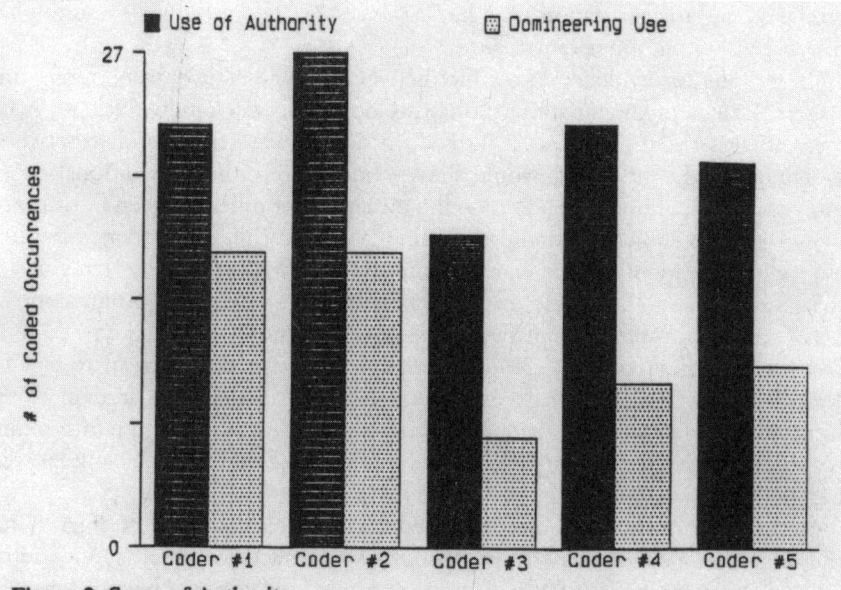

Figure 2. Sums of Authority.

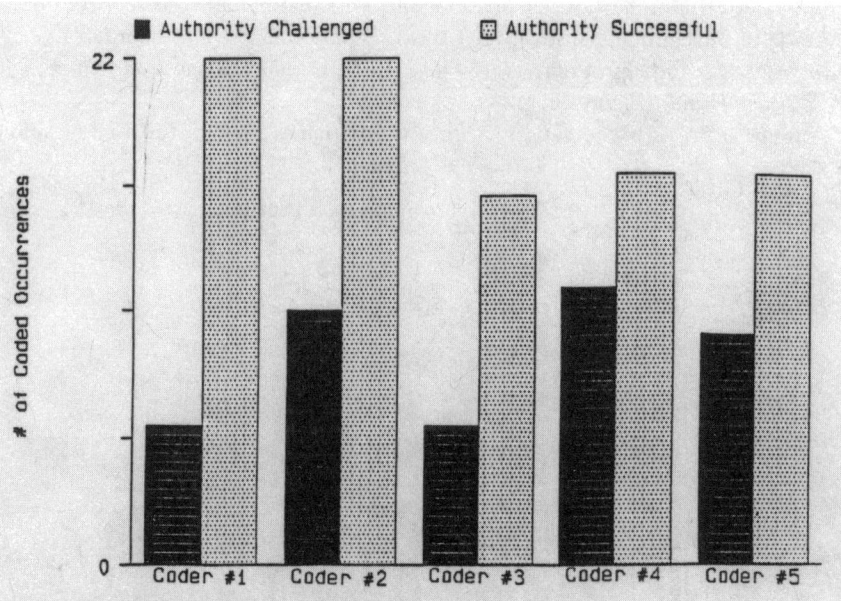

Figure 3. Sums of Responses to Authority.

tempered by the realization that he still loves his deceased wife, resulting in internal questions about remarrying.

In looking for evidence of conflict between individuals, we were not, at this stage, making a judgment about morality. Conflict between individuals, no matter who was right, indicates an individualistic value system. Conflict between individuals and institutions, would show evidence of either a traditional or an individualistic culture, depending on the outcome. Conflict between institutions would tend to indicate a traditional value system. While the coders were not always in agreement concerning the amount of individual vs. internal conflict that was present, they were in agreement on the following point: conflict between two or more individuals was the most commonly reported type of conflict (mean = 28, range = 20 – 38). Internal conflict was reported in an average of 10 segments. There was little disagreement about evidence of individual vs. institutional conflict—four out of five coders saw none at all and the fifth found that plot feature in only three segments. Institutional conflict went unreported by the coders (Figure 4).

Second, our coders were asked to identify beneficiaries of the conflict under the following categories: personal benefit of a character or another individual was being sought, benefit for an institution or organization, and benefit for society as a whole. Coders did not agree on the number of times each beneficiary type was apparent, but they were in agreement that the most common source of conflict was the pursuit of personal benefit. Personal benefit was reported in an average of 38 segments; institutional and societal benefit were recorded in only five programs (these programs were *Full House, Roseanne, Major Dad, Cheers,* and *A Different World*) (Figure 5).

Figure 6 presents the causes of conflict, which were reduced to four basic

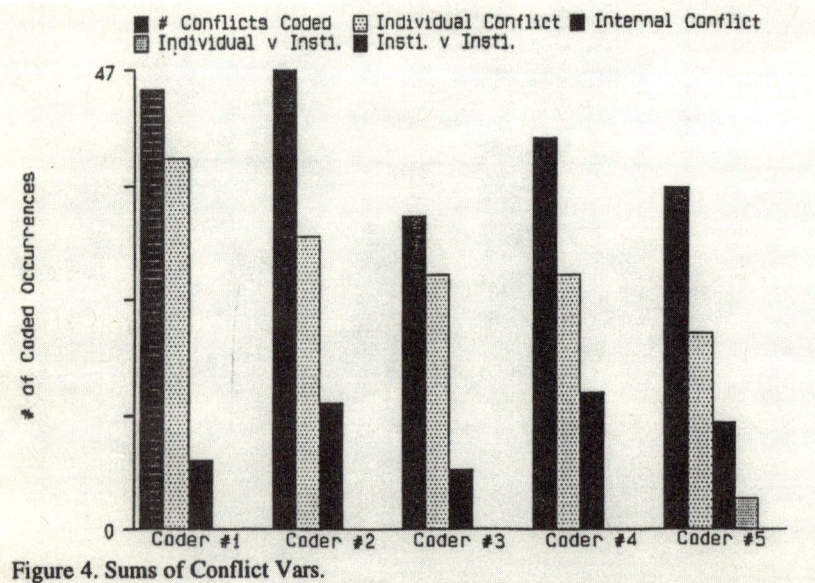

Figure 4. Sums of Conflict Vars.

types, including: tangible benefit, emotional benefit, psychological benefit, or physical welfare. Not surprisingly, emotional benefits (love, friendship) and psychological benefits (power) proved to be difficult to distinguish. There was little evidence apparent to coders, however, that material gain or physical welfare were the sources of conflict in Top 20 programs. Emotional benefits were most often coded as the cause (mean = 21) and psychological benefit was found to be the source of the conflict in an average of 14 segments. As can be seen from Figure 6, the other sources of conflict were negligible.

The final conflict dimension was the manner in which the conflict was resolved, which coders were asked to categorize according to one of the following types: a resolution imposed from above; a resolution found by the *independent* action of the characters; a violent resolution; a resolution by the *cooperative* action of the characters; a resolution by the intervention of a *deus ex machina*. Resolution by imposition turned out to be rare even though authority figures were abundant. The coders found that the characters taking independent action was the primary form of resolution, reported in an average of 12 segments. Resolution by cooperative action was the second most common form with an average reported of 4 segments per coder. Violent solutions and solutions involving a deus ex machina were nonexistent in our sample (Figure 7).

Discussion

We have investigated the existence of three political culture types and have found evidence to support the notion that Elazar's individualistic culture is most prominent of the three, particularly in the realm of conflict and conflict resolution. The conflicts as coded by our coders were largely between individuals who

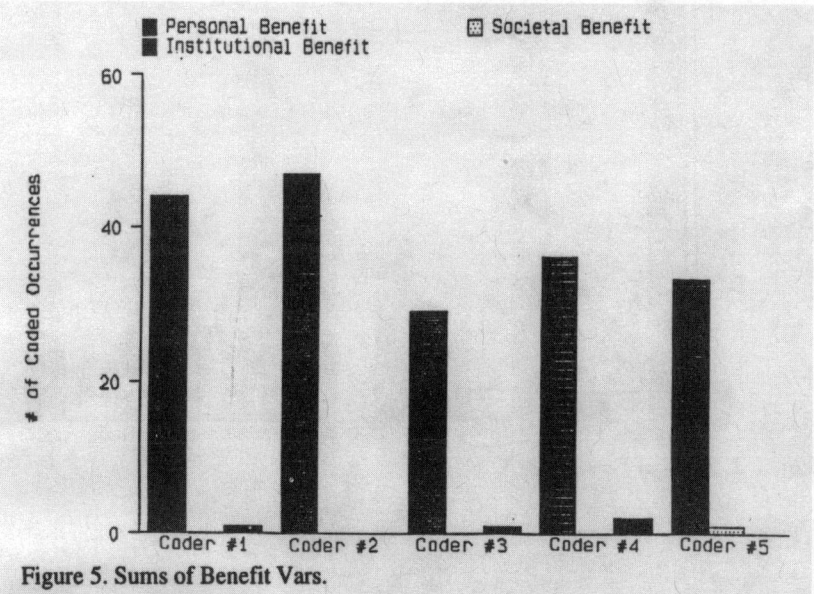

Figure 5. Sums of Benefit Vars.

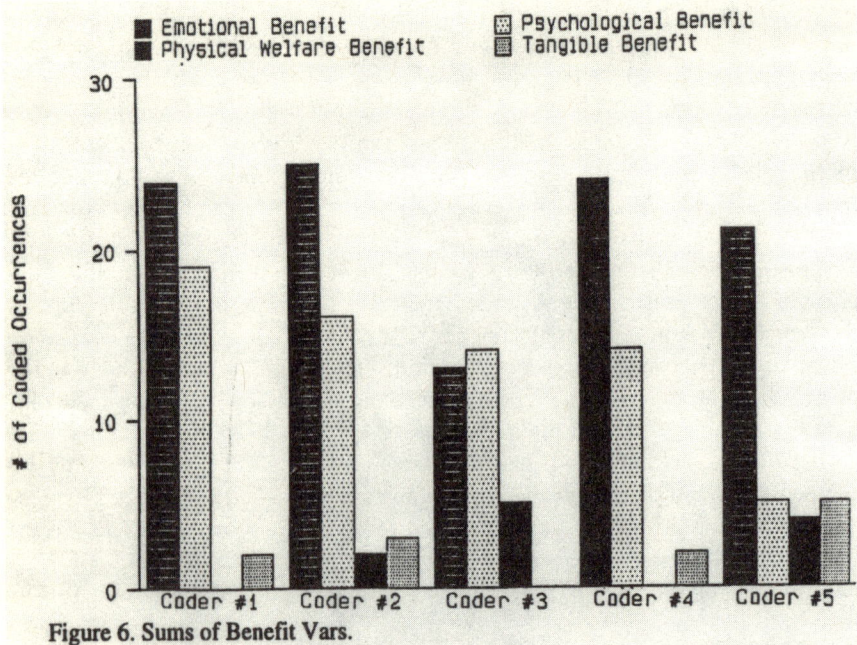

Figure 6. Sums of Benefit Vars.

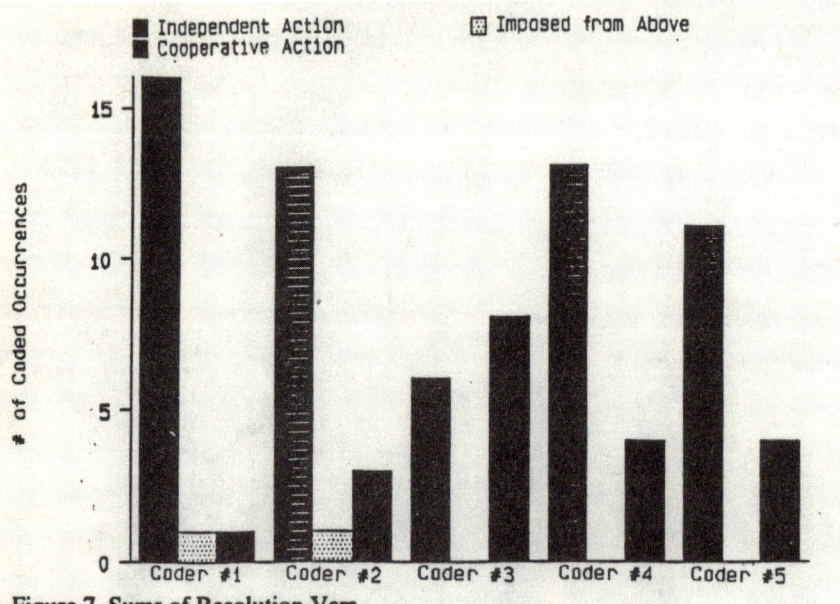

Figure 7. Sums of Resolution Vars.

were seeking personal benefit for themselves or another individual. Emotional and psychological benefit were most prevalent, as characters were wont to establish and retain love/friendship and power relationships. The nearly unanimous agreement by coders on the total lack of institutional/organizational themes as the basis for conflict provides even more striking evidence of the "individualist" nature of the programs. (Conflicts between individual and institution would have provided support for the hypothesis as well, had they been found.)

The widespread presence of authority figures undermines the dominant individualist culture hypothesis to some extent, though not entirely so. The weakness of the individualist hypothesis is also indicated by the failure to find extensive resistance or challenge to authority which is wielded in domineering fashion. Some challenges were reported but only in limited numbers. Although found in each of Elazar's (1984) three cultures, authority figures play a more untrammeled role in the traditional culture, which suggests an alternative hypothesis that the traditional culture is more prominent, at least on the authority dimension. But hierarchically imposed solutions were rare (even though authority figures often attempted and were often successful in wielding their authority), indicating that the power of the authorities was circumscribed.

By the same token there is virtually no evidence of moralistic culture in the programs that were coded. Evidence of a moralistic culture would have included cooperative behavior undertaken to achieve a societal good. Only one coder found evidence of such behavior.

The findings point to an individualist orientation, with evidence of domineering authority figures who, are more likely to be successful than they are to be challenged. Elazar (1984) found that only a few states at the time of his original research fit squarely into the three pure categories of culture, leading Elazar to suggest a continuum including paired cultures in which one type was dominant and another was subordinate. Using this approach as a model we suggest that the paired culture most evident in television entertainment programming is an individualistic/traditionalistic culture.

Implications

Does it matter that there is a dominant cultural form presented on network programming? According to Gerbner it does matter. Television "cultivates" attitudes, values, and world views. For example, he and his co-researchers argue that heavy viewers adopt a "mainstream" perspective of the American political system. According to Gerbner there is an apparent conservative, yet still mainstream, effect from television viewing, particularly in network news programming. Heavy viewers with liberal or left-leaning politics become more likely to show evidence of moderating their political views than those with conservative or right-leaning politics, though both groups tend towards the middle (Gerbner 1977, 1986, 1990).

Further, Morgan and Shanahan (1991) found that Argentine adolescents "who watch more television are significantly more likely to agree that people should obey authority, to approve of limits on free speech, and to think that it is someone's fault if he or she is poor" (88). While Argentina vacillates politically between democracy and authoritarianism, television programming there bears sufficient similarities to American television to allow for comparisons. The values recorded by Morgan and Shanahan indicate a televised culture that shares characteristics of both individualism and traditionalism or hierarchy.

If our conclusions about the nature of political culture are correct, there may be behavioral implications as well. According to Elazar's (1984) model, the type of culture that is prominent in a state results in differing levels of political participation. In 1960, for example, in traditionalistic culture states, the median voter turnout was slightly above 25%. In purely moralistic states, in the same year, the median voter turnout was nearly 80%. States with individualistic cultures fell between these two extremes. Since the 1960 election, however, there has been quite a noticeable moderation within and between the cultural categories. The median turnout in traditionalistic dominant states increased one and a half percentage points between 1960 and 1988, and the median turnout for moralistic dominant states declined by over fourteen points during the same time span. Somewhat surprisingly, the greatest amount of change occurs for individualistic dominant states, with a decline of slightly over 18.32%.

Further, there was greater homogeneity among the states that Elazar grouped as culturally distinctive, in terms of voter turnout. This is most particularly true in the cultures with traditionalistic and individualistic characteristics. The boxplots[1] for individualistic, individualistic/traditionalistic, traditionalistic/individualistic, and traditionalistic cultures all provide evidence of significant diversity in the 1960 turnout rates, but by the 1988 election the level of spread had dropped dramatically (this can be seen in the graph, as the boxes in 1988 appear to be considerably shorter for those cultures than they were in 1960), suggesting homogenization between and within these cultural pockets. A pattern of homogenization in voter turnout was also apparent for the purely moralistic states. Only the individualistic/moralistic culture shows no evidence of a within-culture homogenization pattern.

We are not prepared to conclude that television entertainment programming is responsible for all, or even most of the change towards political participation homogenization. However, we believe that, given the amount of time that Americans spend with television, it would be foolish to assume it has no effect. And given the national character of, and lack of regional variation in, television programming, we would expect that effect to be a homogenizing influence. Our research suggests that the specific direction of such TV-influenced homogenization is toward a more uniformly individualistic culture, which is consistent with the homogenization of turnout (i.e. turnout is more similar from state to state today than it was in 1960) as well.

Habermas (1976) has argued that in the "late stages of capitalism" citizen attention to government and politics is limited to interest in governmental outputs, with only "minor participation in the process of will-formation. . . . Civil privatism thus corresponds to the structures of a depoliticized public" (57). This sort of culture would be like the traditionalistic and individualistic cultures we have discussed above. Citizens in these types of cultures would be less likely to participate in the actual decision-making processes of government, to play some role in the selection of the decision-makers, and, particularly in individualistic cultures, to seek outputs from the system to fulfill personal needs.

As political participation, measured in terms of voter turnout, has declined, political parties have also weakened (the decline really dates back to the late 1800s) (McGerr 1986). However, since the end of the New Deal, which coincided with the widespread availability of commercial television in the United States, there has been a dramatic decline in citizen identification with political parties, and a concurrent increase in the number of citizens who consider themselves politically independent. Individualism, as a political style, is characterized by weakened ties to groups of all types, including political parties. The conventional wisdom is that television campaigning has made the parties superfluous, but we suggest that entertainment programming has created a milieu in which the voters are receptive to second hand campaigning; direct videotaped appeal to voters by candidates, instead of by political parties, is made more attractive as individualistic culture strengthens.

Similarly, as parties have weakened in the electorate, they have become less powerful in Congress, making a government of deadlock more likely. For decades, for all of their apparent abuses, the political parties provided the adhesive that held an intentionally fragmented government on track. As parties have weakened, as candidates have relied more heavily on their own resources, and have built their own bases of power, the government has seemed to become rudderless, blowing with the prevailing political winds.

According to Thompson, Ellis, and Wildavsky (1991), one characteristic of individualism is to blame the individual for his/her failures. Hence, the growth of individualistic culture characteristics may be linked to an increasing intolerance of welfare. The increasing antipathy toward the poor and toward welfare and welfare recipients appears to be generalized (Katz 1989). David T. Elwood (1988) points out that welfare contradicts, for most Americans, cherished values we associate with individualism, independence, hard work, and responsibility for one's own actions (5). Public opinion polls consistently show this individualistic attitude toward welfare. Much of the dislike and criticism of welfare expressed in such polls stems from the belief that welfare keeps people dependent and does not do a good job of helping people stand on their own two feet (41).

Finally, the individualistic hypothesis suggests that, as the individualistic culture becomes dominant, there may be less tolerance for large institutions of any variety. Thompson, Ellis, and Wildavsky (1991) suggest that antiestablishmentarianism is largely a product of egalitarianism (moralism in Elazar's typology), but these authors also suggest that individualism and egalitarianism/moralism share a dislike for overbearing rules that restrict the freedom of individuals to negotiate their own relationships. To the extent that institutions attempt to impose such rules, they will be opposed by both individualistic and egalitarian/moralistic cultures. Robinson (1976) has noted that political cynicism has been more widespread in recent decades, as Americans become more likely to question their political and economic institutional leadership.

Although many features of the political landscape reflect individualistic cultural dominance, others do indicate some traditionalistic elements, as suggested by the paired individualistic/traditionalistic hypothesis. For example, while there has been a decline in trust of political and economic leadership, the institutions of the public and private sectors have grown dramatically.

It is a cultural irony, in fact, that large "private sector" institutions, often organized as formal hierarchies, use the "bully pulpit" of television advertising to intone individualistic themes such as "It's not your car, it's your freedom." So far, this individualistic appeal has allowed private sector institutions to retain the loyalty of the populace, but it also increases the potential for cross cultural pressures and creates a rise in cynicism, as the real performance of the corporation and its products fails to meet the standards of the advertising.

Government has also grown, as citizens turn to hierarchic power in modern society, to solve certain problems. Television reflects and reinforces this traditionalistic modification of individualism. For example, television has been instrumental in posing the problem of crime in the streets and the boardrooms of America. Acquisitive individualism turns to the power of hierarchy in order to stem the presumed flood of criminal behavior, by signing a contract with government to protect private property from the levelers.[2] Today news programs insure that crime against persons and property is a societal focal point, and police shows are a common form of entertainment programming.

While the evidence on these points remains conjectural, the linkages between television and culture are suggestive, and the sheer magnitude and pervasiveness of modern day television broadcasting (including cable), make the cultural bias of entertainment programming a subject worthy of political and social scientists' interest.

References

Adams, W. C., et al. 1985. The power of the right stuff: A quasi-experimental field test of the docudrama hypothesis. *Public Opinion Quarterly* 49: 330-339.
Ball-Rokeach, S. J., J. Grube, and M. Rokeach. 1981. Roots: The next generation—Who watched and with what effect? *Public Opinion Quarterly* 45: 58-68.
Block, F., et al., eds. 1987. *The mean season.* New York: Pantheon.
Carey, J. 1988. *Communication as culture: Essays on media and society.* Boston: Unwin Hyman.
Combs, J. 1984. *Polpop: Politics and popular culture in America.* Bowling Green, KY: Bowling Green State University Popular Press.
Easton, D. 1981. *The political system: An inquiry into the state of political Science.* 2d ed. Chicago: University of Chicago Press.
Elazar, D. 1984. *American federalism.* 3d ed. New York: Harper & Row.
Elwood, D. T. 1988. *Poor support: Poverty in the American family.* New York: Basic Books.
Feldman, S., and L. Sigelman. 1985. The political impact of primetime television: The Day After. *Journal of Politics* 47: 556-578.
Gerbner, G. 1977. Comparative cultural indicators. In *Mass media policies in changing cultures,* edited by G. Gerbner. New York: John Wiley & Sons.
Gerbner, G., et al. 1986. Living with television: The dynamics of the cultivation process. In *Perspectives on media effects,* edited by J. Bryant and D. Zillman. Hillsdale, NJ: Laurence Erlbaum Assoc.
———., et al. 1990. Charting the mainstream: Television's contributions to political orientations. In *Media power in politics,* edited by D. Graber. Washington, D.C.: Congressional Quarterly Press.
Habermas, J. 1976. Problems of legitimation of late capitalism. In *Critical sociology,* edited by P. Connerton. New York: Penguin Books.

Hamilton, L. 1990. *Modern data analysis: A first course in applied statistics.* Pacific Grove, CA: Brooks/Cole.
Katz, M. B. 1989. *The undeserving poor.* New York: Pantheon.
Lenart, S., and K. McGraw. 1989. America watches Amerika: Television docudrama and political attitudes. *Journal of Politics* 51: 697-712.
McGerr, M. 1986. *The decline of popular politics.* New York: Oxford.
Merelman, R. 1989. On culture and politics in America: A perspective from structural anthropology. *British Journal of Political Science* 19: 465-493.
Morgan, M., and J. Shanahan. 1991. Television and the cultivation of political attitudes in Argentina. *Journal of Communication* 41 (1): 88-103.
Morrow, L. 1992. Folklore in a box. *Time.* September 21: 50-51.
Reiner, R. 1981. Keystone to Kojak: The Hollywood cop. In *Cinema, politics, and society in America,* edited by P. Davis and B. Neve. New York: St. Martin's.
Robinson, M. J. 1976. Public affairs television and the growth of political malaise: The case of the "selling of the President." *American Political Science Review* 70: 409-432.
Rubin, A. M. 1986. Uses, gratifications, and media effects research. In *Perspectives on media effects,* edited by J. Bryant and D. Zillman. Hillsdale, NJ: Lawrence Earlbaum Assoc.
Schiltz, T., and R. L. Rainey. 1978. The geographic distribution of Elazar's political subcultures among the mass population: A research note. *Western Political Quarterly* 31: 410-15.
Schultze, W. 1988. *State and local politics: A political economy approach.* St. Paul, MN: West.
Sigelman, L., and C. K. Sigelman. 1973-74. The politics of popular culture: Campaign cynicism and *The Candidate. Sociology and Social Research* 58: 272-77.
Thompson, M., R. Ellis, and A. Wildavsky. 1991. *Cultural theory.* Boulder, CO: Westview.
Wildavsky, A. 1987. Choosing preferences by constructing institutions: A cultural theory of preference formation. *American Political Science Review* 81: 3-21.

CHAPTER 9

The Symbolic Annihilation of Women by the Mass Media
Gaye Tuchman

Originally published as the introduction to
Hearth and Home: Images of women in the mass media, *1978.*

READING INTRODUCTION

In this introduction to a larger edited volume, Tuchman surveys the substantive content of the mass media—television, newspapers, magazines—and the advertising they carry to gather support for her argument that, by largely ignoring women or portraying them in stereotypical roles of victim and/or consumer, the mass media symbolically annihilate women. Tuchman notes that most media portray women, if at all, in traditional roles: homemaker, mother, or, if they are in the paid workforce, clerical and other "pink-collar" jobs. Correspondingly, there are few, if any, depictions of strong female characters in positions of responsibility or authority, even inside the home. Similarly, women's magazines focus on the "domestic" pursuits—marriage, child rearing, and the like—while not encouraging education, training, and other choices that tend to bring individuals into positions of power, authority, and independence. Instead, women generally are shown to be defined in terms of their relationships with men—suggesting that women are, in the end, dependent, incapable of living their own lives without male "guidance."

What makes these patterns particularly troubling for Tuchman is the role that the mass media may play in shaping young girls' wants, needs, and expectations. To the degree that the institutions of mass communication influence behavior and attitudes, consistent repetition of such themes can be expected to encourage the maintenance of women's subordinate position in society. Additionally, because the media *reflect* the dominant values of society, they add a powerful link in the chain of socialization that keeps women dependent. Women as independent, creative actors, then, are annihilated in favor of what Tuchman perceives as a false, repressive "ideal."

The Symbolic Annihilation of Women by the Mass Media

READING TEXT

Americans learn basic lessons about social life from the mass media, much as hundreds of years ago illiterate peasants studied the carvings around the apse or the stained glass windows of cathedrals. As Harold Lasswell (1948) pointed out almost thirty years ago, mass media have replaced yesterday's cathedrals and parish churches as teachers of the young and of the masses. For our society, like any other society, must pass on its social heritage from one generation to the next. The societal need for continuity and transmission of dominant values may be particularly acute in times of rapid social change, such as our own. Then, individuals may not only need some familiarity with the past, if the society is to survive, but they must also be prepared to meet changing conditions. Nowhere is that need as readily identifiable as in the area of *sex roles*—sex roles are social guidelines for sex-appropriate appearance, interests, skills, behaviors, and self-perceptions.

It is in this area, in the past few decades, where social expectations and social conditions have been changing most rapidly. In 1920, twenty-four percent of the nation's adult women worked for pay outside the home and most of them were unmarried. Fifty years later, in 1976, over half of all American women between the ages of eighteen and sixty-four were in the labor force, most of them married and many of them with children who were of preschool age. One-third of all women with children between the ages of three and five were employed in 1970. Such a transformation not only affects women: it affects their families as members make adjustments in their shared life; and as working men in the factory and office increasingly encounter economically productive women who insist on the abandonment of old prejudices and discriminatory behaviors. In the face of such change, the portrayal of sex roles in the mass media is a topic of great social, political, and economic importance.

This book★ concerns the depiction of sex roles in the mass media and the effect of that portrayal on American girls and women. In each chapter, social science researchers ask, what are the media telling us about ourselves? How do they say women and men should behave? How women should treat men? How women should view themselves? What do the media view as the best way for a woman to structure her life? What do they tell a little girl to expect or hope for when she becomes a woman?

Based on original research, each of these chapters helps break a new path in communications research. Not surprisingly, little research appeared on these topics until the modern women's movement gained strength in the late 1960s and early 1970s. Until then, psychology, sociology, economics, and history were mainly written by men, about men, and for men. As Jessie Bernard (1973) points out, the interactions of men were viewed as the appropriate subject for social science research, and upwardly mobile male researchers were fascinated with the topics of power and social stratification. No one considered the way women

---

★In original publication.

experienced the world. Instead, they were seen as men's silent or unopinionated consorts. (The term "unopinionated" is used because studies of attitudes by survey researchers frequently neglected to ask women their opinions, concentrating instead upon the attitudes of men. The most well-known exception to this role is a study of influences upon women's consumer habits, funded by a women's magazine in the 1940s [Katz and Lazarsfeld 1955).

These generalizations are, unfortunately, equally true of communications researchers. Generations of researchers studied the impact of the media upon political life. In the past, the main topic of concern was male voting behavior. (It was assumed women voted like their husbands; women were swayed by a husband's or father's personal influence [see McCormack 1975].) More recently, researchers have become fascinated by agenda setting—the way the media structure citizens' priorities and definitions of political issues. Since the women's movement is not a top priority for the news media, little is known about its place in citizens' political agendas. Nobody seemed to care about the effect of the mass media upon the generation and maintenance of sex-role stereotypes. And why should they? Before the advent of the women's movement these stereotypes seemed natural, "given." Few questioned how they developed, how they were reinforced, or how they were maintained. Certainly the media's role in this process was not questioned.

But the importance of stereotyping was not lost on the women's movement; for stereotypes are confining. Sex-role stereotypes are set portrayals of sex-appropriate appearance, interests, skills, behaviors, and self-perceptions. They are more stringent than guidelines in suggesting persons *not* conforming to the specified way of appearing, feeling, and behaving are *inadequate* as males or females. A boy who cries is not masculine and a young woman who forswears makeup is not feminine. Stereotypes present individuals with a more limited range of acceptable appearance, feelings, and behaviors than guidelines do. The former may be said to limit further the human possibilities and potentialities contained within already limited sex roles.

This volume* hopes to delineate a national social problem—the mass media's treatment of women. It is a crucial problem, because as Lasswell (1948) points out, the mass media transmit the social heritage from one generation to the next. In a complex society, such as ours, the mass media pass on news from one segment of society, classes, regions, and subcultures to another. Additionally, they enable societal institutions to coordinate activities. Like the Catholic Church in the middle ages "that great broadcasting center of medieval Europe" (Baumann 1972, 65), the mass media can disseminate the same message to all classes at the same time, with authority and universality of reception, in a decidedly one-directional flow of information. But, if the stereotyped portrayal of sex roles is out-of-date, the media may be preparing youngsters—girls, in particular—for a world that no longer exists.

Suppose for a moment that children's television primarily presents adult women as housewives, nonparticipants in the paid labor force. Also, suppose that

---

*Original publication.

girls in the television audience "model" their behavior and expectations on that of "television women." Such a supposition is quite plausible for

> what psychologists call "modeling" occurs simply by watching others, without any direct reinforcement for learning and without any overt practice. The child imitates the model without being induced or compelled to do so. That learning can occur in the absence of direct reinforcement is a radical departure from earlier theories that regarded reward or punishment as indispensable to learning. There now is considerable evidence that children do learn by watching and listening to others even in the absence of reinforcement and overt practice. (Lesser, quoted in Cantor 1975, 5)

And psychologists note that "opportunities for modeling have been vastly increased by television" (Lesser, quoted in Cantor 1975, 5). It is then equally plausible that girls exposed to "television women" may hope to be homemakers when they are adults, but not workers outside the home. Indeed, as adults these girls may resist work outside the home unless necessary for the economic well-being of their families. Encouraging such an attitude in our nation's girls can present a problem in the future: As noted, over forty percent of the labor force was female in 1970, and married women dominate the female labor force. The active participation of women in the labor force is vital to the maintenance of the American economy. In the past decade, the greatest expansion of the economy has been within the sectors that employ women. Mass-media stereotypes of women as housewives may impede the employment of women by limiting their horizons.

The possible impact of the mass media sex-role stereotypes upon national life seems momentous. As the studies★ collected here demonstrate, this supposition may accurately predict the future. As an illustration of that possibility, the following sections of this introduction examine the media used by an American girl as she completes school, then becomes a worker and, probably, a spouse and mother.[1] Following the format★ of this book, this introduction starts with an examination of the dominant medium American children and adults watch—television—and then turns to two media especially designed for women—the women's pages of newspapers and women's magazines. But because of the plethora of research about television, we concentrate upon that medium. Finally, we review studies of the impact of the media upon girls and women, again stressing studies of television.

Two related ideas are central to our discussion. These are *the reflection hypothesis* and *symbolic annihilation*. According to the reflection hypothesis, the mass media reflect dominant societal values. In the case of television (see Tuchman 1974, 1976), the corporate character of the commercial variety causes program planners and station managers to design programs for appeal to the largest audiences. To attract these audiences (whose time and attention are sold to commercial sponsors), the television industry offers programs consonant with

★ Original publication.

American values. The pursuit of this aim is solidified by the fact that so many members of the television industry take those very values for granted: Dominant American ideas and ideals serve as resources for program development, even when the planners are unaware of them, much as we all take for granted the air we breathe. These ideas and ideals are incorporated as *symbolic representations of American society, not as literal portrayals.* Take the typical television family of the 1950s: mother, father, and two children living in an upper-middle-class, single-residence suburban home. Such families and homes were not the most commonly found units in the 1950s, but they were the American ideal. Following George Gerbner (1972, 44), we may say that "representation in the fictional world," such as the 1950s ideal family, symbolizes or "signifies social existence"; that is, representation in the mass media announces to audience members that this kind of family (or social characteristic) is valued and approved.

Conversely, we may say that either condemnation, trivialization, or "absence means symbolic annihilation" (Gerbner 1972, 44). Consider the symbolic representation of women in the mass media. Relatively few women are portrayed there, although women are fifty-one percent of the population and are well over forty percent of the labor force. Those working women who are portrayed are condemned. Others are trivialized: they are symbolized as child-like adornments who need to be protected or they are dismissed to the protective confines of the home. In sum, they are subject to *symbolic annihilation.*

The mass media deal in symbols and their symbolic representations may not be up-to-date. A time lag may be operating, for nonmaterial conditions, which shape symbols, change more slowly than do material conditions. This notion of a time lag (or a "culture lag," as sociologists term it) may be incorporated into the reflection hypothesis. As values change, we would expect the images of society presented by the media to change. Further, we might expect one medium to change faster than another. (Because of variations in economic organization, each medium has a slightly different relationship to changing material conditions.)

The reflection hypothesis also includes the notion that media planners try to build audiences, and the audiences desired by planners may vary from medium to medium. For instance, television programmers may seek an audience of men and women, without distinguishing between women in the labor force and housewives. But the executives at women's magazines may want to attract women in the labor force in order to garner advertisements designed *for those women.* (Magazine ads essentially support that medium, since each copy costs much more to produce than it does to purchase. Accordingly, we might expect the symbolic annihilation of women by television to be more devastating than that of *some* women's magazines.

Without further ado, then, let us turn to images of women in the mass media.

Television: The Symbolic Annihilation of Women

To say television is the dominant medium in American life is a vast understatement. In the average American household, television sets are turned on more than six hours each winter day. More American homes have television sets than have private bathrooms, according to the 1970 census. Ninety-six percent of all American homes are equipped with television, and most have more than one set. As Sprafkin and Liebert note in Chapter 15,* by the time an American child is fifteen years old, she has watched more hours of television than she has spent in the classroom. And since she continues watching as she grows older, the amount of time spent in school can never hope to equal the time invested viewing television.

The use of television by children is encouraged because of parental use. The average adult spends five hours a day with the mass media, almost as much time as she or he spends at work. Of these five hours, four are occupied by the electronic media (radio and television). The other hour is taken up with reading newspapers, magazines, and books. Television consumes forty percent of the leisure time of adult Americans. To be sure, despite increased economic concentration there are still 1,741 daily newspapers in this country. And studies indicate that 63,353,000 papers are sold each day. But the nation's nine hundred–odd television stations reach millions more on a daily basis. In 1976, over seventy-five million people watched one event via television, football's annual Super Bowl spectacular (Hirsch 1978); and when "All in the Family" first appeared on Saturday night, it had a weekly audience of over 100,000,000, more than half the people in the nation. Each year, Americans spend trillions of hours watching television.

What are the portrayals of women to which Americans are exposed during these long hours? What can the preschool girl and the school girl learn about being and becoming a woman?

From children's shows to commercials to prime-time adventures and situation comedies, television proclaims that women don't count for much. They are underrepresented in television's fictional life—they are "symbolically annihilated." From 1954, the date of the earliest systematic analysis of television's content, through 1975, researchers have found that males dominated the television screen. With the exception of soap operas where men make up a "mere majority" of the fictional population, television has shown and continues to show two men for every woman. Figure 1.1 indicates the proportion has been relatively constant. The little variation that exists, occurs between types of programs. In 1952 sixty-eight percent of the characters in prime-time drama were male. In 1973, seventy-four percent of those characters were male. Women were concentrated in comedies where men make up "only" sixty percent of the fictional world. Children's cartoons include even fewer women or female characters (such as anthropomorphized foxes or pussycats) than adult's prime-time programs do. The paucity of women on American television tells viewers that women don't matter much in American society.

That message is reinforced by the treatment of those women who do appear on the television screen. As seen in Figure 1.2, when television shows reveal someone's occupation, the worker is most likely to be male. Someone might object that the pattern is inevitable, because men constitute a larger share of the

---

*In original book.

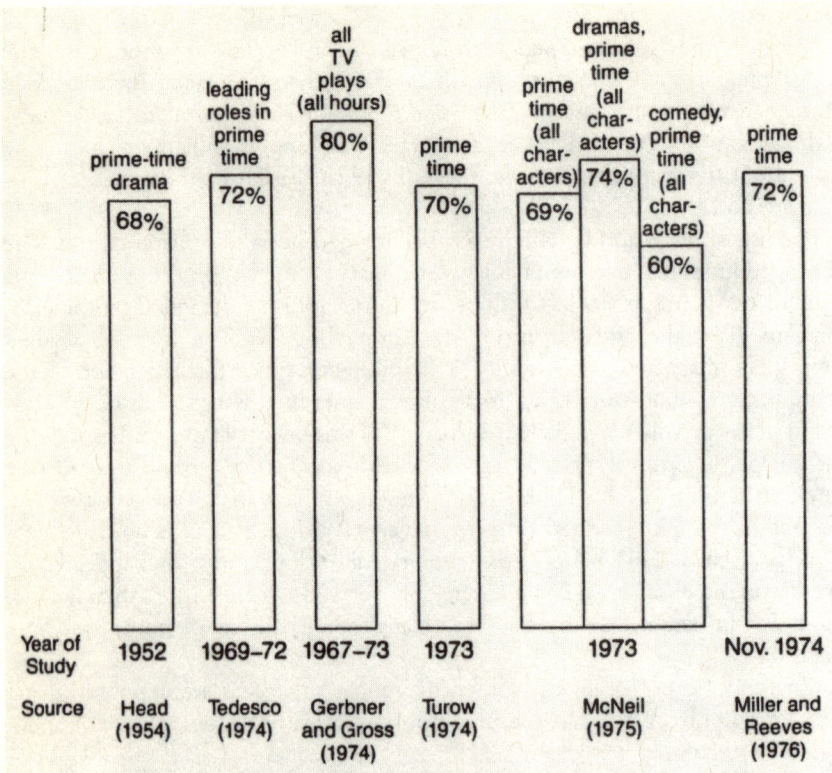

Figure 1.1. Percentage of Males in TV Programs, 1952–1974.

pool of people who can be professionals. But that objection is invalidated by the evidence presented by soap operas, where women are more numerous. But the invariant pattern holds there too, despite the fact that men have been found to be only about fifty percent of the characters on the "soaps" (see Downing 1974; Katzman 1972).

Additionally, those few working women included in television plots are symbolically denigrated by being portrayed as incompetent or as inferior to male workers. Pepper, the "Police Woman" on the show of the same name (Angie Dickinson) is continually rescued from dire and deadly situations by her male colleagues. Soap operas provide even more powerful evidence for the portrayal of women as incompetents and inferiors. Although Turow (1974) finds that soap operas present the most favorable image of female workers, there too they are subservient to competent men. On "The Doctors," surgical procedures are performed by male physicians, and although the female M.D.'s are said to be competent at their work, they are primarily shown pulling case histories from file cabinets or filling out forms. On other soap operas, male lawyers try cases and female lawyers research briefs for them. More generally, women do not appear

Figure 1.2. Percentage of Males Among Those Portrayed as Employed on TV, 1963–1973.

in the same professions as men: men are doctors, women, nurses; men are lawyers, women, secretaries; men work in corporations, women tend boutiques.

The portrayal of incompetence extends from denigration through victimization and trivialization. When television women are involved in violence, unlike males, they are more likely to be victims than aggressors (Gerbner 1972). Equally important, the pattern of women's involvement with television violence reveals approval of married women and condemnation of single and working women. As Gerbner (1972) demonstrates, single women are more likely to be victims of violence than married women, and working women are more likely to be villains than housewives. Conversely, married women who do not work for money outside the home are most likely to escape television's mayhem and to be treated sympathetically. More generally, television most approves those women who are presented in a sexual context or within a romantic or family role (Gerber 1972; cf. Liebert, Neale, and Davidson 1973). Two out of three television-women are married, were married, or are engaged to be married. By way of contrast, most television men are single and have always been single. Also, men are seen outside the home and women within it, but even here, one finds trivialization of women's role within the home.

According to sociological analyses of traditional sex roles (such as Parsons 1949), men are "instrumental" leaders, active workers and decision makers outside the home; women are "affective" or emotional leaders in solving personal problems within the home. But television trivializes women in their traditional role by assigning this task to men too. The nation's soap operas deal with the personal and emotional, yet Turow (1974) finds that on the soap operas, the male sex is so dominant that men also lead the way to solving emotional problems. In sum, following the reasoning of the reflection hypothesis, we may tentatively conclude that for commercial reasons (building audiences to sell to advertisers) network television engages in the symbolic annihilation of women.

Two additional tests of this tentative conclusion are possible. One examines noncommercial American television; the other analyzes the portrayal of women in television commercials. If the commercial structure of television is mainly responsible for the symbolic annihilation of women, one would expect to find more women on public than on commercial television. Conversely if the structure of corporate commercial television is mainly responsible for the image of women that is telecast, one would expect to find even more male domination on commercial ads. To an even greater extent than is true of programs, advertising seeks to tap existing values in order to move people to buy a product.

Unfortunately, few systematic studies of public broadcasting are available. The best of these is Caroline Isber's and Muriel Cantor's work (1975) funded by the Corporation for Public Broadcasting, the source of core programming in the Public Broadcasting System. In this volume, in an adaptation of her report for the CPB, Cantor asks, "Where are the women in public television?" Her answer, based on a content analysis of programming is "in front of the television set." Although a higher proportion of adult women appear on children's programming in public television than is true of commercial television, Cantor finds "both commercial and public television disseminate the same message about women, although the two types of television differ in their structure and purpose." Her conclusion indicates that commercialism is not solely responsible for television's symbolic annihilation of women and its portrayal of stereotyped sex roles. Rather, television captures societal ideas even when programming is partially divorced from the profit motive.[2]

Male domination has not been measured as directly for television commercials, the other kind of televised image that may be used to test the reflection hypothesis. Since so many of the advertised products are directed toward women, one could not expect to find women neglected by commercials. Given the sex roles commercials play upon, it would be bad business to show two women discussing the relative merits of power lawn mowers or two men chatting about waxy buildup on a kitchen floor. However, two indirect measures of male dominance are possible: (1) the number of commercials in which only men or only women appear; and (2) the use of males and females in voice-overs. (A "voice-over" is an unseen person speaking about a product while an image is shown on the television screen; an unseen person proclaims "two out of three doctors recommend" or "on sale now at your local. . . .")

On the first indirect measure, all-male or all-female commercials, the findings are unanimous. Schuetz and Sprafkin (1978), Silverstein and Silverstein (1974) and Bardwick and Schumann (1967), find a ratio of almost three all-male ads to each all-female ad. The second indirect measure—the use of voice-overs in commercials, presents more compelling evidence for the acceptance of the reflection hypothesis. Echoing the findings of others, Dominick and Rauch (1972) report that of 946 ads with voice-overs, "only six percent use a female voice; a male voice was heard on eighty-seven percent." The remainder use one male and one female voice.

The commercials themselves strongly encourage sex-role stereotypes. Although research findings are not strictly comparable to those on television programs because of the dissimilar "plots," the portrayals of women are even more limited than those presented on television dramas and comedies. Linda Busby (1975) summarized the findings of four major studies of television ads. In one study,

- 37.5% of the ads showed women as men's domestic adjuncts
- 33.9% showed women as dependent on men
- 24.3% showed women as submissive
- 16.7% showed women as sex objects
- 17.1% showed women as unintelligent
- 42.6% showed women as household functionaries

Busby's summary of Dominick and Rauch's work reveals a similar concentration of women as homemakers rather than as active members of the labor force:

- Women were seven times more likely to appear in ads for personal hygiene products than not to appear [in those ads]
- 75% of all ads using females were for products found in the kitchen or in the bathroom
- 38% of all females in the television ads were shown inside the home, compared to 40% of the males
- Men were significantly more likely to be shown outdoors or in business settings than were women
- Twice as many women were shown with children [than] were men
- 56% of the women in the ads were judged to be [only] housewives
- 43% different occupations were coded for men, 18 for women.

As Busby notes, reviews of the major studies of ads (such as Courtney and Whipple 1974) emphasize their strong "face validity" (the result of real patterns rather than any bias produced by researchers' methods), although the studies use different coding categories and some of the researchers were avowed feminist activists.

In sum, then, analyses of television commercials support the reflection hypothesis. In voice-overs and one-sex (all male or all female) ads, commercials neglect or rigidly stereotype women. In their portrayal of women, the ads banish females to the role of housewife, mother, homemaker, and sex object, limiting the roles women may play in society.

What can the preschool girl, the school girl, the adolescent female and the woman learn about a woman's role by watching television? The answer is simple. Women are not important in American society, except *perhaps* within the home. And even within the home, men know best, as the dominance of male advice on soap operas suggests. To be a woman is to have a limited life divorced from the economic productivity of the labor force.

Women's Magazines: Marry, Don't Work

As the American girl grows to womanhood, she, like her counterpart elsewhere in industrialized nations, has magazines available designed especially for her use. Some, like *Seventeen,* whose readers tend to be young adolescents, instruct on contemporary fashions and dating styles. Others, like *Cosmopolitan* and *Redbook,* teach about survival as a young woman—whether as a single woman hunting a mate in the city or a young married coping with hearth and home.

This section reviews portrayals of sex roles in women's magazines, seeking to learn how often they too promulgate stereotypes about the role their female readers may take—how much they too engage in the symbolic annihilation of women by limiting and trivializing them. Unfortunately, our analyses of images of women in magazines cannot be as extensive as our discussion of television. Because of researchers' past neglect of women's issues and problems, few published materials are available for review.

Like the television programs just discussed, from the earliest content analyses of magazine fiction (Johns-Heine and Gerth 1949) to analyses of magazine fiction published in the early 1970s, researchers have found an emphasis on hearth and home and a denigration of the working woman. The ideal woman, according to these magazines, is passive and dependent. Her fate and her happiness rest with a man, not with participation in the labor force. There are two exceptions to this generalization: (1) The female characters in magazines aimed at working-class women are a bit more spirited than their middle-class sisters. (2) In the mid-1970s, middle-class magazines seemed less hostile toward working women. Using the reflection hypothesis, particularly its emphasis upon attracting readers to sell advertisements, we will seek to explain the general rule and these interesting exceptions to it.

Like other media, women's magazines are interested in building their audience or readership. For a magazine, attracting more readers is *indirectly* profitable. Each additional reader does not increase the magazine's profit margin by buying a copy or taking out a subscription, because the cost of publication and distribution per copy far exceeds the price of the individual copy—whether it is purchased on the newsstand, in a supermarket, or through subscription. Instead a magazine realizes its profit by selling advertisements and charging its advertisers a rate adjusted to its known circulation. Appealing to advertisers, the magazine specifies known demographic characteristics of its readership. For instance, a magazine may inform the manufacturer of a product intended for housewives that a vast proportion of its readership are homemakers, while another magazine may appeal to the producer of merchandise for young working women by lauding its readership as members of that target group. Women's magazines differentiate themselves from one another by specifying their intended readers, as well as the size of their mass circulation. Additionally, they all compete with other media to draw advertisers. (For example, *Life* and *Look* folded because their advertisers could reach a larger group of potential buyers at a lower price per person through television commercials.) Both daytime television and women's magazines present potential advertisers with particularly appealing audiences, because women are the primary purchasers of goods intended for the home.

Historically, middle-class women have been less likely to be members of the labor force than lower-class women. At the turn of the century, those married women who worked were invariably from working-class families that required an additional income to assure adequate food, clothing, and shelter (Oppenheimer 1970). The importance of this economic impetus for working is indicated by the general adherence of working-class families to more traditional definitions of male and female sex roles (Rubin 1976). Although middle-class families subscribe to a more flexible ideology of sex roles than working-class families, both groups of women tend to insist that the man should be the breadwinner. The fiction in women's magazines reflects this ideology.

Particularly in middle-class magazines, fiction depicts women "as creatures... defined by the men in their lives" (Franzwa 1974a, 106; see also Franzwa 1974b, 1975). Studying a random sample of issues of *Ladies' Home Journal, McCall's,* and *Good Housekeeping* between the years 1940 and 1970, Helen Franzwa found four roles for women: "single and looking for a husband, housewife-mother, spinster, and widowed or divorced—soon to remarry." All the women were defined by the men in their lives, or by their absence. Flora (1971) confirms this finding in her study of middle-class *(Redbook* and *Cosmopolitan)* and working-class *(True Story* and *Modern Romances)* fiction. Female dependence and passivity are lauded; on the rare occasions that male dependence is portrayed, it is seen as undesirable.

As might be expected of characterizations that define women in terms of men, American magazine fiction denigrates the working woman. Franzwa says that work is shown to play "a distinctly secondary part in women's lives. When work is portrayed as important to them, there is a concomitant disintegration of their lives" (1974a, 106). Of the 155 major female characters depicted in Franzwa's sample of magazine stories, only 65 or forty-one percent were employed outside the home. Seven of the 65 held high-status positions. Of these seven, only two were married. Three others were "spinsters" whose "failure to marry was of far greater importance to the story-line than their apparent success in their careers" (106-107). One single woman with a high status career was lauded: She gave up her career to marry.

From 1940 through 1950, Franzwa found, working mothers and working wives were condemned. Instead, the magazines emphasized that husbands should support their spouses. One story summary symbolizes the magazines' viewpoint: "In a 1940 story, a young couple realized that they couldn't live on his salary. She offered to work; he replied, 'I don't think that's so good. I know some fellows whose wives work and they might just as well not be married' " (Frazwa 1974a, 108). Magazines after 1950 are even less positive about work. In 1955, 1960, 1965, and 1970 not one married woman who worked appeared in the stories Franzwa sampled. (Franzwa selected stories from magazines using five-year intervals to enhance the possibility of finding changes.)

Since middle-class American wives are less likely to be employed than their working-class counterparts, this finding makes sociological sense. Editors and writers may believe that readers of middle-class magazines, who are less likely to be employed, are also more likely to buy magazines approving this lifestyle. More likely to work and to be in families either economically insecure or facing downward mobility, working-class women might be expected to applaud effective women. For them, female dependence might be an undesirable trait. Their magazines could be expected to cater to such preferences, especially since those preferences flow from the readers' life situations. Such, indeed, are Flora's findings, presented in Table 1.1.

However, this pattern does not mean that the literature for the working-class woman avoids defining women in terms of men. All the women in middle-class magazines dropped from the labor force when they had a man present; only six percent of the women in the working-class fiction continued to work when they had a man and children. And Flora explained that for both groups "The plot of the majority of stories centered upon the female achieving the proper dependent status either by marrying or manipulating existing dependency relationships to reaffirm the heroine's subordinate position. The male support—monetary, social, and psychological—which the heroine gains was generally seen as well worth any independence or selfhood given up in the process" (1971, 441).

Such differences as do exist between working-class and middle-class maga-

TABLE 1.1. Female Dependence and Ineffectuality by Class, by Percentage of Stories*

	FEMALE DEPENDENCE			FEMALE INEFFECTUALITY		
	Undesirable	Desirable	Neutral	Undesirable	Desirable	Neutral
Working Class	22	30	48	38	4	58
Middle Class	18	51	31	18	33	49
Total	20	41	40	28	19	53

* Adapted from Flora (1971).

zines remain interesting, though. For they indicate how much more the women's magazines may be responsive to their audience than television can be. Because it is the dominant mass medium, television is designed to appeal to hundreds of millions of people. In 1970, the circulation of *True Story* was "only" 5,347,000, and of *Redbook,* a "mere" 8,1173,000. Drawing a smaller audience and by definition, one more specialized, the women's magazines can be more responsive to changes in the position of women in American society. If a magazine believes its audience is changing, it may alter the content to maintain its readership. The contradictions inherent in being women's magazines may free them to respond to change.

A woman's magazine is sex-typed in a way that is not true of men's magazines (Davis 1976). *Esquire* and *Playboy* are for men, but the content of these magazines, is, broadly speaking, American culture. Both men's magazines feature stories by major American writers, directed toward all sophisticated Americans, not merely to men. Both feature articles on the state of male culture as American culture or of male politics as American politics. Women's magazines are designed in opposition to these "male magazines." For instance, "sports" are women's sports or news of women breaking into "men's sports." A clear distinction is drawn between what is "male" and what is "female."

Paradoxically, though, this very limitation can be turned to an advantage. Addressing women, women's magazines may suppose that some in their audience are concerned about changes in the status of women and the greater participation of women in the labor force. As early as 1966, before the growth of the modern women's movement, women who were graduated from high school or college assumed they would work until the birth of their first child. Clarke and Esposito (1966) found that magazines published in the 1950s and addressed to these women *(Glamour, Mademoiselle,* and *Cosmopolitan)* stressed the joys of achievement and power when describing working roles for women and identifying desirable jobs. Magazines addressed to working women were optimistic about these women's ability to combine work and home, a message that women who felt that they should or must work would be receptive to. Indeed, in 1958 Marya and David Hatch criticized *Mademoiselle, Glamour,* and *Charm* as "unduly optimistic" in their "evaluation of physical and emotional strains upon working women." Combining work and family responsibilities may be very difficult, particularly in working-class homes, since working class husbands refuse to help with housework (Rubin 1976). But even working-class women prefer work outside the home to housework (Rubin 1976; Vanek forthcoming) since it broadens their horizons. Wanting to please and to attract a special audience of working women, magazine editors and writers may be freed to be somewhat responsive to new conditions, even as these same writers and editors feature stereotyped sex roles in other sections of their magazines.

Additional evidence of the albeit limited responsiveness of women's magazines to the changing status of women in the labor force is provided by their treatment of sex-role stereotypes since the advent of the women's movement. The modern women's movement is usually said to begin in the mid-1960s with the founding of the National Organization for Women. The date is of consequence for the study of sex roles in women's magazines because of Betty Friedan's involvement in the National Organization for Women. Her book, *The Feminine Mystique,* published in 1963, provided much of the ideology for the young movement. And, its analysis of sexism ("the problem with no name") was based in part on an analysis of the portrayal of sex roles in women's magazines. In an undated manuscript cited in Busby (1975), Stolz and her colleagues compared the image of women in magazines before and after the advent of the women's movement. Like others, they found no changes between 1940 and 1972. However, a time lag ("culture lag") is probably operating since nonmaterial conditions (ideas and attitudes) change more slowly than do material conditions (such as participation in the labor force.)

Several very recent studies affirm that women's magazines may be introducing new conceptions of women's sex roles that are more conducive to supporting the increased participation of women in the labor force. Butler and Paisley[3] note that at the instigation of an editor of *Redbook,* twenty-eight women's magazines published articles on the arguments for and against the Equal Rights Amendment, a constitutional change prompted by the women's movement and the increased participation of women in the labor force. Franzwa's impression of the women's magazines she had analyzed earlier is that they revealed more sympathy with working women in 1975.[4] Sheila Silver (1976) indicates that a "gentle support" for the aims of the women's movement and a "quiet concern" for working women may now be found in *McCall's.* By the terms "gentle support" and "quiet concern," she means to indicate that the magazine approves equal pay for equal work and other movement aims, although it does not approve of the women's movement itself. That magazine and others, such as the *Ladies' Home Journal,* continue to concentrate upon helping women as housewives: They still provide advice on hearth and home. The women's magazines continue to assume that every woman will marry, bear children and "make a home." They do not assume that every woman will work some time in her life.

In sum, the image of women in the women's magazines is more responsive to change than is television's symbolic annihilation and rigid typecasting of women. The sex roles presented are less stereotyped, but a woman's role is still limited. A female child is always an eventual mother, not a future productive participant in the labor force.

Newspapers and Women: Food, Fashion, and Society

Following the argument developed thus far, one might expect the nation's newspapers to be even more responsive than magazines to the changing status of women in American society. With smaller circulations than the magazines and supposedly more responsive to a local population rather than a national one, newspapers might cater to their female readers in order to maintain or even increase the base of their circulation. Such an expectation seems particularly plausible because contemporary newspapers face increased costs and are suffering from the economic competition of the electronic media. But this expectation flies in the face of the actual organization of newswork, for newspapers are *not, strictly speaking, local media.* Rather, local newspapers' dependence upon national news services is sufficiently great for them to be considered *components of a national medium,* designed to appeal to as many Americans as possible. As we have just seen, such a design encourages a rigid treatment of sex roles. An historical review of newspapers' treatment of news about women makes this result clearer.

Unlike the women's magazines, newspapers seek to appeal to an entire family. Historically, they have sought to attract female readers by treating them as a specialized audience, given attention in a segregated women's page, an autonomous or semi-autonomous department whose mandate precludes coverage of the "hard news" of the day. Although women's magazines have been published in the United States since the early nineteenth century, it took the newspaper circulation wars of the 1880s to produce the notion of "women's news." At that time, it appeared that every man who would buy a newspaper was already doing so. To build circulation by robbing each other of readers and attracting new readers, newspapers hired female reporters to write about society and fashion, as well as to expand "news" to include sports and comic strips. Items of potential interest to women were placed near advertisements of goods that women might purchase for their families. The origin of women's news reveals how long newspapers have traditionally defined women's interests as different from men's and how items of concern to women have become non-news, almost oddities. That view continues today. The budget for women's pages rarely provides for updating those pages from edition to edition, as is done for the general news, sports, and financial pages, sections held to be of interest to men. Finally, as is true of other departments as well, women's page budgets are sufficiently restricted to force that department's dependence upon the wire services.

During the nineteenth century's circulation wars, newspapers banded into cooperative services intended to decrease the costs of total coverage for each participating newspaper. A reporter would cover a story for newspapers in different cities, decreasing the need for scattered newspapers to maintain extensive bureaus in a variety of cities, such as Washington and New York. Furthermore, a newspaper in a small out-of-the-way town could be requested to share its story about an important event with newspapers from distant places that would not, under normal circumstances, have a reporter on hand. Aside from playing a limited role in the development of journalistic objectivity (Schudson 1976), since stories were designed to meet the political-editorial requirements of diverse news organizations, the news services encouraged the expansion of definitions of news. Some provided features, such as comics and crossword puzzles. Others provided sports items, financial stories, and features of concern to women, as well as "hard news." Sometimes the women's items were scandalous revelations of the activities of "Society." More often, they were advice for the homemaker, such as recipes and articles about rearing children. In this century, syndicated and wire-service features include gossip columns about the celebrated and the notorious and advice to the lovelorn, such as that fictionalized in Nathanael West's *Miss Lonelyhearts* or that represented by "Dear Abby."

For women's pages, items like these represent more than an economic investment purchased by a newspaper on behalf of its women's department. They are also an investment of space in the paper. Expected by readers to appear on a Monday, the column inches set aside for advice or gossip cannot be withdrawn for news of the women's movement. Similarly, it may be difficult to turn aside essentially prepaid feature stories about clothing and fashions supplied by the Associated Press or some other news syndicate in order to hire additional women's page staff interested in covering the changing status of women in American society. Commitments like these "nationalize" the local media, because the news syndicate or wire service reaches virtually every daily newspaper in the United States. Because the wire services *as businesses* are necessarily committed to pleasing all (or as many as possible) of their subscribing newspapers, they must shrink from advocating vast social changes. As in the case of television, what goes in New York may not go in Peoria, Illinois or Norman, Oklahoma. National in scope, syndicated and wire-service items for the women's page must seek an American common denominator. For the sex stereotyping of the women's pages to cease, the leadership of the Associated Press and the syndicates would have to be convinced that most of their subscribing papers wanted a different kind of story for their women's pages. Only then, it seems safe to say, would the papers serviced by the syndicates run the kinds of news about changes in the status of women that may be found in the *New York Times* and the *Los Angeles Times*, whose women's pages develop their own stories through independent staffs.

For now, a characterization of women's pages provided by Lindsay Van Gelder (1974) seems apt. She speculates thus: Suppose a Martian came to earth and sought to learn about American culture by reading the women's pages. Bombarded by pictures of wedding dresses, the Martian might suppose that American women marry at least once a week. After all, a Martian might reason that newspapers and their women's pages reflect daily life. That view, we might add, would seem justified by the women's pages' intense involvement with the social life of the upper class, because upper-class power is a daily aspect of American life. Women's pages feed upon the parties, marriages, engagements, and clothing and food preferences of the wealthy and the celebrated. In this, like newspapers in general (Lazarsfeld and Merton 1948), the women's pages encourage all citizens to emulate the upper class and to chase after positions of high status and institutionalized importance.

Newspapers' very emphasis upon established institutions and those with institutionalized power may account in part for their denigration of women and the women's movement (Morris 1974). Most information in the general sections of newspapers concerns people in power, and newspapers justify this emphasis by stressing that such people work in or head societal institutions that regulate social intercourse. But communications researchers view the matter somewhat differently. They argue that newspapers exercise social control: By telling stories about such people, newspapers lend status to approved institutions and chastise lawbreakers. Historically, those few women mentioned in the general news pages belonged to the powerful groups in society. Gladys Engel Lang suggests "the most admired woman" list probably reflects the publicity given to specific women. They are mainly wives of the powerful, celebrities and stars, and the few women who are heads of state. But women are mainly seen as the consorts of famous men, not as subjects of political and social concern in their own right.

This situation appears to be changing. Once ignored or ridiculed (Morris 1974), the women's movement has received increasing coverage as it has passed through the stages characteristic of any social movement. As the women's movement became sufficiently routinized to open offices with normal business hours, some newspapers established a "women's movement beat" that required a reporter to provide at least periodic coverage of new developments. When increased legitimation brought more volunteers and more funds to wage successful law suits against major corporations and to lobby for the introduction of new laws, newspapers concerned with major institutions were forced to cover those topics. In turn, these successes increased the movement's legitimation. Legitimation also brought support of sympathizers within other organizations who were not movement members (Carden 1973). Reporters having those other organizations as their beats are being forced to write about the ideas of the women's movement and women's changing status. For instance, the position of women and minorities in the labor force is becoming a required topic for labor reporters and those who write about changing personnel in the corporate world.

On the whole, though, despite coverage of women forcibly induced by the legitimation of the women's movement, newspapers continue to view women in the news as occasional oddities that must be tolerated. Attention to women is segregated and found on the women's page. As a recent survey of women's pages demonstrates (Guenin 1975), most women's pages continue to cater to a traditional view of women's interests. They emphasize home and family, only occasionally introducing items about women at work. And those items are more likely to concern methods of coping with home and office tasks than they are with highlighting problems of sex discrimination and what the modern women's movement has done in combatting it. Like the television industry, appealing to a common denominator encourages newspapers to engage in the symbolic annihilation of women by ignoring women at work and trivializing women through banishment to hearth and home.

The Impact of the Media

As of this writing, women continue to enter the labor force at a faster rate than in the past—a rate that has far exceeded the predictions of demographers and specialists on the labor force. What are we to make of this discrepancy between the sex-role stereotypes reflected in the media and the employment pattern of women? Does the discrepancy mean that because of culture lag, the mass media reflect attitudes discarded by the population and that the mass media have no effect on the behavior of women? That conclusion seems quite seductive, given the patterns we have described. By entering the labor force at increasing rates, women seem to be ignoring the media's message. But that conclusion flies in the face of *every* existing theory about the mass media. Communications theorists agree that the mass media are the cement of American social life. They are a source of common interest and of conversation. Children and adults may schedule their activities around favorite television programs. And the mass media serve to coordinate the activities of diverse societal institutions. To paraphrase Gerbner and Gross (1976), the mass media in general and television in particular have replaced religion as a source of social control in American life. Like the medieval church that broadcast one message to all social classes, all the mass media disseminate the same theme about women to all social classes: They announce their symbolic annihilation and trivialization.

Equally important, all available evidence about the impact of the media upon sex-role stereotyping indicates that the media encourage their audiences to engage in such stereotyping. They lead girls, in particular, to believe that their social horizons and alternatives are more limited than is actually the case. The evidence about the impact of television is particularly compelling.

Aimee Dorr Leifer (1975) points out that television provides many of the same socialization processes as the family. Like the family, television provides examples of good and bad behavior. The family socializes children through the patterning and power of those examples, and television programming also provides variation in the frequency, consistency, and power of examples. Leifer notes some indications that variations in these factors may have an impact on the child viewer (5). Finally, like the family, television can provide reinforcers (rewards and punishments) for behaviors. However, although the family can tailor reinforcers to the individual child, television cannot.

Most of the documentation regarding the impact of television upon children considers the effect of televised violence, primarily because of the national push for such research after the political assassinations and riots of the 1960s. That research is particularly interesting, for our purposes, because of the unanimity of the findings and because of the diverse methods used to analyze the topic.

Social science researchers frequently squabble about which methods of research are appropriate to explore a problem. All seem ready to admit that the ideal way to explore television's impact would be to perform a controlled experiment in a natural setting. Ideally, one would isolate a group that did not watch television, matching characteristics of individuals in that group with the characteristics of others whose viewing was designed by the researchers. The groups would be studied over a period of some years to see whether the effects of television are cumulative. Unfortunately, such a research design is impossible. Virtually all American homes have at least one television set; and so, one cannot locate children for the "control group"—those not exposed to television. To get around this problem, the violence researchers used both laboratory and field experiments. In the former, children were exposed to carefully selected (and sometimes specially prepared) videotapes, lasting anywhere from ten minutes to an hour. Behavior was analyzed before viewing the tape, while viewing it, and after viewing it. By carefully controlling which children would see what tape (designing "control groups"), the experimenters could comment upon the effect of televised violence on the children. Unfortunately, laboratory studies are artificial. For one thing, both sets of children are already dosed with violence in normal viewing, and both watch television under conditions different from their homes or classrooms. Thus, researchers cannot state in any definitive way how the research findings are related to activities in the real world.

The second approach, field experiments, also has difficulties. Such studies are invariably "correlational." The studies demonstrate that two kinds of behavior are found together, but cannot state whether one behavior causes the other or whether both are caused by a third characteristic of the children studied. For instance, in the violence studies, teams of researchers asked youths and children about their viewing habits (and in one case tried to control those habits) and also measured (in a variety of ways) their antisocial behavior. Although viewing aggression and antisocial behavior were invariably found together, it remains possible that some third factor accounts for the variation.

The fact that different research teams interviewed children of different sexes, ages, social classes, and races from different parts of the country makes it fairly certain that a third factor was not responsible for the association of television viewing and antisocial behavior. And this conclusion is strengthened by the evidence provided by the laboratory studies. Furthermore, since the Surgeon General issued his report in 1973, additional field studies have found "that viewing televised or filmed violence in naturalistic settings increases the incidence of naturally-occurring aggression, that long-term exposure to television may increase one's aggressiveness, and that exposure to televised violence may increase one's tolerance for everyday aggression" (Leifer 1975).

Although there are not as many studies, researchers have also established that television programming influences racial attitudes. Again, both laboratory and field studies were used. They demonstrate that white children may take their image of blacks from television (Greenberg 1972), that the longer a white child watches "Sesame Street," the less likely that child will have negative attitudes toward blacks, and that positive portrayals of blacks produce more positive attitudes toward blacks, with negative portrayals producing little attitude changes (Graves 1975). Aimee Leifer (1975) writes of these findings: "Apparently black children increase their [positive] image of their own group by seeing them portrayed on television, while white children are influenced by the portrayal, especially when it is uncomplementary to blacks" (26). The evidence on the impact of the depiction of race is important in assessing television's impact on sex roles because content analyses provide strong documentation that television treats blacks and whites differently. For instance, Schuetz and Sprafkin's analysis of children's commercials and Lemon's analysis of patterns of domination document differential treatment by race as well as by sex.

Since the documentation on violence is extensive and the documentation on race is strong, it seems more than reasonable to expect that the content of television programs leads children to hold stereotyped images of sex roles. The power of the evidence on race and violence is important, because researchers have just started to ask about the impact of television on societal sex roles. What, then, do we know now?

Suppose, we asked earlier, that television primarily presents adult women as housewives. Also suppose that girls in the television audience "model" their behavior and expectations on that of television women. Such a supposition is quite plausible for psychologists note that "opportunities for modeling have been vastly increased by television" (Lesser, quoted in Cantor 1975, 5). It is then equally plausible that girls exposed to television women may hope to be homemakers when they are adults, but not workers outside the home.

Do girls actually model their attitudes and behavior on the symbolically annihilated and dominated television woman?

This general question may be broken down into several component questions:

1. Do girls pay closer attention to female television characters than to male characters?
2. Do girls value the attributes of female characters or those of male characters?
3. Does television viewing have an impact on the attitudes of young children toward sex roles?
4. Do these attitudes continue as children mature?

As in the studies on violence and race, the available evidence includes laboratory and field studies.

1. Do girls pay closer attention to female characters than to male characters?
Joyce Sprafkin and Robert Liebert report the results of three laboratory experiments designed to see whether (a) boys and girls each prefer television programs featuring actors of their own sex; (b) whether the children pay closer attention when someone of the same sex is on the television screen; and (c) whether the children prefer to watch members of their own sex engaging in sex-typed (playing with a doll or a football) or nonsex-typed (as in reading with one's parents) behavior. To gather information, they enabled the tested children to switch a dial, choosing between an episode of "Nanny and the Professor" and one of the "Brady Bunch." (Children like to watch situation comedies [Lyle and Hoffman 1972].) For each program, episodes featuring male or female characters were selected with different episodes showing a boy or a girl engaging in sex-typed or nonsex-typed behavior. The findings are clear: In their viewing habits, children prefer sex-typing. They prefer programs featuring actors of their own sex; they watch members of their own sex more closely; and they also pay more attention when a member of their own sex engages in sex-typed behavior. According to Sprafkin and Liebert (1976), such behavior probably involves learning, for according to psychological theories children prefer to expose themselves to same-sex models as an information-seeking strategy; children are presumed to attend to same-sex peers because they already know that much social reinforcement is sex-typed and must discover the contingencies that apply to their own gender (see also Grusec and Brinker 1972).

2. Do girls value the attributes of female characters or of male characters?
The evidence on evaluation is not as clear. A variety of communications researchers, particularly a group working at Michigan State University, have performed a series of laboratory experiments to determine which specific characters boys and girls prefer, and why they do so. They found that invariably boys identify with male characters. Sometimes though (about thirty percent of the time) girls also identify with or prefer male characters (Miller and Reeves 1976). When girls choose a television character as a model, they are guided by the character's physical attractiveness; boys are guided by strength (Greenberg, Held, Wakshlag, and Reeves 1976; Miller and Reeves 1976). Indeed, even when girls select a male character they appear to be guided by his physical attractiveness (Greenberg et al. 1976). Girls who select male characters do *not* state they are basing their choices on the wider opportunities and fun available to men, although the girls who select female characters state that the characters do the same kind of things as they themselves do (Reeves 1976).

3. Does television viewing have an impact on the attitudes of young children toward sex roles?
Here the evidence is clearer. Frueh and McGhee (1975) interviewed children in kindergarten through sixth grade, asking them about the amount of time they spent watching television and testing the extent and direction of their sex-typing. The children who viewed the most television (twenty-five hours per week) were significantly more traditional in their sex-typing than those who viewed the least (ten hours or less per week). Because this study is correlational, one cannot know whether viewing determines sex-typing or *vice versa*. But television does seem to be the culprit, according to laboratory studies on television viewing and occupational preferences.

Miller and Reeves (1976; see also Pingree 1976) asked children to watch television characters in nontraditional roles and then asked them what kinds of jobs boys and girls could do when they grew up. Children exposed to programs about female police officers, for instance, were significantly more likely to state that a woman could be a police officer than were children who watched more traditional fare.

Beuf (1974) reports similar results from sixty-three interviews with boys and girls between the ages of three and six. Some girls had even abandoned their ambitions:

> One of the most interesting aspects of the children's responses lay in the reaction to the question: "What would you want to be when you grew up, if you were a girl (boy?)" Several girls mentioned that this other-sex ambition was their true ambition, but one that could not be realized because of their sex. Doctor and milkman were both cited in this regard. . . . One blond moppet confided that what she really wanted to do when she grew up was fly like a bird. "But, I'll never do it," she sighed, "Because I'm not a boy." Further questioning revealed that a TV cartoon character was the cause of this misconception. (143)

A boy said, "Oh, if I were a girl, I'd have to grow up and be nothing." Beuf reports, "Children who were moderate viewers appeared to exert a wider range of choice in career selection than heavy viewers. Seventy-six percent of heavy viewers (compared with fifty percent of the moderate viewers) selected stereotyped careers for themselves" (147).

4. Do these attitudes continue as children mature?
It is known that sex-typing increases as children mature. Second graders are more insistent in their sex-typing than first graders are. Adolescent boys and girls insist upon discriminating between behavior by sex. But little is known about the impact of television on this process. A longitudinal study presently underway at the University of Pennsylvania's Annenberg School of Communication is the first attempt to answer this question systematically. Chapter 14,* which contains a summary of that research, indicates that definitive answers are not yet available. However, analyses based on data from the second year of the study do tentatively indicate an association between television viewing and sexist attitudes. The association is weak, but it does suggest that the more a youngster watches television, the more likely the child will be to hold sexist attitudes.

What can we make of all this? The answer is: The mass media perform two tasks at once. First, with some culture lag, they reflect dominant values and attitudes in the society. Second, they act as agents of socialization, teaching youngsters in particular how to behave. Watching lots of television leads children and adolescents to believe in traditional sex roles: Boys should work; girls should not. The same sex-role stereotypes are found in the media designed especially for women. They teach that women should direct their hearts toward hearth and home.

At a time when over forty percent of the American labor force is female and when women with preschool children are entering the labor force in increasing numbers, the mass media's message has severe national consequences. As demographers (for example, Oppenheimer 1970) and economists (for example, Bowen and Finegan 1969) have shown, the maintenance and expansion of the American economy depends upon increasing the rate of female employment. Discouraging women from working presents a national dilemma. Furthermore, it is quite probable that the media's message discourages women from working up to their full capacity in the labor force. And by limiting the *kinds* of jobs held by fictional women, it may encourage the underemployment of women, a severe problem for those working-class families who can barely scrape by with two incomes (Rubin 1976). And rigid sex-role stereotypes make the burden heavier for all working women who must still shoulder the responsibilities of home and family with limited support from their husbands. This problem is particularly acute in blue-collar families (Rubin 1976). For the nation and for individuals, the message "women belong in the home" is an anachronism we can ill afford.

---

*Of original publication.

References

Bardwick, J., and S. Schumann. 1967. Portrait of American men and women in TV commercials. *Psychology* 4 (4): 18-23.

Baumann, Z. 1972. Saturday children's television: A report of television programming and advertising on Boston commercial television. Unpublished monograph.

Bernard, J. 1973. My four revolutions: An autobiographical history of the ASA. *American Journal of Sociology* 78: 773-791.

Beuf, A. 1974. Doctor, lawyer, household drudge. *Journal of Communication* 24 (2): 142-145.

Bowen, W., and T. Finegan. 1969. *The economics of labor force participation*. Princeton, NJ: Princeton University Press.

Busby, L. 1975. Sex-role research on the mass media. *Journal of Communication* 25 (4): 107-131.

Cantor, M. 1975. Children's television: Sex-role portrayals and employment discrimination. In *The federal role in funding children's television programming*. Vol. 2. Edited by K. Mielke et al. United States Office of Education, USOE-074-8674.

Carden, M. 1973. *The new feminist movement*. New York: Russell Sage.

Clarke, P., and V. Esposito. 1966. A study of occupational advice for women in magazines. *Journalism Quarterly* 43: 477-485.

Courtney, A., and T. Whipple. 1974. Women in TV commercials. *Journal of Communications* 24 (2): 110-118.

Davis, M. 1976. The *Ladies' Home Journal* and *Esquire*: A comparison. Unpublished manuscript. Stanford University, Department of Sociology.

DeFleur, M. 1964. Occupational roles as portrayed on television. *Public Opinion Quarterly* 28 (Spring): 57-74.

Dominick, J., and G. Rauch. 1972. The image of women in network TV commercials. *Journal of Broadcasting* 16 (3): 259-265.

Downing, M. 1974. Heroine of the daytime serial. *Journal of Communication* 24 (2): 130-137.

Flora, C. 1971. The passive female: Her cooperative image by class and culture in women's magazine fiction. *Journal of Marriage and the Family* 33 (August): 435-444.

Franzwa, H. 1974a. Working women in fact and fiction. *Journal of Communication* 24 (2): 104-109.

———. 1974b. Pronatalism in women's magazine fiction. In *The myth of motherhood and apple pie*, edited by E. Peale and J. Senderowitz. New York: T. Y. Crowell.

———. 1975. Female roles in women's magazine fiction, 1940-1970. In *Women: Dependent or independent variable*, edited by R. Unger and F. Denmark. New York: Psychological Dimensions.

Frueh, T, and P. McGhee. 1975. Traditional sex role development and amount of time spent watching television. *Development Psychology* 11: 109.

Gerbner, G. 1972. Violence in television drama: Trends and symbolic functions. In *Media content and controls*, edited by G. Comstock and E. Rubinstein. Vol. 1 of *Television and social behavior*. Washington, DC: U.S. Government Printing Office.

Gerbner, G., and L. Gross. 1976. Cultural indicators: The social reality of television drama. Unpublished manuscript. Annenberg School of Communications, University of Pennsylvania.

Graves, S. 1975. How to encourage positive racial attitudes. Paper presented at the biennial meeting of the Society for Research in Child Development, Denver, Colorado.

Greenberg, B. 1972. Children's reaction to TV blacks. *Journalism Quarterly* 49: 5-14.

Greenberg, B., G. Held, J. Wakshlag, and B. Reeves. 1976. TV character attributes, identification and children's modeling tendencies. Paper presented at International Communication Association, Portland, Oregon.

Grusec, J., and D. Brinker, Jr. 1972. Reinforcement for imitation as a social learning determinant with implications for sex-role development. *Journal of Personality and Social Psychology* 21: 149-158.

Guenin, Z. 1975. Women's pages on contemporary newspapers: Missing out on contemporary content. *Journalism Quarterly* 52 (Spring): 66-69, 75.

Hatch, M., and D. Hatch. 1958. Problems of married and working women as presented by three popular working women's magazines. *Social Forces* 37: 148-153.

Head, S. 1954. Content analysis of television drama programs. *Quarterly of Film, Radio and Television* 9: 175-194.

Hirsch, P. 1978. Television as a national medium: Its cultural and political role in American society. In *Handbook of urban life*, edited by D. Street. San Francisco: Jossey-Bass.

Isber, C., and M. Cantor. 1975. *Report of the task force on women in public broadcasting.* Washington, DC: Corporation for Public Broadcasting.

Johns-Heine, P., and H. Gerth. 1949. Values in mass periodical fiction, 1921- 1940. *Public Opinion Quarterly* 13 (Spring):105-113.

Katz, E., and P. Lazarsfeld. 1955. *Personal influence.* New York: Free Press.

Katzman, N. 1972. Television soap operas: What's been going on anyway? *Public Opinion Quarterly* 35: 200-212.

Lasswell, H. 1948. The structure and function of communication in society. In *The communication of ideas,* edited by L. Bryson. New York: Harper Brothers.

Lazarsfeld, P., and R. Merton. 1948. Mass communication, popular taste and organized social action. In *The communication of ideas,* edited by L. Bryson. New York: Harper Brothers.

Leifer, A. 1975. Socialization processes in the family. Paper presented at Prix Jeunesse Seminar, Munich, Germany.

Liebert, R., J. Neale, and E. Davidson. 1973. *The early window: Effects of television on children and youth.* New York: Pergamon.

Lyle, J., and H. Hoffman. 1972. Children's use of television and other media. In *Television in day to day life: Patterns of use,* edited by E. Rubinstein, G. Comstock, and J. Murphy. Vol. 4 of *Television and social behavior.* Washington, DC: U.S. Government Printing Office.

McCormack, T. 1975. Toward a nonsexist perspective on social and political change. In *Another voice: Feminist perspectives on social life and social science,* edited by M. Millman and R. M. Kanter. New York: Doubleday/Anchor.

McNeil, J. 1975. Feminism, femininity, and the television series: A content analysis. *Journal of Broadcasting* 19: 259-69.

Miller, M., and B. Reeves. 1976. Dramatic TV content and children's sex-role stereotypes. *Journal of Broadcasting* 20 (1): 35-50.

Morris, M. 1974. The public definition of a social movement: Women's liberation. *Sociology and Social Research* 57: 526-543.

Oppenheimer, V. 1970. *The female labor force in the United States: Demographic and economic factors governing its growth and changing composition.* Population Monograph Series No. 5. Berkeley: University of California Institute of International Studies.

Parsons, T. 1949. Age and sex in the social structure of the United States. *Essays in sociological theory.* New York: Free Press.

Pingree, S. 1976. The effects of nonsexist television commercials and perceptions of reality on children's attitudes towards women. Paper presented at the annual meetings of the International Communication Association, Portland, Oregon.

Reeves, B. 1976. The dimensional structure of children's perception of TV characters. Ph.D. dissertation. Michigan State University, East Lansing, MI.

Rubin, L. 1976. *Worlds of pain: Life in the working-class family.* New York: Basic.

Schudson, M. 1976. Origins of the ideal of objectivity in the professions: Studies in the history of American journalism and American law, 1830-1940. Ph.D. dissertation. Harvard University, Cambridge, MA.

Seegar, J., and P. Wheeler. 1973. World of work on TV: Ethnic and sex representation in TV drama. *Journal of Broadcasting* 17: 210-214.

Silver, S. 1976. Then and now—content analysis of *McCall's* magazine. Paper presented at the annual meetings of Association for Education in Journalism. College Park, Maryland.

Silverstein, A., and R. Silverstein. 1974. The portrayal of women in television advertising. *FCC Bar Journal* 1: 71-98.

Sprafkin, J., and R. Liebert. 1976. Sex and sex-roles as determinants of children's television program selections and attention. Unpublished manuscript. State University of New York at Stony Brook.

Tedesco, N. 1974. Patterns in prime time. *Journal of Communication* 24 (2): 119- 124.

Tuchman, G. 1974. *The TV establishment: Programming for power and profit.* Englewood Cliffs, NJ: Prentice-Hall.

———. 1976. Media values. *Society* (November/December): 51-54.

Turow, J. 1974. Advising and ordering: Daytime, prime time. *Journal of Communication* 24 (2): 138-141.

Vanek, J. Forthcoming. *Married women and the work day: Time trends.* Baltimore, MD: The Johns Hopkins University Press.

Van Gelder, L. 1974. Women's pages: You can't make news out of a silk purse. *Ms* (November): 112-116.

CHAPTER 10

Deep Play: Notes on the Balinese Cockfight
Clifford Geertz

Originally published in Daedalus *101 (1), 1972.*

READING INTRODUCTION

This reading alerts us that Americans hold no monopoly on popular culture. Geertz relates both the various events surrounding and the deeper cultural meaning of an example of popular culture, cockfighting on a South Pacific island. He contrasts his interpretation of engaging in "deep play" (extremely high stakes activities) with Jeremy Bentham's famous earlier characterization of irrational behavior. For Geertz, cockfighting in Bali engages central cultural values such as honor, dignity, and respect. Thus, rather than seeing Balinese men betting unreasonable amounts of money on a mere game, Geertz portrays what appears as play to be a deadly serious struggle over relative status.

Geertz supports this interpretation with a number of lengthy enumerated conclusions. Roughly these can be reduced to the following two straightforward relationships. First, the closer the contestants are in status, the "deeper" (i.e., the more serious and desperate) the play. Second, the higher the contestants' status, the deeper the play. Geertz then summarizes various other ways in which we might recognize deep play.

At a still higher level of interpretation Geertz contends that the status implications of "deep play" allow the Balinese to tell their story. By this he means that cockfighting epitomizes a concern with relative status that pervades Balinese society.

In contrast to many of the other authors whose work appears in this volume, Geertz has been outspoken about the local character of knowledge. He believes that specific cases lend themselves to interpretation, rather than explanation, only via the type of "participant observation" that he exemplifies here. He is skeptical about going beyond individual cases and constructing anything resembling a social science of empirical generalizations.

READING TEXT

The Raid

Early in April of 1958, my wife and I arrived, malarial and diffident, in a Balinese village we intended, as anthropologists, to study. A small place, about five hundred people, and relatively remote, it was its own world. We were intruders, professional ones, and the villagers dealt with us as Balinese seem always to deal with people not part of their life who yet press themselves upon them: as though we were not there. For them, and to a degree for ourselves, we were nonpersons, specters, invisible men.

We moved into an extended family compound (that had been arranged before through the provincial government) belonging to one of the four major factions in village life. But except for our landlord and the village chief, whose cousin and brother-in-law he was, everyone ignored us in a way only a Balinese can do. As we wandered around, uncertain, wistful, eager to please, people seemed to look right through us with a gaze focused several yards behind us on some more actual stone or tree. Almost nobody greeted us; but nobody scowled or said anything unpleasant to us either, which would have been almost as satisfactory.

If we ventured to approach someone (something one is powerfully inhibited from doing in such an atmosphere), he moved, negligently but definitely, away. If, seated or leaning against a wall, we had him trapped, he said nothing at all, or mumbled what for the Balinese is the ultimate nonword—"yes." The indifference, of course, was studied; the villagers were watching every move we made, and they had an enormous amount of quite accurate information about who we were and what we were going to be doing. But they acted as if we simply did not exist, which, in fact, as this behavior was designed to inform us, we did not, or anyway not yet.

This is, as I say, general in Bali. Everywhere else I have been in Indonesia, and more latterly in Morocco, when I have gone into a new village, people have poured out from all sides to take a very close look at me, and, often an all-too-probing feel as well. In Balinese villages, at least those away from the tourist circuit, nothing happens at all. People go on pounding, chatting, making offerings, staring into space, carrying baskets about while one drifts around feeling vaguely disembodied. And the same thing is true on the individual level. When you first meet a Balinese, he seems virtually not to relate to you at all; he is, in the term Gregory Bateson and Margaret Mead made famous, "away" (Bateson and Mead 1942, 68). Then—in a day, a week, a month (with some people the magic moment never comes)—he decides, for reasons I have never quite been able to fathom, that you are real, and then he becomes a warm, gay, sensitive, sympathetic, though, being Balinese, always precisely controlled, person. You have crossed, somehow, some moral or metaphysical shadow line. Though you are not exactly taken as a Balinese (one has to be born to that), you are at least regarded as a human being rather than a cloud or a gust of wind. The whole complexion of your relationship dramatically changes to, in the majority of cases, a gentle, almost affectionate one—a low-keyed, rather playful, rather mannered, rather bemused geniality.

My wife and I were still very much in the gust-of-wind stage, a most frustrating, and even, as you soon begin to doubt whether you are really real after all, unnerving one, when, ten days or so after our arrival, a large cockfight was held in the public square to raise money for a new school.

Now, a few special occasions aside, cockfights are illegal in Bali under the Republic (as, for not altogether unrelated reasons, they were under the Dutch), largely as a result of the pretensions to puritanism radical nationalism tends to bring with it. The elite, which is not itself so very puritan, worries about the poor, ignorant peasant gambling all his money away, about what foreigners will think, about the waste of time better devoted to building up the country. It sees cockfighting as "primitive," "backward," "unprogressive," and generally unbecoming an ambitious nation. And, as with those other embarrassments—opium smoking, begging, or uncovered breasts—it seeks, rather unsystematically, to put a stop to it.

Of course, like drinking during Prohibition or, today, smoking marihuana, cockfights, being a part of "The Balinese Way of Life," nonetheless go on happening, and with extraordinary frequency. And, as with Prohibition or marihuana, from time to time the police (who, in 1958 at least, were almost all not Balinese but Javanese) feel called upon to make a raid, confiscate the cocks and spurs, fine a few people, and even now and then expose some of them in the tropical sun for a day as object lessons which never, somehow, get learned, even though occasionally, quite occasionally, the object dies.

As a result, the fights are usually held in a secluded corner of a village in semi-secrecy, a fact which tends to slow the action a little—not very much, but the Balinese do not care to have it slowed at all. In this case, however, perhaps because they were raising money for a school that the government was unable to give them, perhaps because raids had been few recently, perhaps, as I gathered from subsequent discussion, there was a notion that the necessary bribes had been paid, they thought they could take a chance on the central square and draw a larger and more enthusiastic crowd without attracting the attention of the law.

They were wrong. In the midst of the third match, with hundreds of people, including, still transparent, myself and my wife, fused into a single body around the ring, a superorganism in the literal sense, a truck full of policemen armed with machine guns roared up. Amid great screeching cries of "pulisi! pulisi!" from the crowd, the policemen jumped out, and, springing into the center of the ring, began to swing their guns around like gangsters in a motion picture, though not going so far as actually to fire them. The superorganism came instantly apart as its components scattered in all directions. People raced down the road, disappeared headfirst over walls, scrambled under platforms, folded themselves behind wicker screens, scuttled up coconut trees. Cocks armed with steel spurs sharp enough to cut off a finger or run a hole through a foot were running wildly around. Everything was dust and panic.

On the established anthropological principle, "When in Rome," my wife and I decided, only slightly less instantaneously than everyone else, that the thing to do was run too. We ran down the main village street, northward, away from where we were living, for we were on that side of the ring. About halfway down another fugitive ducked suddenly into a compound—his own, it turned out—and we, seeing nothing ahead of us but rice fields, open country, and a very high volcano, followed him. As the three of us came tumbling into the courtyard, his wife, who had apparently been through this sort of thing before, whipped out a table, a tablecloth, three chairs, and three cups of tea, and we all, without any explicit communication whatsoever, sat down, commenced to sip tea, and sought to compose ourselves.

A few moments later, one of the policemen marched importantly into the yard, looking for the village chief. (The chief had not only been at the fight, he had arranged it. When the truck drove up he ran to the river, stripped off his sarong, and plunged in so he could say, when at length they found him sitting there pouring water over his head, that he had been away bathing when the whole affair had occurred and was ignorant of it. They did not believe him and fined him three hundred rupiah, which the village raised collectively.) Seeing me and my wife, "White Men," there in the yard, the policeman performed a classic double take. When he found his voice again he asked, approximately, what in the devil did we think we were doing there. Our host of five minutes leaped instantly to our defense, producing an impassioned description of who and what we were, so detailed and so accurate that it was my turn, having barely communicated with a living human being save my landlord and the village chief for more than a week, to be astonished. We had a perfect right to be there, he said, looking the Javanese upstart in the eye. We were American professors; the government had cleared us; we were there to study culture; we were going to write a book to tell Americans about Bali. And we had all been there drinking tea and talking about cultural matters all afternoon and did not know anything about any cockfight. Moreover, we had not seen the village chief all day; he must have gone to town. The policeman retreated in rather total disarray. And, after a decent interval, bewildered but relieved to have survived and stayed out of jail, so did we.

The next morning the village was a completely different world for us. Not only were we no longer invisible, we were suddenly the center of all attention, the object of a great outpouring of warmth, interest, and most especially, amusement. Everyone in the village knew we had fled like everyone else. They asked us about it again and again (I must have told the story, small detail by small detail, fifty times by the end of the day), gently, affectionately, but quite insistently teasing us: "Why didn't you just stand there and tell the police who you were?" "Why didn't you just say you were only watching and not betting?" "Were you really afraid of those little guns?" As always, kinesthetically minded and, even when fleeing for their lives (or, as happened eight years later, surrendering them), the world's most poised people, they gleefully mimicked, also over and over again, our graceless style of running and what they claimed were our panic-stricken facial expressions. But above all, everyone was extremely pleased and even more surprised that we had not simply "pulled out our papers" (they knew about those too) and asserted our Distinguished Visitor status, but had instead demonstrated our solidarity with what were now our covillagers. (What we had actually demonstrated was our cowardice, but there is fellowship in that too.)

Even the Brahmana priest, an old, grave, halfway-to-heaven type who because of its associations with the underworld would never be involved, even distantly, in a cockfight, and was difficult to approach even to other Balinese, had us called into his courtyard to ask us about what had happened, chuckling happily at the sheer extraordinariness of it all.

In Bali, to be teased is to be accepted. It was the turning point so far as our relationship to the community was concerned, and we were quite literally "in." The whole village opened up to us, probably more than it ever would have otherwise (I might actually never have gotten to that priest, and our accidental host became one of my best informants), and certainly very much faster. Getting caught, or almost caught, in a vice raid is perhaps not a very generalizable recipe for achieving that mysterious necessity of anthropological field work, rapport, but for me it worked very well. It led to a sudden and unusually complete acceptance into a society extremely difficult for outsiders to penetrate. It gave me the kind of immediate, inside-view grasp of an aspect of "peasant mentality" that anthropologists not fortunate enough to flee headlong with their subjects from armed authorities normally do not get. And, perhaps most important of all, for the other things might have come in other ways, it put me very quickly on to a combination emotional explosion, status war, and philosophical drama of central significance to the society whose inner nature I desired to understand. By the time I left I had spent about as much time looking into cockfights as into witchcraft, irrigation, caste, or marriage.

Of Cocks and Men

Bali, mainly because it is Bali, is a well-studied place. Its mythology, art, ritual, social organization, patterns of child rearing, forms of law, even styles of trance, have all been microscopically examined for traces of that elusive substance Jane Belo (1970) called "The Balinese Temper." But, aside from a few passing remarks, the cockfight has barely been noticed, although as a popular obsession of consuming power it is at least as important a revelation of what being a Balinese "is really like" as these more celebrated phenomena.[1] As much of America surfaces in a ball park, on a golf links, at a race track, or around a poker table, much of Bali surfaces in a cock ring. For it is only apparently cocks that are fighting there. Actually, it is men.

To anyone who has been in Bali any length of time, the deep psychological identification of Balinese men with their cocks is unmistakable. The double entendre here is deliberate. It works in exactly the same way in Balinese as it does in English, even to producing the same tired jokes, strained puns, and uninventive obscenities. Bateson and Mead (1942) have even suggested that, in line with the Balinese conception of the body as a set of separately animated parts, cocks are viewed as detachable, self-operating penises, ambulant genitals with a life of their own.[2] And while I do not have the kind of unconscious material either to confirm or disconfirm this intriguing notion, the fact that they are masculine symbols par excellence is about as indubitable, and to the Balinese about as evident, as the fact that water runs downhill.

The language of everyday moralism is shot through, on the male side of it, with roosterish imagery. *Sabung,* the word for cock (and one which appears in inscriptions as early as A.D. 922), is used metaphorically to mean "hero," "warrior," "champion," "man of parts," "political candidate," "bachelor," "dandy," "lady-killer," or "tough guy." A pompous man whose behavior presumes above his station is compared to a tailless cock who struts about as though he had a large, spectacular one. A desperate man who makes a last, irrational effort to extricate himself from an impossible situation is likened to a dying cock who makes one final lunge at his tormentor to drag him along to a common destruction. A stingy man, who promises much, gives little, and begrudges that, is compared to a cock which, held by the tail, leaps at another without in fact engaging him. A marriageable young man still shy with the opposite sex or someone in a new job anxious to make a good impression is called "a fighting cock caged for the first time" (Hooykaas 1958, 39).[3] Court trials, wars, political contests, inheritance disputes, and street arguments are all compared to cockfights (Korn 1932, index under *toh*). Even the very island itself is perceived from its shape as a small, proud cock, poised, neck extended, back taut, tail raised, in eternal challenge to large, feckless, shapeless Java.[4]

But the intimacy of men with their cocks is more than metaphorical. Balinese men, or anyway a large majority of Balinese men, spend an enormous amount of time with their favorites, grooming them, feeding them, discussing them, trying them out against one another, or just gazing at them with a mixture of rapt admiration and dreamy self-absorption. Whenever you see a group of Balinese men squatting idly in the council shed or along the road in their hips down, shoulders forward, knees up fashion, half or more of them will have a rooster in his hands, holding it between his thighs, bouncing it gently up and down to strengthen its legs, ruffling its feathers with abstract sensuality, pushing it out against a neighbor's rooster to rouse its spirit, withdrawing it toward his loins to calm it again. Now and then, to get a feel for another bird, a man will fiddle this way with someone else's cock for a while, but usually by moving around to squat in place behind it, rather than just having it passed across to him as though it were merely an animal.

In the houseyard, the high-walled enclosures where the people live, fighting cocks are kept in wicker cages, moved frequently about so as to maintain the optimum balance of sun and shade. They are fed a special diet, which varies somewhat according to individual theories but which is mostly maize, sifted for impurities with far more care than it is when mere humans are going to eat it, and offered to the animal kernel by kernel. Red pepper is stuffed down their beaks and up their anuses to give them spirit. They are bathed in the same ceremonial preparation of tepid water, medicinal herbs, flowers, and onions in which infants are bathed, and for a prize cock just about as often. Their combs are cropped, their plumage dressed, their spurs trimmed, and their legs massaged, and they are inspected for flaws with the squinted concentration of a diamond merchant. A man who has a passion for cocks, an enthusiast in the literal sense of the term, can spend most of his life with them, and even those, the overwhelming majority, whose passion though intense has not entirely run away with them, can and do spend what seems not only to an outsider, but also to themselves, an inordinate amount of time with them. "I am cock crazy," my landlord, a quite ordinary *afficionado* by Balinese standards, used to moan as he went to move another cage, give another bath, or conduct another feeding. "We're all cock crazy."

The madness has some less visible dimensions, however, because although it is true that cocks are symbolic expressions or magnifications of their owner's self, the narcissistic male ego writ out in Aesopian terms, they are also expressions—and rather more immediate ones—of what the Balinese regard as the direct inversion, aesthetically, morally, and metaphysically, of human status: animality.

The Balinese revulsion against any behavior regarded as animal-like can hardly be overstressed. Babies are not allowed to crawl for that reason. Incest, though hardly approved, is a much less horrifying crime than bestiality. (The appropriate punishment for the second is death by drowning, for the first being forced to live like an animal.[5]) Most demons are represented—in sculpture, dance, ritual, myth—in some real or fantastic animal form. The main puberty rite consists in filing the child's teeth so they will not look like animal fangs. Not only defecation but eating is regarded as a disgusting, almost obscene activity, to be conducted hurriedly and privately, because of its association with animality. Even falling down or any form of clumsiness is considered to be bad for these reasons. Aside from cocks and a few domestic animals—oxen, ducks—of no emotional significance, the Balinese are aversive to animals and treat their large number of dogs not merely callously but with a phobic cruelty. In identifying with his cock, the Balinese man is identifying not just with his ideal self, or even his penis, but also, and at the same time, with what he most fears, hates, and ambivalence being what it is, is fascinated by—"The Powers of Darkness."

The connection of cocks and cockfighting with such Powers, with the animalistic demons that threaten constantly to invade the small, cleared-off space in which the Balinese have so carefully built their lives and devour its inhabitants, is quite explicit. A cockfight, any cockfight, is in the first instance a blood sacrifice offered, with the appropriate chants and oblations, to the demons in order to pacify their ravenous, cannibal hunger. No temple festival should be conducted until one is made. (If it is omitted, someone will inevitably fall into a trance and command with the voice of an angered spirit that the oversight be immediately corrected.) Collective responses to natural evils—illness, crop failure, volcanic eruptions—almost always involve them. And that famous holiday in Bali, "The Day of Silence" (*Njepi*), when everyone sits silent and immobile all day long in order to avoid contact with a sudden influx of demons chased momentarily out of hell, is preceded the previous day by large-scale cockfights (in this case legal) in almost every village on the island.

In the cockfight, man and beast, good and evil, ego and id, the creative power of aroused masculinity and the destructive power of loosened animality fuse in a bloody drama of hatred, cruelty, violence, and death. It is little wonder that when, as is the invariable rule, the owner of the winning cock takes the carcass of the loser—often torn limb from limb by its enraged owner—home to eat, he does so with a mixture of social embarrassment, moral satisfaction, aesthetic disgust, and cannibal joy. Or that a man who has lost an important fight is sometimes driven to wreck his family shrines and curse the gods, an act of metaphysical (and social) suicide. Or that in seeking earthly analogues for heaven and hell the Balinese compare the former to the mood of a man whose cock has just won, the latter to that of a man whose cock has just lost.

The Fight

Cockfights (*tetadjen; sabungan*) are held in a ring about fifty feet square. Usually they begin toward late afternoon and run three or four hours until sunset. About nine or ten separate matches (*sehet*) comprise a program. Each match is precisely like the others in general pattern: there is no main match, no connection between individual matches, no variation in their format, and each is arranged on a completely ad hoc basis. After a fight has ended and the emotional debris is cleaned away—the bets have been paid, the curses cursed, the carcasses possessed—seven, eight, perhaps even a dozen men slip negligently into the ring with a cock and seek to find there a logical opponent for it. This process, which rarely takes less than ten minutes, and often a good deal longer, is conducted in a very subdued, oblique, even dissembling manner. Those not immediately involved give it at best but disguised, sidelong attention; those who, embarrassedly, are, attempt to pretend somehow that the whole thing is not really happening.

A match made, the other hopefuls retire with the same deliberate indifference, and the selected cocks have their spurs (*tadji*) affixed—razor-sharp, pointed steel swords, four or five inches long. This is a delicate job which only a small proportion of men, a half dozen or so in most villages, know how to do properly. The man who attaches the spurs also provides them, and if the rooster he assists wins, its owner awards him the spur-leg of the victim. The spurs are affixed by winding a long length of string around the foot of the spur and the leg of the cock. For reasons I shall come to presently, it is done somewhat differently from case to case, and is an obsessively deliberate affair. The lore about spurs is extensive—they are sharpened only at eclipses and the dark of the moon, should be kept out of the sight of women, and so forth. And they are handled, both in use and out, with the same curious combination of fussiness and sensuality the Balinese direct toward ritual objects generally.

The spurs affixed, the two cocks are placed by their handlers (who may or may not be their owners) facing one another in the center of the ring.[6] A coconut pierced with a small hole is placed in a pail of water, in which it takes about twenty-one seconds to sink, a period known as a *tjeng* and marked at beginning and end by the beating of a slit gong. During these twenty-one seconds the handlers (*pengangkeb*) are not permitted to touch their roosters. If, as sometimes happens, the animals have not fought during this time, they are picked up, fluffed, pulled, prodded, and otherwise insulted, and put back in the center of the ring and the process begins again. Sometimes they refuse to fight at all, or one keeps running away, in which case they are imprisoned together under a wicker cage, which usually gets them engaged.

Most of the time, in any case, the cocks fly almost immediately at one another in a wing-beating, head-thrusting, leg-kicking explosion of animal fury so pure, so absolute, and in its own way so beautiful, as to be almost abstract, a Platonic concept of hate. Within moments one or the other drives home a solid blow with his spur. The handler whose cock has delivered the blow immediately picks it up so that it will not get a return blow, for if he does not the match is likely to end in a mutually mortal tie as the two birds wildly hack each other to pieces. This is particularly true if, as often happens, the spur sticks in its victim's body, for then the aggressor is at the mercy of his wounded foe.

With the birds again in the hands of their handlers, the coconut is now sunk three times after which the cock which has landed the blow must be set down to show that he is firm, a fact he demonstrates by wandering idly around the ring for a coconut sink. The coconut is then sunk twice more and the fight must recommence.

During this interval, slightly over two minutes, the handler of the wounded cock has been working frantically over it, like a trainer patching a mauled boxer between rounds, to get it in shape for a last, desperate try for victory. He blows in its mouth, putting the whole chicken head in his own mouth and sucking and blowing, fluffs it, stuffs its wounds with various sorts of medicines, and generally tries anything he can think of to arouse the last ounce of spirit which may be hidden somewhere within it. By the time he is forced to put it back down he is usually drenched in chicken blood, but, as in prize fighting, a good handler is worth his weight in gold. Some of them can virtually make the dead walk, at least long enough for the second and final round.

In the climactic battle (if there is one; sometimes the wounded cock simply expires in the handler's hands or immediately as it is placed down again), the cock who landed the first blow usually proceeds to finish off his weakened opponent. But this is far from an inevitable outcome, for if a cock can walk, he can fight, and if he can fight, he can kill, and what counts is which cock expires first. If the wounded one can get a stab in and stagger on until the other drops, he is the official winner, even if he himself topples over an instant later.

Surrounding all this melodrama—which the crowd packed tight around the ring follows in near silence, moving their bodies in kinesthetic sympathy with the movement of the animals, cheering their champions on with wordless hand motions, shiftings of the shoulders, turnings of the head, failing back en masse as the cock with the murderous spurs careens toward one side of the ring (it is said that spectators sometimes lose eyes and fingers from being too attentive), surging forward again as they glance off toward another—is a vast body of extraordinarily elaborate and precisely detailed rules.

These rules, together with the developed lore of cocks and cockfighting which accompanies them, are written down in palm-leaf manuscripts (*lontar; rontal*) passed on from generation to generation as part of the general legal and cultural tradition of the villages. At a fight, the umpire (*saja komong; djuru kembar*)—the man who manages the coconut—is in charge of their application and his authority is absolute. I have never seen an umpire's judgment questioned on any subject, even by the more despondent losers, nor have I ever heard, even in private, a charge of unfairness directed against one, or, for that matter, complaints about umpires in general. Only exceptionally well trusted, solid, and, given the complexity of the code, knowledgeable citizens perform this job, and in fact men will bring their cocks only to fights presided over by such men. It is also the umpire to whom accusations of cheating, which, though rare in the extreme, occasionally arise, are referred; and it is he who in the not infrequent cases where the cocks expire virtually together decides which (if either, for, though the Balinese do not care for such an outcome, there can be ties) went first. Likened to a judge, a king, a priest, and a policeman, he is all of these, and under his assured direction the animal passion of the fight proceeds within the civic certainty of the law. In the dozens of cockfights I saw in Bali, I never once saw an altercation about rules. Indeed, I never saw an open altercation, other than those between cocks, at all.

This crosswise doubleness of an event which, taken as a fact of nature, is rage untrammeled and, taken as a fact of culture, is form perfected, defines the cockfight as a sociological entity. A cockfight is what, searching for a name for something not vertebrate enough to be called a group and not structureless enough to be called a crowd, Erving Goffman (1961, 9-10) has called a "focused gathering"—a set of persons engrossed in a common flow of activity and relating to one another in terms of that flow. Such gatherings meet and disperse; the participants in them fluctuate; the activity that focuses them is discrete—a particulate process that reoccurs rather than a continuous one that endures. They take their form from the situation that evokes them, the floor on which they are placed, as Goffman puts it; but it is a form, and an articulate one, nonetheless. For the situation, the floor is itself created, injury deliberations, surgical operations, block meetings, sit ins, cockfights, by the cultural preoccupations—here, as we shall see, the celebration of status rivalry—which not only specify the focus but, assembling actors and arranging scenery, bring it actually into being.

In classical times (that is to say, prior to the Dutch invasion of 1908), when there were no bureaucrats around to improve popular morality, the staging of a cockfight was an explicitly societal matter. Bringing a cock to an important fight was, for an adult male, a compulsory duty of citizenship; taxation of fights, which were usually held on market day, was a major source of public revenue; patronage of the art was a stated responsibility of princes; and the cock ring, or *wantilan,* stood in the center of the village near those other monuments of Balinese civility—the council house, the origin temple, the marketplace, the signal tower, and the banyan tree. Today, a few special occasions aside, the newer rectitude makes so open a statement of the connection between the excitements of collective life and those of blood sport impossible, but, less directly expressed, the connection itself remains intimate and intact. To expose it, however, it is necessary to turn to the aspect of cockfighting around which all the others pivot, and through which they exercise their force, an aspect I have thus far studiously ignored. I mean, of course, the gambling.

Odds and Even Money

The Balinese never do anything in a simple way that they can contrive to do in a complicated one, and to this generalization cockfight wagering is no exception.

In the first place, there are two sorts of bets, or *toh*.[7] There is the single axial bet in the center between the principals (*loh ketengah*), and there is the cloud of peripheral ones around the ring between members of the audience (*toh kesasi*). The first is typically large; the second typically small. The first is collective, involving coalitions of bettors clustering around the owner; the second is individual, man to man. The first is a matter of deliberate, very quiet, almost furtive arrangement by the coalition members and the umpire huddled like conspirators in the center of the ring; the second is a matter of impulsive shouting, public offers, and public acceptances by the excited throng around its edges. And most curiously, and as we shall see most revealingly, where the first is always, without exception, even money, the second, equally without exception, is never such. What is a fair coin in the center is a biased one on the side.

The center bet is the official one, hedged in again with a webwork of rules, and is made between the two cock owners, with the umpire as overseer and public witness.[8] This bet, which, as I say, is always relatively and sometimes very large, is never raised simply by the owner in whose name it is made, but by him together with four or five, sometimes seven or eight, allies—kin, village mates, neighbors, close friends. He may, if he is not especially well-to-do, not even be the major contributor; though, if only to show that he is not involved in any chicanery, he must be a significant one.

Of the fifty-seven matches for which I have exact and reliable data on the center bet, the range is from fifteen ringgits to five hundred, with a mean at eighty-five and with the distribution being rather noticeably trimodal: small fights (15 ringgits either side of 35) accounting for about 45 percent of the total number; medium ones (20 ringgits either side of 70) for about 25 percent; and large (75 ringgits either side of 175) for about 20 percent, with a few very small and very large ones out at the extremes. In a society where the normal daily wage of a manual laborer—a brickmaker, an ordinary farmworker, a market porter—was about three ringgits a day, and considering the fact that fights were held on the average about every two-and-a-half days in the immediate area I studied, this is clearly serious gambling, even if the bets are pooled rather than individual efforts.

The side bets are, however, something else altogether. Rather than the solemn, legalistic pactmaking of the center, wagering takes place rather in the fashion in which the stock exchange used to work when it was out on the curb. There is a fixed and known odds paradigm which runs in a continuous series from ten-to-nine at the short end to two-to-one at the long: 10–9, 9–8, 8–7, 7–6, 6–5, 5–4, 4–3, 3–2, 2–1. The man who wishes to back the *underdog cock* (leaving aside how favorites, *kebut,* and underdogs, *ngai,* are established for the moment) shouts the short-side number indicating the odds he wants to be given. That is, if he shouts *gasal,* "five," he wants the underdog at five-to-four (or, for him, four-to-five); if he shouts "four," he wants it at four-to-three (again, he putting up the "three"); if "nine," at nine-to-eight, and so on. A man backing the favorite, and thus considering giving odds if he can get them short enough, indicates the fact by crying out the color-type of that cock-"brown," "speckled," or whatever.[9]

As odds-takers (backers of the underdog) and odds-givers (backers of the favorite) sweep the crowd with their shouts, they begin to focus in on one another as potential betting pairs, often from far across the ring. The taker tries to shout the giver into longer odds, the giver to shout the taker into shorter ones.[10] The taker, who is the wooer in this situation, will signal how large a bet he wishes to make at the odds he is shouting by holding a number of fingers up in front of his face and vigorously waving them. If the giver, the wooed, replies in kind, the bet is made; if he does not, they unlock gazes and the search goes on.

The side betting, which takes place after the center bet has been made and its size announced, consists then in a rising crescendo of shouts as backers of the underdog offer their propositions to anyone who will accept them, while those who are backing the favorite but do not like the price being offered, shout equally frenetically the color of the cock to show they too are desperate to bet but want shorter odds.

Almost always odds-calling, which tends to be very consensual in that at any one time almost all callers are calling the same thing, starts off toward the long end of the range—five-to-four or four-to-three—and then moves, also consensually, toward the short end with greater or lesser speed and to a greater or lesser degree. Men crying "five" and finding themselves answered only with cries of "brown" start crying "six," either drawing the other callers fairly quickly with them or retiring from the scene as their too-generous offers are snapped up. If the change is made and partners are still scarce, the procedure is repeated in a move to "seven," and so on, only rarely, and in the very largest fights, reaching the ultimate "nine" or "ten" levels. Occasionally, if the cocks are clearly mismatched, there may be no upward movement at all, or even a movement down the scale to four-to-three, three-to-two, very, very rarely two-to-one, a shift which is accompanied by a declining number of bets as a shift upward is accompanied by an increasing number. But the general pattern is for the betting to move a shorter or longer distance up the scale toward the, for sidebets, nonexistent pole of even money, with the overwhelming majority of bets falling in the four-to-three to eight-to-seven range.[11]

As the moment for the release of the cocks by the handlers approaches, the screaming, at least in a match where the center bet is large, reaches almost frenzied proportions as the remaining unfulfilled bettors try desperately to find a last-minute partner at a price they can live with. (Where the center bet is small, the opposite tends to occur: betting dies off, trailing into silence, as odds lengthen and people lose interest.) In a large-bet, well-made match—the kind of match the Balinese regard as "real cockfighting"—the mob scene quality, the sense that sheer chaos is about to break loose, with all those waving, shouting, pushing, clambering men is quite strong, an effect which is only heightened by the intense stillness that falls with instant suddenness, rather as if someone had turned off the current, when the slit gong sounds, the cocks are put down, and the battle begins.

When it ends, anywhere from fifteen seconds to five minutes later, all bets are immediately paid. There are absolutely no IOUs, at least to a betting opponent. One may, of course, borrow from a friend before offering or accepting a wager, but to offer or accept it you must have the money already in hand and, if you lose, you must pay it on the spot, before the next match begins. This is an iron rule, and as I have never heard of a disputed umpire's decision (though doubtless there must sometimes be some), I have also never heard of a welshed bet, perhaps because in a worked-up cockfight crowd the consequences might be, as they are reported to be sometimes for cheaters, drastic and immediate.

It is, in any case, this formal asymmetry between balanced center bets and unbalanced side ones that poses the critical analytical problem for a theory which sees cockfight wagering as the link connecting the fight to the wider world of Balinese culture. It also suggests the way to go about solving it and demonstrating the link.

The first point that needs to be made in this connection is that the higher the center bet, the more likely the match will in actual fact be an even one. Simple considerations of rationality suggest that. If you are betting fifteen ringgits on a cock, you might be willing to go along with even money even if you feel your animal somewhat the less promising. But if you are betting five hundred you are very, very likely to be loathe to do so. Thus, in large-bet fights, which of course involve the better animals, tremendous care is taken to see that the cocks are about as evenly matched as to size, general condition, pugnacity, and so on as is humanly possible. The different ways of adjusting the spurs of the animals are often employed to secure this. If one cock seems stronger, an agreement will be made to position his spur at a slightly less advantageous angle—a kind of handicapping, at which spur affixers are, so it is said, extremely skilled. More care will be taken, too, to employ skillful handlers and to match them exactly as to abilities.

In short, in a large-bet fight the pressure to make the match a genuinely fifty-fifty proposition is enormous, and is consciously felt as such. For medium fights the pressure is somewhat less, and for small ones less yet, though there is always an effort to make things at least approximately equal, for even at fifteen ringgits (five days' work) no one wants to make an even money bet in a clearly unfavorable situation. And, again, what statistics I have tend to bear this out. In my fifty-seven matches, the favorite won thirty-three times overall, the underdog twenty-four, a 1.4:1 ratio. But if one splits the figures at sixty ringgits center bets, the ratios turn out to be 1.1:1 (twelve favorites, eleven underdogs) for those above this line, and 1.6:1 (twenty-one and thirteen) for those below it. Or, if you take the extremes, for very large fights, those with center bets over a hundred ringgits the ratio is 1:1 (seven and seven); for very small fights, those under forty ringgits, it is 1.9:1 (nineteen and ten).[12]

Now, from this proposition—that the higher the center bet the more exactly a fifty-fifty proposition the cockfight is—two things more or less immediately follow: (1) the higher the center bet is, the greater the pull on the side betting toward the short-odds end of the wagering spectrum, and vice versa; (2) the higher the center bet is, the greater the volume of side betting, and vice versa.

The logic is similar in both cases. The closer the fight is in fact to even money, the less attractive the long end of the odds will appear and, therefore, the shorter it must be if there are to be takers. That this is the case is apparent from mere inspection, from the Balinese's own analysis of the matter, and from what more systematic observations I was able to collect. Given the difficulty of making precise and complete recordings of side betting, this argument is hard to cast in numerical form, but in all my cases the odds-giver, odds-taker consensual point, a quite pronounced mini-max saddle where the bulk (at a guess, two-thirds to three-quarters in most cases) of the bets are actually made, was three or four points further along the scale toward the shorter end for the large-center-bet fights than for the small ones, with medium ones generally in between. In detail, the fit is not, of course, exact, but the general pattern is quite consistent: the power of the center bet to pull the side bets toward its own even-money pattern is directly proportional to its size, because its size is directly proportional to the degree to which the cocks are in fact evenly matched. As for the volume question, total wagering is greater in large-center-bet fights because such fights are considered more "interesting," not only in the sense that they are less predictable, but, more crucially, that more is at stake in them—in terms of money, in terms of the quality of the cocks, and consequently, as we shall see, in terms of social prestige.[13]

The paradox of fair coin in the middle, biased coin on the outside is thus a merely apparent one. The two betting systems, though formally incongruent, are not really contradictory to one another, but are part of a single larger system in which the center bet is, so to speak, the "center of gravity," drawing, the larger it is the more so, the outside bets toward the short-odds end of the scale. The center bet thus "makes the game," or perhaps better, defines it, signals what, following a notion of Jeremy Bentham's, I am going to call its "depth."

The Balinese attempt to create an interesting, if you will, "deep," match by making the center bet as large as possible so that the cocks matched will be as equal and as fine as possible, and the outcome, thus, as unpredictable as possible. They do not always succeed. Nearly half the matches are relatively trivial, relatively uninteresting—in my borrowed terminology, "shallow"—affairs. But that fact no more argues against my interpretation than the fact that most painters, poets, and playwrights are mediocre argues against the view that artistic effort is directed toward profundity and, with a certain frequency, approximates it. The image of artistic technique is indeed exact: the center bet is a means, a device, for creating "interesting," "deep" matches, not the reason, or at least not the main reason, why they are interesting, the source of their fascination, the substance of their depth. The question of why such matches are interesting—indeed, for the Balinese, exquisitely absorbing—takes us out of the realm of formal concerns into more broadly sociological and social-psychological ones, and to a less purely economic idea of what "depth" in gaming amounts to.[14]

Playing with Fire

Bentham's concept of "deep play" is found in his *The Theory of Legislation*.[15] By it he means play in which the stakes are so high that it is, from his utilitarian standpoint, irrational for men to engage in it at all. If a man whose fortune is a thousand pounds (or ringgits) wages five hundred of it on an even bet, the marginal utility of the pound he stands to win is clearly less than the marginal disutility of the one he stands to lose. In genuine deep play, this is the case for both parties. They are both in over their heads. Having come together in search of pleasure they have entered into a relationship which will bring the participants, considered collectively, net pain rather than net pleasure. Bentham's conclusion was, therefore, that deep play was immoral from first principles and, a typical step for him, should be prevented legally.

But more interesting than the ethical problem, at least for our concerns here, is that despite the logical force of Bentham's analysis men do engage in such play, both passionately and often, and even in the face of law's revenge. For Bentham and those who think as he does (nowadays mainly lawyers, economists, and a few psychiatrists), the explanation is, as I have said, that such men are irrational—addicts, fetishists, children, fools, savages, who need only to be protected against themselves. But for the Balinese, though naturally they do not formulate it in so many words, the explanation lies in the fact that in such play, money is less a measure of utility, had or expected, than it is a symbol of moral import, perceived or imposed.

It is, in fact, in shallow games, ones in which smaller amounts of money are involved, that increments and decrements of cash are more nearly synonyms for utility and disutility, in the ordinary, unexpanded sense—for pleasure and pain, happiness and unhappiness. In deep ones, where the amounts of money are great, much more is at stake than material gain: namely, esteem, honor, dignity, respect—in a word, though in Bali a profoundly freighted word, status.[16] It is at stake symbolically, for (a few cases of ruined addict gamblers aside) no one's status is actually altered by the outcome of a cockfight; it is only, and that momentarily, affirmed or insulted. But for the Balinese, for whom nothing is more pleasurable than an affront obliquely delivered or more painful than one obliquely received—particularly when mutual acquaintances, undeceived by surfaces, are watching—such appraisive drama is deep indeed.

This, I must stress immediately, is not to say that the money does not matter, or that the Balinese is no more concerned about losing five hundred ringgits than fifteen. Such a conclusion would be absurd. It is because money *does,* in this hardly unmaterialistic society, matter and matter very much that the more of it one risks, the more of a lot of other things, such as one's pride, one's poise, one's dispassion, one's masculinity, one also risks, again only momentarily but again very publicly as well. In deep cockfights an owner and his collaborators, and, as we shall see, to a lesser but still quite real extent also their backers on the outside, put their money where their status is.

It is in large part *because* the marginal disutility of loss is so great at the higher levels of betting that to engage in such betting is to lay one's public self, allusively and metaphorically, through the medium of one's cock, on the line. And though to a Benthamite this might seem merely to increase the irrationality of the enterprise that much further, to the Balinese what it mainly increases is the meaningfulness of it all. And as (to follow Weber rather than Bentham) the imposition of meaning on life is the major end and primary condition of human existence, that access of significance more than compensates for the economic costs involved (Weber 1963).[17] Actually, given the even-money quality of the larger matches, important changes in material fortune among those who regularly participate in them seem virtually nonexistent, because matters more or less even out over the long run. It is, actually, in the smaller, shallow fights, where one finds the handful of more pure, addict-type gamblers involved—those who are in it mainly for the money—that "real" changes in social position, largely downward, are affected. Men of this sort, plungers, are highly dispraised by "true cockfighters" as fools who do not understand what the sport is all about, vulgarians who simply miss the point of it all. They are, these addicts, regarded as fair game for the genuine enthusiasts, those who do understand, to take a little money away from—something that is easy enough to do by luring them, through the force of their greed, into irrational bets on mismatched cocks. Most of them do indeed manage to ruin themselves in a remarkably short time, but there always seems to be one or two of them around, pawning their land and selling their clothes in order to bet, at any particular time.[18]

This graduated correlation of "status gambling" with deeper fights and, inversely, "money gambling" with shallower ones is in fact quite general. Bettors themselves form a sociomoral hierarchy in these terms. As noted earlier, at most cockfights there are, around the very edges of the cockfight area, a large number of mindless, sheer-chance-type gambling games (roulette, dice throw, coin-spin, pea-under-the-shell) operated by concessionaires. Only women, children, adolescents, and various other sorts of people who do not (or not yet) fight cocks—the extremely poor, the socially despised, the personally idiosyncratic—play at these games, at, of course, penny ante levels. Cockfighting men would be ashamed to go anywhere near them. Slightly above these people in standing are those who though they do not themselves fight cocks, bet on the smaller matches around the edges. Next, there are those who fight cocks in small, or occasionally medium matches, but have not the status to join in the large ones, though they may bet from time to time on the side in those. And finally, there are those, the really substantial members of the community, the solid citizenry around whom local life revolves, who fight in the larger fights and bet on them around the side. The focusing element in these focused gatherings, these men generally dominate and define the sport as they dominate and define the society. When a Balinese male talks, in that almost venerative way, about "the true cockfighter," the *bebatoh* ("bettor") or *djuru kurung* ("cage keeper"), it is this sort of person, not those who bring the mentality of the pea-and-shell game into the quite different, inappropriate context of the cockfight, the driven gambler (*potét*, a word which has the secondary meaning of thief or reprobate), and the wistful hanger-on, that they mean. For such a man, what is really going on in a match is something rather closer to an *affaire d'honneur* (though, with the Balinese talent for practical fantasy, the blood that is spilled is only figuratively human) than to the stupid, mechanical crank of a slot machine.

What makes Balinese cockfighting deep is thus not money in itself, but what, the more of it that is involved the more so, money causes to happen: the migration of the Balinese status hierarchy into the body of the cockfight. Psychologically an Aesopian representation of the ideal/demonic, rather narcissistic, male self, sociologically it is an equally Aesopian representation of the complex fields of tension set up by the controlled, muted, ceremonial, but for all that deeply felt, interaction of those selves in the context of everyday life. The cocks may be surrogates for their owners' personalities, animal mirrors of psychic form, but the cockfight is—or more exactly, deliberately is made to be—a simulation of the social matrix, the involved system of cross-cutting, overlapping, highly corporate groups—villages, kingroups, irrigation societies, temple congregations, "castes"— in which its devotees live (see Geertz 1959; Korn 1933). And as prestige, the necessity to affirm it, defend it, celebrate it, justify it, and just plain bask in it (but not, given the strongly ascriptive character of Balinese stratification, to seek it), is perhaps the central driving force in the society, so also—ambulant penises, blood sacrifices, and monetary exchanges aside—is it of the cockfight. This apparent amusement and seeming sport is, to take another phrase from Erving Goffman, "a status bloodbath" (Goffmann 1961, 78).

The easiest way to make this clear, and at least to some degree to demonstrate it, is to invoke the village whose cockfighting activities I observed the closest— the one in which the raid occurred and from which my statistical data are taken.

Like all Balinese villages, this one—Tihingan, in the Klungkung region of southeast Bali—is intricately organized, a labyrinth of alliances and oppositions. But, unlike many, two sorts of corporate groups, which are also status groups, particularly stand out, and we may concentrate on them, in a part-for-whole way, without undue distortion.

First, the village is dominated by four large, patrilineal, partly endogamous descent groups which are constantly vying with one another and form the major factions in the village. Sometimes they group two and two, or rather the two larger ones versus the two smaller ones plus all the unaffiliated people; sometimes they operate independently. There are also subfactions within them, subfactions within the subfactions, and so on to rather fine levels of distinction. And second, there is the village itself, almost entirely endogamous, which is opposed to all the other villages round about in its cockfight circuit (which, as explained, is the market region), but which also forms alliances with certain of these neighbors against certain others in various supravillage political and social contexts. The exact situation is thus, as everywhere in Bali, quite distinctive; but the general pattern of a tiered hierarchy of status rivalries between highly corporate but various based groupings (and, thus, between the members of them) is entirely general.

Consider, then, as support of the general thesis that the cockfight, and especially the deep cockfight, is fundamentally a dramatization of status concerns, the following facts, which to avoid extended ethnographic description I shall simply pronounce to be facts—though the concrete evidence, examples, statements, and numbers that could be brought to bear in support of them, is both extensive and unmistakable:

1. A man virtually never bets against a cock owned by a member of his own kingroup. Usually he will feel obliged to bet for it, the more so the closer the kin tie and the deeper the fight. If he is certain in his mind that it will not win, he may just not bet at all, particularly if it is only a second cousin's bird or if the fight is a shallow one. But as a rule he will feel he must support it and, in deep games, nearly always does. Thus the great majority of the people calling "five" or "speckled" so demonstratively are expressing their allegiance to their kinsman, not their evaluation of his bird, their understanding of probability theory, or even their hopes of unearned income.

2. This principle is extended logically. If your kingroup is not involved you will support an allied kingroup against an unallied one in the same way, and so on through the very involved networks of alliances which, as I say, make up this, as any other, Balinese village.

3. So, too, for the village as a whole. If an outsider cock is fighting any cock from your village, you will tend to support the local one. If, what is a rarer circumstance but occurs every now and then, a cock from outside your cockfight circuit is fighting one inside it, you will also tend to support the "home bird."

4. Cocks which come from any distance are almost always favorites, for the theory is the man would not have dared to bring it if it was not a good cock, the more so the further he has come. His followers are, of course, obliged to support him, and when the more grand-scale legal cockfights are held (on holidays, and so on) the people of the village take what they regard to be the best cocks in the village, regardless of ownership, and go off to support them, although they will almost certainly have to give odds on them and to make large bets to show that they are not a cheapskate village. Actually, such "away games," though infrequent, tend to mend the ruptures between village members that the constantly occurring "home games," where village factions are opposed rather than united, exacerbate.

5. Almost all matches are sociologically relevant. You seldom get two outsider cocks fighting, or two cocks with no particular group backing, or with group backing which is mutually unrelated in any clear way. When you do get them, the game is very shallow, betting very slow, and the whole thing very dull, with no one save the immediate principals and an addict gambler or two at all interested.

6. By the same token, you rarely get two cocks from the same group, even more rarely from the same subfaction, and virtually never from the same sub-subfaction (which would be in most cases one extended family) fighting. Similarly, in outside village fights two members of the village will rarely fight against one another, even though, as bitter rivals, they would do so with enthusiasm on their home grounds.

7. On the individual level, people involved in an institutionalized hostility relationship, called *puik,* in which they do not speak or otherwise have anything to do with each other (the causes of this formal breaking of relations are many:

wife-capture, inheritance arguments, political differences) will bet very heavily, sometimes almost maniacally, against one another in what is a frank and direct attack on the very masculinity, the ultimate ground of his status, of the opponent.

8. The center bet coalition is, in all but the shallowest games, *always* made up by structural allies—no "outside money" is involved. What is "outside" depends upon the context, of course, but given it, no outside money is mixed in with the main bet; if the principals cannot raise it, it is not made. The center bet, again especially in deeper games, is thus the most direct and open expression of social opposition, which is one of the reasons why both it and match-making are surrounded by such an air of unease, furtiveness, embarrassment, and so on.

9. The rule about borrowing money—that you may borrow *for* a bet but not *in* one—stems (and the Balinese are quite conscious of this) from similar considerations: you are never at the *economic* mercy of your enemy that way. Gambling debts, which can get quite large on a rather short-term basis, are always to friends, never to enemies, structurally speaking.

10. When two cocks are structurally irrelevant or neutral so far as you are concerned (though, as mentioned, they almost never are to each other) you do not even ask a relative or a friend whom he is betting on, because if you know how he is betting and he knows you know, and you go the other way, it will lead to strain. This rule is explicit and rigid; fairly elaborate, even rather artificial precautions are taken to avoid breaking it. At the very least you must pretend not to notice what he is doing, and he what you are doing.

11. There is a special word for betting against the grain, which is also the word for "pardon me" (*mpura*). It is considered a bad thing to do, though if the center bet is small it is sometimes all right as long as you do not do it too often. But the larger the bet and the more frequently you do it, the more the "pardon me" tack will lead to social disruption.

12. In fact, the institutionalized hostility relation, *puik,* is often formally initiated (though its causes always lie elsewhere) by such a "pardon me" bet in a deep fight, putting the symbolic fat in the fire. Similarly, the end of such a relationship and resumption of normal social intercourse is often signalized (but, again, not actually brought about) by one or the other of the enemies supporting the other's bird.

13. In sticky, cross-loyalty situations, of which in this extraordinarily complex social system there are of course many, where a man is caught between two more or less equally balanced loyalties, he tends to wander off for a cup of coffee or something to avoid having to bet, a form of behavior reminiscent of that of American voters in similar situations (Berelson, Lazarsfeld, and McPhee 1954).

14. The people involved in the center bet are, especially in deep fights, virtually always leading members of their group—kinship, village, or whatever. Further, those who bet on the side (including these people) are, as I have already remarked, the more established members of the village—the solid citizens. Cockfighting is for those who are involved in the everyday politics of prestige as well, not for youth, women, subordinates, and so forth.

15. So far as money is concerned, the explicitly expressed attitude toward it is that it is a secondary matter. It is not, as I have said, of no importance; Balinese are no happier to lose several weeks' income than anyone else. But they mainly look on the monetary aspects of the cockfight as self-balancing, a matter of just moving money around, circulating it among a fairly well-defined group of serious cockfighters. The really important wins and losses are seen mostly in other terms, and the general attitude toward wagering is not any hope of cleaning up, of making a killing (addict gamblers again excepted), but that of the horse-player's prayer: "Oh, God, please let me break even." In prestige terms, however, you do not want to break even, but, in a momentary, punctuate sort of way, win utterly. The talk (which goes on all the time) is about fights against such-and-such a cock of So-and-So which your cock demolished, not on how much you won, a fact people, even for large bets, rarely remember for any length of time, though they will remember the day they did in Pan Loh's finest cock for years.

16. You must bet on cocks of your own group aside from mere loyalty considerations, for if you do not people generally will say, "What! Is he too proud for the likes of us? Does he have to go to Java or Den Pasar [the capital town] to bet, he is such an important man?" Thus there is a general pressure to bet not only to show that you are important locally, but that you are not so important that you look down on everyone else as unfit even to be rivals. Similarly, home team people must bet against outside cocks or the outsiders will accuse them—a serious charge—of just collecting entry fees and not really being interested in cockfighting, as well as again being arrogant and insulting.

17. Finally, the Balinese peasants themselves are quite aware of all this and can and, at least to an ethnographer, do state most of it in approximately the same terms as I have. Fighting cocks, almost every Balinese I have ever discussed the subject with has said, is like playing with fire only not getting burned. You activate village and kingroup rivalries and hostilities, but in "play" form, coming dangerously and entrancingly close to the expression of open and direct interpersonal and intergroup aggression (something which, again, almost never happens in the normal course of ordinary life), but not quite, because, after all, it is "only a cockfight."

More observations of this sort could be advanced, but perhaps the general point is, if not made, at least well-delineated, and the whole argument thus far can be usefully summarized in a formal paradigm:

THE MORE A MATCH IS . . .
1. Between near status equals (and /or personal enemies)
2. Between high status individuals
THE DEEPER THE MATCH.

THE DEEPER THE MATCH . . .
1. The closer the identification of cock and man (or, more properly, the deeper the match the more the man will advance his best, most closely-identified-with cock).

2. The finer the cocks involved and the more exactly they will be matched.
3. The greater the emotion that will be involved and the more the general absorption in the match.
4. The higher the individual bets center and outside, the shorter the outside bet odds will tend to be, and the more betting there will be overall.
5. The less an "economic" and the more a "status" view of gaming will be involved, and the "solider" the citizens who will be gaming.[19]

Inverse arguments hold for the shallower the fight, culminating, in a reversed-signs sense, in the coin-spinning and dice-throwing amusements. For deep fights there are no absolute upper limits, though there are of course practical ones, and there are a great many legendlike tales of great Duel-in-the-Sun combats between lords and princes in classical times (for cockfighting has always been as much an elite concern as a popular one), far deeper than anything anyone, even aristocrats, could produce today anywhere in Bali.

Indeed, one of the great culture heroes of Bali is a prince, called after his passion for the sport, "The Cockfighter," who happened to be away at a very deep cockfight with a neighboring prince when the whole of his family—father, brothers, wives, sisters—were assassinated by commoner usurpers. Thus spared, he returned to dispatch the upstart, regain the throne, reconstitute the Balinese high tradition, and build its most powerful, glorious, and prosperous state. Along with everything else that the Balinese see in fighting cocks—themselves, their social order, abstract hatred, masculinity, demonic power—they also see the archetype of status virtue, the arrogant, resolute, honor-mad player with real fire, the ksatria prince.[20]

Feathers, Blood, Crowds, and Money

"Poetry makes nothing happen," Auden says in his elegy of Yeats, "it survives in the valley of its saying . . . a way of happening, a mouth." The cockfight too, in this colloquial sense, makes nothing happen. Men go on allegorically humiliating one another and being allegorically humiliated by one another, day after day, glorying quietly in the experience if they have triumphed, crushed only slightly more openly by it if they have not. But no one's status really changes. You cannot ascend the status ladder by winning cockfights; you cannot, as an individual, really ascend it at all. Nor can you descend it that way.[21] All you can do is enjoy and savor, or suffer and withstand, the concocted sensation of drastic and momentary movement along an aesthetic semblance of that ladder, a kind of behind-the-mirror status jump which has the look of mobility without its actuality.

As any art form—for that, finally, is what we are dealing with—the cockfight renders ordinary, everyday experience comprehensible by presenting it in terms of acts and objects which have had their practical consequences removed and been reduced (or, if you prefer, raised) to the level of sheer appearances, where their meaning can be more powerfully articulated and more exactly perceived. The cockfight is "really real" only to the cocks—it does not kill anyone, castrate anyone, reduce anyone to animal status, alter the hierarchical relations among people, or refashion the hierarchy; it does not even redistribute income in any significant way. What it does is what, for other peoples with other temperaments and other conventions, *Lear* and *Crime and Punishment* do; it catches up these themes–death, masculinity, rage, pride, loss, beneficence, chance—and, ordering them into an encompassing structure, presents them in such a way as to throw into relief a particular view of their essential nature. It puts a construction on them, makes them, to those historically positioned to appreciate the construction, meaningful—visible, tangible, graspable—"real," in an ideational sense. An image, fiction, a model, a metaphor, the cockfight is a means of expression; its function is neither to assuage social passions nor to heighten them (though, in its playing-with-fire way it does a bit of both), but, in a medium of feathers, blood, crowds, and money, to display them.

The question of how it is that we perceive qualities in things—paintings, books, melodies, plays—that we do not feel we can assert literally to be there has come, in recent years, into the very center of aesthetic theory (see Goodman 1968; Langer 1953; Merleau-Ponty 1964; Wollheim 1968). Neither the sentiments of the artist, which remain his, nor those of the audience, which remain theirs, can account for the agitation of one painting or the serenity of another. We attribute grandeur, wit, despair, exuberance to strings of sounds; lightness, energy, violence, fluidity to blocks of stone. Novels are said to have strength, buildings eloquence, plays momentum, ballets repose. In this realm of eccentric predicates, to say that the cockfight, in its perfected cases at least, is "disquietful" does not seem at all unnatural, merely, as I have just denied it practical consequence, somewhat puzzling.

The disquietfulness arises, "somehow," out of a conjunction of three attributes of the fight: its immediate dramatic shape; its metaphoric content; and its social context. A cultural figure against a social ground, the fight is at once a convulsive surge of animal hatred, a mock war of symbolical selves, and a formal simulation of status tensions, and its aesthetic power derives from its capacity to force together these diverse realities. The reason it is disquietful is not that it has material effects (it has some, but they are minor); the reason that it is disquietful is that, joining pride to selfhood, selfhood to cocks, and cocks to destruction, it brings to imaginative realization a dimension of Balinese experience normally well-obscured from view. The transfer of a sense of gravity into what is in itself a rather blank and unvarious spectacle, a commotion of beating wings and throbbing legs, is effected by interpreting it as expressive of something unsettling in the way its authors and audience live, or, even more ominously, what they are.

As a dramatic shape, the fight displays a characteristic that does not seem so remarkable until one realizes that it does not have to be there: a radically atomistical structure.[22] Each match is a world unto itself, a particulate burst of form. There is the matchmaking, there is the betting, there is the fight, there is the result—utter triumph and utter defeat—and there is the hurried, embarrassed passing of money. The loser is not consoled. People drift away from him, look around him, leave him to assimilate his momentary descent into nonbeing, reset his face, and return, scarless and intact, to the fray. Nor are winners congratulated, or events rehashed; once a match is ended the crowd's attention turns totally to the next, with no looking back. A shadow of the experience no doubt remains with the principals, perhaps even with some of the witnesses of a deep fight, as it remains with us when we leave the theater after seeing a powerful play well-performed; but it quite soon fades to become at most a schematic memory—a diffuse glow or an abstract shudder-and usually not even that. Any expressive form lives only in its own present—the one it itself creates. But, here, that present is severed into a string of flashes, some more bright than others, but all of them disconnected, aesthetic quanta. Whatever the cockfight says, it says in spurts.

But, as I have argued lengthily elsewhere, the Balinese live in spurts (Geertz 1959). Their life, as they arrange it and perceive it, is less a flow, a directional movement out of the past, through the present, toward the future than an on-off pulsation of meaning and vacuity, an arhythmic alternation of short periods when "something" (that is, something significant) is happening, and equally short ones where "nothing" (that is, nothing much) is—between what they themselves call "full" and "empty" times, or, in another idiom, "junctures" and "holes." In focusing activity down to a burning-glass dot, the cockfight is merely being Balinese in the same way in which everything from the monadic encounters of everyday life, through the clanging pointillism of *gamelan* music, to the visiting-day-of-the-gods temple celebrations are. It is not an imitation of the punctuateness of Balinese social life, nor a depiction of it, nor even an expression of it; it is an example of it, carefully prepared.[23]

If one dimension of the cockfight's structure, its lack of temporal directionality, makes it seem a typical segment of the general social life, however, the other, its flat-out, head-to-head (or spur-to-spur) aggressiveness, makes it seem a contradiction, a reversal, even a subversion of it. In the normal course of things, the Balinese are shy to the point of obsessiveness of open conflict. Oblique, cautious, subdued, controlled, masters of indirection and dissimulation—what they call *alus,* "polished," "smooth"—they rarely face what they can turn away from, rarely resist what they can evade. But here they portray themselves as wild and murderous, with manic explosions of instinctual cruelty. A powerful rendering of life as the Balinese most deeply do not want it (to adapt a phrase Frye has used of Gloucester's blinding) is set in the context of a sample of it as they do in fact have it (Frye 1964, 99). And, because the context suggests that the rendering, if less than a straightforward description, is nonetheless more than an idle fancy; it is here that the disquietfulness—the disquietfulness of the fight, not (or, anyway, not necessarily) its patrons, who seem in fact rather thoroughly to enjoy it—emerges. The slaughter in the cock ring is not a depiction of how things literally are among men, but, what is almost worse, of how, from a particular angle, they imaginatively are.[24]

The angle, of course, is stratificatory. What, as we have already seen, the cockfight talks most forcibly about is status relationships, and what it says about them is that they are matters of life and death. That prestige is a profoundly serious business is apparent everywhere one looks in Bali—in the village, the family, the economy, the state. A peculiar fusion of Polynesian title ranks and Hindu castes, the hierarchy of pride is the moral backbone of the society. But only in the cockfight are the sentiments upon which that hierarchy rests revealed in their natural colors. Enveloped elsewhere in a haze of etiquette, a thick cloud of euphemism and ceremony, gesture and allusion, they are here expressed in only the thinnest disguise of an animal mask, a mask which in fact demonstrates them far more effectively than it conceals them. Jealousy is as much a part of Bali as poise, envy as grace, brutality as charm; but without the cockfight the Balinese would have a much less certain understanding of them, which is, presumably, why they value it so highly.

Any expressive form works (when it works) by disarranging semantic contexts in such a way that properties conventionally ascribed to certain things are unconventionally ascribed to others, which are then seen actually to possess them. To call the wind a cripple, as Stevens does, to fix tone and manipulate timbre, as Schoenberg does, or, closer to our case, to picture an art critic as a dissolute bear, as Hogarth does, is to cross conceptual wires; the established conjunctions between objects and their qualities are altered, and phenomena—fall weather, melodic shape, or cultural journalism—are clothed in signifiers which normally point to other referents.[25] Similarly, to connect—and connect, and connect—the collision of roosters with the divisiveness of status is to invite a transfer of perceptions from the former to the latter, a transfer which is at once a description and a judgment. (Logically, the transfer could, of course, as well go the other way; but, like most of the rest of us, the Balinese are a great deal more interested in understanding men than they are in understanding cocks.)

What sets the cockfight apart from the ordinary course of life, lifts it from the realm of everyday practical affairs, and surrounds it with an aura of enlarged importance is not, as functionalist sociology would have it, that it reinforces status discriminations (such reinforcement is hardly necessary in a society where every act proclaims them), but that it provides a metasocial commentary upon the whole matter of assorting human beings into fixed hierarchical ranks and then organizing the major part of collective existence around that assortment. Its function, if you want to call it that, is interpretive: it is a Balinese reading of Balinese experience, a story they tell themselves about themselves.

Saying Something of Something

To put the matter this way is to engage in a bit of metaphorical refocusing of one's own, for it shifts the analysis of cultural forms from an endeavor in general parallel to dissecting an organism, diagnosing a symptom, deciphering a code, or ordering a system—the dominant analogies in contemporary anthropology—to one in general parallel with penetrating a literary text. If one takes the cockfight, or any other collectively sustained symbolic structure, as a means of "saying something of something" (to invoke a famous Aristotelian tag), then one is faced with a problem not in social mechanics but social semantics.[26] For the anthropologist, whose concern is with formulating sociological principles, not with promoting or appreciating cockfights, the question is, what does one learn about such principles from examining culture as an assemblage of texts?

Such an extension of the notion of a text beyond written material, and even beyond verbal, is, though metaphorical, not, of course, all that novel. The *interpretatio naturae* tradition of the middle ages, which, culminating in Spinoza, attempted to read nature as Scripture, the Nietszchean effort to treat value systems as glosses on the will to power (or the Marxian one to treat them as glosses on property relations), and the Freudian replacement of the enigmatic text of the manifest dream with the plain one of the latent, all offer precedents, if not equally recommendable ones (Ricoeur 1970). But the idea remains theoretically undeveloped; and the more profound corollary, so far as anthropology is concerned, that cultural forms can be treated as texts, as imaginative works built out of social materials, has yet to be systematically exploited.[27]

In the case at hand, to treat the cockfight as a text is to bring out a feature of it (in my opinion, the central feature of it) that treating it as a rite or a pastime, the two most obvious alternatives, would tend to obscure: its use of emotion for cognitive ends. What the cockfight says it says in a vocabulary of sentiment—the thrill of risk, the despair of loss, the pleasure of triumph. Yet what it says is not merely that risk is exciting, loss depressing, or triumph gratifying, banal tautologies of affect, but that it is of these emotions, thus exampled, that society is built and individuals are put together. Attending cockfights and participating in them is, for the Balinese, a kind of sentimental education. What he learns there is what his culture's ethos and his private sensibility (or, anyway, certain aspects of them) look like when spelled out externally in a collective text; that the two are near enough alike to be articulated in the symbolics of a single such text; and—the disquieting part—that the text in which this revelation is accomplished consists of a chicken hacking another mindlessly to bits.

Every people, the proverb has it, loves its own form of violence. The cockfight is the Balinese reflection on theirs: on its look, its uses, its force, its fascination. Drawing on almost every level of Balinese experience, it brings together themes—animal savagery, male narcissism, opponent gambling, status rivalry, mass excitement, blood sacrifice—whose main connection is their involvement with rage and the fear of rage, and, binding them into a set of rules which at once contains them and allows them play, builds a symbolic structure in which, over and over again, the reality of their inner affiliation can be intelligibly felt. If, to quote Northrop Frye again, we go to see *Macbeth* to learn what a man feels like after he has gained a kingdom and lost his soul, Balinese go to cockfights to find out what a man, usually composed, aloof, almost obsessively self-absorbed, a kind of moral autocosm, feels like when, attacked, tormented, challenged, insulted, and driven in result to the extremes of fury, he has totally triumphed or been brought totally low. The whole passage, as it takes us back to Aristotle (though to the Poetics rather than the Hermeneutics), is worth quotation:

> But the poet [as opposed to the historian], Aristotle says, never makes any real statements at all, certainly no particular or specific ones. The poet's job is not to tell you what happened, but what happens: not what did take place, but the kind of thing that always does take place. He gives you the typical, recurring, or what Aristotle calls universal event. You wouldn't go to Macbeth to learn about the history of Scotland—you go to it to learn

what a man feels like after he's gained a kingdom and lost his soul. When you meet such a character as Micawber in Dickens, you don't feel that there must have been a man Dickens knew who was exactly like this: you feel that there's a bit of Micawber in almost everybody you know, including yourself. Our impressions of human life are picked up one by one, and remain for most of us loose and disorganized. But we constantly find things in literature that suddenly coordinate and bring into focus a great many such impressions, and this is part of what Aristotle means by the typical or universal human event. (Frye 1964, 63-64)

It is this kind of bringing of assorted experiences of everyday life to focus that the cockfight, set aside from that life as "only a game" and reconnected to it as "more than a game," accomplishes, and so creates what, better than typical or universal, could be called a paradigmatic human event—that is, one that tells us less what happens than the kind of thing that would happen if, as is not the case, life were art and could be as freely shaped by styles of feeling as *Macbeth* and *David Copperfield* are.

Enacted and re-enacted, so far without end, the cockfight enables the Balinese, as, read and reread, *Macbeth* enables us, to see a dimension of his own subjectivity. As he watches fight after fight, with the active watching of an owner and a bettor (for cockfighting has no more interest as a pure spectator sport than does croquet or dog racing), he grows familiar with it and what it has to say to him, much as the attentive listener to string quartets or the absorbed viewer of still life grows slowly more familiar with them in a way which opens his subjectivity to himself.[28]

Yet, because—in another of those paradoxes, along with painted feelings and unconsequenced acts, which haunt aesthetics—that subjectivity does not properly exist until it is thus organized, art forms generate and regenerate the very subjectivity they pretend only to display. Quartets, still lifes, and cockfights are not merely reflections of a pre-existing sensibility analogically represented; they are positive agents in the creation and maintenance of such a sensibility. If we see ourselves as a pack of Micawbers, it is from reading too much Dickens (if we see ourselves as unillusioned realists, it is from reading too little); and similarly for Balinese, cocks, and cockfights. It is in such a way, coloring experience with the light they cast it in, rather than through whatever material effects they may have, that the arts play their role, as arts, in social life.[29]

In the cockfight, then, the Balinese forms and discovers his temperament and his society's temper at the same time. Or, more exactly, he forms and discovers a particular facet of them. Not only are there a great many other cultural texts providing commentaries on status hierarchy and self-regard in Bali, but there are a great many other critical sectors of Balinese life besides the stratificatory and the agonistic that receive such commentary. The ceremony consecrating a Brahmana priest, a matter of breath control, postural immobility, and vacant concentration upon the depths of being, displays a radically different, but to the Balinese equally real, property of social hierarchy—its reach toward the numinous transcendent. Set not in the matrix of the kinetic emotionality of animals, but in that of the static passionlessness of divine mentality, it expresses tranquillity not disquiet. The mass festivals at the village temples, which mobilize the whole local population in elaborate hostings of visiting gods—songs, dances, compliments, gifts—assert the spiritual unity of village mates against their status inequality and project a mood of amity and trust.[30] The cockfight is not the master key to Balinese life, any more than bullfighting is to Spanish. What it says about that life is not unqualified nor even unchallenged by what other equally eloquent cultural statements say about it. But there is nothing more surprising in this than in the fact that Racine and Moliére were contemporaries, or that the same people who arrange chrysanthemums cast swords.[31]

The culture of a people is an ensemble of texts, themselves ensembles, which the anthropologist strains to read over the shoulders of those to whom they properly belong. There are enormous difficulties in such an enterprise, methodological pitfalls to make a Freudian quake, and some moral perplexities as well. Nor is it the only way that symbolic forms can be sociologically handled. Functionalism lives, and so does psychologism. But to regard such forms as "saying something of something," and saying it to somebody, is at least to open up the possibility of an analysis which attends to their substance rather than to reductive formulas professing to account for them.

As in more familiar exercises in close reading, one can start anywhere in a culture's repertoire of forms and end up anywhere else. One can stay, as I have here, within a single, more or less bounded form, and circle steadily within it. One can move between forms in search of broader unities or informing contrasts. One can even compare forms from different cultures to define their character in reciprocal relief. But whatever the level at which one operates, and however intricately, the guiding principle is the same: societies, like lives, contain their own interpretations. One has only to learn how to gain access to them.

References

Bateson, G., and M. Mead. 1942. *Balinese character: A photographic analysis*. New York.
Belo, J. 1970. The Balinese temper. In *Traditional Balinese culture*, edited by J. Belo. New York.
Berelson, B. R., P. Lazarsfeld, and W. N. McPhee. 1954. *Voting: A study of opinion formation in a presidential campaign*. Chicago.
Frye, N. 1964. *The educated imagination*. Bloomington, IN.
Geertz, C. 1959. Form and variation in Balinese village structure. *American Anthropologist* 61: 94-108.
Goffman, E. 1961. *Encounters: Two studies in the sociology of interaction*. Indianapolis.
Goodman, N. 1968. *Languages of art*. Indianapolis.
Hooykaas, C. 1958. *The Lay of the Jaya Prana*. London.
Korn, V. 1933. *De Dorsrepubliek tnganan Pagringsingan*. Santpoort, Netherlands.
———. 1932. *Het Adatrecht van Bali*, 2d ed. The Hague.
Langer, S. 1953. *Feeling and form*. New York.
Merleau-Ponty, M. 1964. The eye and the mind. In *The primacy of perception*. Evanston, IL.
Ricoeur, P. 1970. *Freud and philosophy*. New Haven.
Weber, M. 1963. *The sociology of religion*. Boston.
Wollheim, R. 1968. *Art and its objects*. New York.

PART IV
Civil Society and Social Capital

Introduction

Do different sorts of political arrangements (monarchy, republicanism etc.) require and/or produce a particular type of political culture? Machiavelli, Montesquieu, Rousseau, Tocqueville, and Weber, among others, have thought so. Over thirty years ago, in the context of the cold war, Almond and Verba (1963) conducted a landmark social science study and reported that what they called the "civic culture" fostered democracy. By a civic culture they referred to a competent, self-confident citizenry that was: (1) well informed about political issues; (2) socially interactive in terms of exchanging opinions and devoting some leisure time to social pursuits, such as membership in voluntary associations; and (3) participatory in terms of voting and contacting elected and other public officials about matters of concern. Several contemporary communitarian theorists have recommended even more ambitious conceptions of civil society for invigorating the character of American democracy (Etzioni 1996; Pateman 1971, 1980, 57-102; Sandel 1982, 1996).

Democracy's recent spread across societies and concern for consolidating these democratic gains have renewed American political scientists' interest in the sort(s) of political culture(s) compatible with the development of democracy. The most common term employed to denote a political culture that fits democracy today is "civil society." While different authors attend to different aspects, civil society includes citizens' awareness of the political aspects of social life, favorable evaluations of their political institutions, positive feelings toward these institutions, and a variety of participatory activities (e.g., actively discussing political issues, serving in various voluntary capacities, voting, contacting public officials over matters of concern) presumably prompted by these beliefs and values. Robert Putnam, a prominent researcher in this area, uses the term "social capital" roughly as a synonym for civil society. (See chapter 12.)

Two central issues dominate this area of studies in culture and politics. First, some of the earlier political theorists who developed the ideal of civic virtue (a version of civil society) in their normative exhortations characterized this concept with levels of citizen involvement that appear remarkably altruistic and thus unrealistic against the background of contemporary advanced industrial society or, alternatively, undesirable for various practical reasons. So, is civil society a figment of utopian imagination, or does the concept have sensible, concrete bases? Chapter 11, by Shelley Burtt, takes up some aspects of this issue and argues, to paraphrase Tocqueville, that civic virtue—rightly understood—is in citizens' self-interest.

While Burtt does a nice job of summarizing the "classical" thesis on civic virtue and drawing attention to more realistic contemporary versions, her argument largely sidesteps two practical difficulties. First, as Olson (1965) points out, strong temptations exist for "free ridership" among groups as large and weakly organized as a society's citizens. That is, any one citizen's participation is unlikely to make a difference even at the local level, so—in the absence of impressive organizational pressures—each citizen is apt to opt out of engaging in time-consuming political activities and to ride free on the efforts of others. If a sufficient proportion of the citizenry adopts this individually rational orientation, civil society may fail to emerge. From this perspective civil society appears to be limited to people with especially strong incentives for what are called expressive or symbolic benefits: that is, people with particularly strong needs to signal their support of certain views or who derive intrinsic pleasure from engaging in political activity. Second, some scholars maintain that extensive political participation overloads channels of political communication and possibly state capacities as well. Thus they argue that democracy works better when elected elites are left relatively free from ordinary citizens' claims on their time and other resources. For a discussion of the practical problems of government overload that some associate with an active citizenry, see Huntington, Crozier and Watanuki (1975) and Rose and Peters (1978).

A second issue involves the flow of causation between civil society and democracy. Does civil society foster democracy, or is it a consequence of democratic political institutions? This issue has been hotly contested. Inglehart (1988) argues that civic culture (civil society) fosters democracy, but Muller and Seligson (1994) respond that civil society is the result of democratic political conditions. Inglehart (1997; see also chapter 18 herein by Inglehart and Carballo) clarifies a pattern of reciprocal causation whereby varying levels of economic development foster distinctive orientations toward political life. In turn, these orientations sustain expectations for distinctive political institutions, some of which are decidedly more democratic than others. (With respect to controversies focused on Inglehart's research, see part VI.)

In the following readings, we take up this question in two chapters. In chapter 12, Robert D. Putnam contends that recent decline in American democracy, a subject of concern for numerous analysts, has its roots in the tapering off of social capital (civil society) in the United States. That is, since civil society fosters democracy, when civil society atrophies, democracy suffers (Putnam 1993). In chapter 13, Sidney Tarrow reviews Putnam's more extensive studies on civic republicanism (civil society) and Italian democracy, arguing that Putnam's data suggest civil society is the result of democracy.

References and Further Reading

Ackerman, B. 1984. The Storrs lectures: Discovering the Constitution. *Yale Law Journal* 93: 1013-1072.
Almond, G., and S. Verba. 1963. *The civic culture: Political attitudes and democracy in five nations.* Princeton, NJ: Princeton University Press.
Barber, B. 1984. *Strong democracy: Participatory politics for a new age.* Berkeley: University of California Press.
Bellah, R., R. Madsen, W. Sullivan, A. Swidler, and S. Tipton. 1985. *Habits of the heart: Individualism and commitment in American life.* Berkeley: University of California Press.
Burtt, S. 1993. The politics of virtue today: A critique and a proposal. *American Political Science Review* 87: 360-368..
Elkin, S. 1987. *City and regime in the American republic.* Chicago: University of Chicago Press.
Etzioni, A. 1996. *The new golden rule: Community and morality in a democratic society.* New York: Basic.
Huntington, S., M. Crozier, and J. Watanuki. 1975. *The crisis of democracy: Report to the Trilateral Commission of the task force on governability of democracies.* New York: New York University Press.
Inglehart, R. 1988. The renaissance of political culture. *American Political Science Review* 82: 1203-1230.
———. 1997. *Modernization and postmodernization: Cultural, economic and political change in 43 societies.* Princeton, NJ: Princeton University Press.
Inglehart, R., and M. Carballo. 1997. Does Latin America exist? (And is there a Confucian culture?): A global analysis of cross-cultural differences. *PS: Political Science and Politics* 30: 34-47.
Muller, E., and M. Seligson. 1994. Civic culture and democracy: The question of causal relationships. *American Political Science Review* 88: 635-652.
Olson, M. 1965. *The logic of collective action.* Cambridge, MA: Harvard University Press.
Pateman, C. 1971. Political culture, political structure and political change. *British Journal of Political Science* 1: 291-305.
———. 1980. The civic culture: A philosophic critique. In *The civic culture revisited,* edited by G. Almond and S. Verba. Boston: Little, Brown.
Putnam, R. 1993. The prosperous community: Social capital and public life. *The American Prospect* 13 (Spring): 35-42.
———. 1995a. Bowling alone: America's declining social capital. *Journal of Democracy* 6: 65-78.
———. 1995b. Tuning in, tuning out: The strange disappearance of social capital in America. *PS: Political Science and Politics* 28: 664-683.
Putnam, R., with R. Leonardi and R. Nanetti. 1988. Institutional performance and political culture: Some puzzles about the power of the past. *Governance* 1: 221-242.
———. 1993. *Making democracy work: Civic traditions in modern Italy.* Princeton: NJ: Princeton University Press.
Rose, R., and G. Peters. 1978. *Can government go bankrupt?* New York: Basic.
Sandel, M. 1982. *Liberalism and the limits of justice.* New York: Cambridge University Press.
———. 1996. *Democracy's discontent: America in search of a public philosophy.* Cambridge, MA: Harvard University Press.
Tarrow, S. 1996. Making social science work across space and time: A critical reflection on Robert Putnam's *Making democracy work. American Political Science Review* 90: 389-397.

CHAPTER 11

The Politics of Virtue Today: A Critique and a Proposal
Shelley Burtt

Originally published in
American Political Science Review 87 (2), 1993.

READING INTRODUCTION

Burtt initially distinguishes various strands of thought on civic virtue, particularly a public, participatory republican version (e.g., Rousseau or Tocqueville) and a more private, less participatory liberal orientation (e.g., J. S. Mill). Then, drawing especially on Machiavelli and Rousseau, Burtt argues that classical conceptions of civic virtue simply demand too much from humans who are typically concerned with personal ambition and comfort. Burtt finds that some contemporary versions of civic virtue (Barber 1984; Bellah et al. 1985; Etzioni 1996; Sandel 1982; 1996) are similarly unrealistic. Finally, drawing on the eighteenth-century English classic *Cato's Letters* and two contemporary American political analysts (Elkin 1987; Ackerman 1984), Burtt argues that civic virtue can be envisioned in a much more practical and socially salutary way by basing it on citizen self-interest.

READING TEXT

I argue for a distinction between publicly oriented and privately oriented conceptions of civic virtue. I first provide a critique of two current politics of virtue (liberal and republican), arguing (1) that despite their differences, they are both publicly oriented and (2) that their problems lie in this public orientation. I conclude by arguing for the legitimacy and promise of a privately oriented politics of civic virtue, using as examples of this approach *Cato's Letters* from the early eighteenth century and the work of two contemporary theorists, Bruce Ackerman and Stephen Elkin.

In recent years, political philosophers across the ideological spectrum have rediscovered virtue. In fact, the idea of reinvigorating public life with suitable doses of citizenly devotion has proved so compelling to theorists in recent years that we can identify a range of politics of virtue on offer today, each with its own problems and possibilities.

Proponents of an Aristotelian politics of virtue want to make the cultivation of personal and public virtues the primary end of political life. They argue that modern governments can and should follow the example of Aristotle's best constitution and give "first place to considerations of excellence of character and how it may be cultivated" (Budziszewski 1988, 17). For these neo-Aristotelians, character development is the province not only of Mom, Dad, and the Boy Scouts, but of legislatures and the courts. Nurturing a sense of "rational purposefulness" or "rational self-understanding" in the citizenry and politically rewarding its presence can and should be the primary goal of all good polities, including liberal democratic ones (17, 11).[1]

When it frames the proposed tasks of government with appropriate caution—informed, perhaps, by a liberal skepticism toward political authority—the Aristotelian perspective on virtue can offer a compelling vision of public life. Certainly, advocates of such a politics make a convincing case that some sustained attention to the virtues of the citizen body is both possible and desirable today. Still, to find the Aristotelian approach completely satisfying, one must believe that the end of politics in contemporary constitutional democracies ought to be, or inevitably is, the cultivation of virtue. I want to focus here on an alternate and at least equally influential approach to citizen virtue, one that works within a more conventional understanding of the ends of politics.

We might call this species of virtue politics *instrumental* in that the development of virtuous citizens is not seen as the end or purpose of political life. Rather, the political or civic virtues are praised for being especially good means to the advancement of other worthy political ends, such as liberty, equality, democracy, and order. Thus, communitarians and other participants in the republican revival tend to identify as civic virtues those qualities that would make private individuals more citizenly, involving them more actively in a democratic polity. Liberals willing to broach the topic of virtue at all urge the cultivation or appreciation of character traits that would make citizens better liberals (e.g., personal autonomy, tolerance). While the dispositions recommended in these contexts generally represent certain moral excellences, they are not valued or pursued for this reason. Rather, they are conceived, in more instrumental terms, as those dispositions or characteristics of the person that best fit individuals to contribute to the flourishing of their political community.

Typically, those who have attempted to assess the claims made by this more instrumental politics of virtue have proceeded on two fronts: they debate the relative merits of a particular theorist's conception of civic virtue or argue about which vision of the good citizen is more attractive—the liberals' or republicans'. Such criticism, however, while valuable, fails to go far enough and does not take seriously the *politics* of the politics of virtue. Both the liberal and republican politics of virtue offered today at least implicitly urge a particular course of political action, namely, the cultivation of the desired virtues or character traits in the contemporary citizenry. Any evaluation of the modern politics of virtue must respect these real-world aspirations and judge competing conceptions of political virtue at least partially on whether they make proper allowances for the nature, habits, and spirit of the people they hope to reform.

This standard does not mean rank-ordering political theories according to the chances of their visions' being realized. On the other hand, proposals for the renewal of political life that presuppose resources, capabilities, and political will that until now have been completely absent from any modern polity may properly be criticized for their utopian quality. I suggest a new set of categories by which to judge the politics of virtue, one which moves beyond the standard liberal/republican distinction to a new view of the varieties of political virtue and their relative potentials for political success in contemporary constitutional democracies.[2]

The Varieties of Virtue

Public and Private

For certain modern commentators, the term *civic virtue* stands simply for "the moral and political qualities that make a good citizen," in whatever regime the citizen may be found (Walzer 1980, 55; see also Sinopoli 1987, 344). This conflation of civic and political virtue has the advantage of simplicity yet slights the particularly charged quality that the former term has acquired in recent years. To say that individuals have *civic* virtue seems to say something very definite about the regime in which these virtuous individuals live, the qualities they possess, and the activities in the public realm that these qualities support or to which they dispose. For this reason, I treat civic virtue as a specific sort of political virtue, one particularly appropriate to, and manifested in, a political regime that allows for a civic mode of fife. This civic, as opposed to merely political, mode of life is one grounded in "participatory self-rule." It is bounded on one side by despotism and on the other by extreme forms of "procedural liberalism" (Taylor 1989, 178, 172). Between these poles lie a variety of regimes in which individuals participate, to a greater or lesser extent, in the shaping of their collective destiny.

The accounts of civic virtue with which we are most familiar posit a stark divide between public and private. Within the republican tradition, especially, the qualities praised as virtuous are those that enable or dispose the citizen to privilege the public, political realm over private, personal desires and ambitions.[3] Thus, Carter Braxton, writing during the American Revolution, defines public virtue as "a disinterested attachment to the public good, exclusive and independent of all private and selfish interest" (cited in Wood 1969, 96). Historians of political thought echo this terminology: "For most classical republicans, liberty could only be achieved by each man's willingness to renounce his purely private concerns for the greater good of the community" (Pagden 1987, 10; see also Kramnick 1988, 15; Wood l969, 68). In all these examples, the qualities that make a citizen virtuous, while variously described, hinge on a mind-set in which the goods of the public realm, the world of political action and deliberation, are given priority over private goods—whether from a rational decision to set aside "private interests" or from an intense emotional engagement with the public and its goods (liberty, national honor, political action itself).[4] I call conceptions of political or civic virtue grounded in such a mindset *publicly oriented*.

There is however no necessary identity between the qualities that advance the flourishing of the state and safeguard political liberty and the sort of aggressively public-minded self-sacrificing behavior praised by representatives of the republican tradition. Public spirit, patriotism, love of country, love of equality, and the willingness to subordinate private to public good are simply the particular answers given consistently throughout the republican tradition to the question, What citizen excellences are necessary to preserve a free and flourishing society? But it is at least conceivable that individuals would be able to serve a civic regime without possessing the passionate attachment to the polity and its needs that grounds the more familiar sort of publicly oriented civic virtue just described. This is not to say that such individuals would suddenly have become "perfect privatists," inhabitants of a liberal state that asks nothing from them but that they treat others and others' life goals with equal concern and respect.[5] Rather, their civic virtues would rest on a different basis from the enthusiastic or self-sacrificing "public spirit" characteristic of the republican tradition. Civic virtues of this sort I call *privately oriented*.

Keeping this distinction between publicly and privately oriented virtue in mind, we can now consider more closely the various contemporary liberal and republican politics of virtue on offer today. I want to show both that these politics endorse a publicly oriented form of civic virtue and that this public orientation creates problems for both the possibility and desirability of establishing a politics of virtue today.

Liberal and Republican

Contemporary theorists proposing a republican politics of virtue usually characterize the good citizen as the good deliberator, someone who participates eagerly and competently in the conversations that are central to twentieth-century republicans' understanding of good political life. Interestingly, what makes a good deliberator for these contemporary republicans is not the sort of aggressively public-minded, self-sacrificing behavior praised by earlier representatives of the republican tradition. Rather, the requisite quality is "critical distance from prevailing desires and practices" (Sunstein 1988, 1549), or, the "capacity for reflexively critical reconsideration of [one's] ends and commitments" (Michelman 1988, 1528). To deliberate well about common ends—to exercise republican civic virtue—requires some degree of detachment from self, the subordination of personal interest to the practice of dialogue.

The growing number of liberal theorists prepared to endorse a politics of virtue describe the end of the good polity and the citizen virtues that advance it in a somewhat different way. Stephen Macedo (1990) in his book *Liberal Virtues* argues that the best liberal regime endorses a "situated autonomy," grounded in the free individual's "critical capacity to interpret and shape nature and desire" (213). Rogers Smith (1985) places a similarly demanding conception of individual liberty at the center of the liberal state. A liberal polity, he argues, dedicates itself to "what has always been the deepest concern of liberal thought, the promotion of personal capacities for reflective self-direction" (171).

These passages suggest that liberals, as well as republicans, consider the ability to distance oneself from one's immediate preferences as crucial to good citizenship. But while republican citizens place their critical abilities in the service of an expansive and directed dialogue with their fellow countrymen, good liberal citizens (as befits the liberal satisfaction with representative democracy) are primarily good judges—of the actions of their representatives, of the achievements of their government, of the state of their liberties. Smith, for example, envisions the good citizen as a sort of public ombudsman continually assessing how he or she, as well as society at large, measures up to the goals set by the ideal of rational liberty. Good citizens must, first of all, look inward, cultivating liberal dispositions on a personal level. They must then look outward, judging, urging, and prodding their government to a better realization of liberal ideals: "Particularly when they act as collective deliberative self-governors, through democratic political processes, such liberal citizens should ask whether basic economic, educational and cultural arrangements are working adequately to empower all, or whether some are being systematically neglected or constrained. When such oppressive political and social institutions are found, a liberal polity must seek their reconstruction" (Smith 1985, 291). Macedo (1990) too, identifies the demeanor of the good citizen as one of "critical reflectiveness on public principles," writing that "liberal citizens are called upon to take up the attitude of the ideal judge, Hercules, and to act in politics as critical interpreters of public moral principles" (128, 102).[6]

Both liberals and republicans then offer an account of civic virtue for our consideration, a description of the dispositions needed to keep a regime free and flourishing. Liberals want citizens who judge well, republicans, ones who deliberate well. Despite the difference in context and evidence, these various politics of virtue ground a citizen's excellence—performance of praiseworthy political deeds—in an emotional engagement with the polity and its principles. Whether the mark of civic virtue is the ability to deliberate well or to judge perceptively, the anterior requirement is to embrace, in thought and deed, the public world, to engage in politics for abstractly public reasons.

Thus, Benjamin Barber (1984), after identifying "civility" as the characteristic civic virtue of good democrats, admits that his politics requires "an infusion of communitarian values." Loyalty, fraternity, patriotism, neighborliness, bonding, tradition, mutual affection, and common belief are all necessary to make his strong democrats willing—indeed, eager—to attend neighborhood political assemblies, to inform themselves and vote in national referenda, to explore the content of the country's common good. So the good deliberator must, in fact, possess a very public civic virtue, that is, devotion to the participatory politics that underlies the republican vision of political community (243).

The liberal politics of virtue also envisions a virtue grounded in an emotional commitment to the public realm, a passionate attachment to public goods and practices. Smith (1989) argues that "a liberal polity should be united . . . by a shared political and social purpose: to promote ways of life that advance liberty for all" (290). Macedo (1990), too, calls for "citizens united by their devotion to a public morality," individuals willing to affirm the ideal of liberal justice "as a supreme moral commitment" (273, 255). Good liberals, then, like good republicans, act out of commitment to a very public purpose—in this case, a demanding philosophy of liberty, a desire "to promote ways of life that advance liberty for all," an end they seek not out of any Tocquevillean "enlightened self-interest" but because it is right and good for the community as a whole, since for virtuous citizens, furthering the "commitment [to rational liberty] is what their civic life is really all about" (Smith 1989, 290).

These publicly oriented conceptions of civic virtue receive an eloquent defense in the various works already discussed. But how plausible are any of these accounts when considered as real political proposals? Would an effort actually to cultivate these specific qualities in the modern citizen, to create the political and social institutions needed to nurture virtuous citizens be possible or desirable?

In fact, neither liberal nor republican versions of the politics of virtue hold much promise for engaging the political enthusiasms of the American people or of successfully negotiating the democratic political process. This is not to deny that each presents a challenging and at times compelling vision of what, in ideal circumstances, good citizens of the modern polity might look like. But despite what first appearances might suggest, the theories discussed all advance robustly *public* conceptions of the good citizen and, as such, are subject to a number of difficulties that recommend another sort of civic virtue to our attention.

The Problem with Public Virtue

The precariousness of public virtue in the contemporary world has been observed and lamented before. But I shall propose a different explanation for such precariousness from those usually offered. Those who doubt the possibility of a genuinely civic virtue today often blame the emergence of liberal, commercial society for making a robust involvement with, or dedication to, public ends unlikely or impossible. But whatever the impact of liberal ideals or a market economy on individuals' sense of themselves and their priorities, it is still a mistake to blame the dominance of liberal ideology or the spread of commercial enterprise for placing a politics of public virtue beyond the reach of twentieth-century constitutional democracies.

In this context, it is important to recall just how skeptical the great republican theorists were of the possibility of establishing and maintaining a regime favorable to virtue. Both Machiavelli and Rousseau, for example, insisted that virtuous citizens were products of a virtuous founding and that a virtuous founding required a severe legislator imbued with divine authority who shaped a regime's constitution so as to bind citizens emotionally and materially to the republic. Any such achievement was seen as open to corruption, and both Machiavelli and Rousseau doubted the possibility, except in the most extreme circumstances, of returning a corrupt citizenry to the practice of public virtue.[7] These philosophers, then, did not tie the uncertain prospects for citizen virtue to the emergence of liberal theories of political obligation or of a modern system of commerce and finance. Rather their concern was with certain enduring human passions—self-love, ambition, desire for material comfort—which present a persistent challenge to the realization of any politics of civic virtue, a challenge the contemporary calls for a renewal of civic virtue have ignored almost completely.

To put this point in a different way, given men and women as they are, it is difficult to conceive of the circumstances under which a Western democracy would embrace the changes in popular culture, lifestyle, and political process that would be necessary to make either the liberal or republican version of the politics of virtue a reality. Some may wish to blame our liberal heritage or the commercial ethos for stripping individuals of the potential to be truly civic beings. It seems to me, drawing on the insights of Machiavelli and Rousseau, that the problem is more profound, linked not to particularly modern conditions but to human desires and dispositions with which all political communities have struggled. Public virtue of any sort asks too great an abstraction from self and the parochial interests that conventionally draw citizens into politics to have any chance of being successfully cultivated in a community that must establish its conditions through the legislative process. (The alternative route, contemplated by the great republican thinkers, is to have the sources of virtue imposed from above at the founding of a republic, not an open option at the present time.) Public virtue, then, is a victim not of liberalism or commerce but of politics and the necessary conditions of democratic public life.

Republican Failings
Barber's admirably detailed account of the institutional reforms necessary to transform the United States into a "strong democracy" provides a good example of the failure to think through the *politics* of a politics of public virtue. Central to Barber's "systematic program of participatory reform" is a "national system of *neighborhood assemblies* in every rural, suburban, and urban district in America" (Barber 1984, 269). These assemblies would meet weekly, encouraging the development of "civic competence" from "the discussion of a flexible and citizen-generated agenda" (264-265, 270). Were such assemblies established, I am quite prepared to grant Barber the civic benefits he attributes to them. But what are the odds of realizing such an achievement? To imagine the circumstances in which a reasonably powerful coalition of public activists and community groups would (1) endorse such a proposal and (2) convince Congress to fund it is difficult enough. But imagining the conditions under which a significant number of American citizens would free up their Saturday afternoons or Wednesday evenings (Barber's scheduling suggestions) so that they might examine different legislative positions in detail, assess the local impact of regional and national bills, explore ideological stances in the absence of pressures from special-interest groups, and introduce new questions of interest to the neighborhood" (271) is impossible.[8] These objections are not meant to condemn Americans as beyond civic virtue, unable to muster the dispositions necessary to contribute positively to the flourishing of a democratic state. But they are meant to suggest that a politics of virtue that requires of the good citizen a willingness

to spend long hours debating matters of public concern "in which [citizens'] most immediate interests would be ignored" (265) is destined to fail. I use such strongly determinist language deliberately. Such proposals place far too great a demand on an individual's time and emotional resources to garner much support in any deliberative democratic process. (As a working parent of young children, I call these reservations "the babysitter problem" and the "me-first factor," respectively.)

My critique is not directed against the workability of communitarian proposals per se. Individuals born and raised to civic maturity in a polity characterized by Barber's strong democratic institutions would learn to live with, and perhaps love, such neighborhood assemblies or other trappings of a republican politics. It is not that human beings are incapable of living within strongly participatory political cultures. The question, however, is how one gets there from here without some form of nondemocratic founding moment. By requiring of good citizens a passionate and time-consuming involvement in the public realm, republicans and communitarians articulate a vision of civic virtue that necessarily excludes the hard-working and often undereducated citizens of any truly inclusive democratic polity.[9]

The liberal politics of virtue just surveyed do not call for the participatory virtues envisioned by republicans and thus avoid political difficulty on this account. However, the United States is equally unlikely to produce a race of citizens that make commitment to a liberal public philosophy their primary motive for political action and involvement. To demand such a devotion to liberal justice or rational liberty as the mark of civic virtue sets a standard far beyond the reach of most American citizens, even those with largely liberal sympathies.

Liberal politics that insist on good citizens' embracing a publicly oriented civic virtue run the risk of forgetting one of the most compelling insights of liberal philosophy: what brings us into politics in the first place is the desire to satisfy or protect our personal interests. Indeed, our satisfaction with our leaders and our government is often a function of how well we perceive them to be meeting our interests. Any effort to wean citizens away from an attachment to the commonwealth based on these personal considerations seems not only misguided but unlikely to succeed. What possible plan do liberal theorists possess for convincing citizens that they ought to judge their government not on whether it makes their life better but on whether it fosters particularly liberal sorts of excellences in them and their neighbors?

A democratic or liberal politics of virtue that transcends self-interest is a seductive but illusory ideal. The elusive nature of this option derives not from some fundamental corruption or constitutional idiosyncrasy afflicting modern culture and spared the ancients. The problem dogging the politics of virtue today is the one with which all seekers after civic virtue have had to contend. Tocqueville (1945), for one, understood the problem well:

> It is difficult to draw a man out of his own circle to interest him in the destiny of the state, because he does not clearly understand what influence the destiny of the state can have upon his own lot. But if it is proposed to

make a road cross the end of his estate, he will see at a glance that there is a connection between this small public affair and his greatest private affairs; and he will discover, without its being shown to him, the close tie that unites private to general interest. (2:iii)

Rousseau (1972) is another reliable guide to the necessary limits of virtue. The apostle of the general will, he still believed that "one can make men act only by appealing to their self-interest" (70). Neither Rousseau nor Tocqueville blame liberal ideology or commercial society for the difficulties faced by those who would attach citizens' sentiments more or less exclusively to public ideals. Rather, they recognize that, whatever a polity's constitutional ideals, it will be difficult to persuade citizens to embrace and work to further them from the nobility or justice of the ideals themselves. It can perhaps be done: Rousseau's political writings set out what, for him, were the necessary steps. But a politics of public virtue (whether liberal or republican) that calls on citizens to forsake the private for the public without providing for the sort of political institutions and procedures recommended by classical republican theorists cannot succeed.

Civic Virtues We Can Live With

Is the caricature of modern liberal democracy, then, correct after all? Must we abandon civic virtue for the mere manipulation or accommodation of self-interest? This conclusion is too extreme. It fails to recognize the possibility of a civic virtue that is not publicly oriented. By distinguishing privately from publicly oriented civic virtue as I have proposed, we can recognize and encourage a form of civic virtue well within the reach of contemporary citizens.

An Eighteenth-Century Exemplar

To set out more concretely the nature and necessary preconditions of the sort of privately oriented virtue I have in mind, I want to introduce the account of citizen virtue argued for in *Cato's Letters,* an influential collection of essays penned in England in the 1720s by two Whig opponents to Walpole's ministry, John Trenchard and Thomas Gordon.[10] The good citizen of *Cato's Letters* very much resembles the good judge of the modern liberal vision. He keeps vigilant watch on the behavior of elected officials, inspects public policies for any unjust or tyrannical designs, and protests government activity that harms the public good. However, the motivation for this civic service is not an abstract belief or commitment to the ideals of a liberal polity but a very concrete sense of the benefits to which each individual is entitled in a free society. Government, says Cato, should further the public interest; and the best judge of its success or failure in this end is the citizens' own experience: "The People's Interest is the Public Interest; it signifies the same thing" (1:106). By "people," Cato has in mind what we might call all potentially active citizens. In Cato's day, this class included not only relatively well off enfranchised males but a larger group of men and women whose political grievances might mobilize them to extraconstitutional forms of protest. What I want to emphasize about Cato's account is that it casts self-interest not as an obstacle to civic virtue but as the source of individuals' positive contributions to the public good.

A historical example might help clarify what Cato has in mind. Imagine a disastrous government-sponsored financial scheme in which many small investors are ruined and several prominent government officials implicated. (*Cato's Letters* debuted in the aftermath of just such a scandal, the South Sea Bubble.) Cato calls on his countrymen to demand the public investigation and punishment of those responsible for the debacle regardless of political position. On what basis might individuals be moved to serve the public in this way? One might act to rid government of corrupt speculators out of a sense of public duty or love of country, but this notion of what motivates the virtuous citizen completely misses the point of what brings individuals to political action in the first place. In this example, Cato expects those with a *personal* interest in seeing justice done to be the most motivated and the most effective in advancing the public good—precisely because what satisfies their desire for personal vengeance on a set of corrupt officials also satisfies the public's need to get the same men out of office and in jail. Thus, Cato contends that especially in times of crisis or government malfeasance, ordinary citizens can be counted on to serve the public simply by following their self-interest: "The Whole People, by consulting their own Interest, consult the Publick, and act for the Public by acting for themselves" (*Cato's Letters* 2:41).

One might think also in this context of the extraordinary civic valor of the peoples of Eastern Europe and the former Soviet Union in creating the conditions under which regimes of participatory self-rule became at least thinkable. Their civic virtues were born of intensely personal desires for cultural particularity, freedom from communist rule, and material comfort and convenience. Looking to further (not subordinate) their private ends, they acted with great political courage to create free, self-governing communities, as well. Theirs was, in my sense, a privately oriented civic virtue.

One cannot, however, create virtuous citizens of the sort Cato praises simply by declaring that the public interest and the private interest signify the same thing. For individuals to manifest the sort of civic virtue that Cato recommends, there must first exist a genuine fit between the public good and citizens' private interest. One reason that classical republicans emphasized overcoming or subordinating private interest in their accounts of civic virtue is that historically, they addressed themselves primarily to an ambitious elite whose private interests (a desire for power and prestige) were, indeed, at odds with the republicans' hope for a free polity. One of the strengths, then, of a democratic polity of either the liberal or republican variety is that it expands the political realm to include the vast majority of a nation's inhabitants for whom the fit between personal and public good is tighter than it is with an elite bent on political domination. Ordinary men and women can, in Cato's vision, be counted on to keep a democratic government faithful to its constitutional principles and just and efficient in its operations—not because they harbor any profound loyalty to a public morality or political ideal but because a well-functioning democratic government is most responsive to their personal desires for liberty, security, and material comfort.[11]

In such polities, Cato's willingness to ground civic virtue in the citizens' pursuit of their self-interest makes good sense.

Grounding the Good Citizen

Civic virtue of the sort Cato has in mind also requires individuals who understand themselves as citizens and take seriously the rights and responsibilities that this role implies. When called upon to participate in public political deliberation, they must be able to put aside self-interest narrowly conceived (in which the horizons of interest stop at one's front doorstep) and consider, instead, what is in their self-interest as members of the political community. Not only must they possess an understanding of their polity's constitution (so as to judge when and whether its principles are being violated), but they must understand themselves as possessing rights and privileges worth defending through political action.

To secure this self-understanding requires a considerable amount of explicit and implicit political education, but this education neither makes any unusual demands on the basic impulses of human nature (the scope of self-interest is to be expanded, not narrowed) nor would require an extraordinary commitment of resources by public institutions. In fact, the various institutions through which this education for citizen virtue could take place are already in place in the modern democratic polity. The media, the schools, voluntary associations, local political organizations, family, and church can all reinforce the understanding of self as a bearer of political rights that deserve realization.

Once this self-understanding is achieved, it can provide a powerful impetus to civically virtuous political action. Both the Woman Suffrage and Civil Rights movements provide examples of citizens acting to further both their own interest (inclusion in the political process) and the public good (the achievement of a truly inclusive civic regime). The best possible citizen of a civic regime would also be driven to assure that all individuals had their rights respected and justice done to them. But, because Cato does not envision the ethnic, racial, and religious cleavages that challenge modern democracies, he is willing to rely on a "bootstrap" vision of civic virtue in which each citizen, defending his or her own interests and rights, secures the interests of the polity, as well. An expansive concern for the rights of minorities is not strictly necessary to Cato's vision of virtue.

Here, then, is the beginning of a viable account of civic virtue that is privately, rather than publicly, oriented. Cato's citizens defend and sustain the public good of a political community committed to some form of participatory self-rule (thus, they are civically virtuous), but they act primarily out of concern for their personal welfare (thus, the virtue is privately oriented). *Cato's Letters* does not necessarily provide a prescription for civic virtue in the modern polity, but it does suggest a model on which a contemporary politics of virtue might build.

American Virtues: Two Possibilities

One shortcoming of Cato's particular account of privately oriented civic virtue is its limited sense of the political activities appropriate to the good citizen. The citizen's role remains primarily that of watchdog—to react to danger, to alert the community to malfeasance and pressure the government for its correction. To the extent that we aspire, as well, to a polity in which citizens shape and reshape the political agenda—in which they decide what ends the government should pursue, as well as judge how well it pursues them—more is needed. As it happens, at least two recent works in political philosophy have advanced suggestions for a modern politics of civic virtue that might make good the shortcomings in Cato's analysis while continuing to offer to twentieth-century democrats an attractive and achievable, privately oriented vision of the virtuous citizen.

Elkin's Self-Interested Citizen

Stephen Elkin, in *City and Regime in the American Republic* (1987), proposes a restructuring of city government so as to nurture a citizenry better capable of deliberating upon what he calls the common public interest. Elkin suggests three institutions that could make citizens better deliberators upon the common good: "(1) neighborhood assemblies with significant powers, (2) citywide referenda, and (3) city legislatures, also with significant powers" (171; his focus is on reforms possible at the city level). A politics grounded in these institutions would teach citizens to think of politics as "broadly deliberative" and of political choice as "involving the giving of reasons," not just the aggregation of interests (150, 149). Such an orientation offers the hope of detaching deliberation about the common interest from concern about businesses' bottom line and would encourage citizens to participate constructively in the ongoing task of evaluating, debating, and challenging the policy choices made by city officials so as best to further the common good.

Elkin cites Barber (as well as Rousseau) as the source for his institutional innovations. But the motives he relies on to encourage virtuous public deliberation are quite different. Individuals, he argues, can be brought to act in appropriate, citizenly ways only through the "harnessing of powerful motives": "First, struggle and debate over the public interest must be connected to the day-to-day vital interests of the citizen. Political argument about the public interest must be tied then to specific policy choices ... that involve such things as neighborhood matters, schools, the land-use patterns of their localities, and a variety of features of their work lives" (1987, 153). This passage captures one of the most admirable features of Elkin's politics of civic virtue: citizens are to be brought to civically virtuous activity through reflection on matters of particular interest to them. The point is to expand the individual's sense of personal self-interest, not to expend resources to subordinate or subdue it. Elkin also calls for eliciting our participation as citizens through engaging the "deep interest that each of us has in enjoying the esteem of others" (ibid.).[12] When civic virtue emerges from motives of this sort, it is privately oriented, because it involves less an engagement with the public than a reflection upon the self.

Three features of Elkin's account of citizenship deserve particular emphasis: (1) he focuses on the deliberative abilities of the citizen, intending to nurture individuals capable of reflecting on the public interest; (2) he tries to nurture the deliberative virtues not by stripping men and women of a sense of private interest but by encouraging them to develop a complementary sense of themselves as citizens, who take pride in properly fulfilling the rights and responsibilities of such a public role; and (3) in sketching out how the institutions necessary to cultivate this sort of civic virtue would work, Elkin works with, rather than abstracts from, self-interest. Neighborhood assemblies, city government, and a city referenda process will focus on matters of day-to-day interest for city residents while invoking their concern with winning the esteem of others. Elkin himself is quite pessimistic about the chances of reviving a civic virtue of the sort he describes (1987, 188); but the possibility of instituting his set of suggested reforms seems far less remote than that of most politics of virtue on offer today.

Virtue in a "Dualist Democracy"

Bruce Ackerman is another contemporary theorist articulating a privately oriented conception of civic virtue. His account, in the Storrs Lectures, of a "dualist democracy" envisions an American polity in which an "intermittent and irregular politics of public virtue" pursued during "rare periods of heightened political consciousness" alternates with normal politics, in which interests are brokered and factions predominate (1984, 1022).[13] Like Elkin, Ackerman finds it important to reach an accommodation between the self-interest that so dominates our lives and character and the public regard necessary if a liberal democracy is to flourish. Like Cato, Ackerman grounds this accommodation in a two-track vision of citizenship that recognizes "the ebb and flow of political involvement" for the typical "private citizen" (1035). Cato saw the civic virtue of English citizens surfacing only occasionally, drawn forth in frustration and anger when gross corruption and malfeasance threatened their liberty. Between these times of crisis, politics was a matter appropriately left to parliament and the king's ministers. Ackerman envisions a similarly irregular practice of individuals' civic virtue. Most of the time, Ackerman argues, people can and do leave the business of politics to professional politicians willing to engage in the bartering of interests characteristic of normal liberal politics. There will be times, however, when the "ordinary irresponsibilities of politics sometimes begin to offend in a special way" (1040), when normal politics gives way to what he calls constitutional politics. These sporadic efforts to transform the constitutional order, to invoke the higher lawmaking powers of We the People represent, for Ackerman, an American "politics of public virtue"—historically significant moments "when the mass of American citizens mobilizes itself in a collective effort to renew and redefine the public good" (1023, 1040).

One might argue that on the basis of this description, Ackerman joins Barber and others in advocating a publicly oriented civic virtue. Ackerman himself lays claim to this label, arguing that those who participate in constitutional politics must be understood "to sacrifice their private interests to pursue the common good" (1984, 1020). But the "sacrifice" Ackerman refers to here is simply that of the allocation of time between roles. To expend one's energies on political campaigns to repeal Prohibition, establish the civil rights of America's minorities, or protect unborn children means less time available for everyday obligations and politics, means a sacrifice of private interests. This compartmentalization of personal commitments—what Ackerman calls "the strategy of differential sacrifice" (1041)—is not the sort of sacrifice or subordination of private interest traditionally called for by republican authors. In fact, Ackerman acknowledges that those embarked on the higher lawmaking track will not have "hearts entirely purged of self-interest and minds fully focused upon the rights of citizens and the permanent interests of the community"—such a public orientation of desire and "pristine purity of motive" being, he admits, psychologically impossible (1041).

The features that make Elkin's account an important candidate for a contemporary politics of virtue are present in Ackerman's, too. Like Elkin, Ackerman emphasizes the deliberative responsibilities of the good citizen without falling victim to democratic romanticism: the virtuous citizen's participation is called forth only in exceptional circumstances. Ackerman also avoids demanding the sort of disinterested embrace of the public weal that dooms most politics of public virtue. As with Elkin, the good citizen need not jettison his selfish attachments, only place them properly in perspective. The key is to create the circumstances under which individuals come to define themselves as citizens while developing some understanding of the rights and responsibilities entailed in that role. Thus, Ackerman argues, our culture generally provides for, and encourages, our "self-identification as private citizens, capable of responding in a distinctive voice on questions involving the political community," a sensibility whose cultivation becomes a matter of self-interest for the typical American who does not like to "appear to [his or her] fellows as a selfish person bent solely on egoistic self-aggrandizement" (1984, 1033). Thus, our self-interest leads us to virtuous, citizenly behavior.

Ackerman probably assumes too readily that our self-identification as "private citizen" comes naturally in a democratic polity like the United States. A politics of civic virtue conceived along these lines would have to pay a great deal of attention to cultivating a sense of citizenship among citizens. But again, this end is far more easily and less coercively achieved than any effort to develop a truly publicly oriented civic virtue.

Ackerman and Elkin thus offer complementary visions of what it might mean to be a virtuous citizen in the twentieth century American polity. Their work invites us to think creatively about the enabling conditions of a modern politics of civic virtue—one that is both attractive and achievable, sensitive to the political realities of a mass democracy and alert to the deficiencies of human character.

Conclusion

Some may find it hard to abandon the seductive vision of public virtue—of citizens who manage to make the public (of which they are a part) the center of their reflections and affections. Yet imagine what would be necessary to make such a vision a practical reality. The programs by which a truly publicly oriented civic virtue of either the liberal or republican variety might be nurtured in any citizenry are just too demanding, institutionally and psychologically, to gain the lasting assent of the inhabitants of a democratic polity. Those who find this language too melodramatic are urged to consider the circumstances under which the institutions and laws undergirding Rousseau's or Montesquieu's virtuous republics might become law in the United States. With proposals for compulsory national service still too politically controversial to pursue seriously in Congress and with public schools (an important locus of civic education and training) desperately underfunded, where might we expect to find the political will or interest for any comprehensive politics of public virtue? To put this another way, a public virtue available to a democratic citizenry is not the victim of liberalism or commerce, snagged and left behind at some watershed of modernity. The difficulty with the politics of *public* virtue in any democratic regime is simply political: no one will vote for it.

However, those willing to bracket the pursuit of public virtue (for a better and different world) will discover that another sort of civic virtue remains accessible to the modern citizen, one that links our enduring concern for self to the public life of a deliberative citizen. There are a number of ways in which a civic virtue of this sort might be encouraged or grounded, some of which I have explored. The challenge for any modern politics of virtue is therefore to do more than simply shepherd its vision of the good citizen through the perilous byways of democratic debate: it must transform that debate from an impossible emphasis on public virtue to a focus on developing the sorts of privately oriented civic virtue that can and should ground responsible political deliberation and action in the modern polity.

References

Ackerman, B. 1984. The Storrs lectures: Discovering the constitution. *Yale Law Journal* 93: 1013-1072.
———. 1991. *We the people.* Cambridge: Harvard University Press.
Barber, B. 1984. *Strong democracy: Participatory politics for a new age.* Berkeley: University of California Press.
Budziszewski, J. 1986. *The resurrection of nature: Political theory and human character.* Ithaca, NY: Cornell University Press.
———. 1988. *The nearest coast of darkness: A vindication of the politics of virtues.* Ithaca, NY: Cornell University Press.
Burtt, S. 1990. The good citizen's psyche: On the psychology of civic virtue. *Polity* 23: 23-38.
———. 1992. *Virtue transformed: Political argument in England, 1688-1740.* Cambridge: Cambridge University Press.
Elkin, S. 1987. *City and regime in the American republic.* Chicago: University of Chicago Press.
Kramnick, I. 1988. The "great national discussion": The discourse of politics of 1787. *William and Mary Quarterly* 45: 3-22.
Macedo, S. 1990. *Liberal virtues: Citizenship, virtue, and community in liberal constitutionalism.* Oxford: Clarendon.
MacIntyre, A. 1981. *After virtue: A study in moral theory.* Notre Dame, IN: University of Notre Dame Press.
———. 1990. *First principles, final ends, and contemporary philosophical issues.* Minneapolis, MN: Marquette University Press.
Michelman, F. 1988. Law's republic. *Yale Law Journal* 97: 1493-1537.
Pagden, A., ed. 1987. *The languages of political theory in early modern Europe.* Cambridge: Cambridge University Press.
Pitkin, H. 1981. Justice: On relating public to private. *Political Theory* 9: 327-352.
Rousseau, J. J. 1972. *Government of Poland.* Translated by W. Kendall. Indianapolis: Bobbs-Merrill.
Salkever, S. 1990. *Finding the mean: Theory and practice in Aristotelian political philosophy.* Princeton, NJ: Princeton University Press.

Sinopoli, R. C. 1987. Liberalism, republicanism, and the Constitution. *Polity* 19: 331-352.
Smith, R. M. 1985. *Liberalism and American constitutional law.* Cambridge, MA: Harvard University Press.
———. 1989. "One united people": Second-class female citizenship and the American quest for community. *Yale Journal of Law and the Humanities* 1: 229-293.
Spitz, E. 1986. Citizenship and liberal institutions. In *Liberals on liberalism,* edited by A. J. Damico. Totowa, NJ: Rowman & Littlefield.
Sunstein, C. R. 1988. Beyond the republican revival. *Yale Law Journal* 97: 1539-1590.
Taylor, C. 1989. Cross-purposes: The liberal-communitarian debate. In *Liberalism and the moral life,* edited by N. L. Rosenblum. Cambridge, MA: Harvard University Press.
Tocqueville, A. de. 1945. *Democracy in America.* 2 vols. New York: Vintage Books.
Trenchard, J., and T. Gordon. 1969. *Cato's letters.* 4 vols. Facsimile reprint. 2 vols. New York: Russell and Russell.
Walzer, M. 1980. *Radical principles: Reflections of an unreconstructed democrat.* New York: Basic Books.
Will, G. 1980. *Statecraft as soulcraft.* New York: Simon and Schuster.
Wood, G. 1969. *The creation of the American republic.* New York: Norton.

CHAPTER 12

Bowling Alone: America's Declining Social Capital
Robert D. Putnam

Originally published in Journal of Democracy 6 (1), 1995.

READING INTRODUCTION

After briefly explaining why social capital (civil society) is important to democracy, Putnam devotes the bulk of this chapter to demonstrating social capital's decline in the United States across the last quarter century. (See Putnam 1995 for a similar but more detailed argument.) While he acknowledges that the significance of a few countertrends is difficult to assess without further study, Putnam concludes that crucial factors such as social trust are eroding rapidly in the United States. He offers some possible explanations for this erosion and concludes by outlining the work needed to consider these possibilities more fully.

READING TEXT

Many students of the new democracies that have emerged over the past decade and a half have emphasized the importance of a strong and active civil society to the consolidation of democracy. Especially with regard to the postcommunist countries, scholars and democratic activists alike have lamented the absence or obliteration of traditions of independent civic engagement and a widespread tendency toward passive reliance on the state. To those concerned with the weakness of civil societies in the developing or postcommunist world, the advanced Western democracies and above all the United States have typically been taken as models to be emulated. There is striking evidence, however, that the vibrancy of American civil society has notably declined over the past several decades.

Ever since the publication of Alexis de Tocqueville's *Democracy in America,* the United States has played a central role in systematic studies of the links between democracy and civil society. Although this is in part because trends in American life are often regarded as harbingers of social modernization, it is also because America has traditionally been considered unusually "civic" (a reputation that, as we shall later see, has not been entirely unjustified).

When Tocqueville visited the United States in the 1830s, it was the Americans' propensity for civic association that most impressed him as the key to their unprecedented ability to make democracy work. "Americans of all ages, all stations in life, and all types of disposition," he observed, "are forever forming associations. There are not only commercial and industrial associations in which all take part, but others of a thousand different types—religious, moral, serious, futile, very general and very limited, immensely large and very minute. . . . Nothing, in my view, deserves more attention than the intellectual and moral associations in America" (Tocqueville 1969, 513-517).

Recently, American social scientists of a neo-Tocquevillean bent have unearthed a wide range of empirical evidence that the quality of public life and the performance of social institutions (and not only in America) are indeed powerfully influenced by norms and networks of civic engagement. Researchers in such fields as education, urban poverty, unemployment, the control of crime and drug abuse, and even health have discovered that successful outcomes are more likely in civically engaged communities. Similarly, research on the varying economic attainments of different ethnic groups in the United States has demonstrated the importance of social bonds within each group. These results are consistent with research in a wide range of settings that demonstrates the vital importance of social networks for job placement and many other economic outcomes.

Meanwhile, a seemingly unrelated body of research on the sociology of economic development has also focused attention on the role of social networks. Some of this work is situated in the developing countries, and some of it elucidates the peculiarly successful "network capitalism" of East Asia.[1] Even in less exotic Western economies, however, researchers have discovered highly efficient, highly flexible "industrial districts" based on networks of collaboration among workers and small entrepreneurs. Far from being paleoindustrial anachronisms, these dense interpersonal and interorganizational networks undergird ultramodern industries, from the high tech of Silicon Valley to the high fashion of Benetton.

The norms and networks of civic engagement also powerfully affect the performance of representative government. That, at least, was the central conclusion of my own 20-year, quasi-experimental study of subnational governments in different regions of Italy (Putnam 1993). Although all these regional governments seemed identical on paper, their levels of effectiveness varied dramatically. Systematic inquiry showed that the quality of governance was determined by longstanding traditions of civic engagement (or its absence). Voter turnout, newspaper readership, membership in choral societies and football clubs—these were the hallmarks of a successful region. In fact, historical analysis suggested that these networks of organized reciprocity and civic solidarity, far from being an epiphenomenon of socioeconomic modernization, were a precondition for it.

No doubt the mechanisms through which civic engagement and social connectedness produce such results—better schools, faster economic development, lower crime, and more effective government—are multiple and complex. While these briefly recounted findings require further confirmation and perhaps qualification, the parallels across hundreds of empirical studies in a dozen disparate disciplines and subfields are striking. Social scientists in several fields have recently suggested a common framework for understanding these phenomena, a framework that rests on the concept of social capital.[2] By analogy with notions of physical capital and human capital—tools and training that enhance individual productivity—"social capital" refers to features of social organization such as networks, norms, and social trust that facilitate coordination and cooperation for mutual benefit.

For a variety of reasons, life is easier in a community blessed with a substantial stock of social capital. In the first place, networks of civic engagement foster sturdy norms of generalized reciprocity and encourage the emergence of social trust. Such networks facilitate coordination and communication, amplify reputations, and thus allow dilemmas of collective action to be resolved. When economic and political negotiation is embedded in dense networks of social interaction, incentives for opportunism are reduced. At the same time, networks of civic engagement embody past success at collaboration, which can serve as a cultural template for future collaboration. Finally, dense networks of interaction probably broaden the participants' sense of self, developing the "I" into the "we," or (in the language of rational-choice theorists) enhancing the participants' "taste" for collective benefits.

I do not intend here to survey (much less contribute to) the development of the theory of social capital. Instead, I use the central premise of that rapidly growing body of work—that social connections and civic engagement pervasively influence our public life, as well as our private prospects—as the starting point for an empirical survey of trends in social capital in contemporary America. I concentrate here entirely on the American case, although the developments I portray may in some measure characterize many contemporary societies.

Whatever Happened to Civic Engagement?

We begin with familiar evidence on changing patterns of political participation, not least because it is immediately relevant to issues of democracy in the narrow sense. Consider the well-known decline in turnout in national elections over the last three decades. From a relative high point in the early 1960s, voter turnout had by 1990 declined by nearly a quarter; tens of millions of Americans had forsaken their parents' habitual readiness to engage in the simplest act of citizenship. Broadly similar trends also characterize participation in state and local elections.

It is not just the voting booth that has been increasingly deserted by Americans. A series of identical questions posed by the Roper Organization to national samples ten times each year over the last two decades reveals that since 1973 the number of Americans who report that "in the past year" they have "attended a public meeting on town or school affairs" has fallen by more than a third (from 22 percent in 1973 to 13 percent in 1993). Similar (or even greater) relative declines are evident in responses to questions about attending a political rally or speech, serving on a committee of some local organization, and working for a political party. By almost every measure, Americans' direct engagement in politics and government has fallen steadily and sharply over the last generation, despite the fact that average levels of education—the best individual-level predictor of political participation—have risen sharply throughout this period. Every year over the last decade or two, millions more have withdrawn from the affairs of their communities.

Not coincidentally, Americans have also disengaged psychologically from politics and government over this era. The proportion of Americans who reply that they "trust the government in Washington" only "some of the time" or "almost never" has risen steadily from 30 percent in 1966 to 75 percent in 1992.

These trends are well known, of course, and taken by themselves would seem amenable to a strictly political explanation. Perhaps the long litany of political tragedies and scandals since the 1960s (assassinations, Vietnam, Watergate, Irangate, and so on) has triggered an understandable disgust for politics and government among Americans, and that in turn has motivated their withdrawal. I do not doubt that this common interpretation has some merit, but its limitations become plain when we examine trends in civic engagement of a wider sort.

Our survey of organizational membership among Americans can usefully begin with a glance at the aggregate results of the General Social Survey, a scientifically conducted, national-sample survey that has been repeated 14 times over the last two decades. Church-related groups constitute the most common type of organization joined by Americans; they are especially popular with women. Other types of organizations frequently joined by women include school-service groups (mostly parent-teacher associations), sports groups, professional societies, and literary societies. Among men, sports clubs, labor unions, professional societies, fraternal groups, veterans' groups, and service clubs are all relatively popular.

Religious affiliation is by far the most common associational membership among Americans. Indeed, by many measures America continues to be (even more than in Tocqueville's time) an astonishingly "churched" society. For example, the United States has more houses of worship per capita than any other nation on Earth. Yet religious sentiment in America seems to be becoming somewhat less tied to institutions and more self-defined.

How have these complex crosscurrents played out over the last three or four decades in terms of Americans' engagement with organized religion? The general pattern is clear: The 1960s witnessed a significant drop in reported weekly churchgoing—from roughly 48 percent in the late 1950s to roughly 41 percent in the early 1970s. Since then, it has stagnated or (according to some surveys) declined still further. Meanwhile, data from the General Social Survey show a modest decline in membership in all "church-related groups" over the last 20 years. It would seem, then, that net participation by Americans, both in religious services and in church-related groups, has declined modestly (by perhaps a sixth) since the 1960s.

For many years, labor unions provided one of the most common organizational affiliations among American workers. Yet union membership has been falling for nearly four decades, with the steepest decline occurring between 1975 and 1985. Since the mid-1950s, when union membership peaked, the unionized portion of the nonagricultural work force in America has dropped by more than half, falling from 32.5 percent in 1953 to 15.8 percent in 1992. By now, virtually all of the explosive growth in union membership that was associated with the New Deal has been erased. The solidarity of union halls is now mostly a fading memory of aging men.[3]

The parent-teacher association (PTA) has been an especially important form of civic engagement in twentieth-century America because parental involvement in the educational process represents a particularly productive form of social capital. It is, therefore, dismaying to discover that participation in parent-teacher organizations has dropped drastically over the last generation, from more than 12 million in 1964 to barely 5 million in 1982 before recovering to approximately 7 million now.

Next, we turn to evidence on membership in (and volunteering for) civic and fraternal organizations. These data show some striking patterns. First, membership in traditional women's groups has declined more or less steadily since the mid-1960s. For example, membership in the national Federation of Women's Clubs is down by more than half (59 percent) since 1964, while membership in the League of Women Voters (LWV) is off 42 percent since 1969.[4]

Similar reductions are apparent in the numbers of volunteers for mainline civic organizations, such as the Boy Scouts (off by 26 percent since 1970) and the Red Cross (off by 61 percent since 1970). But what about the possibility that volunteers have simply switched their loyalties to other organizations? Evidence on "regular" (as opposed to occasional or "drop-by") volunteering is available from the Labor Department's Current Population Surveys of 1974 and 1989. These estimates suggest that serious volunteering declined by roughly one-sixth over these 15 years, from 24 percent of adults in 1974 to 20 percent in 1989. The multitudes of Red Cross aides and Boy Scout troop leaders now missing in action have apparently not been offset by equal numbers of new recruits elsewhere.

Fraternal organizations have also witnessed a substantial drop in membership during the 1980s and 1990s. Membership is down significantly in such groups as the Lions (off 12 percent since 1983), the Elks (off 18 percent since 1979), the Shriners (off 27 percent since 1979), the Jaycees (off 44 percent since 1979), and the Masons (down 39 percent since 1959). In sum, after expanding steadily throughout most of this century, many major civic organizations have experienced a sudden, substantial, and nearly simultaneous decline in membership over the last decade or two.

The most whimsical yet discomfiting bit of evidence of social disengagement in contemporary America that I have discovered is this: more Americans are bowling today than ever before, but bowling in organized leagues has plummeted in the last decade or so. Between 1980 and 1993 the total number of bowlers in America increased by 10 percent, while league bowling decreased by 40 percent. (Lest this be thought a wholly trivial example, I should note that nearly 80 million Americans went bowling at least once during 1993, nearly a third more than voted in the 1994 congressional elections and roughly the same number as claim to attend church regularly. Even after the 1980s' plunge in league bowling, nearly 3 percent of American adults regularly bowl in leagues.) The rise of solo bowling threatens the livelihood of bowling-lane proprietors because those who bowl as members of leagues consume three times as much beer and pizza as solo bowlers, and the money in bowling is in the beer and pizza, not the balls and shoes. The broader social significance, however, lies in the social interaction and even occasionally civic conversations over beer and pizza that solo bowlers forgo. Whether or not bowling beats balloting in the eyes of most Americans, bowling teams illustrate yet another vanishing form of social capital.

Countertrends

At this point, however, we must confront a serious counter argument. Perhaps the traditional forms of civic organization whose decay we have been tracing have been replaced by vibrant new organizations. For example, national environmental organizations (like the Sierra Club) and feminist groups (like the National Organization for Women) grew rapidly during the 1970s and 1980s and now count hundreds of thousands of dues-paying members. An even more dramatic example is the American Association of Retired Persons (AARP), which grew exponentially from 400,000 card-carrying members in 1960 to 33 million in 1993, becoming (after the Catholic Church) the largest private organization in the world. The national administrators of these organizations are among the most feared lobbyists in Washington, in large part because of their massive mailing lists of presumably loyal members.

These new mass-membership organizations are plainly of great political importance. From the point of view of social connectedness, however, they are sufficiently different from classic "secondary associations" that we need to invent a new label—perhaps "tertiary associations." For the vast majority of their members, the only act of membership consists in writing a check for dues or perhaps occasionally reading a newsletter. Few ever attend any meetings of such organizations, and most are unlikely ever (knowingly) to encounter any other member. The bond between any two members of the Sierra Club is less like the bond between any two members of a gardening club and more like the bond between any two Red Sox fans (or perhaps any two devoted Honda owners): they root for the same team and they share some of the same interests, but they are unaware of each other's existence. Their ties, in short, are to common symbols, common leaders, and perhaps common ideals, but not to one another. The theory of social capital argues that associational membership should, for example, increase social trust, but this prediction is much less straightforward with regard to membership in tertiary associations. From the point of view of social connectedness, the Environmental Defense Fund and a bowling league are just not in the same category.

If the growth of tertiary organizations represents one potential (but probably not real) counterexample to my thesis, a second countertrend is represented by the growing prominence of nonprofit organizations, especially nonprofit service agencies. This so-called third sector includes everything from Oxfam and the Metropolitan Museum of Art to the Ford Foundation and the Mayo Clinic. In other words, although most secondary associations are nonprofits, most nonprofit agencies are not secondary associations. To identify trends in the size of the nonprofit sector with trends in social connectedness would be another fundamental conceptual mistake.[5]

A third potential countertrend is much more relevant to an assessment of social capital and civic engagement. Some able researchers have argued that the last few decades have witnessed a rapid expansion in "support groups" of various sorts. Robert Wuthnow (1994) reports that fully 40 percent of all Americans claim to be "currently involved in [a] small group that meets regularly and provides support or caring for those who participate in it" (45). Many of these groups are religiously affiliated, but many others are not. For example, nearly 5 percent of Wuthnow's national sample claim to participate regularly in a "self-help" group, such as Alcoholics Anonymous, and nearly as many say they belong to book-discussion groups and hobby clubs.

The groups described by Wuthnow's respondents unquestionably represent an important form of social capital, and they need to be accounted for in any serious reckoning of trends in social connectedness. On the other hand, they do not typically play the same role as traditional civic associations. As Wuthnow emphasizes,

> Small groups may not be fostering community as effectively as many of their proponents would like. Some small groups merely provide occasions for individuals to focus on themselves in the presence of others. The social contract binding members together asserts only the weakest of obligations. Come if you have time. Talk if you feel like it. Respect everyone's opinion. Never criticize. Leave quietly if you become dissatisfied. . . . We can imagine that [these small groups] really substitute for families, neighborhoods, and broader community attachments that may demand lifelong commitments, when, in fact, they do not. (3-6)

All three of these potential countertrends—tertiary organizations, nonprofit organizations, and support groups—need somehow to be weighed against the erosion of conventional civic organizations. One way of doing so is to consult the General Social Survey. Within all educational categories, total associational membership declined significantly between 1967 and 1993. Among the college-educated, the average number of group memberships per person fell from 2.8 to 2.0 (a 26 percent decline); among high-school graduates, the number fell from 1.8 to 1.2 (32 percent); and among those with fewer than 12 years of education, the number fell from 1.4 to 1.1 (25 percent). In other words, at all educational (and hence social) levels of American society, and counting all sorts of group memberships, the average number of associational memberships has fallen by about a fourth over the last quarter-century. Without controls for educational levels, the trend is not nearly so clear, but the central point is this: more Americans than ever before are in social circumstances that foster associational involvement (higher education, middle age, and so on), but nevertheless aggregate associational membership appears to be stagnant or declining.

Broken down by type of group, the downward trend is most marked for church-related groups, for labor unions, for fraternal and veterans' organizations, and for school-service groups. Conversely, membership in professional associations has risen over these years, although less than might have been predicted, given sharply rising educational and occupational levels. Essentially the same trends are evident for both men and women in the sample. In short, the available survey evidence confirms our earlier conclusion: American social capital in the form of civic associations has significantly eroded over the last generation.

Good Neighborliness and Social Trust

I noted earlier that most readily available quantitative evidence on trends in social connectedness involves formal settings, such as the voting booth, the union hall, or the PTA. One glaring exception is so widely discussed as to require little comment here: the most fundamental form of social capital is the family, and the massive evidence of the loosening of bonds within the family (both extended and nuclear) is well known. This trend, of course, is quite consistent with—and may help to explain—our theme of social decapitalization.

A second aspect of informal social capital on which we happen to have reasonably reliable time-series data involves neighborliness. In each General Social Survey since 1974 respondents have been asked, "How often do you spend a social evening with a neighbor?" The proportion of Americans who socialize with their neighbors more than once a year has slowly but steadily declined over the last two decades, from 72 percent in 1974 to 61 percent in 1993. (On the other hand, socializing with "friends who do not live in your neighborhood" appears to be on the increase, a trend that may reflect the growth of workplace-based social connections.)

Americans are also less trusting. The proportion of Americans saying that most people can be trusted fell by more than a third between 1960, when 58 percent chose that alternative, and 1993, when only 37 percent did. The same trend is apparent in all educational groups; indeed, because social trust is also correlated with education and because educational levels have risen sharply, the overall decrease in social trust is even more apparent if we control for education.

Our discussion of trends in social connectedness and civic engagement has tacitly assumed that all the forms of social capital that we have discussed are themselves coherently correlated across individuals. This is in fact true. Members of associations are much more likely than nonmembers to participate in politics, to spend time with neighbors, to express social trust, and so on.

The close correlation between social trust and associational membership is true not only across time and across individuals, but also across countries. Evidence from the 1991 World Values Survey demonstrates the following[6]:

- Across the 35 countries in this survey, social trust and civic engagement are strongly correlated; the greater the density of associational member-

ship in a society, the more trusting its citizens. Trust and engagement are two facets of the same underlying factor—social capital.
- America still ranks relatively high by cross-national standards on both these dimensions of social capital. Even in the 1990s, after several decades' erosion, Americans are more trusting and more engaged than people in most other countries of the world.

The trends of the past quarter-century, however, have apparently moved the United States significantly lower in the international rankings of social capital. The recent deterioration in American social capital has been sufficiently great that (if no other country changed its position in the meantime) another quarter-century of change at the same rate would bring the United States, roughly speaking, to the midpoint among all these countries, roughly equivalent to South Korea, Belgium, or Estonia today. Two generations' decline at the same rate would leave the United States at the level of today's Chile, Portugal, and Slovenia.

Why is U.S. Social Capital Eroding?

As we have seen, something has happened in America in the last two or three decades to diminish civic engagement and social connectedness. What could that "something" be? Here are several possible explanations, along with some initial evidence on each.

The Movement of Women into the Labor Force
Over these same two or three decades, many millions of American women have moved out of the home into paid employment. This is the primary, though not the sole, reason why the weekly working hours of the average American have increased significantly during these years. It seems highly plausible that this social revolution should have reduced the time and energy available for building social capital. For certain organizations, such as the PTA, the League of Women Voters, the Federation of Women's Clubs, and the Red Cross, this is almost certainly an important part of the story. The sharpest decline in women's civic participation seems to have come in the 1970s; membership in such "women's" organizations as these has been virtually halved since the late 1960s. By contrast, most of the decline in participation in men's organizations occurred about ten years later; the total decline to date has been approximately 25 percent for the typical organization. On the other hand, the survey data imply that the aggregate declines for men are virtually as great as those for women. It is logically possible, of course, that the male declines might represent the knock-on effect of women's liberation, as dishwashing crowded out the lodge, but time-budget studies suggest that most husbands of working wives have assumed only a minor part of the housework. In short, something besides the women's revolution seems to lie behind the erosion of social capital.

Mobility: The "Re-Potting" Hypothesis

Numerous studies of organizational involvement have shown that residential stability and such related phenomena as homeownership are clearly associated with greater civic engagement. Mobility, like frequent re-potting of plants, tends to disrupt root systems, and it takes time for an uprooted individual to put down new roots. It seems plausible that the automobile, suburbanization, and the movement to the Sun Belt have reduced the social rootedness of the average American, but one fundamental difficulty with this hypothesis is apparent: the best evidence shows that residential stability and homeownership in America have risen modestly since 1965, and are surely higher now than during the 1950s, when civic engagement and social connectedness by our measures was definitely higher.

Other Demographic Transformations

A range of additional changes have transformed the American family since the 1960s—fewer marriages, more divorces, fewer children, lower real wages, and so on. Each of these changes might account for some of the slackening of civic engagement, since married, middle-class parents are generally more socially involved than other people. Moreover, the changes in scale that have swept over the American economy in these years—illustrated by the replacement of the corner grocery by the supermarket and now perhaps of the supermarket by electronic shopping at home, or the replacement of community-based enterprises by outposts of distant multinational firms—may perhaps have undermined the material and even physical basis for civic engagement.

The Technological Transformation of Leisure

There is reason to believe that deep-seated technological trends are radically "privatizing" or "individualizing" our use of leisure time and thus disrupting many opportunities for social-capital formation. The most obvious and probably the most powerful instrument of this revolution is television. Time-budget studies in the 1960s showed that the growth in time spent watching television dwarfed all other changes in the way Americans passed their days and nights. Television has made our communities (or, rather, what we experience as our communities) wider and shallower. In the language of economics, electronic technology enables individual tastes to be satisfied more fully, but at the cost of the positive social externalities associated with more primitive forms of entertainment. The same logic applies to the replacement of vaudeville by the movies and now of movies by the VCR. The new "virtual reality" helmets that we will soon don to be entertained in total isolation are merely the latest extension of this trend. Is technology thus driving a wedge between our individual interests and our collective interests? It is a question that seems worth exploring more systematically.

What Is to Be Done?

The last refuge of a social-scientific scoundrel is to call for more research. Nevertheless, I cannot forbear from suggesting some further lines of inquiry. We must sort out the dimensions of social capital, which clearly is not a unidimensional concept, despite language (even in this essay) that implies the contrary. What types of organizations and networks most effectively embody—or generate—social capital, in the sense of mutual reciprocity, the resolution of dilemmas of collective action, and the broadening of social identities? In this essay I have emphasized the density of associational life. In earlier work I stressed the structure of networks, arguing that "horizontal" ties represented more productive social capital than vertical ties (Putnam 1993).

Another set of important issues involves macrosociological crosscurrents that might intersect with the trends described here. What will be the impact, for example, of electronic networks on social capital? My hunch is that meeting in an electronic forum is not the equivalent of meeting in a bowling alley—or even in a saloon—but hard empirical research is needed. What about the development of social capital in the workplace? Is it growing in counterpoint to the decline of civic engagement, reflecting some social analogue of the first law of thermodynamics—social capital is neither created nor destroyed, merely redistributed? Or do the trends described in this essay represent a deadweight loss?

A rounded assessment of changes in American social capital over the last quarter-century needs to count the costs as well as the benefits of community engagement. We must not romanticize small-town, middle-class civic life in the America of the 1950s. In addition to the deleterious trends emphasized in this essay, recent decades have witnessed a substantial decline in intolerance and probably also in overt discrimination, and those beneficent trends may be related in complex ways to the erosion of traditional social capital. Moreover, a balanced accounting of the social-capital books would need to reconcile the insights of this approach with the undoubted insights offered by Mancur Olson (1982) and others who stress that closely knit social, economic, and political organizations are prone to inefficient cartelization and to what political economists term "rent seeking" and ordinary men and women call corruption.

Finally, and perhaps most urgently, we need to explore creatively how public policy impinges on (or might impinge on) social-capital formation. In some well-known instances, public policy has destroyed highly effective social networks and norms. American slum-clearance policy of the 1950s and 1960s, for example, renovated physical capital, but at a very high cost to existing social capital. The consolidation of country post offices and small school districts has promised administrative and financial efficiencies, but full-cost accounting for the effects of these policies on social capital might produce a more negative verdict. On the other hand, such past initiatives as the county agricultural-agent system, community colleges, and tax deductions for charitable contributions illustrate that government can encourage social-capital formation. Even a recent proposal in San Luis Obispo, California, to require that all new houses have front porches illustrates the power of government to influence where and how networks are formed.

The concept of "civil society" has played a central role in the recent global debate about the preconditions for democracy and democratization. In the newer democracies this phrase has properly focused attention on the need to foster a vibrant civic life in soils traditionally inhospitable to self-government. In the established democracies, ironically, growing numbers of citizens are questioning the effectiveness of their public institutions at the very moment when liberal democracy has swept the battlefield, both ideologically and geopolitically. In America, at least, there is reason to suspect that this democratic disarray may be linked to a broad and continuing erosion of civic engagement that began a quarter-century ago. High on our scholarly agenda should be the question of whether a comparable erosion of social capital may be under way in other advanced democracies, perhaps in different institutional and behavioral guises. High on America's agenda should be the question of how to reverse these adverse trends in social connectedness, thus restoring civic engagement and civic trust.

Robert Putnam's newest work, Bowling Alone *(New York: Simon and Schuster), is forthcoming in 2000.*

References

Olson, M. 1982. *The rise and decline of nations: Economic growth, stagflation, and social rigidities.* New Haven, CT: Yale University Press.

Putnam, R. 1993. *Making democracy work: Civic traditions in modern Italy.* Princeton, NJ: Princeton University Press.

Tocqueville, A. de. 1969. *Democracy in America,* edited by J. P. Maier, translated by G. Lawrence. Garden City, NY: Anchor Books.

Wuthnow, R. 1994. *Sharing the journey: Support groups and America's new quest for community.* New York: The Free Press.

CHAPTER 13

Making Social Science Work Across Space and Time: A Critical Reflection on Robert Putnam's Making Democracy Work*

Sidney Tarrow

Originally published in
American Political Science Review *90 (2), 1996.*

READING INTRODUCTION

Tarrow initially provides a synopsis of Putnam's widely heralded *Making Democracy Work: Civic Traditions in Modern Italy* (1993 and with Leonardi and Nanetti). He is encouraging about Putnam's early narrower project (see Putnam with Leonardi and Nanetti 1988), which shows how a 1970s central political reform was realized quite differently in the distinctive political cultures of northern and southern Italy. Tarrow agrees that this part of Putnam's study demonstrates that distinctive political cultures are apt to shape initially similar institutions quite differently over time. So in this regard culture shapes political institutions. However, Putnam extended the initial scope of his analysis to inquire into the origins of these distinctive regional cultures, concluding that these regional peculiarities are long-standing, stemming from differences in civic republicanism (social capital or civil society) in the late medieval period that persist into the present. Thus, once again, Putnam portrays culture as shaping political institutions: Civic republicanism produces more thorough democracy. Tarrow disagrees with the causal flow Putnam suggests in his expanded project. Tarrow argues instead that, across this lengthy period, institutional differences shaped distinctive political cultures. Tarrow also thinks that Putnam's operationalization of democracy has limitations, and we might add that Putnam's indices of culture lack a theoretical superstructure.

---

* The author wishes to espress his gratitude to David Blackmer, Mauro Calise, Miriam Golden, Stephen Hellman, David Laitin, Peter Lange, Joseph LaPalombra, Jonas Pontusson, Robert Putnam, Carlo Trigilia, and Alan Zuckerman, as well as two anonymous reviewers, for their unusually helpful comments on this chapter.

READING TEXT

Political scientists are becoming more self-conscious about how they connect quantitative and qualitative data in social science and about the role of systematic country studies in comparative research. As the most striking examples of both practices in recent years, Robert Putnam and collaborators' *Making Democracy Work* deserves more serious criticism than it has received. While Putnam's original project aimed at a precise goal—studying how a new administrative reform is institutionalized—his ultimate project aimed at nothing less than examining how differently democracy works in different sociopolitical contexts, operationalized cross-sectionally in southern and northern Italy. The sources for these differences he found in the two regions' histories, which led him to employ the quantitative interregional data he had collected for one purpose to support a model of historical development North and South. This historical reconstruction rests largely on qualitative data; but it also rests on a set of comparative inferences about individual values and community cohesiveness in the two regions that is of questionable historical validity and innocent of structural grounding. This article applauds Putnam's joining qualitative and quantitative data but attacks his reconstruction of Italian history to fit his model of social capital.

All self-respecting political scientists like to think of themselves as intrigued with what makes democracy work. But what brings a reviewer to risk a critical reflection on one of the most acclaimed recent works in the field?[1] That author and reviewer learned their trade in the same school and have both carried out research in Italy is part of the explanation, but only a small part.[2] A second reason is that we are becoming more self-conscious about the use of quantitative and qualitative data in social science and about the role of systematic country studies in comparative research.[3] And the third is the fact that the study on which Robert Putnam's book was based, which has caused a sensation outside academic circles, was first reported in this *Review* (Putnam and others 1983), a rare linkage between scientific effort and popular success.[4] Moreover, while Putnam's *American Political Science Review* article made modest claims, defining the problem as "institutional success," *Making Democracy Work* aims at a broader target—nothing less than the correlates of democracy.

In his book, Putnam (1993a) attacks two enduring problems in social science: how to marry directly collected quantitative data with historical information from external sources, and how to connect political culture to democracy. The first problem is particularly thorny when the logic of inference from primary data is cross-sectional while the external data are historical; the second is even tougher when political culture is specified and operationalized through past political traditions, while the indicators of democracy are lodged in the present. Since Putnam attempts both of these things, examining *Making Democracy Work* will help understand the problems we face both in joining history to systematic empirical data and in linking political culture to democracy.

Making Social Science Work: The Achievements of Putnam

It is worth underscoring the strategy and main successes of *Making Democracy Work*. Putnam's achievements are three. First, both the *APSR* article (Putnam and others 1983) and the book demonstrate how—and how uneven—institutional innovations are translated into practice. Second, Putnam shows that institutional performance is not policy-specific or idiosyncratic but is coherent among policy sectors and stable over time. Third, he shows how the same seeds of institutional innovation grow differently in different socioeconomic and cultural soils to produce different kinds of institutional plants.[5] Let us examine each of these claims before turning to the problems of explanation sketched above.

Institutional Change and Democratic Politics

"Those who build new institutions," writes Robert Putnam in chapter 2 of his book, "and those who would evaluate them need patience" (1993a, 60). Not the least virtue of Putnam and his collaborators was to have the endurance and creativity to carry out research tasks in the Italian regions since they were created more than twenty years ago.[6] Given the growing tendency in parts of our discipline to substitute affirmations of revealed preferences for observation of behavior, this was no mean feat. But still more impressive is that, without suffering visibly from discontinuity, *Making Democracy Work* reads like a stratified rock formation of U.S. political science over the last three decades: from the behavioral methods and political culture theories of the 1960s to the policy-oriented studies of the 1970s, to the game theoretical perspectives and historical turn of the 1980s and early 1990s.

Putnam's central problem is a classical political culture dilemma[7]: How do traditions of association and civic engagement affect political behavior? He first examines how the regional governments created in Rome in 1970 and implanted over the next two decades in Italy's regions compare in terms of various measures of policy performance that he has constructed. He finds dramatic differences between the regions in North and South, differences that associate with different levels of civic involvement. Next he turns to the histories of each region to seek the sources of these differences in performance. Finally, he interprets the results in terms of the category of "social capital," a property that he finds lacking in southern Italy but flourishing in the North. This he broadens to the problem of democracy anywhere in the world, including the United States (1993a, chapter 6; also see Putnam 1994 and 1995), for where there is no social capital, he argues, democracy cannot flourish.

The first and uncontested success of these decades of research was to provide a magnificent profile of the birth, growth, and institutionalization of new representative institutions (Putnam 1993a, 17). But as the imperfect progress of the Italian regions shows, "that institutional reforms alter behavior is an hypothesis, not an axiom" (18), and the hypothesis was only partially supported by the results of the regional reform. For while the first two decades in the life of the new institutions "transformed elite political culture" (28), the greater efficiency that reformers anticipated from it did not materialize, and some of the classical dysfunctions of Italian public life even appear to have been exacerbated by it (61).[8]

Measuring Political Performance

That some units of government will perform better than others is true by definition; and that Italy's regions are diverse and unevenly endowed is the first law that any student of Italian politics learns.[9] But without systematic measurement and comparison of policy areas, two possibilities follow. First, the aphorism "The South is different" may prove no more than a piece of political folklore. Second, as Theodore Lowi (1985) argues, each policy area may have a distinct politics, leading to the inference that it is the politics of the particular policy regime and not the character of the political unit that is responsible for the outcomes observed (67-68).

Putnam's analysis shows that neither of these is the case for the Italian regional governments. His book documents and quantifies the regional governments' policy performance in twelve distinct policy areas and dimensions, finding the South consistently performing worse in each area and over time (Putnam 1993a, 65-76).

Not only that: The "objective" measures of policy performance that he developed correlate significantly with the assessments made by citizens and community elites of their own region's effectiveness (76-80). In every respect, what we suspected is true after all: The South is different, and this difference is so profound that even the new and formally standardized institutions simultaneously created in North and South were penetrated by it, affecting every aspect of policy performance. But does this difference, and the variations in institutional capacity that it produces, predict democracy? There is a long row to hoe until we get there.

Making Direct Inferences from Paired Comparisons

Although Putnam first set out to study the effects of a new institution on political socialization and recruitment over time (1993a, xiv; Putnam and others 1981), the cross-sectional differences he found led him away from his initial time-series design to a cross-sectional one. Using the North-South cleavage as an analytical lever, he began to ask: What it is about the South that is different (83), and can it be linked to deficiencies observed in its regional governments' performance? And what is it about the Center-North in Italy that helped its regions turn the same new institutions to effective use? After a brief consideration of socioeconomic modernity, which Putnam argues does not explain the differences between North and South,[10] he centers on a construct he calls "the civic community" (enter political culture). This he links intellectually to the tradition of civic humanism (87), which he specifies through four theoretical dimensions: (1) civic engagement, (2) political equality, (3) solidarity, trust, and tolerance, and (4) the social structures of cooperation (87-91).

Putnam spends a good deal of effort fleshing out the political and social correlates of these indicators (96-116) before building his measure of civic community on the first and the fourth: civic engagement, which he measures through newspaper readership and voting in referenda, and associational structures, which he measures through the density of sports clubs and other associations. He then adds another measure whose relation to civic humanism is not so obvious, the voters' use of individual preference voting, which he sees as a surrogate for clientelism and thus for the noncivic community.[11]

Although these measures bring into the analysis data from outside Putnam's primary data set, they were collected in standard form across the regions and are ordinal in form, and thus they can reasonably be associated with the indicators Putnam developed to measure institutional performances.[12] When combined, Putnam's composite index of civic capacity correlates impressively with the institutional performance of the regional governments. Figure 1 [not reproduced—editors' note], which reproduces Putnam's scattergram of the regions, tells the dramatic story. *All* the regions with high institutional performance and high scores on the civic community index are from the Center-North; *all* those that score low on both these measures are in the South. The North is the home of civic competence and institutional performance[13]; the South is the site of neither.[14] "Happiness," concludes Putnam, "is living in a civic community" (113).

It should be noted that in making the case for the North's civic capacity and for the South's civic weakness, Putnam's eye perhaps swept a bit too broadly across the Italian landscape to allow him to catch sight of a few jagged outcroppings which might have given him pause. On the one hand, recent research directed by Carlo Trigilia shows a growth in associational activity in the South, "in part political, but above all cultural, which is shaping new possibilities on the level of democratic growth and the positive use of civic resources" (Ramella 1995, 471).[15] On the other hand, it would have been interesting to learn what Putnam would make of the successive explosions in northern Italian public life that were erupting as *Making Democracy Work* was going to press: of corruption scandals on top of separatism; of Mafia infestation on top of years of terrorism and political kidnappings; of the collapse of the Marxist and Catholic subcultures with their panoply of mass organizations, giving way to a party system whose capillary structures have all but disappeared.

Do Trigilia's findings on associational capacity question Putnam's image of the South? And do the symptoms of crime, separatism, and corruption mark a collapse of the North's vaunted civic capacity? Or does civic capacity have another face, one with less positive implications for democracy (Levi 1996)? Before turning to the democratic implications of civic capacity, let us follow Putnam in searching for its origins.

The Pathways of Putnam: Reaching Beyond Direct Inference into History

For some social scientists, the internal inferences reported above and the startlingly high correlations they produced would have satisfied their urge for viable generalizations. But Putnam wanted to go farther.[16] He thought the differences he had found through cross-sectional analysis of his data transcended his study's initial focus on institutional growth—and on Italy. In fact, he argues, they "had astonishingly deep historical roots" (1993a, xiv). So, from an empirical focus on the cross-sectional variations within the twenty-year period of the Italian regional experience, his analytical lens shifted boldly to interpreting the differences among the regions in terms of longer historical differences. Much longer.

From City-State to Civic Competence

Leaving behind his familiar terrain of quantitative, cross-sectional statistical analysis, Putnam traveled back to the late-medieval origins of north-central Italy's city-state governments and to the simultaneous development of the autocratic Norman regime in the South during the same period. In both cases, he found analogues to the divergent civic capacities he identified in his contemporary data, analogues that he interpreted as their indirect causes. In the history of the South from the eleventh to the thirteenth century, he found a steep social hierarchy that was ever more dominated by a landed aristocracy endowed with feudal powers, while at the bottom of the social pyramid masses of peasants struggled wretchedly close to the limits of physical survival (1993a, 123-124). Meanwhile, in the North, the solution created in these early times was quite different, "relying less on vertical hierarchy and more on horizontal collaboration" (124). By the beginning of the fourteenth century, Putnam argues, Italy had produced not one but two patterns of governance with their associated social and cultural features (130). These syndromes had crucial outcomes for the civic capacity of each region:

> Collaboration, mutual assistance, civic obligation, and even trust . . . were the distinguishing features in the North. The chief virtue in the South, by contrast, was the imposition of hierarchy and order on latent anarchy. (130)

I cannot deal fairly here with the historiographic aspects of Putnam's analysis of southern Italy since the Norman conquest or with the criticisms they have raised.[17] But it is worth pointing out that his image of the late-medieval northern city-state as a paragon of civic republicanism is telescopic, to say the least.[18] That the early Italian city-states had associational origins did not make them inherently civic, or even "horizontal." After a short period as voluntary associations, most of them produced closed urban oligarchies, fought constantly over territory and markets, and left the urban poor vertically compromised.

Moreover, Putnam places within the same general category of civic republicanism some northern regions whose experiences with communal democracy were long, others that were brief, and still others that were subject to continued feudal control or to the extended authority of the pope (Cohn 1994, 317).[19] Finally, in focusing on the golden age of the city-state, he treats the five or six centuries that followed somewhat cavalierly, trolling rapidly through a long and turbulent stretch of history for analogues of the cultural patterns he found in the earlier period without specifying the links either theoretically or empirically.

This is the feature of Putnam's evidentiary structure that has caused the greatest perplexity among historians and others (for example, see Cohn 1994, 319).[20] It would have been interesting to know by what rules of inference he chose the late-medieval period as the place to look for the source of northern Italy's twentieth-century civic superiority.[21] Why not look to the region's sixteenth-century collapse at the hands of more robust European monarchies; at its nineteenth-century conquest of the South (see below); at its 1919-21 generation of fascism; or at its 1980s corruption-fed economic growth.[22] None of these phenomena were exactly "civic"; by what rules of evidence are they less relevant in "explaining" the northern regions' civic superiority over the South than the period 800 years ago when republican governments briefly appeared in (some of) its cities?

But let us not exaggerate the importance of Putnam's speculations on distant historical times. Ever the empiricist, when his quest reached the nineteenth century, for which regional statistical data begin to be available, he developed a statistical index of "civic involvement" for each region which reinforced his image of the two regions. He found that "the same [north-central] Italian regions that sustained cooperatives and choral societies also provided the most support for mutual aid societies and mass parties" and that "citizens in those same regions were the most eager to make use of their newly granted electoral rights" (1993a, 149). In the South, in contrast, "apathy and ancient vertical bonds of clientelism restrained civic involvement and inhibited voluntary, horizontally organized manifestations of social solidarity" (149).

The index of civic participation that Putnam developed for 1860-1920 correlates strongly with his directly observed contemporary indices of civic capacity ($r = .93$) and with the institutional performance of the regional governments ($r = .86$). So, on top of the other achievements in his book, Putnam appears to have demonstrated a correlation and a putative causal link from the communal associations of the early medieval city-state, to the growth of civic capacity in the nineteenth century, to contemporary civic politics and institutional performance. But there are problems with these sequential historical adumbrations of civic capacity.

First, looking backward from the nineteenth century, the fact that associations appear in different periods of a society's history does not give them each a similar function in that society or even make them "horizontal." Here, Putnam makes the same analogical error across time as did his great teacher, Tocqueville, across space, when he saw American voluntary associations as the analogue to the lost world of the French estates. When we look carefully at the intermediate structures that Tocqueville saw as buffers against an overweening Old Regime, they turn out to have been far less "horizontal" and certainly less nurturing of democracy than were the town meetings and local civic associations he found in America. Putnam makes a similar assumption about associations in different periods of Italian history.

Second, looking forward, although Putnam's nineteenth-century statistical measures of civic competence are ingenious and correlate strongly with his findings about contemporary performance and civic competence, it is not clear what these measures signify. To the naked eye, all the elements in this index (mutual aid societies, cooperatives, voting turnout, and unionization) support the thesis of civic competence. But why are they strongest in the areas of the Po Valley in which popular politics, both socialist and Catholic, took hold in the late nineteenth century—what today we would call "the Third Italy" (Bagnasco 1994; Trigilia 1986)? This is no accident: Both socialist and Catholic parties rooted themselves in this soil by a deliberate strategy of creating just the kind of secondary associations that make up Putnam's measures of civic capacity. And these regions happen, for the most part, to be the areas of both effective regional government and progressive politics today.

Thus, the impressive correlations that Putnam displays in chapter 5 (figures 5.3 and 5.4), which he interprets as evidence of a causal link between past civic competence and present regional performance, can also be interpreted as a correlation between progressive politics then and now and between progressive political traditions and civic capacity. In both periods, electorates were deliberately mobilized on the basis of networks of mass organizations and social and recreational associations; and in both, civic competence was deliberately developed after World War II as a symbol of the left-wing parties' governing capacity (Putnam 1993a, 149, Table 5.1, 119). Both progressive politics and civic capacity were correspondingly weak in the South (Tarrow 1967a, chapters 3 and 8).

To some, these may seem like methodological niceties, but they begin to indicate an alternative model: The operative cause of the performance of the regional institutions in both North and South is neither cultural nor associational but political (Pasquino 1994). Expressed in the form of a hypothesis, the historical evidence can be read as support for the idea that the nineteenth-century popular politics of north-central Italy are themselves the source of both the civic community and the positive political performance of its regional governments. But something more than party building was occurring in nineteenth-century Italy—there was also state building and the differential structuring of a public culture.

The Perils of Putnam:
State Building, State Strategy, and Democracy

This takes us to the causes of the civic incapacity that Putnam identifies in the South and to the causes and remedies of the lack of social capital in general. Even agreeing with his depiction of the lack of institutional performance in the Italian South, I wish to raise two sorts of questions about its causes: the role of state structures in making causal inferences about civic capacity and the relations between social capital and democracy.

States as Independent Variables
This is not the place to speculate about the manifold mediations that could have helped explain the correlations Putnam found between civic vitality and regional policy performance. But there is one alternative or complementary explanation for Putnam's findings that he never considers: the effect of the pattern of state building on indigenous civic capacity.[23] The best way to suggest this is with a datum Putnam provides but passes over very quickly: Every regime that governed southern Italy from the Norman establishment of a cen-

tralized monarchy in the twelfth century to the unified government which took over there in 1861 was foreign and governed with a logic of colonial exploitation. Indeed, as he remarks, the last two regimes in the region before it unified with the North in 1861 followed a strategy of promoting "mutual distrust and conflict among their subjects, destroying horizontal ties of solidarity in order to maintain the primacy of vertical ties of dependence and exploitation" (136).

Nor did southern Italy's semicolonial status suddenly disappear with unification. The region was joined to the North by a process of rival conquest, its fragile commercial sector brutally merged with the North's more flourishing economy, a uniform tax system and customs union imposed on its vulnerable industries, and brigandage rooted out by a full-scale military campaign. Politically, the South's communes and provinces were governed by northern administrators who regarded the region as a *terra di missione,* and its economy was penetrated by carpetbaggers in search of new markets and raw materials.

Putnam does not neglect to describe the *trasformismo* that linked the South to national politics after unification.[24] But he says much less about how the region was actually governed: about prefects who bought elections for the government's candidates; about how they often arrested unfriendly candidates and closed down local governments which displeased them; and about the cooptation of the local elite into patron-client chains that began with the day worker standing hat in hand in the daily labor market in the village piazza and ended in the ministries in Rome (1993a, 124).[25] Like the merger of West and East Germany 130 years later, a stronger, richer, more legitimate regime conquered a weaker, poorer, more marginal one, inducting its residents into political life through the tools of patronage, paternalism, and the power of money—and rubbing it in by sending in commissions of experts to shake their heads over their backwardness.

Nor did the differences in state intervention in northern and southern Italy end when the "liberal" state gave way to the corporate and republican ones in the next century. Leaving fascism aside, since the end of World War II, the Italian state has continued to intervene in the South with "extraordinary" initiatives and institutions, interacting with the local elite in ways that are far different from its interactions with north-central Italy (for example, see Trigilia 1992). Putnam gives us a great deal of information about the development of the Italian regions after 1970, but he says much less about the system of center/periphery ties into which the new institutions were inserted.

How could Robert Putnam, who knows the history of Italian unification well, have missed the penetration of southern Italian society by the northern state and the effect this had on the region's level of civic competence? The reason seems to lie in the model with which he turned to history, a model that conceived of civic capacity as a native soil in which state structures grow rather than one shaped by patterns of state building and state strategy. In a comparison between the nineteenth-century unification of Italy and the twentieth-century installation of the regions, Putnam reveals this "bottom-up" model of causation very clearly. He writes:

The new institutions of the unified nation-state, far from homogenizing traditional patterns of politics, were themselves *pulled* ineluctably into conformity with those contrasting traditions, just as the regional governments after 1970 would be *remolded* by these same social and cultural contexts (Putnam 1993a, 145, emphasis added).

"Pulled"? "Remolded"? Who are the agents doing this pulling and remolding? Putnam does not say, and the lack of state agency in the book is one of the major flaws of his explanatory model.

More than thirty years ago, Edward Banfield (1958) went to a village in southern Italy and found a lack of associational activity, which led him to posit a lack of civic capacity, too.[26] With far more theoretical sophistication and more systematic data, Putnam's treatment of the relations between state and civic capacity in the South resembles Banfield's logic. For him, as for Banfield, the character of the state is external to the model, suffering the results of the region's associational incapacity but with no responsibility for producing it. But as Alessandro Pizzorno (1971, 87-98) asked, in the context of a centralized state with a system of Roman law, and a history of marginality, can we be satisfied interpreting civic capacity as a home-grown product in which the state has played no role? The new Italian regions were certainly installed in different soils in northern and southern Italy. But an important part of that difference was a public culture shaped by more than a century of political and administrative dependence.

Political Culture and Democracy

This takes us to my final argument with Putnam's interpretation of his findings. His key causal inference, that a history of vibrant communal government has produced present civic capacity in the North, while autocratic monarchism was the source of the South's lack of civism, is a plausible one that may apply to other countries as well. In fact, Putnam himself is leading an initiative in this direction in the United States.[27] But does this mean we should expect to find a history of communal autonomy and flowering mercantile life everywhere that we encounter contemporary civic competence? And a history of communal weakness and centralized autocracy wherever we find civic incapacity? Putnam at one point quotes Maurice Agulhon's work on sociability in the villages of southern France as a parallel to the associational capacity Putnam found in northern Italy (Putnam 1993a, 137-38; Agulhon 1982). But he is surely aware that the Provençal villagers Agulhon studied organized their *cercles* and *chambrées* in the context of a state which was militantly centralizing and intruded heavily on local life.[28] If associational capacity co-occurs with state centralization in southern France and with local communal traditions in northern Italy, then either the link between communal traditions and civic competence is problematic, or it must be much more mediated than what Putnam describes.

This leads to my final point: How does the chain of causation that Putnam posits relate to the practice of democracy—which, after all, is in the title of his book? Let us summarize Putnam's argument. At the beginning of his causal chain depicting northern Italy's civic virtues are the horizontal associations of the late-medieval city-states; this civic capacity reappears in different form in nineteenth-century mutual aid societies, cooperatives, unions, and voting behavior and, in broader form, in the civic competence of today. This in turn produces the relative success of the regional institutions in the North, the ultimate outcome of which is to make democracy work, and the weak institutional performance of the South. "Tocqueville was right," concludes Putnam: "Democratic government is strengthened, not weakened, when it faces a vigorous civil society" (1993a, 182).

Putnam marshals a good deal of evidence that northern Italy, with greater civic competence, has higher institutional performance and that the citizens in the higher performance regions get results that they like. He regards this finding as a surrogate for democratic government. But is the causal link between the political culture of association and the practice of democracy really as straightforward as this? In the first place, Putnam's operational dependent variable is not democratic practice but policy *performance,* and performance is as likely to be positive in nondemocratic as in democratic states. There is good evidence that the administrative structures of southern and northern Italy worked as differently under fascism as they do today: Would that make fascist northern Italy more democratic than the South in Mussolini's heyday?

Finally, if we define democracy as effective policy performance, we run the risk of falling into an elitist definition of democracy. But if, as this reviewer is inclined to do, we follow the classics and define it as popular sovereignty and individual rights, I am afraid that history gives us little reason to expect a strong association with institutional performance. Putnam's book is good social science across space; its evidence about the historical and political-cultural sources of policy performance, although it can be challenged, is intriguing; but the book has little to say about democracy.

Making Social Science Work Across Space and Time

If the above observations are read as counseling students to stick to their own turf and never try to marry qualitative and historical information to quantitative data, this review will have been seriously misread (Tarrow 1995, reviewing King, Keohane, and Verba 1994). On the contrary, Putnam's achievement is to have gone considerably beyond the statistical model of cross-sectional comparison with which he began and to have integrated both quantitative and qualitative historical sources with his findings on contemporary institutional performance. I want to argue a somewhat different case.

Making History Work Better
History is not a neutral reservoir of facts out of which viable generalizations are drawn. The social scientist looking for validation of research findings goes to history with a theory, or at least with a set of theoretical hunches. Putnam's hunches came from his admiration of civic competence, specified and operationalized mainly through association. From the original twenty-year time frame

of the study and the expectation that explanation would come from direct inference on behavioral variables, his focus shifted to a much longer time frame in order to interpret and explain what he had observed. The key to that door became historically developed traditions of civic competence.

But how can a concept that is derived from contemporary democratic politics be transposed to other periods of history and to other political systems? In the course of his search through history, Putnam's key variable intersected with a wide variety of institutional and sociological contexts. I have pointed to the effect of the national state in the South; another was the rise of popular political traditions in the Po Valley. Social scientists ignore history at their peril; but when we go to history, we must be aware that our models affect what we look for, how we interpret it, and how we conjoin it to our own data. The strength of Putnam's achievement was to go outside the comfort of his data into the less certain terrain of narrative and quantitative history; its main weakness was in the lack of a structural perspective with which to interpret what he found there.

Extending "Social Capital" Carefully

A final note: Some of my readers have found the above arguments so persuasive that they wonder why a reviewer would give the book such extended attention. This is a mistake. Putnam's bold hypothesis about the Italian South's civic incompetence—translated into his broader theory of social capital in chapter 6 and in subsequent publications (Putnam 1993b, 1995)—goes well beyond southern Italy. It parallels both arguments made about the causes of the urban malaise in U.S. society today and the developmental problems of the Third World. According to these arguments, the source of the personal anomie and social disintegration in U.S. urban ghettos and the weakness of development in parts of the Third World is a lack of social capital. This leads to a Tocquevillian policy prescription to policy makers: Work to develop networks of social capital in the cities and cooperative arrangements among Third World small farmers.

But if this reviewer is correct, and if the absence of civic capacity is the by-product of politics, state building, and social structure, then the causes of the malaise in U.S. cities or in Third World agriculture are more likely to be found in such structural factors as the flight of real capital, in the first case, and the instability of commodity prices and the presence of exploitative governments, in the second. In north Philadelphia and the Sahel, as in southern Italy, while the indicators of malaise may be civic, the causes are structural. If my critique of Putnam in southern Italy can be extended as far as his theory, then policy makers who attack the lack of social capital by encouraging association would be attacking the symptoms and not the causes of the problem.

But the achievements of *Making Democracy Work* are as impressive as its problems. After years in which the country was regarded as a kind of Potemkin democracy, Putnam has placed Italy squarely back among the industrial democracies of the West with important lessons to teach students of comparative politics. Through an ingenious strategy of controlled paired comparison, he demonstrated how institutional reform intersects with different contextual styles of politics to produce different plants from the same seeds. He has interpreted his results in such catholic terms that students of cultural interpretation and public choice—who differ in so many ways—can find common ground in the outcome. Scholars coming from a structuralist persuasion, like this reviewer, will be less easily convinced, but even they receive satisfaction from the fact that Putnam's concept of social capital has a structural as well as a normative dimension. If the results can be criticized, it is because Putnam dared to traverse the gap between the presentism of much social science work and the less certain terrain of history and culture. *Making Democracy Work* is a milestone in the marriage of quantitative and qualitative cultural and policy research and should inspire researchers for years to come.

References

Agulhon, M. 1982. *The republic in the village: The people of the Var from the French Revolution to the Second Republic.* New York: Cambridge University Press.
Bagnasco, A. 1994. Regioni, tradizione civica, modernizzazi-one italiana: Un commento alla ricerca di Putnam. *Stato e mercato* 40 (April): 93-104.
———. 1995. Regions, civic tradition and Italian modernization. *APSA-CP* (Newsletter of the APSA Organized Section in Comparative Politics) 6 (Summer): 4-5.
Banfield, E. C. 1958. *The moral basis of a backward society.* Chicago: Free Press.
Bizzocchi, R. 1987. Chiesa e potere nella Toscana del Quattrocento. Bologna: Il Mulino.
Cohn, S. K., Jr. 1994. La storia secondo Robert Putnam. *Polis* 8 (August): 315-324.
della Porta, D. 1992. *Lo scarnbio occulto. Casi di corruzione politica in Italia.* Bologna: II Mulino.
Feltrin, Paolo. 1994. Review of *La tradizione civica nelle regioni italiane. Rivista italiana di scienza politica* 24 (April): 169-172.
Fried, R. 1963. *The Italian prefects: A study in administrative politics.* New Haven, CT: Yale University Press.
Goldberg, E. 1996. Thinking about how democracy works. *Politics and Society* 4 (March): 7-18.
King, G., R. Keohane, and S. Verba, 1994. *Designing social inquiry: Scientific inquiry in qualitative research.* Princeton, NJ: Princeton University Press.
Laitin, D. 1994. The civic culture at thirty. *American Political Science Review* 89 (March):168-173.
LaPalombara, J. 1965. Italy: Fragmentation, isolation, alienation. In *Political culture and political development*, edited by L. W. Pye and S. Verba. Princeton, NJ: Princeton University Press.
———. 1993. Review of *Making Democracy Work. Political Science Quarterly* 108 (3): 549-550.
Leonardi, R., and R. Y. Nanetti, eds. 1990. *The regions and European integration: The case of Emila-Romagna.* New York: Pinter.
Levi, M. 1996. Social and unsocial capital. *Politics and Society* 24 (March): 45-55.
Lipset, S. M. 1995. Malaise and resiliency in America. *Journal of Democracy* 6(3): 2-16.
Lowi, T. J. 1985. The state in politics: The relation between policy and administration. In *Regulatory Policy and the Social Sciences,* edited by R. G. Noll. Berkeley: University of California Press.
Molho, A. 1994. *Marriage alliances in late medieval Florence.* Cambridge, MA: Harvard University Press.
Mutti, A. 1995. Paths of development. *APSA-CP* (Newsletter of the APSA organized Section in Comparative Politics) 6 (Summer): 6-8.
Nanetti, R. Y. 1988. *Growth and territorial policies: The Italian model of social capitalism.* New York: Pinter.
Pasquino, G. 1994. La politica eclissata dalia ttadizione civica. *Polis* 8 (August): 307-313.
———. 1995. The politics of civic tradition eclipsed. *APSA-CP* (Newsletter of the APSA Organized Section in Comparative Politics) 6 (Summer): 8-9.
Pizzorno, A. 1971. Amoral familism and historical marginality. In *European politics: A reader*, edited by M. Dogan and R. Rose. Boston: Little, Brown.
Putnam, R. D., with R. Leonardi and R. Y. Nanetti. 1993a. *Making democracy work: Civic traditions in modern Italy.* Princeton, NJ: Princeton University Press.
Putnam, R. D. 1993b. The prosperous community. *American Prospect* 13 (Spring): 35-42.
———. 1994. Lo storico e l'attivista. *Polis* 8 (August): 325-328.
———. 1995. Bowling alone: America's declining social capital. *Journal of Democracy* 6 (l): 65-78.

Putnam, R. D., R. Leonardi, and R. Y. Nanetti. 1981. Devolution as a political process: The case of Italy. *Publius* 11 (l):95-117.

———. 1985. *La pianta e le radici: Il radicamento dell'istituto regionale nel sisterna politico italiano.* Bologna: Il Mulino.

Putnam, R. D., R. Leonardi, R. Y. Nanetti, and F. Pavoncello. 1983. Explaining institutional success: The case of Italian regional government. *American Political Science Review* 77 (March): 55-74.

Ramella, F. 1995. Mezzogiorno e societa civile: Ancora l'epoca del familismo? *Il Mulino* 44 (May-June): 471-480.

Review symposium, the qualitative-quantitative disputation: Gary King, Robert 0. Keohane, and Sidney Verba's *Designing Social Inquiry. American Political Science Review* 89 (July): 45-81.

Sabetti, F. 1996. Path dependency and civic culture: Some lessons from Italy about interpreting social experiments. *Politics and Society* 24 (March):19-44.

Salvemini, G. 1955. *Scritti sulla questione meridionale, 1896-1955.* Turin: Einaudi.

Tarrow, S. 1967a. *Peasant communism in southern Italy.* New Haven, CT: Yale University Press.

———. 1967b. Political dualism and Italian communism. *American Political Science Review* 61 (March): 39-53.

———. 1995. Bridging the quantitative-qualitative divide in political science. *American Political Science Review* 89 (June): 471-474.

Trigilia, C. 1986. *Grandi partiti e piccole irnprese.* Bologna: Il Mulino.

———. 1992. *Sviluppo senza autonomia. Effetti perversi delle politiche nel Mezzogiorno.* Bologna: Il Mulino.

———. 1994. Dai comuni medievali alle nostre regioni. *L'indice,* No. 3 (March): 36.

Trigilia, C., ed. 1995. *Cultura e sviluppo. L'associazionismo nel mezzogiorno.* Rome: Donzelli.

Ventura, A. 1964. *Nobilta e popolo nella societa veneta del '400 e '500.* Bari: Laterza.

PART V

Social Movements, Collective Identity, and Political Culture

Introduction

Social movements and the formation of collective identities associated with them provide the basis for one of the most interesting and complex literatures in the area of political culture. One reason for this is that the circumstances in which social movements form are often controversial. The civil rights, gender rights, and gay rights movements of contemporary American political life offer supportive examples. Additionally, such movements may cluster in time and foreshadow shifts in societal trajectory. The hectic American reform period of the late 1960s and early 1970s, for example, combined elements of the gender, race, and antiwar movements into a quilt that challenged many of the dominant norms of society. Therefore, the social consequences of collective identity formation and social movement activity make these phenomena important areas of study.

Research into social movements and the formation of collective identities focuses on several core questions. Dominant issues include: how and why individuals decide that social change is desirable and so form groups with particular shared goals, what conditions promote or undermine social movement formation and outcomes, what internal dynamics hold movements together or tear them apart, and what long-term effects social movements have within a given polity.

Crucial to understanding and evaluating relations among social movements, collective identities, and political culture is a concept examined with some care in part VII, "Culture and Rationality." For the moment and briefly, some theorists think of rationality as an instrumental concept involving an evaluation of the efficiency with which particular actions realize given ends. *Why* people want what they do is beyond the bounds of their explanatory concerns. Thus spending discretionary income on candy bars can be seen as rational if the individual seeks to satisfy a craving for sweets. From the standpoint of wanting to build a large investment portfolio, however, the same behavior is irrelevant and would represent an irrational choice of means. Other social theorists are concerned as well with how particular goals are formed from certain social experiences. For them, different "thick" rationalities (Ferejohn 1991, 279-305) reflect varying life experiences by seeking to realize efficiently the distinctive values and associated practical interests fostered by disparate experiences.

One strain of social movement–collective identity research essentially mirrors the instrumental approach to rationality and is known as either structuralism or resource mobilization (hereafter resource mobilization). For researchers with this orientation, social movements form when the dominant social order develops "cracks": problems emerge that the established order cannot solve, the ruling groups suffer some major setback in their authority, or tensions emerge between what people claim to believe and what they actually do. That is, the social order remains relatively stable and potential social movements are virtually invisible until the system develops cracks. Then, in response to the opportunities made available by various contingencies, social movements form. In some cases these movements may repair the cracks in some fashion. In other instances revolutionary movements may expand the cracks, attempting to topple the existing society and construct a new social order in its place. In either case, movements rise in response to certain societal flaws which provide opportunities that movements can exploit in order to achieve their goals. The sources and nature of these goals are not subjects of careful study. Representative examples of such studies include Tilly (1978), Tarrow (1994), McAdam (1982), Skocpol (1979), Goldstone (1991), Kriesi (1990), Kitschelt (1986), Fireman and Gamson (1979, 8-44), McCarthy and Zald (1987), and Freeman (1979, 167-89).

Alternatively, other theorists consider rationality in terms of the appropriateness of reactions to particular contexts. While these analysts may agree that rationality also reflects relations between means and ends, they insist on examining as well how individuals and movements form their goals in the first place. This is a broader conception of rationality than that employed in the resource mobilization approach. This broader view requires explicit consideration of cultural factors in order to ascertain how and why *particular* social movements and collective identities form in response to certain cracks in existing social structures. From this contextual perspective, the resource mobilization approach cannot explain the specific character of various movements and collective identities.

Many studies examine the question of social movement and collective identity formation from an explicitly cultural perspective. In these studies, a movement's specific beliefs and values (its culture) are perceived as helping to shape the particular form, internal dynamics, and ultimate influence it exhibits. For example, studies examine the ways that cultural framing (Snow and Benford 1988, 197-217; Snow et al. 1986), contradictions (Evans 1980; Fishel and Quarles 1970, 218-32; Sitkoff 1978), dramatizations of system vulnerability (Gerber 1962; McAdam 1982), and the appearance of suddenly imposed grievances (Useem 1980; Molotch 1970; Walsh 1981) shape the emergence of social movements and collective identities. The relationship between the broader culture from which a social movement sharing a collective identity emerges and the movement itself is another avenue of research (cf. Bellah et al., 1985; Huntington 1981; Klatch 1995, 74-89; Meyer 1975; Reinarman 1995, 90-109). Other studies examine the unique cultures individual social movements develop and the ways these cultures help to account for these movements' relative success or failure (cf. Freeman 1973; Hunt 1984; Johnston 1991; Mannheim 1952, 276-320). Additional studies of collective identity and social movements have focused on the roles previous movements play in the lives of current efforts (cf. Aveni 1977; Granovetter 1983; Morris 1984; Rupp and Taylor 1987). Finally, another group of studies have analyzed the cultural consequences of social movements (cf. Clemens 1993; McAdam 1988; C. Smith 1991; Snow et al., 1986).

Our reading selections in this part clearly fall into the relatively culturalist strand of analyses of social movements and collective identity formation. Each focuses on the ways that the broader culture helps to shape particular instances of social movement development and collective identity formation. As we argue in part VII, these contextual studies do not reject the resource mobilization approach. Instead, they treat questions of group formation and identity more broadly by inquiring why social movements take specific forms and act in support of particular values and practical interests. Taken together, these readings present an overview of the central issues that direct current research about relations among collective identity, social movements, and political culture.

References and Further Reading

Aveni, A. 1977. The not-so-lonely crowd: Friendship groups in collective behavior. *Sociometry* 40: 96-110.

Bellah, R., R. Madsen, W. Sullivan, A. Swidler, and S. M. Tipton. 1985. *Habits of the heart: Individualism and commitment in American life.* New York: Harper and Row.

Clemens, E. 1993. Organizational repertoires of institutional change: Women's groups and the transformation of U.S. politics, 1890-1920. *American Journal of Sociology* 98: 755-798.

Evans, S. 1980. *Personal politics.* New York: Vintage Books.

Ferejohn, J. 1991. Rationality and interpretation: Parliamentary elections in early Stuart England. In *The economic approach to politics: A critical reassessment of the theory of rational action,* edited by K. R. Monroe. New York: HarperCollins.

Fireman, B., and W. Gamson. 1979. Utilitarian logic in the resource mobilization perspective. In *The dynamics of social movements: Resource mobilization, social control, and tactics,* edited by M. Zald and J. McCarthy. Cambridge, MA: Winthrop.

Fishel, L., Jr., and B. Quarles. 1970. In the New Deal's wake. In *The segregation era, 1863-1954,* edited by A. Weinstein and F. O. Gattell. New York: Oxford University Press.

Freeman, J. 1973. The origins of the women's liberation movement. *American Journal of Sociology* 78: 792-811.

———. 1979. Resource mobilization and strategy: A model for analyzing social movement organization actions. In *The dynamics of social movements: resource mobilization, social control, and tactics,* edited by M. Zald and J. McCarthy. Cambridge, MA: Winthrop.

Gerber, I. 1962. The effects of the Supreme Court's desegregation decision on the group cohesion of New York City's Negroes. *Journal of Social Psychology* 58: 295-303.

Goldstone, J. 1991. The comparative and historical study of revolution, *Annual Review of Sociology* 8: 187-207.

Granovetter, M. 1983. The strength of weak ties: A network theory revisited. In *Sociological theory,* edited by R. Collins. San Francisco: Jossey-Bass.

Hunt, L. 1984. *Politics, culture, and class in the French Revolution.* Berkeley: University of California Press.

Hunter, J. D. 1990. Cultural conflict in America. In *Culture wars: The struggle to define America.* New York: Basic.

Huntington, S. 1981. *American politics: The promise of disharmony.* Cambridge, MA: Harvard University Press.
Johnston, H. 1991. *Tales of nationalism: Catalonia, 1939-1979.* New Brunswick, NJ: Rutgers University Press.
Kitschelt, H. 1986. Political opportunity structures and political protest. *British Journal of Political Science* 16: 57-85.
Klatch, R. 1995. The counterculture, the New Left, and the New Right. In *Cultural politics and social movements,* edited by M. Darnovsky, B. Epstein, and R. Flack. Philadelphia: Temple University Press.
Kriesi, H. 1990. The political opportunity structure of the Dutch peace movement. *Western European Politics* 12: 295-312.
Laraña, E., H. Johnston, and J. Gusfield, eds. 1994. *New social movements: From ideology to identity.* Philadelphia: Temple University Press.
Mannheim, K. 1952. The problem of generations. In *Essays on the sociology of knowledge.* London: Routledge and Kegan Paul.
McAdam, D. 1982. *Political process and the development of Black insurgency, 1930-1970.* Chicago: University of Chicago Press.
———. 1988. *Freedom Summer.* Chicago: University of Chicago Press.
———. 1990. Culture and social movements. In *New social movements: From ideology to identity,* edited by E. Laraña, H. Johnston, and J. Gusfield. Philadelphia: Temple University Press.
McCarthy, J., and M. Zald. 1987. Resource mobilization and social movements: A partial theory. In *Social movements in an organizational society: Collected essays.* New Brunswick, NJ: Transaction Publishers.
Meyer, D. 1975. *The positive thinkers.* Garden City, NY: Doubleday.
Molotch, H. 1970. Oil in Santa Barbara and power in America. *Sociological Inquiry* 40: 131-141.
Morris, A. 1984. *The origins of the Civil Rights Movement.* New York: The Free Press.
Reinarman, C. 1995. The twelve-step movement and advanced capitalist culture: The politics of self-control in postmodernity. In *Cultural politics and social movements,* edited by M. Darnovsky, B. Epstein, and R. Flacks. Philadelphia: Temple University Press.
Rupp, L., and V. Taylor. 1987. *Survival in the doldrums: The American women's rights movement, 1945 to the 1960s.* New York: Oxford University Press.
Sitkoff, H. 1978. *A New Deal for blacks.* New York: Oxford University Press.
Skocpol, T. 1979. *State and social revolutions.* New York: Cambridge University Press.
Smith, C. 1991. *The emergence of liberation theology: Radical religion and social movement theory.* Chicago: University of Chicago Press.
Snow, D., and R. Benford. 1988. Ideology, frame resonance, and participant mobilization. In *From structure to action: Comparing social movement research across cultures,* edited by B. Klandermans, H. Kriesi, and S. Tarrow. Vol. 1 of *International social movement research.* Greenwich, CT: JAI Press.
Snow, D., E. B. Rochford, Jr., S. Worden, and R. Benford. 1986. Frame alignment processes, micromobilization, and movement participation. *American Sociological Review* 51: 464-481.
Swidler, A. 1995. Cultural power and social movements. In *Social movements and culture,* edited by H. Johnson and B. Klandermans. Vol. 4 of *Social movements, protest, and contention,* edited by B. Klandermans. Minneapolis: University of Minnesota Press.
Tarrow, S. 1994. *Power in movement: Social movements, collective action, and mass politics in the modern state.* New York: Cambridge University Press.
Tilly, C. 1978. *From mobilization to revolution.* Reading, MA: Addison-Wesley.
Useem, B. 1980. Solidarity model, breakdown model, and the Boston anti-busing movement. *American Sociological Review* 45: 357-369.
Walsh, E. 1981. Resource mobilization and citizen protest in communities around Three Mile Island. *Social Problems* 29:1-21.

CHAPTER 14

Culture and Social Movements*

Doug McAdam

Originally published in
New Social Movements: From Ideology to Identity, *1994*.

READING INTRODUCTION

McAdam presents a good example of focusing on the questions discussed in the introduction to this section, explaining: why groups form, why they adopt the characteristics they do, what factors shape their success and failure, and how cultures broadly influential in their societies shape their identity and opportunities. Key among the points in his analysis is the concept of "frames." McAdam uses this term to refer to packets of shared assumptions through which particular social movements can be categorized. Frames also highlight common elements through which movements' purposes can be understood. A core belief of the civil rights movement, for example, was that American society was denying African Americans the equality in which the broader society professed to believe. Subsequent movements, such as women's and gay rights movements, have largely adopted the same approach as their members pursue their goals. Social movements, in McAdam's analysis, are embedded in the cultures within which they act and should be understood in relation to both the broader culture and each other across time.

READING TEXT

Over the past two decades, the study of social movements has been among the most productive and intellectually lively subfields within sociology. But, as with all emergent paradigms, the recent renaissance in social movement studies has highlighted certain aspects of the phenomenon while ignoring others. Specifically, the dominance, within the United States, of the "resource mobilization" and "political process" perspectives has privileged the political, organizational,

---

* Acknowledgments: This chapter was completed while I was a Fellow at the Center for Advanced Study in the Behavioral Sciences. Partial support for the year at the Center was provided by the National Science Foundation (BNS-8700864). I would also like to thank Dick Flacks, Hank Johnston, Enrique Laraña, Dieter Rucht, and Sidney Tarrow for their extremely helpful comments on various drafts.

and network/structural aspects of social movements while giving the more cultural or ideational dimensions of collective action short shrift.

From a sociology of knowledge perspective, the recent ignorance of the more cultural aspects of social movements is the result of the rejection of the classical collective behavior paradigm, which emphasized the role of shared beliefs and identities but whose hints of irrationality and pathology (Klapp 1969; Lang and Lang 1961; Smelser 1962) made it unattractive to a new generation of scholars whose own experiences led them to view social movements as a form of rational political action. Whatever the reason, the absence of any real emphasis on ideas, ideology, or identity has created, within the United States, a strong "rationalist" and "structural" bias in the current literature on social movements. At the most macro level of analysis, social movements are seen to emerge in response to the "expansion in political opportunities" that grant formal social movement organizations (SMOs) and movement entrepreneurs the opportunity to engage in successful "resource mobilization." At the micro level, individuals are drawn into participation not by the force of the ideas or even individual attitudes but as the result of their embeddedness in associational networks that render them "structurally available" for protest activity. Until recently, "culture," in all of its manifestations, was rarely invoked by American scholars as a force in the emergence and development of social movements. The renewed interest in the topic has been spurred, in part, by the European "new social movement" perspective, which has made cultural and cognitive factors central to the study of social movements (Brand 1990; Eyerman and Jamison 1991; Melucci 1985, 1989).

This chapter broadens the discourse among movement scholars by focusing on some of the links between culture and social movements. Specifically, I address three broad topics: the cultural roots of social movements, the emergence and development of distinctive "movement cultures," and the cultural consequences of social movements.

The Cultural Roots of Social Movements

The "structural bias" in movement studies is most evident in recent American work on the emergence of social movements and revolutions. With but a few exceptions, recent theorizing on the question has located the roots of social movements in some set of political, economic, or organizational factors. While acknowledging the importance of such factors, I add cultural factors and processes to this list as important constraints or facilitators of collective action. There are three distinct ways in which culture can be said to facilitate movement emergence.

Framing as an Act of Cultural Appropriation

Drawing on the work of Erving Goffman (1974), David Snow and various of his colleagues (Snow et al. 1986; Snow and Benford 1988) have developed the concept of "frame alignment processes" to describe the efforts by which organizers seek to join the cognitive orientations of individuals with those of social movement organizations. The task is to propound a view of the world that both legitimates and motivates protest activity. The success of such efforts is determined, in part, by the *cultural resonance* of the frames advanced by organizers. In this sense, framing efforts can be thought of as acts of cultural appropriation, with movement leaders seeking to tap highly resonant ideational strains in mainstream society (or in a particular target subculture) as a way of galvanizing activism.

Much has been made of Martin Luther King, Jr.'s use of Gandhian nonviolence as an ideological cornerstone of the civil rights movement. In fact, King's interest in and advocacy of Gandhi's philosophy was largely irrelevant to the rapid emergence and spread of the civil rights struggle. Far more significant was King's appropriation and powerful evocation of highly resonant cultural themes, not only in the southern black Baptist tradition, but in American political culture more generally.

> Consider King's "I Have a Dream" speech. Juxtaposing the poetry of the scriptural prophets—"I have a dream that every valley shall be exalted, every hill and mountain shall be made low"—with the lyrics of patriotic anthems—"This will be the day when all of God's children will be able to sing with new meaning, 'My country 'tis of thee, sweet land of liberty, of thee I sing'"—King's oration reappropriated that classic strand of the American tradition that understands the true meaning of freedom to lie in the affirmation of responsibility for uniting all of the diverse members of society into a just social order. (Bellah et al. 1985, 249)

Indeed, this was King's unique genius: to frame civil rights activity in a way that resonated not only with the culture of the oppressed but with the culture of the oppressor as well. King successfully mobilized Southern blacks while he generated considerable sympathy and support for the movement among whites as well.

The student democracy movement in Beijing in the spring of 1989 also drew on deeply resonant cultural themes and traditions in the early days of the struggle. The initial march on April 27 that stimulated the movement was ostensibly organized to mark and mourn the death of former premier Yu Yaobang. Such public displays of respect and veneration for departed leaders (and the dead more generally) have deep roots in Chinese political culture. By framing the march as an act of public mourning, movement organizers appropriated long-standing cultural symbols in the service of the movement. This helps explain both the large size of the initial march and the surprising restraint exercised by Communist party leaders in dealing with the students. The cultural legitimacy that attached to the march encouraged participation while constraining official efforts at social control.

Expanding Cultural Opportunities as a Stimulus to Action
Scholars such as Charles Tilly (1978), Sidney Tarrow (1994), Doug McAdam (1982), Theda Skocpol (1979), Jack Goldstone (1991), Hanspeter Kriesi (1990), and Herbert Kitscheit (1986), among others, have established the notion that

social movements/revolutions often emerge in response to an expansion in the "political opportunities" available to a particular challenging group. The argument is that movements are less the product of meso level mobilization efforts than they are the beneficiaries of the increasing political vulnerability or receptivity of their opponents or of the political and economic system as a whole.

Although I generally concur with this view, I think it betrays a "structural" or "objectivist" bias in many of its specific formulations. It is extremely hard to separate these objective shifts in political opportunities from the subjective processes of social construction and collective attribution that render them meaningful. In other words, "expanding political opportunities . . . do not, in any simple sense, produce a social movement. . . . [Instead] they only offer insurgents a certain objective 'structural potential' for collective political action. Mediating between opportunity and action are people and the subjective meanings they attach to their situations" (McAdam 1982, 48).

The causal importance of expanding political opportunities, then, is inseparable from the collective definitional processes by which the meaning of these shifts is assigned and disseminated. Given this linkage, the movement analyst has two tasks: accounting for the structural factors that have objectively strengthened the challenger's hand, and analyzing the processes by which the meaning and attributed significance of shifting political conditions is assessed. This latter task prompts speculation about the existence and significance of expanding cultural opportunities in the emergence of collective action. By "expanding cultural opportunities" we have in mind specific events or processes that are likely to stimulate the kind of collective framing efforts mentioned above. A close reading of the historical literature on social movements suggests that framing efforts may be set in motion by at least four distinct types of expanding cultural opportunities.

Ideological or Cultural Contradictions
The first type of cultural opportunity involves any event or set of events that dramatize a glaring contradiction between a highly resonant cultural value and conventional social practices. Many such examples can be found in the social movement literature. For example, the contrast between the egalitarian rhetoric and the sexist practices of the early American abolitionist movement have long been regarded as an important impetus in the development of the nineteenth-century women's rights movement. As Sara Evans (1980) and others have argued, much the same thing happened in regard to the women's liberation movement of the 1960s and 1970s. In this case, it was the egalitarian rhetoric and forms of sexual discrimination evident within the civil rights movement and the white student Left that fueled the development of a radical feminist "frame" legitimating protest activity.

One final example of the facilitating effect of this kind of ideological or cultural contradiction can be seen in regard to the threatened 1940 march on Washington. A. Philip Randolph, the president of the American Association of Sleeping Car Porters, organized a mass march on Washington to protest discriminatory labor practices in the defense industries. The apparent spur to action in this case was the glaring contradiction between President Franklin D. Roosevelt's growing anti-Nazi rhetoric—especially its "master race" philosophy—and his own tactic acceptance of racial discrimination at home (Fishel and Quarles 1970; Sitkoff 1978).

Suddenly Imposed Grievances
Another cognitive stimulus to framing processes comes from what Edward Walsh (1981) has called "suddenly imposed grievances." The term describes those dramatic, highly publicized, and generally unexpected events—human-made disasters, major court decisions, official violence—that increase public awareness of and opposition to previously accepted societal conditions. As an example of this process, Walsh (1981) cites and analyzes the generation of antinuclear power activity in the area of Three Mile Island following a 1979 accident there. Bert Useem's (1980) analysis of a movement in Boston during the mid 1970s aimed at stopping the busing of school children to achieve school desegregation leaves little doubt that the resistance was set in motion by a highly publicized court order mandating busing. Harvey Molotch (1970) documents a similar rise in protest activity among residents of Santa Barbara, California, in the wake of a major oil spill that took place in 1969. The initial verdict in the Rodney King beating case (Los Angeles, California, April 1992) is as another example of a highly dramatic event spurring protest activity.

Dramatizations of System Vulnerability
Another "cultural" or "cognitive opportunity" that may stimulate increased framing and other mobilization efforts are those events or processes that highlight the vulnerability of one's political opponents. For example, the unanimous 1954 U.S. Supreme Court decision in *Brown v. Board of Education* declaring racially segregated schools unconstitutional convinced many in the black community of the political and legal vulnerability of the southern system of segregation and, in turn, accelerated the pace of civil rights organizing nationwide (Gerber 1962; McAdam 1982).

The collapse of Communist party rule in Poland and the unwillingness of Mikhail Gorbachev to use military force to suppress the Solidarity movement was widely interpreted throughout Eastern Europe as a sign that all Communist regimes in the region were in trouble. This is not to deny the deep structural roots of the crisis in the Soviet Union (see Tarrow 1991), but a crisis needs to be transparent if it is to serve as a cue for collective action. The end of communist rule in Poland served as just such a cue. This pivotal event led, in turn, to increased framing and other mobilization activities by reformers in all of the Warsaw Pact countries.

Finally, the ineffectual 1991 coup attempt by Soviet hard-liners made it clear just how weak and out of touch the once formidable Communist party bosses had become, thus emboldening citizens from across the USSR to step up demands for political independence and economic reform.

The Availability of Master Frames

Finally, one other cultural opportunity has the potential to set in motion framing efforts and mobilization more generally. This is the availability of what David Snow and Robert Benford (1988) term "master protest frames" legitimating collective action. Movement scholars continue to err in viewing social movements as discrete social phenomena. Instead, movements tend to cluster in time and space precisely because they are not independent of one another (McAdam and Rucht 1993). To illustrate, the major movements of the 1960s in the United States were not so much independent entities as offshoots of a single broad activist community with its roots squarely in the civil rights movement (McAdam 1988). One of the things that clearly linked the various struggles during this period was the existence of a "master protest frame" that was appropriated by each succeeding insurgent group. The source of this frame was the civil rights movement, but in short order the other major movements of the period used the ideological understandings and cultural symbols of the black struggle as the ideational basis for their efforts as well. Evans (1980) has documented the ideological/cultural links between the women's liberation and civil rights movements, while Doug McAdam (1988) has done the same for the black struggle and the antiwar and student movements. The ideological imprint of the civil rights movement is also clear in regard to the gay rights, American Indian, farmworkers, and other leftist movements of the period. All of these groups, drawing heavily upon the "civil rights master frame," came to define themselves as victims of discrimination and, as such, deserving of expanded rights and protection under the law. They mapped their understandings of their own situations on the general framework first put forward by civil rights activists.

The same point applies with equal force to other periods of heightened movement activity. The rash of student movements that flourished around the globe (for example, in Spain, Mexico, Japan, France, Italy, Germany, and the United States) in 1968 were clearly attuned to and influenced by one another, resulting in the development and diffusion of a "student left master frame" (Caute 1988; Katsiaficas 1987).

In similar fashion, the success of Solidarity in finally breaking the Communist party's forty-four-year monopoly on power in Poland encouraged other Eastern European dissidents to adopt prodemocracy frames in their own countries. The same process can be seen in the former Soviet Union, with the success of independence movements in the Baltic states encouraging the rise of ideologically similar ethnic nationalist movements in many of the other former Soviet republics.

The more general theoretical point is that successful framing efforts are almost certain to inspire other groups to reinterpret their situation in light of the available master frame and to mobilize based on their new understanding of themselves and the world around them. Thus, the presence of such a frame constitutes yet another cultural or ideological resource that facilitates movement emergence.

The Role of Long-Standing Activist Subcultures in Movement Emergence

Movement scholars have focused a great deal of attention on the role of existing organizations or associational networks in the emergence of protest activity (Freeman 1973; Gould 1991; McAdam 1982, 1986; Morris 1984; Oberschall 1973; Rosenthal et al. 1985). This literature betrays the "structural bias" of the field as a whole. Virtually all of these authors attribute the importance of prior organization to the concrete organizational resources, that is, leaders, communication networks, and meeting places, that such groups provide. Established organizations, however, are the source of cultural resources as well.

In other words, what is too often overlooked in structural accounts of movement emergence is the extent to which these established organizations/networks are themselves embedded in long-standing activist subcultures capable of sustaining the ideational traditions needed to revitalize activism following a period of movement dormancy. These enduring activist subcultures function as repositories of cultural materials into which succeeding generations of activists can dip to fashion ideologically similar, but chronologically separate, movements. To use Ann Swidler's (1986) term, these subcultures represent the specialized "tool kits" of enduring activist traditions. The presence of these enduring cultural repertoires frees new generations of would-be activists from the necessity of constructing new movement frames from whole cloth. Instead, most new movements rest on the ideational and broader cultural base of ideologically similar past struggles. To assert such continuity is to take issue with certain new social movement theorists (Melucci 1989) who hold that the movements of the 1960s and 1970s represented a total break with past activism. That these movements extended and modified existing activist traditions is undeniable. At the same time, it seems clear that they were initially rooted in the very traditions they subsequently transcended. Examples of these kinds of cross-generational continuities in movement activity are numerous.

In all western industrial nations, for example, the tradition of labor activism has served as a broad cultural template available to succeeding generations of workers as a resource supporting mobilization. In similar fashion, several generations of American peace movements have drawn on a rich pacifist tradition, as nurtured and sustained by a combination of religious denominations (for example, Quakers and Unitarians) and secular-humanist organizations (for example, American Friends Service Committee and Fellowship of Reconciliation). At the other end of the political spectrum, an enduring tradition of antiimmigrant and white supremacist activism has served as a broad "tool kit" encouraging American right-wing movements over many generations. Finally, in Spain, long-standing separatist traditions in both Catalonia and the Basque region have served as the wellspring from which several cycles of nationalist movements have flowed.

Although the role of such long-standing activist subcultures has received little attention in studies of movement emergence, their imprint seems apparent. In his definitive study of the structural origins of the American civil rights movement, Aldon Morris (1984) documents the critical contribution made by what he terms "movement halfway houses." These were such established organizations as the Highlander Folk School and the Fellowship of Reconciliation that, despite intense repression, sustained earlier traditions of civil rights activism. They were available to play the role of organizational and cultural "midwives" in the "birth" of the new movement.

Leila Rupp and Verta Taylor (1987) provide a rich, detailed portrait of the survival of another enduring activist subculture—that of American feminism—during the long hiatus between the decline of the suffrage movement and the emergence of the contemporary women's movement. Like Morris, Rupp and Taylor focus on the crucial role of organizations and specific individuals in nurturing and sustaining an activist subculture during a period of movement dormancy. The result was the survival of a set of ideas, organizational practices, and activist traditions that served as one of the important "tool kits" shaping the cultural contours of modern American feminism.

Enrique Laraña offers another example of cultural continuity in activist traditions. He documents the historical persistence of Marxist discourse and images of struggle in one of the two wings of the Spanish student movement. Howard Kimmeldorf's (1989) comparative study of unionism among East and West Coast dockworkers has continued to shape the ideology and practices of the union to the present. Finally, the imprint of long-standing traditions of student activism are evident on a number of American college or university campuses. For example, one of the best predictors of which colleges and universities contributed student volunteers to the 1964 Mississippi Freedom Summer project was the presence of an active socialist or communist student organization on campus during the 1930s. It should come as no surprise that Berkeley and other colleges such as Antioch and Oberlin sent large contingents of volunteers to Mississippi in 1964. In doing so they were merely drawing on and perpetuating the localized activist subcultures that have long existed on and around those campuses.

Movement emergence, then, is never simply the result of some fortuitous combination of macropolitical opportunities and meso level organizational structures. While important, these factors only afford insurgents a certain structural potential for successful protest activity. Mediating between opportunities and concrete mobilization efforts are the shared meanings people bring to their lives. These meanings, in turn, are expected to be shaped by the cultural resources and opportunities mentioned above.

The Emergence and Development of a Movement Culture

An interest in the relationship between social movements and culture clearly transcends the emergent phase of collective action. Indeed, that relationship becomes more complicated and potentially more interesting as the movement develops because the direction of causal influence in the relationship can run both ways. Not only will the movement bear the imprint of the broader cultural context(s) in which it is embedded but insurgents are also likely to develop a distinctive movement culture capable of reshaping the broader cultural contours of mainstream society.

That such cultures do exist is intuitively clear to anyone who has participated in any but the most ephemeral of movements. Social movements tend to become worlds unto themselves that are characterized by distinctive ideologies, collective identities, behavioral routines, and material cultures. The more thoroughgoing the goals of the movement are, the more likely it is that a movement culture will develop. This is not surprising. Having dared to challenge a particular aspect of mainstream society, there is implicit pressure on insurgents to engage in a kind of social engineering to suggest remedies to the problem. The challenge is to actualize within the movement the kind of social arrangements deemed preferable to those the group is opposing. Again, the more thoroughgoing the changes proposed, the more the tendency to conceive of the movement as an oppositional subculture—a kind of idealized community embodying the movement's alternative vision of social life.

Movement cultures are not static over time. Having opened up the question of the restructuring of social arrangements, there is no guarantee that insurgents will confine their attention to the specific issues or institutions originally targeted. When this happens, movements can take on the character of hothouses of cultural innovation. Anything and everything is open to critical scrutiny. Change becomes the order of the day.

At the moment, we lack any real theoretical or empirical understanding of the processes that shape the ongoing development of distinctive movement cultures, and such an understanding is beyond the scope of this chapter. We can begin to move in that direction by calling attention to two factors that would seem to influence the shifting character of a movement's culture.

Shifts in the Social Locus of the Movement

Social movements typically develop within particular social and generational strata or geographic locations. The expectation is that the culture of the movement will, at least initially, reflect these social, generational, and geographic origins. Movements are hardly the property of those population segments who gave them life in the first place. On the contrary, it is not uncommon for the locus of protest activity to shift over the life of a movement. As such shifts occur, we should see a shift in the ideational and material culture of the movement that reflects the new class, regional, generational, or other social loci of the movement.

One example of this process comes from Lynn Hunt's (1984) definitive study, *Politics, Culture, and Class in the French Revolution*. Hunt's work documents the dramatic shift in the dominant ideology and material symbols of the Revolution that accompanied the change in the class composition of the movement between 1789 and 1795. Dominated at the outset by the emerging bourgeoisie, intellectuals, and even elements of the aristocracy, by 1794-1795 control of the Revolution had passed to artisans, shopkeepers, lawyers, and other less class-privileged elements of French society.

An equally dramatic shift in the cultural content of a movement occurred in the American civil rights movement during the decade of the 1960s as a result of a fundamental shift in the class and geographic loci of protest activity. While the movement initially developed within the churches and other institutions of the Southern, urban, black middle class, by the late 1960s its "home" had shifted to the urban ghettos of a poorer and more secular Northern black community. Partly in response to this shift, the ideational and material culture of the movement became less religious in nature, more explicitly political, and more aggressively focused on the assertion of a shared and distinctive "cultural nationalism" among black Americans. This is not to say that these shifts were solely the product of the geographic and social changes, but they clearly played a part in the broader cultural transformation that occurred during these years.

Nancy Whittier (1993) provides a final example of the shifting cultural content of a movement in her analysis of generational replacement in the contemporary women's movement. Whittier argues persuasively that the very real differences in the cultural content and "tone" of the current movement have come about not because the pioneering feminists of the 1960s and 1970s have changed their collective identities but because new "activist cohorts" have entered the movement and brought distinctive cultural styles and identities to the struggle.

Perceived Effectiveness of the Movement's Dominant Core

Successful movements tend to be fairly heterogeneous, drawing adherents from a variety of subgroups within the population. These subgroups will vie for cultural as well as strategic political influence over the movement. At any one time, however, it is usually possible to identify a particular segment within the movement as dominant. To the extent that this segment is widely perceived as substantively effective, its cultural "package" will likely be privileged as well. To the extent it is seen as ineffective, strategic and organizational control of the movement will likely shift (often following a period of conflict) to some other contender, thereby enhancing the importance of its cultural package.

The contemporary women's movement in the United States affords a prime example of this phenomenon. Initially, the movement coalesced around radical feminists with roots in both the American "New Left" and the "counterculture" of the 1960s. Eschewing formal organization and leadership, this wing of the movement pioneered the use of consciousness-raising groups as a form of activism. As effective as these groups were in drawing new recruits into the movement, they came to be seen by many as ineffective vehicles for pursuing political and economic change (Freeman 1973). Partly as a result of this critique, influence over the movement gradually shifted to an older, more politically and organizationally conventional group of women who were affiliated with the National Organization for Women (NOW). The results of this shift were cultural as much as political and organizational, with the countercultural affinities of the radical wing gradually giving way to the more conventional, professionalized ethos of NOW loyalists.

The Cultural Consequences of Movements

In assessing the impact of social movements, scholars have tended to focus their attention narrowly on political or economic consequences. Given the central importance attached to political or economic change by most social movements, this is certainly an important topic for systematic investigation. At the same time, resistance to significant political or economic change is likely to be sufficiently intense as to mute the material effects of all but the most successful movements. As many commentators have noted, even a movement as broad based and widely supported as the American civil rights movement failed to effect the fundamental redistribution in political and economic power that it ultimately sought. The opposition of the political and economic establishment to such a redistribution was simply too strong and too united to permit its occurrence.

Given the entrenched political and economic opposition movements are likely to encounter, it is often true that their biggest impact is more cultural than narrowly political and economic. Although the topic has never been systematically studied, the examples of movement-based cultural change would seem to be numerous and extraordinarily diverse. What follows is an impressionistic survey of some of these many changes. It is not exhaustive; it merely reflects the richness and diversity of the forms of cultural innovation that may be the result of movement dynamics.

As Ralph Turner reminds us, social movements have been the source of some of the most transformative ideologies or belief systems the world has ever known. We would do well to remember that Christianity, Islam, the Protestant Reformation, and subsequent sectarianism began life as the organizing frames for specific social movements. In many other cases, movements served as the principal vehicles by which belief systems, derived elsewhere, were modified and extended. So, for example, Marxist thought was profoundly shaped and deepened by figures associated with both the Russian (Lenin, Trotsky), Chinese (Mao Zedong, Jou Enlai, Lin Biao), and Cuban (Castro, Che Guevara) Revolutions. Through such figures as Voltaire and Rousseau in France and Thomas Paine and Thomas Jefferson in the American colonies, the French and American Revolutions had a similar impact on Enlightenment thinking.

Specific social movements can also give rise to what Snow and his colleagues (1986) call "master protest frames"; that is, ideological accounts legitimating protest activity that come to be shared by a variety of social movements. So, as noted earlier, the civil rights movement advanced a "civil rights" master frame that was, in turn, adopted by other movements as the ideological grounding for their efforts. These movements include the women's, gay rights, handicapped rights, and animal rights movements. The various revolutions in Eastern Europe have appropriated the "democracy frame" first advanced by the Solidarity movement in Poland.

Social movements have also served historically as the source for new collective identities within society. For example, the identities Christian and Muslim emerged in the context of social movements. So, too, did that of the "working class" via the labor movement. In a more contemporary vein, the identity of "feminist" grew out of the modern women's movement. Indeed, many proponents of the new social movements perspective (Inglehart 1981, 1990; Melucci 1980, 1989; Offe 1985; Touraine 1981) argue that what is "new" about the new social movements—including the women's movement—is the central importance they attach to the creation of new collective identities as a fundamental goal of the movement. In fact, social movements have always served this function, whether it was an explicit goal of the movement or an unintended consequence of struggle.

Social movements have also been a force for innovation in strategic action forms. What began as emergent and often illegal tactics in yesterday's movements often become legitimate, institutionalized forms of politics in later years. The strike and the sit-in are two examples. Both tactics were pioneered in the labor movement, but later came to be recognized as legitimate forms of action by various groups. Elisabeth Clemens (1993) argues that the contemporary importance of lobbying owes historically to its successful and legitimating use by women activists in the period from 1880 to 1920.

Throughout history, social movements have also functioned as a source of new material cultural items. Hunt's (1984) cultural analysis of the French Revolution makes clear the extent to which popular symbols and the material culture of France were transformed during the Revolution. Virtually all political revolutions usher in cultural revolutions as well. The Chinese Revolution, for example, set in motion a thoroughgoing state effort to fashion a popular culture compatible with the ideals of the movement. The same thing has occured more recently in Iran, with the Islamic Revolution ushering in a period of intense anti-Western feeling leading to the wholesale rejection of Western-style consumer goods and other cultural items. Ironically, the reverse process is currently underway in the Soviet Union, with the popular rejection of the Communist party encouraging a simultaneous process of Western-style cultural liberalization and experimentation.

Revolutions are not the only force that exert a powerful transformative effect on the material culture of a society. For example, the 1964 Mississippi Freedom Summer Project gave early expression to a number of specific cultural items that came to be associated with the 1960s counterculture (McAdam 1988). In general, as authors such as Morris Dickstein (1989) have shown, the counterculture and the movements of the 1960s had a profound effect on American popular culture. Dress and hairstyles, popular music, movies, dance, and theater were powerfully affected by the political turbulence of the era. The roots of the "drug culture" can also be found in the political and cultural movements of the 1960s. Language was affected; "black English" made inroads into popular English, and the feminist critique of the traditional vernacular prompted efforts to fashion more gender-neutral modes of expression.

Similar linguistic "insurgencies" are currently under way elsewhere. In the Canadian province of Quebec, French-speaking separatists affiliated with the Parti québécois have succeeded in making French the official provincial language. In Catalonia, separatists continue to press for the same designation for Catalan, underscoring their resolve by painting over street signs in Castilian with the equivalent word or phrase in Catalan.

To round out this survey, mention should be made of the effect of social movements on the culture and practices of mainstream institutions in society. In his thorough study of the impact of liberation theology on the Latin American

Catholic church, Christian Smith (1991) provides a fascinating example of this process. Inspired in part by the spread of communist movements in the region, the liberation theology movement spawned a kind of revolution within the church that is still being waged today. In the United States, the movements of the 1960s have had a dramatic effect on the structure and curricular content of higher education in the United States. Structurally, the political turbulence of the era led to the establishment of African American, Native American, Hispanic, and women's studies programs on many college and university campuses. In addition, the heightened awareness of minorities spawned by the movements has resulted in far more curricular attention to minority groups in social science and humanities courses.

The forms of cultural change that flow from social movements are many and varied, and we know little about which factors or characteristics of movements account for the extent of their cultural impact. As a first approach to the question, I would emphasize the role of four factors in mediating the cultural consequences of social movements. These factors are: the extensiveness of the movement's goals, the movement's success in attaining those goals, the extent to which the movement results in prolonged and meaningful contact between two previously segregated groups, and the extent of the movement's access to existing cultural elites in society.

Breadth of the Movement's Goals
All other things being equal, the more extensive its goals, the more likely that a movement will be a force for cultural change. Given this understanding, it is not surprising that all of the examples of cultural change mentioned in the previous section are the products of movements whose goals were very broad. Revolutionary movements have the broadest goals; they seek nothing less than the replacement of an existing political, economic, and social order. Accordingly, of all types of movements, revolutions typically have the greatest potential for stimulating significant cultural change. Given their fundamental interest in replacing the old regime, insurgents will almost invariably seek to destroy the cultural expressions of the old order and substitute a new revolutionary culture in its place (Gramsci 1971). At the other end of the revolution to reform continuum, movements of the narrow reform variety typically exert little cultural force. For example, the current anti-drunk driving movement has but a few if any cultural, as opposed to legal or political, implications. Its goals are simply so narrow and so specific as to rule out any broader cultural critique of American society.

The Degree of Success Achieved by the Movement
History, as the old saying goes, is written by the winners. The same is true for all major forms of cultural expression. A second determinant, therefore, of the cultural impact of a movement is the degree to which the movement is successful politically. Following Marx (1977), it would seem to be the case that cultural dominance rests, to a large extent, on a firm political and economic base. Accordingly, I hypothesize that the cultural impact of a movement will be commensurate with the substantive political and economic success it achieves. Again,

this is most evident in the case of successful revolutions, wherein the victors move to eradicate the cultural, as well as political, vestiges of the old regime and to popularize cultural forms expressive of the new revolutionary order. At the other extreme, movements that fail to achieve any political leverage typically leave few cultural traces behind.

Contact between Previously Segregated Groups
Those movements that have been especially important as sources of cultural innovation would seem to be those that resulted in meaningful, that is, egalitarian, contact between previously segregated social strata. The significance of this kind of contact—the interaction between what Harrison White (1991) calls two "value streams"—is its potential to produce a new cultural hybrid based on the two subcultures present in the movement. Movements of this type have been among the most important in human history.

The early Christian movement represented a unique cultural hybrid based on a merger of a rural ascetic Jewish tradition with that of urban Hellenized Jews and Romans throughout the eastern Mediterranean. The Indian independence movement facilitated unprecedented contact between the untouchables and the most privileged Indian castes. The result was not simply political success but a period of unusual cultural ferment as well. Finally, for a brief period of time, the American civil rights movement encouraged egalitarian contact between black civil rights activists and the white student left. In large measure, the roots of the 1960s counterculture are found in the distinctive cultural hybrid that grew out of this contact (McAdam 1988).

Ties to Established Cultural Elites
The final factor that can be expected to shape the broader cultural impact of a movement is the extent to which it is linked to established cultural elites in society. One of the commonplace observations concerning the cultural ferment of the 1960s was that it represented "culture from the bottom up." Instead of cultural innovation flowing, as it normally does, from an established cultural elite downward through society, it seemed to emanate from groups whose impact on mainstream culture is ordinarily quite small. What this observation misses is the fact that the groups in question had unusually strong ties to established cultural elites, thus granting them more access to the means of cultural production than they ordinarily would have had. The ties forged in the early days of the movement between civil rights activists and segments of the Northern intellectual and cultural elite afforded blacks increased opportunities for cultural influence. The white student left, dominated as it was by middle- and upper-middle-class youth, enjoyed considerable access to the means of cultural expression via their parents and other influential adults to whom they were directly or indirectly linked. Generally, those movements that are either rooted in culturally privileged classes or that are able to forge such links are likely to have a greater impact on the cultural contours of mainstream society than those movements that remain fundamentally isolated from the established means of cultural production.

Conclusion

What I offer here is the most preliminary statement of the relationship between culture and social movements. The topic is complex and multifaceted. These are the beginnings of what I hope will be an ongoing discourse on the subject by both movement scholars and cultural analysts. Only by encouraging such a discourse can we hope to move toward a fuller understanding of this relationship and move beyond the current structural and rationalist biases evident in the contemporary movement literature.

References

Bellah, R. N., R. Madseti, W. M. Sullivan, A. Swidler, and S. M. Tipton. 1985. *Habits of the heart*. New York: Harper and Row.
Brand, K. 1990. Cyclical aspects of new social movements: Waves of cultural criticism and mobilization ycles of new middle-class radicalism. In *Challenging the political order: New social and political Movements in western democracies*, edited by R. Dalton and M. Kuechler. New York: Oxford University Press.
Caute, D. 1988. *The year of the barricades*. New York: Harper and Row.
Clemens, E. 1993. Organizational repertoires of institutional change: Women's groups and the transformation of U.S. politics, 1890-1920. *American Journal of Sociology* 98: 755-798.
Dickstein, M. 1989. *Gates of Eden*. New York: Penguin Books.
Evans, S. 1980. *Personal politics*. New York: Vintage Books.
Eyerman, R., and A. Jamison. 1991. *Social movements: A cognitive approach*. University Park, PA: Pennsylvania State University Press.
Fishel, L. H., Jr., and B. Quarles. 1970. In the New Deal's wake. In *The segregation era, 1863-1954*, edited by A. Weinstein and F. Gatell. New York: Oxford University Press.
Freeman, J. 1973. The origins of the women's liberation movement. *American Journal of Sociology*. 78: 792-811.
Gerber, I. 1962. The effects of the Supreme Court's desegregation decisions on the group cohesion of New York City's Negroes. *Journal of Social Psychology* 58: 295-303.
Gitlin, T. 1987. *The sixties: Years of hope, days of rage*. New York: Bantam.
Goffman, E. 1974. *Frame analysis: An essay on the organization of experience*. New York: Harper.
Goldstone, J. 1982. The comparative and historical study of revolutions. *Annual Review of Sociology* 8: 187-207.
———. 1991. *Revolution and rebellion in the early modern world*. Berkeley: University of California Press.
Gould, R. 1991. Multiple networks and mobilization in the Paris Commune, 1871. *American Sociological Review* 56: 716-729.
Gramsci, A. 1971. *Selection from the prison notebooks of Antonio Gramsci*. Edited by Q. Hoare and G. N. Smith. New York: International Publishers.
Hunt, L. 1984. *Politics, culture, and class in the French Revolution*. Berkeley: University of California Press.
Inglehart, R. 1981. Post-materialism in an environment of insecurity. *American Political Science Review* 75: 880-900.
———. 1990. *Culture shift in advanced industrial society*. Princeton, NJ: Princeton University Press.
Katsiaficas, G. 1987. *The imagination of the new left*. Boston: South End Press.
Kimmeldorf, H. 1989. *From Reds to rackets*. Berkeley: University of California Press.
Kitschelt, H. 1986. Political opportunity structures and political protest. *British Journal of Political Science* 16: 57-85.
Klapp, O. 1969. *Collective search for identity*. New York: Holt, Rinehart, and Winston.
Kriesi, H. 1989. The political opportunity structure of the Dutch peace movement. *West European Politics* 12: 295-312.
———. 1990. The political opportunity structure of new social movements: Its impact on their mobilization. Paper presented at Social Movements, Framing Processes, and Opportunity Structures, a conference held at Wissenschaftszentrum, Berlin, July.
Lang, K., and G. Lang. 1961. *Collective dynamics*. New York: Crowell.

Laraña, E. 1975. A study of student political activism at the University of California, Berkeley. Master's thesis, University of California, Santa Barbara.
Marx, K. 1977. *Selected writings.* Edited by D. McLelland. Oxford: Oxford University Press.
———. 1979. *The essential Marx: The non-economic writings.* Edited and Translated by S. K. Padover. New York: New American Library.
McAdam, D. 1982. Political process and the development of Black insurgency, 1930-1970. Chicago: University of Chicago Press.
———. 1986. Recruitment to high-risk activism: The case of Freedom Summer. *American Sociological Review* 92: 64-90.
———. 1988. *Freedom summer.* New York: Oxford University Press.
McAdam, D., and D. Rucht. 1993. The cross-national diffusion of movement ideas. *Annals of the American Academy of Political and Social Science* 527 (May): 56-74.
Melucci, A. 1980. The new social movements: A theoretical approach. *Social Science Information* 19: 199-226.
———. 1985. The symbolic challenge of contemporary movements. *Social Research* 52: 789-816.
———. 1989. *Nomads of the present: Social movements and individual needs in contemporary society.* Philadelphia: Temple University Press.
Molotch, H. 1970. Oil in Santa Barbara and power in America. *Sociological Inquiry* 40: 131-141.
Morris, A. 1984. The origins of the Civil Rights Movement. New York: Free Press.
Oberschall, A. 1973. *Social conflict and social movements.* Englewood Cliffs, N.J.: Prentice-Hall.
Offe, C. 1985. New social movements: Challenging the boundaries of institutional politics. *Social Research* 52: 817-868.
Rosenthal, N., M. Fingrutd, M. Ethier, R. Karant, and D. McDonald. 1985. Social movements and network analysis: A case study of nineteenth-century women's reform in New York State. *American Journal of Sociology* 90: 1022-1055.
Rucht, D. 1990. The strategies and action repertoires of new movements. In *Challenging the political order: New social and political movements in western democracies,* edited by R. Dalton and M. Kuechler. New York: Oxford University Press.
Rupp, L., and V. Taylor. 1987. *Survival in the doldrums: The American women's rights movement, 1945 to the 1960s.* New York: Oxford University Press.
Sale, K. 1973. *SDS.* New York: Random House.
Sitkoff, H. 1978. *A New Deal for blacks.* New York: Oxford University Press.
Skocpol, T. 1979. *States and social revolutions.* New York: Cambridge University Press.
Smelser, N. 1962. *Theory of collective behavior.* New York: Free Press.
Smith, C. 1991. *The emergence of liberation theology: Radical religion and social movement theory.* Chicago: University of Chicago Press.
Snow, D. A., and R. D. Benford. 1988. Ideology, frame resonance, and participant mobilization. In *From structure to action: Comparing social movement research across cultures,* edited by B. Klandermans, H. Kriesi, and S. Tarrow. Vol. 1 of *International social movement research.* Greenwich, CT: JAI Press.
Snow, D. A., E. B. Rochford, Jr., S. K. Worden, and R. D. Benford. 1986. Frame alignment processes, micromobilization, and movement participation. *American Sociological Review* 51: 464-481.
Swidler, A. 1986. Culture in action: Symbols and strategies. *American Sociological Review* 51: 273-286.
Tarrow, S. 1989. *Democracy and disorder: Protest and politics in Italy, 1965-1975.* Oxford: Clarendon Press.
———. 1991. "Aiming at a moving target": Social science and the recent rebellions in Eastern Europe. *Political Science and Politics* 29: 12-20.
———. 1994. *Power in movement: Social movements, collective action, and mass politics in the modern state.* New York: Cambridge University Press.
Tilly, C. 1978. From mobilization to revolution. Reading, MA: Addison-Wesley.
Touraine, A. 1981. *The voice and the eye: An analysis of social movements.* New York: Cambridge University Press.
Useem, B. 1980. Solidarity model, breakdown model, and the Boston anti-busing movement. *American Sociological Review* 45: 357-369.
Walsh, E. J. 1981. Resource mobilization and citizen protest in communities around Three Mile Island. *Social Problems* 29: 1-21.
White, H. 1991. Values come in styles, which mate to change. Paper presented at the interdisciplinary conference Toward a Scientific Analysis of Values, Tucson, AZ, February 1-4, 1989.
Whittier, N. 1993. Feminists in the "post-feminist" age: Collective identity and the persistence of the women's movement. Unpublished paper.

CHAPTER 15

Cultural Power and Social Movements

Ann Swidler

Originally published in Social Movements and Culture, *vol. 4, 1995.*

READING INTRODUCTION

In several ways, Swidler provides a more developed analysis of the relationship between culture and social movements than does McAdam. First, she focuses on the ways culture shapes individual beliefs and desires. Thus, culture provides a means by which people make sense of the world. Second, Swidler examines the ways culture provides repertoires of public symbols that structure the kinds of expected responses that individuals develop from their social interactions. A handshake on first meeting a person could be seen as such a symbol: Failure to shake hands once another has been extended is a deliberate insult. Thus, once they have offered it, most people expect that their hand will be shaken. Such an expectation represents cultural knowledge that exists even when no handshake is ongoing. Such assumptions may shape how a social movement acts even if its members are ideologically divided and its contention with the broader society sharp. Third, Swidler pays attention to the ways social institutions shape movement activities: If official organizations and others try to integrate or co-opt a group, for example, the movement is likely to behave differently than if it faces aggressive, perhaps violent, repression. Culture, then, is more than just the private beliefs of individual group members, and it is more than a set of broad principles that can be used for group purposes. It involves a dynamic interaction that shapes private and public acts together.

READING TEXT

Culture has always been important for the kinds of processes students of social movements study. But as culture moves to the forefront of social movement research, it is important to address directly the theories, methods, and assumptions different approaches to the sociology of culture carry with them.

I begin by reviewing the basic theoretical approaches in the sociology of culture and go on to suggest that traditional Weberian approaches, which focus on powerful, internalized beliefs and values held by individual actors (what I call culture from the "inside out") may ultimately provide less explanatory leverage than newer approaches that see culture as operating in the contexts that surround individuals, influencing action from the "outside in."

The sociology of culture contains two basic traditions, one deriving from Max Weber and the other from Emile Durkheim. Weber focused on meaningful action, and for him the fundamental unit of analysis was always the individual actor. Ideas, developed and promoted by self-interested actors (rulers seeking to legitimate their rule, elites attempting to justify their privileges, religious entrepreneurs seeking followers), come to have an independent influence on social action. People find themselves constrained by ideas that describe the world and specify what one can seek from it. Thus culture shapes action by defining what people want and how they imagine they can get it. Cultural analysis focuses on the complex systems of ideas that shape individuals' motives for action. In Weber's famous "switchman" metaphor:

> Not ideas, but material and ideal interests, directly govern men's conduct. Yet very frequently the "world images" that have been created by "ideas" have, like switchmen, determined the tracks along which action has been pushed by the dynamic of interest. "From what" and "for what" one wished to be redeemed and, let us not forget, "could be" redeemed, depended on one's image of the world. (1946, 280)

Weber (1968; 1958) analyzed culture by trying to understand typical worldviews, like the Protestant one, that had shaped the motives of historically important groups. Identifying how a worldview motivates action—how one committed to it would act under its sway—is explanation in Weberian terms.

The second crucial strand in the sociology of culture comes from Durkheim. For Durkheim (1933, 1965), culture is constituted by "collective representations." These are not "ideas" in the Weberian sense. Collective representations may range from the vivid totemic symbol to moral beliefs to modern society's commitment to reason and individual autonomy (Durkheim 1973). Collective representations are not ideas developed by individuals or groups pursuing their interests. Rather, they are the vehicles of a fundamental process in which publicly shared symbols constitute social groups while they constrain and give form to individual consciousness (Durkheim 1965; Bellah 1973). Durkheim writes not of "ideas" and "world images" but of representations, rituals, and symbols. Symbols concretize "collective consciousness," making the animating power of group life palpable for its members. Symbols do not reflect group life; they constitute it.[1]

Talcott Parsons (1937) made a heroic attempt to synthesize Weber and Durkheim, taking from Weber the image of action as guided by culturally determined ends and from Durkheim the notion of culture as a shared, collective product. The end result was the Parsonian theory of "values," a term that played no important role for either Weber or Durkheim. For Parsons (1951; 1961), "values" are collectively shared ultimate ends of action. "Norms" are shared cultural rules that define appropriate means to attain valued ends. Parsons sees shared values as defining societies, making them what they are, just as Durkheim saw the totem as constituting the Aboriginal clan, making it a society. At the same time, Parsons sees values as governing action in very much the way Weber saw ideas as switchmen. But unlike Weber's concept of "ideas," Parsonian values are very general, abstract orientations of action, rather than the specific, historically grounded doctrines and worldviews that Weber thought shaped action (see Swidler 1986).

Despite its logical appeal and distinguished theoretical ancestry, the Parsonian theory of values was never very successful as a guide to research.[2] Renewed interest in culture emerged from the Parsonian legacy but moved in a different direction. Clifford Geertz (1973), a student of Parsons, followed Weber in much of his substantive work but broke with the Weberian foundations of Parsons's theory of action.[3] He did so by altering both the question and the methods of cultural studies. Influenced by semiotic approaches to language and symbols, Geertz argued that culture should be studied for its meanings and not for its effects on action. He also shifted methodological focus, arguing that the proper object of cultural study is not meanings in people's heads but publicly available symbols—rituals, aesthetic objects, and other "texts."

Despite Geertz's debt to Weber, the effect of the Geertzian revolution in anthropology, history, and literary studies has been to break with the Weberian problematic. Rather than looking at the ideas that motivate individual actors (or even collections of individual actors), Geertz's followers examine public symbols and ritual experiences (see Keesing 1974). Culture cannot be used to explain individual action or even group differences in behavior. Attention does not focus primarily on ideas, belief systems, or dogmas, but on other properties of culture, especially the mood or tone that a "cultural system" gives to daily life through its symbolic vocabulary and through the ritual experiences it makes available (Geertz 1973, 1976). Culture constitutes "humanness" itself as well as the social world: "Man is an animal suspended in webs of significance he himself has spun" (Geertz 1973, 5). If culture influences action, then, it is not by providing the ends people seek, but by giving them the vocabulary of meanings, the expressive symbols, and the emotional repertoire with which they can seek anything at all.

The Revolution in Cultural Studies

Since the mid-1960s, when Geertz's influence began to be felt (with the original publication of "Religion as a Cultural System" in 1966), three dramatic developments have transformed cultural studies. They can best be summarized as publicness, practices, and power.

Culture as Public Symbols
Geertz's work fundamentally redefined the object of cultural analysis, revitalizing the practice of cultural studies.[4] Geertz shifted attention from a question that cultural analysts could rarely answer satisfactorily—How does a person's culture

actually influence his or her actions?—to one that was guaranteed to produce satisfying and even dazzling results: What does this cultural text, ritual, or practice mean to the people who use, perform, or live it? From Geertz's (1973) unpacking of the multistranded meanings of a Balinese cockfight to a historian unraveling the meaning of a ritual or folk tale (Davis 1975; Darnton 1984) to a literary critic finding deeper cultural patterns that animated Shakespeare's plays (Greenblatt 1980), the technique is similar. Identify a cultural text and then situate it in the rich web of associated cultural practices, beliefs, social structural realities, folk experiences, and so forth that allow its hearers, practitioners, or devotees to find it meaningful. Meaning itself is defined as context, as the other practices in which a text or ritual is embedded. This redefinition of the object of cultural analysis subtly altered what culture was understood to be. The focus on public vehicles of meaning reduced the need to investigate what any given individual or group actually felt or thought. Indeed, public symbols displayed a system of meanings, what some would call a semiotic code, rather than ideas that were in any person's head. The semiotic code was in some sense external to, or at least independent of, the minds of particular individuals. No longer the study of an ineffable subjectivity, the study of culture could now be grounded in accessible public objects.

The focus on public symbols also avoided the question of whether culture is necessarily shared or consensual. Durkheim and Parsons had been forced by the logic of their arguments to claim that cultural meanings were universally shared. But this claim did not hold up empirically. Public symbols, on the other hand, are clearly shared by the people who use them or form around them, and the question of whether these symbols' wider context of meaning is really shared seems unimportant. The analyst's task is to understand a formerly opaque ritual or practice through its context, and that exercise itself seemingly confirms that the context that has made its meaning comprehensible to the analyst also accounts for the ritual's ability to animate its practitioners or devotees.

Focusing on public ideas or texts also reshapes how one describes culture's influence on history. Rather than looking, as Weber did, for the ideas that motivated particular historical actors, the analyst traces changes in the cultural context within which all actors operated. Weber looked for ideas that directed the operation of "material and ideal interests." Contemporary culture analysts trace shifts in "discourses," the larger contexts of meanings within which any particular ideas or interests can be formulated (see Wuthnow 1987; 1989).

Practices

Cultural analysts have externalized the locus of culture in another way, by moving it from the mind's interior (ideas and mental representations) to social practices. The focus on practice has been widespread, from the attempt to revise the Marxian model of culture as "superstructure" (Williams 1973) to the efforts of Pierre Bourdieu and Michel Foucault to locate culture in embodied and institutionalized practices. Indeed, along with the terms *text* and *discourse,* the concept of "practice" is the hallmark of the new approaches in the sociology of culture.[5]

The concept of practice or practices differs from older conceptions of culture in two important ways. First, in reaction against the Durkheimian tradition, it emphasizes human agency. Pierre Bourdieu's *Outline of a Theory of Practice* (1977) conceives of culture not as a set of rules, but as deeply internalized habits, styles, and skills (the "habitus") that allow human beings to continually produce innovative actions that are nonetheless meaningful to others around them. For Bourdieu, active human beings continually recreate culture. They do not dutifully follow cultural rules, but energetically seek strategic advantage by using culturally encoded skills. Because access to those skills is differentially distributed, people's strategic efforts reproduce the structure of inequality (even if the players of the game are slightly rearranged.)

Second, locating social practices ties the study of culture to the analysis of institutions. Here the most important innovator is Michel Foucault. Foucault (1965, 1978) analyzes how systems of categories and distinctions are enacted and made real in institutional practices. For example, the practices that, after the sixteenth century, came to differentiate the sane from the mad—exclusion and confinement in asylums, or the diagnostic criteria later used by psychologists and others in the human sciences—are sets of cultural rules made real by being used to categorize and control human beings.

Foucault's arguments resemble Durkheim's insistence that rituals demarcate cultural boundaries and make symbolic truths real. But Foucault does not emphasize exotic ritual and symbol, nor the shared mental representations that unify a society's members. Rather, Foucault (1983) shifts attention to institutions, which use power to enact rules that construct human beings ("the subject") and the social world.

Power

The third important element in rethinking culture is a focus on power and inequality (Lamont and Wuthnow 1990). Max Weber (1968) always noted how the struggle for power shaped ideas, arguing that the interests of powerful groups had lasting influence on the shape of a culture. But he was interested in how ideas originally created to serve the powerful came to have a life of their own, constraining rulers as well as those they ruled, forcing elites to preserve their legitimacy by making good on their status claims and leading religious specialists to become preoccupied with distinctively religious problems.

Contemporary theorists instead see culture as itself a form of power. Foucault (1980), for example, analyzes how new kinds of knowledge and associated practices (such as measuring, categorizing, or describing objects of knowledge) in effect construct new sites where power can be deployed. New disciplines, such as psychoanalysis, construct new loci such as the unconscious, new subjectivities, where power can be exercised (and also where resistance can emerge). Foucault (1977, 1983) eliminates the question of who has power, leaving aside the role of interested agents, to emphasize instead that each cultural formation, each technique of power, has a history of its own, and that different actors adopt these techniques for different purposes. Since cultural practices, categories, and rules are enactments of power, Foucault does not think of culture as being used by the powerful to maintain their power. Rather, he thinks of power itself as practices that deploy knowledge to constitute human beings as the subjects of that knowledge.

Pierre Bourdieu focuses less on power than on inequality. He emphasizes that people differ not only in their cultural resources but also in the skill with which they deploy those resources. Bourdieu's (1984) special contribution is to show how deeply inequalities between the more and less privileged penetrate persons, constituting the fundamental capacities for judgment, aesthetic response, social ease, or political confidence with which they act in the world. Actors use culture in creative ways to forward their own interests in a system of unequal power, but the effect of that struggle is to reproduce the basic structure of the system.

Culture and Social Movements

Both opportunities and difficulties await researchers who look to the sociology of culture for fruitful new approaches to social movement questions. On the one hand, as others have noted (Cohen 1985; Tarrow 1992), culture has always been central to the kinds of processes social movements researchers study, such as formulating grievances, defining a common identity, or developing solidarity and mobilizing action. Indeed, social movements are the sites where new cultural resources, such as identities and ideologies, are most frequently formulated (Friedman and McAdam 1992). Addressing such processes more directly, as several recent researchers have done (see Klandermans, Kriesi, and Tarrow 1988; Morris and Mueller 1992), can only invigorate the field.

On the other hand, the traditional concern of social movement theory with activists and their motives fits naturally with the Weberian focus on how individuals develop understandings that guide their action. Researchers such as Doug McAdam (1988) who study activists, theorists such as David Snow (Snow et al. 1986; Snow and Benford 1988) who analyze the cultural preconditions for activism, and scholars such as William Gamson (1992) who study how ordinary people talk about politics all focus on individuals and their motives. They try to understand actors' experience and the larger forces that shape their motives, ideas, and identities. While such approaches have already proved fruitful, it is important that social movement researchers not become wedded to an implicitly Weberian image of culture just as cultural theory is moving in the other direction—toward more global, impersonal, institutional, and discursive assertions of cultural power.

Turning Culture Inside Out

There is now an abundance of work—that of Foucault and Bourdieu, but also many others (Wuthnow 1987; Sewell 1985, 1990, 1992)—arguing that culture constitutes social experience and social structure, that culture should be seen as socially organized practices rather than individual ideas or values, that culture can be located in public symbols and rituals rather than in ephemeral subjectivities, and that culture and power are fundamentally linked. Yet these more global approaches to the study of culture can also be difficult to grasp firmly, either theoretically or empirically. It would be ideal to marry Weber's concrete, grounded style of causal argument to Durkheim's understanding of the irreducibly collective, encompassing nature of culture.[6]

One new approach to understanding how culture shapes social movements involves rethinking how culture works. Most culture theory assumes that culture has more powerful effects where it is deeper—deeply internalized in individual psyches, deeply integrated into bodies and habits of action, or deeply embedded in taken-for-granted "mentalities." But at least some of the time, culture may have more powerful effects when it is on the "outside," not deeply internalized or even deeply meaningful. Variations in the ways social contexts bring culture to bear on action may do more to determine culture's power than variations in how deeply culture is held. And study of these social contexts may prove a fruitful direction for integrating culture into social movement research.

For Weber's actor-based sociology of ideas, culture has more influence when it is clearer, more coherent, and more deeply held. Protestantism had more influence on economic action than any other faith because its rationalized doctrine cut off "magical paths" to salvation, because it held that salvation was demonstrated in worldly action, and because it demanded that the intensely believing faithful rigorously regulate every aspect of daily life. Although Durkheim's model of culture was different from Weber's, he also held that culture had its greatest effects when it was most deeply part of the collective consciousness. Only universally shared, actively practiced, vivid symbols could constrain individual passions and impose a social reality on individual consciousness.

To analyze culture's power to affect action, independent of whether it is deeply held (either in the sense of deeply internalized, taken-for-granted practices like the habitus or in the sense of deeply held beliefs like those of Weber's Protestant saints), we may focus on three sources of cultural power: codes, contexts, and institutions. In each case we will see how the culture's effects on action can operate from the outside in, as social processes organize and focus culture's effects on action.

Codes

The notion of culture as a semiotic code has been one of the hallmarks of the new cultural studies. But the notion of semiotic code, by analogy with the deep structures that organize language, usually refers to deeply held, inescapable relationships of meaning that define the possibilities of utterance in a cultural universe. Deep, unspoken, and pervasive equals powerful.

Some codes are not deep, however, and not in the least invisible. A perfect example is provided by Theodore Caplow's (1982, 1984) study of Christmas gift giving in Middletown. In an article with the compelling title "Rule Enforcement without Visible Means," Caplow (1984) makes the point precisely. Caplow finds that middle-class Americans do not "believe in" Christmas gift giving. They criticize the commercialization of Christmas; they consider buying Christmas gifts an unpleasant burden; they think most gifts are a waste of money; they often do not like the gifts they receive; and they are unhappy with much of what they buy for others. Thus, Caplow asks, why do they give Christmas gifts, spending a considerable share of their disposable income, if they do not believe in it? Why does the practice persist without normative support and even in the face of widespread criticism?

Caplow uses data on actual gift giving to argue that Christmas gift giving constitutes a semiotic code (that is, a set of relationally defined meanings) in which the relative value of the gifts a person gives others signals the relative importance with which she or he holds those others. Not to give a gift would, independent of the intentions of the giver, be interpretable as a sign that one did not value the (non)recipients. What governs action in this case, then, is not individuals' internalized beliefs, but their knowledge of what meanings their actions have for others.[7]

Speaking of semiotic codes may seem to take us right back into the thickets of French structuralist theories or into a search for the deep underlying meanings that animate Geertzian "cultural systems." But semiotic codes can be much more discrete, more superficial, and sometimes more contested or political than semioticians usually imply. For example, when florists and confectioners try to increase their business by announcing National Secretaries' Week, few are presumably moved by deep belief in the principles that lie behind the announcement. But if every newspaper in the country is for weeks blanketed with advertisements implying that bosses who appreciate their secretaries will give them flowers and take them out to lunch, both secretaries and their employers may be, at the least, uncomfortable about what signals their actions will send. An employer may well think that for twenty-five dollars it is not worth the risk of hurting the secretary's feelings; and even a secretary who has disdain for the occasion may feel offended, or at least ambivalent, if it is ignored.

Much of our cultural politics is fought out on precisely such terrain. Let us imagine that a national secretaries' union launches a "Bread Not Roses" campaign, so that for employers to offer flowers without a raise is redefined as a sign of contempt. This would be a direct use of culture to influence action, not so much by shaping beliefs as by shaping the external codes through which action is interpreted. These are cultural power struggles, in which publicity can be a potent weapon even if no deeper persuasion occurs.

Even without conscious efforts at publicity, one of the most important effects social movements have is publicly enacting images that confound existing cultural codings. From the punk subculture's deliberate embrace of "ugly" styles (meant to muddle standard status codings [Hebdige 1979]) to the Black Panthers' display of militant, disciplined, armed black revolutionaries to the New Left spectacle of middle-class college students being beaten by police (Gitlin 1980), altering cultural codings is one of the most powerful ways social movements actually bring about change.

Recent American gender politics exhibit similar redefinitions of the cultural codes that signal masculinity and femininity. Increasingly in films (a perfect example is *Working Girl*) toughness and ambition are coded as part of earthy, sexy femininity, while classical feminine weakness, lace, and fluffy pillows are identified with a manipulative, dishonest antifeminity. In the same spirit, the very word *macho* makes the traditional hallmarks of masculinity seem suspect—signs of insecurity or weakness. The recent Disney classic *Beauty and the Beast* offers a wonderfully muscled, powerful, handsome antihero, Gaston, who is made utterly ridiculous as he carefully examines his appearance in every mirror he passes. In contrast, the Beast wins Beauty's love through his gentle awkwardness, his eagerness to please her, his love of books, and his distaste for violence. These cultural reworkings may sometimes change people's values or give them new role models. But more important, such cultural recodings change understandings of how behavior will be interpreted by others. If traditional feminine helplessness starts to look manipulative and controlling, and if masculine dominance starts to look pathetically self-absorbed, then men and women do not have to convert to find themselves meeting a new standard. Men may continue to aspire to masculinity and women to femininity, but the content those ideals encode has changed.

The agendas of many social movements revolve around such cultural recodings. Indeed, since most movements lack political power (this is precisely why they use unconventional political tactics) they can reshape the world more effectively through redefining its terms rather than rearranging its sanctions. And of course opponents employ the giant machinery of publicity that defines antiwar activists as unpatriotic, feminists as man haters, and the wealthy as beleaguered taxpayers to subvert social movements and their goals, precisely by winning the battle for symbolic encoding.

Since many of the enduring accomplishments of social movements are transformations in culture—in the legitimacy of specific demands, but also in the general climate of public discourse (see McAdam 1982)—theoretical ideas that focus on global properties of cultural systems may be more valuable than approaches that focus primarily on specific actors or even specific gains.[8] Such analyses would emphasize the flamboyance or visibility of a movement's tactics rather than either its success in mobilization or its gains in more conventional terms (see J. Gamson 1989). Researchers might then seek to understand why *some* cultural offensives succeed and others fail.

Contexts
One of the persistent difficulties in the sociology of culture is that culture influences action much more powerfully at some moments than at others. I have argued elsewhere (Swidler 1986), for example, that explicit cultural ideologies emerge during "unsettled" historical periods when such coherent, systematic worldviews can powerfully influence their adherents. But sometimes even fully articulated ideologies do not predict how people will act (as the many examples of co-optation, of movements that sell out their principles, or of leaders who betray revolutions attest). And at other times, even inchoate or contradictory worldviews powerfully affect action. To better understand such variations in culture's influence, we need to think more carefully about the specific contexts in which culture is brought to bear.

The contexts in which ideas operate can give them coherence and cultural power. "Context" in the first instance means the immediate, face-to-face situation—whether actors are meeting in public forums such as mass meetings or legislatures where issues are debated and decided. In such settings, the dynamics of the meeting itself can give ideas a coherent, systematic influence, even when the individual participants are confused and ambivalent. Second, context can mean the more general situation of conflict or accommodation, polarization and alliance formation, crisis or politics as usual.

The effect of context is evident in many ordinary political and work activities. In academia, for example, one may be confused or ambivalent about an issue—how good a job candidate's work is, whether a colleague merits tenure, whether a departmental decision is genuinely feminist. But in a meeting where sides polarize, where one group defines the issue one way and their antagonists define it in another, these ambiguities fall by the wayside. When politics polarize and alliances are at stake, the public culture crystallizes. Ideas that may have had only loose associations become part of a unified position; other ideas, which may originally have been intermingled with the first set, become clearly opposed. To back the side one supports comes to mean holding a particular ideological line, casting one's lot with a given framing of the situation. It is the conflict itself, the need to separate allies from foes and the need to turn general predispositions into specific decisions, that structures ideological debate.

Certain contexts, particularly those that are important in many social movements, give culture a coherent organization and consistent influence that it normally lacks in the minds of most individuals. This accounts for some of the difficulty in trying to pin down just where and why culture makes a difference in social action (see, for an example, the revealing debate between Sewell [1985] and Skocpol [1985] on the role of culture in the French revolution). If we think of culture either in the Weberian sense, as ideas deeply internalized in individual psyches, or in the more recent semiotic sense as broad, encompassing discourses that shape all social discussion in a given historical era, we will miss the more specific ways cultural power varies by context.

Social movements play out in contexts such as revolutionary committees, public meetings, and constituent assemblies, where stakes are high, risks are great, and political alliances are both essential and uncertain. When activists demand ideological purity to undermine their enemies and consolidate their alliances, they make ideas powerful from the outside in. When a political meeting decides that individual leadership violates its principles, or that fetal tissue research threatens the right to life, ideas can acquire a power to affect action that they normally lack. Of course there is a relation between such context-specific amplifications and clarifications of ideological effects and the wider beliefs, commitments, and values that individuals use to think about their lives in ordinary times. But ordinary culture is fluid, multistranded, and often inconsistent. Specific contexts turn inchoate individual beliefs and broad cultural idioms into particular demands for action. To use contemporary jargon, political actors know the "correct line" even if they remain uncertain about their personal beliefs. And specific political contexts lead actors to draw lines of ideological division sharply, to develop the action implications of their ideological stances, and to make adherence to one side or another of a debate an important sign of alliance or opposition. As the song says, "Which side are you on?"

Institutions

To explain how culture can have consistent effects on action even when people's beliefs are inconsistent, ambiguous, or lightly held, I have suggested that semiotic codes and political contexts can make ideas and symbols culturally constraining, irrespective of whether people believe them. Institutions can have similar effects, by another route.

Institutions are well-established, stable sets of purposes and rules backed by sanctions. One example is legally structured marriage. Others, less formal but no less powerful, are the employment relationship and the established norms about buying and selling that define consumer transactions.[9]

Institutions create obdurate structures that are both constraints and opportunities for individuals. For sociologists of culture, what is interesting about institutions is that individuals create culture around their rules. Individuals can then come to act in culturally uniform ways, not because their experiences are shared, but because they must negotiate the same institutional hurdles.[10]

For example, in a college where students must have a major in order to graduate, they need to be able to answer the question, What do you plan to major in? They may also ask themselves and each other, What am I interested in? because the institution contains the presumption that focused interests guide the choice of major. Moreover, students may develop cultural lore about how to select a major, identities based around the choice of major and categorizations of others ("techies" versus "fuzzies") on the basis of their majors. In a similar way, the American institution of voting presumes that citizens have ideas or opinions about public issues. Those who do not have opinions or ideas may feel that they are missing some crucial ingredient of selfhood. The tasks an institution requires make sense only if people have or can develop corresponding orientations. Widely shared cultural accounts for those orientations ensue, creating collective consistencies and resonances that the actors might not possess otherwise.

Similarly, the cultures of social movements are shaped by the institutions the movements confront. Different regime types and different forms of repression generate different kinds of social movements with differing tactics and internal cultures. Dominant institutions also shape the movements' deeper values. The most obvious case is the institution of suffrage itself. From Chartism to women's suffrage to the civil rights movement, Western democracies have witnessed the drama of people denied suffrage organizing extralegal protest to batter their way into the system, making claims for equal dignity and equal moral personhood. In such systems, to be a legitimate political actor is to be one who can vote.

Social movements develop their cultures to fit extant institutions in other ways as well. Where, for example, the state is responsible for public order, movements can induce state action by threatening the public peace. French workers, for example, protested against employers, not directly, but by barricading streets, marching to the town square, and demanding state involvement (Reddy 1984).

In the weaker American state, with powerful market institutions but weak centralized police powers, workers defined their battles as struggles with employers over benefits and wages.

Institutions affect the formulation of social movement identities and objectives in yet more central ways. Where the state enshrines "rights" as the crucial legal claim that trumps all others, both individuals and social movements will conceive of the claims they make as "rights" (Glendon 1991). And where legal claims are tied to group identities, as they long have been for American Indians (Cornell 1988) and increasingly have become for women, the disabled, and members of many ethnic and racial groups, identity becomes a central focus for social movements. When institutions make questions of group identity salient, they generate identity-oriented movements and a quest for identity on the part of individuals.

If institutions shape cultural responses in these ways, then the "frame alignment" of which David Snow and his colleagues (Snow et al. 1986; Snow and Benford 1988) have written is not just a matter of individuals' getting their frames in sync. Rather, individuals develop common scripts in response to the features of the institutions they confront. Commonalities in movement cultures are, at least in part, responses to the institutions the movements are trying to change.

The implication of all this for social movement researchers is in part to change the ordering in their implicit causal models. Gamson's *Talking Politics* (1992), for example, looks carefully at discourse—at what ordinary people say about politics when they are stimulated to think about it in a group situation. Gamson is interested in delineating the elements from which an active, oppositional culture could be built. But on the evidence of the ways people in Gamson's focus groups talk, one might well conclude that social movements in contemporary America are a near impossibility. While respondents demonstrate intelligence and occasional indignation over social wrongs, their information is fragmentary, their conversation meandering, and their worldviews concatenations of numerous overlapping frames, many of which are nearly self-canceling. But perhaps this search for a popular culture that could support activism starts in the wrong place. How people organize the cultural resources at their disposal depends very much on the kinds of institutional challenges they face.

Conclusion

I began this essay by stressing the two great wellsprings from which much of contemporary culture theory derives. In a sense Weber and Durkheim still define the range of alternatives available to sociologists who want to use culture to explain things. I have suggested that while the Weberian image of culture as belief carried by committed individual actors seems easier to work with, recent developments in cultural studies have moved in a more Durkheimian direction, seeing culture as constitutive, inherently collective, imbedded in symbols and practices, and necessarily infused with power (see Alexander 1988). But culture in this sense—public practices infused with power—can also be extremely hard to grasp concretely. Indeed, too-easy embrace of the notion that culture is ubiquitous and constitutive can undermine any explanatory claims for culture. Then emphasis on culture becomes a species of intellectual hand waving, creating a warm and cozy atmosphere, while other factors continue to carry the real explanatory weight.

I have tried to offer four concrete suggestions about how culture might be conceived as a global, collective property without becoming only a diffused mist within which social action occurs. I have argued first that, to think more powerfully about culture, we must entertain the possibility that culture's power is independent of whether or not people believe in it. I have then gone on to suggest that culture can have powerful influence if it shapes not individuals' own beliefs and aspirations, but their knowledge of how others will interpret their actions.

My third suggestion is that students of culture in general, and social movement scholars in particular, need to pay close attention to the public contexts in which cultural understandings are brought to bear. Reminding ourselves of the power that meetings and other group forums have to crystallize ideological splits and recode public speech and action, I suggest that culture can have consistent, coherent effects on action in particular contexts even if individuals and groups are divided and inconsistent in their beliefs.

Finally, I have suggested that institutions structure culture by systematically patterning channels for social action. In a sense this simply reinforces the insights of the "political process" model of social movements, which notes that movements respond to the wider structure of political constraints and opportunities (McAdam 1982). But I have tried to push the cultural dimension of such processes, arguing that even cultural patterns that appear to be independent inventions (or innate needs) of individuals or groups can be produced or reproduced by the challenges with which institutions confront actors. Thus many movements may invent simultaneously what seem to be common cultural frames (like the many rights movements of the 1960s or the identity movements of the 1980s). But these need not be matters either of independent discovery or of cultural contagion. Rather, they may be common responses to the same institutional constraints and opportunities.

Rethinking how culture might work from the outside in is a large task. I do not think the suggestions I have made here about codes, contexts, and institutions are the only ways the issue might be approached. But I am convinced that if interest in culture is restricted to studying the inner meaning systems of deeply committed activists, or if culture is relegated to a vague—if "constitutive"—penumbra, we will sacrifice more incisive ways of thinking about its power.

References

Alexander, J. C., ed. 1988. *Durkheimian sociology: Cultural studies*. New York: Cambridge University Press.
Bellah, R. N. 1973. Introduction. In *Emile Durkheim on morality and society*, edited by R. N. Bellah. Chicago: University of Chicago Press.
Bourdieu, P. 1977. *Outline of a theory of practice*. Cambridge: Cambridge University Press.

———. 1984. *Distinction: A social critique of the judgment of taste.* Translated by R. Nice. Cambridge, MA: Harvard University Press.
Caplow, T. 1982. Christmas gifts and kin networks. *American Sociological Review* 47: 383-392.
———. 1984. Rule enforcement without visible means: Christmas gift giving in Middletown. *American Journal of Sociology* 89: 1306-1323.
Cohen, J. L. 1985. Strategy or identity: New theoretical paradigms and contemporary social movements. *Social Research* 52 (4): 663-716.
Collins, R. 1981. On the microfoundations of macrosociology. *American Journal of Sociology* 86: 984-1014.
———. 1988. The micro contribution to macro sociology. *Sociological Theory* 6 (Fall): 242-253.
Cornell, S. 1988. *The return of the native.* New York: Oxford University Press.
Darnton, R. 1984. *The great cat massacre and other episodes in French cultural history.* New York: Basic Books.
Davis, N. Z. 1975. *Society and culture in early-modern France.* Stanford, CA: Stanford University Press.
Durkheim, E. 1933. *The division of labor in society.* New York: Free Press.
———. 1965. *The elementary forms of the religious life.* Translated by J. W. Swain. New York: Free Press.
———. 1973. Individualism and the intellectuals. In *Emile Durkheim on morality and society*, edited by R. N. Bellah. Chicago: University of Chicago Press.
Foucault, M. 1965. *Madness and civilization: A history of insanity in the age of reason.* New York: Random House.
———. 1978. *The history of sexuality*, Vol. 1. London: Penguin.
———. 1980. *Power/knowledge: Selected interviews and other writings, 1972-1977*, edited by C. Gordon. New York: Pantheon.
———. 1983. Afterword: The subject and power. In *Michel Foucault: Beyond structuralism and hermeneutics*, edited by H. Dreyfus and P. Rabinow. Chicago: University of Chicago Press.
Friedman, D., and D. McAdam. 1982. Collective identity and activism: Networks, choices, and the life of a social movement. In *Frontiers in social movement theory*, edited by A. Morris and C. Mueller. New Haven, CT: Yale University Press.
Gamson, J. 1989. Silence, death, and the invisible enemy: AIDS activism and social movment "newness." *Social Problems* 36: 351-367.
Gamson, W. 1992. *Talking politics.* Cambridge: Cambridge University Press.
Geertz, C. 1960. *The religion of Java.* New York: Free Press of Glencoe.
———. 1966. Religion as a cultural system. In *Anthropological approaches to the study of religion*, edited by M. Banton. London: Tavistock.
———. 1968. *Islam observed: Religious development in Morocco and Indonesia.* New Haven, CT: Yale University Press.
———. 1973. *The interpretation of cultures.* New York: Basic Books.
———. 1976. Art as a cultural system. *Modern Language Notes* 91: 1473-99.
Gitlin, T. 1980. *The whole world is watching.* Berkeley: University of California Press.
Glendon, M. A. 1991. *Rights talk: The impoverishment of political discourse.* New York: Free Press.
Greenblatt, A. D. 1980. Comprehensive discourse analysis: An instance of professional peer interaction. *Language in Society* 11: 15-47.
Hebidge, D. 1979. *Subculture: The meaning of style.* London: Methuen.
Jepperson, R. L. 1991. Institutions, institutional effects, and institutionalism. In *The new institutionalism in organizational analysis*, edited by W. W. Powell and P. DiMaggio. Chicago: University of Chicago Press.
Keesing, R. M. 1974. Theories of culture. In *Annual Review of Sociology* 3. Palo Alto, CA: Annual Reviews.
Klandermans, B., H. Kriesi, and S. Tarrow. 1988. *International social movement research.* Vol. 1, *From structure to action: Comparing movement participation across cultures.* Greenwich, CT: JAI Press.
Kluckhohn, F. R., and F. Strodtbeck. 1961. *Variations in value orientations.* New York: Row, Peterson.
Lamont, M., and R. Wuthnow. 1990. Betwixt and between: Recent cultural sociology in Europe and the United States. In *Frontiers of social theory: The new synthesis*, edited by G. Ritzer. New York: Columbia University Press.
McAdam, D. 1988. *Political process and the development of Black insurgency 1930-1970.* Chicago: University of Chicago Press.
Morris, A. D., and Mueller, C. M., eds. 1992. *Frontiers in social movement theory.* New Haven, CT: Yale University Press.
Ortner, S. 1984. Theory in anthropology since the sixties. *Comparative Studies in Society and History* 26: 126-166.

Parsons, T. 1937. *The structure of social action*. New York: Free Press.

———. 1951. *The social system*. Glencoe, IL: Free Press.

———. 1961. An outline of the social system. In *Theories of society*, edited by T. Parson et al. New York: Free Press.

Reddy, W., Jr. 1984. *The rise of market culture: The textile trade and French society, 1750-1900*. Cambridge: Cambridge University Press.

Rokeach, M. 1973. *The nature of human values*. New York: Free Press.

Scott, W. R. 1992. Institutions and organizations: Toward a theoretical synthesis. Unpublished paper, Department of Sociology, Stanford University.

Sewell, W. H., Jr. 1985. Ideologies and social revolutions: Reflections on the French case. *Journal of Modern History* 57: 57-85.

———. 1990. Collective violence and collective loyalties in France: Why the French Revolution made a difference. *Politics and Society* 18 (4): 527-552.

———. 1992. A theory of structure: Duality, agency, and transformation. *American Journal of Sociology* 98: 1-29.

Skocpol, T. 1985. Cultural idioms and political ideologies in the revolutionary reconstruction of state power: A rejoinder to Sewell. *Journal of Modern History* 57: 86-96.

Snow, D. A., and R. D. Benford. 1988. Ideology, frame resistance, and participant mobilization. In *International social movement research: From structure to action*, edited by B. Klandermans, H. Kriesi, and S. Tarrow. Greenwich, CT: JAI Press.

Snow, D. A., E. B. Rochford Jr., S. K. Worden, and R. D. Benford. 1986. Frame alignment processes: Micromobilization and movement participation. *American Sociological Review* 51: 456-481.

Swidler, A. 1986. Culture in action: Symbols and strategies. *American Sociological Review* 51: 273-286.

———. Forthcoming. *Talk of love: How Americans use their culture*. Chicago: University of Chicago Press.

Tarrow, S. 1992. Mentalities, political cultures, and collective action frames: Constructing meanings through action. In *Frontiers in Social Movement Theory*, edited by A. Morris and C. Mueller. New Haven, CT: Yale University Press.

Weber, M. 1946. The social psychology of the world religions. In *From Max Weber*, edited by H. H. Gerth and C. W. Mills. New York: Oxford University Press.

———. 1958. *The Protestant ethic and the spirit of capitalism*. New York: Scribner's.

———. 1968. *Economy and society: An outline of interpretive sociology*. Berkeley: University of California Press.

Williams, R. 1973. Base and superstructure in Marxist cultural theory. *New Left Review* 82 (November-December): 3-16.

Wuthnow, R. 1987. *Meaning and moral order: Explanations in cultural analysis*. Berkeley: University of California Press.

———. 1989. *Communities of discourse: Ideology and social science structure in the Reformation, the Enlightenment, and European socialism*. Cambridge, MA: Harvard University Press.

CHAPTER 16

Cultural Conflict in America

James Davison Hunter

Originally published in
Culture Wars: The Struggle to Define America, *1990.*

READING INTRODUCTION

Hunter provides an analysis of contemporary group conflict in America that focuses on the presence of two distinct collective identities in political debate. For Hunter, Americans tend to cleave into two groups, especially at the extremes: the progressives and the orthodox. Progressives derive their sense of political authority from a vision of morality that is evolutionary, malleable, and subject to change as circumstances shift. There are few, if any, absolute standards of right and wrong; instead, social practices that made sense at one point in human history may be absurd at another. The traditional place of the woman in the home as child-rearer serves as a useful example of progressive thought: While this practice may once have made sense, contemporary circumstances make it possible for women to leave the home and enter the paid workforce as equal partners with men. Thus the traditional role for women represents a time-bound conception of "rightness": It may have once made sense, but times change.

For the orthodox, in contrast, moral authority is fixed and permanent. There are absolute standards of right and wrong that do not change simply because the economic structure of society changes. Again, the traditional role for women stands as a useful example: Women, for the orthodox, should be at home because they are best at child rearing and lack talent for public life, whether in the paid workforce or political activity. The recent Southern Baptist Convention dictate that women ought to "submit" to their husbands in matters concerning the family represents this orthodox "impulse." It expresses an orthodox vision of what is right is right for all time, regardless of contemporary pressures.

What makes the progressive and orthodox impulses interesting for Hunter is the way they play out on the political stage. On many of the issues currently wracking American society—abortion, gay rights, the death penalty, euthanasia, and so on—Hunter finds that representatives of these rival identities come into conflict as a consequence of their disparate interpretations of moral authority. Extremists in both groups talk past each other as they use cultural symbols to try to win the "great middle" of American political life. Depending on which choices Americans make—which, if any, impulse they choose to follow—the structure of American society is likely to face remarkable changes.

READING TEXT

The various conflicts presented in the prologue,* and the lives that give them flesh and blood, will not be totally strange to most Americans. All of these stories, and the particular voices that tell them, relate to larger issues that are widely recounted on the front pages of newspapers and weekly news and opinion magazines, in the accounts and commentaries of television news anchors, and in the topical dialogue of radio talk-show celebrities: "I have Alan from Blue Ash, Ohio, on the line. Our question tonight is, 'Should there be a Constitutional amendment prohibiting flag burning in America?' What is your view, Alan?" The stories themselves and, more importantly, the issues that underlie them are the topics of dispute at the corporate cocktail party and the factory cafeteria alike, in the high school civics classroom, in the church lounge after the weekly sermon, and at the kitchen table over the evening meal. Few of us leave these discussions without ardently voicing our own opinions on the matter at hand. Such passion is completely understandable. These are, after all, discussions about what is fundamentally right and wrong about the world we live in—about what is ultimately good and what is finally intolerable in our communities.

The views of the six people presented in the previous dispatches[†] illustrate only a few of the voices heard in public debate today. Yet their few stories nevertheless show that the debates on these issues are not made up simply of abstract and disembodied statements but express views rooted in real lives unfolding in real communities all across the nation. The voices heard here, as well as those that make up the larger forum of public debate and discussion in America, cannot be easily caricatured; in the details, each point of view is novel, indeed incomparable.

Though these voices are distinctive, they are not, in the end, extraordinary. Indeed, they share much that is common and familiar within American life, echoing thoughts and themes that resonate with many of our own experiences. All six people are basically middle-class Americans who are actively involved in their own neighborhoods and cities. In each case, their involvement is born out of a deep concern for the character of life—first and foremost in the places where they live, but also very much within the country as a whole. Each of them was able to draw out the implications of the particular controversy at hand for the character of life in the nation. In the very best sense of the term, then, each is a responsible and engaged citizen; words and phrases such as truth, justice, the public good, and national purpose have important personal meanings for them.

Looking at their backgrounds and current careers, it would be inaccurate to call any of these people "intellectuals." It is certainly fair to say, however, that

---

*Of original publication.
†In original publication.

they are all philosophically or religiously reflective. All would recognize that their own lives and world views form part of a larger community of moral understanding and commitment that is distinct from yet integrated within their involvement in neighborhood, city, and region. For Chuck McIlhenny, that community of moral commitment is the Reformed wing of Evangelical Christianity; for Richmond Young, it is a Catholic fellowship within a gay subculture; for Yehuda Levin, it is the traditional world of Orthodox Judaism; for Bea Blair, it is the social justice wing of mainline Protestantism; for Mae Duggan, it is, as she put it, "old-fashioned" Catholicism; and for Harriet Woods, it is the policy establishment of secular liberalism. These attachments are singularly important: all six find themselves thrust into controversy and into long-term community involvement not because they are quarrelsome by nature but rather because their prior moral commitments—to what they personally believe is true, just, good, and in the public interest—have compelled them to become involved. Chuck's calling as an Evangelical Christian; Richmond's commitment as a liberal Catholic; Yehuda's obligations as an Orthodox Jew; Bea's responsibility as an Episcopal clergywoman; Mae's commitment to the imperatives of traditional Catholic teaching; and Harriet's allegiances to the humanistic ideals of stewardship to the human family—these commitments oblige them to speak out as they do. Remove these commitments and you take away that which engages them as neighbors and citizens; separate them from these understandings and you take away their hearts and souls.

On his or her own terms, we find each of the six individuals profiled to be reasonable, engaging, and even appealing. In the details of their lives they are so normal and human: they all have great qualities as well as a few quirks, high and noble hopes as well as deep worries, personal triumphs as well as disappointments. Yet this personal and human face of public debate is one we rarely if ever see. In most cases, our sources of information about the controversies of the day are the media of mass communications: the radio and television, the daily newspaper and the weekly news magazine. By their very nature, these media can only give superficial coverage; they are incapable of delving into or rising above the personalities and events of the moment. As a consequence, the individuals who inspire various forms of social action tend to be presented as extremists, demagogues, and even opportunists for their own personal causes and special interests. Angry at what they see as injustice, they have decided to stand defiantly against what seem to be the givens of history. Likewise, the events themselves tend to be presented as flashes of political insanity—spasmodic symptoms of civic maladjustment against the routine conduct of public affairs. Such events are rarely related to one another, but appear to be merely "disparate" outbursts by disparate (and sometimes "desperate") individuals and groups. Commentators make little effort to explain and interpret these stories and the issues that underlie them, to place them in a broader frame of reference. Those who *do* present events as interrelated often raise the specter of a dark and shadowy conspiracy. Most Americans reply, "Bosh" to conspiracy theories—and they do so quite rightly. Yet they also, perhaps unwisely, tend to overlook the possibility that these "disparate" events may nevertheless be related to each other in complex and important ways.

The question we face is simply this: What if these events are not just flashes of political madness but reveal the honest concerns of different communities engaged in a deeply rooted cultural conflict? What if the voices of public argument—the McIlhennys and Youngs, the Levins and Blairs, the Duggans and Woodses—are not just the cranky utterances of America's political fringe but the articulation of concerns that are central to the course and direction of the mainstream of American public culture?

The argument of this book is that these voices and events *are* related to each other in complex ways—that America is in the midst of a culture war that has had and will continue to have reverberations not only within public policy but within the lives of ordinary Americans everywhere. In understanding the character of this conflict, we will see that important differences often separate the personal from the public. As Chuck and Richmond, Yehuda and Bea, and Mae and Harriet have shown us, the personal disagreements that fire the culture war are deep and perhaps unreconcilable. *But these differences are often intensified and aggravated by the way they are presented in public.* In brief, the media technology that makes public speech possible gives public discourse a life and logic of its own, a life and logic separated from the intentions of the speaker or the subtleties of arguments they employ.

In this book★ we will also see just how high the stakes of this war are. They reach far beyond the biographies of those who give voice to conflicting concerns, and far beyond the immediate policy outcomes news media accounts describe. *At stake is how we as Americans will order our lives together.*

An Absence of Categories

How are we to make sense of all this? Certainly there are disagreements from time to time about matters of community interest and even of public policy. These are to be expected. Yet a "culture war" in America? The very thought or possibility of a deeply rooted and historically pivotal cultural conflict in America strains our imagination.

Our difficulty in coming to terms with the idea of such a conflict in contemporary America arises largely from the absence of conceptual categories or analytical tools for understanding cultural conflict. We simply lack ways of thinking about the subject. The predominant images of contemporary cultural conflict focus on religious and cultural hostilities played out in other parts of the world: the suppression of the Kurds in Iraq; the struggle of Sikh nationalists to establish their own homeland in northwest India; the political offensive of Gush Emunim, the political organ of Jewish fundamentalism in Israel, in its efforts to maintain the purity of orthodoxy in a pluralistic society; and the continuing hostilities between the Hindu Tamil minority and the Sinhalese Buddhist majority

---

★Original publication.

in northern Sri Lanka. As vivid and arresting as these images may be, they are foreign to the everyday experience of most Americans, distant from us both spatially and culturally. Thus, few Americans can relate personally, much less passionately, to the interests and concerns these images represent.

These images should not be seen as so remote, however, for they can provide metaphors for our thinking about religious and cultural conflict in our country. Of course, the particular cast of cultural players on the American scene is different from those found in other countries. Likewise, the character of the actual cultural conflict played out in the United States is very distinctive. Nevertheless, the story underlying cultural conflict in numerous places throughout the world—a story about the struggle for power—resonates with narratives found in America's not-so-distant past. An understanding of that past is essential for coming to terms with the unfolding conflict of the present.

Cultural Conflict: The American Story

The memory need only be prodded lightly to recall that Protestant hostility toward Catholicism (and, to a far lesser extent, Catholic resentment of Protestantism) provides one of the dominant motifs of early modern American history.[1] Understanding the American experience even as late as the nineteenth century requires an understanding of the critical role played by anti-Catholicism in shaping the character of politics, public education, the media, and social reform.

Of course, the mutual hostility of Protestants and Catholics had been implacable since the time of the Reformation and Counter-Reformation in the sixteenth century. For their rejection of church tradition and ecclesiastical authority, Protestants were regarded by Catholics as infidels who had abandoned the true faith; for their elevation of "arcane rituals" to the status of scriptural truth and for their elevation of papal authority to the status of the authority of Christ, Catholics were regarded by Protestants as heretics who had perverted the true faith.

Needless to say, these tensions were not only religious or theological in nature. Indeed, the split between Catholics and Protestants during the Reformation generated one of the most enduring and consequential *political* divisions in Western experience. More than a century (between 1559 and 1689) of religious warfare within and among the nations of Western Europe can be attributed to these interreligious hostilities. And even after the age of religious wars had formally come to an end, the political tensions between these religious and cultural traditions continued to affect the institutional fabric of Western life. Prejudice, discrimination, and even physical violence were commonplace for the Protestant minorities in southern Europe (France, Spain, Italy, and Portugal) and the Catholic minorities in the north (Britain, Germany, Holland, and Scandinavia).

America, of course, was colonized primarily by emigrating European Protestants of one stripe or another. It is not surprising, then, that anti-Catholic sentiment emigrated to American shores as well, and became woven into the unofficial political and cultural traditions of the colonists. In fact, anti-Catholicism in America reached something of an apex in the nineteenth century. For one, many of the major urban daily newspapers displayed a prominent anti-Catholic prejudice: the *Chicago Tribune,* for example, played a significant role in inciting anti-Catholic agitation through the 1840s and 1850s (Keefe 1975). There was also an enormous literature exclusively devoted to discrediting the Catholic presence. Between 1800 and 1860, American editors published at least 25 daily, weekly, or bimonthly newspapers and 13 monthly or quarterly magazines opposing Catholicism, while American publishing houses published more than 200 anti-Catholic books.[2] The most titillating and popular of this literature presented accounts of priests and nuns who had abandoned their faith because of their experiences of torture, mental brutality, and even sexual offense. One of the first and certainly the most famous of these accounts, Maria Monk's *Awful Disclosures of the Hotel Dieu Convent: The Secrets of Black Nunnery Revealed* (1836), sold over 300,000 copies. Others published around the same time included Rebecca Reed's *Six Months in a Convent* (1835), Rosamond Culbertson's *A Narrative of the Captivity and Sufferings of an American Female Under the Popish Priests in the Island of Cuba, with a Full Disclosure of Her Manners and Customs* (1836), Andrew Steinmetz's *The Novitiate, or a Year Among the English Jesuits* (1846), and Josephine Bunkley's *The Testimony of an Escaped Novice from the Sisterhood of St. Joseph* (1856). The Protestant suspicion and fear that fueled widespread interest in these tales formed a pretext for riots in Boston, New York, Philadelphia, St. Louis, Louisville, and other cities east of the Mississippi, as well as numerous attacks on convents, churches, and seminaries (such as the burning of the Ursuline Convent of Charlestown in Boston in 1834, and of St. Michael's Church and St. Augustine's Church in Philadelphia in 1844).[3]

Anti-Catholicism also ignited the great school wars of the mid-nineteenth century, visible in Philadelphia and Boston but particularly in New York, due to the outspoken views of John Hughes, an Irishman and the presiding bishop in that city. Because skills, values, and habits of life are passed on to children in school, it was inevitable that the schools would be an arena of cultural conflict, where the majority would assert its power and minority cultures would struggle to maintain a voice. Despite advocates' claims that the common schools of New York were nonsectarian, the Public School Society of New York retained textbooks that contained numerous overt anti-Irish and anti-Catholic statements. They also maintained the practice of a daily reading and recitation of the (Protestant) King James version of the Bible. When the Public School Society refused to accommodate Catholic interests either by allowing Catholic religious instruction after hours or by providing public funds to be used for the establishment of public schools of a Catholic nature, the Catholic community suffered.

Yet perhaps the most vociferous expressions of anti-Catholicism came from anti-Catholic societies (such as the American Protestant Association, the Christian Alliance, the American and Foreign Christian Union, the American Protective Association, and American Alliance) and anti-Catholic political parties (such as the Native American parties of the 1840s, the Know-Nothing party of the 1850s, and the Republican party of the 1850s and 1860s). Importantly, these organizations were most successful in precisely the states where Catholics were most numerous. Thus, they became significant not only for organizing and voicing both popular and elite resentment against Catholics but for mobilizing electoral opinion against the interests of a rapidly expanding Catholic community that remained both severely disadvantaged and largely powerless.

But Catholics are not the only religious minority that has endured hardship in America. The memory only needs to be prodded a bit further to recall the ways in which interreligious hostility has extended to Judaism. Christianity has long held Jews in the ambivalent status of being both God's chosen people, who had been miraculously sustained throughout the generations, and an unfaithful people who suffered deservedly for their betrayal of the Messiah. This was no less true for the Evangelical pietism that prevailed through the nineteenth century. In America, the remnants of Puritan culture retained a deep sympathy with the "People of the Book" and an identification with the Old Testament imagery of a people "in covenant with God." Still, in their view, the sufferings of the diaspora were the just punishments of a vengeful God for a people who had rebelled against His purposes.

Yet while the religious component was never absent, the secular and specifically economic behavior of Jews received the most vicious exploitation in stereotypes. Jews were portrayed as crude, aggressively greedy Shylocks whose conduct in business was always opportunistic and very often unscrupulous. Jews were the pawnbrokers, petty white-collar criminals, and merchants of the big cities, perennially in pursuit of the bargain and conspicuous in their display of new wealth. Such was the imagery presented in popular dramas featuring Jews (like Melter Moss in *The Ticket-of-Leave Man* [1864], Mo Davis in *Flying Scud* [1867], Dicey Morris in *After Dark* [1868], and Mordie Solomons in *The Lottery of Life* [1867]. Popular novels of the period echoed the theme; at least three of Horatio Alger's stories, for example, contain Jews of this cast as minor characters (Alger 1966; 1870; 1871). The portrait was reinforced throughout dozens of inexpensive and sensationalized dime novels written at the end of the century. Herman Stoll, the unscrupulous German-Jewish Wall Street broker in Albert Aiken's *The White Witch* (1871) and the shady operator Aaron Mosenstein in Aiken's *Dick Talbot and the Ranch King* (1892) are just two examples. Jews were similarly stereotyped in the works of Gilbert Jerome, Prentiss Ingraham, H. P. Halsy, and J. R. Coryell, the author of the popular Nick Carter stories.[4]

Despite the vulgar stereotyping and the popular concern about the "Hebrew conquest of the financial centers of New York," anti-Semitism was never greatly politicized in the way that anti-Catholicism had been. Jews never appeared to present a cultural or demographic threat equivalent to that posed by the Catholics. Nevertheless, various forms of anti-Jewish discrimination did characterize the last two decades of the nineteenth century and the first three decades of the twentieth in particular.[5] For one, quotas limited the admission of Jews to private schools, colleges, and medical schools as late as the 1920s. As an upwardly mobile Jewish population began to migrate out of its ethnic and religious enclaves, restrictive covenants were placed in the deeds of homes, allowing real estate agents to refuse to rent apartments to Jews, and landlords to hang "To Let" signs with the addendum "No Jews." These practices extended to membership in social clubs and to the enjoyment of summer and weekend resorts. At Saratoga, Manhattan Beach, and Coney Island, in the Catskills and other resorts throughout New York and New Jersey, placards were raised that stated, "No Jews or Dogs Admitted Here." In retaliation, Jews purchased several prestigious hotels in most of the resort towns and formed their own elite clubs in New York, Baltimore, Rochester, Detroit, and other major cities. In sum, the discrimination faced by Jews in the last decades of the nineteenth century and the first decades of the twentieth, while in many ways different from that experienced by the mainly Irish Catholics, was no less hostile. The net effect was to exclude and control.

Less visible motifs of cultural conflict in American history include hostility toward Mormons. From the founding of the Mormon Church in 1830, Mormons were subject to harassment and persecution. The governor of Missouri stated in 1838, "The Mormons must be treated as enemies and must be exterminated or driven from the state, if necessary, for the Public good" (Hofstadter and Wallace 1971, 302). And in several states, mainly in the South, they were. Joseph Smith and his brother were jailed and then killed by a mob in Illinois in 1844; four Mormon missionaries were killed by a mob in Cane Creek, Tennessee, in 1884; and numerous others became victims of murder, beatings, tar-and-featherings, and other acts of violence.[6]

In all of these instances cultural tension arose not simply from academic disagreement over the proper form of ecclesiastical structures or a theoretical argument over doctrinal truths. Rather, America's uneasy pluralism implied a confrontation of a deeper nature—a competition to define social reality. Through the nineteenth and early twentieth century cultural discord was kindled, in general, by two competing tendencies. On one hand, there was the quest on the part of various minority cultures to carve out a space in American life where they could each live according to the imperatives of conscience and the obligations of community without harassment or reprisal. Such a space would provide the base from which to expand their own legitimate interests as a distinct moral community. On the other hand, there was the endeavor of Protestants and a largely Protestant-based Populism to ward off any challenges—to retain their advantage in defining the habits and meaning of American culture.

The End of an Age?

The conflicts involving Protestants, Catholics, Jews, and Mormons are indeed a prominent part of the American heritage, and yet even these experiences are largely removed from contemporary American experience. The reason for this is that all signs would seem to point to a growing sense of tolerance among Protestants, Catholics, and Jews (as well as Mormons and others too).

One series of national surveys conducted between 1966 and 1984, for example, showed that strong prejudicial feeling both for and against different religious faiths declined. Neutrality (what may actually be mutual indifference) among Catholics, Protestants, and Jews generally increased while antipathy toward various groups declined.[7] Another general indication of growing interreligious tolerance is found in the answers to questions about the suitability of presidential candidates who personally identify with one or another religious tradition. In 1958 one of every four Americans (25 percent) claimed to be opposed to a nominee who was Catholic, but by 1987 that number had decreased to only 8 percent. Likewise, in 1958, 28 percent said that they would not vote for a candidate who was Jewish. By 1987, this figure had dropped to only 10 percent.[8]

The research on anti-Semitism in post–World War II America points in the same direction. Once again, the trends point to a rapid *decrease* in the proportion of the population holding negative perceptions of Jews.[9] For example, non-Jews are now far less likely to believe that Jews "have a lot of irritating faults," or are "unscrupulous," or "more willing than others to use shady practices to get what they want," that they "always like to be at the head of things," or that they are "objectionable neighbors." Non-Jews are also now far less likely to believe that Jews "have too much power," that they "don't care what happens to anyone but their own kind," and that they "are more loyal to Israel than to America."

Even among white Evangelical Protestants, the sector of the population that has historically been most hostile to Jews, anti-Semitic feeling is quite low. According to one survey conducted in 1986 for the Anti-Defamation League of B'nai B'rith, there is no longer any "strong direct evidence" to suggest that "most Evangelical Christians consciously use their deeply held Christian faith and convictions as justification for anti-Semitic views of Jews."[10] Indeed, 90 percent of the Evangelicals disagreed with the statement that "Christians are justified in holding negative attitudes toward Jews since the Jews killed Christ," and less than one in ten agreed that "God doesn't hear the prayer of a Jew." The study concluded that many of the negative attitudes of Evangelicals toward Jews are best interpreted as a measure of "general particularism" than of specific anti-Semitism per se. Indeed, the study further noted that "There is some evidence to suggest that Evangelical Christians may have more positive attitudes toward Jews than [toward] other non-Christians because of the interrelationship between the Christian and Jewish tradition throughout the Old and New Testaments."

The expansion of cultural tolerance, it is important to point out, is not an isolated event. It coincides with the slow but steady expansion of political and ideological tolerance (such as tolerance of communists and atheists), racial tolerance (of blacks and Hispanics), and sexual tolerance (of homosexuals and those cohabitating outside of marriage).[11]

No one would say that interreligious and interideological tension of the kind that prevailed in the nineteenth and early twentieth centuries has disappeared altogether—nor, in all likelihood, will it ever disappear entirely. The voices of prejudice can continue to be heard by those who warn against "the Jewish Menace," or like the leadership of the World Congress of Fundamentalists who claimed in 1983 that the Roman Catholic Church is "the mother of harlots and abominations of the earth."[12] Even so, overwhelming evidence demonstrates that the social ethos of the late twentieth century reflects dramatic change.

Social and historical tendencies as important as these compel us to confront a momentous possibility. The Enlightenment *philosophes* long ago predicted that as societies advanced, modern individuals would outgrow their need for the comfort of religious "superstitions." One of the long-dreamed-for consequences of this would be the end to religiously motivated violence and division in society. If religion was deteriorating, its passions could no longer be linked with the tremendous power of the state. All such conflict would come to an end. Though the Enlightenment thinkers held out this hope universally, they were particularly anxious to see the end of hostilities between Protestants and Catholics and between Christians and Jews in their own societies. It was the political disruption and human suffering generated by these particular cleavages that were most immediate to their own time and experience.

The evidence just reviewed provides still another compelling explanation of why the very idea of cultural conflict in contemporary America is so implausible to most Americans. When we look all around the social and political landscape, we see a general harmony among the traditional faiths of the United States; by and large, Protestants get along well with Catholics, Christians get along better with Jews, and even the small number of religious cults are more of a curiosity than a source of widespread resentment and antagonism. If one can argue anything on the basis of scholarly study, it is that the predictions of the Enlightenment age are coming true after all.

But are they? Is the age of cultural and, in particular, religious conflict in America coming to a close?

The answer must be no. The reason is that cultural conflict is taking shape along new and in many ways unfamiliar lines.

New Lines of Conflict: The Argument in Brief

Let me begin to make sense of the new lines of cultural warfare by first defining what I mean by "cultural conflict." I define cultural conflict very simply as political and social hostility rooted in different systems of moral understanding. The end to which these hostilities tend is the domination of one cultural and moral ethos over all others. Let it be clear, the principles and ideals that mark these competing systems of moral understanding are by no means trifling but always have a character of ultimacy to them. They are not merely attitudes that can change on a whim but basic commitments and beliefs that provide a source of identity, purpose, and togetherness for the people who live by them. It is for precisely this reason that political action rooted in these principles and ideals tends to be so passionate.

So what is new about the contemporary cultural conflict? As we have seen, the cultural hostilities dominant over the better part of American history have taken place *within* the boundaries of a larger biblical culture—among numerous Protestant groups, and Catholics and Jews—over such issues as doctrine, ritual observance, and religious organization. Underlying their disagreements, therefore, were basic agreements about the order of life in community and nation— agreements forged by biblical symbols and imagery. But the old arrangements have been transformed. The older agreements have unraveled. The divisions of political consequence today are not theological and ecclesiastical in character but the result of differing worldviews. That is to say, they no longer revolve around specific doctrinal issues or styles of religious practice and organization but around our most fundamental and cherished assumptions about how to order our lives—our own lives and our lives together in this society. Our most fundamental ideas about who we are as Americans are now at odds.

Because this is a culture war, the nub of political disagreement today on the range of issues debated—whether abortion, child care, funding for the arts, affirmative action and quotas, gay rights, values in public education, or multiculturalism—can be traced ultimately and finally to the matter of moral authority. By moral authority I mean the basis by which people determine whether something is good or bad, right or wrong, acceptable or unacceptable, and so on. Of course, people often have very different ideas about what criteria to use in making moral judgments, but this is just the point. It is the commitment to different and opposing bases of moral authority and the world views that derive from them that creates the deep cleavages between antagonists in the contemporary culture war. As we will see, this cleavage is so deep that it cuts *across* the old lines of conflict, making the distinctions that long divided Americans—those between Protestants, Catholics, and Jews—virtually irrelevant.

At this point let me introduce a critical word of qualification. Though competing moral visions are at the heart of today's culture war, these do not always take form in coherent, clearly articulated, sharply differentiated world views. Rather, these moral visions take expression as *polarizing impulses* or *tendencies* in American culture. It is important, in this light, to make a distinction between how these moral visions are institutionalized in different organizations and in public rhetoric, and how ordinary Americans relate to them. In truth, most Americans occupy a vast middle ground between the polarizing impulses of American culture. Many will obviously lean toward one side while many others will tilt toward the other. Some Americans may seem altogether oblivious to either. The point is that most Americans, despite their predispositions, would not embrace a particular moral vision wholly or uncritically. Where the polarizing tendencies in American culture tend to be sharpest is in the organizations and spokespeople who have an interest in promoting a particular position on a social issue. It is they who, perhaps unwittingly, give voice to the competing moral visions. (Even then, I might add, the world views articulated are often less than coherent!) These institutions possess tremendous power in the realm of public discourse. They almost seem to have a life of their own: an existence, power, and agenda independent of the people for whom they presumably speak.

Polarizing Impulses: The Orthodox and the Progressive
To come right to the point, the cleavages at the heart of the contemporary culture war are created by what I would like to call *the impulse toward orthodoxy* and *the impulse toward progressivism*. The terms are imperfect, but each aspires to describe in shorthand a particular locus and source of moral truth, the fundamental (though perhaps subconscious) moral allegiances of the actors involved in the culture war as well as their cultural and political dispositions. Though the

terms "orthodox" and "progressive" may be familiar to many, they have a particular meaning here that requires some elaboration.

Let me acknowledge, first off, that the words, orthodox and progressive, can describe specific doctrinal creeds or particular religious practices. Take orthodoxy. Within Judaism, orthodoxy is defined mainly by commitment to Torah and the community that upholds it; within Catholicism, orthodoxy is defined largely by loyalty to church teaching—the Roman Magisterium; and within Protestantism, orthodoxy principally means devotion to the complete and final authority of Scripture. Substantively, then, these labels can mean vastly different things within different religious traditions.

But I prefer to use the terms orthodox and progressive as *formal properties* of a belief system or world view. What is common to all three approaches to orthodoxy, for example (and what makes orthodoxy more of a formal property), *is the commitment on the part of adherents to an external, definable, and transcendent authority.* Such objective and transcendent authority defines, at least in the abstract, a consistent, unchangeable measure of value, purpose, goodness, and identity, both personal and collective. It tells us what is good, what is true, how we should live, and who we are. It is an authority that is sufficient for all time. Thus, as different as Chuck McIlhenny, Yehuda Levin, and Mae Duggan are in their personal faith commitments, all three believe that moral authority comes from above and for all time. This is seen clearly in Yehuda's statement that what the Torah says about abortion is "the beginning and the end of the subject." Chuck and Mae, in their own ways, would say something similar. This fundamental commitment, then, is what these three share in common and one reason why, in the current climate, their voices tend to resonate with each other.

Within cultural progressivism, by contrast, moral authority tends to be defined by the spirit of the modern age, a spirit of rationalism and subjectivism.[13] Progressivist moral ideals tend, that is, to derive from and embody (though rarely exhaust) that spirit. From this standpoint, truth tends to be viewed as a process, as a reality that is ever unfolding. There are many distinctions that need to be made here. For example, what about those progressivists who still identify with a particular religious heritage? For them, one may note a strong tendency to translate the moral ideals of a religious tradition so that they conform to and legitimate the contemporary *zeitgeist*. In other words, what all Progressivist world views share in common *is the tendency to resymbolize historic faiths according to the prevailing assumptions of contemporary life.* This is seen, for example, in Bea Blair's rejection of biblical literalism and her conviction that, as she put it, "people have to interpret the Scripture for themselves." The same theme is illustrated by stories Chuck McIlhenny tells of ministers he has debated, some of whom, Chuck says, reinterpret Scripture to justify homosexuality, while others recognize what the biblical texts say about the immorality of homosexuality but reject its authority over one's life. From Chuck's point of view, progressivist church leaders base their views on the belief that "the Bible is just a human document, no different from any other book." The general point both Bea and Chuck make here is that the traditional sources of moral authority, whether scripture, papal pronouncements, or Jewish law, no longer have an exclusive or even a predominant binding power over their lives. Rather, the binding moral authority tends to reside in personal experience or scientific rationality, or either of these in conversation with particular religious or cultural traditions.

I have been talking about the contemporary cultural divide in the context of religious communities in order to highlight the historical novelty of the contemporary situation. But what about the growing number of "secularists"?[14] These people range from the vaguely religious to the openly agnostic or atheistic. While they would probably claim no affiliation with a church or religious denomination, they nevertheless hold deep humanistic concerns about the welfare of community and nation. (Of those we met in the prologue,* Harriet Woods of St. Louis would most closely match this description. She was raised in the Reform movement of Judaism but has for many years maintained only the loosest attachments to that tradition. Instead, she thinks of herself as a humanist.) Secularists like Harriet are central to this discussion for the obvious reason that their presence and perspectives have become so prominent in American life. How then do secularists relate to the matter of moral authority?

Like the representatives of religious communities, they too are divided. Yet public opinion surveys show that a decided majority of secularists are drawn toward the progressivist impulse in American culture.[15] For these people religious tradition has no binding address, no opinion-shaping influence. Some secularists, however, (particularly many secular conservative and neo-conservative intellectuals) are drawn toward the orthodox impulse. For them, a commitment to natural law or to a high view of nature serves as the functional equivalent of the external and transcendent moral authority revered by their religiously orthodox counterparts.

In sum, the contemporary cultural conflict turns upside down (or perhaps inside out) the way cultural conflict has long been waged. Thus, we see those with apparently similar religious or cultural affiliations battling with one another. The culture war encompasses all Americans, religious and "non-religious," in very novel ways.

Political Dispositions: Cultural Conservatives Versus Cultural Progressivists
The orthodox and progressivist impulses in American culture, as I have described them, contrast sources of moral truth and also the allegiances by which people, drawn toward one or the other, live and interpret the world. They also express, somewhat imperfectly, the opposing social and political dispositions to which Americans on opposing sides of the cultural divide are drawn. Here, though, a word of elaboration.

It nearly goes without saying that those who embrace the orthodox impulse are almost always cultural conservatives, while those who embrace progressivist moral assumptions tend toward a liberal or libertarian social agenda. Certainly, the associations between foundational moral commitments and social and polit-

---
*Of the original publication.

ical agendas is far from absolute; some people and organizations will cross over the lines, taking conservative positions on some issues and liberal views on others. Yet the relationship between foundational moral commitments and social and political agendas is too strong and consistent to be viewed as coincidental. This is true for most Americans (as seen in public opinion surveys), but it is especially true for the organizations engaged in the range of contemporary disputes. For the practical purposes of naming the antagonists in the culture war, then, we can label those on one side cultural conservatives or moral traditionalists, and those on the other side liberals or cultural progressives. These are, after all, the terms that the actors in the culture war use to describe themselves. The danger of using these "political" labels, however, is that one can easily forget that they trace back to prior moral commitments and more basic moral visions: We subtly slip into thinking of the controversies debated as political rather than cultural in nature. On political matters one can compromise; on matters of ultimate moral truth, one cannot. This is why the full range of issues today seems interminable.

New and Unlikely Alliances
The real novelty of the contemporary situation emerges out of the fact that the orthodox and progressivist communities are not fighting isolated battles. Evangelical Protestants, for example, are not locked in an isolated conflict with liberal Protestants. Nor are theologically progressive Catholics struggling in isolation with their theologically conservative counterparts in the Roman hierarchy. The contemporary culture war is much larger and more complicated. *At the heart of the new cultural realignment are the pragmatic alliances being formed across faith traditions.* Because of common points of vision and concern, the orthodox wings of Protestantism, Catholicism, and Judaism are forming associations with each other, as are the progressive wings of each faith community—and each set of alliances takes form in opposition to the influence the other seeks to exert in public culture.

These institutional alliances, it should be noted, are not always influential in terms of the joint power they hold. Some of the groups, after all, are quite small and have few resources. But these institutional alliances are *culturally* significant, for the simple reason that ideological and organizational associations are being generated among groups that have historically been antagonistic toward one another. Had the disagreements in each religious tradition remained simply theological or ecclesiastical in nature, these alliances would have probably never developed. But since the divisions have extended into the broader realm of public morality, the alliances have become the expedient outcome of common concerns. In other words, although these alliances are historically "unnatural," they have become pragmatically necessary. Traditional religio-cultural divisions are superseded—replaced by the overriding differences taking form out of orthodox and progressive moral commitments.

These unlikely alliances are at the center of a fundamental realignment in American culture and, in turn, identify the key actors in an emerging cultural conflict. It is in this realignment that we find the real significance of the stories recounted at the opening of this book.* Each one illustrated the shifting alliances: at the Police Academy on East 20th Street in Manhattan stood Orthodox rabbis, Evangelical pastors, and Catholic priests, all being charged with disorderly conduct. There in the offices of Bea Blair's Religious Coalition for Abortion Rights and in Mae Duggan's Citizens for Educational Freedom an array of faiths (progressive in Bea's case and orthodox in Mae's case) are represented. There in San Francisco, there in Hartford, there in Cleveland, there in Boise, there in Birmingham, there in towns and cities all across America.

Points of Clarification
The first mistake we should guard against is to view the culture war as merely the accumulation of social issues debated today (such as abortion, values in schools, homosexuality, or the meaning of Columbus's discovery of America). The culture war encompasses these issues, but the source of the conflict is found in different moral visions. For this reason, it would also be a mistake to view the culture war as merely a social referendum on Ronald Reagan, George Bush, or other presidents and their political legacies. If this were the case, the present conflict would simply be a dispute between political "liberals" and "conservatives." The cleavages run much deeper. For the same reasons, it would be inaccurate to describe this as a collision between "religious liberals" and "religious conservatives."[16] Nor is it a clash between what one scholar described as "New Protestants" and "Old Protestants," "New Catholics" and "Old Catholics," and by extension, "New Jews" and "Old Jews" (Noll 1987). In a similar vein, it would be wrong to confuse the contemporary culture war with the ambitions of Protestant Fundamentalism and the New Christian Right and the backlash it created among such secular activists as feminists in the National Organization for Women (NOW) or attorneys of the American Civil Liberties Union (ACLU). It is true that Evangelical and Fundamentalist Protestants are the most vocal and visible actors on the orthodox side of the new cultural divide and that the secular activists of NOW, the ACLU, or the People for the American Way are among the most visible actors on the progressive side of the divide. But to frame the contemporary culture war in this way ignores the central role played by a wide range of other cultural actors on both sides who are neither Fundamentalists on the one hand nor secular activists on the other. Besides, many of the organizations of the New Christian Right (for instance, such as the Moral Majority, Christian Voice, the Religious Roundtable) have either disappeared from public sight or gone out of business. Yet the cultural conflict continues—and it continues without any sign that it will soon abate.

The Struggle to Define America

RANDALL TERRY (spokesman for the pro-life organization Operation Rescue): The bottom line is that killing children is not what America is all about. We are not here to destroy our offspring.

---
*Original publication.

FAYE WATTLETON (president of Planned Parenthood): Well, we are also not here to have the government use women's bodies as the instrument of the state, to force women into involuntary servitude.

RANDALL TERRY (laughing): Oh come on, Faye.

FAYE WATTLETON: I think that as Americans celebrate the Fourth of July, our independence, and when we reflect on our personal liberties, this is a very, very somber time, in which the courts have said that the most private aspects of our lives are now . . . not protected by the Bill of Rights and the Constitution. And I believe that that is a time for Americans to reflect on the need to return to the fundamentals, and the fundamentals of personal privacy are really the cornerstones upon which our democracy is built.

RANDALL TERRY: I think that to assume or even suggest that the founding fathers of this country risked their lives and many of them died so that we can kill our offspring is pathetic.[17]

Although Randall Terry and Faye Wattleton were debating the morality and legality of abortion, what they said goes far beyond the abortion controversy. First, the contemporary culture war is not just an expression of different "opinions" or "attitudes" on this or that issue, like abortion. If this were all there was to it, the conflict I refer to would be, as someone once suggested, the "politics of distraction"—a trivial pursuit that keeps Americans from settling more important matters.[18] No, the conflict is deeper than mere "differences of opinion" and bigger than abortion, and in fact, bigger than the culmination of all the battles being waged. As suggested earlier, the culture war emerges over fundamentally different conceptions of moral authority, over different ideas and beliefs about truth, the good, obligation to one another, the nature of community, and so on. It is, therefore, cultural conflict at its deepest level. This is why the differences between Chuck McIlhenny and Richmond Young, between Yehuda Levin and Bea Blair, and between Mae Duggan and Harriet Woods are so intense and seem so unresolvable.

Though the conflict derives from differences in assumptions that are philosophical and even theological in nature, the conflict does not end as a philosophical dispute. This is a conflict over how we are to order our lives together. This means that the conflict is inevitably expressed as a clash over national life itself. Both Randall Terry and Faye Wattleton acknowledge this in their exchange. Hearing them invoke the Bill of Rights, the "founding fathers," "what America is really all about," and so on, we come to see that the contemporary culture war is ultimately a struggle over national identity—*over the meaning of America,* who we have been in the past, who we are now, and perhaps most important, who we, as a nation, will aspire to become in the new millennium. Importantly, Randall Terry and Faye Wattleton are not the only ones who see a larger relationship between a single issue in the culture war and the American character. A well-known photographer whose work has been scrutinized by the FBI claims, "We are not going down without a fight. We're not going to go down without a voice that's saying loudly and clearly, 'this is not what we think

America is about.'"[19] A young mother and activist near Sacramento, who protests the content of schoolbooks in California's public schools, said, "The battle we are fighting here is being fought all around the state and around the nation. We as parents get involved because our children are affected but in the end it is our country that is at stake."[20] A video store owner who was prosecuted for violating pornography laws stated, "I feel like I'm fighting for America. I feel like I'm fighting for our rights as Americans. That's what I feel like."[21] And each of the individuals we met in the prologue believes that the battle they wage has consequences for America—its institutions and its ideals. And the list goes on. Arguably, our national identity and purpose has not been more a source of contention since the Civil War.

Though intellectuals and activists of various sorts play a special role in this cultural conflict, it would be very wrong to assume that this conflict is really just the lofty and cerebral machinations of squirrelly academic types who roam the corridors of think tanks and universities. To the contrary, this culture war intersects the lives of most Americans, even those who are or would like to be totally indifferent. This is so because this conflict has an impact on virtually all of the major institutions of American society. As the "stories from the front" suggest, this conflict has a decisive impact on the *family*—not just on the critical issues of reproduction and abortion but on a wide range of other issues such as the limits (if any) of legitimate sexuality, the public and private role of women, questions of childraising, and even the definition of what constitutes a family in the first place. The cultural conflict concerns the structure and content of public *education*—of how and what American children will learn. Also affected is the content of the popular media—from the films that are shown to the television shows that are aired to the books that are read and to the art that is exhibited. It has a critical effect on the conduct of *law,* particularly in the ways in which Americans define rights—who should have them and who should not and with whose interests the state should be aligned. Not least, this cultural clash has tremendous consequences for electoral *politics,* the way in which Americans choose their leaders. The contemporary culture war even has a bearing on the way in which public discussion is carried out—in the way people with opposing ideals and agendas try to resolve their differences in the public forum.

Once again, what seems to be a myriad of self-contained cultural disputes actually amounts to a fairly comprehensive and momentous struggle to define the meaning of America—of how and on what terms will Americans live together, of what comprises the good society. The purpose of this book is to explore the nature, depth, and consequences of this struggle. Part II★ describes the historical and societal sources that have given rise to the new cultural strains as well as the nature and historical significance of the new cleavages that divide American public culture. Part III† explores the mechanisms by which cultural conflict is carried out. In particular, this section explores the *nature* of public discussion about national life and purpose, and how the technologies that mediate

---

★ Part numbers refer to sections of the original publication.
† Part numbers refer to sections of the original publication.

public discourse aggravate the differences and intensify the polarities. In this way we see how most Americans are eclipsed from public debate. Part IV* examines the various fields of conflict—the symbolic territory over which the larger culture war actually takes place. The key areas surveyed are the family, education, media and the arts, law, and electoral politics. Finally, Part V† attempts to assess the status of the conflict today and traces the implications of this conflict for the unfolding of American democracy as it embarks upon its third century.

The first task, however, is to explore the general character of cultural conflict. The topic is somewhat theoretical but its implications are far from abstract. From it we will discern the tangible principles by which the contemporary American culture war takes shape.

References

Alger, H. 1870. *Ben, the luggage boy, or among the wharves.* Boston: Loring.

———. 1871. *Paul the peddler, or the adventures of a young street merchant.* Boston: Loring.

———. 1966. *Adrift in New York, and the world before him.* Edited by W. Coyle. New York: Odyssey Press.

Hofstadter, R., and M. Wallace, eds. 1971. *American violence.* New York: Vintage Books.

Keefe, T. M. 1975. The Catholic issues in the *Chicago Tribune* before the Civil War. *Mid-America* 57 (October): 227-245.

Noll, M. 1987. The eclipse of old hostilities. In *American violence,* edited by R. Hofstadter and M. Wallace. New York: Vintage Books.

---

*Part numbers refer to sections of the original publication.
†Part numbers refer to sections of the original publication.

PART VI

Culture and Political Change

Introduction

Culture is frequently considered to be inertia-bound and relatively resilient to change. Such views are common, not only for everyday conceptions of culture, but among social scientists as well, including some who study culture. Thus as the initial enthusiasm for the postwar, Almond-led political development research (Almond and Coleman 1960; Almond and Powell 1966) faded, political scientists began to evince, in spite of Verba's (1965, 512-60) powerful argument to the contrary, increased reluctance to rely on culture for explaining change. For instance, Johnson (1982) argues that, since Japanese public sector efforts to foster economic development change across time, it is difficult to attribute them to presumably stable cultural variables. Rogowski (1974) offers an incisive statement of this view. He points out that German enthusiasm for Hitler's regime in the late 1930s was widely attributed to authoritarian German cultural orientations. Yet by the early 1970s the Federal Republic had acquired a quarter century's experience as a democracy with broad popular support. If individual cultural orientations are as resistant to change as some political culture theorists claim, how then, Rogowski wonders, can culture be important to the explanation of rapid, thorough German societal transformation or political change generally? Rogowski thinks that rational-choice theory, which portrays humans as adept at adjusting their behavior to realize their interests under shifting circumstances, offers a conception of human motivation that fits better with the empirical evidence and thus provides a more compelling explanation of political change.

Rogowski's characterization of cultural inertia is drawn from the work of Eckstein and other major figures of the first wave of post–World War II political culture theory in the United States. This conception of culture is concisely detailed by Eckstein in chapter 17. It is a view of "cumulative socialization" by which early learning acts as a filter for later learning. Earlier learning becomes deeply rooted and resilient to change. Further, these filters help to construct orientations that fit various pieces of learning into larger coherent patterns. Culture amounts, then, to established patterns of attending to and interpreting a complex ambiguous world. Such cultures shape people's beliefs and values and carry inertia that makes rapid adjustment unlikely. Eckstein shares with Rogowski the position that political culture theories and rational-choice theory are rivals for explaining human motivation and political change, an issue on which we offer alternative views in part VII. (See also Wildavsky 1994.)

Yet various arguments suggesting culture's lack of usefulness for explaining political change, while influential, are not the only voices on this matter, and increasingly across the last couple of decades, scholars interested in political change have employed culture as an explanatory variable. For instance, Baker, Dalton, and Hildebrandt (1981) reveal substantial intergenerational differences among contemporary Germans, with later generations demonstrating more support for democracy than earlier ones. They conclude that rapid development of German support for democracy is attributable to sharply revised themes of early socialization. (See also Conradt 1980, 212-72.) Drawing on Thompson, Ellis, and Wildavsky (1990), Lockhart (1999) argues that German society, like others, is not composed of a single national character or culture. Rather, multiple rival cultures—egalitarian socialists, liberal individualists, and hierarchical statists—contend in social life. He explains the rapid transition from Nazi to democratic society in part through an externally initiated and supported change in relations between the components of the cultural coalition that has dominated German society for over a century. With the help of Western allies, German individualists came to dominate their coalition with hierarchists, whereas previously individualists had been the distinctly junior partners in this coalition. So the instance of postwar German transformation no longer appears to be the death knell for culture's ability to explain political change that it once appeared.

Dalton, Flanagan, and Beck (1984) trace the shifting political consequences of cultural change more broadly across Europe. Additionally, several scholars argue that cultural orientations help to explain prominent instances of political change such as revolutions (Foran 1997, 203-226; Goldstone 1991; and particularly Taylor 1989)—see also part V, "Social Movements, Collective Identity, and Political Culture." But the issue of culture's usefulness for political explanation is open to questions from different directions. For instance, Steinmo (1994, 106-131), who recognizes that societies are composed of multiple cultures whose influence shifts across time, argues—contra Johnson (1982)—that culture cannot explain enduring features of societies such as the persistent absence of socialist influence on the character of American political institutions.

The other two chapters in this part offer instances of culture contributing to political change. In chapter 18 Inglehart and Carballo, drawing on Inglehart (1988, 1997) argue that distinctive cultural orientations predominate under various socioeconomic conditions: traditional, industrial or modern, and advanced-industrial or postmodern. As socioeconomic conditions shift, young people are socialized to different cultural orientations, so progressive generations adopt distinctive views appropriate for different circumstances. Further, as the cultural orientations of societal populations change, so too do citizens' demands on and expectations of government. Cultural change thus leads to alterations in the character of political institutions and public policies.

Various aspects of Inglehart's thesis about culture and political change have been vigorously challenged by a number of critics, particularly Flanagan, who, drawing on his research on Japan, offers an alternative conception of the sort of cultural change occurring in advanced industrial societies. For more on this controversy see, in addition to the Inglehart citations in the previous paragraph, Flanagan (1979, 1982a, 1982b, 1987), Inglehart (1971, 1977, 1982, 1990), Inglehart and Abramson (1994), and particularly the exchange between Inglehart and Flanagan (1987).

Huntington's (1981) *American Politics: The Promise of Disharmony*, from which chapter 19 is drawn, focuses on the reappearance at roughly sixty-year intervals of periods of what he calls "creedal passion" in American political life: the revolution, the Jacksonian era, the Populist/Progressive era and the 1960s-1970s. Huntington, similarly to Free and Cantril (1967), argues that Americans have divided ideological or cultural loyalties. On one (abstract) hand, they are antistatist individualists, holding liberty, equality (of opportunity), individualism, democracy, constitutionalism, and limited, local government as values. On the other (more practical) hand, they are citizens of the world and use or want to use government, at least periodically, to defend themselves from foreign threats and to provide against various social hazards, such as aging and disability. This latter orientation produces a more substantial state that threatens or actually violates various conceptions of liberty, equality, individualism and democracy, fitting better overall with an hierarchical cultural orientation. Huntington argues that Americans go through a cycle in which they periodically reaffirm their abstract anti-statist creed but then gradually drift again into more hierarchical practices. Recently Huntington (1993) has offered another culturally based perspective through which international conflict—and the political changes flowing from it—is organized along persistent lines of cultural division among regions of the world.

References and Further Reading

Almond, G., and J. Coleman. 1960. *The politics of developing areas.* Princeton, NJ: Princeton University Press.

Almond, G., and G. B. Powell, Jr. 1966. *Comparative politics: A developmental approach.* Boston: Little, Brown.

Baker, K., R. Dalton, and K. Hildebrandt. 1981. *Germany transformed: Political culture and the new politics.* Cambridge, MA: Harvard University Press.

Conradt, D. 1980. Changing German political culture. In *The civic culture revisited,* edited by G. Almond and S. Verba. Boston: Little, Brown.

Dalton, R., S. Flanagan, and P. Beck, eds. 1984. *Electoral change in advanced industrial democracies: Realignment or dealignment?* Princeton, NJ: Princeton University Press.

Eckstein, H. 1988. A culturalist theory of political change. *American Political Science Review* 82: 789-804.

Flanagan, S. 1979. Value change and partisan change in Japan: The silent revolution revisited. *Comparative Politics* 11: 253-278.

———. 1982a. Changing values in advanced industrial societies: Inglehart's silent revolution from the perspective of Japanese findings. *Comparative Political Studies* 14: 403-444.

———. 1982b. Measuring value change in advanced industrial societies: A rejoinder to Inglehart. *Comparative Political Studies* 15: 99-128.

———. 1987. Value change in industrial societies. *American Political Science Review* 81: 1303-1319.
Foran, J. 1997. Discourses and social forces: The role of culture and cultural studies in understanding revolutions. In *Theorizing revolutions*. London: Routledge.
Free, L., and H. Cantril. 1967. *The political beliefs of Americans: A study of public opinion*. New Brunswick, NJ: Rutgers University Press.
Goldstone, J. 1991. Ideology, cultural frameworks, and the process of revolution. *Theory and Society* 20: 405-453.
Huntington, S. 1981. *American politics: The promise of disharmony*. Cambridge, MA: Harvard University Press.
———. 1993. The clash of civilizations. *Foreign Affairs* 72 (3): 22-49.
Inglehart, R. 1971. The silent revolution in Europe: Intergenerational change in post-industrial societies. *American Political Science Review* 65: 991-1017.
———. 1977. *The silent revolution: Changing values and political styles among Western publics*. Princeton, NJ: Princeton University Press.
———. 1982. Changing values in Japan and the West. *Comparative Political Studies* 14: 445-479.
———. 1988. The renaissance of political culture. *American Political Science Review* 82: 1203-1230.
———. 1990. *Culture shift in advanced industrial society*. Princeton, NJ: Princeton University Press.
———. 1997. *Modernization and postmodernization: Cultural, economic and political change in 43 societies*. Princeton, NJ: Princeton University Press.
Inglehart, R., and P. Abramson. 1994. Economic security and value change. *American Political Science Review* 88: 336-354.
Inglehart, R., and M. Carballo. 1997. Does Latin America exist? (And is there a Confucian culture?): A global analysis of cross-cultural differences. *PS: Political Science and Politics* 30: 34-47.
Inglehart, R., and S. Flanagan. 1987. Value change in industrial societies. *American Political Science Review* 81: 1289-1319.
Johnson, C. 1982. *MITI and the Japanese miracle*. Stanford, CA: Stanford University Press.
Lockhart, C. 1999. Cultural contributions to explaining institutional form, political change and rational decisions. *Comparative Political Studies* 32.
Rogowski, R. 1974. *Rational legitimacy: A theory of political support*. Princeton, NJ: Princeton University Press.
Steinmo, S. 1994. American exceptionalism reconsidered: Culture or institutions? In *Dynamics in American politics*, edited by L. Dodd and C. Jillson. Boulder, CO: Westview.
Taylor, M. 1989. Structure, culture and action in the explanation of social change. *Politics and Society* 17: 115-162.
Thompson, M., R. Ellis, and A. Wildavsky. 1990. *Cultural theory*. Boulder, CO: Westview.
Verba, S. 1965. Comparative political culture. In *Political culture and political development*, edited by L. W. Pye and S. Verba. Princeton, NJ: Princeton University Press.
Wildavsky, A. 1994. Why self-interest means less outside of a social context: Cultural contributions to a theory of rational choices. *Journal of Theoretical Politics* 6: 131-159.

CHAPTER 17

A Culturalist Theory of Political Change

Harry Eckstein

Originally published in
American Political Science Review, 82 (3), 1988.

READING INTRODUCTION

Eckstein introduces the political cultural approach as one of two viable options for theory in political science, the other being rational-choice theory. He then explains why the "cumulative socialization" process that he associates with culture leads to what he calls "expectations of continuity." In short, since earlier learning builds on later learning, people acquire considerable inertia to their orientations toward the world and cannot easily accommodate rapid, extensive change. But, Eckstein acknowledges, if the cultural approach fails to incorporate change, it offers little help in explaining a world in which change is ubiquitous. Instead political culture theory predicts that certain changes are likely while others are not. For instance, people routinely alter their actions in efforts to maintain their preferred social patterns in moderately new situations. Particularly among the members of modern societies, for whom such new situations are common, Eckstein thinks that social patterns capable of accommodating considerable flexibility gradually develop. But new situations that confront people with large-scale contextual changes likely will overwhelm culture-bound creatures. Faced with such circumstances, people are apt to lapse into various forms of incoherent and fragmented reactions rather than deftly revising their actions in ways that maintain their social patterns. Thus revolutionary transformations through which societies attempt to realize unprecedented objectives are not likely to achieve their intended outcomes.

READING TEXT

The most telling criticism of political culture theory is that it has coped very inadequately with political change. There is a good reason for this: the assumptions of the political culture approach in fact lead to the expectation of continuity. But continuity can be reconciled with changes, though only changes of particular kinds. The nature of political changes consistent with culturalist assumptions and with the culturalist expectation of continuity are here specified by hypotheses about (1) the effects of changes in social context, whether "normal" or involving abrupt discontinuity, and (2) the effects of attempted revolutionary transformation.

The political culture approach to building positive political theories and to political explanation has been with us since about 1960, and has been much described abstractly and much applied to concrete cases. The seminal works are Almond and Coleman's (1960) and Almond and Verba's (1963). Applications of the approach are covered comprehensively in a retrospective on the influence of their work by Almond and Verba (1979). Explications of it as a contender for paradigmatic status in political science, so to occur in numerous works (e.g., Bill and Hardgrave 1973; Dawson and Prewitt 1969; Merkl 1970; Putnam 1973; and Pye and Verba 1965). My own use of the concept of culture, which I consider more precise than that of others is discussed in the Appendix.*

Political culture theory may plausibly be considered one of two still viable general approaches to political theory and explanation proposed since the early fifties to replace the long-dominant formal-legalism of the field—the other being political rational choice theory. Indeed, determining which of the two modes of theorizing and explaining—the "culturalist" or the "rationalist"—is likely to give the better results may be the single most important item now on the agenda of political science (Eckstein 1979a).

Whether or not it is advisable to take the culturalist road to theory depends above all on the ability to produce a cogent culturalist theory of political change: a theory consistent with the assumptions (postulates) of the approach and confirmed by experience. Criticisms of culturalist political theories certainly have emphasized the occurrence of certain changes in political structures, attitudes, and behavior and culturalist accounts of their occurrence in order to impugn the approach. Rogowski (1974), for example, has argued that political culturalists have been very offhand in dealing with change—that they have tended to improvise far too much in order to accommodate political changes into their framework. They have done so, he writes, to the point that they no longer have a convincing way to treat political change at all. His argument is directed at culturalist theory in general, but he singles out Almond's work with Powell (1966) as especially indicative of the sins that culturalists commit.

This argument—and others to similar effect—strikes me as cogent criticism of how culturalists have in fact dealt with political changes. Furthermore, difficulties accounting for change in general and for certain kinds of change especially seem to me inherent in the assumptions on which the political culture approach is based.

Difficult, however, does not mean impossible, nor implausible. It is quite possible to deduce from these assumptions a logically cogent account of how political change, and every kind of such change, occurs. My purpose here is to provide such an account, as remedy for the "ad hocery" Rogowski rightly criticizes.

---

*Of original publication.

The Postulates of Culturalist Theories and the Expectations of Continuity

The basic reason why a culturalist account of change is intrinsically difficult to construct (hence, why culturalists have in fact tended to waffle in explaining political change) is simple: the postulates of the approach all lead to the expectation of political continuity; they make political continuity the "normal" state.

The Postulates of Culturalism

To see why this is so we must first make explicit the fundamental assumptions from which culturalist theory proceeds—its "axiomatic" basis, so to speak. These assumptions unfortunately have been left implicit in culturalist writings. It is necessary to make them explicit if one is compellingly to specify what experiences are "normal" in a culturalist world and what conditions culturalist theory can and cannot accommodate.

The touchstone of culturalist theory is the *postulate of oriented action:* actors do not respond directly to "situations" but respond to them through mediating "orientations." All else either elaborates or follows from that postulate. What exactly, then, does the postulate assert?

"Orientations to action" are general dispositions of actors to act in certain ways in sets of situations. Such general dispositions pattern actions. If actors do not have them, or if orientations are ill formed or inconsistent, actions will be erratic: patternless, anomic. The idea of "orientations to action" follows a particular psychological stimulus-response model: not the simple "single-stage" behaviorist model in which nothing "subjective" intervenes between the experience of situations and responses to it (actions) but "mediational" models in which responses to stimuli (actions in situations) are considered results both of the experience of objective situations and actors' subjective processing of experience. "Orientations" do the processing. We may call them, as did Bentley, soul-stuff, or mind-stuff. The critical methodological task of studies based on such models is, of course, to penetrate reliably and with validity into the subjective.

Orientations are not "attitudes": the latter are specific, the former *general,* dispositions. Attitudes themselves derive from and express orientations; though attitudes may, through their patterning, help us to find orientations. If orientations frequently occur in collectivities they may be called "culture themes," as by Mead and Metraux (1954). Pye (Pye and Verba 1965) has distinguished four sets of such "themes" that he considers useful for making cultural comparisons on the societal level: trust-distrust, hierarchy-equality, liberty-coercion, parochial-national identifications. Putnam (1973) considers the theme of conflict or its counterpart, harmony, critical for cross-cultural analysis. These "themes" exemplify how "orientations" are general dispositions that pattern sets of actions and sets of specific attitudes. It is conventional to regard orientations as having three components: cognitive elements that, so to speak, decode experience (give it meaning); affective elements that invest cognition with feelings that "move" actors to act; and evaluative elements that provide goals toward which actors are moved to act (Pye and Verba 1965).

The assumption of oriented actions would be vacuous without the addition of a second postulate, which we might call the *postulate of orientational variability:* orientations vary and are not mere subjective reflections of objective conditions. The significance of this postulate lies particularly in this: if the processing of experiences into actions were uniform—if it were fixed at the biological level or if it always involved "rationalist" cost-benefit calculation—then mediating mind-stuff could simply be left out of theory. In Hempel's terms, we would only need to know "initial conditions" (situations, structures) to explain actions, since we already know the universal covering law needed to complete an *explanandum*. No doubt ingenuity is required in relating conditions to actions via uniform orientations: the rational choice theories we have provide more than enough cases in point. But this does not alter the logic of the argument that without orientational variability we remain in a strictly behaviorist world. Similarly, if actions are merely "superstructural," we manifestly need only to know situations to explain actions. In that case, only the explanation of deviant cases (like false class consciousness) would require the use of mediating variables.

If orientations are not inherent in actors but variable, then something that is variable must form them. And if orientations are not simply subjective reflections of varying objective situations, then the variable conditions through which they are formed must themselves be cultural. Orientations are not acquired in some automatic way; they must be learned. Thus, a *postulate of cultural socialization* must hold if the first and second assumptions hold: orientations are learned through the agency of external "socializers." The repertoire of cognitions, feelings, and schemes of evaluation that process experience into action must be imparted by the socialized carriers of culture. The process can be direct, by "teachers" who are culturally variable actors; or it can occur indirectly simply through the experience of variable cultures.

"Rationalist" theorists do not, of course, reject the notion of political socialization. That would be silly. What divides culturalist and rationalist theorists here involves the issue of late-in-life learning, or resocialization.

In regard to that matter, culturalists proceed from a *postulate of "cumulative" socialization*. This means two things. First, although learning is regarded as continuous throughout life (which is not likely to be questioned) early learning—all prior learning—is regarded as a sort of filter for later learning: early learning conditions later learning and is harder to undo. Second, a tendency is assumed toward making the bits and pieces of cognitive, affective, and evaluative learning form a coherent (consistent, consonant) whole.

The postulate of cumulative learning provides the culturalist account of how two fundamental needs of actors in societies are satisfied: the need for economy of action and the need for predictability in interaction. Life would hardly be bearable, even possible, if one had to think out every action, taking into account all pertinent information and lack of information. Orientational schemata thus save virtually all decision costs. Social life, similarly, would hardly be possible without reliable preknowledge of others' actions and of the effect of one's own actions on those of others. Without such preknowledge social life would tend to be entropic. As Crozier (1964) has cogently argued, "uncertainty" of action also begets power—arbitrary power.

Both economy of action and predictability in interaction are diminished to the extent that individual orientations are inconsistent and that early learning may readily be undone. These conditions have effects similar to a lack of orientations to actions and of socially shared orientations altogether. They lead to erratic, incoherent behavior by individuals and in social aggregates: anomie in the former; the absence of anything like a stable *conscience collectif* in the latter.

It should be pointed out that the culturalist solution of the problems of economy of action and social predictability is not a unique solution, however plausible it may seem. Thus, in the rationalist perspective, economy of action is provided by "ideologies" or by the sensible delegation of decision-making powers (Downs 1957). The fixity required for predictability in social life follows from the very fact that rational choice is considered a fixed disposition. If this is so, one can anticipate the actions of others and adjust one's own behavior to the anticipation. Social predictability may also be achieved through rationally formulated and enforced contractual arrangements or general legal rules. (It should be apparent that the two accounts of economy of action and social predictability provide a good basis for evaluating the relative power of culturalist and rationalist perspectives.)

To summarize, "cultural" people process experience into action through general cognitive, affective, and evaluative predispositions; the patterns of such predispositions vary from society to society, from social segment to social segment; they do not vary because objective social situations or structures vary but because of culturally determined learning; early learning conditions later learning and learning involves a process of seeking coherence in dispositions. And this is so in order to "economize" in decisions to act and to achieve predictability in social interactions.

The Expectation of Continuity

When the postulates of the political culture approach are made explicit, it should be evident why political culture theorists *should* have difficulties in accounting for political change. The assumptions of culturalist theory manifestly lead to an expectation of continuity, even in cases of changes in the objective contexts of political actions.

The expectation of continuity in aggregate (and individual) orientations follows most plainly from the assumption that orientations are not superstructural reflections of objective structures, but themselves invest structures and behavior with cognitive and normative meaning.

Cultural continuity also manifestly follows from the assumption that orientations are formed through processes of socialization. To the extent that socialization is direct (by precept), generational continuity must occur, the socializers being formed, "cultural men." To the extent that socialization is indirect (by experience), generational continuity still follows; experience with authority occurs first in the family, then in schools, where unformed children encounter formed adults. In either case, what is true of one generation should continue substantially to be true in the next. This applies as much to cultural divisions in a society as to more general culture types and themes—if any exist in the first place. This, incidentally, makes the political culture perspective quite compatible with the holding that political regimes typically are short-lived (Gurr 1974).

The expectation of continuity in political cultures follows, most obviously, from the assumption of orientational cumulativeness, namely, that earlier learning conditions later learning and that actors tend to seek orientational consonance. The first allows some room for adult socialization and resocialization—but not much. The second makes unlikely the internalization of piecemeal orientational change that might increase dissonance.

But if change in culture patterns and themes were categorically excluded, political culture theory must immediately be thrown out as obvious nonsense: changes happen, including cultural changes. The saving grace of culturalist theory here is that continuity is, so to speak, an ideal-typical expectation—one that holds in an *abstract,* parsimonious cultural world. It is an expectation akin to that of inertia in the Galilean conception of motion. Physical inertia does not rule out changes of direction or rest, acceleration, and deceleration. It does make such phenomena depend on contingent factors that may or may not impinge on objects in motion. Continuity is the inherent lawful expectation and so, therefore, is resistance to change of motion: exceptionally great forces are needed to induce great changes in direction or velocity. The notion of continuity as inertia in motivations (the psychological counterpart of physical motion) thus opens the door to culturalist accounts of change.

Through that door, however, the tendency toward improvised, post hoc accounts of political change may enter—may be bound to enter. If one's preferred theoretical approach implies a strong bias toward the continuity of culture or resistance to cultural change, then it is always tempting to extemporize theory-saving "special" conditions, or adjustments in concepts or theory to handle occurrences of change—especially major change. If, say, theoretical difficulties arise from emphasizing early socialization, then why not just relax that emphasis and assign more scope for late socialization or adult resocialization? If the assumption of a tendency toward orientational consonance makes it awkward to explain certain observations, then why not simply posit more toleration for dissonance? Or why not redefine consonance? In that way, however, one is likely to end with the term continuity meaning nothing more than "not completely (or instantaneously) changeable"—which drains the term of all reasonable meaning. This is exactly the point of Rogowski's criticism of how culturalists have in fact accounted for political change.

The remedy is to develop an explicit general culturalist theory of change, consistent with culturalist assumptions, in order to prevent ad hoc tinkering with culturalist postulates and their implications. Such a theory should state, prior to explanations of specific changes, the characteristics of change that the political culture approach can logically accommodate and those that do not fit its constraints.

To formulate such a theory, I will consider two broad types of cultural changes: those arising "naturally" from changes in situations and structural conditions and those that result from "artifice"—deliberate attempts to transform political structures and behavior.

Situational Change

Pattern-Maintaining Change

Actors must often face novel situations with which their dispositional equipment is ill suited to deal. The world changes or presents us with experiences that are unfamiliar for other reasons (say, the penetration of peasant societies by market forces). The unfamiliar is encountered routinely in maturation, as one proceeds from family to school, from lower schools to higher ones, and from schools to participation in adult institutions. At the level of society and polity, novel situations also arise from internal "development," however development may be conceived. Novel situations also arise from socially internal discontinuities (economic crises or political disruptions, like those caused by governmental instability or collapse, or from changes brought about by protest movements), or from externally imposed changes. Immigration brings actors into unfamiliar situations. So does internal migration and social mobility. The encounter of novel situations will, no doubt, occur much more frequently among individuals than on the macro level, but it also occurs in groups and societies.

Novel situations may be short-lived results of ephemeral upheavals. In that case no cultural adjustments are needed, nor are they likely to occur. What, however, should one if such situations persist?

If cultures exhibit inertia then it should be expected that changes in culture patterns and themes will occur so as to maintain optimally such patterns and themes; that is to say, changes in culture are perfectly consistent with culturalist postulates if they occur as adaptations to altered structures and situations and if the function of change is to keep culture patterns in existence and consonant. "Pattern maintenance" (Parsons' concept) can take that form just as well as strict cultural continuity.

The French have a half-facetious adage for this sort of pattern maintenance: The more things change, the more they remain the same. The saying no doubt fits (used to fit?) France. The pragmatic masters at pattern maintaining change, however, have been the British. Tory concessions to British working class voters and interests are the usual case in point. Their function—sometimes "latent" but in the case of Disraeli's Tory democracy quite explicit—was to maintain Tory hegemony in the face of considerable sociopolitical change through the maintenance of as much as possible of what the Young England Circle considered the feudalistic virtues: the disposition to defer to one's betters and action by the betters on behalf of the lower orders. The point applies to reforms of the suffrage and also to the less well known role of the Tories in the evolution of the British welfare state, which Tory governments not only have kept virtually intact but much of which they pioneered.

An alternative to pattern-maintaining change is to subject unfamiliar experience to procrustean interpretation in order to obviate cognitive or normative change. "Perceptual distortion" has turned up frequently in experiments on how individual cognitive dissonance is handled (see Brehm and Cohen 1962). We know at least a little about the same way of dealing with the unfamiliar on the political macro level. To give just one example: party political elections in Northern Nigeria were initially regarded as a version of long-familiar elections to chieftaincy, in which the "candidates" were a small number of ascriptively defined eligibles (Whitaker 1970). The extent to which perceptual distortion can be adaptive to unfamiliar experience no doubt is highly limited. However, where institutions like elections to chieftaincy exist in traditional cultures, the adaptation of dispositions to other kinds of elections should be easier than in other cases.

Change Toward Flexibility

Highly modern societies have traits that make it especially likely that actors and aggregates of actors will frequently confront novel situations. Social mobility, vertical and horizontal, is the most obvious cause. Because any changes in dispositions are costly (dysfunctional) in the culturalist perspective, one should expect as a correlate to the expectation of pattern-maintaining cultural change, that the more modern societies are, the more the elements of their cultures will be general, thus flexible. No doubt there are considerable limits upon how general and flexible orientations can be and still perform their functions of making experience meaningful, actions economical, and interactions predictable. In more modern societies one should not expect culture to change as readily as situations and structures. Situational and structural change tend to occur with great frequency and rapidity in modern societies, and the assumption of orientational inertia postulates resistance to frequent, swift reorientation. Rather one should expect that the rigidity of cultural prescription will relax, so that culture can accommodate much social fluidity.

The tendency toward cultural flexibility can be regarded itself as a way to maintain cultural patterns and themes. As societies become more changeable, the elements of culture increasingly become "forms" that can subsume a variety of "contents." It is probably no coincidence that some sociologists early in the twentieth century (especially Simmel [1950]) adapted the Kantian distinction between form and content to social analysis. Durkheim argued much the same point directly. In early societies, he wrote, "the collective environment is essentially concrete . . . [and] the states of conscience then have the same character." ("Culture" is not a bad translation of his notion of a *conscience collectif*.) As societies develop, the "common conscience" is obliged to rise above diversity and "consequently to become more abstract. . . . General ideas necessarily appear and become dominant" (Durkheim 1960, 287-291).

I want to make three other points pertinent to the expectation that cultural abstractness and flexibility will grow with social development. First, the disposition to act "rationally" introduces just the kind of general and flexible culture trait that inherent social fluidity requires. (Durkheim [1960] already associated rational attitudes and behavior with the abstractness of thought necessary in highly developed societies.) The rationalization of modern life—which Weber considered to be its governing trait—thus may be an accommodation to structural conditions rather than, contra Weber, their underlying cause.

Second, the obviously difficult problem of finding a proper trade-off between two warring imperatives in modern societies, that of cultural flexibility and that of cultural fixity, is bound to be a practical difficulty, not just a theoretical one. Reconciling fixity with flexibility, abstractness, and formality may be a crucial element in what has widely been perceived as growing malaise in highly modern societies. Anomie will follow not only from lack of internal guides to action but from guidelines too general and loose to serve in the relentless particularity of experience. Highly modern society thus may be intrinsically acultural and, for that reason, transitory or susceptible to *surrogates* for culture—including cults and dogmas.

The expectation of cultural flexibility, finally, should apply to *all* highly modern societies. It thus pertains to polities initially based on rigid dogma (like communist societies) that have successfully pursued modernization. In such societies, the first expectation, that of cultural inertia, should hold. Old culture should resist new dogma. The expectation of pattern-maintaining change (or perceptual distortion) should hold as well. So one should expect also that as culture changes in such societies, it will change toward greater flexibility—and therefore to reinterpretations of dogma that make it increasingly pliable.

Cultural Discontinuity

Contextual changes can be so considerable or rapid or both that neither pattern-maintaining changes nor changes that gradually relax cultural rigidity to deal with social fluidity are possible. Rapid industrialization is the case in point usually cited. Changes resulting from war or from the formation of new polities also generally involve upheavals in social contexts. Such upheavals may result as well from economic traumas like the great inflation of 1923 in Germany (which led to far greater social disruption than the Great Depression—or possibly even the Black Death). And traumatic change sometimes strikes special segments of society rather than the whole.

We must deal, therefore, with social discontinuity, as well as "normal" change. Culturalists have tended either to avoid the matter or, worse, to treat cases of social trauma simply as "deviant cases" in which the theoretical constraints of their perspective are off—not least, the expectation of cultural inertia.

Obviously, traumatic social discontinuity will have cultural consequences different from contextual stability or less rapid, less pervasive change. Even in such cases, however, we may not simply improvise. If the assumptions of culturalists are correct, then traumatic social discontinuity should have logically expectable consequences, no less than other change.

The one consequence of social trauma absolutely precluded by culturalist assumptions is rapid reorientation. Social upheaval may overcome cultural inertia, but if so, actors should be plunged into a collective infancy in which cognitions that make experience intelligible and normative dispositions (affect, evaluative schemes) must be learned again, and learned cumulatively. No culturalist may expect, for instance, a democratic political culture to form, in a few short years, in a society like Germany after World War II, or "national" orientations to form rapidly in postcolonial tribal societies. Instead, changes in political cultures that occur in response to social discontinuity should initially exhibit considerable formlessness. For *formlessness* one may substitute other terms, like Durkheim's anomie or Merton's *deinstitutionalization*. The essence of the matter is that culture loses coherent structure. It becomes highly entropic.

The idea that rapid, large-scale contextual changes are personally disorienting and culturally disruptive is hardly new. Lipset (1960) argued a generation ago that rapid economic development is associated with political "extremism" ("anomic protest movements" like anarchism and syndicalism), despite the fact that high levels of such development are related to political stability. Huntington (1968) later made much the same point, and Olson (1963) has probably developed it most cogently.

To say that formlessness under conditions of socioeconomic discontinuity should be "considerable" is not mere hedging. Cultural entropy can never be complete. If it were, no patterned action or interactions would be possible at all. In any case, social discontinuity never is total—intimate social units, like the family, survive the greatest upheavals (may, indeed, be strengthened by them, as refuges of predictable order); so too do structures that are supposedly merely instrumental—for example, bureaucracies. As well, if learning is cumulative, older people should exhibit a good deal of orientational inertia even when traumatic socioeconomic change occurs. We may surely suppose that the more ingrained orientations are and the more they are consonant systems, the less susceptible they are to "disorientation"—the more mechanisms like perceptive distortion will used to invest experience with accustomed meaning.

Governmental authority will, of course, survive cultural discontinuity. In fact, it is likely to become more powerful to the extent that internalized dispositions cannot govern actions and interactions. How then do people act politically if political culture is highly formless?

We can get useful clues to answers from the growing literature on an analogous experience: how children adapt to novel situations that they enter in highly discontinuous ways—going to school, for instance, or going from one to another type or level of schooling. Much of the literature on this subject (like Wakeford 1969 and Woods 1979) has been informed by Merton's (1949) path-breaking study of the bases of deviant behavior, which dealt in general terms with behavior under more or less "anomic" conditions.

Under conditions of cultural discontinuity, conformity with authority is still likely to occur, but it will tend to have certain characteristics. In Merton's technology, it will tend to be *ritualistic* or else *self-serving* (opportunistic and of dubious morality, as general culture defines morality). Ritual conformity is compliance without commitment. One does what the rules or rulers prescribe, not for any discernible reason but (quoting from a lower-class British pupil interviewed by Woods) "because I behave meself...I just do what I'm told... [I] ain't got much choice." Conformity of this sort may be supposed to occur frequently in cases in which the former political cultures and subcultures prescribed high compliance ("subject cultures," as Almond and Verba called them). Self-serving, opportunistic conformity bends norms and rules for private advantage—including that of getting ahead in the competition for political power. Charles Dickens observed a lot of that sort of behavior in his travels in America as he reports them in his *American Notes*. Thus, in regard to a very successful businessman, " 'He is a public nuisance, is he not?' 'Yes sir,' . . . 'And he is utterly dishonest, debased, and profligate?' 'Yes, sir.' 'In the name of wonder, then, what is his merit?' 'Well, sir, he is a smart man' " (1957, 246). I mention Dickens because one should especially expect "smart" conformity in immigrant societies or immigrant segments of society, where (as in schools) discontinuity occurs through movement into an unfamiliar but intact culture. Perhaps one should expect it even more in cultures greatly unsettled by upheaval. Thus, Burke presciently remarked (in 1790) that when cultural constraints are off, "the worst rise to the top" (1923, 45).

More commonly than conformity, one should expect what Merton called *retreatism* under conditions of cultural discontinuity. Retreatism involves withdrawing from the "alien" larger society into the smaller, more familiar worlds of family, neighborhood, village, and the like. In Almond and Verba's scheme of concepts, it should show up as increased "parochialism." In the small worlds of schools, retreatism tends to involve self-imposed isolation—for instance, into remote places and daydreams or what Woods calls removal activities—"unserious pursuits which are sufficiently engrossing . . . [to make participants] oblivious for the time being of [their] actual situation"—or both.

Rebellion against, and intransigent resistance to, authority are also likely responses to the experience of cultural decay. A voluminous literature links social, economic, and political discontinuities to political violence—from Marx to Moore and Skocpol. Rebellion and intransigence, however, are always likely to be costly and call for much energy; retreatist behavior into parochial worlds or ritualistic conformity are thus more likely, especially where governing power—if not authority—is strong.

What should follow over time from contextual and cultural discontinuity? If economy of action and predictability indeed are imperatives in individual and collective life, one should expect new culture patterns and themes to emerge. But if dispositions are formed by cumulative learning, they should emerge only slowly (over generations) and, in the transitional period, at great costs resulting from raw power, withdrawal, and (because of withdrawal) forced mobilization and rebelliousness against it. Thus, the process of reformation of political cultures should be prolonged and socially costly. This is all the more likely to be the case if parochial units remain intact refuges from discontinuities in society, economy, or polity.

The expectation is logical also if older people, as is likely, cling to long-fixed dispositions even in face of strong forces that might unsettle inertia. We might thus posit as a general expectation that in the process of cultural reformation considerable age-related differences should occur. In fact, age, in cases of pronounced discontinuity, might even be expected to be a major basis for subcultural differentiation. If indeed this were found to be so, the cultural perspective upon theory would be enormously strengthened over alternatives. Empirical work pertinent to the expectation, however, is oddly lacking; and as culturalists have built adult learning increasingly into their approach in order to accommodate ill-fitting facts, the incentive to inquire into age-related cultural differences, in both established and transitional contexts, has regrettably declined.

I want to make another point about the reformation of dispositions and culture patterns, more briefly. As the young should be more susceptible to reorientation than the old, so one should expect to find in social macrostructures particular segments that have traits especially conducive or susceptible to reorientation. By "conducive traits" I mean structural or dispositional traits readily accommodated to new culture patterns or, indeed, anticipations of them. In Western traditional societies, for instance, there always existed a large island of achievement in a sea of ascription—the celibate clergy, which hardly could be ascriptively recruited. The clergy, in fact, played a considerable role in the emergence of modern political institutions—despite its stake in the distribution of traditional privileges. Similarly, socially "marginal" groups—groups that occupy the fluid interstices of established cultures—should be highly susceptible to reorientation, thus "vanguards" in the reorienting of unsettled societies. There is a good deal of literature making the case that this is indeed so (e.g., Rejai and Phillips 1979, Wolf 1973).

Political Transformation

By *transformation* I mean the use of political power and artifice to engineer radically changed social and political structures, thus culture patterns and themes: to set society and polity on new courses toward unprecedented objectives. Transformation, typically, is the objective of modern revolutions. It can also be the objective of military conquerors and of nation builders or other modernizers. Revolutions, however, provide the most unambiguous and dramatic cases. I will therefore confine my remarks to them—though what is said about them should also apply to transformation attempted in other ways.

Hannah Arendt (1963) undoubtedly was right in arguing that attempts at revolutionary transformation are distinctively modern—that revolutions as we think of them (not mere rebellious attacks on authorities or their actions) begin with the French and American revolutions. As long as political and social structures were considered divinely ordained, or natural, or simply the ways of a folk, the idea of their deliberate transformation hardly could occur. "History" then could only be endless repetition or an intrinsic progress toward a preordained end. Societies and polities could no more be "transformed" than the heavenly bodies set upon new orbits. One of the decisive traits of modern societies then is the belief that a "new beginning"—a felicitous and not redundant expression—could be made in political and social life.

Initially, making a new beginning did not seem to call for much artifice—no more, perhaps, than a proper constitution. Achieving liberty or equality throughout society simply called for setting polities and societies on their inherently right course—right, given human nature. For reasons not necessary to sketch in the age of the "God that failed," *really* making revolution—not seizing power but the accomplishment of transformation—came increasingly to be seen as a task, and a difficult task, for political artificers. Unfortunately, systematic studies of that process are few, although the exceptions often have been notable: for instance, Massell's study of Soviet attempts to bring Soviet Central Asia into modernity (1974) and Kelley and Klein's study of the effects on inequality of the Bolivian Revolution of 1951 (1981). Inquirers into revolution still are hooked on the issue of their etiology.

Since revolutions are themselves major discontinuities and since they generally occur in periods of social or political upheavals, not least governmental breakdown (Edwards 1927; Brinton 1965), the expectations listed in the preceding section should apply to transformation. But I want to state here some expectations that follow from the culturalist perspective especially for processes of revolutionary transformation. Intrinsic interest and contemporary relevance aside, these processes seem to me especially critical for evaluating culturalist theories and their bases. After all, transformative processes involve not only adjustment to necessity but also the deliberate engineering of great change, and they are typically backed by great power and control.

As a first expectation we may posit that revolutionary transformation is strictly impossible in the short run. Revolutions certainly bring upheaval. They may also be expected to bring about movement in the direction of their professed goals by readily accomplished actions—instituting wide suffrage, kicking out the landlords and redistributing land, ending feudal privileges and obligations, and the like. But if discontinuity begets "formlessness" of culture, then revolutionaries can hardly do much to reorient people in the short run (say, in a generation or so). Reorientation is, of course, the less likely the more intact is the prerevolutionary culture: the more it provides parochial refuges from transformative power or institutional centers of resistance to it. But even if revolution only reflects discontinuity instead of engendering it, the expectation stated still should hold.

If the conventional norms and practices of political life are disrupted by revolution, what can be put in their place? We may posit the answer that revolutionary transformation will initially be attempted by despotic or legalistic means. What, after all, can "order" societies and polities in place of conventional, internalized culture? Only brute power, or else the use of external legal prescriptions as a surrogate for internal orientational guides to behavior. "Revolutionary legalism" was in fact a device used early after the Bolshevik seizure of power, and it overlapped a good deal (even before Stalin) with attempts to "storm" society (especially its more backward parts) with head-on "administrative assault." Neither, according to Massell (1974), accomplished much toward the realization of transformation; responses to it, he writes, included "avoidance," "selective participation," "evasion," "limited retribution," and "massive backlash."

"Legalism," it might be noted here, is likely to be a general response to massive cultural disruption, whether revolutionary or situational or both. Indeed, it can become, in highly unusual cases, a persistent surrogate for normative culture—indeed, a culture form. I have argued this elsewhere (1979b), defining "legalist" cultures as cultures in which legal rules are widely known, such rules are widely used (instead of justice or prudence) to justify political standpoints or decisions, legal actions are the normal mode of dealing with conflicts and disputes, and therefore laws deal in highly detailed—if possible comprehensive—ways with social interaction and tend to be punctiliously adhered to. Durkheim (1960) argued the even more general, related proposition that in the course of development civil law (which regulates social interactions) constantly grows, while criminal, or restitutive, law declines. His argument makes sense if indeed development "loosens" normative cultural prescription, as I argued, and lessens cultural similitude, as Durkheim argues.

The case I used to make this argument is contemporary West Germany. That, we should note, also is the case Rogowski (1974) mainly relies on to argue that reorientation can occur rapidly—the crucial point in his critique of culturalist theory. Rogowski seems to me to miss the read import of "deviant cases"—that through their very abnormal characteristics they can be used to shed light upon the factors that condition typical cases.

What of the long-run prospects of revolutionary transformations? I suggest the expectation that the long-run effects of attempted revolutionary transformation will diverge considerably from revolutionary intentions and resemble more the prerevolutionary condition of society. The expectation is not that little change in "content" will occur: in who holds power, gets privilege, and so on. No inevitable Thermidorean Reaction is posited. The argument is somewhat less categorical: reconstructed culture patterns and themes will diverge widely from revolutionary visions and will tend to diverge from them in the direction of the patterns of the old society and regime. The degree to which the expectation holds obviously depends on the extent to which the old culture was already in disarray.

Several points made earlier lead to this expectation. Culture must still be learned on a comprehensive scale, as in all societies; and although revolutionary teaching can no doubt play a considerable role in shaping the young, it can hardly replace socialization in small parochial units. Nor are teachers or role models likely to be, extensively, the sort of marginal individuals who are steeped in revolutionary dogma as a surrogate for convention—or people for whom the revolutionary vision has much meaning at all. Sheer cultural inertia will also play a role in the process of revolutionary decay; so will the tendency toward turning change into pattern maintenance—perhaps by a progressive transformation of revolutionary visions into mere revolutionary rhetoric; so—to the extent that the new rulers succeed in modernizing—will the tendency of modern cultures to be general, abstract, and (especially pertinent here) flexible; so will "retreatist" and "ritualist" responses to discontinuity; and so will the tendency of opportunistic conformists to get ahead, by scheming or approval, in unfamiliar contexts.

In fact, it may well be the case that the short-run effects of attempted transformation are greater than the longer-run effects. More can be done in upheaval than when life again acquires fixity. Kelley and Klein (1981) have argued precisely this point, on the basis of generalizing the case of the Bolivian Revolution of 1951.

Whether all this also entails the expectation that in the longer run incremental change will accomplish more than attempts at radical transformation we can perhaps leave an open question here. But note that the rulers of the Soviet

Union came increasingly to view the achievement of cultural change as a matter for what they called "systematic social engineering" for—as Massell (1974) describes it—"a pragmatic commitment to relatively patient and systematic social action, wherein at least as much time and effort would be devoted to the building of bridges to traditional society . . . as to actual and direct confrontation with the traditional system."

Conclusion

It may well be the case that the political culture approach has been used to explain political changes in the sort of ad hoc and post hoc manner that saves—and thus weakens—theories rather than testing and strengthening them. Culturalists hardly have a monopoly on such theoretical legerdemain—certainly not when compared to rational choice theorists—when discomfiting facts confront them. But I have tried to show here that culturalists must have a strong propensity toward improvised theory saving when dealing with political change, since their assumptions lead, necessarily, to an expectation of cultural continuity—at any rate in a "pure" (abstract, ideal-typical) cultural world, where all matters falling under "ceteris paribus" are in fact "equal."

Nevertheless, it should be evident that a cogent, potentially powerful theory of political change can be derived from culturalist premises. The theory sketched here specifies that changes in dispositions, in response to contextual changes, should be pattern-maintaining changes or—if the contextual changes involve modernization—changes toward normative generality and flexibility; that in response to abrupt social discontinuities cultural dispositions should, for a considerable period, be "formless"—incoherent in individuals and fragmented in aggregates; that in such cases retreating into intact parochial structures occurs, while conformity should become ritualistic or opportunistic; that revolutionary artifice cannot accomplish cultural transformation in the short run; that such transformation will be attempted by despotic power or (mainly hopeful) legal prescriptions; and that, in the longer run, attempts at revolutionary transformation will tend to be regressive or at least have quite unintended outcomes. Note, however, that nothing here rules out engineered change, so to speak—attempted structural reforms of politics. In the modern world, political tinkering, on small or grand scales, is endemic. The theory simply states what should result from such tinkering.

The problem of testing the theory against experience obviously remains, as do problems of operationalizing concepts for that purpose. But obviously theory comes first.

If the power of a culturalist account of political change is to be compared with that of different approaches to political theory and explanation, then general accounts of change, derived from noncultural postulates and similar to that presented here, are needed. Political culture theories, admittedly, have not heretofore met the challenge of developing a general theory of change; but neither have others.

Appendix: Culture

The term *culture,* unfortunately, has no precise, settled technical meaning in the social sciences, despite its centrality in them. The variable and ambiguous use of key concepts generates unprofitable arguments that are merely definitional. Hence I append a note that places my use of the term, as sketched in the first section, in its conceptual context. [See Figure A-1, editor's note.]

My use of the term *culture* tries to make explicit, at the axiomatic level, what is implicit (occasionally almost explicit) in the works of Almond and his various collaborators (Coleman 1960; Powell 1966; Verba 1963; Verba 1979). Their use of the concept seems to be based squarely on Talcott Parsons' "action frame of reference." Parsons first worked out that "frame of reference" as a way of synthesizing four apparently diverse, all highly influential, early modern social scientists: Marshall, Pareto, Durkheim, and Weber (Parsons 1937). He and collaborators developed action theory in a large series of works, the most useful of which probably is the multiauthored book, *Toward a General Theory of Action* (Parsons and Shils 1951).

The action frame of reference is based, at the microlevel, on Parsons' notion of an interaction, societies being complexes of interactions (some earlier sociologists called them acts of "sociation"). The notion is depicted on Figure A-1. In brief translation, (1) ego (an actor) is in a "situation"—an objective context; (2) ego cognitively decodes that context and invests it with feeling (cathexis)—thus

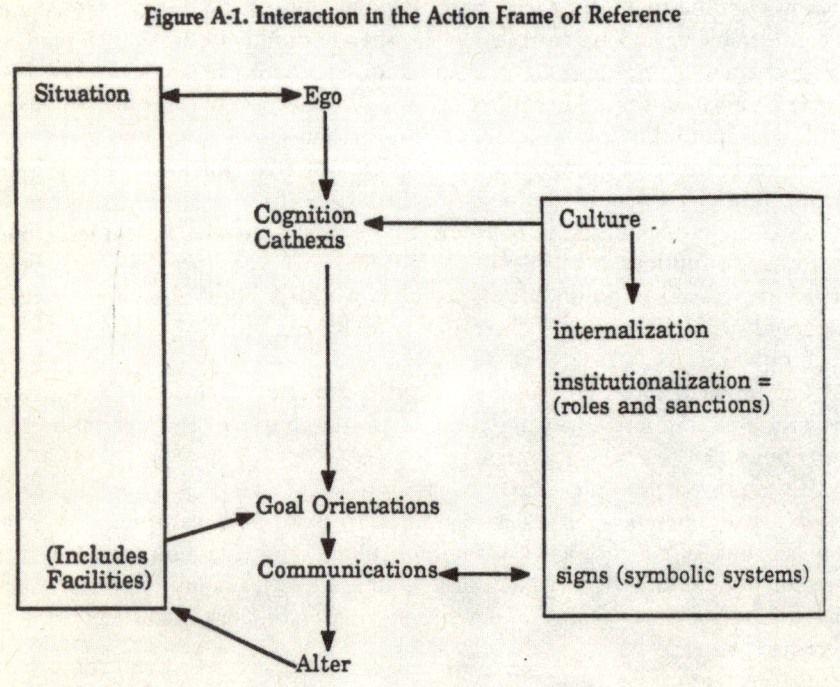

Figure A-1. Interaction in the Action Frame of Reference

the context comes to have meaning for the actor; (3) the manner of investing situations with meaning is acquired through socialization, which consists mainly of early learning—this imparts the modes of understanding and valuing prevalent in societies or subsocieties or both. In aggregate, these may be called a society's "culture"; (4) socialization leads to the internalization of cognitive and affective meanings (viz., the cultural becomes personal) and their institutionalization (the definition of expected behavior in social roles and that of sanctions in case of deviation from expected behavior—these make smooth and regular patterns of interaction possible; (5) cognitions and affective responses to them define goals and ways to pursue them; (6) cognitions, feelings, and goals are communicated to alter (another actor) through the use of "signs" (symbolic expressions of culture that make ego's actions intelligible to alter)—but actions also depend on objective facilities that are part of any actor's situation and that independently affect the choice of goals; (7) alter responds, changing the situation in some so that the process resumes.

Note especially that the action frame of reference emphasizes neither subjective nor objective factors but rather how the two are linked in interactions. Culturalists focus on the matters in the box on the right, but they should also bring that on the left into interpretation and theories. This I have tried to do throughout this essay, emphasizing how culture conditions change in varying contexts of objective change.

Alternatives to the notion of culture I use come chiefly from cultural anthropology. I use the plural intentionally, because the meanings of culture vary a great deal in that field. One can probably subsume these meanings under four categories: (1) culture is coterminous with society: it is the whole complex of the ways of a "folk," of human thought and action among particular people—Park (1937) comes close to that view; (2) culture is social life in its subjective aspects: the knowledge, beliefs, morals, laws, customs, habits of a society—one finds this meaning (and these illustrative words) in the seminal work of Tyler (1871) and, later, Benedict (1934) and Kluckhohn (1962); (3) culture is what differentiates societies from one another, for the purpose of idiographic description but also for theorizing through comparisons and contrasts (agreements and differences)—I take the seminal work here to be Malinowski's (1944); (4) culture is the distinctive, variable set of ways in which societies normatively regulate social behavior (Goodenough 1968; Sumner 1906).

The fourth set of meanings comes closest to that used here. My use of the concept of culture here seems to be justified by usage in political science and, more important, by its suitability to testing theories through the catholic deduction of unknowns once it postulates are explicitly stated. Anyway, my version of the concept is that about which theoretical conflicts have thus far occurred in political inquiry.

References

Almond, G. A., and J. S. Coleman. 1960. *The politics of the developing areas*. Princeton: Princeton University Press.

Almond, G. A., and G. B. Powell. 1966. *Comparative politics: A developmental Approach.* Boston: Little, Brown.
Almond, G. A., and S. Verba. 1963. *The civic culture.* Boston: Little, Brown.
———. 1979. *The civic culture revisited.* Princeton, NJ: Princeton University Press.
Arendt, H. 1963. *On revolution.* New York: Viking.
Benedict, R. 1934. *Patterns of culture.* New York: Houghton.
Bill, J., and R. L. Hardgrave. 1973. *Comparative politics: The quest for theory.* Columbus: Merrill.
Brehm, J. W., and A. R. Cohen. 1962. *Explorations in cognitive dissonance.* New York: Wiley.
Brinton, C. 1965. *The anatomy of revolution.* New York: Vintage.
Burke, E. 1923. *Reflections on the French Revolution.* London: Methuen.
Crozier, M. 1964. *The bureaucratic phenomenon.* Chicago: University of Chicago Press.
Dawson, R. E., and K. Prewitt. 1969. *Political socialization.* Boston: Little, Brown.
Dickens, C. 1957. *American notes & pictures from Italy.* London: Oxford.
Downs, A. 1957. *An economic theory of democracy.* New York: Harper & Row.
Durkheim, E. 1960. *The division of labor in society.* Glencoe, IL: Free Press.
Eckstein, H. 1979a. *Support for regimes.* Research Monograph no. 44. Princeton, NJ: Center of International Studies.
———. 1979b. On the "science" of the state. *Daedalus* 108 (4): 1-20.
Edwards, L. P. 1927. *The natural history of revolutions.* Chicago: University of Chicago Press.
Goodenough, W. 1968. *Description and comparison in cultural anthropology.* Chicago: Aldine.
Gurr, T. 1974. Persistence and change in political systems. *American Political Science Review* 68: 1482-1504.
Huntington, S. 1968. *Political order in changing societies.* Cambridge, MA: Harvard University Press.
Kelley, J., and H. Klein. 1981. *Revolution and the rebirth of inequality.* Berkeley: University of California Press.
Kluckhohn, C. 1962. *Culture and behavior.* New York: Free Press.
Lipset, S. M. 1960. *Political man.* Garden City, NY: Doubleday.
Malinowski, B. 1944. *A scientific theory of culture.* New York: Oxford University Press.
Massell, G. 1974. *The surrogate proletariat.* Princeton, NJ: Princeton University Press.
Mead, M., and R. Metraux. 1954. *Themes from French culture.* Stanford, CA: Stanford University Press.
Merkl, P. 1970. *Modern comparative politics.* New York: Holt, Rinehart, & Winston.
Merton, R. K. 1949. *Social theory and social structure.* Glencoe, IL: Free Press.
Olson, M., Jr. 1963. Rapid economic growth as a destabilizing force. *Journal of Economic History* 23: 529-552.
Park, R. 1937. Introduction to *The marginal man,* by E. V. Stonequist. New York: Scribners.
Parsons, T. 1937. *Toward a general theory of action.* New York: McGraw-Hill.
Parsons, T., and E. Shils, eds. 1951. *Toward a general theory of action.* Cambridge, MA: Harvard University Press.
Putnam, R. 1973. *The beliefs of politicians.* New Haven, CT: Yale University Press.
Pye, L. W., and S. Verba. 1965. *Political culture and political development.* Princeton, NJ: Princeton University Press.
Rejai, M., and K. Phillips. 1979. *Leaders of revolutions.* Beverly Hills, CA: Sage.
Rogowski, R. 1974. *Rational legitimacy.* Princeton, NJ: Princeton University Press.
Simmel, G. 1950. *The sociology of George Simmel.* Translated by K. Wolf. Glencoe, IL: Free Press.
Sumner, W. 1906. *Folkways.* Boston: Ginn.
Tyler, E. 1871. *Primitive culture.* 2 vols. London: John Murray.
Wakeford, J. 1969. *The cloistered elite.* London: Macmillan.
Whitaker, C. S. 1970. *The politics of tradition: Continuity and change in northern Nigeria 1946-1966.* Princeton, NJ: Princeton University Press.
Wolf, E. 1973. *Peasant wars in the twentieth century.* London: Faber & Faber.
Woods, P. 1979. *The divided school.* London: Routledge & Kegan Paul.

CHAPTER 18

Does Latin America Exist? (And Is There a Confucian Culture?): A Global Analysis of Cross-Cultural Differences

Ronald Inglehart and Marita Carballo

Originally published in
PS: Political Science and Politics, *30 (1), 1997*

READING INTRODUCTION

Inglehart and Carballo's first task in this article is to introduce the two underlying dimensions that, they argue, explain a good deal of the variation in people's attitudes toward a broad range of questions (see Figure 1) across a number of societies. These dimensions contrast: traditional conceptions of authority characteristic of some of the least technologically developed societies with secular-rational conceptions of authority prevalent among most European and East-Asian societies as well as concerns about physical and economic survival typical of industrializing or "modern" societies in Eastern Europe and East Asia and quality-of-life concerns (opportunities for participation in politics and the workplace, meaningful leisure and environmental protection) found more commonly among advanced-industrial or "postmodern" societies in northwestern Europe. The average or mean scores of citizens of 43 societies on the broad range of questions Inglehart and Carballo ask produce clusters of societies (in Figures 4-6) that roughly duplicate geographic relationships. Thus the authors show that Latin America (or any other geographic region from other clusters in Figure 4) exists in terms of attitudinal similarities in addition to being a set of geographically proximate societies.

Inglehart and Carballo's fundamental explanation for societies' positions with respect to the dimensions of Figures 4-6 draws on their socioeconomic position. That is, extensive, thorough economic development requires increased secular-rational authority and produces quality-of-life concerns. The poorest societies, characterized by traditional survival orientations, are found in the lower left-hand corner of the concept space. The most actively industrializing societies ("modern" ones for Inglehart and Carballo), in which secular-rational survival orientations predominate, are found in the upper left-hand corner of the concept space. The most advanced (and wealthiest) societies ("postmodern" for Inglehart and Carballo), found in the upper right-hand corner of the concept space, have the largest proportions of citizens with secular-rational, quality-of-life orientations. So societal movement across time tends to be toward the top and then toward the right-hand side of the concept space. (See Figure 6.)

Inglehart and Carballo depict a reciprocal flow of influence between institutions and culture. First, different economic institutions (or at least their practical consequences) foster distinctive cultures. Then rival cultures form and sustain different political institutions, including public policies. For instance, "postmodern" values produce policy orientations distinctly more tolerant of diversity than either modern or traditional values. (See Figure 3.) Inglehart (1997) offers a more extensive explanation for societies' positions with respect to these two dimensions, but an additional factor discussed in this chapter is variation in religious traditions. (See Figure 5.)

READING TEXT

Does Latin America Exist?[1]

Latin American studies centers (like African, or Middle Eastern or West European studies centers) are based on the assumption that Latin America (and Africa, the Middle East, etc.) are more than arbitrary geographic expressions: they define coherent cultural regions, having people with distinctive values and worldviews that make them think differently and behave differently from people of other cultures.

The most powerful challenge to this view currently comes from the rational choice school, whose practitioners occasionally mention the importance of cultural differences but whose models almost always ignore them, implicitly assuming that in a given situation all people will make the same "rational" choices regardless of cultural perspectives. But if major differences exist between the worldviews and motivations of people in different cultural zones, a rational choice model that applies to the United States may not accurately describe the behavior of people in other cultures.

The existence of meaningful cultural areas has been challenged on other grounds as well. Modernization theory focuses on the differences between "traditional" and "modern" societies, each of which are characterized by distinctive economic, political, and cultural institutions. This perspective tends to attribute any differences between Latin America and highly industrialized societies to differences in their levels of economic development: with economic development, these differences will tend to disappear. Differences between various "traditional" cultures tend to be ignored.

The usefulness of "Latin America" as a meaningful cultural boundary could also be disputed on various other grounds. Geographically, Latin America extends over an enormous range. One could argue that its coherence depends on the persisting influence of its Hispanic cultural heritage, which is the main thing these diverse societies have in common. But this implies that Spain and Portugal—the source of this common heritage—should also be included. Instead of focusing on Latin America, the meaningful cultural entity should be the Hispanic cultural zone.

Still another influential school of thought would argue that it is not their linguistic heritage so much as their Roman Catholic religious heritage that has shaped the societies of Latin America most decisively. This implies that the crucial cultural boundary really is that between the historically Catholic societies and the rest of the world.

Yet another interpretation would stress the fact that certain Latin American societies such as Mexico and Peru, have been heavily influenced by indigenous American cultures; while others such as Argentina have been less influenced by them, but have had relatively large amounts of recent European immigration. If these are decisive influences, one might expect to find such countries as Argentina to be culturally closer to Southern Europe including Italy, than to their Latin American neighbors.

The World Values Surveys

Do coherent cultural patterns exist in given regions such as Latin America? And if so, do they mainly reflect that region's level of economic development? Or do they reflect its linguistic, religious, or historical heritage? The World Values Surveys (WVS) enable us to answer these questions for the first time, on the basis of data from representative national surveys covering most (70%) of the world's population.[2] The WVS provides an unprecedentedly rich cross-cultural data base exploring orientations toward religion, politics, work, economic growth, family values, sexual norms, and gender roles. These surveys cover the full range of variation, from societies with per capita incomes as low as $300 per year, to societies with per capita incomes up to $30,000 per year; and from long-established democracies with market economies, to authoritarian states and communist societies.

Because the World Values Surveys provide data from nearly 50 societies, the characteristics of the society itself can be used as variables in the analysis, making it possible to perform statistically significant analyses that move from the individual level to the societal level. This article examines linkages between the value systems of given societies and their economic, linguistic, religious, geographical, and political characteristics. Does the evidence reveal distinct and coherent cultural zones?

Do Constrained Belief Systems Characterize Given Cultural Zones? If So, Why?

The first question we must answer is: do coherent cultural patterns exist among these peoples? It would not be surprising to find that the various Latin America peoples had relatively similar views on some topic or other, but it would not be very meaningful. The concept of a common culture implies that a given group tends to share an entire worldview, manifesting a coherent and distinctive pattern of values across a wide range of topics.

It is not self-evident that a given group does share a common worldview. A generation ago, Converse (1963) demonstrated that the belief systems of mass publics do not show much constraint: mass attitudes toward various issues are only weakly related to each other. Knowing a given individual's attitude toward one issue does not enable us to predict his or her position on other issues. This finding was controversial, but has held up fairly well during succeeding decades. If mass attitudes don't show much constraint, how could the people of a given cultural zone such as Latin America show constrained worldviews that distinguish them from the people of other cultural zones?

In fact, they do, as we will see. Survey data from scores of societies reveal an astonishingly high degree of constraint between the basic values held by peoples of different societies. Furthermore, we find huge *differences* between the basic values of peoples in different cultural groups. Though individual-level constraint is relatively low, given *societies* have highly constrained and highly distinctive worldviews. We believe that this is true because, in a given economic and technological environment, certain cultural components tend to go together. They do so because they are mutually supporting and conducive to the survival of the given society (see Inglehart, forthcoming).

This interpretation is based on a revised version of modernization theory. The World Values Survey was designed to test the hypothesis that economic development leads to specific, functionally related changes in mass values and belief systems. We do not assume that *all* elements of culture will change, leading to a uniform global culture. We see no reason to expect that the Chinese will stop using chopsticks in the foreseeable future, or that Brazilians will learn to polka. But certain cultural and political changes do seem to be logically linked with the dynamics of a modernization process involving urbanization, industrialization, occupational specialization, and the spread of mass literacy.

This implies that economic development, cultural change, and political change go together in coherent and even, to some extent, predictable patterns. This is a controversial claim. It means that some trajectories of socio-economic change are more likely than others—and consequently, that certain changes are foreseeable. Once a society has embarked on industrialization, a whole syndrome of related changes, from mass mobilization to diminishing differences in gender roles, are likely to occur.

hough any simplistic version of modernization theory has long since been exploded, we do endorse the idea that some scenarios of social change are far more probable than others–and we will present empirical evidence that supports this proposition. Modernization theory implies:

1. That various cultural elements tend to go together in coherent patterns. For example, do societies that place relatively strong emphasis on religion, also tend to favor large families (or respect for authority, or other distinctive attitudes)? If each culture goes its own way, elements such as these would be uncorrelated, and one would find no consistent patterns of constraint.

2. Coherent cultural patterns exist, and they are linked with economic and technological development.

Postmodernization: Changing Values and a Changing Political Agenda
At the same time, it seems clear to us that modernization is not linear. In advanced industrial societies, the prevailing direction of development has

changed in the last quarter century and the change in what is happening is so fundamental that it seems appropriate to describe it as "postmodernization," rather than "modernization." For modernization is not the final stage of history. The rise of advanced industrial society has led to another fundamental shift in basic values—one that de-emphasizes the instrumental rationality that characterized industrial society. When postmodern values become prevalent, they bring a variety of societal changes, from equal rights for women to democratic political institutions and the decline of state socialist regimes.

The rise of postmodern values changes the political agenda throughout advanced industrial society, moving it away from an emphasis on economic growth at any price, toward increasing concern for its environmental costs. It has also brought a shift from political cleavages based on social class conflict, toward cleavages based on cultural issues and quality-of-life concerns.

Once industrialization became possible, modernizing societies focused on rapid economic growth as the best way of maximizing well being. But no strategy is optimal for all circumstances. Modernization was dramatically successful in raising life expectancies, but it has begun to produce diminishing returns in advanced industrial societies. Postmodernization is a shift in survival strategies, moving from maximizing economic growth to maxim izing survival and well being, through lifestyle changes. We believe that each of these processes has given rise to a major dimension of cross-national variation in basic beliefs and values.

Cross-Cultural Variation in Global Perspective: Empirical Findings

We have outlined the patterns of cross-cultural variation we expect to find, and why. Now let us examine cross-cultural variation empirically, as it is reflected in survey data from societies around the world. Our first question is whether the various religious, social, economic, and political components of given cultures are randomly related; or whether they go together, with certain coherent combinations being more probable than others. Figure 1 shows the results of a principal components factor analysis of the data from representative national surveys in the 43 societies included in the 1990-1991 World Values survey. The responses to each of the variables used here are boiled down to a mean score for each country; using the society as the unit of analysis, we can examine cross-cultural variation in a wide range of norms and values.

Figure 1 sums up an immense amount of information. It presents an overview of findings from the World Values surveys, showing the relationships between scores of items, based on responses from almost 60,000 respondents in 43 societies. We do not provide the full text of each question used here. A short phrase as "Abortion OK" is used to convey the gist of each item on Figure 1 (for the full text, see Inglehart, forthcoming). The 43 variables used here reflect a much larger number of questions. Some of them are based on responses to whole batteries of questions. "*Affect balance,*" for example, sums up each respondent's answers to the ten questions in the Bradburn Affect Balance Scale; "*Postmaterialist Values*" sums up the responses to a series of questions through which each respondent ranks a set of 12 basic goals; and "*Achievement Motivation*" sums up

FIGURE 1

Variation in the values emphasized by different societies: Traditional authority vs. Rational-legal authority and Survival values vs. Well-being values.

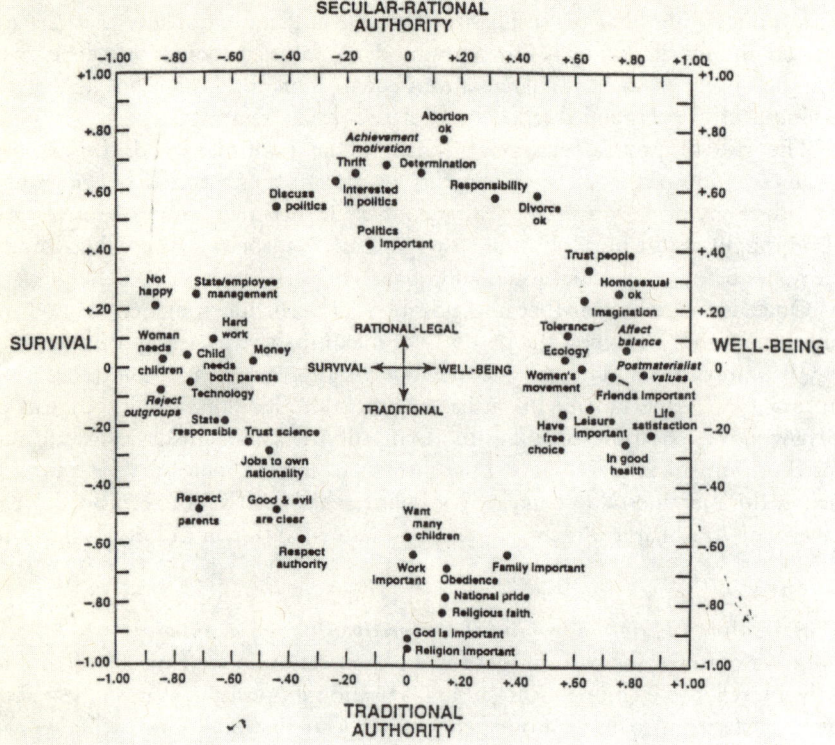

Source: 1990–1991 World Values survey. This figure shows the first and second principal components emerging from a factor analysis of data from representative national surveys of 43 societies, aggregated to the national level. The scales on the margins show each item's loadings on the two respective dimensions. The items in italics ("reject outgroups," "achievement motivation," "postmaterialist values," and "affect balance") are multi-item indices.

responses to four items concerning important values for a child to learn; "*Reject outgroups*" also sums up the responses to several questions.

Furthermore, these variables were chosen to reflect a considerably larger number of related items that show similar patterns. "God is important," for example, taps a cluster of more than 30 items that measure the extent to which religion is, or is not, an important part of the respondent's life. Similarly, "Life satisfaction," "Affect balance" and "Not happy" reflect a larger cluster of additional items that tap subjective well-being. To avoid redundancy, and to limit Figure 1 to a readable size, we have only included the most sensitive indicators of each cluster. Figure 1 depicts the structure underlying responses to more than 100 questions dealing with many aspects of life in 43 societies, providing a global overview of basic cultural patterns.

Figure 1 shows the relationships between scores of variables covering a wide variety of topics ranging from religion to politics to sexual norms to attitudes toward science. These diverse orientations tend to go together in coherent patterns. For example, certain societies place relatively heavy emphasis on religion—and the people of these societies also show high levels of national pride, and prefer to have relatively large families, and would like to see more respect for authority, and tend to rank relatively low on achievement motivation and political interest, and oppose divorce, and have a number of other distinctive cultural orientations. The people of other societies consistently fall toward the opposite end of the spectrum on all of these orientations, giving rise to a vertical dimension that reflects "Traditional" versus "Secular-Rational" orientations. This dimension reflects cross-national linked with the modernization process.

Our first major finding is that there is a great deal of constraint among cultural systems. The pattern found here is anything but random. The first two dimensions that emerge from the principal components factor analysis depicted in Figure 1 account for fully 51% of the cross-national variance among these variables! In other words, over half of the cross-national variation among these variables can be explained by two dimensions that reflect the modernization and postmodernization process respectively. Additional dimensions explain relatively small amounts of variance. Moreover, these two main dimensions are robust, showing little change when we drop given items, even high-loading ones. The vertical axis reflects the polarization between "Traditional Authority" and "Secular-Rational Authority"; the horizontal axis depicts the polarization between a cluster of items labeled "Survival" values and another cluster labeled "Well-being" values. The scales on the borders of Figure 1 indicate each item's loadings on these two dimensions.

Just two dimensions account for over half of the cross-national variance among these items. But this also means that about half of the variance in these values and orientations is *not* explained by the modernization and postmodernization dimensions. It is important to keep this in mind. Cross-cultural variation does not simply reflect the changes linked with the modernization and postmodernization processes: to a great extent, each society works out its history in its own unique fashion, influenced by the culture, leaders, institutions, climate, geography, situation-specific events, and other unique elements that make up its own distinctive heritage. General explanatory factors can not account for everything in cross-cultural research. Just as each individual is unique, each society is unique. Thus, while we find the metaphor of evolution useful in describing how social change works, we do not equate evolution with determinism. Certain strategies for coping with a given environment are far more probable than others: such a strategy represents a mutually supportive combination of economic, technological, political and cultural factors, and one that is likely to survive, while other almost limitless numbers of dysfunctional combinations are likely to prove abortive. But social change also involves less systematic factors that make each society unique.

Religion plays a much more important role in some societies than in others. In Nigeria, 85% of the population said that religion is "very important" in their lives; in South Africa, the figure was 66%; in Turkey, 61%; in both Poland and the United States, 53%; in Italy, the figure was only 34%; in Great Britain, France and Germany, the figures were 16%, 14%, and 13% respectively; in Russia, it was 12%; in Denmark, 9%; in Japan it was 6% and in China 1%.

We asked, "Do societies that place relatively strong emphasis on religion, also tend to favor large families?" The answer is an unequivocal "Yes," as the proximity of "Religion important" and "Want many children" near the bottom of Figure 1 suggests: the correlation between these two items is r = .51 (significant at the .001 level). Moreover, societies characterized by an emphasis on religion also tend to place relatively strong emphasis on work, as the proximity between "Work important" and "Religion important" suggests (r = .62, significant at the .0000 level). The emphasis here is on *having* work, for the sake of survival; in economically more developed societies, people place much greater emphasis on work as a source of *personal satisfaction*. Relatively traditional societies also tend to stress "Obedience" as an important quality to teach a child (r = .58), and to view the family as relatively important ("Family important," r = .56). And, as one would expect, those societies in which the public considers "Religion important" also tend to be those in which the public believe that "God is important," and to say that religious faith is an important quality to teach a child ("Religious faith"); these are almost 1:1 relationships (r = .95 and r = .87, respectively). These last two linkages are obvious; the others, though intuitively plausible, are not. All of these items have high loadings on the vertical dimension, labeled "Traditional Authority" vs. "Secular-Rational Authority."

Societies that place relatively strong emphasis on religion are characterized by very distinctive norms concerning sexual behavior, child rearing, the role of women, and fertility rates; they have distinctive attitudes toward divorce, abortion, and homosexuality; they also place relatively strong emphasis on deference to authority; and they have distinctive norms concerning economic achievement and distinctive motivations for work. These differences involve one's sense of identity. For example, societies in which religion is important are characterized by much higher levels of national pride than those in which it is not, as Figure 2 demonstrates. Here, the horizontal axis shows the percentage in each society who say that God plays an important role in their lives. The people of societies that rank high on this variable show much higher levels of national pride than those that rank low. China is a deviant case, with a high level of national pride despite being overwhelming secular, and West Germany deviates in the opposite direction, showing a lower level of national pride than her level of religiosity would predict. But the overall linkage is remarkably strong and significant at the .0000 level.

High levels of constraint exist between various cultural attributes. For example, if we know that a society ranks high on national pride, we can pretty accurately predict its position on child-rearing practices, religiosity, and a number of other important attributes. But the pattern extends even further. Societies that emphasize the importance of religion tend to attach low importance to politics, as the locations of "Religion important" and "Politics important" (far apart from each other on the vertical dimension) suggests: the correlation between the two is -.39. And these same societies tend to place low emphasis on "Thrift"

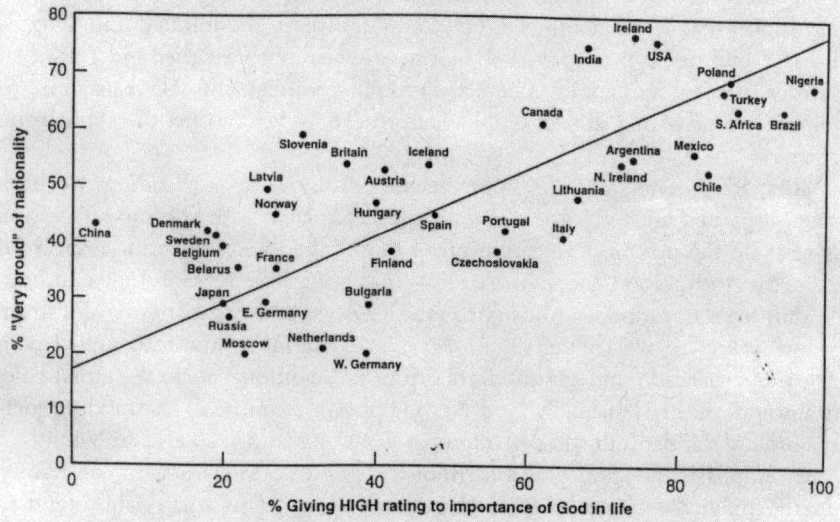

FIGURE 2
Coherent values patterns on the Traditional vs. Secular-Rational authority dimension: the linkage between religiosity and national pride. Horizontal dimension shows percentage ranking importance of God in their lives as relatively high (i.e., scores of 7–10 on a 10-point scale from "not at all important" to "very important"). $r = .71$, significant at .0000 level.

and "Determination" as important qualities to teach a child ($r = -.57$ and $-.59$, respectively). Emphasis on the latter two values is part of an Achievement Motivation syndrome that is strongly linked with the economic growth of given societies.

Coherent Value Patterns: The Postmodernization Dimension

In the postmodernization phase of development, emphasis shifts from maximizing economic gains—the central goal of modernization—to maximizing subjective well-being. This gives rise to another major dimension of cross-cultural variation, on which a wide range of orientations are structured. This dimension taps "Survival" Values vs. "Well-being" values. A very sensitive indicator of this dimension is "Postmaterialist" values (located near the right-hand pole of the horizontal axis on Figure 2). This is a central element in a much broader cultural configuration.

Societies with large numbers of postmaterialists tend to be characterized by a relatively strong sense of subjective well-being. Their publics tend to express high levels of satisfaction with their lives as a whole ("Postmaterialist values" has a .68 correlation with "Life satisfaction"). Moreover, they report relatively high levels of positive affect on the Bradburn "Affect balance" scale. Furthermore, the publics of societies with high levels of postmaterialism are likely to rate themselves as "In good health," ($r = .58$) and are not likely to describe themselves as "Not happy" (the correlation with "Postmaterialist values" is $-.71$).

The publics of societies with high proportions of postmaterialists do *not* emphasize "Hard work" as one of the most important qualities to teach a child (reflected in a loading of $-.67$ on the Scarcity-Security dimension); instead, they emphasize "Tolerance" and "Imagination." Similarly, their publics do not view more emphasis on "Money" as a desirable change. The polarization between "Survival" values and "Well-being" values extends to family values as well. The publics of societies with high proportions of Postmaterialists tend to reject the proposition that a "Woman needs children" in order to be fulfilled, and disagree that a "Child needs both parents," in a home with both a father and a mother, in order to grow up happily. There is a growing emphasis on self-realization for women, linked with a shift of emphasis from the role of mother to emphasis on careers.

"Respect parents" and "Respect authority" show strong loadings on both dimensions in Figure 2. Their loadings indicate that both the modernization process and the postmodernization process are linked with declining respect for authority. And "Good and Evil are clear" has a negative relationship with both the shift from traditional authority to rational-legal authority; and the shift from survival values to well being values. A growing moral relativism is linked with both modernization and postmodernization. In traditional societies, moral rules are absolute truths, revealed by God. At the opposite extreme, in postmodern society, absolute standards dissolve, giving way to an increasing sense of ambiguity.

An emphasis on science and technology was a core element of modernity. But the publics of societies with high proportions of postmaterialists tend to have little confidence that scientific advances will help, rather than harm, humanity ("Trust science" has a negative correlation with "Postmaterialist values" significant at the .001 level); similarly, they tend to doubt that more emphasis on "Technology" would be a good thing. Conversely, these same societies have relatively high levels of support for the "Ecology" movement. The fact that societies shaped by security tend to reject science and technology, is a major departure from the basic thrust of modernization—another reason why this dimension reflects change in a postmodern direction.

Societies influenced by postmodern or well-being values tend to be far more tolerant than those characterized by survival values. These societies emphasize "Tolerance" as an important quality to teach a child; and their publics are less likely to "Reject outgroups," saying that they would not like to have foreigners, people with AIDS, or homosexuals as neighbors; and they are relatively likely to feel that homosexuality is acceptable ("Homosexual OK"). Both of these correlations with "Postmaterialist values" are significant at the .001 level. Moreover, societies with relatively high levels of subjective well-being rank relatively low on intolerance of outgroups, as Figure 3 illustrates. The outgroup dealt with here is homosexuals, but the same pattern applies to rejection of other outgroups. In Russia and Belarus, where subjective well-being was extremely low in 1990, 80% of the public said they would not like to have homosexuals as neighbors. In such societies as Denmark or The Netherlands, where overall life satisfaction was much higher, only about 10% of the public were unwilling to have homosexuals as neighbors. Numerous other orientations are closely related to whether a society has high or low levels of subjective well-being.

No culture is immune to xenophobia, but it tends to be most intense where insecurity is most severe. Conversely, at the individual level, Postmaterialists—

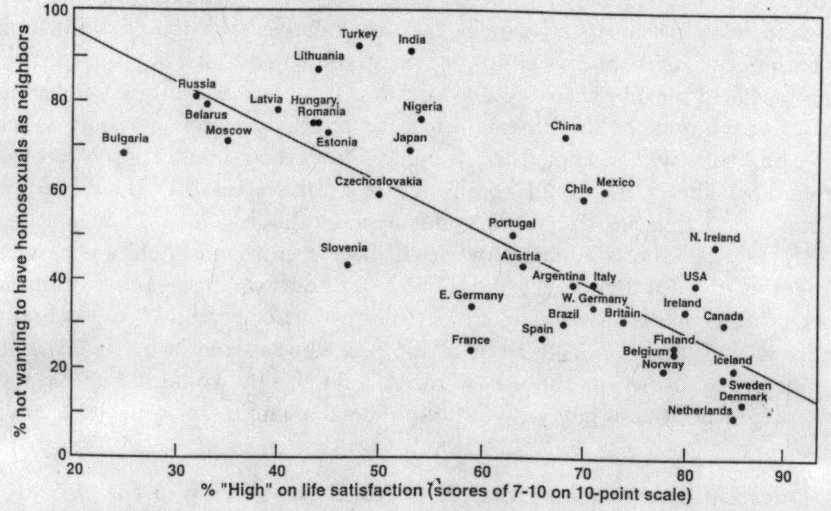

FIGURE 3
Coherent value patterns on the Survival vs. Well-being dimension: life satisfaction vs. rejection of homosexuals (part of the "Reject Outgroups" cluster). r = −.75, significant at .0000 level.

those who have grown up under conditions of relative economic and physical security—tend to be relatively tolerant of people with different ethnicity or sexual orientations. Similarly, they are relatively supportive of the "Women's movement". The rise of security values seems conducive to increasing tolerance of diversity, an essential component of democracy.

An environment of security and subjective well-being seems to foster not only tolerance, but a whole cluster of traits that are conducive to democracy. For example, "Well-being" values are linked with high levels of interpersonal trust (as reflected in the .66 loading of "Trust people" on this dimension). Moreover, a participant public is an essential component of democracy-and one of the defining characteristics of postmaterialist values is the fact that they give a high priority to self-expression and participation in decision-making at all levels, including the political. Postmaterialism constitutes a central component of postmodern values. As Inglehart (forthcoming) demonstrates, these values are closely linked with the persistence of stable democracy.

In addition to its emphasis on science and technology, another key characteristic of modernization was its tendency to bureaucratize all aspects of life, with the biggest bureaucracy of all resulting from the seemingly inexorable growth of government. But postmodern values are linked with *declining* support for big government: believing that the state (rather than the individual) should take more responsibility to ensure that everyone is provided for ("State responsible") is linked with "Survival" values, and not with "Well-being" values; the same is true of support for "State/employee management" rather than owner management. Support for big government was a central component of modernization. It does *not* go with postmodern values, which reflects a fundamental change of direction from the modernization trajectory.

Do our questions have comparable meaning to people from 43 widely varying societies, who were interviewed in 31 different languages? Our questionnaire was, of course, designed to cope with this problem. Building on extensive previous cross-national survey research and extensive pilot testing, with input from social scientists on five continents, it was designed to ask questions that do have a shared meaning across many cultures. If we had asked questions about nation-specific issues, the cross-cultural comparability almost certainly would have broken down. In France, for example, a hot recent political issue revolved around whether girls should be allowed to wear scarves over their heads in school (a reaction against Islamic fundamentalism). This question would have had totally different meanings (or would have seemed meaningless) in many other societies. On the other hand, a question about whether religion is important in one's life is meaningful in virtually every society on earth, including those in which most people say it is not. The same is true of questions about respect for authority; or about how many children one would like to have; or whether or not one is satisfied with one's life as a whole.

Does Latin American Exist? A Cultural Geography of the World

We have found that coherent patterns of cross-cultural variation exist, with the peoples of given societies taking highly distinctive positions, in a highly constrained fashion, across a wide range of orientations from politics to religion to sexual norms. This means we can now answer the question: do the peoples of Latin America have relatively similar worldviews?

Figure 4 shows the location of each society on these two dimensions. To locate them in this space, dummy variables were created for each of the 43 societies surveyed in 1990-1993; these variables were mapped onto the two dimensions shaped by the worldviews of the respective publics. Because these dummy variables are extremely skewed, the correlations with the cultural dimensions are modest; but if we combine countries into larger groups (such as the Nordic group or the Latin American group) the correlations with the ideological space become quite strong. The societies that show similar cultural orientations in our surveys are near each other on this figure. And they fall into intuitively meaningful clusters.

First, it is clear that the value systems of richer countries differ systematically from those of poorer countries. The poorer countries tend to be located toward the lower left on Figure 4, with the richer ones falling into the upper right hand quadrant. Though there are some deviant cases (the United States having more traditional values than her GNP per capita would predict), the overall correlation between values and economic development is very strong.

But the pattern is coherent in many additional respects. For example, all four of the Latin American societies included in the 1990 World Values survey fall into one compact cluster, reflecting the fact that in global perspective they have relatively similar value systems. If we had found that the Brazilian people's worldview was closest to that of Sweden or China; or if Russia had fallen into the middle of the Latin American cluster, then the concept of a Latin American

FIGURE 4

Where given societies fall on two key cultural dimensions.

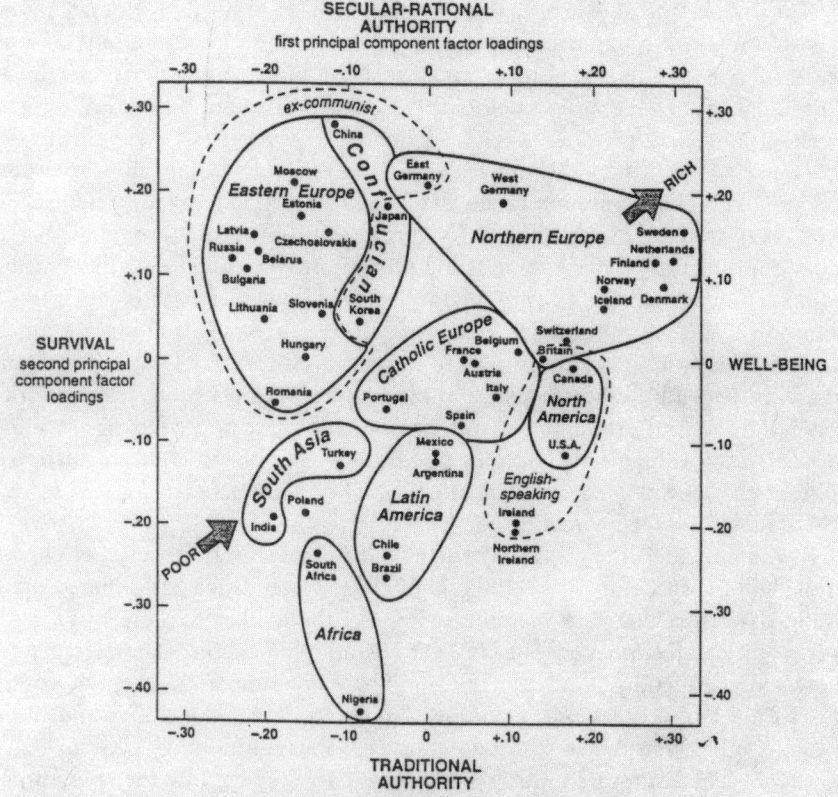

Source: 1990–1991 World Values survey. Positions are based on the mean scores of the publics of the given nation on each of the two dimensions.

culture would be difficult to sustain. But in fact, the peoples of the four Latin American societies consistently show relatively similar values across a wide range of topics.

Similarly, the two African societies fall into another relatively compact cluster. And the three Confucian-influenced societies of East Asia fall into another cluster which partly overlaps with another cluster containing the former communist societies. The historically Catholic societies of Western Europe fall into another compact cluster. Although church attendance in Western Europe has collapsed in recent years, the historically Protestant societies of Northern Europe fall into another cluster (with East Germany located at the intersection of the Northern European cluster and the ex-communist cluster, as her historical experience might suggest). The United States and Canada constitute a North American cluster—and it could be expanded to include the other English-speaking societies. Poland is an outlier, having more traditional values than the other ex-communist societies of eastern Europe. But on the whole, the value systems of a majority of the world's people are anything but random: though shaped by a variety of factors, they manifest remarkably coherent patterns that must be interpreted very carefully.

Norway, Iceland, Denmark, Finland and Sweden—the five Nordic countries—form a compact sub-cluster within the Northern European group on Figure 4. All five have related histories and similar cultures, ranking moderately high on the cultural outlook associated with rational-legal authority, and leading the world on Postmodern values. To some extent, these countries are geographically proximate, but the fact that they are prosperous and traditionally-Protestant welfare states seems more important than their geographic proximity. Thus The Netherlands, which is not a Nordic country but is historically Protestant and is today a prosperous welfare state, falls squarely into the middle of the Nordic group. Though she is geographically located next door to Belgium and shares a common language with half of Belgium, The Netherlands is culturally much closer to the Nordic countries than to Belgium. Historically, The Netherlands has been shaped by Protestantism; even the Dutch Catholics today are remarkably Calvinist. And although the churches themselves are now a fading influence in West European society, religious traditions helped shape enduring national cultures that persist today. Thus, culturally, The Netherlands is located somewhere between Norway and Sweden.

Belgium, France, Italy, Spain, Portugal and Austria constitute another cluster in the cultural space of Figure 4. Though church attendance has declined drastically, all of these countries were historically Catholic. Furthermore, this cluster is adjacent to a Latin American (an overwhelmingly Catholic) cluster containing Mexico, Argentina, Chile, and Brazil. These predominantly Catholic countries form a fairly coherent group. One could even expand the cluster to include the four other historically Catholic countries, Poland, Hungary, Slovenia, and Lithuania. The last four countries are outliers, probably because the rising prosperity experienced by West European Catholic countries in recent decades did not extend to them, and they are more permeated by Survival values than the rest of the Catholic group. On the modernization dimension, however, their values are almost as traditional as those of other Catholic countries (and they have more traditional values than the other ex-socialist countries). As Basanez (1993) demonstrates, the Protestant-Catholic differences do not simply reflect the fact that the historically Protestant countries tend to be richer than the historically Catholic ones: controlling for GDP/capita, the value differences between them remain significant at the .001 level.

The former West German and East German regions of Germany were still independent states when these surveys were carried out and were thus sampled separately. Though West Germany falls into the upper right-hand quadrant with the other West European societies, and East Germany into the upper left-hand quadrant containing most of the historically communist societies, the two societies are relatively close to each other on the two main cultural dimensions. From 1945 to 1990, the communist regime made a massive effort to reshape East German culture to support a Marxist and atheistic authoritarian regime. Simultaneously, the Western powers launched massive efforts to remake political culture to support a market-oriented Western liberal democracy. It seems that 45 years under radically different regimes did have an impact: by 1990, the two societies were some distance apart, especially along the Postmodernization dimension. But even more impressive is the fact that, in global perspective, the basic cultural values of the two societies were still relatively similar. This natural experiment indicates that, even when it makes a conscious and concerted effort to do so, the ability of a regime to reshape its underlying culture is limited. After 45 years under radically different political and economic institutions, in their basic values East Germany and West Germany remained about as similar to each other as the United States and Canada.

Almost all of the socialist or ex-socialist societies fall into the upper left-hand quadrant. They are characterized by (1) survival values, and (2) a strong emphasis on state authority, rather than traditional authority. Poland is an outlier, distinguished from the other socialist societies by her strong traditional-religious values. China is an outlier in the opposite direction—the least religious and most state-oriented society for which we have data. These societies' positions reflect their distinctive cultural heritages. On one hand, adherence to the Catholic church has been a mainstay of the Polish struggle for independence since 1792. The church continued to play a vital role in this struggle throughout the 1980s, revitalizing the role of religion in the national culture.

China, on the other hand, has had a relatively secular cultural system for two thousand years, and bureaucratic authority developed within the Confucian system long before it reached the West. Thus China and the other Confucian-influences societies of East Asia have possessed the bureaucratic component of modern culture for a very long time. Until recently, they lacked the emphasis on science and technology and the esteem for economic achievement that are its other main components; but their secular, bureaucratic heritage probably helped to facilitate rapid economic development once these were attained. China's traditional emphasis on the state was probably reinforced by four decades of socialism. Japan, another Confucian-influenced society; and both East and West Germany are also characterized by relatively strong emphasis on rational-legal authority.

Most of the socialist and ex-socialist societies are oriented toward rational-legal, rather than traditional-religious authority. Their people have experienced four to eight decades of socialist regimes in which religion has been systematically repressed and in which it is perfectly realistic to consider politics important because economic life, cultural life, and even one's chances of survival depend on the state. The socialist states were probably the most heavily bureaucratized, centralized and secularized societies in history, and they held science and technology in such esteem that their elites legitimated their power by the claim that they ruled not through the unscientific and fallible process majority rule, but according to the principles of scientific socialism. By these standards, the socialist states represented the culmination of modernization—and the fact that, on Figure 4, they are located near the Modernization pole of the Traditional Authority-Rational-legal Authority dimension seems appropriate.

We find that a Latin American culture does exist. But reality is multi-layered.

The points at which each society is located on Figure 4 are determined by empirical research. But the boundaries drawn around these points reflect theoretical considerations, and could be drawn in a number of alternative ways. Empirically, a Latin American cluster does exist—but it would be easy to extend the boundaries of this cluster to include Spain and Portugal. We would then have an Hispanic cluster, for Spain and Portugal are as close to Mexico and Argentina as the latter are to Chile and Brazil. Furthermore, Italy (a major source of immigration to Latin America) is also located nearby.[3] Finally, we could also merge the Latin American cluster with the Catholic Europe cluster and parts of Eastern Europe, to create a broad yet reasonably compact Catholic cluster containing all of the historically Catholic societies. Both theoretically and empirically, all of these clusters overlap. Latin America exists—but it reflects the intersection of a variety of economic, religious, and historical influences.

Do Institutions Determine Culture?

Across a wide range of basic values, the historically Protestant countries of both Northern Europe and North America form one large group; similarly, the historically Catholic countries of Western Europe, Latin America, and Eastern Europe form another broad but reasonably cohesive cluster. Despite the enormous recent changes linked with economic and social modernization, and despite the tremendous sociopolitical changes linked with communist domination of several historically Catholic societies throughout the Cold War, in global perspective the historically Catholic societies still have relatively similar cultural values—as do the historically Protestant societies. As Figure 5 illustrates, the Catholic societies form a group characterized by more traditional values, and by greater emphasis on survival values, than holds true of most Protestant societies. On this figure Poland and Ireland are no longer outliers. They fit into a broad cluster of societies historically shaped by Roman Catholicism.

At first glance, this might seem to constitute strong evidence for an institutional determinist interpretation. If institutional determinism is simply taken to mean that a society's institutions are among the factors that help shape its culture, it is undoubtedly correct. But institutional determinism is often pushed to a much more extreme claim. It is taken to mean that institutions alone determine a society's cultural values, so one needn't really take cultural factors into account: if one changes the institutions, the culture automatically changes to fit it. Examining the evidence more closely, it is clear that this position is untenable.

There are major cultural differences between Protestant and Catholic societies, but for the most part they do not reflect the direct influence of the Catholic and Protestant churches today. For the direct influence of the church today is very slight in many of these countries. Though church attendance remains high in Poland and Ireland (and the United States), it has fallen drastically in most of the historically Catholic countries; and it has fallen even more drastically in most historically Protestant European societies, to the point where some observers now speak of the Nordic countries as post-Christian societies. The societies that are historically Catholic still show very distinct values from

FIGURE 5

Where given societies fall on two key cultural dimensions.

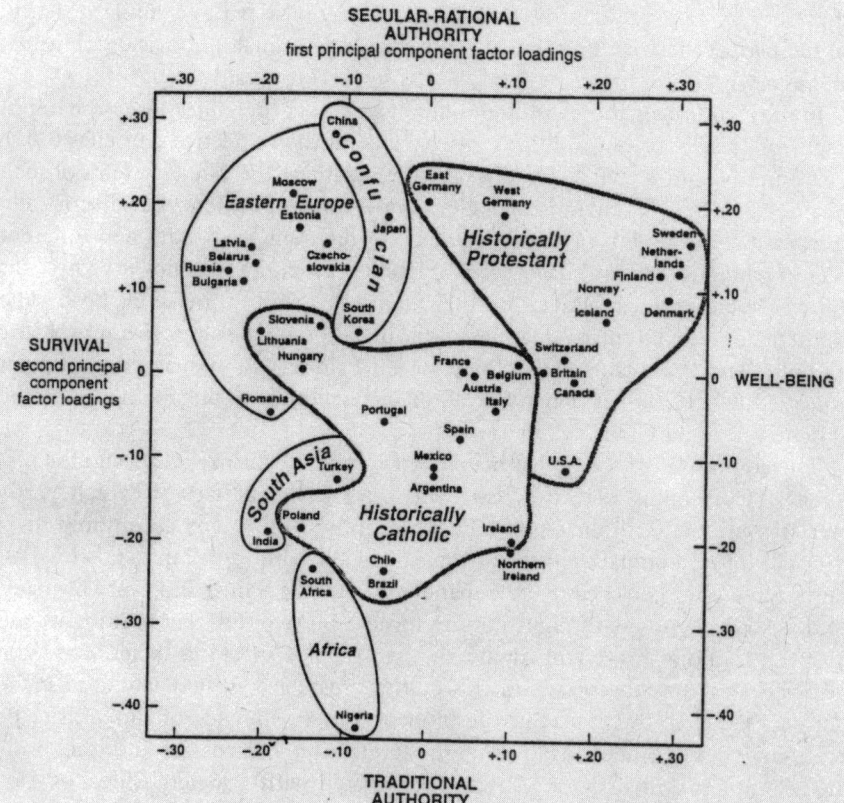

Source: 1990–1991 World Values survey. Positions are based on the mean scores of the publics of the given nation on each of the two dimensions.

those that are historically Protestant—even among segments of the population who have no contact with the church today. These values persist as part of the cultural heritage of given nations, and not through the direct influence of religious institutions. This cultural heritage has been shaped by the economic, political, and social experience of the given people, including the fact that the Protestant societies industrialized earlier than most of the Catholic societies—which at an even earlier stage of history may, in turn, have been linked with religious differences (as Weber suggests), but is certainly not a case of direct institutional determinism.

There is a remarkable degree of coherence to these cross-cultural differences. On Figure 4, forty of the 43 societies fall into compact clusters with coherent cultural heritages, such as Latin America or Eastern Europe or East Asia. There are only three outliers on this figure: Poland, Ireland, and Northern Ireland. Both Poland and Ireland might be described as hyper-Catholic societies, for both societies were occupied and dominated for centuries by more powerful non-Catholic neighbors, and both responded to pressures toward cultural assimilation by an intense re-emphasis of their Roman Catholic heritage as a means of preserving national identity. Ironically, this may have led to a similar reaction on the part of the Irish Protestants, who constitute a small minority within Ireland as a whole and might be described as hyper-Protestants.

In most countries, these cultural differences reflect the entire historical experience of given societies, and *not* the influence of the respective churches today. This point becomes vividly evident when we examine the values systems of such societies as The Netherlands and Germany—both of which were historically Protestant societies, but (as a consequence of different birth-rates and different rates of religious attrition) have about as many practicing Catholics as Protestants today. Despite these changes in their current religious makeup, both The Netherlands and Germany manifest typically Protestant values. Moreover, the Catholics and Protestants *within* these societies do not show markedly different values: Dutch Catholics today are about as Calvinist as the members of the Dutch Reformed Church.

The communist ideology has been described as a secular religion, and the historically Communist societies also make up a coherent cluster, which partly overlaps with the Catholic cluster. Thirteen of the 14 formerly communist societies fall into a compact cluster in the upper left-hand quadrant, and this East European cluster could easily be expanded to include China and East Germany. And as we have noted, though they are located on two different continents and span the Catholic-Protestant divide, the five English-speaking societies are also relatively near to each other on this cultural map; a common language is the unifying factor in this case. But the most pervasive influence of all seems to be economic development. Both the modernization dimension and the postmodernization dimension are strongly correlated with a society's level of economic development. The values of richer societies differ systematically from those of poorer societies. Clearly, institutional determinism would be a far too simple interpretation of the evidence. Though the impact of religious institutions is evident, economic, political, geographic, linguistic, and other factors also play major roles. The worldview of a given people reflects its entire historical heritage.

Stability and Change in the Worldviews of Given Societies

The World Values Survey has carried out two waves of fieldwork, which enables us to examine the stability of the worldviews of given societies over time. Our theoretical framework implies that we should find gradual changes, linked with economic development. At the same time, the overall configuration should be stable, with coherent cultural zones persisting over time. Cultural differences are relatively stable; though the basic values of a given society can change over time, they do so gradually, largely through intergenerational population replacement. This implies that the cultural locations that we have just charted should be reasonably stable over time, and a recognizable Latin American cluster (and African or Confucian clusters) should persist from one decade to the next.

But our theoretical framework implies that gradual cultural changes are occurring, linked with the processes of modernization and postmodernization. Industrialization and all the concomitant processes of change are driving the transition from traditional to secular-rational values. Similarly, the economic miracles and welfare states that emerged in the post–World War II era have produced societies in which very few die of starvation; this is giving rise to an intergenerational shift from survival values to well-being values.

Intergenerational population replacement is not the only factor involved. Current economic and political conditions also have a predictable impact. Since our theory holds that changes are driven by rising levels of security, we would expect a major decline in economic and physical security to retard or reverse the effects of intergenerational population replacement. On the other hand, periods of exceptional prosperity would tend to magnify the effects of generational change.

Figure 6 shows the empirical results. This figure maps each society on the Modernization and Postmodernization dimensions respectively. This map is similar to Figures 4 and 5 but goes beyond them, presenting a dynamic perspective. With every society for which we have valid data from both 1981 and 1990, we show its position at both time points. Thus, Figure 6 shows two dots for Sweden, labeled "Sweden 81" and "Sweden 90" showing the position of the Swedish public as measured in the 1981 and 1990 surveys, respectively.[4]

This graph is based on a factor analysis that utilizes only about half as many variables as the one underlying Figures 4 and 5, since we could only use only those indicators of the modernization and postmodernization dimensions that were included in both surveys. Though it uses 22 more surveys and 20 fewer variables than the corresponding analysis based on the 1990 data only, the resulting factor structure is a close approximation of the one shown in Figure 1. And on the whole, the positions of the given societies are similar to those they had in 1990.

The massive data base underlying Figure 6 (based on 65 surveys, carried out in 44 societies), indicates that we are dealing with coherent and stable cross-cultural differences. Though we are particularly interested in the changes that occur from 1981 to 1990, the position of each society in 1981 is relatively close to its position in 1990. Thus, "Sweden 81" is located relatively near to "Sweden 90"; and "USA 81" is relatively close to "USA 90"; as are "South Korea 81" and "South Korea 90." and "Spain 81" and "Spain 90," and so on.

Moreover, these societies fall into coherent clusters. The same basic pattern emerges as the one we saw earlier in Figures 4 and 5. The locations of these societies reflect their levels of economic development, with the poorer societies located toward the lower left-hand corner and the richer ones near the upper right hand corner of Figure 6. But a society's religious heritage, language, geographic location, and whether or not it experienced communist domination also seem to influence the cultural locations of these societies. Thus, the Nordic societies constitute a coherent cluster near the upper right, and they form part of a broader (historically Protestant) Northern European cluster. The countries of

FIGURE 6

Positions of given societies on two cultural dimensions in 1981 and 1990 Surveys.

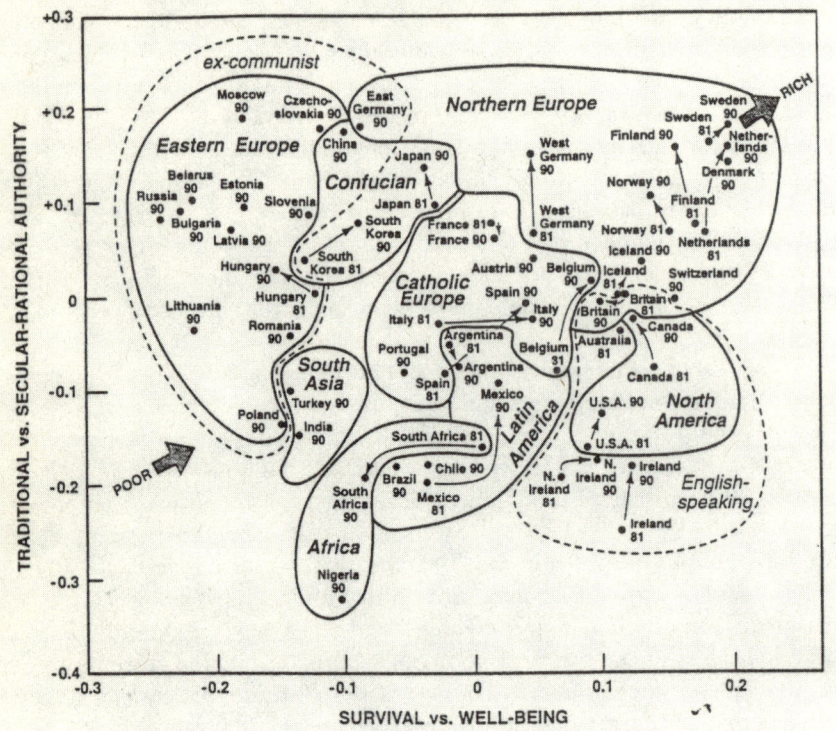

Source: 1981–1993 World Values survey. Positions are based on the mean scores of the publics on each of the two dimensions.

Catholic Europe form another coherent cluster, as do the Confucian-influenced societies of East Asia. Eastern Europe forms another cluster; and it falls into a broader ex-communist zone that incorporates Eastern Europe, plus culturally adjacent positions of Northern Europe and East Asia. The United States and Canada form a compact North American cluster into which all four surveys fall; but this is part of a broader English-speaking zone that includes Great Britain (at both time points), the Republic of Ireland and Northern Ireland (in both 1981 and 1990). "Australia 81" also falls into this English-speaking zone. (Australia was not included in the 1990 survey, and so did not appear in our previous analyses—but she *was* surveyed in 1981, and the data indicate that, despite great geographical distance, Australia is culturally a close neighbor of Britain and Canada.) We find a coherent pattern of cross-cultural differences in which continuity is far more prominent than change.

But significant cultural changes have been taking place, and they are visible on Figure 6. The most striking aspect of this map of cultural change is the fact that most of the arrows point upward or to the right. This means that most of the changes are moving away from the "Traditional authority" pole toward the "Secular-rational authority" pole—or from "Survival" values toward the "Well-being" values. In other words, the main shift is from the cultural values linked with low levels of economic development, toward the values linked with *higher* levels of economic development.

But some of these shifts move in the opposite direction, toward traditional values, and the pattern is far from random. Three of these societies experienced economic stagnation and political collapse during the period from 1981 to 1990, and all three of them show shifts that are mainly downward or to the left. In the case of Argentina, the movement is minimal. In the case of Hungary, it is more substantial, with the main component of change being toward stronger emphasis on survival values and a secondary component of secularization. The South African public shows the largest changes of all, with a sizable shift toward "Survival" values and a lesser movement toward "Traditional" authority.

The 18 remaining societies for which we have data on cultural change, experienced relatively normal conditions. In 16 of these 18 cases the main shift is upward or to the right (or both)—that is, in the direction linked with economic development. We find two exceptions: the British shifted toward greater emphasis on "Survival" values from 1981 to 1990; and the French public showed a slight movement toward emphasis on "Traditional" authority (though the shift is so small that it may simply reflect sampling error). But in South Korea, Japan, West Germany, Norway, Iceland, Finland, Sweden, The Netherlands, Ireland, Northern Ireland, Belgium Italy, Spain, Canada, the United States and Mexico, the main shift is either upward or to the right or both. Some of these shifts are minimal, but some are rather large. Cultural change has been moving in the direction of Modernization and Postmodernization: cultural change shows some degree of predictability.

Data from the third wave of the WVS have begun to come in, permitting some further tests. This third wave is being carried out in a number of Latin American societies, in addition to the four that were analyzed here; and the data from three of them (Venezuela, the Dominican Republic, and Puerto Rico) have been received at the time of this writing. Do they fit into the "Latin American" cluster—or is it really only a "Mexico-Argentina-Brazil-Chile" cluster? In fact, the three new countries fit into the Latin American cluster quite well. When we add Venezuela to the analysis in Figure 6, she falls into a position just below "Brazil 90," while the Dominican Republic falls slightly to the Right of that point. Puerto Rico takes a position about halfway between "Venezuela 95" and "Ireland 81." Puerto Rico is relatively near to the English-speaking group, but can still be included in the Latin American cluster-a finding that seems to reflect her unique historical heritage. Data from Taiwan had also arrived, providing another test of the Confucian cultural zone. When added to the analysis in Figure 6, "Taiwan 95" takes a position to the right of "South Korea 81," and also falls into the right ball park.

Figure 6 is already packed to a density that strains the eye, and when we add a third time point for each society (some of them showing relatively large movements over time, like Spain and Italy) we will inevitably find increasing amounts of overlap in this finite space. Nevertheless, the pattern is far from random and we expect that it will continue to be so. Despite considerable variation between the societies of Latin America, and considerable changes over time, a coherent Latin American cultural zone manifests itself in comparative data representing most of the world's population. And a distinctive Confucian cultural zone is also evident. Thus, the answer to both of the questions in our title is positive.

Conclusion

We should point out that this analysis has imposed a difficult test of whether Latin American (or Confucian or English-speaking) culture exists. One can readily imagine that a study designed to focus on the distinctive feature of Hispanic culture versus Confucian or Anglo-Saxon culture might come up with far more striking contrasts between the worldviews of the respective peoples. But the analysis presented here is based on a dataset that was designed to focus on concerns that are *not* region specific, but are meaningful in virtually any society around the world. Nevertheless, we find clear and distinct cultural zones.

Furthermore, this investigation was motivated by an interest in developmental concepts and was designed to examine the extent to which economic development gives rise to systematic cultural changes linked with the modernization and postmodernization processes, respectively. We do indeed find evidence that each of these processes is linked with major dimension of cross-cultural variation. But it is worth emphasizing that even in an analysis designed to focus on developmental processes, we find coherent and distinctive cultural patterns that can readily be described as Latin American (or Hispanic), African, Confucian, English-speaking, ex-Communist, and so forth.

Our research has mainly focused on broad patterns of global chance and will probably continue to do so. But we must respect what the data are telling us. One finding that emerges clearly is the fact that distinctive cultural zones exist—even *apart* from the fact that these societies have widely differing levels of economic development and different levels of modernization and postmodernization.

The World Values Surveys reveal huge differences between the basic values of people in different cultural zones. These cross-cultural differences are coherent and relatively stable. And they have important behavioral consequences. To demonstrate the latter claim would require far more space than is available here, but a large body of supporting evidence indicates that the cultural variables we have just examined are closely linked with a variety of important societal characteristics ranging from the persistence of stable democracy, to economic growth and fertility rates (Inglehart, 1997). The obvious rational choice for the typical American, may not be the rational choice for an Islamic fundamentalist. To understand a given people's worldview and its implications requires a detailed knowledge of that society's history and culture.

Though the importance of economic factors is evident, in keeping with modernization (and postmodernization) theory, a society's religious institutions, political experience, language, geographic location and other factors also play important roles in shaping its value system. Economic factors alone do not determine what people want and how they behave. The worldview of a given people reflects its entire historical heritage.

References

Basanez, M. 1993. Protestant and Catholic ethics: An empirical comparison. Paper presented at conference on Changing Social and Political Values: A Global Perspective, Complutense University, Madrid, September 27-October 1.

Basanez, M., R. Inglehart and A. Moreno. 1997. *Human beliefs* and values: A cross-cultural sourcebook. *Ann Arbor: University of Michigan Press.*

Converse, P. E. 1963. The nature of belief systems in mass publics. In *Ideology and discontent,* edited by D. Apter. New York: The Free Press.

Inglehart, R. 1997 (forthcoming). *Modernization and postmodernization: Cultural, economic and political change in 43 societies.* Princeton, NJ: Princeton University Press.

CHAPTER 19

Patterns of Response

Samuel P. Huntington

Originally published in
American Politics: The Promise of Disharmony, *1981*.

READING INTRODUCTION

For Huntington, American society is intrinsically conflictual. His reason for thinking so is not the presence of antagonistic social classes, but the incompatibility between what he calls the "American creed" (a political culture of antistatist values including liberty, equality of opportunity, individualism, democracy, constitutionalism and limited local government) and the requirements of running a society. Coping with the various historical contingencies that confront the United States from abroad (e.g., the Nazi challenge) and within (e.g., disability and aging in an increasingly urban society of nuclear households) routinely produces actions destructive of the values of this antistatist American political culture, particularly a large, more active (e.g., large standing military forces and social security) national government. These practical challenges simply require the coping mechanisms (institutions) of a more hierarchical political culture. This creates what Huntington calls the "IvI gap"—a tension between American ideals (the first "I") and the institutions (the second "I") that are necessary to practice modern government. As a consequence of this IvI gap, the United States experiences roughly sixty-year cycles of "creedal passion" involving attacks on authority (hierarchy) in general and central political authority in particular designed to bring political life back into conformance with creedal values. Yet life inevitably returns to hierarchical practices that violate these values. In the pages selected here Huntington provides a brief description of this pattern in terms of a four-stage cycle: moralism, cynicism, complacency, and finally hypocrisy that breeds a return to moralism. In brief, each peak of creedal passion exhausts the citizenry so that a lengthy process of perceptual clarification and value reaffirmation is required before the passion can be repeated. In the final few pages Huntington shows that particular social groups are predisposed toward particular responses or periods of the cycle.

READING TEXT

Patterns of Response

What are the ways in which Americans cope with their cognitive dissonance? Consensus and stability have generally characterized American political values, and the IvI gap is always present. Variations do occur, however, in the intensity with which groups of Americans hold to their beliefs in American political ideals—that is, the level of creedal passion in American society—and in the clarity with which Americans perceive the gap to exist. Differences in these two variables can yield the four major responses set forth in Table 2.

1. *Moralism*. If Americans intensely believe in their ideals and clearly perceive the IvI gap, they moralistically attempt to *eliminate* the gap through reforms that will bring practice and institutions into accord with principles and beliefs.
2. *Cynicism*. If intensity of belief is low and perception of the gap is clear, Americans will resort to a cynical willingness to *tolerate* the gap's existence.
3. *Complacency*. If intensity of belief is low and their perception of the gap is unclear, Americans can attempt to *ignore* the existence of the gap by in effect reducing its cognitive importance to themselves through complacent indifference.
4. *Hypocrisy*. If they are intensely committed to American ideals and yet *deny* the existence of a gap between ideals and reality, they can alter not reality but their perceptions of reality through an immense effort at "patriotic" hypocrisy.[1]

At various times social critics, including foreign observers of the American scene, have seized upon one or another of these four responses as *the* typical American response. In fact, however, all four have been present throughout most of American history, interacting, with one another in mutually reinforcing and mutually counterbalancing ways (Albert 1963; Williams 1951). Complacency is probably the most prevalent response, but it is also the least noted and least notable one. The others have all left a definite mark on American culture.

Table 2: American responses to the IvI gap.

	Perception of gap	
Intensity of belief in ideals	Clear	Unclear
High	Moralism (eliminate gap)	Hypocrisy (deny gap)
Low	Cynicism (tolerate gap)	Complacency (ignore gap)

The tolerance of the IvI gap which is the essence of the cynical response is, for instance, a major source of American humor. Comedy depends on incongruity, and the sources of incongruity vary from one society to another. It has been observed that "nearly all the greatest British comedy rests on class differences. From *The Country Wife* to *The Diary of a Nobody,* from P. G. Wodehouse to Anthony Powell, or from Chaucer to Nancy Mitford, few writers have set out to amuse their readers without going straight to the class structure" (Blythe 1966). In America the source of comedy is not the incongruity between classes, but, as Louis Rubin argued, "the incongruity between the ideal and the real . . . [that] lies at the heart of the American experience." This incongruity provides the central theme of most American humor, manifested most notably, perhaps, in the work of that most American of humorists, Mark Twain. "Out of the incongruity between mundane circumstance and heroic ideal," Rubin goes on to observe, "material fact and spiritual hunger . . . theory of equality and fact of social and economic inequality, the Declaration of Independence and the Prohibition Act, the Gettysburg Address and the Gross National Product, the Battle Hymn of the Republic and Dollar Diplomacy, the Horatio Alger ideal and the New York Social Register—between what men would be and must be, as acted out in American experience, have come a great deal of pathos, no small bit of tragedy, and also a great deal of humor." This was what Robert Penn Warren identified as the "burr under the metaphysical saddle of America," the problem of living in the same house with "a big promise—a great big one: the Declaration of Independence."[2] The gap between how Americans ideally should behave and how they actually behave furnishes an inexhaustible lode for the ridicule of moral pretense. The Americans delight in being "debunked"— "bunk" itself being an American word (Samson 1932, 13). Humor becomes one way of coping with the national problem of cognitive dissonance. The promise of American life is transformed into "the great American joke."

Not surprisingly, foreign observers have often pointed to hypocrisy as a distinctive characteristic of American culture. Although there is no reason to assign it a predominant role, there can be little doubt that it occupies a central place in American politics. Americans want to believe that their liberal-democratic ideals are reflected in their institutions. This belief is often expressed to foreigners and engenders the view abroad that Americans are given to hypocritical, moralistic cant. As Irving Kristol (1972) suggested, this public hypocrisy has its roots in the "deep emotional commitment" of Americans "to the idea that government— all government, everywhere—should be subservient to the citizen's individual life, his personal liberty, and his pursuit of happiness" (130). Americans find it congenial to believe that at least their government and political system meet this standard. In this respect, hypocrisy, defined by the dictionary as the "false pretense of moral excellence," is a product not just of practice deviating from one's principles, but also of asserting principles that cannot be practiced. Americans thus reduce their cognitive dissonance by clouding their perception of the realities of power, inequality, hierarchy, and constraints in American life.

All ruling classes must in some measure be hypocritical. This is especially true of modern liberal democracies, and the eruption of democracy in America during the Jacksonian years led writers such as Nathaniel Hawthorne to seize upon hypocrisy as the pervasive characteristic of American society. In a democracy, leaders such as Lincoln and Franklin Roosevelt are open to "endless accusations of hypocrisy" because they gave "a new vigor to flagging political principles and loyalties" and "raised the level of moral and political expectations," but were unable "to fulfill the standards they had themselves revived" (Shklar 1979, 11, 14-16, 24). The most distinguished spokesmen of the American Establishment mouth the clichés of American liberalism as if they were realistic descriptions rather than pious aspirations. Ashamed of their power, their ability to wield it is constrained by their felt need to pretend that it does not exist. Yet although Americans may relish the exposure of hypocrisy, they are not comfortable when it is absent in their leaders. People demand high-mindedness in their public figures, and if "you are extraordinarily high-minded in your political pronouncements, you are bound in the nature of things to be more than ordinarily hypocritical" (Kristol 1972, 130).

In the United States, indeed, public figures may be attacked for not being hypocritical enough—a point well illustrated by the reactions of some political figures to the earthy realism, vulgarity, and pathos revealed in the Nixon Watergate tapes. "There's no reference throughout the whole transcription," observed Senator Bob Packwood sanctimoniously, "to what is good for the American people. There are not even any token clichés about what is good for the people." In similar tones, Chairman Robert Strauss of the Democratic Party felt moved to complain: "It's sadder and sicker than I ever imagined. I keep looking for some mention of the American people, some concern for the nation."[3] Along with his other misdoings, Nixon was guilty of not carrying over into his private conversations with his aides the hypocritical clichés demanded of public rhetoric.

In similar fashion, moralism is also often pointed to as a peculiarly American trait. "Americans are eminently prophets," Santayana (1956) once observed. "They apply morals to public affairs; they are impatient and enthusiastic. . . . They are men of principles, and fond of stating them" (3). Others have noted how this leads to a penchant, almost perverse in European eyes, for self-criticism, and have pointed to this attitude as the distinguishing characteristic of Americans. Gunnar Myrdal (1944), indeed, defended Americans against the charge of hypocrisy and insisted upon their devotion to the moralistic exposure of evil:

> The *popular* explanation of the disparity in America between ideals and actual behavior is that Americans do not have the slightest intention of living up to the ideals which they talk about and put into their Constitution and laws. Many Americans are accustomed to talk loosely and disparagingly about adherence to the American Creed as "lip-service" and even "hypocrisy." Foreigners are even more prone to make such a characterization.
>
> This explanation is too superficial. To begin with, the true hypocrite sins in secret; he conceals his faults. The American, on the contrary, is strongly and sincerely "against sin," even, and not least, his own sins. He investigates his faults, puts them on record, and shouts them from the

housetops, adding the most severe recriminations against himself, including the accusation of hypocrisy. If all the world is well informed about the political corruption, organized crime, and faltering system of justice in America, it is primarily not due to its malice but to American publicity about its own imperfections. (21)

Myrdal's statement about the passion of Americans for exposing their sins is perfectly true. But it is equally true that at various times some Americans may tolerate, ignore, or deny their sins. Moralism, cynicism, complacency, and hypocrisy are all familiar ways by which Americans respond to their cognitive dissonance problem. The role and importance of these responses, however, differ from time to time and from group to group.

Response Dynamics
The propensity of American society as a whole to resort to one response or another, or some combination of responses, varies. The national mood can at different times be described as predominantly one of complacency, hypocrisy, moralism, or cynicism. Experience suggests that recourse to one of these responses may generate consequences that encourage recourse to another response. No one response, however, provides a lasting satisfactory solution to the problem of cognitive dissonance. Each is tried for a while and then abandoned in a never-ending search for a way out of the national dilemma. The logical dynamics of such a cyclical pattern of response are as follows.

1. *Moralistic reform (eliminating the gap).* Since cognitive dissonance cannot be eliminated by changing fundamental principles, changes must occur in institutions and behavior. The moralistic response occurs when people feel intensely committed to American political values, clearly perceive the gap between ideals and reality, and attempt to restructure institutions and practices to reflect these ideals. The combination of intensity and perception furnishes the moral motive to reform, "The history of reform," Emerson (1870) said, "is always identical; it is the comparison of the idea with the fact" (149). Major groups in American society become obsessed with the facts of inequality, lack of freedom, arbitrary power. They dramatize those facts and force them upon the public consciousness, making it impossible for decision makers and the attentive public to ignore the extent to which the actuality of political life contradicts American beliefs. The moral indignation of the few stimulates public outrage from the many. Institutions and practices that had been accepted as part of the way things are lose their legitimacy. Demands for curtailing power and reforming the system sweep to the top of the political agenda: reality must be made to conform to the ideal. During such creedal passion periods, the latent disharmonic qualities of American society come to the surface.

2. *Cynicism (tolerating the gap).* Large bodies of people can sustain high levels of moral indignation for only limited periods of time. The unveiling of evil, which was first the instrument by which moralism laid bare hypocrisy, later furnishes the vindication of cynicism against moralism. The perception of the IvI

gap remains, but the expectation that anything can be done to close the gap dwindles. Those who had expounded the Creed in order to change reality find themselves increasingly divorced from reality. The exposers of hypocrisy become the exemplars of hypocrisy.

Reform begins with the assumption that the elimination of evil can be achieved by the elimination of evil men-in-power. It moves on to the assumption that some restructuring of institutions is necessary. It comes to an end with the realization that neither of these will suffice. Some reformers conclude that the "system" itself must be totally changed and advocate revolution. Others let the intensity of their commitment to reform values decline and lapse into at least temporary cynical toleration of the gap. The feeling that the gap must be eliminated is replaced by the feeling that nothing can be changed. Moral indignation is replaced by moral helplessness. All politicians are crooks, all institutions corrupt. The gap must be accepted—and perhaps even enjoyed, as its role in American humor suggests.

3. *Complacency (ignoring the gap).* Cynicism is an effort to live with cognitive dissonance. But just as most people cannot maintain moral intensity indefinitely, neither can they indefinitely sustain toleration of the gap between ideal and practice. "Cognitive dissonance is a noxious state," and the "severity or the intensity of cognitive dissonance varies with the importance of the cognitions involved and the relative number of cognitions standing in dissonant relation to one another" (Zajonc 1968, 618). Whereas the escape from creedal passion to cynicism involves a dulling of moral sensibility, the escape from cynicism to complacency involves a dulling of perceptual clarity. The importance of the dissonant cognitions is reduced simply by turning attention to other matters. During such periods of creedal passivity and perceptual opaqueness, Americans may, if compelled to do so, admit the existence of a gap between ideal and reality—as they did for years with respect to the role of black people in American life—but then shunt it off into a back corner of their consciousness and simply not become terribly concerned about it. The dilemma, as Myrdal argued, exists but it does not trouble people nor lead them to become intensely and passionately concerned with resolving it. Cognitive dissonance lurks uneasily beneath the surface of conscience but is not sufficiently commanding to trouble people seriously. There is no intense concern with American ideals or with the discrepancy between ideal and reality.

4. *Hypocrisy (denying the gap).* The ideological nature of their national identity means that Americans cannot indefinitely eschew the affirmation of the basic values and principles of the national Creed. Responding to the need to articulate these values, however, they may still be reluctant to acknowledge the existence of the IvI gap. They may view themselves through filtering lenses. American institutions are seen to be open and democratic; America is the land of opportunity; the equality of man is a fact in American life; the United States is the land of the free and the home of the brave; it is the embodiment of government of the people, by the people, and for the people. During these periods, Americans so shape their perceptions that they cannot see any gap between the unpleasant facts of political institutions and power in the United States and the

values of the American Creed. Reality is hailed as the ideal. The discrepancies are strained out and avoided. The United States not only should be the land of liberty, equality, and justice for all; it actually is.

In due course, however, the intense assertion of American ideals leads to renewed perception of the IvI gap. New individuals and groups begin to use the affirmation of the ideals as a means not of glorifying the American way of life but of exposing it. The hypocritical identification of reality with ideal gives way to the moralistic denunciation of reality in terms of the ideal. The way is cleared for another wave of creedal passion directed toward reform.

This sequence of responses is designed as a model and not as a representation of empirical reality. History does not necessarily develop according to logical patterns. Some measure of psychological dissatisfaction is, however, the inevitable result of the IvI gap and some combination of moralism, cynicism, complacency, and hypocrisy is required to reduce that dissatisfaction. Particular phases in American history often tend to be colored more by one response than by the others, and one response often creates conditions favorable to the rise of another. History does not follow a logical model, but neither is the logical model irrelevant to the understanding of history.

Group Propensities

Just as different responses may predominate in different historical phases, so also different groups in society may have propensities toward different responses. Age and socioeconomic status appear to have a significant effect upon people's choices.

The American educational system, particularly at the elementary-school level, indoctrinates its students in American ideals and minimizes the disparity between ideal and reality. As a result, grade-school children generally have highly positive and benign images of the political system, the government, and particularly of the President.[4] They are, in short, educated in the hypocritical response. These attitudes provide the basis for their subsequent adult acceptance of the legitimacy of the political system. Secondary-school children have more "realistic" and, in some respects, more cynical attitudes toward politics. There still remains, however, a substantial difference between their views and those of young adults who have been out of school for several years. In addition, high-school seniors have considerably lower levels of political cynicism than do their parents who went to high school. Among those who leave school after high school, increasing exposure to the unpleasant realities of political life combines with feelings of limited political efficacy to produce a significantly more cynical approach to the political process. Among those who go on to college, on the other hand, an increasingly clear perception of the IvI gap encourages more of a shift toward moralism. The educational system that minimizes the distinction between ideal and reality for young children maximizes the impact of perceptions of that gap among college-age youth. "Societies teach youth to adhere to the basic values of the social system in absolute terms.... Compromises which are dictated by contradictory pressures and are justified in the eyes of many adults are viewed by idealistic youth as violations of basic morality. Young people tend to be committed to ideals rather than institutions. Hence, events which point up the gap between ideals and reallty often stimulate them to action, though cynicism and withdrawal occur as well if they see no appropriate way to act" (Lipset 1971, 744-745). As people age, however, the intensity of belief necessary for either hypocrisy or moralism tends to decline, and among adults a high correlation exists between cynicism and age.[5]

Socioeconomic status plays an even more important role in shaping responsive propensities. The available evidence suggests two significant tendencies. First, almost all groups in American society favor the basic liberal-democratic values of the American Creed. People who are better educated, who are of higher socioeconomic status, and who occupy positions of social or political leadership are, however, more likely to support those values than are other people. That is, the proportion of such groups affirming support for these values may be 85 percent rather than 65 percent or 70 percent (Devine 1972, 260-265). This difference in breadth of support does not necessarily demonstrate anything about the relative intensity of support from these two groups, but it does suggest the probability that intensity of support will be greater among those of higher socioeconomic position. In addition, people with more education and of higher socioeconomic status are more likely to support the application of liberal-democratic values in specific instances than are other people (Prothro and Grigg 1960; Stouffer 1955). Such evidence would clearly seem to indicate greater commitment to and intensity of belief in those liberal-democratic values. In short, there is reason to believe that higher-status people are more likely to be hypocritical or moralistic, and lower-status people cynical or complacent.

A second difference among groups according to socioeconomic status is even more clearly documented by the evidence. People who have less income and less education and who do not occupy leadership roles are more likely than others to have a critical view of the political process and to perceive a significant gap between American ideal and American reality. People of higher status, position, and education are less likely to perceive a wide gap between the two. As Table 3 indicates [editor's note—not reproduced], Herbert McClosky (1964) found substantial differences in political cynicism between "political influentials," that is, people who had been delegates or alternates to a national party convention, and a cross-section of the general electorate. Overall, 10.1 percent of the influentials scored "high" on the cynicism scale, compared with 31.3 percent of the general population. Similarly, a study of political ideology in Muskegon, Michigan, found that "the higher their income, the more people believe that the ideology of pluralism accurately describes the way the system works and, as a corollary, the lower their income, the less symmetry people see between normative and actualized aspects of the ideology. . . . Higher income strata tend to equate normative and existential statements about political pluralism, while lower income strata tend to deny their symmetry and to support action to make them more congruent" (Huber and Form 1973, 132-33). In similar fashion, black children and poor Appalachian children see the President as deviating significantly more from idealistic norms than do white middle-class children (Greenberg 1969; 1970; Jarros, Hirsch and Fleron, Jr. 1968). In short, higher-status people are more likely to be hypocritical or complacent, lower-status people to be cynical or moralistic.

These two conclusions on the relation of socioeconomic status to intensity of creedal beliefs and to clarity of perception of the IvI gap combine to suggest one broad generalization. People of higher socioeconomic status are more likely than people of lower status to believe intensely in the values of the Creed and are less likely to perceive a major gap between those values and political reality. They consequently are likely to have a propensity toward the hypocritical response. People of lower socioeconomic status are less likely to have intense beliefs in the Creed. A large number of lower-status people probably do not concern themselves with politics and hence do not perceive a significant gap between ideal and reality. They are thus likely to have a propensity toward complacency. Insofar as lower-status people become politically aware, however, they will tend toward a cynical response.

This pattern of group propensities underlies the stability of the political system. Those who most intensely believe in the values of the system are less likely to see a gap between those values and political reality. Those who see such a gap are less likely to have the moralistic fervor to do anything about it. Upper-class and upper-middle-class hypocrisy combines with working-class and lower-class cynicism to perpetuate the status quo. At least this seems to be the predominant tendency for much of the time. To be sure, some people within the higher-status groups are ever sensitive to the gap between ideal and reality and regularly attempt to do something about it. Their success, however, is dependent upon their ability to mobilize additional support from those who are either hypocritical or cynical. Change in the system—or, if one views it unfavorably, instability—occurs when those who perceive the gap develop moralistic passion or when those who feel such passion come to perceive the gap. The latter shift, which normally involves significant changes in the perceptions of the upper middle class, has historically been the most important source of change in American political institutions and practices. Shifts in either perceptions or intensity may also affect different groups in the population differently. In the 1960s, for example, higher-status and lower-status groups both developed clearer perceptions of the gap between political ideals and political reality. As a result, higher-status groups became less hypocritical and more moralistic, furnishing the impetus for wide-ranging reforms of institutions and practices; at the same time, lower-status groups became less complacent and more cynical, causing a massive decline in popular trust and confidence in government, as reflected in public opinion polls.

If Americans do not blind themselves to reality, they have a choice between moralism and cynicism. If Americans do not falter in the intensity of their belief in American ideals, they have a choice between moralism and hypocrisy. Moralism is thus the one response that, in some sense, combines both realism and idealism. It involves the effort to remove the fundamental cause of American cognitive dissonance by reducing or eliminating the gap between promise and practice. In this sense it is the most positive American political response. As

American history demonstrates, however, it can be not only the reformer but the destroyer of American institutions. Henry Stimson, at the end of an extraordinarily distinguished career of public service, concluded his memoirs with the words: "The only deadly sin I know is cynicism" (Stimson and Bundy 1947, 672). As a central figure of the American Establishment, Stimson focused on the popular sin of cynicism and did not recognize the Establishment sin of hypocrisy. More important, he also failed to note that in America the only deadly virtue is moralism.

References

Albert, E. 1963. Conflict and change in American values: A culture-historical approach. *Ethics* 74 (October).
Blythe, R. 1966. Introduction. *Emma* by Jane Austen. Harmondsworth: Penguin Books.
Devine, D. 1972. *The political culture of the United States.* Boston: Little, Brown.
Emerson, R. W. 1870. *Prose works.* Boston: Fields, Osgood & Co.
Huber, J., and W. Form. 1973. *Income and ideology.* New York: The Free Press.
Jarros, D., H. Hirsch, and F. Fleron, Jr. 1968. The malevolent leader: Political socialization in American subculture. *American Political Science Review* 62 (June).
Kristol, I. 1972. *On the democratic ideal in America.* New York: Harper & Row.
Lipset, S. M. 1971. Youth and politics. In *Contemporary social problems,* 3d ed., edited by R. Merton and R. Nisbet. New York: Harcourt Brace Jovanovich.
McCloskey, H. 1964. Consensus and ideology in American politics. *American Political Science Review* 58 (June).
Myrdal, G. 1944. *An American dilemma.* New York: Harper & Row.
Prothro, J. W. and C. Grigg. 1960. Fundamental principles of democracy: Bases of agreement and disagreement. *Journal of Politics* 22 (February): 284-291.
Samson, L. 1932. *The American mind.* New York: Jonathan Cape and Harrison Smith.
Santayana, G. 1956. *Character and opinion in the United States.* Garden City, NY: Doubleday Anchor.
Shklar, J. 1979. Let us not be hypocritical. *Daedalus* 108 (Summer).
Stimson, H. and M. Bundy. 1947. *On active service in peace and war.* New York: Harper & Bros.
Stouffer, 1955. *Communism, conformity and civil liberties.* Garden City, NY: Doubleday.
Williams, R. 1951. *American society.* New York: Knopf.
Zajonc, R. 1968. Thinking: Cognitive organization and processes. In *International encyclopedia of the social sciences,* ed. David L. Sills. New York: Macmillan Co. and Free Press.

PART VII
Culture and Rationality

Introduction

Perspectives on the relations between culture and rationality are wide-ranging, swiftly changing, and hotly disputed. Near one end of a range of perspectives, Eckstein (1997, 21-44) expresses a view widely held by political scientists until recently: culture and rationality denote distinct, even opposing, orientations toward political life and its analysis. From this perspective culture represents a hodgepodge of "irrational feelings, tradition and values" (Swedberg, chapter 21 herein) sharing little, if any, common ground with rationality. Chapter 20 offers another expression of this view. Yet near the opposing end of this range of perspectives Wildavsky (1994) argues that culture and rationality are complementary and reinforce one another in producing a more complete theory of rational action. Our Chapters 21 and 22 provide background on these conflicting perspectives and an example of what Wildavsky has in mind, respectively. We shall return to Wildavsky's argument near the end of this introduction. Let us begin, however, by examining the concept of rationality and then see how culture might be related to it.

Among ancient philosophers (e.g., Plato and Aristotle), rationality was associated with the pursuit of particular objectives considered to be appropriate for a person's telos, or ultimate end. Thus rational people were distinguished by pursuing what these philosophers saw as their true ends. But for the last couple of centuries, with the major exception of Immanuel Kant, rationality has been viewed as instrumental. That is, rational behavior involves the consistent, efficient pursuit of, generally, whatever ends people prefer. The modifier "generally" serves to separate rational behavior from extreme cases based on highly idiosyncratic and likely erroneous conceptions of the world (i.e., a person who thinks that everyone else is out to get her and consequently takes unreasonable security precautions). In everyday terms, such a person would be considered irrational, however consistently and efficiently she organized her security, by virtue of the discrepancy between her view of the world and that of other people.

Across the last century economists have relied increasingly on an instrumental conception of rationality as an analytic device for predicting, and thus explaining, human behavior. Over the last few decades, this orientation toward social science has found growing favor in other academic disciplines, particularly political science. Similar orientations are known by distinctive names in various fields (e.g., neoclassical economics, public choice, and rational-choice theory). The last term is generally employed in contemporary political science. Rational-choice theorists routinely rely on two basic and simple assumptions: 1) persons can rank-order, and thus state consistent preferences among, various objectives; and 2) they choose alternative courses of action so as to maximize their satisfaction (Riker 1990, 172; related versions are offered by Wildavsky 1994, 133; Taylor 1989, 149-50; and Monroe 1995, 2; see especially Monroe 1991b, 1-31).

While some exceptions occur (Sugden 1989; Young 1996), rational-choice theorists generally do not examine why people have the preferences or interests they do. Frequently, rational-choice theorists assume both an intersubjective reality and egoistic, material ("economic man") motivation (Taylor 1989, 149-150). In ordinary terms, they consider humans to be materially self-interested. (While it is surely possible to make finer distinctions, in this section we use the terms "values" and "motives" as rough synonyms for the origins of humans' preferences for particular objectives and their associated practical political interests.) Accordingly, "rational choice" is generally employed as a theory of preference implementation. That is, its practitioners assume that people agree as to how the world works and want to do as well for themselves as they can in terms of personal, material benefits. Rational-choice theorists then derive predictions about the courses of action that people will follow from these assumptions. Sometimes these predictions are accurate and insightful; occasionally they are surprising and reveal as rational practices heretofore not perceived as rationally explicable (Axelrod 1984). In other instances rational-choice predictions are either difficult because of uncertainty as to how the world works (Denzau and North 1994, 9-12) or clearly wide of the mark because the people in question employ motives that are not egoistic and material (Etzioni 1988).

As Mansbridge (1990, 3-22) suggests, attributions of egoistic, material motives are either false in some instances or, if egoism and materialism are defined broadly enough to make the assumptions correct, vacuous. Macaulay (1852) probably makes this point most effectively:

> One man goes without a dinner that he may add a shilling to a hundred thousand pounds: another runs in debt to give balls and masquerades. One man cuts his father's throat to get possession of his old clothes: another hazards his own life to save that of an enemy. One man volunteers on a forlorn hope: another is drummed out of a regiment for cowardice. Each of these men has, no doubt, acted from self-interest. But we gain nothing by knowing this, except the pleasure, if it be one, of multiplying useless words. (200)

Clearly more attention needs to be paid to how distinctive motivations arise and why they take the forms they do. Otherwise, as Sen (1979, 317-344) suggests, social science falsely portrays humans as "rational fools," unable to recognize and act on concerns that are understandably important, even crucial, to actual people.

Interest in preference formation introduces culture into our discussion. One source for varying conceptions of how the world works and what values are worth realizing lies in differences among the cultures that various organizations produce. It is frequently the case, for instance, that a political actor's policy preference depends on where that person "sits" (i.e., her or his organizational position). Several contemporary political scientists demonstrate that variations in organizational responsibilities and histories produce different patterns of preferences (Kreps 1990, 90-143; Legro 1996; Lichbach and Zuckerman 1997). Thus organizational cultures become one means of constraining and thus predicting the particular practical political interests that people will seek to realize efficiently. Greif (1992, 1994) considers a broader range of human experience as constitutive of constrained preferences that facilitate the development of distinctive institutions.

Greif's contribution directs attention once again to Wildavsky's argument in our opening paragraph. Following Hume (1951, 168-176), Mansbridge (1990, 3-22) and Jencks (1990, 53-67) argue that people routinely employ duty and love as well as egoism as motives for instrumentally rational action. (See also Etzioni 1988; Sen 1979, 1-25; Taylor 1989). Thompson, Ellis and Wildavsky (1990) show that these three distinctive motivations (egoism, duty, and love) are associated with and socially embedded in three rival cultures: individualism, hierarchy, and egalitarianism. In this view culture and rationality are complementary and contribute (as theories of preference formation and implementation respectively) to what Wildavsky (1994) calls a "theory of rational choices." (See also Chai forthcoming; Lockhart and Coughlin 1992; Lockhart and Wildavsky 1998, 113-131; and various selections in the excellent collections edited by Monroe 1991a and Zey 1992). Each culture has its own way of looking at the world (metaphysical or ontological preferences), its distinctive value clusters (motivational preferences), and its preferred institutions (goal implementation preferences). The resulting theory of rational action explains not only how people go about acquiring what they want but why people want what they do, surely a desirable objective for the social sciences.

References and Further Reading

Axelrod, R. 1984. *The evolution of cooperation*. New York: Basic.
Chai, S. Forthcoming. *Choosing an identity: A general model of preference and belief formation and its applications to comparative development*. Ann Arbor: University of Michigan Press.
Denzau, A., and D. North. 1994. Shared mental models: Ideologies and institutions. *Kyklos* 47: 3-31.
Douglas, M., ed. 1982. *Essays in the sociology of perception*. London: Routledge and Kegan Paul.
Eckstein, H. 1988. A culturalist theory of political change. *American Political Science Review* 82: 789-804.

———. 1997. Social science as cultural science; Rational choice as metaphysics. In *Culture matters: Essays in honor of Aaron Wildavsky,* edited by R. Ellis and M. Thompson. Boulder, CO: Westview.
Elster, J. 1989a. *The cement of society: A study of social order.* Cambridge, UK: Cambridge University Press.
———. 1989b. Social norms and economic theory. *Journal of Economic Perspectives* 3: 99-117.
Etzioni, A. 1988. *The moral dimension: Toward a new economics.* New York: Free Press.
Ferejohn, J. 1991. Rationality and interpretation: Parliamentary elections in early Stuart England. In *The economic approach to politics: A critical reassessment of the theory of rational action,* edited by K. R. Monroe. New York: HarperCollins.
Greif, A. 1992. Institutions and international trade: Lessons from the commercial revolution. *American Economic Review* 82: 128-133.
———. 1994. Cultural beliefs and the organization of society: A historical and theoretical reflection on collectivist and individualist societies. *Journal of Political Economy* 102: 912-950.
Hume, D. 1951 [1777]. Of parties in general. In *Hume: Theory of politics,* edited by F. Watkins. London: Nelson.
Jencks, C. 1990. Varieties of altruism. In *Beyond self-interest,* edited by J. Mansbridge. Chicago: University of Chicago Press.
Kreps, D. 1990. Corporate culture and economic theory. In *Perspectives on positive political economy,* edited by J. Alt and K. Shepsle. New York: Cambridge University Press.
Legro, J. 1996. Culture and preferences in the international cooperation two-step. *American Political Science Review* 90: 118-137.
Lichbach, M., and A. Zuckerman, eds. 1997. *Comparative politics: Rationality, culture, and structure.* New York: Cambridge University Press.
Lockhart, C., and R. Coughlin. 1992. Building better comparative social theory through alternative conceptions of rationality. *Western Political Quarterly* 45: 793-809.
Lockhart, C., and A. Wildavsky. 1998. The social construction of cooperation: Egalitarian, hierarchical, and individualistic faces of altruism. In A. Wildavsky's *Culture and social theory,* edited by S. Chai and B. Swedlow. New Brunswick, NJ: Transaction.
Macaulay, T. B. 1852. Mill's essay on government [1829]. In *Critical and miscellaneous essays,* vol. 5. Philadelphia: Hart, Carey and Hart.
Mansbridge, J. 1990. The rise and fall of self-interest in the explanation of political life. In *Beyond self-interest.* Chicago: University of Chicago Press.
Monroe, K. R., ed. 1991a. *The economic approach to politics: A critical reassessment of the theory of rational action.* New York: HarperCollins.
———. 1991b. The theory of rational action. In *The economic approach to politics: A reassessment of the theory of rational action.* New York: HarperCollins.
Monroe, K. R. 1995. Psychology and rational actor theory. *Political Psychology* 16: 1-22.
Riker, W. 1990. Political science and rational choice. In *Perspectives on positive political economy,* edited by J. Alt and K. Shepsle. New York: Cambridge University Press.
Sen, A. 1979. Rational fools: A critique of the behavioral foundations of economic theory. In *Scientific models and man,* edited by H. Harris. London: Oxford University Press.
Sugden, R. 1989. Spontaneous order. *Journal of Political Perspectives* 3: 85-97.
Swedberg, R. 1990. Socioeconomics and the new 'Battle of the Methods': Towards a paradigm shift?" *Journal of Behavioral Economics* 19: 141-154.
Taylor, M. 1989. Structure, culture and action in the explanation of social change. *Politics and Society* 17: 115-162.
Thompson, M., R. Ellis, and A. Wildavsky. 1990. *Cultural theory.* Boulder, CO: Westview.
Wildavsky, Aaron. 1994. Why self-interest means less outside of a social context: Cultural contributions to a theory of rational choices. *Journal of Theoretical Politics* 6: 131-159.
Young, P. 1996. The economics of conventions. *Journal of Economic Perspectives* 10: 105-122.
Zey, M., ed. 1992. *Decision-making alternatives to rational choice models.* Newbury Park, CA: Sage.

CHAPTER 20

Social Norms and Economic Theory

Jon Elster

Originally published in
Journal of Economic Perspectives *3 (4), 1989.*

READING INTRODUCTION

Elster contrasts two distinct and frequently opposing social science traditions. One was fostered by Adam Smith and is carried forward today by neoclassical economists and rational-choice theorists in political science. It views humans as "economic men," that is, as motivated by egoistic material concerns. The other tradition has its roots in the work of the French sociologist Emile Durkheim, provides the basis for much contemporary sociology and has adherents among political scientists, particularly political culture theorists such as Eckstein (1988). It views humans as social creatures, having duty-based and other obligations to their fellows. "Sociological man's" activity is thus constrained by shared social (cultural) norms. Elster is skeptical that these cultural norms generally realize individual self-interest as this is understood in the rational-choice tradition. Indeed, elsewhere he distinguishes "economic man" rationality and "nonrational" cultural norms even more sharply than he does in this chapter (Elster 1989b). Overall, Elster holds that, for the most part, cultural norms neither arise from rationality, as neoclassical economists understand it, nor do they serve it.

READING TEXT

One of the most persistent cleavages in the social sciences is the opposition between two lines of thought conveniently associated with Adam Smith and Emile Durkheim, between *homo economicus and homo sociologicus*. Of these, the former is supposed to be guided by instrumental rationality, while the behavior of the latter is dictated by social norms. The former is "pulled" by the prospect of future rewards, whereas the latter is "pushed" from behind by quasi-inertial forces (Gambetta 1987). The former adapts to changing circumstances, always on the lookout for improvements. The latter is insensitive to circumstances, sticking to the prescribed behavior even if new and apparently better options become available. The former is easily caricatured as a self-contained, asocial atom, and the latter as the mindless plaything of social forces. In this paper I characterize this contrast more fully, and discuss attempts by economists to reduce norm-oriented action to some type of optimizing behavior.[1]

Rational action is concerned with outcomes. Rationality says: If you want to achieve Y, do X. By contrast, I define social norms by the feature that they are *not outcome-oriented*. The simplest social norms are of the type: Do X, or: Don't do X. More complex norms say: If you do Y, then do X, or: If others do Y, then do X. More complex norms still might say: Do X if it would be good if everyone did X. Rationality is essentially conditional and future-oriented. Social norms are either unconditional or, if conditional, are not future-oriented. For norms to be *social*, they must be shared by other people and partly sustained by their approval and disapproval. They are also sustained by the feelings of embarrassment, anxiety, guilt and shame that a person suffers at the prospect of violating them. A person obeying a norm may also be propelled by positive emotions, like anger and indignation. Djilas (1958, 107) refers to the feeling of a person enacting the norms of vengeance in Montenegro as "the wildest, sweetest kind of drunkenness." Social norms have a grip on the mind that is due to the strong emotions they can trigger.

This initial statement somewhat exaggerates the mechanical, unreflective character of norm-guided behavior. Social norms offer considerable scope for skill, choice, interpretation and manipulation. For that reason, rational actors often deploy norms to achieve their ends. Yet there are limits to the flexibility of norms, otherwise there would be nothing to manipulate.

Social norms must be distinguished from a number of other, related phenomena. First, social norms differ from moral norms. Some moral norms, like those derived from utilitarian ethics, are consequentialist. Secondly, social norms differ from legal norms. Legal norms are enforced by specialists who do so out of self-interest: they will lose their job if they don't. By contrast, social norms are enforced by members of the general community, and not always out of self-interest (see below). Thirdly, social norms are more than the convention equilibria described in Robert Sugden's accompanying article.* As Sugden explains, the evolution of a convention equilibrium is guided by whether the conventions lead to a substantively better outcome. I argue below, however, that many social norms do not benefit anyone. Fourthly, social norms differ from private norms, the self-imposed rules that people construct to overcome weakness of will (Ainslie 1982, 1984, 1986). Private norms, like social norms, are non-outcome-oriented and sustained by feelings of anxiety and guilt. They are not, however, sustained by the approval and disapproval of others since they are not, or not necessarily, shared with others. Finally, norm-guided behavior must be distinguished from habits and compulsive neuroses. Unlike social norms, habits are private. Unlike private norms, their violation does not generate self-blame or guilt. Unlike neuroses and private norms, habits are not compulsive. Unlike social norms, compulsive neuroses are highly idiosyncratic. Yet what in one culture looks like a compulsive neurosis may, in another society, be an established

---

*In original publication, not included here.

social norm (Fenichel 1945, 586). Compulsive revenge behavior could be an example (Djilas 1958).

To fix our ideas, let me give some examples of social norms. *Consumption norms* regulate manners of dress, manners of table and the like. As shown by Proust's masterful account of life in the Guermantes circle, conformity with such norms can be vitally important to people, in spite of the fact that nothing of substance seems to be at stake. Pierre Bourdieu (1979) has extended the notion of consumption norms to cover cultural behavior: which syntax, vocabulary and pronunciation do you adopt? which movies do you see? which books do you read? which sports do you practice? what kind of furniture do you buy?

Norms against behavior "contrary to nature" include rules against incest, cannibalism, homosexuality and sodomy. The rule against cannibalism allows, however, for exceptions in case of *force majeure* (Edgerton 1985, 51). The point obtains quite generally: Whenever there is a norm, there are often a set of adjunct norms defining legitimate exceptions. Often, these are less explicit than the main norm, and rely heavily on judgment and discretion.

Norms regulating the use of money often become legal, like the law against buying and selling votes. Often, however, they remain informal, like the norm against buying into a bus queue or the norm against asking one's neighbor to mow one's lawn for money. I discuss both of these cases later.

Norms of reciprocity enjoin us to return favors done to us by others (Gouldner 1960). Gift-giving is often regulated by these norms. There may not be an unconditional norm of giving Christmas presents to a first cousin, but once the cousin begins to give me a gift I am under an obligation to return it.

Norms of retribution enjoin us to return harms done to us by others. Rules regulating revenge are often highly elaborate (Hasluck 1954; Boehm 1984; Miller forthcoming). Nevertheless, revenge often seems to be contrary to self-interest: "Who sees not that vengeance, from the force alone of passion, may be so eagerly pursued as to make us knowingly neglect every consideration of ease, interest, or safety?" (Hume 1751, Appendix II).

Work norms. The workplace is a hotbed for norm-guided action. There is a social norm against living off other people and a corresponding normative pressure to earn one's income from work (Elster 1988). At the workplace one often finds informal norms among the workers that regulate their work effort. Typically, these set lower as well as upper limits on what is perceived as a proper effort: neither a chiseler nor a ratebuster be (Roethlisberger and Dickson 1939, 522). Akerlof (1980) argues that employed workers have a "code of honor" that forbids them to train new workers who are hired to do the same job for lower wages.[2]

Norms of cooperation. There are many outcome-oriented maxims of cooperation. A utilitarian, for instance, would cooperate if and only if his contribution increases the average utility of the members in the group. There are also, however, non–outcome-oriented norms of cooperation. One is what one may call "everyday Kantianism:" cooperate if and only if it would be better for all if all cooperated than if nobody did. Another is a "norm of fairness": cooperate if and only if most other people cooperate. Among the phenomena based on norms of cooperation one may cite voting (Barry 1979) and tax compliance (Laurin 1986).

Norms of distribution regulate what is seen as a fair allocation of income or other goods. In democratic societies, the norm of equality is especially strong. As Tocqueville (1969, 505) wrote: "the passion for equality seeps into every corner of the human heart, expands and fills the whole. It is no use telling them that by this blind surrender to an exclusive passion they are compromising their dearest interests; they are deaf." People may be willing to take a loss rather than accept a distribution they find unfair (Kahneman, Knetsch, and Thaler 1986). The solution concept for cooperative bargaining proposed by Kalai and Smorodinsky (1975) embodies a norm of fair distribution (McDonald and Solow 1981, 905-906).

Drawing on these examples, I shall consider a number of arguments that have been made to the effect that social norms are "nothing but" instruments of individual, collective or genetic optimization. First, however, I want to make two brief remarks.

To accept social norms as a motivational mechanism is not to violate methodological individualism. True, many sociologists who have stressed the importance of social norms have also advocated methodological holism (e.g. Durkheim 1958), but there is no logical connection between these views. Social norms, as I understand them here, are emotional and behavioral propensities of individuals.

To accept social norms as a motivational mechanism is not to deny the importance of rational choice. One eclectic view is that some actions are rational, others are norm-guided. A more general and more adequate formulation would be that actions typically are influenced both by rationality and by norms. Sometimes, the outcome is a compromise between what the norm prescribes and what rationality dictates. The subjects in the experiment of Kahneman, Knetsch and Thaler (1986) who rejected very unfair distributions, preferring to take nothing rather than to be exploited by others, did accept mildly skewed distributions. At other times, rationality acts as a constraint on social norms. Many people vote out of civic duty, except when the costs become very high. Conversely, social norms can act as a constraint on rationality. Cutthroat competitiveness in the market can go together with strict adherence to norms of honesty (Coleman 1982).

Are Norms Rationalizations of Self-Interest?

Is it true, as argued by early generations of anthropologists and sociologists, that norms are in the saddle and people merely their supports? Or is it true, as argued by more recent generations, that rules and norms are just the raw material for strategic manipulation or, perhaps, for unconscious rationalization?

Sometimes, people will invoke a social norm to rationalize self-interest. Suppose my wife and I are having a dinner party for eight, and that four persons have already been invited. We discuss whether to invite a particular couple for the last two places, and find ourselves in disagreement, for somewhat murky reasons. I like the woman of the couple, and my wife doesn't like it that I like her.

But we don't want to state these reasons. (Perhaps there is a social norm against doing so.) Instead we appeal to social norms. I invoke the norm of reciprocity, saying, "Since they had us over for dinner, it is our turn to invite them now." My wife invokes another norm: "Since we have already invited two single men, we must invite two women, to create a balance."

In wage negotiations, sheer bargaining power counts for much. Appeals to accepted social norms can also have some efficacy, however. There is a norm of fair division of the surplus between capital and labor. Employers will appeal to this norm when the firm does badly, workers when it does well. There is a norm of equal pay for equal work. Workers will appeal to this norm when they earn less than workers in similar firms, but not when they earn more. The norm of preservation of status, or wage differences, can also be exploited for bargaining purposes.

Social psychologists have studied norms of distribution to see whether there is any correlation between who subscribes to a norm and who benefits from it. Some findings point to the existence of a "norm of modesty:" high achievers prefer the norm of absolute equality of rewards, whereas low achievers prefer the norm of equity, or reward proportionally to achievement (Mikula 1972; Kahn, Lamm and Nelson 1977; Yaari and Bar-Hillel 1988). More robust, however, are the findings which suggest that people prefer the distributive norms which favor them (Deutsch 1985, Ch. 11; Messick and Sentis 1983). This corresponds to a pattern frequently observed in wage discussions. Low-income groups invoke a norm of equality, whereas high-income groups advocate pay according to productivity.

Conditional norms lend themselves easily to manipulation. There is, for instance, a general norm that whoever first proposes that something be done has a special responsibility for making sure that it is carried out. This can prevent the proposal from ever being made, even if all would benefit from it. A couple may share the desire to have a child and yet neither may want to be the first to lance the idea, fearing that he or she would then get special child-caring responsibility.[3] The member of a seminar who suggests a possible topic for discussion is often saddled with the task of introducing it. The person in a courtship who first proposes a date is at a disadvantage (Waller 1937). The fine art of inducing others to make the first move, and of resisting such inducements, provides instances of instrumentally rational exploitation of a social norm.

Some have said that this is all there is to norms: they are tools of manipulation, used to dress up self-interest in more acceptable garb. But this cannot be true. Some norms, like the norm of vengeance, obviously override self-interest. In fact, the cynical view of norms is self-defeating. "Unless rules were considered important and were taken seriously and followed, it would make no sense to manipulate them for personal benefit. If many people did not believe that rules were legitimate and compelling, how could anyone use these rules for personal advantage?" (Edgerton 1985, 3). Or again, "if the justice arguments are such transparent frauds, why are they advanced in the first place and why are they given serious attention?" (Zajac 1985, 120). If some people successfully exploit norms for self-interested purposes, it can only be because others are willing to let norms take precedence over self-interest. Moreover, even those who appeal to the norm usually believe in it, or else the appeal might not have much power (Veyne 1976).

The would-be manipulator of norms is also constrained by the need—in fact, the social norm—to be consistent. Even if the norm has no grip on his mind, he must act as if it had. Having invoked the norm of reciprocity on one occasion, I cannot just dismiss it when my wife appeals to it another time. An employer may successfully appeal to the workers and get them to share the burdens in a bad year. The cost he pays is that in a good year he may also have to share the benefits. By making the earlier appeal, he committed himself to the norm of a fair division of the surplus (Mitchell 1986, 69). The Swedish metal workers in the 1930s successfully invoked a norm of equality to bring about parity of wages with workers in the construction industry. Later, when they found themselves in a stronger bargaining position, their previous appeal to equality forced them to pull their punches (Swenson 1989, 60). Finally, the manipulator is constrained by the fact that the repertoire of norms on which he can draw is, after all, limited. Even if unconstrained by earlier appeals to norms, there may not be any norm available that coincides neatly with his self-interest.

When I say that manipulation of social norms presupposes that they have some kind of grip on the mind since otherwise there would be nothing to manipulate, I am not suggesting that society is made up of two sorts of people: those who believe in the norms and those who manipulate the believers. Rather, I believe that most norms are shared by most people—manipulators as well as manipulated. Rather than manipulation in a direct sense, we are dealing here with an amalgam of belief, deception and self-deception. At any given time we believe in many different norms, which may have contradictory implications for the situation at hand. A norm that happens to coincide with narrowly defined self-interest easily acquires special salience. If there is no norm handy to rationalize self-interest, or if I have invoked a different norm in the recent past, or if there is another norm which overrides it, I may have to act against my past self-interest. My self-image as someone who is bound by the norms of society does not allow me to pick and choose indiscriminately from the large menu of norms to justify my actions, since I have to justify them to myself no less than to others. At the very least, norms are soft constraints on action. The existence of norms of revenge shows that sometimes they are much more than that.

Are Norms Followed Out of Self-Interest?

When people obey norms, they often have a particular outcome in mind: they want to avoid the disapproval—ranging from raised eyebrows to social ostracism—of other people. Suppose I face the choice between taking revenge for the murder of my cousin and not doing anything. The cost of revenge is that I might in turn be the target of a counter-vengeance. At worst, the cost of not doing anything is that my family and friends desert me, leaving me out on my own, defenselessly exposed to predators. At best, I will lose their esteem and my ability to act as an autonomous agent among them. A cost-benefit analysis is likely to tell me that revenge (or exile) is the rational choice. More generally, norm-guided behavior is supported by the threat of social sanctions that make it rational to obey the norms. Akerlof (1976) argues, along these lines, that in India it is rational to adhere to the caste system, even assuming that "tastes" are neutral.

In response to this argument, we can first observe that norms do not need external sanctions to be effective. When norms are internalized, they are followed even when violation would be unobserved and not exposed to sanctions. Shame or anticipation of it is a sufficient internal sanction. I don't pick my nose when I can be observed by people on a train passing by, even if I am confident that they are all perfect strangers whom I shall never see again and who have no power to impose sanctions on me. I don't throw litter in the park, even when there is nobody around to observe me. If punishment was merely the price tag attached to crime, nobody would feel shame when caught. People have an internal gyroscope that keeps them adhering steadily to norms, independently of the current reactions of others.

A second answer to the claim that people obey norms because of the sanctions attached to violations of norms emerges if we ask why people would sanction others for violating norms. What's in it for them? One reply could be that if they do not express their disapproval of the violation, they will themselves be the target of disapproval by third parties. When there is a norm to do X, there is usually a "meta-norm" (Axelrod 1986) to sanction people who fail to do X, perhaps even a norm to sanction people who fail to sanction people who fail to do X. As long as the cost of expressing disapproval is less than the cost of receiving disapproval for not expressing it, it is in one's rational self-interest to express it. Now, expressing disapproval is always costly, whatever the target behavior. At the very least it requires energy and attention that might have been used for other purposes. One may alienate or provoke the target individual, at some cost or risk to oneself. Opportunities for mutually beneficial transactions are lost when one is forbidden to deal with an ostracized person. By contrast, when one moves upwards in the chain of actions, beginning with the original violation, the cost of receiving disapproval falls rapidly to zero. People do not usually frown upon others when they fail to sanction people who fail to sanction people who fail to sanction people who fail to sanction a norm violation.[4] Consequently, some sanctions must be performed for other motives than the fear of being sanctioned.

Do Norms Exist to Promote Self-Interest?

I believe that for many economists an instinctive reaction to the claim that people are motivated by irrational norms would be that on closer inspection the norms will turn out to be disguised, ultrasubtle expressions or vehicles of self-interest. Gary Becker (1976, 5, 14) argues, for example, that the "combined assumptions of maximizing behavior, market equilibrium and stable preferences, used relentlessly and unflinchingly . . . provides a valuable unified framework for understanding all human behavior." This view suggests that norms exist because they promote self-interest, over and above the avoidance of sanctions.

Some social norms can be individually useful, such as the norm against drinking or overeating. Moreover, people who have imposed private norms on their own behavior may join each other for mutual sanctioning, each in effect asking the other to punish him if he deviates, while being prepared to punish them if they do not punish him. Alcoholics Anonymous provide the best-known example (Kurtz 1979, 215): "Each recovering alcoholic member of Alcoholics Anonymous is kept constantly aware, at every meeting, that he has *both* something to give *and* something to receive from his fellow alcoholics." Most norms, however, are not social contracts of this kind.

It might also be argued that social norms are individually useful in that they help people to economize on decision costs. A simple mechanical decision rule may, on the whole and in the long run, have better consequences for the individual than fine-tuned search for the optimal decision. This argument, however, confuses social norms and habits. Habits certainly are useful in the respect just mentioned, but they are not enforced by other people, nor does their violation give rise to feelings of guilt or anxiety.

A further argument for the view that it is individually rational to follow norms is that they lend credibility to threats that otherwise would not be believable. They help, as it were, to solve the problem of time inconsistency. Vendettas are not guided by the prospect of future gain but triggered by an earlier offense. Although the propensity to take revenge is not guided by consequences, it can have good consequences. If other people believe that I invariably take revenge for an offense, even at great risk to myself, they will take care not to offend me. If they believe that I will react to offense only when it is in my interest to react, they need not be as careful. From the rational point of view, a threat is not credible unless it will be in the interest of the threatener to carry it out when the time comes. The threat to kill oneself, for instance, is not rationally credible. Threats backed by a code of honor are very effective, since they will be executed even if it is in the interest of the threatener not to do so.

This observation, while true, does not amount to an explanation of the norm of vengeance. When a person guided by a code of honor has a quarrel with one who is exclusively motivated by rational considerations, the first will often have his way. But in a quarrel between two persons guided by the code, both may do worse than if they had agreed to let the legal system resolve their conflict. (Mafiosi seem to do better for themselves in the United States than in Sicily.) Since we are talking about codes of honor that are shared social norms, the latter case is the typical one. The rationality of following the code then reduces to the desire to avoid sanctions, discussed above.

In any case, one cannot rationally decide to behave irrationally, even when one knows it would be in one's interest to do so. To paraphrase Max Weber, a social norm is not like a taxi from which one can disembark at will. Followers of a social norm abide by it even when it is not in their interest to do so. In a given situation, following the norm may be useful, but that is not to say that it is always useful to follow it. Moreover, there is no presumption that its occasional usefulness can explain why it exists.

The distinction between the usefulness of norms and their rationality can also be brought out by considering Akerlof's explanation of why workers refuse to train new workers who are hired at lower wages. In an analysis of wage rigidity, Assar Lindbeck and Dennis Snower (1986) argue that the explanation is to be sought in the self-interest of the employed workers. By keeping potential entrants out, they can capture a greater deal of the benefits of monopoly power. The weapons at their disposal for keeping the unemployed at bay include the following:

> First, by being unfriendly and uncooperative to the entrants, the insiders are able to make the entrants' work more unpleasant than it otherwise would have been and thereby raise the wage at which the latter are willing to work. In practice, outsiders are commonly wary of underbidding the insiders. This behavior pattern is often given an *ad hoc* sociological explanation: "social mores" keep outsiders from "stealing" the jobs from their employed comrades. Our line of argument, however, suggests that these mores may be traced to the entrants' anticipation of hostile insider reaction and that this reaction may follow from optimisation behavior of insiders. Second, insiders are usually responsible for training the entrants and thereby influence their productivity. Thus insiders may be able to raise their wage demands by threatening to conduct the firm's training programs inefficiently or even to disrupt them. . . . In sum, to raise his wage, an insider may find it worthwhile to threaten to become a thoroughly disagreeable creature.

The insider may, to be sure, make this threat, *but is it credible?* If an outsider is hired, would it then still be in the insider's interest to be unfriendly and uncooperative? Since Lindbeck and Snower (1988, 171) believe that "harassment activities are disagreeable to the harassers," they ought also to assume that outsiders will recognize this fact and, in consequence, will not be deterred by fear of harassment. I believe Akerlof is right in arguing that it takes something like a social norm to sustain this behavior. While useful, the ostracism is not rational.

Do Norms Exist to Promote Common Interests?

Among economists, those who do not subscribe to the individual rationality of norms will mostly argue for their collective rationality, claiming that social norms have collectively good consequences for those who live by them and that, moreover, these consequences explain why the norms exist. Most writers on the topic probably use the term "socially useful" to mean that a society with the norm is at least as good for almost everybody and substantially better for many than a society in which the norm is lacking, perhaps with an implied clause that no other norm could bring further Pareto-improvements.

Among those who have argued for the collective optimality of norms, Kenneth Arrow (1971, 22) is perhaps the most articulate and explicit:

> It is a mistake to limit collective action to state action. . . . I want to [call] attention to a less visible form of social action: norms of social behavior,

including ethical and moral codes. I suggest as one possible interpretation that they are reactions of society to compensate for market failure. It is useful for individuals to have some trust in each other's word. In the absence of trust, it would become very costly to arrange for alternative sanctions and guarantees, and many opportunities for mutually beneficial cooperation would have to be foregone. Banfield has argued that the lack of trust is indeed one of the causes of economic underdevelopment.

It is difficult to conceive of buying trust in any direct way (though it can happen indirectly, e.g. a trusted employee will be paid more as being more valuable); indeed, there seems to be some inconsistency in the very concept. Non-market action might take the form of a mutual agreement. But the arrangement of these agreements and especially their continued extension to new individuals entering the social fabric can be costly. As an alternative, society may proceed by internalization of these norms to the achievement of the desired agreement on an unconscious level.

There is a whole set of customs and norms which might be similarly interpreted as agreements to improve the efficiency of the economic system (in the broad sense of satisfaction of individual values) by providing commodities to which the price system is inapplicable.[5]

I shall adduce three arguments against this view. First, not all norms are Pareto-improvements. Some norms make everybody *worse* off, or, at the very least, they do not make almost everybody better off. Secondly, some norms that would make everybody better off are not in fact observed. Thirdly, even if a norm does make everybody better off, this does not explain why it exists, unless we are also shown the feedback mechanism that specifies how the good consequences of the norm contribute to its maintenance.

To support the first argument I shall consider a number of norms that do not appear to be socially useful in the sense defined. The social sciences being what they are, no conclusive proof can be given, but I hope the overall impact of the counterexamples will be persuasive.

Consumption norms do not appear to have any useful consequences. If anything, norms of etiquette seem to make everybody worse off, by requiring wasteful investments in pointless behaviors. Let me, nevertheless, mention three possible arguments for the social usefulness of these norms, together with corresponding objections.

First, there is the argument that norms of etiquette serve the useful function of confirming one's identity or membership in a social group. Since the notion of social identity is elusive, the argument is hard to evaluate, but one weakness is that it does not explain why these rules are as complicated as they often are. To signal or confirm one's membership in a group one sign should be sufficient, like wearing a badge or a tie. Instead, there is often vast redundancy. The manner of speaking of an Oxford-educated person differs from standard English in many more ways than what is required to single him out as an Oxford graduate.

Secondly, there is the argument that the complexity of the rules serves an additional function, that of keeping outsiders out and upstarts down (Bourdieu

1979). It is easy to imitate one particular behavior, but hard to learn a thousand subtly different rules. But that argument flounders on the fact that working-class life is no less norm-regulated than that of the upper classes. Whereas many middle-class persons would like to pass themselves off as members of the upper class, few try to pass themselves off as workers.

Thirdly, one might combine the first and the second position, and argue that norms simultaneously serve functions of inclusion and exclusion. Evans-Pritchard's (1940, 120) classical argument about the Nuer can help us here. "A man of one tribe sees the people of another tribe as an undifferentiated group to whom he has an undifferentiated pattern of behavior, while he sees himself as a member of a segment of his own group." Fine-tuned distinction and gamesmanship within a group is consistent with "negative solidarity" towards outsiders. This view is more plausible, but it does not really point to social benefits of norm following. It is not clear why the working-class as a whole would benefit from the fact that it contains an infinite variety of local subcultures, all of them recognizably working-class and yet subtly different from each other in ways that only insiders can understand. Nor is it clear that the local varieties provide collective benefits to members of the subculture. One might say, perhaps, that norms are useful in limiting the number of potential interaction partners to a small and manageable subset, thus making for greater focus and consistency in social life. A community of norms would then be a bit like a conventional equilibrium, since it is important that one's partners limit *their* partners by the same device. This explanation, however, fails to account for the emotional tonality of norms and for their capacity to induce self-destructive behavior.

Consider, as a second example, the social norms against behavior "contrary to nature." Some of these norms like those against cannibalism and incest, are good candidates for collectively beneficial norms. Everybody benefits from a norm that forces people to look elsewhere than to other people for food.[6] Norms against incest may well be optimal from a number of perspectives: individual, collective or genetic. Norms against sodomy, by contrast, involve only harmful restrictions of freedom and no benefits. They make everybody worse off. Norms against homosexuality might also, under conditions of overpopulation, make everybody worse off.

Many social norms against various uses of money do not appear to be collectively rational either. Consider the norm against walking up to a person in a bus queue and asking to buy his place. Nobody would be harmed by this action. Other people in the queue would not lose their place. The person asked to sell his place is free to refuse. If the forbidden practice were allowed, some would certainly gain: the norm does not create a Pareto-improvement. Yet I cannot assert that it makes everybody worse off, since some individuals could lose from its abolition. That question can only be answered in a general-equilibrium model which, to my knowledge, does not exist.

The norm that prevents us from accepting or making offers to mow other people's lawn for money seems more promising. Consider a suburban community where all houses have small lawns of the same size.[7] Suppose a houseowner is willing to pay his neighbor's son ten dollars to mow his lawn, but not more. He would rather spend half an hour mowing the lawn himself than pay eleven dollars to have someone else do it. Imagine now that the same person is offered twenty dollars to mow the lawn of another neighbor. It is easy to imagine that he would refuse, probably with some indignation. But why is mowing one lawn worth $10 or less, while mowing an identical lawn is worth $20 or more?

Thaler (1980) has suggested, as one possible explanation, that people evaluate losses and gains foregone differently. (Credit card companies exploit this difference when they insist that stores advertise cash discounts rather than credit card surcharges.) The houseowner is more affected by the out-of-pocket expenses that he would incur by paying someone to mow his lawn, than by the loss of a windfall income. But this cannot be the full story, because it does not explain why the houseowner should be indignant at the proposal. Part of the explanation must be that he doesn't think of himself as the kind of person who mows other people's lawns for money. It *isn't done,* to use a revealing phrase that often accompanies social norms.

One may argue that the norm serves an ulterior purpose. Social relations among neighbors would be disturbed if wealth differences were too blatantly displayed, and if some treated others as salaried employees. An unintended consequence of many monetary deals among neighbors could be the loss of the spontaneous self-help behavior that is a main benefit from living in a community. By preventing deals, the norm preserves the community.

The norm could also have a more disreputable aspect, however. The norm against flaunting one's wealth may just be a special case of a higher-order norm: *Don't stick your neck out.* "Don't think you are better than us, and above all don't behave in ways that make us think that you think you are better than us" (Sandemose 1936). This norm, which prevails in many small communities, can have very bad consequences. It can discourage the gifted from using their talents, and may lead to their being branded as witches if nevertheless they go ahead and use them (Thomas 1973, 643-644). By preserving the community, the norm stifles progress.

It is plausible that norms of reciprocity do, on the whole, have good consequences. Even in this case, however, there are counterexamples, since these norms can become the object of strategic manipulation. An extreme example of such ambiguous altruism is found in Colin Turnbull's (1972, 8) description of gift and sacrifice in this society among the miserable Ik of Uganda:

> These are not expressions of the foolish belief that altruism is both possible and desirable: they are weapons, sharp and aggressive, which can be put to divers uses. But the purpose for which the gift is designed can be thwarted by the non-acceptance of it, and much Icien ingenuity goes into thwarting the would-be thwarter. The object, of course, is to build up a whole series of obligations so that in times of crisis you have a number of debts you can recall, and with luck one of them may be repaid. To this end, in the circumstances of Ik life, considerable sacrifice would be justified, to the very limits of the minimal survival level. But a sacrifice that

can be rejected is useless, and so you have the odd phenomenon of these otherwise singularly self-interested people going out of their way to "help" each other. In point of fact they are helping themselves and their help may very well be resented in the extreme, but it is done in such a way that it cannot be refused, for it has already been given. Someone, quite unasked, may hoe another's field in his absence, or rebuild his stockade, or join in the building of a house that could easily be done by the man and his wife alone. At one time I have seen so many men thatching a roof that the whole roof was in serious danger of collapsing, and the protests of the owner were of no avail. The work done was a debt incurred. It was another good reason for being wary of one's neighbors. Lokeléa always made himself unpopular by accepting such help and by paying for it on the spot with food (which the cunning old fox knew they could not resist), which immediately negated the debt.[8]

Similarly, I may try to benefit from the conditional norm that if I give something to a friend for Christmas, he has an obligation to reciprocate. Suppose the friend is wealthy, and that there is a norm that wealthier people should give more in absolute terms (although allowed to give less in relative terms). I can then exploit the situation to my advantage by making the initial gift.

Norms of retribution are often said to serve the social function of resolving conflicts and reducing the level of violence below what it would otherwise have been. There will be fewer quarrels in societies regulated by codes of honor, since everybody knows that they can have disastrous consequences (Boehm 1984, 88). But it is not clear that this is a good thing. One could probably get rid of almost all criminal behavior if all crimes carried the death penalty, but the costs of creating this terror regime would be prohibitive. Also, it is not clear that there is less violence in a vendetta-ridden society than in an unregulated state of nature. In the state of nature, people are supposed to be rational. Hence there would be less violence because people would not harm others just to get even. Also, codes of honor generate quarrels, because honor is attained by brinksmanship and demonstrated willingness to run the risk of initiating a feud (146). On the other hand, the state of nature could be even more violent, since people need not fear that others might retaliate just to get even. The net effect is anybody's guess, since the state of nature is not really a well-defined notion.

Consider next Akerlof's analysis of the norm against two-tiered wage systems. This norm does not seem to benefit the employed workers, while harming both employers and the unemployed who have a common interest in such systems. If the employed workers have good reasons to think that the new workers would drive their wages down, the code of honor makes good collective sense, at least with respect to the short-run interests of the local group of workers. Society as a whole might, however, suffer because of the unemployment generated by the practice. In that case, codes of honor would embody solutions to local collective action problems while also creating a higher-order problem.

Somewhat similar arguments apply to the norm against rate-busting. It has been argued that this norm is due to sheer conformism (Jones 1984) or to envy

(Schoeck 1987, 31, 310). The obvious alternative explanation is that the norm is a collectively optimal response to the constant pressure of management to change piece-rates. Workers often express the view that any increase in effort will induce management to reduce rates. It remains to be shown, however, that this argument is more than rationalization of envy. In the words of one notorious rate-buster: "There are three classes of men: (1) Those who can and will; (2) those who can't and are envious; (3) those who can and won't—they're nuts!" (Dalton 1948, 74). The third category, presumably, are moved by solidarity and norms of justice.

The question cannot be treated separately from the behavior of management. On the one hand, management has a clear incentive to make it clear that they will never cut rates as a result of increased efforts. "Changes in piece rates at the Western Electric Company...are not based upon the earnings of the worker. The company's policy is that piece rates will not be changed unless there is a change in the manufacturing process" (Roethlisberger and Dikson 1939, 534).

On the other hand, how can management make this promise credible? They cannot commit themselves to never introducing new methods of production, nor easily prove that a new method is not just a subterfuge for changing rates. A knowledgeable engineer wrote, "I was visiting the Western Electric Company, which had a reputation of never cutting a piece rate. It never did; if some manufacturing process was found to pay more than seemed right for the class of labor employed on it—if, in other words, the rate-setters had misjudged—that particular part was referred to the engineers for redesign, and then a new rate was set for the new part" (Mills 1946, 9, cited after Roy 1952). Knowing that management has the capability of taking actions of this kind, workers have good reasons to be skeptical.

Three conclusions emerge. First, both management and workers would benefit if a way was found to distinguish "good" from "bad" changes in the piece rates. Second, the worker collective as a whole may well benefit from the norm against rate-busting, given that management cannot credibly commit itself to maintain rates. Third, however, the norm may work against the interest of society as a whole, including the working-class as a whole, if the loss of productivity caused by the norm is sufficiently serious.[9] Even granting that the norm represents the successful solution of a collective action problem within the enterprise, it might create a new problem among enterprises.

At the very least, I believe these examples demonstrate that the social usefulness of social norms cannot be taken for granted. In fact, I think I have shown more than that. Even though each of my claims about non-optimality could be contested and the facts be represented and explained in different ways, I believe that the cumulative impact of the claims is very difficult to refute.

A second strategy for attacking the claim that social norms spring from collective rationality is to imagine some socially useful norms that do not, in fact, exist. If public transportation was widely chosen over private driving, the roads would be less congested and everyone would spend so much less time commuting that the loss of comfort would be offset. Yet there is no social norm to use public transportation in crowded cities. In many developing countries private insurance motives create an incentive to have large families, although the aggregate effect is overpopulation and pressure on resources. Yet there is no social norm against having many children. Japan has apparently imposed the norm "Buy Japanese," but other countries have been less successful. The small Italian village described by Edward Banfield (1958) would certainly have benefited from a social norm against corruption. Instead it had what appears to have been a norm against public-spirited behavior. Nobody would frequent a person stupid enough not to violate the law when he would get away with it. Criminals could benefit from a minimum of solidarity among themselves. A book about the Brooklyn wiseguys suggests, however, that as soon as you're in trouble, you're forgotten: there is no honesty among thieves (Pileggi 1986). The reader is encouraged to think of other examples.

A third strategy is to criticize the explanatory impact of the collective benefits of social norms. In the absence of a mechanism linking the benefits to the emergence or perpetuation of the norm we cannot know if they obtain by accident. Social scientists should be suspicious of theories of society that deny the possibility of accidental benefits. Moreover, and perhaps more importantly, the beneficial or optimal nature of the norm is often controversial. It is only a slight exaggeration to say that any economist worth his salt could tell a story—produce a model, that is, resting on various simplifying assumptions—which provides the individual or collective benefits derived from the norms. The very ease with which such "just-so stories" can be told suggests that we should be skeptical about them. We would be much more confident about the benefits if a mechanism could be demonstrated.

There are not many plausible candidates for a feedback mechanism. Individual reinforcement could not work here, since the benefits are collective rather than individual. Chance variation and social selection might seem a better alternative.[10]

On this account, social norms arise by accident. Societies which happen to have more useful norms thrive, flourish and expand; those which do not disappear or imitate the norms of their more successful competitors. Whether the successful societies proceed by military conquest or economic competition, the end result is the same. The argument is popular, but weak. The norms of the strong are not as a rule taken over by the weak, nor do the weak always disappear in competition with the strong. Greece was conquered by Rome, but Rome assimilated more Greek norms than the other way around. When China was conquered by the barbarians, the latter ended up assimilating and defending the culture they had conquered. Today, few developing countries are taking over the norms and work habits that were a precondition for Western economic growth, nor is there any sign of these countries going out of existence.

These arguments do not add up to a strong claim that the social usefulness of norms is irrelevant for their explanation. I find it as hard as the next man to believe that the existence of norms of reciprocity and cooperation has *nothing* to do with the fact that without them civilization as we know it would not exist. Yet it is at least a useful intellectual exercise to take the more austere view, and to entertain the idea that civilization owes its existence to a fortunate coincidence. On this view, social norms spring from psychological propensities and dispositions that, taken separately, cannot be presumed to be useful, yet happen to interact in such a way that useful effects are produced.

Do Norms Exist to Promote Genetic Fitness?

The final argument against the autonomy of norms is that they owe their existence to their contribution to genetic fitness. I do not know of explicit statements of this view. Several writers have, however, taken this position on the closely related issue of the emotions of guilt and shame that sustain norm-guided behavior (Trivers 1971; Hirschleifer 1987; Frank 1988). Chagnon (1988) argues that revenge can be explained as fitness-maximizing behavior, but he does not explicitly consider norms of revenge. I know too little about evolutionary biology to evaluate these claims. I would like, nevertheless, to record my skepticism and make a few general remarks, largely inspired by Kitcher (1985).

Evolutionary explanations do not take the narrow form "Feature X exists because it maximizes the genetic fitness of the organism." Rather, their general form is "X exists because it is part of a package solution that at some time maximized the genetic fitness of the organism." The latter form allows for two facts that the former excludes. First, there is the omnipresent phenomenon of *pleitropy*. A tendency to conform to a social norm might detract from genetic fitness and yet be retained by natural selection if it is the by-product of a gene whose main product is highly beneficial. Secondly, the general form allows for time lags. A social norm may be maladaptive today and yet have been adaptive at the stage in history when the human genome evolved and, for practical purposes, was fixed.

When I said that norms might owe their existence to "psychological propensities and dispositions," a natural reply would be to say that these in turn must be explicable in terms of genetic fitness. Let me concede the point, provided that the explanation is allowed to take this general form. Advocates of evolutionary explanations, however, usually have the narrower form in mind. I am not saying that in doing so they are always wrong, only that they cannot take it for granted that an explanation of the narrow form always exists. What is true, is that a plausible story of the narrow form can almost always be told. Again, however, the very ease with which just-so stories are forthcoming should make us wary of them.

Let me summarize the discussion in a diagram:

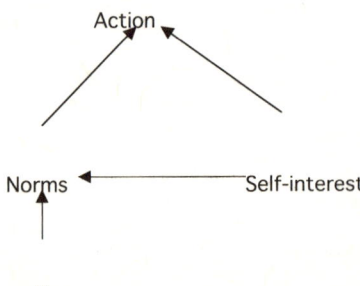

I believe that both norms and self-interest enter into the proximate explanations of action. To some extent, the selection of the norm to which one subscribes can also be explained by self-interest. Even if the belief in the norm is sincere, the choice of one norm among the many that could be relevant may be an unconscious act dictated by self-interest. Or one might follow the norm out of fear of the sanctions that would be triggered by violation. But I do not believe that self-interest provides the full explanation for adherence to norms. There must be some further explanation, X, of why norms exist. I have discussed various candidates for X and found them wanting. I have no positive account of my own to offer. In particular, I have no suggestion as to how norms emerge and disappear. I suggest, however, that a good research strategy might be to investigate the role of emotions in maintaining social norms. Also, the often-ignored phenomena of envy and honor might repay further study. Finally, the psychological theory of conformism should be brought to bear on the subject.

References

Abreu, D. 1988. On the theory of informally repeated games with discounting. *Econometrics* 56: 383-396.
Ainslie, G. 1982. A behavioral economic approach to the defense mechanisms: Freud's energy theory revisited. *Social Science Information* 21: 735-779.
———. 1984. Behavioral economics II: Motivated involuntary behavior. *Social Sciences Information* 23: 247-274.
———. 1986. Beyond microeconomics. In *The multiple self*, edited by J. Elster. Cambridge: Cambridge University Press.
Akerlof, G. 1976. The economics of caste and of the rat race and other woeful tales. *Quarterly Journal of Economics* 90: 599-617.
———. 1980. A theory of social custom, of which unemployment may be one consequence. *Quarterly Journal of Economics* 94: 749-775.
Arrow, K. 1971. Political and economic evaluation of social effects and externalities. In *Frontiers of qualitative economics*, edited by M. Intriligator. Amsterdam: North-Holland.
Axelrod, R. 1986. An evolutionary approach to norms. *American Political Science Review* 80: 1095-1111.
Banfield, E. G. 1958. *The moral basis of a backward society*. New York: Free Press.
Barry, B. 1979. *Sociologists, Economists and Democracy*, 2d ed. Chicago: University of Chicago Press.
Becker, G. 1976. *The economic approach to human behavior*. Chicago: University of Chicago Press.
Boehm, C. 1984. *Blood revenge: The anthropology of feuding in Montenegro and other tribal societies*. University of Kansas Press.
Bourdieu, P. 1979. *La Distinction*. Paris: Editions de Minuit.
Chagnon, N. 1988. Life histories, blood revenge, and warfare in a tribal population. *Science:* 23-9, 985-92.
Coleman, J. S. 1982. Systems of trust. *Angewandte Sozialforschung* 10: 277-300.
Dalton, M. 1948. The industrial "rate-buster:" A characterization. *Applied Anthropology* (Winter): 5-18.
Deutsch, M. 1985. *Distributive justice*. New Haven, CT: Yale University Press.
Djilas, M. 1958. *Land without justice*. London: Methuen.
Durkheim, E. 1958. *The rules of sociological method*. Glencoe, IL.: Free Press.
Edgerton, R. 1985. *Rules, exceptions and the social order*. Berkeley: University of California Press.
Elster, J. 1988. Is there (or should there be) a right to work? In *Democracy and the welfare state*, edited by A. Guttman. Princeton, NJ: Princeton University Press.
———. 1989. *The cement of society*. Cambridge: Cambridge University Press.
Engel, H. 1986. *A city called July*. New York: Penguin Books.
Evans-Pritchard, E. 1940. *The Nuer*. Oxford: Oxford University Press.
Faia, M. A. 1986. *Dynamic functionalism*. Cambridge: Cambridge University Press.
Fenichel, O. 1945. *The psychoanalytic theory of neurosis*. New York: Norton.
Frank, R. K. 1988. *Passions within reason*. New York: Norton.

Gambetta, D.1987. *Did they jump or were they pushed?* Cambridge: Cambridge University Press.
Gouldner, A. 1960. The norm of reciprocity. *American Sociological Review* 25: 161-178.
Hasluck, M. 1954. *The unwritten law in Albania.* Cambridge: Cambridge University Press.
Hirschleifer, J. 1987. On the emotions as guarantors of threats and promises. In *The latest on the best,* edited by J. Dupre. Cambridge, MA: MIT Press.
Hume, D. 1751. *An enquiry concerning the principles of morals.*
Jones, S. F. 1984. *The economics of conformism.* Oxford: Blackwell.
Kahn, A., H. Lamm, and R. Nelson. 1977. Preferences for an equal or equitable allocator. *Journal of Personality and Social Psychology* 35: 837-844.
Kahneman, D., J. Knetsch, and R. Thaler. 1986. Fairness and the assumptions of economics. *Journal of Business* 59: 5285-5300.
Kitcher, P. 1985. *Vaulting ambition.* Cambridge, MA: MIT Press.
Kurtz, E., 1979. *Not-God: A history of Alcoholics Anonymous.* Center City, MN: Hazelden Educational Services.
Laurin, U. 1986. *Pa heder och samvette.* Stockholm: Norstedts.
Lindbeck, A., and D. J. Snower. 1986. Wage rigidity, union activity and unemployment. In *Wage rigidity and unemployment,* edited by W. Beckerman. London: Duckworth.
———. 1988. Cooperation, harassment and involuntary unemployment. *American Economic Review.* 78: 167-188.
McDonald, I. M., and R. Solow. 1981. Wage bargaining and employment. *American Economic Review* 71: 896-908.
Messick, D. M., and K. Sentis. 1983. Fairness, preference and fairness biases. In *Equity theory,* edited by D. M. Messick and K. Cook. New York: Praeger.
Mikula, G. 1972. Gewinnaufteilung in dyaden bei variiertem leistungsverhaltnis. *Zeitschrift für Sozialpsychologie* 3: 126-133.
Miller, W. forthcoming. *Bloodtaking and peacemaking: Society and the disputing process in medieval Iceland.* Chicago: University of Chicago Press.
Mills, J. 1946. *The engineer in society.* New York: Nostrand.
Mitchell, D. J. 1986. Explanations of wage inflexibility. In *Wage rigidity and unemployment,* edited by W. Beckerman. London: Duckworth.
Pileggi, N. 1986.*Wiseguy.* New York: Pocket Books.
Roethlisberger, F. J., and Dickson, A. 1939. *Management and the Worker.* Cambridge, MA: Harvard University Press.
Roy, D. 1952. Quota Restriction and Goldbricking in a Machine Shop. *American Journal of Sociology* 62: 427-442.
Sandemose, A. 1936. *A fugitive crosses his track.* New York: Knopf.
Schoeck, H. 1987. *Envy.* Indianapolis: Liberty Press.
Swenson, P. 1989. *Fair shares.* Ithaca, NY: Cornell University Press.
Thaler, R. 1980. Towards a positive theory of consumer behavior. *Journal of Economic Behavior and Organization* 1: 39-60.
Thomas, K. 1973. *Religion and the decline of magic.* Harmondsworth: Penguin.
Tocqueville, A. de. 1969. *Democracy in America.* New York: Anchor Books.
Trivers, R. E. 1971. The evolution of reciprocal altruism. *Quarterly Review of Biology* 46: 35-57.
Turnbull, C. 1972. *The mountain people.* New York: Simon and Schuster.
Tversky, A., and Kahneman, D. 1981. The psychology of choice and the framing of preferences. *Science* 211: 4353-4358.
Ulmann-Margalit, E. 1977. *The emergence of norms.* Oxford: Oxford University Press.
Veyne, P. 1976. *Le pain et le cirque.* Paris: Editions du Seuil.
Waller, W. 1937. The rating and dating complex. *American Sociological Review* 2: 727-734.
Yaari, M., and Bar-Hillel, M. 1988. Judgments of justice. Unpublished manuscript.
Zajac, E. P. 1985. Perceived economic justice: The example of public utility regulation. In *Cost allocation,* edited by H. P. Young. Amsterdam: North Holland.

CHAPTER 21

Socioeconomics and the New "Battle of Methods": Toward a Paradigm Shift?

Richard Swedberg

Originally published in
Journal of Behavioral Economics *19 (2), 1990*

READING INTRODUCTION

Swedberg traces the history of conflict between "economic man" analysis (largely neoclassical economics) and cultural analysis (largely in sociology) in the social sciences. He focuses particularly on two relatively recent developments: 1) the growing introduction of "economic man" analysis into other social sciences, particularly political science and sociology over the last three decades (a process he labels "economic imperialism"); and 2) Etzioni's (1988) renewed call for socioeconomics, that is, an orientation toward social science analysis recognizing not only egoistic material motives, but as well motivation arising from recognition of duties toward and/or love of others. Etizoni's objectives in this regard are similar to those we associated in the introduction of this section with Thompson, Ellis, and Wildavsky (1990) in that he sees rationality employed instrumentally to achieve a range of ends broader than those involving material self-interest.

READING TEXT

ABSTRACT: During the last ten or fifteen years the old separation between economics and other social sciences has increasingly been challenged by economists applying the neoclassical paradigm to problems that traditionally concern the other social sciences. The main thesis of this paper is that this so-called "economic imperialism" threatens to unleash a new paradigmatic struggle in the social sciences, which is likely to be just as destructive as the old *Methodenstreit*. It is in this situation that socioeconomics emerges as a viable alternative, since it emphasizes the need for a synthesis of the findings of several social science when an economic problem is analyzed. The article stresses the original battle of the methods at the turn of the [twentieth] century that gave birth to a set of ideas, analogous to those of Etzioni on socioeconomics, namely what Max Weber called *Sozialökonomik*. The emergence of "economic imperialism" is described, and the essay ends with a plea for a socioeconomics in the sense of a broad, overarching approach to economic analysis. Economic imperialism, it is concluded, threatens to close the door to new developments in economics; socioeconomics, on the other hand, tries to keep it open.

In order to understand what socioeconomics really is—in the version of Amitai Etzioni as well as in its earlier, less well-known Weberian version—one clearly has to look at the historical circumstances in which it has made its appearance. This is generally true for any complex of ideas, but in this case it is especially true. The reason for this is that socioeconomics is basically a response to something else, namely the narrow vision of mainstream economics. In his recent book on socioeconomics, *The Moral Dimension: Toward A New Economics,* Etzioni (1988) writes, "We are now in the middle of a paradigmatic struggle. Challenged is . . . the neoclassical paradigm which is applied not merely to the economy but also increasingly to the full array of social relations, from crime to the family."

What is at the center of this new "paradigmatic struggle" is in other words the relationship of economic analysis to other kinds of social analysis. This relationship can be divided into several, fairly distinct periods.

1. *The Time of Political Economy (late eighteenth century to late nineteenth century)*
During these years there was an easy mingling in the works of the economists of institutional analysis, philosophical reflections, and straightforward economic analysis. According to John Stuart Mill, "A person is not likely to be a good economist who is nothing else. Social phenomena acting and reacting on one another, they cannot rightly be understood apart" (Mill as cited in Marshall [1891]).

2. *The Methodenstreit or the First Paradigmatic Battle Between Economics and the Other Social Sciences (1880-1910)*
his is the period when the transition from "political economy" to "economics" is made. This entailed the radical separation of economics from history as well as from sociology; and it also led to the birth of economic history as a separate science. The motto of this period could well be, "A person is likely to be a good economist who is nothing else."

3. *Mutual Ignorance and Distortion in the Social Sciences (1920-1960)*
During these years modern economics come into its own. The nonexisting relationship between economics and the other social sciences, which had been proclaimed in the *Methodenstreit,* is now routinized. Interdisciplinary interest among economists is replaced by ignorance of the other social sciences. The noneconomic social scientists, in their turn, stay away from economics. All of this has a distorting influence on the social disciplines.

4. *Economic Imperialism and the Challenge of Redrawing the Boundaries in the Social Sciences (1970-)*
Today we are witnessing two tendencies in the mainstream economic community vis-à-vis the other social sciences. On the one hand economic analysis is turning even further inwards. But on the other hand, the economic approach is being used to analyze a host of topics, which by tradition only the other social

sciences have dealt with. This so-called "economic imperialism," which represents a radical attempt to redraw the boundaries in the social sciences, is today becoming increasingly accepted by mainstream economists, who at first were skeptical and hostile to it.

Now, what Etzioni calls "socioeconomics" belongs to the last of these periods and can be seen as both a response to the aggressive inroads of economic imperialism into the other social sciences and as a reaction to the incapacity of economics to include any kind of genuine social dimension in its analyses of economic phenomena. The rest of this article devotes much space to economic imperialism, since this movement represents something of a revolution in the history of economics: namely the first attempt since the turn of the [twentieth] century, insofar as economics is concerned, to redraw the map of the social sciences and to end the isolation between economics and its scientific neighbors. Through the aggressive way in which it proposes to do this, it also threatens to unleash a new *Methodenstreit* or paradigmatic battle. *The three main theses of this paper are (1) that such a new battle of the methods is on the horizon, (2) that this battle can easily become as destructive for the social sciences as the original Methodenstreit, and (3) that socioeconomics represents a creative and reasonable response to this threat.* In order to show this I shall first take a brief look at the German *Methodenstreit*. In doing this, particular attention will be paid to Max Weber's position. It was namely during the original battle of the methods that the idea of a broad synthesis of the social sciences called "socioeconomics" was for the first time formulated. More precisely, it was Max Weber who invented "socioeconomics" or *"Sozialökonomik,"* to use the original German term. Weber's thoughtful comments on the destructive potential of the *Methodenstreit* and the need for a new synthesis of neoclassical economics and the other social sciences, are part of the tradition of modern social science and should therefore be taken into account today when we are on the verge of a new *Methodenstreit*.

The First *Methodenstreit*—and the First Appearance of Socioeconomics

In hindsight, it has been argued that the *Methodenstreit* should never have taken place. People like Knut Wicksell, Joseph Schumpeter and others who have studied the battle of the methods, all feel that what was to become the key issue—should one only use abstractions or rather rely on detailed historical facts when doing economics?—was really a pseudoissue (see Wicksell 1904; Schumpeter 1954; Hansen 1968; Bostaph 1976). Still, the fight between the neoclassical economists and the historically oriented economists *did* take place, and with quite disastrous consequences for economics and the other social sciences.

The *Methodenstreit* started in the early 1880s with an exchange between Carl Menger and Gustav von Schmoller which very quickly got out of hand. Menger basically accused Schmoller of trying to destroy economic theory by turning it into history, and according to Schmoller, Menger was destroying economic theory by turning it into unreal abstractions. Menger and Schmoller stopped their violent exchange already in the mid-1880s but their disciples kept the fight going for several decades. Till at least the 1910s the *Methodenstreit* kept polarizing scholars into the two opposite camps.

The most important effect of the battle of the methods was clearly that Schmoller's one sided defense of the historical method in economics succeeded in discrediting it in a most fateful manner. Versions of the battle of the methods were soon reproduced in other countries, such as England and the United States; and everywhere historical economics, by squarely opposing recent developments in economic theory, helped to polarize economics (Swedberg 1987; Mongiovi 1988). As a result, history was totally out of economics and ended up as its own academic discipline—economic history—which had no interest in economic theory. In addition, the hostility to history was also extended to sociology, which meant that economists to became suspicious of sociology and vice versa. This, for example, was the case in England and the United States, where it was common that advocates of the historical approach saw their own approach as a form of sociology.

In Germany, the role of sociology was to be somewhat different, at least in so far as Max Weber was concerned. Weber was horrified by the *Methodenstreit* and how it had created "two sciences of economics" (Weber 1949). As a way of getting out of this deadlock Weber suggested a synthesis of the neoclassical and the historical approach. This synthesis he tried to accomplish in various ways and the term he used for his project was *"Sozialökonomik"* or *"socioeconomics."* The term itself had been introduced into German academic discourse in the 1890s, and Weber seized on it as a suitable replacement for the term "political economy" which was becoming outmoded in Germany (as in other countries) around the turn of the [twentieth] century.[1] It was also Weber who more than any other scholar tried to popularize the term "socioeconomics" in Germany, according to Schumpeter (1954).

To Weber, socioeconomics had both an intellectual side and a practical side. The intellectual program of socioeconomics is most clearly outlined in his essays on methodology, especially "'Objectivity' in Social Science and Social Policy." Weber here argues that socioeconomics is part of the cultural sciences *(Kulturwissenschaften),* and that it draws not only on "economic theory" but also on "economic sociology" and "economic history" (Weber 1949; see also Wegener 1962). One of Weber's key ideas was actually centered around the proposition that real progress in economics could only be made by drawing on both historical economics and theoretical economics *simultaneously.* A synthesis between the two approaches is in other words what is needed. Weber's famous notion of "ideal types" exemplifies what he had in mind when he spoke about synthesis in this context. Ideal types, according to Weber (1949), must be based on solid historical data; but they also imply an "analytical accentuation of certain elements of reality."

Weber also tried to use socioececonomics in a practical way to reconcile the two warring camps in the battle of the methods. Weber thus approached the Schmoller camp as well as the Menger camp in a conciliatory fashion, sometimes praising the one, sometimes the other.[2] He tried to break down the personal animosities between the two camps in several different ways and used whatever institutional resources he had for this purpose. His major attempt in this direction was no doubt the giant handbook of economics, *Grundriss der Sozialökonomik,* which he had started to edit around the turn of the [twentieth] century. This is an extremely important and interesting work, which unfortunately has fallen into oblivion. In any case, Weber here got representatives from the two warring factions in the *Methodenstreit to* work together on a collective project.

Mutual Ignorance and Distortion in the Social Sciences (1920s-1960s)

After the battle of the methods there comes a period when the economists show practically no interest in the other social sciences, which in their turn avoid economic problems. During this "heroic period of neoclassical economics," as the Norwegian sociologist Gudmund Hernes (1978) has called it, the following simplifying assumptions were made: (1) The actors—firms, households, and so on—are unitary or "black boxes"; (2) The actors are rational and have consistent preferences in the sense that the firms maximize profit and the households maximize utility; (3) The actors are fully informed about their surroundings and they also have perfect knowledge about all possible alternatives; (4) The actors have no costs of calculation; they instantaneously pick the best alternative or the best combination of alternatives; (5) The transactions between the actors are free; (6) The consumers decide over the producers, and any change in their needs or desires is automatically taken into account through the price mechanism; (7) Economics is about production and consumption, and how scarce means with alternative uses are utilized to reach a social optimum; (8) Ideally this optimum is described with the help of the notion of general equilibrium; and such an equilibrium is reached when all the direct and indirect effects of the myriads of mutual decisions by consumers and producers become stabilized or so-to-speak settle down. A few more simplifying assumptions should be added to Hernes' list. The actors in neoclassical theory from this period are as a rule not connected to each other except through momentary exchange. This means that most social bonds and networks are ignored. The economy is also seen as basically independent of the rest of society. Or, alternatively, the major social institutions are so stable that they for all practical purposes can be taken for granted. This means, among other things, that most forms of power are ignored. And finally, the fact that the economist is part of the reality that he or she studies, is of no particular consequence since positive knowledge is perfectly possible.

All of this resulted in a distorted type of economics, where simply too much of the social dimension was ignored. It also led to a distortion of the other social sciences, such as sociology, which in their turn completely ignored economics. During this period we therefore get a series of pseudoindependent social sciences, which are really distorted mirror images of each other. In the sociology and economics of the 1950s homo economicus is, for example, always *an individual actor* while homo sociologicus is *a collective actor.* The motive action of homo economicus is exclusively *rational calculation,* while that of homo sociologicus is *irrational feelings, tradition, and values*. We find homo economicus only *in the market*, and homo sociologicus *everywhere but the market*, and so on (see Table 1).[3]

Economic Imperialism and the Threat of a New *Methodenstreit*

During 1920-1960 there existed a certain balance between economics and the other social sciences in the sense that economists only dealt with economic topics and the other social scientists stayed away from economic subjects. Today, however, this is not the case. *Instead we are witnessing a major attempt to redraw the boundaries between economics and the other social sciences.* This claim is made in the name of "economic imperialism"; and the general idea is that the old division of labor between the social sciences is outmoded and needs to be replaced by a new division, where the economic approach is recognized as the master model for all the other social sciences. Economic imperialism is often advancing its ideas and claims to solve age-old problems in a provocative manner. It is thereby threatening to set off a new major battle about methodology in the social sciences, which may well end up being as destructive as the original *Methodenstreit*.

Given the key role that is attributed to economic imperialism in the argument of this article, it is important to pause here for a while and describe it in more detail; where it comes from, what it wants, and what it has accomplished thus far. The term "economic imperialism" seems actually to have made its first appearance in the 1930s, more precisely in a book by a young economist at Columbia

Table 1: The Neoclassical Paradigm and the Sociological Paradigm as Mirror Images of Each Other (Mid-Twentieth Century)

	Homo Economicus	*Homo Sociologicus*
Actor	individual actor	collective actor
Principle of action	freedom of action	constraint of social structure
Motive of action	rational calculation	irrational feelings, tradition, and values
Arena of action	the market	all society but the market
Steering principle	multiple, decentralized decisions	decisions involving social and political power
Type of concepts used	analytical and abstract	empirical and descriptive
Goal of the analysis	prediction as explanation	description as explanation
Image in relation to the other science	self-sufficient	self-sufficient

Source: *Samuelson 1947; Schumpeter 1954; Parsons and Smelser 1956; Dahrendorf 1958; Wrong 1961; Granovetter 1985; Hirsch, Michaels, and Friedman 1987.*

University, Ralph William Souter.[4] The book in question had the somewhat awkward title *Prolegomena to Relativity Economics: An Elementary Study in the Mechanics and Organics of an Expanding Economic Universe*. The relevant part, for our purposes, is hinted at in the last few words of the subtitle: "*an expanding economic universe.*" In his book Souter introduces the geopolitical imagery, which was to become so popular with today's economists. His main argument can be found in the following passage:

> The salvation of Economic Science in the twentieth century lies in an enlightened and democratic "economic imperialism," which invades the territories of its neighbors, not to enslave them or to swallow them up, but to aid and enrich them and promote their autonomous growth in the very process of aiding and enriching itself.
>
> Under such circumstances, occasional armed conflict among the sciences is inevitable. Such conflicts must be conducted according to the rules of civilised warfare: and it is the duty of each science to subordinate its strategy, as best it knows how, to the ultimate goal of the harmonious unification of knowledge. Mistakes and injustices are bound to occur from time to time; but the "science" which cannot maintain its integrity and vitality in such an environment deserves to pefish. And, for any science, a cowardly isolationist pacifism which cries peace! peace! when there is no peace is the stigma of intellectual disintegration and decay (Souter 1933).

Souter's book was published by a well-known press, Columbia University Press, but was not reviewed in any of the major economic journals. It was, however, still to leave some traces behind. It was, for example, drawn into the debate around Lionel Robbins's book *On the Nature and Significance of Economic Science* (1932) by another young economist, Talcott Parsons, who was fascinated by questions of this type. Parsons carefully went through Souter's argument about economic imperialism in an article in *The Quarterly Journal of Economics* from 1934 and concluded that, "Economic imperialism . . . results not only in enriching these neighboring 'countries,' which of course it does, but in putting some of them into a strait jacket of economic categories which is illsuited to their own conditions" (Parsons 1934). If pushed far enough, Parsons argued, economic imperialism will lead to the extinction of the other social sciences. It is a tendency, he stressed, "*against which the sociologist, as well as other scientists, must stand up and fight for his scientific life*" (Parsons 1934, emphasis added).

Souter's book is today mainly interesting because it is the first place where the term "economic imperialism " is mentioned. The fact that it was published in the 1930s, is also a reminder that economic imperialism has its intellectual roots in the economics of this period. It was, however, not until many years later—more precisely in the late 1950s—that we find the first attempts by economists to actually practice economic imperialism and take on topics from other social sciences. Why this was happening just in the 1950s is not clear. George Stigler (1984) has suggested that it is perhaps related to the fact that it was by about this time that young American economists had for the first time been trained in seeing economics as "a general analytical machine": "The abstraction increased the distance between economic theory and empirical economic phenomena ... and made the extension to other bodies of phenomena easy and natural."

The pioneer works from the late 1950s include Gary Becker's Ph.D. thesis, *The Economics of Discrimination* (1957), Anthony Downs' *An Economic Theory of Democracy* (1957), and A. H. Conrad and J. R. Meyer's article "The Economics of Slavery in the Antebellum South" (1958). These three works signaled the introduction in the 1950s of the economic model into three new disciplines: sociology, political science, and economic history. During the 1950s a fight also broke out in anthropology over the use of the economic approach, the so-called formalist-substantivist controversy. During the 1960s and 1970s the neoclassical model was extended to law (including criminology), demography, education, and Organization theory (Becker 1960; Coase 1960; Calabresi 1961; Becker 1964; Buchanan and Tullock 1962; Posner 1973; Ehrlich 1975; Williamson 1976). It was also during the 1970s that economic imperialism really acquired its own identity. The term "economic imperialism" was for the first time applied to the works by Becker, Buchanan and so on in an article by Gordon Tullock from the early 1970s (Tullock 1972; see also note 5). A few years later the first textbook in the field appeared, entitled *The New World of Economics* (Tullock and McKenzie 1975). At about this time the movement also got its intellectual program, Gary Becker's *The Economic Approach to Human Behavior* (1976). Becker here makes a frontal attack on the old division of labor in the social sciences, according to which economics is the science of wealth and production. This usually means, Becker says, that all noneconomic forms of human behavior were labeled irrational, traditional, and value oriented, so that they could be handed over to the other social sciences without any bad feelings. Economic imperialism or the "economic approach" as Becker prefers to call it, is presented in the following way: "The combined assumptions of maximizing behavior, market equilibrium, and stable preferences, used relentlessly and unflinchingly, form the heart of the economic approach." The definition of economics in this quote is not particularly novel, but that the economic approach should be used *"relentlessly and unflinchingly"* gives a hint of the new tone of discourse. The same is true for Becker's remark that the economic approach is applicable to "all human behavior."

In the mid-1970s, when Becker wrote his programmatic statement about the economic approach, economic imperialism was still a minority movement. Becker[5] thus complains that "many economists" are openly hostile to all but "traditional applications" of economics and keep insisting that there exist irrational behavior, ad hoc shifts in the values of people, and the like. During the few years that have elapsed since the publication of Becker's book, economic imperialism has however advanced very quickly. Buchanan has, for example, received the Nobel Prize and Becker has been made president of the AEA. This means that mainstream economics basically accepts economic imperialism today. Maybe sensing the impending change of opinion in the economic profession toward the economic approach, Jack Hirschleifer published a particularly bombastic article on economic imperialism in 1985 in *The American Economic Review*, entitled "The Expanding Domain of Economics." Economics is here described as "the universal grammar of social science," and it is prophesized that the noneconomic social sciences will soon become "increasingly indistinguishable from economics."

Besides Hirschleifer's article, there are several other signs that the temperature is rising in and around economic imperialism. During the 1980s there has, for example, been a minor flood of books on the advantages of using the concept of rationality in social science in general (see the works as cited in Elster 1986). These have in general been well received, even if there are also some exceptions (Etzioni 1987a; 1987b). The debate around public choice has intensified, as empirical findings keep accumulating which contradict the theories of Downs et al. (see the works as cited in Lewin 1988). A new conquest—Marxism—has been made, which has angered the more traditional marxists (Roemer 1982; Hindess 1984). And finally, a major confrontation between traditional sociology and "rational choice sociology," is about to take place. A concerted effort is presently being made at the University of Chicago to introduce the economic approach into sociology. The two leading figures behind this are James Coleman and Gary Becker. The latter has had a joint appointment at the departments of economics and history since 1983. Coleman and Becker have put together a graduate program in rational choice sociology. They are planning a book series on this topic, and they are starting up a new sociological magazine, called *Rationality and Sociology. By the summer of 1989, when the first issue of this magazine appeared, a major theoretical treatise on rational choice sociology by James Coleman, Foundations of Social Theory,* was also scheduled to be published (see Swedberg 1990).

The Need for a Socioeconomic Approach

Economic imperialism has had a positive impact on the social sciences in the sense that the borders between economics and its neighbors are now much more open. But even if we grant the economic imperialists the merit of having ended much of the artificial separation between economics and other social sciences, it is also clear that they have a very specific vision of what the relationship between economics and its neighbors should be like. And this vision amounts, for all practical purposes, to a closing of the borders again.

What is needed instead of economic imperialism is therefore an approach that can steer the situation in the social sciences, as it exists today, into the kind of renaissance in the study of economics that many of us think is possible. Such an approach would as a minimum have to fulfill certain demands. These would, in my mind, be the following: There should be multiple approaches to economic problems *(Condition 1);* the borders between economics and the other social sciences must be kept open *(Condition 2);* and allowance must be made for the complexity of human behavior and culture *(Condition 3).*

What Weber at the turn of the [twentieth] century called socioeconomics fits these three conditions. And socioeconomics, in its present day version, does it too. This is clear from the programmatic statements in socioeconomics which Etzioni has produced this far: "Making Policy for Complex Systems" (1985), in which socioeconomics is presented as a kind of policy science for economics; "Founding a New Socio-economics" (1986), in which the major research tasks of socioeconomics are outlined; and *The Moral Dimension* (1988), which is a major social-philosophical treatise on socioeconomics.

In all of these works it is emphasized that not only one but several approaches are needed to successfully solve economic problems (Condition 1). In socioeconomics, as in medicine or in policy science, one needs to use "findings from a variety of basic sources" (Etzioni 1985). This would include, for example, mainstream economics, political science, experimental psychology, and quantitative sociology. The reason for drawing on several sciences is simply that most economic problems are extremely complex, and that no single science exists which can handle all of them on its own. One therefore has to be pragmatic, use second best solutions, and rely on different sciences in each concrete case.

Implicit in the first condition—that multiple approaches are used in economics—is also the fact that the boundaries between economics and the other social sciences have to be kept open (Condition 2). People need to be able to communicate freely across the boundaries in order to have access to the findings in the various sciences. There is also the argument that the boundaries between the social sciences should be left a bit unclear since, if drawn too sharply, this tends to separate problems in an arbitrary manner into the different sciences. There is finally the fact that many essential problems in the social sciences seem to be situated exactly at the boundaries of a science.

There is finally the need for complexity (Condition 3). Socioeconomics, as Weber pointed out, is a member of the family of *Kulturwissenschaften;* and this means that the complexities of culture and history have to be taken into account. "Culture" should here be understood first of all in terms of intersubjective meanings—meanings constructed and communicated between people in and around economic interaction. Involved in this, as Etzioni makes clear in *The Moral Dimension,* is also the question of human values: Social action is always structured in various ways around values and ethical issues of different kinds.

In conclusion, it can be said that there is presently going on a redefinition of the division of labor in the social sciences which is focused on economics. This process represents a unique opportunity to end the lack of communication between economics and the other social sciences, which has characterized much of the twentieth century, but which was really alien to the founders of economic theory such as Adam Smith and John Stuart Mill. Today there exists a clear chance to steer things in a positive direction. Economic imperialism, however, does not represent a good alternative in this regard, since it is basically trying to impose a new single-minded vision on economics and its scientific neighbors. It, thereby, threatens to close the door to the new and promising developments of a multidisciplinary economics. Socioeconomics, on the other hand, tries to keep the door open.

References

Arndt, P. 1935. Heinrich Dietzel (1857-1935). *Economic Journal* 45: 797-794.
Becker, G. 1957. *The economics of discrimination.* Chicago: University of Chicago Press.
———. 1960. An economic analysis of fertility. In *The economics of discrimination.* Chicago: University of Chicago Press.
———. 1964. *Human capital: A theoretical and empirical approach.* New York: Columbia University Press.
———. 1976. *The economic approach to human behavior.* Chicago: University of Chicago Press.
Bostaph, S. 1976. Epistemological foundations of methodological conflict in economics: The case of the nineteenth-century "methodenstreit." Ph.D. thesis, Southern Illinois University.
Boulding, K. 1969. Economics as a moral science. *American Economic Review* 59: 1-12.
Buchanan, J., and G. Tullock. 1962. *The calculus of consent.* Ann Arbor: University of Michigan Press.
Calabresi, G. 1961. Some thoughts on risk distribution and the law of torts. *Yale Law Journal* 70: 499-533.
Coase, R. 1960. The problem of social cost. *Journal of Law and Economics* 3: 1-44.
Conrad, A. H., and J. R. Meyer. 1958. The economics of slavery in the Antebellum South. *Journal of Political Economy* 66: 95-130.
Dahrendorf, R. 1958. Homo Sociologicus. In *Essays in the theory of society.* Stanford, CA: Stanford University Press, 1958/1968.
Dietzel, H. 1883. Der ausgangspunkt der sozialwirtschaftsiehre und ihr grundbegriff. *Zeitschrift für die gesamte Staatswissenschaft,* 39: 1-80.
———. 1895. *Theoretische sozialökonomik.* Leipzig: C. F. Wintersche Verlagshandlung.
Downs, A. 1957. *An economic theory of democracy.* New York: Harper & Row.
Ehrlich, I. 1975. Capital punishment: A case of life and death. *American Economic Review* 65: 397-417.
Elster, J., ed. 1986. *Rational choice.* New York: New York University Press.
Etzioni, A. 1985. Making policy for complex systems: A medical model for economics. *Journal of Policy Analysis and Management* 4: 383-395.
———. 1986. Founding a new socio-economics. *Challenge* 29(5): 13-18.
———. 1987a. How rational are we? *Sociological Forum* 2: 1-20.
———. 1987b. On thoughtless rationality (rules-of-thumb). *Kyklos* 40: 496-514.
———. 1988. *The moral dimension: Toward a new economics.* New York: Free Press.
Granovetter, M. 1985. Economic action and social structure: The problem of embeddedness. *American Journal of Sociology* 91: 481-510.
Hansen, R. 1968. Der methodenstreit in den sozialwissenschaften zwischen Gustav Schmoller und Karl Menger. Seine wissenschaftshistorische und wissenschaftstheoretische bedeutung. In *Beitrdge zur Entwicklung der Wissenschaftstheorie im 19. Jahrhundert,* edited by A. Diemer. Melsenheim am Glan: Veriag Anton Hain.
Hernes, G. 1978. Mot en institutionell oekonomi. In *Forhandlingsoekonomi og blandingsadministrasjon.* Bergen: Universitetsforlaget.
Hindess, B. 1984. Rational choice theory and the analysis of political action. *Economy and Society* 13: 255-277.
Hirsch, P., S. Michaels, and R. Friedman. 1987. "Dirty hands" versus "clean models": Is sociology in danger of being seduced by economics?" *Theory and Society* 16: 317-336.
Hirschleifer, J. 1985. The expanding domain of economics. *American Economic Review* 75(6): 53-68.
Lewin, L. 1988. *Det gemensamma bästa: om egenintresset och allmänintresset i västerländsk politik (The common good: On private interests and the common good in western politics).* Borås, Sweden: Carlssons.
Marshall, A. 1891. *Principles of economics.* London: Macmillan and Company.
Mill, J. S. 1838. On the definition of political economy: And on the method of investigation proper to it. In *Essays on some unsettled questions of political economy.* London: John W. Parker.
Mongiovi, G. 1988. The American methodenstreit. *History of Economic Society Bulletin,* 10(l): 57-66.
Parsons, T. 1934. Sociological elements in economic thought, I-II. *Quarterly Journal of Economics* 49: 414-453, 645-667.
Parsons, T., and N. Smelser. 1956. *Economy and society: A study in the integration of economic and social theory.* London: Routledge and Kegan Paul.
Posner, R. 1973. *Economic analysis of law.* Boston: Little, Brown.
Roemer, J. 1982. *A general theory of exploitation and class.* Cambridge, MA: Harvard University Press.
Samuelson, P. 1947. *Foundations of economic analysis.* Cambridge, MA: Harvard University Press.
Schön, M. 1989. Gustav Schmoller and Max Weber. In *Max Weber and his contemporaries,* edited by W. J. Mommsen and J. Osterhammel. London: Allen & Unwin.

Schumpeter, J. A. 1954. *History of economic analysis.* London: George Allen & Unwin.
Souter, R. 1933. *Prolegomena to relativity economics: An elementary study in the mechanics and organics of an expanding economic universe.* New York: Columbia University Press, 1933.
Stigler, G. 1984. Economics—the imperial science? *Scandinavian Journal of Economics* 96:301-313.
Swedberg, R. 1987. Economic sociology: Past and present. *Current Sociology* 35(l): 1-221.
———. 1990. *Economics and sociology: Redefining their boundaries.* Princeton, NJ: Princeton University Press, 1990.
Tullock, G. 1972. Economic imperialism. In *Theory of political choice,* edited by J. M. Buchanan and R. D. Tollison. Ann Arbor: University of Michigan Press.
Tullock, G., and R. McKenzie. 1975. *The new world of economics: Explorations into the human experience.* 4th ed. Homewood, IL: Richard D. Irwin.
Weber, Max. 1949. *The methodology of the social sciences.* New York: Free Press.
———. 1975. Marginal utility theory and the fundamental law of psychophysics. *Social Science Quarterly,* 56: 21-36.
Wegener, W. 1962. *Die quellen der wissenschaftsauffassung Max Webers und die problematik der wertuheilsfreiheit der nationalökonomie.* Berlin: Duncker & Humblot.
Wicksell, K. 1904. Måi och medel i nationalekonomien (Ends and means in economic theory). *Ekonomisk tidskrift* (Sweden) 6: 457-474.
Williamson, O. 1976. *Markets and hierarchies: Analysis and antitrust implications.* New York: The Free Press.
Winkelmann, J. 1986. *Max Webers hinterlassenes hauptwerk: Die wirtschaft und die gesellschaftlichen ordnungen und Mächte.* Tübingen: J.C.B. Mohr.
Wrong, D. 1961. The oversocialized conception of man in modern sociology. *American Sociological Review* 26: 183-193.

CHAPTER 22

Rationality and Interpretation: Parliamentary Elections in Early Stuart England

John Ferejohn

Originally published in The Economic Approach to Politics:
A Critical Reassessment of the Theory of Rational Action, *1991*.

READING INTRODUCTION

Ferejohn contrasts two interpretations of English parliamentary "elections" in the early seventeenth century. The "Whig" interpretation, based on the increasing incidence of competition between candidates, is similar to that which we might offer for many elections in contemporary democracies. It focuses on competition between representatives of distinct ideological groupings, each seeking the authority to formulate public policy that supports his personal material interests, which are—presumably—largely shared by other members of his group. The "revisionist" interpretation perceives instead a high degree of consensus among constituencies during this period as to which members of leading families merited parliamentary office. This interpretation further views the activities surrounding many uncontested elections as celebrations of a unified society, whereas occasional competition among candidates represents, in this view, a lamentable breakdown of societal consensus, frequently based on the personal foibles of a particular candidate.

Ferejohn characterizes both of these interpretations as incomplete. He portrays the "Whig" version as consistent with conventional rational-choice theory in positing maximizing behavior among egoistic, materially oriented actors. The incompleteness associated with this perspective is that, depending on the circumstances, either contesting elections or negotiating particular compromises (having the representatives of rival groupings alternate terms) might be optimal. The revisionist account characterizes early seventeen-century Englishmen as in agreement that certain outstanding members of leading families merited parliamentary seats. The incompleteness of this perspective, which Ferejohn refers to as "thick" rationality because it is based on a particular set of values, lies in the lack of an explanation for the superiority of these values over alternatives.

It is useful to read this article against the background provided by Thompson, Ellis, and Wildavsky (1990), particularly as extended by Wildavsky (1994), whereby each of these portrayals represents a version of "thick rationality" and neither is privileged. Arguably each interpretation applies for different people during this period. The life experiences of some people resulted in their becoming adherents of an individualistic culture focused on egoistic hedonistic motivations and employing competitive institutions (e.g., markets and elections) to organize social life among what they perceived as broadly equal capable people. The life experiences of others, in contrast, resulted in their becoming adherents of an hierarchical culture focused on deferential collective motivations among people perceived as differing sharply in their moral and practical capacities. Such a culture employs hierarchical institutions through which honorable ordinary people defer to the merits of exceptionally moral and capable members of the community. Wildavsky would agree with Ferejohn that each of these orientations exhibits instrumental rationality, given the divergent and distinctive set of values from which they begin, but Wildavsky's theory offers an explanation of how these two rival "thick" rationalities—and two others as well—arise from distinctive social experiences and become socially embedded.

READING TEXT

Introduction

It is sometimes thought that rational choice and interpretive explanation are intrinsically opposed to each other in the sense that if one is successful in accounting for something, the other must be either wrong or superfluous. In this essay I try to show why this view is not only incorrect but is also profoundly unproductive in helping us to a richer understanding of social life.

I shall argue that rational accounts and interpretive accounts are or can be complementary in an important sense. Both interpretive and rational explanations are inherently incomplete as accounts of action. At best either type of explanation can eliminate certain patterns of action as inconsistent, but they cannot fully account for social action. Fortunately, the incompleteness of each kind of explanation can be (partly) overcome by appeal to the other.

To demonstrate this claim, I examine the institutions and practices of parliamentary selection as they operated in early seventeenth-century England. There are two broad historical accounts of these practices and institutions: Whig and revisionist. Whig history sees parliamentary elections of that period as similar to elections anywhere, anytime: elections are simply contests for votes among politicians ambitious to obtain office and implement their policies. In order to win office, competing politicians devise programs, aimed at attracting support, develop organizations to mobilize this support, and attempt to manipulate the franchise to their advantage. Seventeenth-century practices and institutions were, to be sure, imperfect versions of more modern ones. Electoral institutions were young then and easily subverted or deflected in practice. Thus they were more tarnished by corruption, ineptness, and casualness; but once account is taken of these superficial imperfections, the logics of electoral competition was pretty much the same then as now.

The revisionist account of this period rejects this view as anachronistic and constructs in its place a self-consciously "interior" (or cultural) interpretation of the perceptions, identities, and meanings of the seventeenth-century English in order to understand the practices by which members of Parliament were chosen. For the revisionists, these practices were not aimed at winning or holding office or implementing rival policies but were aimed, instead, at recognizing and reinforcing local social solidarity by suppressing competition in an ordered hierarchical society. Thus seventeenth-century electoral practices are really best seen as vestiges of a recent medieval past and not as harbingers of an era: of democratic Enlightenment.

These two accounts, the one anachronistic, the other antiquarian, are sometimes thought to stand as irreconcilable alternatives in the historiography of the period. I shall show that each approach contains both rational and interpretive aspects and that each is necessary for an understanding of the practices of the period, and specifically for a richer understanding of how these practices changed in the course of the "long century."

Rational and Cultural Explanation

If, as I claim, rational and interpretive accounts are complementary, why is it that practitioners of each see them in conflict? Part of the reason lies in their differing conceptions of the feasible aims of social science. Generally speaking, rational choice theorists aim at developing theories that can explain and predict observed patterns of behavior and practice. They are committed to a particular kind of philosophy of science, one which attempts to produce lawlike claims about measurable phenomena and in which one theory is judged better than another only if it provides a coherent account of a wider range of observed data.

Interpretivists,[1] on the other hand, reject the possibility of prediction in this sense.[2] For them the proper aim of social science is to interpret practices, behaviors, and institutions by reconstructing the meanings that infect them, by understanding how the agents constitute themselves, their values, and their preferences, in relation to their actions. Charles Taylor, one of the most articulate defenders of this approach and one who is at pains to emphasize the differences between culturalist-interpretivist and positivistic approaches (with which he would place rational choice theory), argues that social sciences cannot hope to predict behavior. At best, social science is an ex post enterprise in which we can hope only to come to some understanding of events and practices after the fact.[3]

Nevertheless, there are criteria for judging among cultural accounts. For example, one account of an event, practice, or institution—one construction of meanings and understandings—is better than another if it can explain (in the sense of making more comprehensible) more aspects of the event, practice, or institution than another.[4] Thus, at minimum, interpretivists seem committed to a coherence test, but, insofar as the demand of comprehensibility is fleshed out, they might endorse a larger set of comparative criteria for judging theories.

Leaving aside issues of measurement, there is nothing in this comparative principle that should seem inhospitable to the rational choice theorist. Rational choice theory is, in this sense, an interpretive theory that constructs explanations by "reconstructing" patterns of meanings and understandings (preferences and beliefs) in such a way that agents' actions can be seen as maximal, given their beliefs. In this sense the logic of rational choice and the interpretivist or culturalist approaches are similar: start with observed data (behavior including documents and letters, practices, institutions) and reconstruct actors and their inner attributes (meanings, beliefs, values) in such a way that the data are as fully explained or accounted for possible. As Jon Elster (1983) argues, both are forms of intentional explanation and are at least formally similar in that respect. Moreover, cultural or interpretive accounts, if they are to ring true to us, must have some aspect of rationality embedded in them. To understand someone's actions implies at minimum that if we had their goals, beliefs, and opportunities, their actions would be plausible choices for us.[5]

The main differences between the approaches seems to lie elsewhere. At the most abstract level, rational choice theorists are committed to a principle of universality: (all) agents act always to maximize their well-being as they understand it, based on their beliefs, preferences, and strategic opportunities. This commitment to a universal description of agents is what permits rational choice theorists to believe in the possibility of prediction as well as ex post explanation. Culturalists argue either that this commitment is so weak as to be without meaning, or that it is merely an article of faith and that there is no a priori reason to believe that the similarity of human agents is particularly extensive.[6] Humans are simply too reflexive, too self-conscious, and too malleable for such universalistic claims to have much truth or power. Instead, interpretivists proceed by taking the data of a given situation, event, or practice and reconstruct meanings and understandings specific to agents in those circumstances. This "thick" description of an event or "text" and its meanings to participants is supposed to stand as an explanation of the event or practice.

At a more concrete level, it is necessary to distinguish among various types of accounts offered by rational choice theorists. In what I call a "thin-rational" account, the theorist assumes only that agents are (instrumentally) rational, that they efficiently employ the means available to pursue their ends. In a "thick-rational" account, the analyst posits not only rationality but some additional description of agent preferences and beliefs. Thick-rational choice theorists generally assume that agents in a wide variety of situations value the same sorts of things: for example, wealth, income, power, or the perquisites of office. A substantial part of the power of a rational choice approach comes from (thickly) specifying the "objective function" of the agents in a way that is separable from the context of decision.

For example, neoclassical consumer theory is essentially a thin-rational account, since it is based only on the assumption that individuals act as though they are maximizing something, although that thing is specified formally only under the name of "utility." The other component of neoclassical economics, the theory of the firm, is based on the thick-rational assumption that firms act as profit maximizers.[7]

While culturalists criticize thin-rational accounts on the grounds that they seem empty, their criticism of thick-rational accounts is that they are anachronistic (when applied to distant times) or ethnocentric (when applied to distant places or peoples). Thick-rational accounts, even where they might seem plausible, are flawed because they contain no theory determining the selection of agent identities, values, beliefs, and strategic opportunities. Without such a theory, there is no (nonethnocentric) reason to make the types of universal assumptions found in thick-rational accounts: that economic actors are wealth maximizers, that politicians are eager to pursue office, and so forth. These things may all be true of the world we live in, but, without further justification, there is no warrant for exporting such assumptions across expanses of time and space.[8]

Two Kinds of Incompleteness

Interpretivists are characteristically suspicious of general claims about human nature, preferring to see individuals as plastic and malleable and as possessed of a wide range of capacities. Thus they often limit attention to the self-interpretations of the agents and ignore other information about human agents that may be available to the analyst. But by restricting the range of observations to a specific time and place and by resisting the urge to attribute universal attributes to actors, they inevitably expand the range of defensible alternative theories or understandings of a given situation. While the domain of observations that can be employed to discriminate among theories is fixed and finite, the set of theories that can be "fit" to these observations is infinite.

This inability to eliminate alternative accounts is the price of the interpretivist's "open-mindedness." Interpretivists sometimes deal with this indeterminacy by trying to explain social action in terms of intersubjective meanings embedded in institutions and practices.[9] Intersubjective or cultural meanings limit the beliefs, self-interpretations, and values available to individuals so that many logically conceivable patterns of practice and behavior may be eliminated. Of course, such accounts leave open two questions: first, how does the analyst arrive at, or "infer," an interpretation or cultural description (the hermeneutical circle)? Second, how fully can such a description delimit agent characteristics and choices?

None of this is to say that culturalists never propose specific interpretations. Often they do. However, the jump to a specific account is not dictated by their method at all but is driven instead by some intuition external to it. Taylor (1985) asks how we can convince another person of the correctness of our interpretation of a text. He says that we must

> try to show him how it makes sense of the original nonsense or partial sense. But for him to follow us he must read the original language as we do. . . . If he does not, what can we do? The answer, it would seem, can only be more of the same. . . . Success here requires that he follow us in these other readings, and so on, it would seem, potentially forever. We cannot escape an ultimate appeal to a common understanding of the expressions. (17)

Taylor seems to suggest that if different analysts consider the same event, and they come to different coherent interpretations, there would be no criterion within the approach to decide between them. Taylor calls this appeal to the intuition of the interpreter the "hermeneutical circle"; I call it incompleteness.[10]

If interpretive methods are weak in failing to discriminate sharply among alternative explanations, rational choice theories share a similar indeterminacy, though for different reasons. A rational choice account of an interaction—a rational reconstruction—aims to explain a social action by reconstructing the agents' beliefs, values, and strategic opportunities (everything there is that is relevant to choice) and showing that the outcome corresponds to equilibrium behavior in this situation or game. An account of an interaction is completely successful if the outcome can be shown to be the unique equilibrium in the resulting game.

Recent work in game theory, however, has shown that in a very wide class of situations of strategic interaction—indeed, in virtually any game that takes place over time or in which there is a nontrivial informational structure—almost any outcome can occur in some game-theoretical equilibrium. This indeterminacy, often called the "folk theorem" by game theorists, suggests that unless we substantially enrich the concept of rationality itself, or supplement it with extra assumptions about human nature, rationality by itself cannot fully account for the selection of one outcome rather than another. In this sense, the naive hope of complete rational reconstruction—the reductionist project—cannot work. At best, rational reconstruction may be necessary for an explanation of social action; it cannot be sufficient.

It is useful to give an example of the reach of the folk theorem to show how it applies to an apparently familiar and misunderstood problem: the infinitely repeated Prisoners' Dilemma game. In the one-shot or stage game, there is a unique equilibrium in which neither player cooperates. As is well known, under pretty general conditions in repeated play there is another equilibrium in which both players cooperate each time. People sometimes conclude from this observation that repeated play leads to cooperation and that the cooperative outcome is a prediction of the repeated-play Prisoners' Dilemma. The folk theorem, however, says that in fact there are a lot of other (indeed, infinitely many) equilibrium outcomes sustainable in this game: specifically, any outcome in which both players receive more than they would in the noncooperative outcome. For instance (assuming that the values attached to outcomes satisfy a certain condition), the players could take turns cooperating and defecting.[11] There is nothing internal to game theory or rational choice theory that allows the analyst to predict the play of one such equilibrium rather than another, so that the prediction of cooperation in this setting does not follow from principles of rationality but from some other (nonrational) assumption about how the game will be played.

To obtain a unique prediction, we need to appeal to an auxiliary principle that would allow the agents to coordinate their behavior on a specific equilibrium. In the Prisoners' Dilemma, for example, the game is usually presented in a symmetric form in which the analyst's eye is drawn to the symmetric equilibrium in which both players cooperate. Obviously, this symmetry is artificial in the sense that it has nothing intrinsically to do with the characteristic feature of Prisoners' Dilemmas—that equilibrium play is not efficient—and would not be expected to occur naturally in many situations.

While there is little agreement among game theorists as to what kinds of auxiliary assumptions are most plausible for selecting among equilibria, many theorists, beginning with Thomas Schelling (1960), have appealed to intersubjective or cultural understandings which permit the actors to focus on one equilibrium among many. In effect, in order to carry out a complete game-theoretical analysis of a game with multiple equilibria, one must assume that somehow it is common knowledge among the agents exactly which equilibrium is being played.[12] Nothing internal to the theory of games, or in the nature of rationality, will accomplish this.

While each approach is plagued by characteristic indeterminacy, these indeterminacies can be partially alleviated by appeal to the other approach. The culturalist can narrow the range of plausible interpretations of an event or practice by appealing to (universal or at least shared) principles of consistent purposive action implied by the possibility of intersubjective comprehensibility. The rational choice theorist may be able to select among equilibria by appealing to culturally shared understandings and meanings necessary to select among strategic equilibria.[13]

The source of this theoretical complementarity is found not in sheer coincidence but in the nature of the relationship between the sphere of action or choice and the sphere of meanings or understandings.[14] In social action, human agents make strategic or allocative choices while simultaneously enacting (ontologically) prior understandings about the nature of the strategic situation in which they find themselves, the characteristics or identities of the players (including themselves), and the common understandings or expectations as to how the game will be played. Thus, when it comes to explaining action, rational accounts, no less than interpretive ones, must appeal to principles external to the individual agents. That appeal may be to historical practice or to cultural expectations, but in any case it remains ad hoc and external to the theory.

Thus neither rational nor interpretive accounts can wholly succeed in explaining social events and practices. Because human practices and institutions are located on the boundary between the sphere of action—where they are constrained by the logic of rational choice and calculation—and the sphere of meanings—which is constrained by subtler ideational logics—they cannot be completely understood without taking both spheres into account. In the end, while neither rational nor interpretive approaches can offer sufficient accounts of institutions and practices, each can claim to offer necessary components of an adequate explanation.

Obviously, this account of the differences and similarities between rational and cultural accounts is stylized and overemphasizes their differences. For that reason, it is useful to see how these approaches might work together in a practical case. The example is drawn from the literature on electoral institutions and practices in early seventeenth-century England, a period in which institutions associated with elections were varied and unsystematized, in which the franchise was ambiguous and unclear, and in which the practices associated with nominations and voting were diverse.

The central controversies in the historiographical literature on this period turn on the question of whether we should look at the elections of this period as forerunners or precursors of present elections (in which candidates compete for office by bidding for votes with policies and ideologies, the franchise is well defined; and the practices of voting are legally codified and enforced) or whether, instead, we should recognize from the outset that these practices really had little to do with what we think of as electoral politics, but were aimed at reinforcing local hierarchical social structures.

As I construe it, this debate is really between nascent thick-rational choice theorists—Whig historians[15]—and culturalist (interpretive) revisionists. I shall claim that both of their accounts are intrinsically incomplete in the sense outlined above and that each would be improved by recognizing a contribution from the other perspective.[16] In the next section I shall set out what I understand to be an agreed upon description of electoral practices in the period and then briefly summarize the interpretations of the Whigs and the revisionists, with which I shall be concerned.

Elections in Early Stuart England

In early seventeenth-century England, elections to the House of Commons were rarely contested: in the first two elections of the century, less than 20 of the more than 400 seats were fought.[17] In most constituencies, there were the same number of aspirants for seats as there were seats available. Typically, these aspirants possessed certain social characteristics. In the larger and more prestigious county seats, they were typically high gentry, ranking just below the peerage. In the boroughs and towns, they were often magistrates, candidates nominated by patrons or neighboring gentry. In all cases, they were men of social distinction. Moreover, they were not anonymously drawn from the upper class; virtually everyone who stood for election (correctly) expected to win the seat based on the specific social characteristics of his family and his place within it.

Parliamentary seats in the counties were largely kept in families while in the boroughs they often adhered to the family of a patron or a local office such as that of recorder or high steward. In virtually every constituency, expectations as to who had the right to be "selected" for Commons were settled and consensual and for that reason contests seldom arose.

Where a contest threatened, somehow one or more of the candidates would somehow be induced to withdraw, presumably to prevent the contest from occurring. A number of institutional devices existed which helped organize this phenomenon. The least visible but most widespread was of course the shared understandings and expectations of the aspirants themselves. Men did not stand for seats that someone else "deserved." But where these understandings were unclear or contested, officials intervened and employed rotation, lot, and other forms of negotiation as ways of rationing access to office. Only where aspirants could not agree on such a method was there resort to contest, or, to use a more evocative phrase, "trial by election."

Historians hold divergent views of elections in the early seventeenth century. From the Whig perspective—stripped of its apologetic and celebratory aspects—elections, then, as now, were contests for valuable political office among ambitious power and wealth seekers. For Whig historians, there was much at stake in elections, even in the early part of century. Those who attained office were able to influence the course of the king's (expensive) foreign policy through the revived use of impeachment and withholding of subsidies, persecute (or prevent the persecution of) Catholics, affect royal grants of monopoly and patent, obtain patronage from the Court or from high-ranking peers, or manipulate tax assessments for their own benefit or that of their neighbors. If the level of competition was low, Whiggish historians tried to explain it by appeal to the manipulation of elections or of Parliament, or by alleging the coercion of the electorate by the Court, powerful families, or oligarchies.

For Whig historians, the Stuart years were marked by a growing opposition between the Court and the Parliament, particularly the House of Commons. The Parliaments of those years, it is claimed, faced with impecunious and ambitious monarchs who required more and more money to carry out foreign adventures or to indulge in extravagant vices, bargained for increased control of their own membership and agenda. The pulling and hauling of this bargaining, the struggles over the right to lay taxes and to influence courts of law, the extent of the royal prerogative in foreign policy, are what characterize the politics of the early Stuart years.

Whig accounts emphasize the growing importance of the electorate as an increasingly legitimate arbiter of disputes over office, the growth in the franchise in both counties and boroughs, and the increase in the frequency of contests over the early part of the century (Hirst 1975). They emphasize, too, the seizure by the House of Commons of the right to settle election disputes. As J. H. Plumb (1969) says, "the Commons took upon themselves the more fundamental questions of parliamentary franchises, the revival of representation in boroughs where it had lapsed, and even the question of new enfranchisement, matters hitherto falling within the prerogatives of the Crown" (95).

Whigs showed that the electorate underwent steady and dramatic expansion, partly as the result of the effects of inflation on the ancient 40-shilling freehold requirement, and partly as the result of parliamentary actions aimed directly at widening the borough franchise.[18] This larger electorate was much less controllable by patrons or courtiers and was therefore more often appealed to in disputes about office. Wallace Notestein (1924), focusing on internal parliamentary developments, emphasizes the creation of new institutions in the House of Commons, particularly the Committee of the Whole,[19] as a barrier to Court influence. He argues that the Committee of the Whole was a device that permitted Parliament to appoint its own presiding officer, to make its own rules of debate, and more efficiently to conduct its business.[20] And, as Parliament gained increasing control over legislation and over the conduct of its own affairs, as it gained increasing control over election disputes, as, in brief, it became a regular and somewhat independent part of government, the value of office increased and the level of competition increased as well. Thus, for the Whigs, we may see in this period the emergence of modern parliamentary forms, of the electorate as an institution, of contests, and of insulation of Parliament from the executive.

For the Whigs, to the extent that elections in this period fail to resemble their modern successors, the reasons are to be found either in an extensive social and political consensus, the tiny size and relative homogeneity of the electorate, or in the imperfect institutions and practices of the time.[21] These institutions and practices still permitted coercion, manipulation, and confusion, and, as these institutional defects were remedied,[22] elections (and other institutions) came to resemble modern ones more closely.

Revisionist Interpretation

Revisionists argue that the Whig view of seventeenth-century parliamentary electoral practices fails for several reasons. Fundamentally, it is claimed, the Whig account employs a misleading and extraneous teleology[23] and imposes on past institutions and practices false and foreign readings. Whig teleology led historians to explain the absence of petition, the infrequency of genuine contests, and the invisibility of elections themselves, by appealing to underlying or latent forces: Court influence through patronage, electoral corruption, and the like. The revisionists claim that direct evidence of these phenomena are either weak or lacking. Revisionists argue that citizens were neither manipulated nor coerced into electing their betters to parliamentary seats. Patronage practices, for example, are not evidence of the capture of unwilling boroughs by powerful aristocrats. Rather, boroughs sought patrons for the services they could provide and generally entered voluntarily into the protection of corrupt courtiers. As to electoral corruption, revisionists generally see the alleged occurrences as instances in which socially legitimate actors undertook to forestall divisive electoral contests.

Revisionists emphasize that Parliament was still, at this period, only an occasional assembly in which seats were not considered especially valuable; that sometimes seats would go unfilled because of the absence of nominations. Indeed, the surviving correspondence suggests that candidates felt more a sense of obligation to serve than an ambition to do so.

For revisionists, the cause of electoral quiesence is found instead in the (real or ideal) fundamental unity of society and in the consensual recognition of the merit of certain people or families. Revisionists deny that much was at stake in the making of policy by Parliament; indeed, they see Parliament as an episodic social event more than as an institution: "Parliaments, if they are to be seen in perspective, should not be seen as the makers of the major historical events of the 1620s, but as *ad hoc* gatherings of men reacting to events taking place elsewhere" (Russell 1979, 1). The members were not struggling to make their mark on policy; that right they freely accorded to the king. Instead, they met to give substance to the king's requests and to make the voice of the "country" heard.

In any case, if policy is conceded to the king, there was little left in Westminster to fight over; electoral politics was all about local social recognition rather than control over legislation. The lack of electoral competition was the result primarily of the broad agreement over who deserved office, to the underlying appeal of the ideal of unity, and not to manipulation, coercion, or any such thing.

Revisionists also deny that there was much opposition between the Court and the Parliament, emphasizing instead the willingness of Parliament men to play their accustomed supporting role for the king's policies. They do not see any real growth in partisanship or ideology until well into the 1640s, and interpret Whiggish accounts of partisanship as placing an ex post facto interpretation on what was really a succession of isolated disputes, traceable more to strong personalities or to simple misunderstandings or miscalculations than to any coherent sense of party.

Mark A. Kishlansky (1986) argues that we should not try to understand this period through contemporary eyes at all; such an attempt would mislead us into thinking that elections of this period were sufficiently like present-day elections that they should be understood as mere precursors, or pale reflections, of our contemporary versions. Instead, we should interpret the past in terms of contemporaneous meanings. We should recognize that there was nothing predetermined about the way modern elections are conducted, that the past might have led to many different histories. We should reconstruct the meanings that contemporaries brought to the choice of members of the Commons. We should strip away the interpretative baggage of nearly four centuries and try to see how the process looked and felt to those who might have been candidates or constituents then. We should be careful not to assume just because the same or similar words are used to describe a phenomenon, that contemporaries understood those words as we do.

Thus the practices of that period should not be seen as imperfect or unperfected versions of modern practices. In the case of voting, for example, most parliamentary selections in the early Stuart period were settled by what was called "giving voices" or the "shout." People assembled at an announced location and shouted, sometimes for hours, the name of their preferred candidates, after which a magistrate would declare a winner or winners. This practice looks similar to the voice vote of modern Parliaments, but Kishlansky cautions us that "giving voice meant giving assent, agreeing to something rather than choosing it. Actually giving voices meant appearing at the place of election to shout or say aye to the proposal of the nominee's name. The shout was a ritual of affirmation and celebration. As a process, it was both anonymous and unanimous. It was the very opposite of voting" (1986, 10-11). Obviously, much rests on the observation that there were very few contests. What, after all, could all these people have been doing except celebrating, out there in a field shouting at the top of their lungs, drinking ale and wine supplied by the nominees, when there was no contest, no alternative candidates, no choice?

And what were they celebrating? The answer to this question provides a key to Kishlansky's interpretation of the selection of members for the Commons.

English society of that period was marked by hierarchy and associated notions of honor, deference, and merit. Access to Parliament and other office was held as a matter of right by those deserving of social distinction. This was clearest in the case of the House of Lords but was almost as true in the case of Commons. Selection to the House of Commons was, according to Kishlansky, a public recognition of social merit, not the outcome of a contest among ambitious aspirants to public office. "In the counties the keynotes of parliamentary selection were honor and deference. Men were chosen members of Parliament or given the right to nominate on the basis of criteria largely social in nature" (Kishlansky 1986, 14). He goes on: "[I]n the early modern world, there was no separation between the social and the political. Authority was integrated. Personal attributes, prestige, standing, godliness—were all implicit in office holding" (15-16).

Elections, Kishlansky says, had little to do with what policy was made, and ideology played no role in selection because the men who were sent to Parliament were not sent there in order to do anything specific. They were sent because of who they were, not because of what they or their supporters wanted to accomplish. "There is almost no evidence upon which to base the assumption that there was a connection between the selection of members to Parliament and the activities of members of Parliament." Thus electoral contests were not struggles over alternative policies but were instead "bitter personal or local feuds that rent the social fabric of the community." Contests were marked by social dislocation, riots, ambushes, lawsuits, and "were a catastrophe for the community and were seen as such" (1986, 16,17,18).

Contests were dangerous because they "could become a vehicle for widening local and familial feuds and an open challenge to the magistracy" (Kishlansky 1986, 71). When candidates undertook to bid for votes, to "labour for voices," they risked not only humiliating rejection but also the social peace:

> [A]n electoral contest would divide county society into warring groups; such a duel could only leave disfiguring scars. To cast down this gauntlet was to place high value on family honor, for the innocent would be victimized with the guilty.... An electoral contest might become an occasion for sedition and treason. (95-96)

Kishlansky sees the rare occurrence of a poll—a recording of each eligible individual's vote—which is indisputable evidence of a contest, as a violation of deeply held social norms. "By counting each man as one, the meanest freeholder equal to the worthiest gentleman, the community violated every other social norm by which it operated." The regression from the voice to the "view" (in which partisans gathered in separate groups to be viewed) to the poll or vote was degenerative: the voice or shout was a celebration, rather than a method of determining majorities; the view was "equally useless as a means of fixing size, as exceedingly helpful if those taking it wanted to know candidate had the support of county leaders." "A poll was good for one thing only ... it was a somber affair. It was a solution akin to Solomon's judgement—equitable but not efficacious." In his discussion in which a sheriff went to great lengths to resolve a contest, Kishlansky noted that, "as always, the sheriff was exceedingly reluctant to hold a poll" (Kishlansky 1986, 61, 62, 71.)

Thus, on Kishlansky's theory, the celebration marked the unity of a social order that was reflected once again in the uncontested selection of candidates in the constituency. While the candidates supplied the wine and the food and the people freely supplied their voices, it was not an exchange and certainly not a competition. The "conventions of selection process were not shadows behind which lurked ambition and the hunger for power" (1986, 23). Indeed, service in Parliament was neither widely nor deeply desired.[24] The commitment of resources by the candidates normally had nothing to do with persuading citizens to vote one way or another. Instead, an election was a festive affirmation of unified social and political order in which honor and merit were recognized in voluntary deference, and in which those of high social standing—the candidates and their families—simply did their part by providing food and drink.

What is important here is to see that the uncontested selection was the normal case not only in the sense that this was what ordinarily occurred, but also in the sense that it was the normatively desired, healthy, peaceful method by which communities recognized rather than chose their representatives. Contests were breakdowns, symptoms of failure, of uncontrolled tensions and hostilities.

For Kishlansky, parliamentary selection in the early part of the seventeenth century contrasts strikingly with the more modern practices of election after the Restoration. Under the later Stuarts, contests were frequent and were routinely expected, campaign expenditures escalated dramatically,[25] the franchise was steadily widened and clarified,[26] the rules of election were codified, and ideology became more central to the choice of members. Elections became more what we would think of as choices of representatives. Older social meanings began to decay and even seemed archaic.

According to Kishlansky, the cause of this shift was the shattering of English social unity during the Civil War. Localities no longer possessed a consensual unified hierarchy of desert and merit, but simply divided along religious and ideological lines. Old institutional forms and practices could no longer contain social conflict and disagreement, and so these institutions and practices began to atrophy. Formal political institutions and practices—elections, Parliament, administration, legal systems—began to separate from and become more autonomous of a deeply divided social world, because the older hierarchy-based mechanisms would no longer serve.

In the end, the empirical-basis revisionist response to the Whigs rests importantly on the observation that there is simply too little contestation for office for the Whig account to be sustained. While it is true that the number of contested seats increased sixfold, from 15 in 1604 to 91 in the Long Parliament,[27] even this number represents much less than a quarter of the available places. If office was valuable, officers ambitious, and electorates relatively large and hard to control, why were there still so few electoral contests?[28] Why, instead, did so many parliamentary seats remain uncontested in the same families that had held them under Elizabeth? The revisionists undercut the Whig attempt to invoke corruption, coercion, and patronage by interpreting these as accepted and legitimate social practices which, while possibly limiting competition, actually point to the necessity for another interpretation of electoral practices altogether.

A Rational Choice Account: Whiggery Revived

To the modern cephologist, an era without competition for seats is not incomprehensible. A good deal of empirical and theoretical effort has gone into trying to understand the relatively low level of competition for congressional seats in the last 30 years, and it has become clear that even where national office is valuable, the franchise is relatively broad and clearly defined, and politicians ambitiously seek election—in other words, where standard Whiggish assumptions hold—the level of competition need not be very high.

While this is not the place to develop a fully specified model of elections, it is useful to give a very simple model that illustrates the main lines of a revised Whig account. I shall assume only that a parliamentary office has some value to whoever holds it and construct a game-theoretical model in which electoral contests are rare. Specifically, I shall argue that we can understand electoral phenomena in this period as the realization of an implicit form of collusion in which potential aspirants for office agree not to contest seats.

Suppose, for the purposes of argument, that there is a constituency with one seat and two potential candidates and that (for both candidates) the costs of running a campaign is c and the benefits of office, b, where $b/2 < c$. Furthermore, assume that election is symmetric in the sense that if two candidates enter the race, each has the same expectation of winning. Then, if only one candidate enters the race, his or her expectation is $b - c > 0$, while if both enter, each expects $b/2 - c < 0$. In a noncooperative analysis of this game, in which the players make their choice independently, there are two pure strategy equilibria: each with exactly one candidate entering, and one mixed-strategy equilibrium in which each candidate enters with probability $2(1 - c/b)$. Thus, in this model, even though office is valuable and politicians are ambitious, competition for office will not necessarily occur.

In the mixed-strategy equilibrium, competition may occur, but if c is large (compared to b), the probability of a contest would be very low. Moreover, the presence of a mixed-strategy equilibrium in which there is competition is the result of the assumption that strategies are announced simultaneously, surely an artificial feature of the example. If announcements are sequential, this equilibrium disappears and all that remains are pure strategy equilibria. In fact, if the candidates have full information about the strategic structure of the game, it is difficult to construct situations in which competition can be observed in equilibrium.

While this example leaves out nearly everything that an actual rational choice account would wish to include (variable campaign costs, private information as to the value of office to each of the candidates, consideration of timing, and the like), it is rich enough to illustrate the indeterminacy of the rational choice explanation. There is nothing internal to the account that explains why one equilibrium rather than another is observed. When, as always, there are more candidates and more strategic opportunities, this indeterminacy becomes even more substantial.

Now suppose, to change the example slightly, that b/2–c > 0. In a (noncooperative) Nash equilibrium, both candidates will surely enter and competition will be observed. Of course, if the situation of the candidates is not symmetric, so that one candidate is much more likely to win than the other, then only the advantaged candidate may enter. Thus we see that (at least in a thick-rational account of this type) competition will occur in some circumstances and not in others. In fact, by comparing this case with the previous one, we might conclude that if the value of political office increases or if the costs of running decreases, the amount of competition will increase.

However, the structure of the model suggests another possibility. In any equilibrium in which there is competition, campaign expenditures are simply thrown away by the candidates. If the two candidates could somehow "agree" (whether explicitly or tacitly) not to compete with each other and, instead, to rotate in office so that only one would enter at each election, it is easy to see (as long as elections are sufficiently frequent) that both would be better off than in any of the noncooperative equilibria described above.

Thus if there is a way for the candidates to arrange to "collude," or to come to an enforceable agreement as to who shall stand and who shall stand down, each can avoid costly campaigning. If methods permitting such collusion are available, the model suggests that they will be used in order to realize gains from exchange. Indeed, it seems that agreements would be resorted to more frequently when the value of office is relatively high and the candidates symmetrically situated, since otherwise the candidates might easily come to their own implicit understandings as to who will enter and under which circumstances.

The claim that early seventeenth-century elections can be understood as collusive outcomes raises two issues: How are collusive arrangements agreed to? How are they enforced? Put another way, we might ask about which conditions are most propitious for the formation and enforcement of such collusive arrangements. In our discussion of the revisionists, we have already seen evidence of enforcement mechanisms. Kishlansky and others document the fear of social disorder that is expected to attend electoral contests, and the possibility—indeed the likelihood—of prolonged feud among powerful families, leading to fighting and deaths following the violation of electoral understandings. The chain of dismal consequences that might be expected to follow the failure to carry out such an understanding is documented as well in John Neale's (1949, 122-131) account of a contest in Rutland.

While enforcement mechanisms would seem to be abundantly available in a closed hierarchical society, it is less obvious how they would work in practice. The possibility of enforcing collusion depends on the availability of beliefs, practices, and institutions permitting the enforcement of understandings when they threaten to break down.[29] Kishlansky demonstrates that both formal institutions and informal normative structures geared to enforcing collusive arrangements of the sort suggested here existed during this period. He gives a number of examples from both counties and boroughs of local officials arranging collusive outcomes when a contest threatened. "No parliamentary selection that threatened to degenerate into a contest was without plans for settling the issue peaceably.... [A]ttempts at composing potential contests were made initially by an appeal to the community's leadership.... [I]f noblemen or magistrates could not successfully intervene to compose potential conflicts, then responsibility fell to the returning officer in the boroughs and to the sheriff in the counties" (1986, 55-57).

Even if enforcement mechanisms are available, it is less obvious just how contestants might be expected to come to an understanding as to who shall stand for the seat in the first place. After all, there is a pervasive distributional issue of who shall share the gains from office, one in which there is a genuine possibility of conflict. Here again, shared expectations associated with a hierarchical society would seem to play the key role. Kishlansky argues that, early in the century, each locality had its own consensually recognized social hierarchy and that only families near the top of that hierarchy were thought to have a legitimate expectation of a seat in the House of Commons. Neale too illustrates the fact that very few families were thought to have a historic claim on a seat and, even within families with legitimate claims, the (socially valued or disvalued) attributes of the individual aspirants imposed further restrictions on potential candidates. Thus I argue that the interior understandings of early Stuart England had the effect of allowing costly contests to be avoided.

While the game-theoretical model is an alternative interpretation of the practices and institutions associated with early Stuart elections, it can also be employed to suggest hypotheses as to the conditions under which we might expect contests to arise. For example, the ease with which collusive outcomes can be "agreed upon" depends on the restriction of the set of potential candidates to a small number. If there are a great number of candidates who may (legitimately) declare their intention to stand for office, and thereby demand some sort of satisfaction in exchange for "standing down," it may be impossible to prevent contests from occurring. Any collusive arrangement would be subject to entry by another candidate demanding satisfaction.

This raises questions as to how the field of candidates is restricted: Is the distribution of wealth so skewed that only a few could afford to run? Or is there some sort of (cultural) expectational phenomenon that restricts the number of "legitimate" aspirants to a small set of families? How does this set of expectations relate to the religious divisions of the period? If parliamentary office became more valuable during the century, or if consensual beliefs and expectations as to existence and legitimacy of local hierarchy declines, we would expect that more candidates would wish to stand in every sort of seat and this would make collusion more difficult to arrange and enforce. If the costs of defeat became more onerous, and here the evidence is more ambiguous, incentives to collude would increase and the level of competition should fall.[30]

To take another example, insofar as rotation or lot—both of which depend on repeated elections rather than wealth transfers as the method of inducing potential challengers to withdraw—are the main "coins" of exchange in preventing contests, collusive outcomes would be more likely when elections are frequent than when they are not. Thus, after Charles refused to call Parliaments for the 11 years after 1629, it is not surprising that the number of contests doubled.

Perhaps, too, different types of constituencies arrived at different sorts of equilibria. It may be the case that the value of office varied according to the type of constituency or that entry barriers—whether rooted in an intersubjectively agreed upon claim to the seat or in the distribution of wealth, in the size or diversity of the constituency, or in some other factors—were stronger in some places than others.

So far I have assumed that the agents face no informational problems in executing collusive arrangements; if information as to the costs and benefits of all courses of action is commonly known to all agents, none would have any reason to depart from the agreement. But if information as to the benefits and costs of actions is privately held by individuals, someone may rationally defect from the arrangement. Such failures to keep to accepted arrangements can arise as a part of equilibrium play in a game of incomplete information. These occasional departures from expected behavior would then be punished by other agents. The punishments, if they are costly to carry out, would have to be severe enough to deter too frequent violations.

Thus Kishlansky's description of the disruptive social consequences of a contest can be given a game-theoretical interpretation. A collusive outcome is based on an (implicit) promise or contract among potential candidates. Some candidates are supposed to stand aside in the expectation of future rewards. Thus the low levels of competition could be evidence not of the relative unattractiveness of office (as Kishlansky argues) but of successfully executed collusion instead.

Indeed, on the rational account, the occurrence of a contest is evidence that someone has broken a promise. Thus it is not surprising (even to moderns) that the matter is understood or interpreted by participants as a question of honor or integrity. It is a question of honor. An important social norm has been violated; someone has been, or appears to have been, dishonest and so others are right to cast doubt upon his word or his character. In the rational account, this is exactly the interpretation that agents should give to the outbreak of a contest. Moreover, these natural feelings of outrage provide support for the retaliatory actions that must be undertaken to deter future occurrences of this sort. The point is that the rational account provides an "interior" description of the significance and meanings of events, and this account is consistent with the documentary evidence found in Kishlansky's book.

Discussion

At one level, the revisionist account can be seen simply as a thick–rational choice explanation. The revisionist takes hierarchical values as given and unproblematic for most people in the early part of the century and interprets their actions as optimal, given these values. If contests are considered disastrous not merely to the candidates but to the whole of local society, then perhaps it is not too surprising that great collective efforts would be spent in avoiding and suppressing them. But that seems to be only a small part of the real value of the revisionist story.

The more important contribution of revisionism is in its narrative aspect: the reconstruction of a worldview in which not only hierarchy, order, and solidarity are valuable, but a world lacking them is inconceivably chaotic and disorienting. The interpretive reconstruction of this world requires the incorporation of religious or sacred values at the center of ordinary life; it requires that we see the local stakes of political disruption as vastly more significant to most people than distant and abstract goings-on in London or Europe. And, most important for our purposes here, it helps us to see how natural and how "unchosen" local society and social expectations were or appeared to be to people of that time.

Neo-Whig theory is aimed at explaining exactly the same facts described by the revisionists. It is aimed at showing that nothing in the revisionist interpretation excludes the possibility that elections in the early seventeenth century were fundamentally similar to those today. This does not imply that a Whiggish account is either better or more plausible: it is a different reconstruction of institutions, practices, meanings, and even of self-understandings—a forward-looking rather than backward-looking one—from the one that Kishlansky proposes.

The rationally reconstructed Whig account is, however, incomplete in certain important ways. Centrally, it lacks any way of selecting which of the many possible equilibria will be played. Indeed, it contains no internal reason to believe that collusive equilibria could be reached or sustained. It does not say who will stand and who will not; it makes no unique prediction as to the level of competition: it is as consistent with high levels of competition as with lower ones.

The weakness of Whig accounts is exactly what is endemic in any rational choice or reconstructive explanation. Such accounts cannot, even in principle, explain why one set of intersubjective or cultural understandings prevailed at a given time rather than some other, or why, among all of the possible equilibria, the specific collusive equilibrium I have identified ex post is the one that occurred rather than some other. Such accounts cannot say, for example, why the rivalry in Sommersetshire was between the Phelips and the Pouletts or why that in Rutland involved the Noels and the Harringtons, and not other families. They cannot explain why these families claimed seats, why others generally deferred to their claims, or why, when contests occurred, they took the form they did. They cannot explain why there were contests in these places and times and not in others. There are many different equilibrium outcomes, each of which seem plausible, ex ante, and which cannot be reduced on purely game-theoretical grounds. Like Taylor's hermeneutics or like Kishlansky's historical description, the game-theoretical analysis is stronger as an ex post account than as prediction.

It is here that an interpretivist approach offers a valuable and unique contribution. There is something in the meanings shared by members of that time and place, in their identities and self-understandings that make some equilibrium outcomes not just plausible but more natural, and even more inevitable than others. Interpretivists are right to suggest the self-understandings of members of a hierarchical and unified society as the likely source of this selection. But if appeals to tradition and to the internal norms of an ordered society are essential components of explanation, they do not exclude that part of explanation that results from principles of rationality, thin or thick. However they construct their worlds, agents' actions must make sense to themselves as in some way not merely appropriate but as representing the best actions they could choose.[31]

But this is only part of what the interpretivist has to offer. The fact that cultural or intersubjective understandings may select among equilibria might be called an exterior or formal relationship between theories of interpretation and choice. Intersubjective understandings happen to play the part of the auxiliary hypothesis, or "focal point," permitting agents to coordinate their strategic behavior in complex social interactions. There is as well the possibility of interior or substantive connections between the two approaches: What is the structure of the set of ideas and interpretations that can be held by actors? Do these intersubjective understandings obey an autonomous dynamic, or is their evolution affected by how they affect the choice of actions? Reciprocally, does the choice of an action in one circumstance somehow limit ensuing cultural or intersubjective understandings?

I think that the debate between neo-Whigs and revisionists helps us to explore some of these interior issues. The revisionist description suggests a view in which intersubjective understandings are given or evolve relatively autonomously and in which the relationship between culture and action is unidirectional. Culturally constituted agents interpret their situations and actions in terms of an autonomously generated and sustained systems of values, beliefs, and understandings. The neo-Whig account envisions more of a symbiotic relationship between interpretation and action. Actor preferences, beliefs, and identities may be given (by biological, social, or cultural processes or by the structure of the strategic setting), but the structure of cultural understandings that permit social coordination—the identification and value of hierarchy and one's place in it—may also be partially determined by the nature of the coordination problem itself.

It seems as wrong to overemphasize the differences among cultures and historical milieus as to overemphasize their similarities. There is much in the revisionist or interpretivist account of seventeenth-century elections that cannot be explained by traditional Whig theory, but we do not need to see the early seventeenth century as a separate world existing on the other side of a fundamental and radical divide in English history in order to comprehend its electoral practices. We do not need to deny that office was valuable, that Parliament was becoming an important source of policy and saw itself so, or that motivations of politicians then were similar to those of today. These claims may all be true or false, of course; the revisionist interpretation remains plausible. But it is not inevitable, and more important, it is not inconsistent with a deeper reconstruction of Whig theory.

References

Elster, J. 1983. *Explaining technical change.* Cambridge: Cambridge University Press.
Geertz, C. 1973. *The interpretation of cultures.* New York: Basic Books.
Hadari, S. 1989. *Theory in practice: Tocqueville's new science of politics.* Stanford, CA: Stanford University Press.
Hirst, D. 1975. *The representative of the people?* Cambridge: Cambridge University Press.

Johnson, J. 1988. Symbolic action and the limits to strategic rationality. *Political Power and Social Theory* 7: 211-248.

———. 1990. Rational choice and culture: Skeptical remarks on "the renaissance of political culture." Northwestern Working Paper.

Kishlansky, M. A. 1986. *Parliamentary selection: Social and political choice in early modern England*. Cambridge: Cambridge University Press.

MacIntyre, A. 1981. *After virtue*. Notre Dame, IN: University of Notre Dame Press.

Neale, J. 1949. *The Elizabethan House of Commons*. Harmondsworth: Penguin.

Notestein, W. 1924. *The winning of the initiative by the Commons*. London: Oxford University Press.

Plumb, J. H. 1969. The growth of the electorate in England from 1600 to 1715. *Past and present*, vol. 42.

Russell, C. 1979. *Parliaments and English Parliaments, 1621-1629*. Oxford: Oxford University Press.

Schelling, T. 1960. *Strategy of conflict*. Cambridge, MA: Harvard University Press.

Taylor, C. 1985. Interpretation and the sciences of man. *Philosophy and the human sciences, philosophical papers*, Vol. 2. Cambridge: Cambridge University Press.

Vincent, J. 1966. *The formation of the British Liberal Party*. New York: Scribner.

NOTES

Chapter 2

1. We speak of "assumptions" rather than "beliefs," "values," "norms," or similar phrases because this terms carries fewer connotations within this field of study. We can use it, therefore, in a very general way, similar to its meaning in logic.
2. The analogy with "passing" was suggested by Ward Goodenough, "Cultural Anthropology and Linguistics," in *Language, Culture, and Society*, edited by Dell Hymes (New York, 1964), esp. p. 36.
3. "I'd like to know whether epochs that possessed culture knew the word at all, or used it. Naiveté, unconsciousness, taken-for-grantedness, seems to me to be the first criterion of the constitution to which we give this name" Adrian Leuerkuehn, in Thomas Mann, *Dr. Faustus* (New York, 1968), p. 61.
4. What we call "structural explanation" is quite similar to (though more broadly conceived than) what is called "demographic explanation" by Arthur L. Stinchcombe, *Constructing Social Theories* (New York, 1968), pp. 57-79.
5. Note, therefore, the sharp difference between our concept and a standard definition of "value" (which has often been considered and elementary unit if culture): "A value is a conception, explicit or implicit, distinctive of an individual or characteristic of a group, of the desirable which influences the selection from available modes, means, and ends of action." Clyde Kluckhohn, "Values and Value-Orientations in the Theory of Action," in Talcott Parsons and Edward A. Shils, eds., *Toward a General Theory of Action* (New York, 1962), p. 395. Values, in other words, direct one's choice among the alternative presented by the [political] culture.
6. For a systematic review of conceptualizations of personality, see Paul M. Sniderman, *Personality and Democratic Politics* (Berkeley, 1975), pp. 9-17, 65-115. He argues that personality affects political behavior primarily by its influence on social learning conditions.
7. See, for example, Garry Wills, *Nixon Agonistes* (New York, 1971), esp. part I; and James David Barber, *Presidential Character* (Englewood Cliffs, NJ, 1972), especially chapter 1 and part five. Note also that "character" and situation collaborate, in Barber's framework, to produce presidential behavior, just as we posit a collaborative relationship between political culture and structure in understanding political behavior more generally.
8. Our logic parallels that developed by Jae-on Kim, John R. Petrocik, and Stephen N. Enokson, "Voter Turnout Among the American States: Systemic and Individual Components," *American Political Science Review* LXIX (March 1975), 107-23. They asked what proportion of variation in turnout was due to the sociodemographic composition of the electorate and to two "system-level" or institutional factors (competitiveness and legal restrictions on voting). Since these two sets of variables accounted for most of the variance, political culture appears to be a relatively unimportant component of the explanation in this instance.

9. A similar argument, though for a different purpose, has been made by Adam Przeworski and Henry Teune, "Equivalence in Cross-National Research," *Public Opinion Quarterly* 30 (Winter 1966-67): 564, fn. 10.
10. Brian Barry, *Sociologists, Economists, and Democracy* (London, 1970); and Carole Pateman, *Political Participation and Democratic Theory* (London, 1970) provide detailed criticisms of explanations at this level of analysis.
11. For example, see Kinhide Mushakoji, "The Strategies of Negotiation: An American-Japanese Comparison," in J. A. Laponce and P. Smoker, eds., *Experimentation and Simulation in Political Science* (Toronto, 1972).

Chapter 3

1. It is possible to identify differences within culturalist approaches to politics in terms of methods, levels of analysis, substantive questions, and willingness to compare and generalize across cases. In this essay, in distinguishing between what I call weak and strong cultural understandings, I emphasize what I view as the useful core of the approach much more than differences within it.
2. Among the issues that divide anthropologists are relativism, the importance of searching for generalizations, the possibility of comparison, and the role of psychological mechanisms in cultural explanations.
3. Taylor uses the term "common reference world" (1985, 38) to refer to what members of a culture know.
4. D'Andrade (1984, 88) points out that the radical shift from the view of culture as behavior that could be understood within a stimulus-response framework to culture as systems of meaning is found in a number of fields. For a complete discussion of culture as meanings and symbols see the excellent discussions in Schweder and LeVine (1984).
5. I use worldview to include affective elements, whereas often the concept of social schema only emphasizes cognitive elements. Anthony Wallace's (1970) concept of mazeway is parallel to worldview.
6. Laitin (1986, 1988) describes "the two faces of culture," referring to culture as a system of meaning on the one hand and culture as a resource for instrumental action on the other. While I find the distinction useful and his analysis very consistent with my own, the twofold distinction is too brief for my purposes here.
7. Certainly the comparative analysis of state-building has long recognized the role of cultural practices and political control over them, as well as the role of political leaders who become cultural icons, linking previously disparate groups in a single state and in the process defining newer, broader identities.
8. This sort of rich understanding of culture is not one that is possible to develop exclusively from survey data. Although such data can make a significant contribution to what I have called subjective cultural analysis, the data by themselves are insufficient for building an intersubjective cultural account.
9. There have been efforts to identify a fixed number of human motives such as Murray's (1938) and McClelland's (1961) work on three particular motives—achievement, affiliation, and power. It is important to recognize that in both of these cases—especially in McClelland's—the relative importance of any single motive varied both cross-culturally and across individuals.
10. However, see Levi and her recognition of early rational choice theory's lack of interest in this question and current attention to it, including an interest in the role of culture as a source of interests (e.g., Greif 1994).
11. An important question is the extent to which any culture characteristically exhibits generalizing of differentiating behaviors in encounters with outsiders, at least in certain domains. In a cross-cultural study of internal and external conflict and violence, I found that in some cultures the levels of internal and external conflict are quite similar (generalizers) while in others they are highly differentiated. The differences between the two groups of societies are quite clear: Differentiating societies are characterized by many ties that link diverse groups in the society and that clearly mark them off from outsiders, while generalizing societies are those without strong mechanisms of internal integration. Probably a key reason why insiders and outsiders are treated somewhat the same is because whether one is an insider or an outsider vis-à-vis a group is defined contextually and not in absolute terms.

12. Cohen's analysis is quite compatible with one resource mobilization theorists offer in their discussion of social movements, especially in their willingness to consider cultural as well as material resources (McAdam, Tarrow, and Tilly this volume).
13. Much of the critique of national character research was also relevant to studies in small-scale societies typically studied by anthropologists. For example, Wallace (1970, 152-54) argued that while culture and personality theories would predict a large proportion of the people in a small society would exhibit a similar personality profile, when he administered standardized tests to a community of Tuscarora Indians only 37% fit the modal pattern. Also see Inkeles and Levinson (1968) and LeVine (1973).
14. An additional criticism of the civic culture tradition is the impoverished, generally implicit, unilineal view of the world's political cultures on a single continuum with the United States at the high end, rather than a multidimensional, more complex image of cultural difference.
15. In another interesting example using a cultural indicator of collective political orientations, Regan (1994) relates sales of war toys and popularity of war movies to U.S. militarization.
16. There has been extensive discussion of Putnam's (1993) work and its relevance beyond Italy, which is not my focus here. For two critical views of his theory pertinent to my discussion of culture, see Laitin (1995b) and Tarrow (1996).
17. Gluckman, for example, wrote about the importance of studying what he called "trouble cases" in his work on African law, but it is clear that he saw this as a much more general methodological strategy as well.
18. In many ways his argument is similar to fraternal interest group theory in anthropology, which says that in the absence of centralized authority, coresident males are likely to defend what they see as their core interests through organized violence (Paige and Paige 1981; Ross 1993a).
19. Galton's Problem refers to the fact that in cross-cultural (and cross-national) samples, assumptions about the independence of units are often inappropriate and that substantive correlations among culture traits can reflect diffusion and borrowing rather than functional association. The most useful response is not to ignore this problem but to build diffusion hypotheses into models to test the relative power of each pattern (Ross and Homer 1976).
20. Another answer comes from Thompson, Ellis, and Wildavsky (1990), who argue that culture is seen in distinct ways of life, which they define in terms of Mary Douglas's grid-group analysis. Group refers to the extent to which an individual is incorporated into bounded units, whereas grid refers to the degree to which a person's behaviors are circumscribed by externally imposed restriction. Different individuals or states can, in their view, exhibit different degrees of each of the five combinations they identify over time. However, viable social units, they argue, are not characterized by the presence of only one culturally defined way of life. While I find much of their analysis of the interaction between values and social structure quite useful, it is less evident to me that making the way of life the unit of analysis provides a guideline easy for researchers to use, since they say multiple orientations can exist in the same culture or subculture and that individuals may have different orientations across time and situations.
21. This does not mean that such a list of societies that represent the world's cultures, such as one of the samples developed in cross-cultural research, is not useful in many research situations.
22. Pye (1991) says that national character analyses tended to treat "personality and culture as opposite sides of the same coin. Character for them was the generalized personality of a people, in the sense that the modal personality of a people was their culture, and thus culture and personality were essentially identical factors shaping behavior" (494).
23. The point here is similar to Przeworski and Teune's (1970), that comparative political analysts should strive to replace proper names with variable names. While some interpretivists only want to consider the uniqueness of each culture and context, others are comfortable making comparisons while recognizing the potential problems inherent in any comparison and the generalizations derived from it.
24. Beatrice Whiting (1980) discusses the importance cross-culturally of the placement of individuals in particular contexts, e.g., girls take care of younger siblings more than boys and boys are more likely to take care of animals in all the cultures for which she has data. Her data also show that cultures vary in the settings they "make available" to individuals, and she distinguishes between behaviors seen as "mundane" and those domains that are "projective" and infused with great emotional significance.
25. In anthropology where this debate has been particularly heated, two issues—evaluation of different cultures (cultural relativism) and comparison of cultures—are often fused. The relativism

debate concerns the appropriateness of evaluating cultures other than one's own, while the comparison question turns on the issue of whether it is possible to compare cultures and develop meaningful generalizations. Edgerton (1992) describes the anti-comparison position as "asserting far more than the self-evident point that people in different societies live in somewhat different worlds of meaning. They are claiming that each of these worlds is truly unique—incommensurable and largely incomprehensible—and that the people who inhabit them have different cognitive abilities . . . [and] various postmodern relativists and interpretivists postulate fundamental differences from one culture to the next in cognitive processes involving logic, causal inferences, and information processing" (28).

26. Here the subjectivity of different social scientists and varying theoretical interests will certainly produce variation in the accounts that are rendered. Often this will reflect differences in emphasis. This is not necessarily a sign of the method's failure but of its complexity; as with other methods, efforts to obtain inter-subjective reliability among observers are important.

27. This is the same claim that many students of the U.S. Congress have made over the years.

28. Taylor (1985) proposes an interesting test of the utility of an interesting test of the utility of an interpretation when he writes, "We make sense of action when there is coherence between the actions of the agent and the meaning of his situation" (24).

29. The term psychocultural brings together the psychological processes central to the construction of these interpretations and cultural dynamics, emphasizing that these orientations are not just personal but, rather, are nurtured and socially reinforced, linking individuals in a collective process, amplifying what is shared, and emphasizing differences among groups (Mack 1983).

30. While there is no room to develop the point here, it is important to understand that in contemporary society, the media became politically significant as creators and interpreters of events (Dayan and Katz 1992, 83).

31. For example in Northern Ireland, Protestant Unionists find great meaning in the story of William of Orange and the Battle of the Boyne in 1689, while Catholic accounts really say little about King Billy or the battle. In contrast, Catholic Nationalists emphasize the meaning of the 1916 Easter Uprising, which for Protestants is far less significant than their sacred pact committing themselves to resist Irish self-rule four years earlier. Even when an event enters into the stories of both sides, such as the Hunger Strikes of Nationalist prisoners in 1980-81, the metaphors and meanings associated with them can be so different that it is hard to realize one is hearing about the same events in two different ways.

32. See the special issue of *Mind and Human Interaction* (1992) devoted to the question of ethnic and nationalistic traumas, and Volkan (1996) for a discussion of the meaning of Kosovo for the Serbs.

33. The flip side is the *chosen glory* in which a group perceives triumph over the enemy; this is seen clearly in the Northern Irish Protestant celebration of the Battle of the Boyne in 1689 every July 12 (Cecil 1993).

34. What is validated is the meaning of the story to the participants on each side. This does not necessarily mean the acceptance of such accounts as accurate. The notion of empathy is useful here. It suggests an acceptance of the account as meaningful to the recounter without necessarily implying agreement on the part of the listener.

35. Carol Hager (personal communication) suggests that critical theory provides a set of guidelines for the empirical study of interpretations in political research with its attention to communication processes and concerns with the problems of mediating between a researcher's own interpretations and those of the people being studied.

36. The issue of how local actors react to an interpretation has several components. One is the extent to which they or the social scientist have provided it. If it is the latter, to what extent do they see it as plausible? Another issue is how local actors react to a social scientist's interpretation. For example, Nancy Scheper-Hughes (1982, v-xi), writing about the severe personal and social dysfunctionality associated with the very high rates of schizophrenia in rural Ireland, reports how upset villagers were with her book describing this pattern. Interestingly, they didn't say she was wrong; rather, they chastised her for making public what were regarded locally as private matters.

Chapter 5

1. See, for example, Immanuel Wallerstein, *The Politics of the World Economy* (Cambridge: Cambridge University Press, 1984); Nigel Harris, *The End of the Third World* (New York: Penguin Books,

1987); Kenichi Ohmae, *The Borderless World: Power and Strategy in the Interlinked Economy* (London: HarperCollins, 1990); Martin Carnoy, Manuel Castells, and Stephen S. Cohen, eds., *The Global Economy in the Information Age* (University Park, PA: Penn State University Press, 1993); Gary Gereffi and Miguel Korzeniewicz eds., *Commodity Chains and Global Capitalism* (Westport, CT: Praeger, 1994); and Saskia Sassen, *Globalization and Its Discontents* (New York: The New Press, 1998).
2. See, for example, Anthony Giddens, *The Consequences of Modernity* (Cambridge: Polity Press, 1990); Mike Featherstone, ed., *Global Culture* (London: Sage, 1990); H. Holm and G. Sorenson, *Whose World Order: Uneven Globalization and the End of the Cold War* (Boulder, CO: Westview Press, 1995); and Robert J. Holton, *Globalization and the Nation-State* (New York: St. Martin's Press, 1998).
3. See, for example, Anthony Giddens, *Beyond Left and Right: The Future of Radical Politics* (Stanford, CA: Stanford University Press, 1994), pp. 4-5; Benjamin R. Barber, *Jihad Vs. McWorld: How Globalism and Tribalism Are Reshaping the World* (New York: Ballantine Books, 1996), pp. 4-5; and Cesare Poppi, "Wider Horizons with Larger Details: Subjectivity, Ethnicity and Globalization," in *The Limits of Globalization: Cases and Arguments,* ed. Alan Scott (London: Routledge, 1997), p. 285.

Chapter 6

1. Almost invariably Western leaders claim they are acting on behalf of "the world community." One minor lapse occurred during the run-up to the Gulf War. In an interview on *Good Morning America,* December 21, 1990, British Prime Minister John Major referred to the actions "the West" was taking against Saddam Hussein. He quickly corrected himself and subsequently referred to "the world community." He was, however, right when he erred.
2. Owen Harries has pointed out that Australia is trying (unwisely in his view) to become a torn country in reverse. Although it has been a full member not only of the West but also of the ABCA military and intelligence core of the West, its current leaders are in effect proposing that it defect from the West, redefine itself as an Asian country and cultivate close ties with in neighbors. Australia's future, they argue, is with the dynamic economics of East Asia. But, as I have suggested, close economic cooperation normally requires a common cultural base. In addition, none of the three conditions necessary for a torn country to join another civilization is likely to exist in Australia's case.

Chapter 7

1. Rather than study the motives of people who seemingly "didn't want to be free"—for whom tyranny appeared to be "more welcome than liberty"—the Greek historian Herodotus was content to attribute such anomalies to the servility natural to barbarians or those descended from them. See Pericles Georges, *Barbarian Asia and the Greek Experience: From the Archaic Period to the Age of Xenophon* (Baltimore: Johns Hopkins University Press, 1994), 39, citing Herodotus. One may compare this with the Marxists' use of "false consciousness" to label the failure of workers to behave as expected. For that attribution too begs deeper questions.
2. Lingle has also discussed his case in his review of Francis Seow's *To Catch a Tartar: A Dissident in Lee Kuan Yew's Prison* (New Haven, CT: Yale Center for International and Area Studies, 1994). The review, entitled "Trouble in Paradise," appeared in the *Journal of Democracy* 6 (July 1995): 172-175.
3. Bowring and the *Tribune* lost the case and were assessed $678,000.
4. "But there is neither East nor West, Border, nor Bread, nor Birth, when two strong men stand face to face, though they come from the ends of the earth!" Rudyard Kipling, "The Ballad of East and West," in *Rudyard Kipling: The Complete Verse* (London: Kyle Cathie, 1990), 190. That Kipling's culture-dissolving ethos is elitist, masculinist, and Westernizing illustrates the risk of asserting the absolute universality of one's own preferred values.
5. The East Asian countries covered were China, Indonesia, Japan, Malaysia, the Philippines, Singapore, South Korea, and Thailand. Respondents were selected neither randomly nor in sufficient quantity to make the results more than suggestive.

Chapter 8

1. Boxplots are a diagnostic tool that provide visual evidence of four elements of a distribution: center, spread, symmetry, and outliers. The box itself represents the interquartile range (the upper boundary = Q3 and the lower boundary = Q1). The median is represented by the line through the middle of the box. The two letter codes that appear near to some of the boxes are state abbreviations for cases that may be considered outliers in relation to other state is the culture (Hamilton 1990, Chap.5).
2. See Madison's classic explanation of the sources of faction in the Federalist #10.

Chapter 9

1. Government data indicate that at age twenty, American women are more likely to be members of the labor force than to be married. U.S. Department of Labor, 1976.
2. Sponsors do play a role in public broadcasting. As underwriters of programs, they may refuse to fund controversial materials. Some critics claim the Corporation for Public Broadcasting has avoided controversial topics to maintain corporate grants, and has designed dramatic series to appeal to corporations and foundations. According to informants at WNET, corporate underwriters object when the station delays airing their programs to squeeze in public appeals for contributions to the station.
3. Matilda Butler and William Paisley. Personal communication, Fall 1976.
4. 1976, personal communication.

Chapter 10

1. The best discussion of cockfighting is again Bateson and Mead's *Balinese Character*, pp. 24-25, 140; but it, too, is general and abbreviated.
2. The cockfight is unusual within Balinese culture in being a single-sex public activity from which the other sex is totally and expressly excluded. Sexual differentiation is culturally extremely played down in Bali and most activities, formal and informal, involve the participation of men and women on equal ground, commonly as linked couples. From religion, to politics, to economics, to kinship, to dress, Bali is a rather "unisex" society, a fact both its customs and its symbolism clearly express. Even in contexts where women do not in fact play much of a role—music, painting, certain agricultural activities—their absence, which is only relative in any case, is more a mere matter of fact than socially enforced. To this general pattern, the cockfight, entirely of, by, and for men (women—at least *Balinese* women—do not even watch), is the most striking exception.
3. The lay has a stanza (no. 17) with the reluctant bridegroom use. Jaya Prana, the subject of a Balinese Uriah myth, responds to the lord who has offered him the loveliest of six hundred servant girls: "Godly King, my Lord and Master / I beg you, give me leave to go / such things are not yet in my mind; / like a fighting cock encaged / indeed I am on my mettle / I am alone / as yet the flame has not been fanned."
4. There is indeed a legend to the effect that the separation of Java and Bali is due to the action of a powerful Javanese religious figure who wished to protect himself against a Balinese culture hero (the ancestor of two Ksatria castes) who was a passionate cockfighting gambler. See C. Hooykaas, *Agama Tirtha* (Amsterdam, 1964), p. 184.
5. An incestuous couple is forced to wear pig yokes over their necks and crawl to a pig trough and eat with their mouths there. On this, see J. Belo, "Customs Pertaining to Twins in Bali," in *Traditional Balinese Culture,* ed. J. Belo, p. 49; on the abhorrence of animality generally, Bateson and Mead, *Balinese Character*, p. 22.
6. Except for unimportant, small-bet fights (on the question of fight "importance," see below) spur affixing is usually done by someone other than the owner. Whether the owner handles his own cock or not more or less depends on how skilled he is at it, a consideration whose importance is again relative to the importance of the fight. When spur affixers and cock handlers are someone other than the owner, they are almost always a quite close relative—a brother or cousin—or a very intimate friend of his. They are thus almost extensions of his personality, as the fact that all three will refer to the cock as "mine," say "I" fought So-and-So, and so on, demonstrates.

Also, owner-handler-affixer triads tend to be fairly fixed, though individuals may participate in several and often exchange roles within a given one.

7. This word, which literally means an indelible stain or mark, as in a birthmark or a vein in a stone, is used as well for a deposit in a court case, for a pawn, for security offered in a loan, for a stand-in for someone else in a legal or ceremonial context, for an earnest advanced in a business deal, for a sign placed in a field to indicate its ownership is in dispute, and for the status of an unfaithful wife from whose lover her husband must gain satisfaction or surrender her to him. See Korn, *Het Adatrecht von Bali;* Th. Pigeaud, *Javaans-Nederlands Handwoordenboek* (Groningen, 1938); H. H. Juynboll, *Oudjavaansche-Nederlandsche Woordenlijst* (Leiden, 1923).

8. The center bet must be advanced in cash by both parties prior to the actual fight. The umpire holds the stakes until the decision is rendered and then awards them to the winner, avoiding, among other things, the intense embarrassment both winner and loser would feel if the latter had to pay off personally following his defeat. About 10 percent of the winner's receipts are subtracted for the umpire's share and that of the fight sponsors.

9. Actually, the typing of cocks, which is extremely elaborate (I have collected more than twenty classes, certainly not a complete list), is not based on color alone, but on a series of independent, interacting, dimensions, which include—besides color—size, bone thickness, plumage, and temperament. (But not pedigree. The Balinese do not breed cocks to any significant extent, nor, so far as I have been able to discover, have they ever done so. The *asil,* or jungle cock, which is the basic fighting strain everywhere the sport is found, is native to southern Asia, and one can buy a good example in the chicken section of almost any Balinese market for anywhere from four or five ringgits up to fifty or more.) The color element is merely the one normally used as the type name, except when the two cocks of different types—as on principle they must be—have the same color, in which case a secondary indication from one of the other dimensions ("large speckled" v. "small speckled," etc.) is added. The types are coordinated with various cosmological ideas which help shape the making of matches, so that, for example, you fight a small, headstrong, speckled brown-on-white cock with flat-lying feathers and thin legs from the east side of the ring on a certain day of the complex Balinese calendar, and a large, cautious, all-black cock with tufted feathers and stubby legs from the north side on another day, and so on. All this is again recorded in palm-leaf manuscripts and endlessly discussed by the Balinese (who do not all have identical systems), and a full-scale componential-cum-symbolic analysis of cock classifications would be extremely valuable both as an adjunct to the description of the cockfight and in itself. But my data on the subject, though extensive and varied, do not seem to be complete and systematic enough to attempt such an analysis here. For Balinese cosmological ideas more generally see Belo, ed., *Traditional Balinese Culture,* and J. L. Swellengrebel, ed., *Bali: Studies in Life, Thought, and Ritual* (The Hague, 1960).

10. For purposes of ethnographic completeness, it should be noted that it is possible for the man backing the favorite—the odds-giver—to make a bet in which he wins if his cock wins or there is a tie, a slight shortening of the odds (I do not have enough cases to be exact, but ties seem to occur about once every fifteen or twenty matches). He indicates his wish to do this by shouting *sapih* ("tie") rather than the cock-type, but such bets are in fact infrequent.

11. The precise dynamics of the movement of the betting is one of the most intriguing, most complicated, and, given the hectic conditions under which it occurs, most difficult to study, aspects of the fight. Motion picture recording plus multiple observers would probably be necessary to deal with it effectively. Even impressionistically—the only approach open to a lone ethnographer caught in the middle of all this—it is clear that certain men lead both in determining the favorite (that is, making the opening cock-type calls which always initiate the process) and in directing the movement of the odds, these "opinion leaders" being the more accomplished cockfighters-cum-solid-citizens to be discussed below. If these men begin to change their calls, others follow; if they begin to make bets, so do others and—though there are always a large number of frustrated bettors crying for shorter or longer odds to the end—the movement more or less ceases. But a detailed understanding of the whole process awaits what, alas, it is not very likely ever to get: a decision theorist armed with precise observations of individual behavior.

12. Assuming only binomial variability, the departure from a fifty-fifty expectation in the sixty-ringgits-and-below case is 1.38 standard deviations, or (in a one direction test) an eight in one hundred possibility by chance alone; for the below-forty-ringgits case it is 1.65 standard deviations, or about five in one hundred. The fact that these departures though real are not extreme merely indicates, again, that even in the smaller fights the tendency to match cocks at least reasonably

evenly persists. It is a matter of relative relaxation of the pressures toward equalization, not their elimination. The tendency for high-bet contests to be coin-flip propositions is, of course, even more striking, and suggests the Balinese know quite well what they are about.

13. The reduction in wagering in smaller fights (which, of course, feeds on itself; one of the reasons people find small fights uninteresting is that there is less wagering in them, and contrariwise for large ones) takes place in three mutually reinforcing ways. First, there is a simple withdrawal of interest as people wander off to have a cup of coffee or chat with a friend. Second, the Balinese do not mathematically reduce odds, but bet directly in terms of stated odds as such. Thus, for a nine-to-eight bet, one man wagers nine ringgits, the other eight; for five-to-four, one wagers five, the other four. For any given currency unit, like the ringgit, therefore, 6.3 times as much money is involved in a ten-to-nine bet as in a two-to-one bet, for example, and, as noted, in small fights betting settles toward the longer end. Finally, the bets which are made tend to be one- rather than two-, three-, or in some of the very largest fights, four- or five-finger ones. (The fingers indicate the multiples of the stated bet odds at issue, not absolute figures. Two fingers in a six-to-five situation means a man wants to wager ten ringgits on the underdog against twelve, three in an eight-to-seven situation, twenty-one against twenty-four, and so on.)

14. Besides wagering there are other economic aspects of the cockfight, especially its very close connection with the local market system which, though secondary both to its motivation and to its function, are not without importance. Cockfights are open events to which anyone who wishes may come, sometimes from quite distant areas, but well over 90 percent, probably over 95, are very local affairs, and the locality concerned is defined not by the village, nor even by the administrative district, but by the rural market system. Bali has a three-day market week with the familiar "solar-system"-type rotation. Though the markets themselves have never been very highly developed, small morning affairs in a village square, it is the microregion such rotation rather generally marks out—ten or twenty square miles, seven or eight neighboring: villages (which in contemporary Bali is usually going to mean anywhere from five to ten or eleven thousand people) from which the core of any cockfight audience, indeed virtually all of it, will come. Most of the fights are in fact organized and sponsored by small combines of petty rural merchants under the general premise, very strongly held by them and indeed by all Balinese, that cockfights are good for trade because "they get money out of the house, they make it circulate." Stalls selling various sorts of things as well as assorted sheer-chance gambling games (see below) are set up around the edge of the area so that this even takes on the quality of a small fair. This connection of cockfighting with markets and market sellers is very old, as among other things, their conjunction in inscriptions [R. Goris, *Prasasti Bali,* 2 vols. (Bandung, 1954)] indicates. Trade has followed the cock for centuries in rural Bali, and the sport has been one of the main agencies of the island's monetization.

15. The phrase is found in the Hildreth translation, International Library of Psychology (1931), note to p. 106; see L. L. Fuller, *The Morality of Law* (New Haven, 1964), p. 6 ff.

16. Of course, even in Bentham, utility is not normally confined as a concept to monetary losses and gains, and my argument here might be more carefully put in terms of a denial that for the Balinese, as for any people, utility (pleasure, happiness . . .) is merely identifiable with wealth. But such terminological problems are in any case secondary to the essential point: the cockfight is not roulette.

17. There is nothing specifically Balinese, of course, about deepening significance with money, as Whyte's description of corner boys in a working-class district of Boston demonstrates: "Gambling plays an important role in the lives of Cornerville people. Whatever game the corner boys play, they nearly always bet on the outcome. When there is nothing at stake, the game is not considered a real contest. This does not mean that the financial element is all-important. I have frequently heard men say that the honor of winning was much more important than the money at stake. The corner boys consider playing for money the real test of skill and, unless a man performs well when money is at stake, he is not considered a good competitor." W. F. Whyte, *Street Corner Society,* 2d ed. (Chicago, 1955), p. 140.

18. The extremes to which this madness is conceived on occasion to go—and the fact that it is considered madness—is demonstrated by the Balinese folk tale *I Tuhung Kuning.* A gambler becomes so deranged by his passion that, leaving on a trip, he orders his pregnant wife to take care of the prospective newborn if it is a boy but to feed it as meat to his fighting cocks if it is a girl. The mother gives birth to a girl, but rather than giving the child to the cocks she gives them a large

rat and conceals the girl with her own mother. When the husband returns, the cocks, crowing a jingle, inform him of the deception and, furious, he sets out to kill the child. A goddess descends from heaven and takes the girl up to the skies with her. The cocks die from the food given them, the owner's sanity is restored, the goddess brings the girl back to the father, who reunites him with his wife. The story is given as "Geel Komkommertje" in J. Hooykaas-van Leeuwen Boomkamp, *Sprookjes en Verhalen van Bali* (The Hague, 1956), pp. 19-25.

19. As this is a formal paradigm, it is intended to display the logical, not the causal, structure of cockfighting. Just which of these considerations leads to which, in what order, and by what mechanisms, is another matter—one I have attempted to shed some light on in the general discussion.

20. In another of Hooykaas-van Leeuwen Boomkamp's folk tales ("De Gast," *Sprookjes en Verhalen van Bali*, pp. 172-180), a low caste *Sudra*, a generous, pious, and carefree man who is also an accomplished cockfighter, loses, despite his accomplishment, fight after fight until he is not only out of money but down to his last cock. He does not despair, however—"I bet," he says, "upon the Unseen World."

    His wife, a good and hard-working woman, knowing how much he enjoys cockfighting, gives him her last "rainy day" money to go and bet. But, filled with misgivings due to his run of ill luck, he leaves his own cock at home and bets merely on the side. He soon loses all but a coin or two and repairs to a food stand for a snack, where he meets a decrepit, odorous, and generally unappetizing old beggar leaning on a staff. The old man asks for food, and the hero spends his last coins to buy him some. The old man then asks to pass the night with the hero, which the hero gladly invites him to do. As there is no food in the house, however, the hero tells his wife to kill the last cock for dinner. When the old man discovers this fact, he tells the hero he has three cocks in his own mountain hut and says the hero may have one of them for fighting. He also asks for the hero's son to accompany him as a servant, and, after the son agrees, this is done.

    The old man turns out to be Siva and, thus, to live in a great palace in the sky, though the hero does not know this. In time, the hero decides to visit his son and collect the promised cock. Lifted up into Siva's presence, he is given the choice of three cocks. The first crows: "I have beaten fifteen opponents." The second crows, "I have beaten twenty-five opponents." The third crows, "I have beaten the king." "That one, the third, is my choice," says the hero, and returns with it to earth.

    When he arrives at the cockfight, he is asked for an entry fee and replies, "I have no money; I will pay after my cock has won." As he is known never to win, he is let in because the king, who is there fighting, dislikes him and hopes to enslave him when he loses and cannot pay off. In order to insure that this happens, the king matches his finest cock against the hero's. When the cocks are placed down, the hero's flees, and the crowd, led by the arrogant king, hoots in laughter. The hero's cock then flies at the king himself, killing him with a spur stab in the throat. The hero flees. His house is encircled by the king's men. The cock changes into a Garuda, the great mythic bird of Indic legend, and carries the hero and his wife to safety in the heavens.

    When the people see this, they make the hero king and his wife queen and they return as such to earth. Later their son, released by Siva, also returns and the hero-king announces his intention to enter a hermitage. ("I will fight no more cockfights. I have bet on the Unseen and won.") He enters the hermitage and his son becomes king.

21. Addict gamblers are really less declassed (for their status is, as everyone else's, inherited) than merely impoverished and personally disgraced. The most prominent addict gambler in my cockfight circuit was actually a very high caste *satria* who sold off most of his considerable lands to support his habit. Though everyone privately regarded him as a fool and worse (some, more charitable, regarded him as sick), he was publicly treated with the elaborate deference and politeness due his rank.

22. British cockfights (the sport was banned there in 1840) indeed seem to have lacked it, and to have generated, therefore, a quite different family of shapes. Most British fights were "mains," in which a preagreed number of cocks were aligned into two teams and fought serially. Score was kept and wagering took place both on the individual matches and on the main as a whole. There were also "battle Royales," both in England and on the Continent, in which a large number of cocks were let loose at once with the one left standing at the end the victor. And in Wales, the so-called Welsh main followed an elimination pattern, along the lines of a present-day tennis tournament, winners proceeding to the next round. As a genre, the cock fight has perhaps less

compositional flexibility than, say, Latin comedy, but it is not entirely without any. On cockfighting more generally, see A. Ruport, *The Art of Cockfighting* (New York, 1949); G. R. Scott, *History of Cockfighting* (London, 1957); and L. Fitz-Barnard, *Fighting Sports* (London, 1921).

23. For the necessity of distinguishing among "description," "representation," "exemplification," and "expression" (and the irrelevance of "imitation" to all of them) as modes of symbolic reference, see Goodman, *Languages of Art,* pp. 61-110, 45-91, 225-241.

24. There are two other Balinese values and disvalues which, connected with punctuate temporality on the one hand and unbridled aggressiveness on the other, reinforce the sense that the cockfight is at once continuous with ordinary social life and a direct negation of it: what the Balinese call *ramé,* and what they call *paling.* *Ramé* means crowded, noisy, and active, and is a highly sought-after social state: crowded markets, mass festivals, busy streets are all *ramé,* as, of course, is, in the extreme, a cockfight. *Ramé* is what happens in the "full" times (its opposite, *sepi,* "quiet," is what happens in the "empty" ones). *Paling* is social vertigo, the dizzy, disoriented, lost, turned-around feeling one gets when one's place in the coordinates of social space is not clear, and it is a tremendously disfavored, immensely anxiety-producing state. Balinese regard the exact maintenance of spatial orientation ("not to know where north is" is to be crazy), balance, decorum, status relationships, and so forth, as fundamental to ordered life (*krama*) and *paling,* the sort of whirling confusion of position the scrambling cocks exemplify as its profoundest enemy and contradiction. On *ramé,* see Bateson and Mead, *Balinese Character,* pp. 3, 64; on *paling,* ibid., p. 11, and Belo, ed., *Traditional Balinese Culture,* p. 90 ff.

25. The Stevens reference is to his "The Motive for Metaphor"[. . . .]; the Schoenberg reference is to the third of his *Five Orchestral Pieces* (Opus 16), and is borrowed from H. H. Drager, "The Concept of 'Tonal Body,'" in *Reflections on Art,* ed. S. Langer (New York, 1961), p. 174. On Hogarth, and on this whole problem—there called "multiple matrix matching"—see E. H. Gombrich, "The Use of Art for the Study of Symbols," in *Psychology and the Visual Arts,* ed. J, Hogg (Baltimore, 1969), pp. 149-170. The more usual term for this sort of semantic alchemy is "metaphorical transfer," and good technical discussions of it can be found in M. Black, *Models and Metaphors* (Ithaca, NY, 1962), p. 25 ff; Goodman, *Language as Art,* p. 44 ff; and W. Percy, "Metaphor as Mistake," *Sewanee Review* 66 (1958): 78-99.

26. The tag is from the second book of the *Organon, On Interpretation.* For a discussion of it, and for the whole argument for freeing "the notion of text . . . from the notion of scripture or writing" and constructing, thus, a general hermeneutics, see P. Ricoeur, *Freud and Philosophy* (New Haven, 1970), p. 20 ff.

27. Levi-Strauss' "structuralism" might seem an exception. But it is only an apparent one, for, rather than taking myths, totem rites, marriage rules, or whatever as texts to interpret, Levi-Strauss takes them as ciphers to solve, which is very much not the same thing. He does not seek to understand symbolic forms in terms of how they function in concrete situations to organize perceptions (meanings, emotions, concepts, attitudes); he seeks to understand them entirely in terms of their internal structure, *independent de tout suiet, de tout objet, et de toute contexte.*

28. The use of the, to Europeans, "natural" visual idiom for perception—"see," "watches," and so forth—is more than usually misleading here, for the fact that, as mentioned earlier, Balinese follow the progress of the fight as much (perhaps, as fighting cocks are actually rather hard to see except as blurs of motion, more) with their bodies as with their eyes, moving their limbs, heads, and trunks in gestural mimicry of the cocks' maneuvers, means that much of the individual's experience of the fight is kinesthetic rather than visual. If ever there was an example of Kenneth Burke's definition of a symbolic act as "the dancing of an attitude" [*The Philosophy of Literary Form,* rev. ed. (New York, 1957), p. 9] the cockfight is it. On the enormous role of kinesthetic perception in Balinese life, Bateson and Mead, *Balinese Character,* pp. 84-88; on the active nature of aesthetic perception in general, Goodman, *Language of Art,* pp. 241-244.

29. All this coupling of the occidental great with the oriental lowly will doubtless disturb certain sorts of aestheticians as the earlier efforts of anthropologists to speak of Christianity and totemism in the same breath disturbed certain sorts of theologians. But as ontological questions are (or should be) bracketed in the sociology of religion, judgmental ones are (or should be) bracketed in the sociology of art. In any case, the attempt to deprovincialize the concept of art is but part of the general anthropological conspiracy to deprovincialize all important social concepts—marriage, religion, law, rationality—and though this is a threat to aesthetic theories which regard certain works of art as beyond the reach of sociological analysis, it is no threat to the conviction, for

which Robert Graves claims to have been reprimanded at his Cambridge tripos, that some poems are better than others.

30. For the consecration ceremony, see V. E. Korn, "The Consecration of the Priest," in Swellengrebel, ed., *Bali Studies,* pp. 131-154; for (somewhat exaggerated) village communion, R. Goris, "The Religious Character of the Balinese Village," ibid., pp. 79-100.
31. That what the cockfight has to say about Bali is not altogether without perception and the disquiet it expresses about the general pattern of Balinese life is not wholly without reason is attested by the fact that in two weeks of December 1965, during the upheavals following the unsuccessful coup in Djakarta, between forty and eighty thousand Balinese (in a population of about two million) were killed, largely by one another—the worst outburst in the country. [J. Hughes, *Indonesian Upheaval* (New York, 1967), pp. 173-183. Hughes' figures are, of course, rather casual estimates, but they are not the most extreme.] This is not to say, of course, that the killings were caused by the cockfight, could have been predicted on the basis of it, or were some sort of enlarged version of it with real people in the place of the cocks—all of which is nonsense. It is merely to say that if one looks at Bali not just through the medium of its dances, its shadow-plays, its sculpture, and its girls, but—as the Balinese themselves do—also through the medium of its cockfight, the fact that the massacre occurred seems, if no less appalling, less like a contradiction to the laws of nature. As more than one real Gloucester has discovered, sometimes people actually get life precisely as they most deeply do not want it.

Chapter 11

1. Budziszewski (1986, 1988) and Will (1980) are two authors that explicitly advocate an Aristotelian politics of virtue. Alasdair MacIntyre (1981, 1990) and Salkever (1990) explore the same territory somewhat less directly.
2. Much of the criticism I shall make applies equally to at least some versions of an Aristotelian politics of virtue. Any criticisms of the neo-Aristotelians, however, would have to begin with their conception of the ends of the politics, a project I do not undertake here. For my comment on the historical fate of Aristotelian politics of virtue, see Burtt (1990).
3. For the various meanings of public and private in political argument, see Pitkin 1981, 327-352. I use *public* here in a strongly political sense, to refer to the goods and concerns of *res publica* as considered separately from both the personal and the broadly social.
4. I discuss these separate psychological groundings of civic virtue in Burtt 1990.
5. The phrase "perfect privatist" is Bruce Ackerman's, used with somewhat different connotations in Ackerman 1984, 1033.
6. For a similar argument, see Spitz 1986, 193, 198.
7. On founding, see, esp., Machiavelli's *Discourses* 1.1-10 and Rousseau's *Social Contract* 1.7-10. On corruption, see, esp., Machiavelli's *Discourses* and Rousseau's *Letter to D'Alembert* and *On the Government of Poland*.
8. Barber argues that participation in his program of "civic renewal" can be elicited through "persuasion, through the self-education yielded by democratic participation itself, and through the logic of political priority, which demonstrates that even in a privatistic politics dominated by economic interests, it is the autonomy of politics and the rights of citizens that give modern women and men the real power to shape their common lives. The taste for participation is whetted by participation: democracy breeds democracy" (p. 265). This final statement may well be true, but does not reach the problem of getting people to participate in the first place.
9. The exception that proves this rule may be aristocratic (i.e., noninclusive) politics where, with the business of every-day life taken care of by slaves, serfs, and women, a select number of men were able to devote themselves either to the practice of politics or to contemplative life. The classic articulation of this possibility is, of course, Aristotle's *Politics.*
10. The account that follows draws on my argument in Burtt 1992, chap. 4.
11. Popular authoritarian regimes of the twentieth century might seem to provide a counterexample of this claim. But Cato's virtuous citizens do not exist in a vacuum. They, too, require a politics of civic virtue, whose conditions are discussed in the next section.
12. See Rousseau 1972, Chap. 13.
13. Ackerman 1991 restates and refines this argument.

Chapter 12

1. On social networks and economic growth in the developing world, see Milton J. Esman and Norman Uphoff, *Local Organizations: Intermediaries in Rural Development* (Ithaca, NY: Cornell University Press, 1984), esp. pp. 15-42 and pp. 99-180; and Albert O. Hirschman, *Getting Ahead Collectively: Grassroots Experiences in Latin America* (Elmsford, NY: Pergamon Press, 1984), esp. pp. 42-77. On East Asia, see Gustav Papanek, "The New Asian Capitalism: An Economic Portrait," in *In Search of an East Asian Development Model,* eds. Peter L. Berger and Hsin-Huang Michael Hsiao (New Brunswick, NJ: Transaction, 1987), pp. 27-80; Peter B. Evans, "The State as Problem and Solution: Predation, Embedded Autonomy and Structural Change," in *The Politics of Economic Adjustment,* eds. Stephan Haggard and Robert R. Kaufman (Princeton, NJ: Princeton University Press, 1992), pp. 139-181; and Gary G. Hamilton, William Zeile, and Wan-Jin Kim, "Network Structure of East Asian Economies," in *Capitalism in Contrasting Cultures,* eds. Stewart R. Clegg and S. Gordon Redding (Hawthorne, NY: De Gruyter, 1990), pp. 105-129. See also Gary G. Hamilton and Nicole Woolsey Biggart, "Market, Culture, and Authority: A Comparative Analysis of Management and Organization in the Far East," *American Journal of Sociology* 94 (Supplement 1988): S52-S94; and Susan Greenhalgh, "Families and Networks in Taiwan's Economic Development," in *Contending Approaches to the Political Economy of Taiwan,* eds. Edwin Winckler and Susan Greenhalgh, (Armonk, NY: M.E. Sharpe, 1987), pp. 224-245.
2. James S. Coleman deserves primary credit for developing the "social capital" theoretical framework. See his "Social Capital in the Creation of Human Capital," *American Journal of Sociology* 94 (Supplement 1988): S95-S120, as well as his *The Foundations of Social Theory* (Cambridge, MA: Harvard University Press, 1990), pp. 300-321. See also Mark Granovetter, "Economic Action and Social Structure: The Problem of Embeddedness," *American Journal of Sociology* 91 (1985): 481-510; Glenn C. Loury, "Why Should We Care About Group Inequality?" *Social Philosophy and Policy* 5 (1987): 249-271; and Robert D. Putnam, "The Prosperous Community: Social Capital and Public Life," *American Prospect* 13 (1993): 35-42. To my knowledge, the first scholar to use the term "social capital" in its current sense was Jane Jacobs, in *The Death and Life of Great American Cities* (New York: Random House, 1961), p. 138.
3. Any simplistically political interpretation of the collapse of American unionism would need to confront the fact that the steepest decline began more than six years before the Reagan administration's attack on PATCO. Data from the General Social Survey show a roughly 40 percent decline in reported union membership between 1975 and 1991.
4. Data for the LWV are available over a longer time span and show an interesting pattern: a sharp slump during the Depression, a strong and sustained rise after World War II that more than tripled membership between 1945 and 1969, and then the post-1969 decline, which has already erased virtually all the postwar gains and continues still. This same historical pattern applies to those men's fraternal organizations for which comparable data are available—steady increases for the first seven decades of the century, interrupted only by the Great Depression, followed by a collapse in the 1970s and 1980s that has already wiped out most of the postwar expansion and continues apace.
5. Cf. Lester M. Salamon, "The Rise of the Nonprofit Sector," *Foreign Affairs* 73 (July-August 1994): 109-122. See also Salamon, "Partners in Public Service: The Scope and Theory of Government-Nonprofit Relations," in *The Nonprofit Sector: A Research Handbook,* ed. Walter W. Powell (New Haven, CT: Yale University Press, 1987), pp. 99-117. Salamon's empirical evidence does not sustain his broad claims about a global "associational revolution" comparable in significance to the rise of the nation-state several centuries ago.
6. I am grateful to Ronald Inglehart, who directs this unique cross-national project, for sharing these highly useful data with me. See his "The Impact of Culture on Economic Development: Theory, Hypotheses, and Some Empirical Tests" (unpublished manuscript, University of Michigan, 1994).

Chapter 13

1. The immediate assessments in the United States were ebullient. See, for example, David Laitin's commentary in this *Review* (1995) and Joseph LaPalombara's praise-filled review (1993). Professional reviewers in Italy have not, for the most part, shared this enthusiasm. Representative exam-

ples are Bagnasco (1994), Cohn (1994), Feltrin (1994), Pasquino (1994), Ramella (1995), and Trigilia (1994). More critical assessments began to appear in English in 1995. See the set of brief reviews by Arnaldo Bagnasco, Antonio Mutti, and Gianfranco Pasquino in APSA-CP, the newsletter of the Organized Section in Comparative Politics, June 1995, and the more probing analyses by Ellis Goldberg, Margaret Levi, and Filippo Sabetti in *Politics and Society,* March 1996.
2. See Tarrow (1967a, b) for two deeply out-of-date efforts to compare northern and southern Italy, about which Putnam has kind words to say in his book. More up-to-date works on the South that touch on some of the same bases as *Making Democracy Work* are by Trigilia (1992, 1995).
3. On qualitative and quantitative methods, see the path-breaking volume by King, Keohane, and Verba (1994) and the symposium on that book in *American Political Science Review* (1995). For an alternative qualitative approach to similar issues as raised by Putnam, carried out in the same country, see Sabetti 1996.
4. Among the press reviews that this author has scanned, the most enthusiastic were found in the *Times Literary Supplement,* February 1993, followed by *The Economist* in October 1993, *The Nation* in November 1993, and *The New York Times Book Review* in January 1995. The Italian media have been wildly enthusiastic but the tone of many of these reactions leads one to suspect an unfortunate attempt to enlist Putnam as an ally in the game of trashing the South, a game which became fashionable with the rise of the separatist Northern League in the early 1990s. For a reflection on this unfortunate coincidence, see Trigilia (1994).
5. The botanic metaphor is no accident; it was even more explicit in another report on the work in Italian by Putnam and others (1985).
6. Almost from the beginning, Putnam was associated in the early study with Robert Leonardi and Raffaella Nanetti, who had primary responsibility for the field research, collaboratively authored several publications with him, and produced several books on their own. See, in particular, Leonardi and Nanetti (1990), Nanetti (1988), and Putnam, Leonardi, and Nanetti (1981, 1983, 1985). For fuller citations, see notes 1 and 2 in Putnam (1993a, 207).

To summarize briefly, they carried out four waves of interviews with regional councilors in six regions in Italy; three waves of interviews in these same regions and a nationwide mail survey with community leaders; six nationwide surveys of voters; extended regional statistical analysis; a "unique experiment" that tested the responsiveness of regional governments to citizen inquiries; and case studies of institutional politics which helped them "marinate" themselves (their term) in Italy's diverse regional realities. See Putnam (1993a, 12-14 and Appendix A).
7. It is only fair to remark that Robert Putnam, in commenting on a draft version of this article, asserts that his book is not a political cultural interpretation of Italian regions. He points out that virtually all his indicators of "civicness" are behavioral or structural, not attitudinal or cultural. Putnam and his collaborators certainly do not engage in symbolic or ritualistic forms of cultural analysis or use the "thick" description that some culturalists favor (Laitin 1995, 173). Reading their article in the Review (1983, 63-67), however, argues otherwise. The model of causation, which goes from civic capacity to political behavior, is in the main line of political culture research from the pioneering studies of Almond and Verba onward (Putnam 1993a, 11) and picks up on crucial arguments of that superb culturalist, Alexis de Tocqueville (Putnam 1993a, 89-91, 182, and 221, note 28). I can only say that, if Making Democracy Work is not a cultural interpretation, then Putnam and his collaborators fooled not only this critic but also many of their admirers, one of whom considers is "a stunning breakthrough in political culture research" (Laitin 1995, 171).
8. For example, Putnam and his collaborators (1993a) found that the regional governments' procedures were often reminiscent of the practices of the central administration (49); that in many cases, clientelism and party affiliation, rather than expertise and experience, were the main criteria for recruitment (50); and that by the late 1980s the initial euphoria of the regional councilors had been replaced by "a grimly realistic assessment of the practical challenges of making the new government work" (57).
9. The first aphorism this reviewer ever heard (from a northerner) about the Italian Communist party that he studied in southern Italy was that it resembled Pirandello's *Six Characters in Search of an Author.* For a more scholarly synthesis on southern and northern political cultures on which many students of Italy cut their teeth, see LaPalombara (1965).
10. Jonas Pontusson, in a personal communication with the author, finds the following contradiction in Putnam's treatment of economic development. In his discussion of the North in the fif-

teenth century, Putnam points out that "the prosperity of the communal republics was arguably the consequence, as much as the cause, of . . . civic engagement" (Putnam 1993a, 152). But subsequently Putnam observes that different levels of economic development were not significantly different in the nineteenth century from the fifteenth. If northern Italian civicness produced economic development—and was produced by it—in the fifteenth century and again in the twentieth, why did it not have similar effects in the intervening period? I am grateful to Pontusson for pointing this out to me and regret that I have been unable to give sufficient attention to the relations between economic development, civicness, and institutional performance in this essay.

11. Those who follow Italian politics will understand empirically how preference voting can be used as a measure of clientelism, but this does not help explain how it relates to the civic virtues that Putnam elucidates theoretically. One might argue intuitively, contra Putnam, that since preference voting is based on knowing the individual candidates, it is a *positive* element in civic involvement. Putnam points out that the preference vote is used in Italy to assure individual benefits, not to anchor a policy preference, and in that sense "preference voting can be taken as an indicator for the absence of civic community" (1993a, 94). I do not find the justification convincing because the absence of personal ties between voters and officials is not an obvious element of civic virtue. It is what usually accompanies preferences in southern Italy—corruption and clientelism—that makes it inimical to what Putnam sees in the civic community. If so, then it would have been more correct to use these factors as (negative) indicators of civic virtue.

12. It should be noted that the four measures are also highly intercorrelated (Putnam 1993a, 96, Table 4.4). The problem with these measures is that they are also highly correlated with the size of the Communist vote, a party which was particularly anxious to have its supporters turn out, as Alan Zuckerman reminded me in a comment on the first draft of this essay.

13. Putnam's correlations are dramatic enough, but his verbal inferences about Italy's civic Center-North verge on chamber-of-commerce enthusiasm. "Some regions of Italy," he writes, "have many choral societies and soccer teams and bird-watching clubs and Rotary clubs. Most citizens in those regions read eagerly about community affairs in the daily press. They are engaged by public issues, but not by personalistic or patron-client politics. Inhabitants trust one another to act fairly and obey the law. Leaders in these regions are relatively honest. They believe in popular government, and they are predisposed to compromise with their political adversaries (1993a, 115).

14. Putnam's prose in describing the South is as bleak as his language about the Center-North was elegiac: "Public life in these regions is organized hierarchically, rather than horizontally. . . . Few people aspire to take partake in deliberations about the commonweal, and few such opportunities present themselves. Political participation is triggered by personal dependency or private greed, not by collective purpose. Engagement in social and cultural associations is meager. Private piety stands in for public purpose. Corruption is widely regarded as the norm, even by politicians themselves, and they are cynical about democratic principles. . . . Trapped in these interlocking vicious circles, nearly everyone feels powerless, exploited, and unhappy" (115).

15. Working with organizational registers in the early 1990s, Trigilia and his collaborators found an impressive total of 6,400 cultural associations in the South, three for every 10,000 inhabitants, and more than two-thirds of them created since 1980 (Ramella 1995, 473). "There emerges," in their view, "a picture that differs in many ways from the opaque and static image of the associational phenomena in the South" (473-474). See Trigilia (1995) for the full report of these findings.

16. It is only fair to point out that Putnam devotes only nineteen pages to the historical roots of civic capacity in the North and to civic incapacity in the South. For some of his critics, this is evidence of scholarly superficiality (see, for example, Cohn 1994, 315), while Putnam, responding to Cohn, writes that if he "had known that the reviewers of [his] book would have applied themselves so devotedly to the nineteen pages . . . [he] dedicated to the history of Italy before unification, [he] would have perhaps lost twenty years frequenting the historians to understand the intricate mechanisms that govern their shifting professional agreements and disagreements" (1994, 325).

17. Cohn (1994, 318) writes: "Although Putnam admits that, moving from place to place within a single southern region, great differences in civic virtue can be found . . . he abandons every restraint when he looks at the period before unification. The South of Putnam is an undiffer-

entiated whole, from the Arab-settled western coast of Sicily up to the region of Rome, despite the fact that the southern regions presented very different situations in terms of the level of urbanization, agrarian systems, industrial development, the diffusion of banditism and the formation of the first mafias."

It would have been interesting to know, as Ellis Goldberg asks in his review of the book, whether Norman kingdoms established elsewhere in Europe left a similar heritage. Based on the regimes that followed the Norman conquest of England, he finds reason for skepticism. See Goldberg (1996) for this and other arguments that are not taken up in this essay.

18. For one thing, Putnam has the merchants and bankers of these early northern communes supplanting the power of the church (1993a, 148), when recent research (for example, Bizzocchi 1987) shows that "an important dimension of the power base of the Medici in republican Florence came from . . . the church hierarchy" (Cohn 1994, 326). For another, contrary to Putnam's paean to their relative social equality, early capitalist cities such as Florence and Venice produced enormous differences in stratification (see Ventura 1964; Molho 1994). This is no more than saying that the birth period of "civic society" was at the same time the birth period of bourgeois society, with all the patterned inequalities that capitalism produced.

19. Putnam does not ignore the "uncivic" features of the city-states (see, for example, 1993a, 129). In a personal communication to the author, he argues that, "however uncivic they were in absolute terms, they were still more civic than the Norman kingdom." By Putnam's reasoning, two things should follow. First, intraregional differences in the independent variable should correlate significantly with intraregional differences in the outcomes he predicts (see Goldberg 1996 for this line of argument). Second, consistent differences in civicness can be traced over time for all the regions. On the scant evidence presented in the book, I do not find sufficient support for either test.

20. And not only historians: As political scientist Gianfranco Pasquino (1994) writes, it is one thing to identify the political origins of contemporary political patterns in a period eight centuries ago, but it is quite another to skim through most features of the politics of the next 500 years (309). For Putnam's reply, see Putnam (1994).

21. I am grateful to Suzanne Berger for this observation, which she first made at a panel dedicated to Putnam's book at the 1994 American Political Science Association meeting.

22. Contra Putnam on the greater corruption of the South and the clean government of the Center-North, the spectacular corruption scandals that have shaken the Italian First Republic since 1990 began and were centered in the North. On corruption in Italy, see della Porta 1992.

23. Putnam does entertain a state-centric model, but the states in question emerged and disappeared many centuries ago. As David Laitin (1994) notes, this is a "big bang" interpretation of history. Putnam is right to point out, in a personal communication to the author, that his focus on early states is consistent with his path-dependent model and does not ignore state building; rather, the criticism is that—once states were formed in northern and southern Italy—there were crucial changes in state building and in state strategy that find no place in his account.

24. Strictly speaking, since the elections of 1876, the term *transformismo* has meant the shift of opposition deputies to support of the government in return for favors, but it has become a general catch-phrase for corruption, clientelism, and the politics of exchange.

25. The sources on the forced economic integration and on prefectoral interference in local elections are legion. See Fried (1963); Salvemini (1955, 73-74); and Tarrow (1967a, 21-28).

26. But see the critiques of method and conception in Pizzorno (1971) and Sabetti (1996). It would appear from Sabetti's account of the village in which Banfield worked that, even in the early 1950s, there were forms of associational capacity which are remembered even today.

27. See Putnam (1993b; 1995) for his thinking about the weakening of social capital in the United States. But here, beginning at the other extreme of associational capacity, he sees a decline in sociability with a resulting weakening of social capital remarkable what he found in southern Italy. For recent data on U.S. associational life and a skeptical view of Putnam's interpretation, see Lipset (1995, 13-14).

28. Indeed, much of what we know about the Provençal *chambrées* comes from the secret reports of the central government's powerful prefects.

Chapter 15

1. See the analysis of Durkheim's view of symbols as constitutive in Bellah 1973.
2. The two major lines of empirical work on values are anthropological, comparing values of different social groups (Kluckhohn and Strodtbeck 1961), and the social-psychological, comparing the values of individuals (Rokeach 1973).
3. Geertz's early classic, *The Religion of Java* (1960), is overtly Weberian in inspiration and execution, tracing the influence of differing religious ethics on economic action. Geertz (1966) also emphasizes the problem of theodicy (explaining suffering and injustice in the world God controls), which was central to Weber's analysis of the dynamics of religious change. And Geertz has returned repeatedly to the problem of rationalization in non-Western religious traditions (1968, 1973).
4. See Keesing 1974 for a detailed treatment of this issue.
5. See Sherry Ortner's (1984) insightful and entertaining analysis of shifts in culture theory, "Theory in Anthropology Since the Sixties."
6. This is the theoretical strategy Randall Collins (1981, 1988) has called "microtranslation." The theorist attempts to provide concrete, individual-level causal imagery even for macro or global causal processes, without making the micro reductionist claim that the underlying causal dynamics operate at the micro level.
7. Careful readers of Weber will note that such an explanation of action is perfectly compatible with his theoretical orientation. "Social action" is, after all, action whose "subjective meaning takes account of the behavior of others and is thereby oriented in its course" (Weber 1968, 4). Weber (1946b) also argued clearly that the Protestant sects continued to influence action long after intense belief had faded because members knew that sect membership gave visible social testimony to their worthiness. Nonetheless, Weber and most of his followers have been preoccupied with the inner workings of the religious psyche rather than with more external forms of cultural power.
8. William Sewell, Jr. (1985, 1990) analyzes how dramatic social movements shift an entire pattern of public discourse and thus remake future forms of collective action.
9. See Jepperson 1991 and Scott 1992 for fuller treatments of institutions and problems of institutional analysis.
10. I develop this argument more fully for the case of marriage in *Talk of Love: How Americans Use Their Culture,* forthcoming from the University of Chicago Press.

Chapter 16

1. See J. Dolan, "Catholic Attitudes Toward Protestants," in *Uncivil Religion,* ed. R. N. Bellah and F. E. Greenspahn (New York: Crossroad, 1987), pp. 72-85, for a brief review of Catholic resentment toward Protestantism and the reasons why it was relatively muted.
2. These figures come from R. A. Billington, "Tentative Bibliography of Anti-Catholic Propaganda," *Catholic Historical Review* 18 (1932): 492-513. Among the newspapers and magazines were *The Protestant Vindicator, The Anti-Romanist, The Protestant Banner, Priestcraft Unmasked, The Native American, The Reformation Defended Against the Errors of the Times, The American Protestant Magazine, The Spirit of the XIX Century,* and *The North American Protestant Magazine,* or, as it was called, *The Anti-Jesuit.* Among the books published were such evocative titles as *Jesuit Juggling: Forty Popish Frauds Detected and Disclosed* (1834), *The Papal Conspiracy Exposed and Protestantism Defended in the Light of Reason, History and Scripture* (1855), *Popery Stripped of Its Garb* (1836), *The Papacy: the Anti-Christ of Scripture* (1854), and *Book of Tracts on Romanism: Containing the Origin and Progress, Cruelties, Frauds, Superstitions, Miracles and Ceremonies of the Church of Rome.*
3. Through the 1840s and 1850s the Committee for the Inspection of Convents was established and operated by the Commonwealth of Massachusetts. See R. A. Billington, *The Protestant Crusade* (Gloucester, MA: Peter Smith, 1963), and T. Maynard, *The Story of American Catholicism* (New York: Macmillan, 1942).
4. This literature is summarized in some depth in M. N. Dobkowski, "American Anti-Semitism," *American Quarterly* 29 (Summer 1977): 166-181. See also Louis Harap, *The Image of the Jew in American Literature: From Early Republic to Mass Immigration* (Philadelphia: Jewish Publication Society of America, 1974).
5. A number of important sources explore the nature of anti-Semitism at the end of the nineteenth and beginning of the twentieth centuries. See, for example, O. Handlin, "American Views of the

Jews," *American Jewish Historical Society* 40 (June 1951): 323-345; J. Higham, "Social Discrimination Against Jews," *American Jewish Historical Society* 47 (September 1957): 1-33; J. Higham, "Anti-Semitism in the Gilded Age," *Mississippi Valley Historical Review* 43 (March 1957): 559-578; and G. Stember, ed., *Jews in the Mind of America* (New York: Basic Books, 1966).

6. An account of these experiences is given in G. Sessions, "Myth, Mormonism, and Murder in the South," *South Atlantic Quarterly* 75 (Spring 1976): 212-225. See also T. O'Dea, *The Mormons* (Chicago: University of Chicago Press, 1957); and D. B. Davis, "Some Themes of Counter-Subversion," *Mississippi Valley Historical Review* 47 (1960): 205-225.

7. Interestingly, while neutrality increased and antipathy declined, close identification among various denominations (as measured by "feelings of warmth") did not increase. These findings are a part of the University of Michigan surveys on American Presidential Politics. The "feeling thermometer" they employed was a 100 point scale along which respondents were asked to locate themselves according to coldness and warmth they felt for different groups. Coldness was measured as a score between 1 and 40, neutrality between 41 and 69, and warmth between 70 and 100. For the general population, coldness toward Catholics decreased from 13 percent of the population in 1966 to 9.9 percent in 1984. (Comparable figures were not available for Protestants and Catholics, but for blacks, the figure dropped from 15 percent to 11 percent.) Those neutral toward Catholics grew from 39 percent in 1966 to 46 percent in 1984; those neutral towards Protestants rose from 27 percent in 1966 to 47 percent in 1976; and for Jews, from 47 percent in 1966 to 56 percent in 1984. Protestants and Jews were omitted from the 1984 survey.

8. The earlier figures were taken from a 1958 Gallup Poll while the more current figures come from J. D. Hunter and O. Guiness, eds., *The Williamsburg Charter Survey on Religion and Public Life*, a survey conducted in December 1987 (Washington, DC: Williamsburg Charter Foundation, 1988).

9. The single most comprehensive summary of the data on non-Jewish beliefs about Jews from the 1930s to the mid-1960s is Steber, "The Recent History of Public Attitudes," in his *Jews in the Mind of America*, pp. 310-336. For the data produced between the mid-1960s and the early 1980s, see G. Rosenfield, "The Polls: Attitude Toward American Jews," *Public Opinion Quarterly* 46 (1982): 431-443. Studies that should be reviewed in their own right and that collectively support this general thesis are C. Glock and R. Stark, *Christian Beliefs and Anti-Semitism* (New York: Harper & Row, 1966); G. Selznick and S. Steinberg, *The Tenacity of Prejudice* (New York: Harper & Row, 1969); H. Quinley and C. Glock, *Anti-Semitism in America* (New York: The Free Press, 1979); and G. Martire and R. Clark, *Anti-Semitism in the United States* (New York: Praeger, 1982).

10. See the "Nationwide Attitudes Survey—September 1986, a Confidential Report Presented to the Anti-Defamation League of B'nai B'rith," by Tarrance, Hill, Newport, and Ryan. The report received a great deal of media play as well. See Bruce Bursma, "Anti-Semitism Fading for Some," *Chicago Tribune*, January 9, 1987; and Marjorie Hyer, "Poll Finds No Rise in Anti-Semitism: Most Evangelicals Reject Jewish Stereotypes," *Washington Post*, January 10, 1987, p. G8.

11. See J. L. Sullivan, J. Piereson, and G. Marcus, *Political Tolerance and American Democracy* (Chicago: University of Chicago Press, 1982), for a summary of some of these data. The General Social Survey performed annually by the National Opinion Research Center has asked questions about the free speech rights of atheists, communists, and homosexuals since 1972 and even since that time the overall trend has been toward greater toleration. In 1973, for example, 41 percent of the American population agreed that a communist should be allowed to teach in public schools. By 1987 this had increased to 49 percent. Likewise, in 1973, 49 percent of the general population agreed that a homosexual should be allowed to teach but by 1987, that percentage had increased to 58. (From the author's analysis of the General Social Survey.)

12. Kate DeSmet, "Shotgun Approach: Congress of Fundamentalists Labels Catholic Church 'Mother of Harlots,'" *Detroit News*, August 20, 1983. The anti-Catholic and anti-Semitic invectives of the pentecostal televangelist Jimmy Swaggart have been especially pronounced. He has called Catholics "poor pitiful individuals that think they have enriched themselves by kissing the Pope's ring" (reported by the Associated Press, March 9, 1985) and has claimed that a "large segment of the Jewish community within the entertainment industry . . . is doing everything in its power to *destroy* the very element that has *produced* . . . freedom" (reported in *The Evangelist*, July 1985; emphasis in the original).

13. The term "progressive" is somewhat imprecise but it is suggestive. The word is not totally satisfactory because of its association with the political movement and ideology. It also connotes a positive development which many would find debatable. Yet the search for alternate terms leads to other problems. The antonyms of orthodoxy—heterodoxy or heresy—connote too much.

"Revisionism" is problematic, too, as it implies a departure from the truth. The problem is not truth versus falsehood but between different interpretations of truth—interpretations that differ because the criteria (or authority) established to measure correct interpretation differ.

14. Secularists are represented in such organizations as the American Humanist Association (founded in 1941), the Council for Democratic and Secular Humanism (founded 1980), the National Service Conference of the American Ethical Union (founded 1929), Gay and Lesbian Atheists (founded 1978), Libertarians for Gay and Lesbian Concerns (founded 1981), and the Association of Libertarian Feminists (founded 1975).
15. Their agreement is confirmed in the Religion and Power Survey in James Davison Hunter, John Jarvis, and John Herrmann, "Cultural Elites and Political Values," unpublished paper, University of Virginia, 1988.
16. Robert Wuthnow's book, *The Restructuring of American Religion* (Princeton, NJ: Princeton University Press, 1988), is the most exhaustive statement on the developments described in this book to date. Those familiar with Wuthnow's treatment should see my book not just as a validation of his general argument but as an extension of it as well. Where Wuthnow focuses upon Protestantism, I focus on interfaith dimensions of the problem. Where he views the tensions as those that exist between "religious liberals" and "religious conservatives," I view the tensions as both deeper and more significant.
17. "The Webster Decision," *Nightline,* ABC-TV broadcast, July 3, 1989.
18. There is little doubt that the controversy over abortion is a central part of the larger conflict. Indeed, it has crystallized the antagonism between the orthodox and progressive as no other issue has. Yet once again, the moral propriety and legality of abortion is just one of many issues over which this war is being fought. David Broder, "Trivial Pursuits," editorial, *Washington Post,* June 17, 1990, p. D7.
19. This comment was made by photographer Jock Sturgis, taken from a transcript of "48 Hours," CBS News, June 27, 1990.
20. Ibid.
21. From an anonymous video store owner interviewed on "48 Hours," ibid.

Chapter 18

1. This article is based on material from Ronald Inglehart, *Modernization and Postmodernization: Cultural, Economic and Political Change in 43 Societies* (Princeton, NJ: Princeton University Press, 1997—forthcoming).
2. The data from both the 1981 and 1990 World Values Surveys are available from the ICPSR survey data archive.
3. The notion that Argentina is uniquely close to Southern Europe does not hold up very well, however, since Mexico is just as close to the Southern European societies as is Argentina.
4. The "1981" surveys were actually carried out in 1981-1983; and the "1990" surveys were actually carried out in 1990-1993. In both cases, most of the surveys were carried out in the initial year, however. The third wave began fieldwork in Fall, 1995 and will continue through the end of 1996.

Chapter 19

1. Some may observe that the labels I have given these four responses all carry unfavorable connotations—and this is certainly true. One could, perhaps, find euphemisms and talk about morality rather than moralism, realism rather than cynicism, satisfaction rather than complacency, and patriotism rather than hypocrisy. Yet these pleasant alternative labels obscure the critical point: that each response is, in some measure, unsatisfactory and cannot be maintained for long by substantial numbers of people. They tend to hide the problem of the gap rather than to highlight it.
2. Louis D. Rubin, Jr., "The Great American Joke," *South Atlantic Quarterly* 72 (Winter 1973), pp. 83-87, where the Robert Penn Warren quote appears. Harold J. Laski, *The American Democracy* (New York: Viking, 1948), p. 740. See generally Walter Blair and Hamlin Hill, *America's Humor: From Poor Richard to Doonesbury* (New York: Oxford University Press, 1979).
3. *New York Times,* May 4, 1974, pp. 1, 24.

4. For analyses supporting the conclusions summarized in this paragraph, see: Fred I. Greenstein, *Children and Politics* (New Haven, CT: Yale University Press, 1965), esp. pp. 31-45; David Easton and Jack Dennis, *Children in the Political System* (New York: McGraw-Hill, 1969), esp. pp. 111-143; M. Kent Jennings and Richard G. Niemi, "Patterns of Political Learning," *Harvard Educational Review* 38 (Summer 1968): 463-465; and idem, "The Transmission of Political Values from Parent to Child," *American Political Science Review* 62 (March 1968): 169-184. For the effects of Watergate on children's attitudes toward politics, see F. Christopher Arterton, "Watergate and Children's Attitudes toward Political Authority Revisited," *Political Science Quarterly* 90 (Fall 1975): 477ff.
5. See, for example, Robert E. Agger, Marshall N. Goldstein, and Stanley A. Pearl, "Political Cynicism: Measurement and Meaning," *Journal of Politics* 23 (August 1961): 487-492, and the data on trust in government for the years 1958-1978 collected by the University of Michigan Center for Political Studies, in Warren E. Miller, Arthur H. Miller, and Edward J. Schneider, *American National Election Studies Data Sourcebook, 1952-1978* (Cambridge, MA: Harvard University Press, 1980), p. 269).

Chapter 20

1. A fuller account of norms, with applications to collective action and bargaining problems, is found in Elster (1989).
2. This was written before the introduction of two-tiered wage systems in several American airlines.
3. I am indebted to Ottar Brox for this example.
4. The argument in Akerlof (1976, 610) seems to rest on the assumption that sanctions can go on forever, without losing any of their force. Anyone who violates any rule of caste, including anyone who fails to enforce the rules, automatically becomes and outcaste. Abreu (1988) offers a formal analysis built on a similar assumption. I know too little about the caste system to assess the validity of the assumption in this case, but I am confident that it is false in the cases about which I have some knowledge. Sanctions tend to run out of steam at two or three removes from the original violation.
5. See also Ullmann-Margalit 1977, 60.
6. Note that the norm cannot be justified by individual "Tit for tat" rationality: if I eat someone I have no reason to fear that he may eat me on a later occasion.
7. I am indebted to Amos Tversky for suggesting this to me as an example of social norms.
8. These strategies are universally employed. As I was completing this paper, I came across a passage in a crime novel (Engel 1986, 155) making the same point: "I decided to make a fast getaway. I had done Pete a favour and it didn't pay to let him thank me for doing it. It was more negotiable the other way. I heard him calling after me but I kept going."
9. As a participant observer in a machine shop Roy (1952) found substantial losses due to deliberately suboptimal efforts.
10. Faia (1986) has a good discussion of the (severely limited) range of cases in which social selection arguments make good sense.

Chapter 21

1. The term "Sozialökonomik" is primarily associated in German economics with the name of Heinrich Dietzel (1857-1935), who was professor in economics at the University of Bonn (see Arndt 1935). Dietzel introduced the term first through an article in 1883 and then in *Theoretische Sozialökonomik* (1895), which was published as a volume in Wagner's handbook of political economy (Winkelmann 1986; see Dietzel 1883, 1895). Dietzel (1895) himself traces the term "Sozialökonomik" to some early Italian economists and especially to Jean-Baptiste Say, who uses it in the introduction to *Cours complet d'economic politique* (1828-1829). Also John Stuart Mill (1838), who introduced the term "social economy" into English, traces this expression to Say. In Mill's opinion, Say defines "social economy" as "every part of man's nature, in so far as influencing the conduct constitution of man in society." Dietzel himself, however, defined

"Sozialökonomik" somewhat differently. He was first of all interested in finding a substitute for the terms "Nationalökonomik" and "politische Ökonomik," which he felt misrepresented economics by connecting it to "the nation" and to "politics." In his own work Dietzel defined "Sozialökonomik" in an organic and wholistic manner.

2. According to Weber (1975), Menger had proposed "excellent views." On Schmoller's 70th birthday, Weber wrote to him that "at a time of the most barren economic rationalism you have created a home for *historical* thought in our science" (Weber as cited in Schön 1989). A few years earlier Weber had recommended that Bohm-Bawerk be given an honorary doctorate at the University of Heidelberg with the motivation that "he would make a particularly happy complement to the strictly historically inductive work by Professor Schmoller, whose promotion has been recommended by the other side" (Weber as cited in Schön 1989).
3. Space does not allow me to properly describe an attempt to reorient economics during these years in a more interdisciplinary direction. This attempt was spearheaded by Herbert Simon and includes such scholars as James March and Richard Cyert.
4. The idea of economic imperialism (if not the term) should probably be credited to Alfred Marshall (see Parsons 1934).
5. The term "economic imperialism" was no doubt also popularized by the fact that Kenneth Boulding used it in his presidential address to the AEA in 1968. Boulding (1969) here defined "economic imperialism" as "an attempt on the part of economics to take over all the other social sciences.

Chapter 22

1. In this essay I will identify the culturalist position with interpretivist or hermeneutical ones. In fact, there are a wide range of alternative positions which can be distinguished. For present purposes the critical feature of these approaches is in what I will call the ethnographic starting point: the proper place to begin social analysis is with the meanings embedded in the social practices in question. These intersubjective meanings, or cultural elements, form the basis for the identification of actors and their choices. The main differences among different schools seems to be in how deeply (beyond the meanings shared consciously by the actors) the interpretation can or must go. That question is unimportant for this essay and is, therefore, left in this note.
2. To take just one prominent example, MacIntyre rejects the widely accepted Hempelian covering law vertion of social science on the grounds that social phenomena are inherently unpredictable. See Chapter 8 of Alasdair MacIntyre (1981).
3. The "most fundamental reason for the impossibility of hard prediction is that man is a self-defining animal" (Taylor 1985, 55).
4. Taylor (1985) says that "a successful interpretation is one which makes clear the meaning originally present in a confused, fragmentary, cloudy form" (17). He goes on to say that the test of the correctness or adequacy of an interpretation is that it "makes sense of the original text: what is strange, mystifying, puzzling, contradictory, is no longer so, is accounted for" (17). I read this statement to imply the criterion for ranking interpretive theories given in the text.
5. I believe that a somewhat stronger claim than this can be defended—namely, that an adequate interpretation of behavior must satisfy the requirement that actors are behaving as though they are trying to maximize something. If this is not true of an interpretation, it must be the case that the explanation can account, for the choice of some action from a set of alternative actions, {a1, a2, . . . ak) such that the actor prefers ai to ai + 1, for all i and ak to a1. In my view such an account does not permit us to understand the agent's actual choices by appeal to his or her values or beliefs. For if the agent made any choice from this set of actions, there would have been some other action that was preferable but which, for some reason, wasn't chosen. The explanation must rest on what that reason is and not on the agent's preferences among actions.
6. Clifford Geertz (1973) rejects the search for universals among anthropologists on the grounds that such "universals" will necessarily be so empty as to tell us little about humans in society. He asks, "What, after all, does it avail us to say . . . that 'morality is a universal, and so is enjoyment of beauty, and some standard for truth,' if we are forced . . . to add that 'the many forms these concepts take are but products of the particular historical experience of the societies that manifest them?"(41).
7. Theorists regard thin-rational accounts, when available, as more fundamental than thick-rational ones. Thus theoretical developments in the theory of the firm have been aimed at constructing

Notes   433

a thin justification of the profit-maximizing assumption. This has proceeded on two levels: externalist theories of "natural selection" and internalist theories of agency relationships in the organization of economic enterprises.

8. Ironically, once these claims are stripped of their pejorative tone, rational choice theorists generally accept them in the sense that they regard thick assumptions as in need of justification. While some theorists move immediately to Friedman's pragmatic justification that if a theory "works," there is no need to question its assumptions, most others recognize that assumptions are predictions of theory too and try to justify thick-rational assumptions either as approximations or as "placeholders" for some deeper (i.e., thinner) theory that will appear later on. See Almond for alternative views of thin and thick rational choice explanations.

9. Some interpretivists stop short of attributing unambiguous causal force to cultural meanings: Geertz (1973) writes that the central problem of his approach is "to conceptualize the dialectic between the crystallization of such directive 'patterns of meaning' and the concrete course of social life" (250).

10. This stance seems to leave interpretivists with little more than a coherence test in comparing different explanations. Indeed, Geertz (1973) acknowledges that there are "serious problems of verification . . . of how you can tell a better account from a worse one. . . . The force of our interpretations cannot rest, as they are now so often made to do, on the tightness with which they hold together. . . . Nothing has done more, I think, to discredit cultural analysis than the construction of impeccable descriptions of formal order in whose actual existence nobody can quite believe" (16, 18).

11. Technically, in a repeated Prisoners' Dilemma game, any outcome which guarantees the players more than they would receive in the "'defect-defect" equilibrium can be supported in an equilibrium.

12. By "common knowledge" I mean the following: X is common knowledge among a set of agents if each knows X; each one knows that each knows X; each knows that each knows that each knows X; and so on, "all the way down."

13. Admittedly, this use of culture within rational choice explanation is functionalist: culture performs the function of selecting among alternative equilibria. Obviously, the account is incomplete as it stands and requires a deeper investigation of "selection" principles among cultural elements or meanings, something I am unable to do in the present essay. The question is this: is it the case that cultural elements that permit coordination in (game-theoretical) social interaction are "selected over" or survive longer than those that do not?

14. I do not mean to imply by this terminology that I regard these domains as in any sense autonomous. Indeed, the larger point of this essay is precisely that the two spheres are interconnected in ways that have to be better understood if we are to understand either of them. See James Johnson 1988, 1990.

15. Derek Hirst (1975) puts the Whig perspective thus: "The corollary of the assertion that the electoral system . . . was forming in this period is that these were its early days. A normal accompaniment of the initial stages of any development is a measure of uncertainty and confusion. . . . But, for our purposes, the important point about elections is that they should be contested" (12).

16. While I focus on divergent explanations of seventeenth-century electoral practices, the reader should be aware that this debate recurs in other periods. For a revisionist account of Victorian elections, for example, see Vincent 1966.

17. Historians of the period disagree as to what constitutes evidence of a contest but, as far as I can tell, most would probably agree that the number of contests was not far from this estimate. This number of contests represents a modest increase from the estimated number in the Elizabethan period. The number of contests began to increase more rapidly in the 1620s and 1640s.

18. Revisionists argue that these attempts must be seen as piecemeal accommodations and not as part of a coherent program aimed at franchise expansion.

19. "By the twenties nearly all important questions are referred to this Committee" (Notestein 1924, 37).

20. "Whether or not there was any connexion between the development of this new procedure and the close relations between the King and Speaker, it is certain that the Commons found it a convenience of the Committee plan that the Speaker could no longer regulate debates. The Committee of the Whole House usually chose men who were not Privy Councillors as chairmen" (Notestein 1924, 37).

21. "Political consensus and the more or less effective workings of the patronage system averted both elections and the open agitation of issues" (Hirst 1975, 1).

22. Plumb and others describe electoral manipulation by sheriffs, biased polling practices, and other procedures conducive to manipulated elections.
23. Even modern Whigs exhibit this tendency. Hirst (1975) betrays a tendency to look toward the future when he argues that "a reluctance to come to terms with integral parts of the electoral process was visible in this period. Contests were uncommon, unpopular, and not fully accepted for what they were. Even the straightforwardly numerical proposition of a majority was not wholly clear of doubt" (16). Or, again: "[P]eople were only beginning to feel their way towards an appreciation of the existence of elections and an electorate" (21).
24. "[S]essions were of uncertain duration; and the preparations and pains of travel could be repaid by sudden dissolution as in 1584 or 1614" (Kishlansky 1986, 24).
25. "Costs increased ten- or twenty-fold, with no logical limit based on competition or constituency. Rising costs were simply the result of the presence of free-spending competitors trying to feed an insatiable electorate" (Kishlansky 1986, 20).
26. "Once majorities were the requirement for selection then the question of who held rights of participation became paramount" (Kishlansky 1986, 20).
27. These numbers are computed from a table in Hirst (1975, 216-222).
28. Kishlansky (1986) writes that "in itself, an increase or decrease in the number of contested elections provides little guidance to the social and political changes of the early seventeenth century. Those who count contests inhabit the same sort of dream world as those who counted manors" (76).
29. The connection of collusive opportunities with institutions is not necessary from a game-theoretical view, though it seems natural enough in the present case. In repeated play situations, "collusive" outcomes can be sustained through "tacit" coordination, which entail the threat of punishment for deviation from collusive behavior. Indeed, it is not clear, in repeated play settings, just what observational difference there is between what we ordinarily think of as an institution and tacit collusive equilibria.
30. Kishlansky reports two offsetting tendencies over the course of the century. On the one hand, the actual amounts spent on campaigning increased because of the increased frequency of contests. On the other, the humiliation of suffering an electoral rejection diminished as the contests came to seem more "normal."
31. In this we must take account of informational limitations and the intersubjective understandings of the strategic structure of interaction.

INDEX

Ackerman, Bruce, 207, 219–20, 423n5, 423n13
Agulhon, Maurice, 244
Akbar, M.J., 106
Akerlof, G., 369, 371, 375, 431n4
Almond, Gabriel, ix, 1, 5, 17–19, 24, 29, 43, 51–2, 303, 308, 316, 322
American Politics: The Promise of Disharmony, 305, 430n1
Arendt, Hannah, 43, 318
Aristotle, 6, 198, 199–200, 208, 359, 423n1, 423n2
Arrow, Kenneth J., 371–2
Axelrod, Bruce, 369

Banfield, Edward, 43, 50, 244
Barber, Benjamin, 83, 211, 213–4, 219, 423n8
Barber, James David, 28–9
Barry, Brian, 10, 35
Becker, Gary, 369, 388, 389
Benedict, Ruth, 9, 50, 51, 323
Benford, Robert, 258, 274, 280
Bentham, Jeremy, 175, 189, 420n16
Bernard, Jessie, 151–2
Bordieu, Pierre, 273, 274
Brown, Murphy, 134
Buchanan, James, 388
Burtt, Shelley, 204, 207

Caplow, Theodore, 275–6
Carballo, Marita, 304–05, 325–6
Carver, Terrell, 84
Cato's Letters, 207, 215–7, 219, 423n11
City and Regime in the American Republic, 218–9
Civic Culture, The, 11–12, 51–2, 57
civic engagement, 224, 225, 234, 239, 240–1, 242
  alternatives to decline, 232–4
  change in, 228–30
  see also civic participation
  decline of, 225–8
  sources of decline, 232–4
civic virtue, 207–22, 423n2, *see also* public virtue, private virtue
civilization
  and conflict, 100–18
  definitions, 101
  and identity, 102, 103, 114
  and rallying, 108–11
civil society, *see* culture and social capital
Cohen, Raymond, 55
Coleman, James, 389
communitarianism, 208, 214
comparative politics, *see* culture and comparison
Converse, Philip, 327–8
Cox, Harvey, 80–1

Cox, Robert W., 87
creedal passion, 305, 348, 349, 352–7
culture
    and action, 21–2, 45–8, 48–9, 60, 271, 309–10, 322, 361, 364–6, 379, 410–11
    and anthropology, 9, 23, 61, 175, 415n18, 415n19, 428n2
    and assumptions, 22–3, 26–8, 31–2, 308, 413n1
    and authority, 16, 43, 137–8, 139–40, 284–5, 287, 294–8, 325
    and change, xviii-xix, 6, 11–17, 59, 102, 103, 237–8, 303–6, 307–24, 326–47, 356–7
    and citizenship, 203–5, 207–20, 223, 224, 225, 233–4
    and civilizations, 100–01, 102–04
    and civil society, xvii, 2, 81, 95–7, 120, 203–05, 223, 233–4
    and codes, 23, 36, 275–7
    and cognitive dissonance, 349–52
    and collective identity, 44, 45, 53–4, 65, 85, 102, 103, 113–15, 163–4, 249–52, 253–67, 274, 284–5
    and collective representation, 270
    and comparison, 16–17, 43, 46–7, 223–34, 235–48, 336–40, 343–6, 414n11, 415n19, 423n23
    and complacency, 349, 353
    and conflict, 54–5, 62–3, 100–18, 137, 138, 140–3, 287–301, 309
    and context, 43–4, 48–9, 61, 119–28, 277–9, 281, 415n24, 418n2
    and continuity, 311–3, 342–6
    critiques of, xvi, 10–11, 31, 34–5, 40–1, 55–61, 71–4, 235, 326–7, 376–8, 415n20
    and cumulative socialization, 303–4, 310–11, 311–13
    and cynicism, 349, 352, 357
    definitions of, xv, 1–3, 5, 7, 10, 21–22, 22–23, 25, 28, 31, 33, 39–40, 41, 42–3, 56–7, 65, 129, 198, 201, 235, 269–74, 309–13, 322, 390
    and democracy, xvii, 27, 76–7, 79–81, 104–05, 121, 123, 127, 146, 203, 204, 213, 216, 233–4, 236, 244–5, 355
    and demographics, 106
    and economics, 14, 80–1, 86–7, 89–91, 92–3, 103–4, 336, 356, 415n14
    effects of, 15–17, 28–31, 32, 33–7, 45, 60–1, 86–93, 122, 123, 135, 136, 145–8, 259, 262–7, 280–1, 288–91, 292–8, 305, 309, 310, 336–40, 352–7, 413n8
    and egalitarianism, 361
    Elazar's theory of, 133, 134, 135, 136, 137, 138, 143, 145, 146
    and explanations, xvi, 2, 21–2, 24, 26, 34–7, 40, 42, 43–9, 59–64, 66–7, 71–4, 304, 311, 366–79, 406–11
    frames, 250, 253, 254–5, 258, 280
    and geography, 101–18, 261–2, 326–7, 336–40, 346–7
    and globalization, xvi, 75–8, 79–97, 99–100, 102, 103–04
    and government capacity, 224, 242–4
    and hierarchy, 361, 394
    and humor, 350, 430n2
    and hypocrisy, 349, 350–1, 353–4
    and ideology, 8, 79, 83, 84–5, 86–9, 89–91, 92–3, 94, 100, 108, 112, 127, 147, 259, 263, 274, 284–301, 330–9
    and individualism, 147–8, 270, 274, 304–05, 350, 361, 394
    and institutions, xvii, 1–2, 21, 30–3, 35–6, 142, 237–8, 242–4, 264–5, 269, 279–80, 281, 326, 340–2, 348, 352–4, 361, 397
    and interpretation, 33–6, 41, 58–9, 61–5, 83, 175, 180, 187–8, 189–95, 195–201, 243–4, 244–5, 271–2, 322–3, 394–411, 416n34, 416n36, 433n10
    and inter-subjectivity, 40, 41, 42, 45–7, 48, 61, 390, 397, 399, 410, 411, 414n8, 432n1, 434n31
    and methodology, *see* methodology
    models of, 17–19, 136, 237–9, 322–3, 348
    and modernization theory, 325–6, 328, 329, 343, 346–7

INDEX

and moralism, 349, 350–1, 352, 357
and motives, 45–8, 414n9
non-Western, 100–01, 103, 105–08, 111–12, 119, 120, 121–6
and norms, 31, 45, 47, 126–8, 270–1, 363, 364–6, 366–8, 368–9, 377–9, 409, 431n1, 431n6
and orientational variability, 310
and orientations, 309–11
orthodox, 285–5, 287, 294–8
and personality, 28–9, 50, 413n6, 413n7, 415n13
and political process, 17–19, 52–3, 147, 281
popular, *see* popular culture
and postmaterialism, 13, 333–6
and postmodernism, 41, 146–7
and postmodernization, 325–6, 328–9, 333–6, 343, 346–7
and power, 273–4
and practices, 272–3, 274–5, 280–1, 397
and preference formation, 361, 369–79, 399, 410–11, 415n15
progressive, 284–5, 287, 294–8, 429n13
and psychology, 1, 9, 10, 43–4, 50, 62–4, 179–82, 378, 416n29, 428n2
and public symbols, 271–2, 280–1
and rationality, xix, 2, 35, 40, 46, 47, 225, 249–50, 254, 307, 308, 310, 311, 359–62, 363–79, 381–90, 393–411, *see also* rationality
and religion, 14–15, 48–49, 99–100, 101, 104, 105–08, 108–11, 115–6, 226, 287–91, 291–3, 327, 331–3, 337, 338, 340–2, 428n5, 428n6, 429n7, 429n9, 429n10, 429n12
and repertoires, 259
and social capital, 203–05, 223, 223–34
and socialization, 310, 312
and social movements, xvii–xviii, 249–52, 253–67, 269–83, 284–301; *see also* social movements
and socioeconomics, 325–6, 355, 382–3, 384–5, 389–90
and sociology, 9, 35, 254, 270–1, 273, 363

and structure, 21, 24, 25, 29–30, 246–7, 256, 259–60, 413n4
and subcultures, 259–60, 260–1, 264–5, 284–301, 304
and subjectivity, 40
and values, 9–10, 36, 40, 101–18, 119–28, 130, 270–1, 288–301, 304–5, 328–9, 329–47, 348, 352–4, 356–7, 361, 393–4, 409–11, 413n5, 428n2
Western, xv, 99–100, 101, 105–08, 111–12, 116–18, 119, 120, 121–6

deep play, 175, 188, 189–95
deep structures, 134, 137
democracy, *see* culture and democracy
Democracy in America, 223
Devine, Donald, 355
Dittmer, Lowell, 17
Douglas, Mary, 415n20
Downs, Anthony, 311, 388
dualist democracy, 219–20
Durkheim, Emile, 2, 9, 270, 272, 273, 275, 280, 314, 316, 322, 363, 366, 428n1

Eckstein, Harry, xviii, 1, 14, 59, 303, 304, 307, 308, 319, 359, 363
economic imperialism, 97, 382–3, 386–9, 390, 432n4, 432n5
economic theory, 81, 86–93, 360–1, 383–4, 385, 386–9, 389–90, 396
Edelman, Murray, 53–4
Eimermann, Tom, ix
Elazar, Daniel, 133, 134, 135, 136, 137, 143–4, 145, 146
Elkins, David, 1, 21–2, 24, 32, 39
Elkin, Stephen, 207, 218–9, 220
Ellis, Richard, ix, 361, 381, 393, 415n20
Elster, Jon, 363, 396, 431n1
Emmerson, Donald K., 77, 119
Engels, Friedrich, 95
Etzioni, Amitai, 360, 381, 382, 383, 390

Fagen, Richard, 11
Feminine Mystique, The, 164
Ferejohn, John, 250, 393–4
focused gathering, 184

Foucault, Michel, 273, 274
free-rider problem, 204
Friedan, Betty, 163–4
Fukuyama, Francis, 76, 79–80, 94

game theory, *see* rationality and game theory
Gamson, William, 274, 280
Gandhi, Mohandas K., 255
Geertz, Clifford, 23, 42, 43, 46, 51, 57, 85, 130, 175, 191, 271–2, 428n3, 432n6, 433n9, 433n10
Gerbner, George, 135, 136, 137, 145, 154, 157
Gift Relationship, The, 28
Giles-Sims, Jean, x
Gill, Stephen, 82, 87, 96
Gingrich, Newt, 88–9
Goffmann, Erving, 184, 191, 254
gullible other effect, 126

Habermas, Jurgen, 146
Hanerz, Ulf, 83
Hartz, Louis, 32
Holton, Robert, 83, 97
Hormats, Robert, 89–90
Hunt, Lynn, 261, 264
Hunter, James Davison, 284–5
Huntington, Samuel, xvi, xviii, xix, 56, 99–100, 305, 316, 348

Inglehart, Ronald, xviii, 12–13, 51, 204, 263, 304–05, 325–6, 346, 424n6, 430n1
international relations, conditions of, xvi, 75–6, 99–100, 100–118, 417n1, 417n2

Jihad v. McWorld, 83

Kant, Immanuel, 314, 359
Keesing, Roger, 23
Kimmeldorf, Howard, 260
kin-country syndrome, 108–11
King, Martin Luther, xviii, 255
Kishlansky, Mark, 403–5, 407–8, 409, 434n28, 434n30
Kline, Steven, 92–3

Koc, Mustafa, 80
Kristol, Irving, 350

Lang, Gladys Engel, 166–7
Laraña, Enrique, 260
Lasswell, Harold, 151, 152
Lewis, Bernard, 106–07
liberalism, 8, 80, 90, 208, 209, 210–12, 214–15, 215–17, 218–19, 219–20, 243, 305
Liberal Virtues, 210
Liefer, Aimee Dorr, 168, 169
Limerick, Patricia Nelson, 3, 71
Lipset, Seymour Martin, 316, 355
Lockhart, Charles, 304, 361
Lowi, Theodore, 238

Macedo, Steven, 210, 211, 212
Machiavelli, Niccolo, 2, 7, 207, 212, 423n7
Mahbubani, Kishore, 112, 122
Making Social Science Work Across Space and Time, 235, 236, 239, 246, 247, 425n7, 425n8, 426n13, 426n14, 426n16, 426n17, 427n18, 427n19, 427n23, 427n27
Manzer, Ronald, 28
Marxism, 7, 8, 11, 85, 263, 265, 389
Marx, Karl, 8, 85, 95, 265
McAdam, Doug, 253, 255, 256, 257, 258, 264, 266, 274, 277
McBride, Allen, 133
McCloskey, Herbert, 355
media
  and agenda setting, 152
  cultural significance of, 133–49, 150, 151–74
  effects of, 145–49, 150, 151–74, 416n30
  impact on women of, 150, 151–74
  and reflection hypothesis, 150, 153–4
  magazines, 160–4
  newspapers, 164–7
  television, 16–17, 134–6, 154–60
  and symbolic annihilation, 153–4, 154–60, 164, 167–8
Menger, Carl, 383–4, 432n2
Merelman, Richard, 41, 51, 57, 130, 134

Merton, Robert K., 35, 316, 317
methodology, 2, 5, 6, 9, 14, 18–19,
    24–25, 28, 31–3, 55–61, 61–5,
    125, 126, 130, 136, 137–8, 168–9,
    185–6, 238–9, 239–42, 245–8,
    309, 329, 381, 381–92, 395–6,
    414n1, 414n8, 425n6
Mill, John Stuart, 207, 390
Mittleman, John, 82, 97
Molotch, Harvey, 257
Montesquieu, Baron de, 2, 7
Moral Dimension, The, 382, 390
Morris, Aldon, 259–60
Myrdal, Gunnar, 351–2, 353

Nassar, Jamal, ix
norms, *see* culture and norms

Olson, Mancur, 204, 316
Outline of a Theory of Practice, 273

Parsons, Talcott, 9, 270, 272, 322, 387
Pateman, Carol, 18
Pizzorno, Alessandro, 244
Plato, 6, 359
Plutarch, 6–7
policy culture, 18
political change, *see* culture and change
political culture, *see* culture
political socialization, 6, 7, 16, 204,
    431n4
politics, *see* culture
Politics, Culture, and Class in the French Revolution, 261, 264
Popkin, Samuel, 11
popular culture, xvi-xvii, 76, 93, 124–6,
    129–31, 134–48, 264
Powell, G. Bingham, 17–18
Pride, Richard, ix
private virtue, 207, 209–10, 215–17,
    218, 220
process culture, 18
public choice, *see* rationality
public virtue, 207, 209–10, 212,
    212–15, 215–17, 217–18, 219–20,
    220–1
Putnam, Robert, ix, 92, 203, 204–05,
    223, 224, 235, 236, 237, 238, 239,
    240, 242, 242–3, 244, 245, 246,
    308, 309, 425n4
Pye, Lucien, 50, 101, 309, 415n22

Quayle, Dan, 134

rational choice, *see* rationality
rationality, xv, 40, 46, 47, 208, 307, 308,
    359–62, 364, 366–8, 368–9,
    369–79, 385–6, 393–4, 394–411,
    433n8
  critiques of, 385–6, 414n10
  and game theory, 27, 35, 398–9,
    406–9, 411n12, 411n13, 411n29
  and instrumentalism, 359, 360,
    366–79, 381 thick rationality, 250,
    393, 394, 396–7, 409, 433n8
  thin rationality, 396–7, 432n7
republicanism, 208, 209, 210–12,
    213–15, 219–20, 220, 240
resource mobilization, *see* social movements and resource mobilization
Ricoeur, Paul, 85, 199
ritual, 53–4
Robertson, Ronald, 83
Rogowski, R., 11, 303, 308, 320
Ross, Marc Howard, 2–3, 39, 55, 62, 67
Rousseau, Jean-Jacques, 2, 7, 207, 212,
    215, 423n12
Rupp, Leila, 260

Santayana, George, 351
Schmoller, Gustav von, 383–4, 432n2
Simeon, Richard E. B., 1, 21–2, 24, 39
Smith, Adam, 363, 390
Smith, Rogers, 210–11
Snow, David, 254–5, 258, 274, 280
social capital, *see* culture and social capital
socialism, 90–1, 93–7
  and democracy, 93–4
social movements, 96–7
  and cultural framing, 250, 253,
    254–5, 258–9, 263, 280
  and cultural contradictions, 256–7
  effects of, 262–7
  emergence of, 259–62

social movements, (*continued*)
  and new social movements, 254, 263–4
  and political process, 253, 256, 281
  and prior movements, 259–60
  and resource mobilization, 250, 253–4, 255–6, 415n2
  and suddenly imposed grievances, 250, 256, 263
  and system vulnerability, 257
social networks, 224, 254, 424n1
Souter, Ralph William, 387
Steger, Manfred, ix, 79, 95
Stigler, George, 387–8
Sugden, Robert, 364
Swedberg, Richard, 359, 381
Swidler, Ann, 259, 269, 277
Symbolic Uses of Politics, The, 53–4
system culture, 17–18

Tarrow, Sidney, xvii, 204–05, 235, 245, 255, 257, 425n2
Taylor, Charles, 395, 397–8, 410
Taylor, Verta, 260
television, *see* media and television
Theory of Legislation, The, 189
Theses on Feuerbach, 95
Titmuss, Richard, 28
Toburen, Robert K., 133
Tocqueville, Alexis de, 2, 7, 204, 214–15, 223, 224, 245, 246, 366
torn countries, 113–15
Toynbee, Arnold, 101
Trigilia, Carlo, 239, 242, 243, 425n2, 426n15

Tuchman, Gaye, 150
Tucker, Robert, 11
Tullock, Gordon, 388
Turner, Ralph, 261
Turner, Victor, 52–3

Useem, Bert, 257

values, *see* culture and values
Van Gelder, Lindsay, 166
Verba, Sidney, ix, 2, 24, 43, 51–2, 303, 316, 322
virtue
  civic, *see* civic virtue
  and politics, 207–21
  private, *see* private virtue
  public, *see* public virtue

Walsh, Edward, 257
Weber, Max, 2, 9, 45, 85, 270, 273, 274, 275, 278, 314, 322, 370, 381–2, 383, 384–5, 389–90, 428n7, 432n2
  and ideal types, 384–5
  and objectivity, 384
Weidenbaum, Murray, 104
White, Harrison, 266
White, Stephen, 11
Whittier, Nancy, 262
Wiatr, Jerzy, 11
Wildavsky, Aaron, ix, 46, 130, 304, 359, 360, 361, 381, 393–4, 415n20
World Values Surveys, 230–1, 327, 328, 329, 342–3, 345, 430n2, 430n4
Wuthnow, Robert, 229, 272, 274, 430n16